The Life of Mencius

by Qu Chunli

Foreign Languages Press Beijing

First Edition 1998

The present volume is a translation of the first Chinese edition of *The Life of Mencius* published in 1992 by the Shandong Friendship Press. The illustrations are drawn by Ma Ji specially for the English edition of the book.

Translated by Zhang Zengzhi

Hardcover: ISBN 7-119-01460-9

© Foreign Languages Press, Beijing, China, 1998
Published by Foreign Languages Press
24 Baiwanzhuang Road, Beijing 100037, China

Distributed by China International Book Trading Corporation
35 Chegongzhuang Xilu, Beijing 100044, China
P.O. Box 399, Beijing, China

Printed in the People's Republic of China

The portrait of Mencius

Preface to the Chinese Edition

It has been scarcely two years since Mr. Qu Chunli published his *Life of Confucius*, and now its companion-piece *Life of Mencius* is produced from under his pen. I would like to take this opportunity to offer my hearty congratulations.

Over the past ten years, Mr. Qu has been engaged in the work of foreign affairs and tourism at Jining City, Shandong Province, the historical site of the ancient states of Zou and Lu and the homeland of Confucius and Mencius. Inspired by an immense admiration and veneration for the sages and philosophers of old, Mr. Qu has read a great amount of historical documents relevant to their lives and deeds, and this he often did by snatching every leisured hour he could from a very active public life. He made long and arduous journeys uphills and down dales, collecting folklore about these sages and philosophers so dear to his heart. As a result, he has gained such an intimate knowledge of the local milieus—historical relics, institutions, customs and folklore—that he can almost recount them one by one upon his fingers. The reason that he could produce his two creative works on Confucius and Mencius in such a rapid succession is simply because he had a rich store of knowledge at his command, to say nothing of his literary talent. As Mr. Kuang Yaming pointed out, in writing his *Life of Confucius*, Mr. Qu had time, place and people in his favour. I would say, the same is true of his writing of *Life of Mencius*.

In the sphere of Confucianism Mencius ranks second only to its founder Confucius; hence posterity looks up to him as the Second Sage. In the book *Mencius* he is quoted as saying, "I have not had the good fortune to have been a disciple of Confucius, I have learned indirectly from him through others." In the *Records of the Historian*, Mencius is said to have studied under a disciple of Zi Si; as Zi Si was Confucius' grandson, so he may be counted as Confucius' disciple fourth removed. After Confucius' death, few people were able to carry forward his thought and theory in spite of the fact that he had so many disciples in his lifetime. By the Warring States period, Confucianism had been in a fair way to decline, so much so that, to quote from Mencius, "The teachings current in the Empire are those of either the school of Yang or the school of Mo Di." Undaunted by such a grim situation, Mencius, who avowed himself to be an orthodox follower of Confucius, came forward to repudiate Yang Zhu and Mo Di while at the same time expounding the thought and theory of Confucius, thereby drawing a large following to him. He went lobbying among the feudal princes, sometimes going so far as to criticize and reprimand them to their faces as if he alone had the last word to say on any problem at issue. We have every reason to believe that it was precisely because Mencius inherited and further developed Confucius' thought and theory that the banner of Confucianism was not laid down and that Confucianism could hold its own without being crowded out by the many schools of thought that had one after another emerged on the philosophical scene.

Mencius was confronted with a much more difficult and grim situation than Confucius had been when the feudal rulers of the bigger states competed with one another in a race for hegemony while the rulers of the lesser states could do nothing more than keep themselves and their people out of harm's way. Faced with such a situation, Mencius should go and preach his doctrine of following the examples of the former kings and of practising benevolence and righteousness. This cannot but be regarded as impractical, not to say pedantic. Such is Sima Qian's comment on Mencius in his *Records* when he describes about his life: "This was the time when Qin was employing Lord Shang to enrich the state and strengthen the army, Chu and Wei were employing Wu Qi to defeat their weaker enemies, King Wei and King Xuan of Qi were employing men like Sun Bin and Tian Ji, while all the other states turned east to pay homage to Qi. The whole empire was divided into alliances with or against Qin and fighting was held in high regard. Mencius, who spoke of the virtues of Yao and Shun and the Three Dynasties, could not get on with these rulers." Thus, throughout his life, Mencius only managed to tour through the states like Qi, Wei, Song and Teng and it was impossible for him to realize his political ideal of bringing the whole empire to peace and order in the end. He had to retire to Zou, his homeland, where he spent his last years, expounding the *Book of Songs* and *Book of Documents*, transmitting the teachings of Confucius and, with Wan Zhang and other disciples, collecting his sayings into seven books, known to history as the *Mencius*.

In political practice, Mencius may not have accomplished anything worthy of note, but this can in no way detract from him as a great philosopher. His teachings in the *Mencius* exert far-reaching and important influence on later generations, even though they contain certain ideas which cannot be considered positive. Although his philosophy is tinged heavily with idealism, sometimes bordering on mysticism, yet it nurtured and encouraged many people with noble ideals and high aspirations over the past ages. To this day not a few of his sayings have been cherished by the Chinese people as the golden rule.

Benevolent government forms the corner-stone of Mencius' political philosophy. There is no denying the fact that his theory of benevolent government is based on the class viewpoint, that is, "There are those who use their minds and there are those who use their muscles. The former rule; the latter are ruled," (*Teng Wen Gong* Part I) and "There will be men in authority and there will be the common people. Without the former, there will be none to rule over the latter; without the latter, there will be none to support the former." (*ibid*) It is true, such a viewpoint is not without its justification when humanity entered upon its initial period of civilization, with different classes coming into being; but unfortunately it played into the hands of all the subsequent exploiting classes which used this theory to justify their rule. However, Mencius' theory of benevolent government still contains things that hold true for all times. For instance, his thesis on the important role of the common people. He points out, "The people are of supreme importance; the altars to the gods of earth and grain come next; last comes the ruler." (*Jin Xin* Part II) This, of course, is not to say that the people must necessarily be more important than the ruling prince but that the ruling prince must take the people fully into account. What Mencius actually means by this is that to distinguish a benevolent government from a tyrannical one, the ultimate criterion should be whether or not the ruler can ensure that "his people always have sufficient food in good years and escape starvation in bad." (*King Hui of Liang* Part I) In his interview with King Hui of Liang, Mencius demanded of the king, "What is the point of mentioning the word 'profit'?" We must not take him to mean that he is opposed to all profits and gains without discrimination; what he is opposed to is the fact that a ruler should seek profits at the expense of the people, such as waging war on neighbouring states, exacting heavy tax from his people etc., etc. According to him, "There is a way to win the Empire; win the people and you will win the Empire." On the contrary, "If a ruler ill-uses his people to an extreme degree, he will be murdered and his state annexed; if he does it to a lesser degree, his person will be in danger and his territory reduced. Such rulers will be given the posthumous names of 'You' (benighted) and "Li' (tyrannical)." (*Li Lou* Part I) From this Mencius further propounds his point of argument that the relationship between the ruler and his subjects is determined by how the former treats the latter, to wit, "If a prince treats his subjects as his hands and feet, they will treat him as their belly and heart. If he treats them as his horses and hounds, they will treat him as a stranger. If he treats them as mud and weeds, they will treat him as an enemy." (*ibid*) Hence, there is no absolute or permanent rule for any ruler on the throne. If the ruler practises no benevolence and if he ill-uses his subjects, then his subjects will have the right to disown him as their sovereign. And that is why when King Xuan of Qi asked Mencius "Is regicide permissible?" his answer was "A man who mutilates benevolence is a mutilator, while one who cripples righteousness is a crippler. He who is both a mutilator and a crippler is an 'outcast'. I have indeed heard of the punishment of the 'outcast Zhou', but I have not heard of any regicide." (*King Hui of Liang* Part II) The meaning implied is obvious. Implicit in this oblique answer of Mencius is indeed a veiled threat to the feudal ethical code so much sanctified by the Confucians themselves. No wonder that Zhu Yuan Zhang, the founder of the Ming Dynasty, once he was firmly in the saddle, hastened to have the concerned text of the *Mencius* bowdlerized in every possible way by his Confucians-ministers. For an ancient philosopher of Mencius' calibre, it is indeed worthwhile to write something about him.

But it is more difficult to write of the life of Mencius than the *Life of Confucius*, since Confucius enjoys greater reputation than does Mencius and there exist documents and materials galore about his life and deeds; even in the *Records of the Historian*, the pages devoted to the life of Confucius are several dozen times more than those devoted to Mencius; and there is no lack of books on Confucius by later generations, either. Not so in the case of Mencius, however. Today, the only authentic material available for the writing of his biography can be found chiefly in the book *Mencius* itself, which records mainly Mencius' disputations with different characters; there are seldom dramatic events mentioned there (as is the case of Confucius) for the development of a good story. Be that as it may, it is significant for Mr.

Qu to portray Mencius as a man with a strong sense of justice, who always stood by the interests of the people and attached importance to their role as material goods producers; a man whose moral courage induced him to criticize the ruling princes without any scruple, so much so that his scathing remarks made one of his victims so embarrassed that he "looked to the right and left, and spoke of other matters." In all this, it can be said that the author has captured the spirit of the man. Furthermore, Mr. Qu can make a good use of the various literary devices, such as imagination, montage and exaggeration, to characterize Mencius as an eloquent speaker with a propensity for disputation, and the book is thus made highly readable. I think, therefore, this *Life of Mencius* will receive a warm reception from the readership just as its companion-piece *Life of Confucius* does.

Yuan Shishuo
April 20,1992

Contents

CONTENTS

CONTENTS

Chapter One

Champion of Justice Mengsun Rescues a Man in Peril; Greedy by Nature Fu Puren Amasses Ill-Gotten Wealth

Legend has it that along the east side of the broad highway leading from the capital of the State of Lu to the capital of the State of Zou there stretched a mountain chain of medium height and breadth which meandered from south to north for some ten *li**. With its nine towering peaks of similar shape, ranged at almost equal distances from each other along the ridge, the mountain resembled nine huge dragons flying south, their heads raised in the air. Hence the local people called it Nine-Dragon Mountain.

On its western side, close to the highway, was a hillock shaped like a saddle, known locally as Saddle Hill. Nestled at the foot of this hill to the west was a community of some hundred households called Wild Duck Village.

At the western end of the village stood an imposing, spacious courtyard with walls of rammed earth. Inside was a tall locust tree with a mass of branches and leaves. It was early autumn in 382 B.C., and the leaves of the tree were beginning to turn yellow.

The door opened and out came a young woman of 24 or so. With a slim figure and fine, delicate features, she looked anything but common, despite her coarse attire. She gazed at the sun sinking in the west, shading her eyes with one hand as she did so. She heaved a long sigh, and her face clouded over with anxiety.

The woman was surnamed Zhang, and she was the wife of Mengsun Ji. The latter, being of the Mengsun clan, was related to the eminent family of the Duke of Lu. The woman was waiting anxiously for the return of her husband, who had been out the whole day.

At the moment Ji was on his way home, walking briskly, his heart full of expectation. He had been to the capital of the State of Zou, where he had been collecting rent from his tenants. With five *yi*** of

---

* *Li*, a Chinese unit of length, equal 1/2 kilometre.
** *Yi*—ancient measure of gold, approximately equivalent to 24 ounces.

fine gold nestling in his bosom, he hastened his pace, all the while figuring in his mind how he would spend it. Once out of the city gate, he headed north, and having covered about six *li*, he found himself in a big market place. There his attention was drawn to an imposing mansion by the roadside. Massive stone-paved steps led up to a lofty arch over a gateway, presenting a sharp contrast to the sordid dwellings of the common people in the vicinity. It was the house of Fu Puren.

Just at that moment a piercing cry, as of somebody suffering great pain, came faintly to his ears. He listened for a moment and soon discovered that it came from the backyard of Fu's house. As he popped his head in over an opening in the wall there appeared before his eyes the horrible scene of a big fellow bound to the trunk of a tall locust tree, his body covered with wounds, bruises and bloodstains.

Fu Puren, aged 40, dressed in silks and satins, was shouting commands to his servants in a most ferocious manner, every inch of his brutal face working convulsively.

"Beat him! beat him! Beat him to death!" he shouted.

Four fierce-looking underlings, whips in hand, each in his turn did as he was ordered. Whack! whack! Whack! Whipping after whipping was administered to the victim.

"Stay your hand!" yelled Ji. He was consumed with righteous indignation.

This command, coming as if out of the blue, had a stunning effect on both servants and master. The thugs desisted for a moment and stared agape at the intruder. Fu, after he recovered from his surprise, stalked up to Mengsun Ji and addressed him arrogantly:

"Mr. Mengsun, I beg your pardon," he said. "Have I ever done anything wrong, to have you poke your nose into my business? What concern is this of yours?" A cynical smirk played about his lips.

"What wrong has he done to you, I should like to know?" Ji retorted in a stern voice, full of the force of justice, and pointing an accusing finger at the bullies. "Why beat him so hard as if you want to kill him? This is sheer murder!"

"He let ten of my slaves escape," said Fu, shrugging his shoulders in disdain. "And I asked him to pay for my loss, but he couldn't afford to, so I am punishing him. Isn't that fair?"

Without much ado, Ji thrust his right hand inside his jacket for the ten pounds of gold there.

"How much did you pay for the ten servants when you bought

them?" Ji demanded.

"Five *yi* of fine gold," was the reply.

"You can have this five *yi* if you let the man go. How's that?"

"You really mean it?" Fu responded eagerly.

"What is said cannot be unsaid," said Ji loudly. "A gentleman never goes back on his word."

"In that case, will you be kind enough to hand over the sum as promised?" Fu drawled out the words contemptuously as he held out his hand for the money.

"Take it!" Ji tossed the packet of gold to Fu.

Fu caught the packet in both hands, and taking an ingot out of it examined it closely.

"Mr Mengsun is indeed a generous man," Fu said to himself. "One must say that for him."

Ji gave Fu a withering glance, which made the latter wince. Immediately Fu waved his hand to his servants with the command: "Let Gongsun Bengzhen go free!"

Gongsun Bengzhen hobbled painfully over to Mengsun Ji and fell to his knees. "Thank you for your timely rescue, Mr. Mengsun," he gasped.

Mengsun invited Gongsun to his home to recuperate; but the latter declined with thanks and staggered away.

Back home, Mengsun told his wife all that had happened. She felt greatly relieved.

"It was very noble of you to save Gongsun Bengzhen from being murdered by those ruffians," she said affectionately. "You could not have made a better use of the five *yi* of gold.

"But our plan to enlarge our house will have to be dropped for the time being, I'm afraid," said Mengsun, not without a sense of guilt, "now that the five *yi* is gone."

"'As long as the green hills are there, one need not worry about firewood,' as the saying goes," said Zhang with a smile, trying to comfort her husband. "Since you are in good health and I'm good at needlework what is there to prevent us from making more money in the days to come? There's no need to worry, my dear."

It was getting dark. Zhang lit the oil lamp. Then she brought the bronze washbasin filled with warm water to her husband for him to wash, as supper was ready.

At the supper table Mengsun Ji suddenly enquire about their son

Meng Ke.

"S—sh!" Zhang made a gesture to silence him, and lowered her voice: "He has been running around all day and is now sound asleep in his room."

She had hardly finished speaking when her son stealthily slipped out of his room in the west wing of the house. He was only three years old, round-faced and large-eyed, quite an attractive boy. He tiptoed up behind his father and threw his arms around him.

"Daddy! Here I am," he piped aloud with a giggle.

Turning round, Mengsun Ji lifted Meng Ke up, holding him close to his breast, and kissed him on both cheeks.

"Were you thinking of your Dad?" he asked.

"Yes, I was," replied Meng Ke straightaway, his large, intelligent eyes dancing with childish delight.

"Where, eh?" teased his father.

"In my heart," said Meng Ke. His right hand first went to his chest. Then on second thoughts, he shifted it to point to his head. "No. In my brain."

"My darling child," Mengsun Ji gave Meng Ke a warm, lingering kiss. "How I love you!"

Suddenly Meng Ke grew serious and made as if he were going to interrogate his father: "Well, what about the toys you promised to buy for me?"

This sudden question caught the father quite unprepared, and for a time he did not know what to say. Under his son's yearning gaze he was overwhelmed with a deep sense of shame as a father who had failed to fulfill his paternal duty.

His wife cast him a glance of mild reproach. "See how thoughtless you are! Call yourself a father!" she said.

"Forgive your dad, son," he said to Meng Ke. "Next time I won't forget. I give you my word."

Meng Ke gave a grudging nod, his eyes already filling with tears of disappointment. Then his father pulled him into his lap and caressed him until the boy smiled.

After supper Mengsun suddenly felt weak in all four limbs, while a draft of autumn wind from outdoors made him shiver and threw him into a fit of coughing. His wife thought that he must have caught a cold due to a change of weather. So she hastened to prepare worm wood and ginger soup, which, it was believed, was a cure for a cold.

The medicine, however, proved of no avail, and the next day Ji seemed to be getting worse. He coughed interminably. His wife felt uneasy. Then a famous doctor was sent for and expensive medicine taken. But a fortnight passed without the patient getting the least bit better. Zhang got into a panic and sought out her neighbor Old Fucheng for help. Fucheng enjoyed great popularity among his neighbors for his honest and upright character.

Fucheng's brows wrinkled the moment he saw the patient, and for a long while he could not bring himself to say anything. This was not lost on Zhang, sensitive and observant creature that she was. From then on, a heavy load weighed on her mind.

A month had elapsed and Mengsun's condition was going from bad to worse; he was emaciated, a mere shadow of his former self. Every time he coughed fresh blood could be detected in the phlegm and saliva he had thrown up. One night, he was found prostrate in bed, waxen-faced, his dull eyes expressing profound despair, looking at the blood-stained white silk handkerchief he held in his hand, by the dim light of the burning oil-lamp. He struggled to raise himself to a sitting position, but failed for lack of strength. Then, following a fit of coughing that seemed to rack his whole frame, his wife rushed in, all in a fluster, a bowl of steaming soup in her hands.

Ji shook his head ever so slightly and mouthed words with difficulty: "Help me to sit up, will you?"

Zhang set the bowl of soup on the window-sill, and gently helped her husband up by tucking a cotton quilt against his back.

"Do have some hot soup to ease your coughing, please," she said imploringly.

"I'm dying..." Ji passed the tip of his tongue over his parched, cracked lips and moaned. "Only I can't die content leaving you, mother and child, with no means of support."

"Don't let that worry you, please!" Zhang pleaded, tears welling in her eyes. Taking up the bowl again, she handed it to her husband. "Have some soup now," she pleaded.

The mere sight of the soup made him feel like retching, and he frowned in disgust. "I can't swallow a thing."

Two streams of tears flowed down her cheeks.

Another paroxysm of coughing seized Ji. Zhang laid down the bowl and picked up a handkerchief, with which she wiped his mouth.

Into it he disgorged a mouthful of blood, the effort of which left him panting and gasping.

"Quick! Bring Ke'er here," he gasped. "I want to have a look at him."

Zhang hurried to the west wing and came back with the boy in her arms. He was still sound asleep.

At the sight of his son, Mengsun Ji choked with sobs.

"My plan was for my son to get a good schooling," he said, amid sobs, "so that one day he might become a great scholar as learned and worldly-wise as Confucius—and that like Confucius he might become a great statesman who could bring peace and stability to the country and reflect glory on our ancestors. Now that I'm dying all my plans will come to nothing. Alas! Such is Heaven's will..." He continued amid sighs and groans: "We have no close relatives—neither the Mengsuns nor the Zhangs. And we have no family fortune, either. What is there for you, mother and child, to depend on for a living? How is it possible for you to carry on? Oh, my..." Upon this, he broke down in a flood of tears, desperately beating both his breast and the bed the while.

Zhang dabbed away her tears and tried hard to comfort her husband. "I can spin and weave to earn a living," she said. "Please rest assured that I can bring our son up all on my own."

At these words, a weak smile flitted across his face, but then suddenly he closed his eyes in a dead swoon.

After Zhang's repeated attempts to arouse her husband by loudly calling his name, he finally came round, only to relapse into unconsciousness again. And thus he remained the whole night and into the next day, in spite of a lot of fuss made over him. It was not until the next evening that he came round again, which made Zhang's heart rejoice immensely.

The moment Ji opened his eyes he glanced frantically around as if searching for something.

Zhang understood straightaway what this meant, and she immediately went to fetch their son Meng Ke, who was then playing under the locust tree in the courtyard. When the boy had been brought into his presence he put his arms around his son's neck and rubbed his cheek against the child's. While he seemed to have a world of things to tell, all he could manage to croak in his exhaustion were the words: "Ke'er...Dad...let..t..you...down...I for...got...to buy..." Suddenly his hands relaxed, his head jerked to one side, and life left him, his sunken eyes still brimming with tears.

Zhang wailed loud and long over the corpse of her husband, lamenting her bereavement which had come all to soon.

Having cried for a long while, she suddenly pulled herself together, as it occurred to her that she had to make arrangements for the funeral. At her request, the neighbors, including Old Fucheng, came to help. In time, the corpse was encoffined and a tiny plot somewhere in the valley between Nine-Dragon Mountain and Saddle Hill was selected for the burial site.

On the day of the funeral many of her neighbors came as mourners but soon left as the last shovelful of earth was scattered over the coffin. Widow and orphan, left alone, knelt in front of the hastily-heaped-up grave mound. They kowtowed, prayed and wept.

From the bare tree-tops came the mournful cawing of a solitary crow, which sent cold shivers down the spine. As Zhang looked up, she saw a young man coming up the path along the southern side of Saddle Hill. He was wearing a black silk gown and a pair of cloth shoes. As he drew near, he walked with a jaunty step twirling a twig in his hand, which he whisked this way and that. He stopped abruptly in front of Zhang with a whistle, shrill and lascivious.

Zhang turned away from him in disgust, and grabbing her son by the hand, tried to force her way past the stranger.

The young man, however, took a step forward and blocked her way. With a deep bow he said, "Here's Lang Xin with his heartfelt condolences, Madam."

Zhang returned his salutation, though rather reluctantly.

"Excuse me, Madam," He enquired, shifty-eyed, "but may I presume that this is Esquire Mengsun Ji's grave?"

"You may," was the matter-of-fact answer.

"In that case, you must be his wife, Madam Zhang, if I'm not mistaken?" queried Lang Xin in a facetious tone.

The woman preserved a stubborn silence.

Lang Xin began to prance about, his heart dancing with glee.

"I say, what a ravishing beauty! You're the Moon Goddess Chang'e come down to earth, I dare say!"

The man's flirtatious manner infuriated Zhang so much that, her eyes round with hatred, she gave an angry shake of her flowing sleeves, scooped up Meng Ke and stalked away.

Lang Xin quickened his steps to catch up with her. Shading his eyes, he pretended to commiserate: "'A good man seldom enjoys a long life', as the saying goes. Your late husband was a case in point. Alas! The pity of it! The pity of it!"

Without so much as turning her head, much less giving a word in reply, Zhang took a short cut and headed for home with all speed.

Flustered as she was, however, she made sure she was aware of the least movement that could spell danger to her. Once, as she looked around, she had a fleeting glimpse of a bulky, shadowy figure lurking in a juniper grove by the roadside. The man seemed to be watching her. Terror struck into her heart; she was forced to double her pace, even though Meng Ke in her arms impeded her progress.

All the while, Lang Xin kept up his chase after Madam Zhang. He stamped his foot from time to time as he ran, calling for her to stop and to listen to what he had to say, but Zhang paid not the least attention.

Safely home, Zhang lost no time in taking precautionary measures against intrusion, seeing that every door of her house was securely bolted. And by the time she got to seating herself on the bed she felt she was almost broken into pieces, what with fright and the dash homeward.

On reaching home, Meng Ke ran into the east room first and called for his father, but as soon as he found that the bed was empty, he burst into tears. "Daddy...Where are you?" he wailed, and then turned back and went straight to his mother, burying his face in her arms: "Mommy, where's Dad?" he damanded tearfully.

Grief-stricken, mother and son fell to sobbing together.

Dusk had fallen. Madam Zhang tucked Meng Ke, who was already fast asleep, into bed, and then went to light the oil-lamp. As she did so, she found herself looking into the bronze mirror on the dressing-table: Hair dishevelled, face wan and sallow, it was no longer the face of her old self. Stupefied, she looked and looked, and then pushed the mirror away with an unchanged blank expression on her face. As she leaned against the head of the bed, lost in thought, she seemed to see her husband come back to life again, with his tall, sturdy figure, handsome face, free-and-easy manner, and, to crown it all, a pair of bright and piercing eyes which, as usual, brightened up with tender love at the sight of his dear one. She closed her eyes, indulging herself in the memory of the beautiful past.

The day their baby Meng Ke came into the world the father held up the new-born baby with both hands, and, darting his caressing eyes all over the little thing, said to himself: "What a handsome baby! With his broad forehead and clear-cut features, he is sure to have a great future before him."

A sunlit and enchanting scene of spring. Birds sang and flowers sent forth delicate fragrances. In the front garden the fullblown roses were a riot of color, with butterflies fluttering around them. Two magpies danced and chattered on the branches of the locust tree. Madam Zhang was teaching her son Meng Ke how to walk. Face to face, hand in hand, she helped the toddler along as she moved back in step with him, two steps at a time, giving the count, "One, two, that's right! One, two, good! Try again, one, two..." Watching nearby, her husband could hardly contain himself. He stepped forward to take Meng Ke's hands. "Come on, let me have a try." This time Meng Ke succeeded in moving three steps all at once, to the great joy of his father, who lifted him up high over his head and turned him round and round. "Try and call me 'Daddy'. Do try!" he demanded of Meng Ke. It was only with much difficulty that Meng Ke at last enunciated "Dad-d-di". This threw Mengsun into a frenzy of joy. He rained kisses on his son's face, as he repeatedly muttered, "My darling boy! You can walk! And you know your dad too!

Carried away by this scene of domestic bliss in her mind's eye, Zhang broke into a smile in spite of herself. But soon she was brought back with a jolt to the harsh reality before her: The room was shrouded in complete darkness as the oil lamp had already burnt out, and from outside the window came the mournful sound of the autumn wind soughing in the trees. The thought of the imminent cold winter made her shiver inwardly.

Next morning a violent wind was howling; the locust tree in the courtyard was stripped almost bare of its leaves. Zhang was sweeping up the fallen leaves. She came to a standstill, gazing at the locust tree in a trance.

Meng Ke could be heard crying for his mother in the house. Getting no answer, his cries turned into shrieks. With a stifled sob, Zhang turned round to go back to the house, her eyes streaming with tears.

Meng Ke stood in front of the bed on which his father used to lie when ill. "Daddy! Daddy! Where are you?" he cried. Seeing his mother, he rushed forward and clasped her legs, wailing, "Mommy! Where's my daddy? I want my daddy!"

His mother gave him a tight hug and soothed him in every way she could until he quietened down.

Soon breakfast was ready. But no sooner had Meng Ke settled down than he sprang up. "I'll go and fetch the chopsticks," he said.

Back with three pairs of chopsticks, he started to lay them out on the table, lisping in his childish way the while: "These are for Daddy. These are for Mommy. And these are mine."

With tears gathering in her eyes, his mother said weakly and yet in a tone full of tenderness: "Darling, eat your breakfast, quick!"

Like the spoiled child that he usually was, he protested coyly: "No, I won't! Not before I see Daddy and Mommy eat theirs."

However much his mother tried to coax him, Meng Ke would not succumb to her entreaties. Finally, she had to lift him up and put him down on the heap of locust leaves in the courtyard, which she had just finished sweeping up.

There, Meng Ke mused a while before he started on a game of his own invention, which consisted in throwing up the golden leaves into the air by the armful, and then turning somersaults among them. He was so carried away by his game that he burst out into a series of inarticulate gasps and hiccoughs in sheer delight.

This brought some relief to the grieved heart of his mother, who had been watching him all the while. She had brought out her spinning wheel and, making an effort to cheer herself up, was now starting to work. As it so happened, this time the wheel did not work as smoothly as it usually did. It turned out uneven silken yarn, with one section coarse and thick, another too fine and flimsy. This went on for some time until at last she got impatient and gave the wheel one violent twist. The silken yarn snapped! She pushed the machine away from her and was just about to take up some other work when she heard someone knocking at the outside gate. Hurriedly she smoothed down her hair and gave her jacket and skirt a pat or two before she went to open it.

The gate opened to a smartly dressed Lang Xin, with his mouse-like eyes fixed on her in a lustful stare.

His sudden appearance threw her into a fluster; for a moment she did not know what to do.

Lang Xin stepped forward and bowed deeply, with an ingratiating smile on his face. "My gracious lady, please accept my respects," he wheedled.

Zhang was so utterly disconcerted that she had to support herself by gripping the doorpost. "You villain...!" she gasped.

Lang Xin, however, was by no means discountenanced. He hastened to interrupt, the same ugly smile on his face: "Come on, dearie, let's have a nice chat. No time like the present, you know."

Zhang could stand no more of such nonsense. She repulsed his advances by adopting a stern tone of voice: "You know I'm a widow," she said, "and as a widow I must keep my widowhood unsullied. Please behave yourself, for your own sake as well as for mine."

Lang Xin switched his tone to one of appeal. "My respectable lady," he said. "I've been so...so... overwhelmed by...since I saw you the other day on the outskirts. Could you be so cruel as to keep me outside your door this long? Oh, good lady, I beg you to let me in."

"No, I can't! I beg your pardon. Please go away!" With this she banged the door shut in his face.

The moment Lang Xin recovered from his surprise at the rebuff he went and knocked at the door over and over again.

Zhang rushed into her bedroom in a huff after she had bolted the door securely. She collapsed into a chair, paying no heed to the incessant knocking and calling from outside.

Fucheng, full of righteous indignation, stalked straight up to Lang Xin and upbraided the latter loudly.

"What do you think you are doing here? Making a row in front of a widow's house. Call yourself a man, do you? Disgraceful!" The people in the neighborhood all came flocking round when they heard the hubbub and when they learned what was going on they all joined in unanimous condemnation of Lang Xin, cursing him as a "snake" and a "beast", while praising Zhang as a "well-cultivated gentle lady" and a "chaste woman".

Finding himself completely isolated, Lang Xin beat a hasty retreat.

It was not until all had quietened down outside that Zhang heaved a long sigh of relief.

That night a northwest wind was blowing high and with ever-increasing force, while black clouds blotted out all the stars in the sky. Zhang, with her son Meng Ke in her arms, tried hard to get to sleep. But her blood-shot eyes hurt her like a bunch of needles, which added to her mental anguish; she simply could not get a wink of sleep. Fear struck into her heart whenever she recalled the ugly face of Lang Xin. She got up, taking care that Meng Ke was snugly covered, and went to inspect all the windows and doors for the last time before she lay down to sleep.

Outside the high mud wall which enclosed the house a figure prowled about, looking this way and that. A moment later he scurried to the foot of the wall, and, as if he had run out of wind, he tried to steady himself for a while before he jumped up in an attempt to climb over the wall and into the courtyard.

Simultaneously from behind the house emerged another figure, who, on approaching the wall, leaped in one bound to alight right on the hands of the former, which were clinging to the edge of the wall's top.

There was a yell of pain.

The newcomer, who was now standing erect on the top of the wall, demanded in a booming voice: "Who are you?"

The other, shaken, replied weakly: "I'm Lang Xin."

Upon this, the fellow roard with laughter, saying: "You deserved it! Lang Xin—that's what you are. You've got a wolf's heart.*"

"You're right. Perfectly right. The name fits me to a nicety. I'm no better than a wolf. But may I ask your name?"

"No more nonsense! Let me put this to you: Will you dare try any nasty tricks again?"

"Oh, no! No!"

The man set Lang's hands free, and so the latter fell on his back on the ground with a thud, accompanied by shrill cries of fright and pain.

Lang Xin struggled to his feet, and no sooner had he done so than he flopped on to his knees, asking further for mercy. "Spare me this once, sir. I won't dare commit wrongs any more."

"Don't let me see your ugly mug again. Or I'll smash you to smithereens. Now, get out of my sight!"

Crestfallen, Lang Xin slunk away without so much as looking back once.

While the above scene was being enacted Zhang had been sitting by her window listening. Every word exchanged by the two men had reached her ears distinctly. Every now and then she had peeped

---

* Lang Xin is Chinese homonym for "wolf's heart".

through the window to see how things would transpire. She had been wondering who could have been the chivalrous man who had come to save her in the nick of time, and it was not until the two men disappeared from view that she left her perch. The event further alerted her to the necessity of guarding herself. So, she made a further investigation of the windows and doors, ensuring once again that they were firmly bolted. Only after this did she lie down to sleep—fully clothed. But sleep would not come to her. As she stared long into the pitch darkness of the room all sorts of poignant feelings came rushing into her mind: loneliness, forlornness, bitterness and grief. She dared not picture to herself what the future might hold for her, and the hardships and privations she would have to go through. All the beautiful things she had once envisioned for herself had suddenly vanished like soap bubbles. She hugged her son closer, and yet closer —the only dear one she could count on in this world.

When Fu Puren learned about Mengsun Ji's death he called his servants into his presence.

"Bah! It served him right," Pu said gloatingly, an ugly smile playing around his lips. "Who asked him to meddle in my business? Showing off his generosity in front of me! Me of all people! Humph! Those who plot against me will certainly come to no good end. Now Mengsun Ji has died; doesn't this bear out what I say?"

"Your lordship," said one servant, trying to curry favor with his master, "I was told that the young gentleman Lang Xin has had his eye on the young widow for some time..."

Fu Puren wrinkled his brows irritably and rebuked the servant: "What has this to do with me?"

"Since your lordship has just now said," the servant continued, "that you were glad to hear the news of Mengsun Ji's death, why, you can't say it's no concern of yours."

"Don't beat about the bush," Fu grew impatient. "Say straight out what you want to say."

"Since Lang Xin is interested in the young widow," the servant cringed and smiled obsequiously and said, "you might as well act as a go-between, don't you think? Once the marriage tie is made, all her ties with the Mengsun family would have to be cut off and with both wife and son gone, the line of Mengsun family discontinued, wouldn't this be the best way to avenge yourself, sir?"

Fu Puren looked pleased for quite some time before he emitted an inarticulate plosive sound from his nose to express his appreciation.

"This is but advantage one..." the servant continued.

"What about the second, and the third?" Fu Puren grasped the servant by the shoulder and urged impetuously. "What are they? Go ahead, go ahead!"

The servant, very pleased with himself by now, cleared his throat with a little cough before saying: "Suppose you have succeeded in this match-making, you can be sure that Lang Xin will reward you handsomely in token of his gratitude."

"Excellent! Well, that is the second; Tell me the third, then?" Fu Puren grinned from ear to ear. He recalled to mind the liberal way Mengsun gave away his money the other day, and he tried to guess just how large a family fortune the man must have owned so that he could afford to be so generous with his money.

"That is all, sir!" The menial smiled sheepishly.

After a moment's reflection, Fu Puren told the servant to invite Lang Xin to come "for something urgent".

Before long, the servant returned with Lang Xin.

Lang Xin joined his hands together and raised them to his brow by way of curtsy, saying: "Here's Lang Xin's salute to Your Lordship!"

Fu Puren looked the young man over, calculating how much profit he could make out of the present deal.

"Don't stand on ceremony, Mr Lang," he said absent-mindedly. "Please be seated."

Lang Xin appeared quite ill at ease. He now pulled at the hem of his coat, now pulled down his sleeve in an effort to cover his hand, which was swollen.

Cunning and evil-minded as he was, Fu certainly knew where Lang's vulnerable spot lay. He squinted, with a sneering look in the corners of his eyes, and said knowingly: "You're looking pale. And in low spirits, too. Could you be ill?"

Lang Xin blushed to the roots of his hair and was tongue-tied for the moment.

Why make a pretence of innocence, you poor devil? thought Fu. See if I will not touch you to the quick! However, for the moment he only gave a smirk, and said probingly: "Surely you don't have something which it would be awkward for you to disclose?"

Lang Xin, guilt-stricken, was too timid to open his lips. All he did was hang his head and sigh.

Fu was bent on driving his victim to the wall, and so he pressed him further with the query: "Don't tell me you've something you want to hide from me?"

Lang Xin lifted his head slowly, but the moment he caught Fu's searching eyes he propmtly ducked his head again.

"Oh my!" Fu stood up impulsively. "You've got no manhood in you. What difficult situation, I wonder, could it be that gets you into such a pitiable state?"

His head still hanging down, Lang Xin summoned up enough courage to stammer out, "I'm badly smitten with Madam Zhang, a lovelorn fool am I."

"Who is this Madam Zhang?"

"The widow of Mengsun Ji in Wild Duck Village."

"A widow?" Fu broke into a guffaw. "I thought you might have taken a fancy to some maiden from a rich and distinguished family." He continued, drawing his chair forward, with his eyes fixed upon Lang. "Is she so attractive as to make you lose your head over her like this?"

"To be frank with you, I'm like a dead man, unable to bring myself to eat or to sleep for thinking of her. She's really a ravishing beauty, you know."

No sooner was this said than Lang Xin fell on his knees at the feet of Fu Puren, pleading earnestly: "Please use your prestige and influence to get this Zhang woman for me. I beseech you."

Fu threw his head back and said with dancing eyebrows and radiant face, "What's so difficult about that? I'm sure I can manage it. But what if I get this done for you..."

Lang Xin was overjoyed at this and immediately scrambled to his feet, saying, "Please give me your enlightened instructions. I promise that I will repay you with a handsome sum once my heart's desire is fulfilled."

Fu put his mouth near Lang's ear and said in a whisper: "You've only to...."

Lang, stupefied, said with trembling lips, "You don't mean..."

Fu gave a sweep of his hand in a gesture of impatience and said loudly: "Call yourself a man, do you? Remember what our ancestors taught us."

Lang looked blank.

Fu stamped his foot: "One who is not broad-minded enough

cannot be called a gentleman; one who dare not act relentlessly when occasion demands cannot be called a great man."

Lang stood nonplussed for a little while before it dawned on him what he was meant to do, and immediately he sallied forth.

He went straight to Wild Duck Village. People passing him all turned back to point accusing fingers at him; wherever he turned to look, he met only contempt and hatred. He felt like a rat running across the street when everybody cries, "Kill it." He had to cut and run to escape the hostility that was closing in on him.

Presently he came to the foot of a hill, with towering pine trees all around. He had never been here before. Curiosity led him on, until he came in view of a thatched cottage. He was just wondering who the owner of the house could be, when there came out a man, broad-shouldered and solidly built.

Coming out into the open, the man deftly picked up a pole with a single upward movement of his foot and at the same time flipped the dust off it with one hand. Then he started to practice martial arts: staff, sabre, spear, sword and stone-throwing. Now and then he would pick up a stone from the ground and aim it at a twig some 20 paces away, and would invariably hit his target every time.

The man's superb skill with weapons so impressed Lang Xin that he thought, with a sinking heart: If I were one day to fall into the hands of this fellow what would happen? No earthly chance for me to stay alive, that's for sure! Terror-stricken, he took to his heels and fled from the spot without more ado.

It was getting dark. At first he intended to make straight for home. Yet Zhang's image kept haunting him, and before he realized where he was heading, he found himself already at the foot of the wall around the Mengsun family courtyard. Quickly he stretched up his hands to the top of the wall. As he did so, there flashed into his mind the terrible scene of his hands being crushed under the feet of the hefty fellow that day. So he quickly withdrew his hands. He hesitated a bit but in the end his bestial instinct overpowered him, and with a defiant air he clambered up onto the top of the wall.

Chapter Two

Influenced by an Unwholesome Environment,
Meng Ke Neglects His Studies;
Concerned About Her Son's Education,
Madam Zhang Moves House Three Times

When Lang Xin had clambered onto the top of the wall of the Mengsun house he squatted there, trembling with fear, like a mouse that has ventured out of its hole. With a quick glance around, he made sure that nobody had noticed him and, congratulating himself that he was safe, was about to jump down inside the courtyard, when, all of a sudden, a stone hit him right on the shoulder. Frightened out of his wits, he fell headlong to the ground outside. He scrambled up, feeling at the same time that there was something about his face hotly clammy to the touch. Then he realized he had bruised himself in the fall. He was dazed for a moment. Then fear seized him as he thought of the hefty fellow practicing marksmanship in the pine grove. He started to run for all he was worth.

Meanwhile, Madam Zhang was preoccupied with weaving by the light of an oil lamp. Completely oblivious of everything that happened in the outside world, she worked day and night, spinning and weaving, in order to earn a living for the family.

She began to teach her son Meng Ke to read and write. The boy was clever and quick to learn. He was gifted with a good memory, too. His mother cherished him as the apple of her eye. Every now and then she would put down her work and take up the coaching of her son in reading and writing. This continued without interruption for six years, until Meng Ke reached nine years of age.

One day, while Zhang was at her wheel under the locust tree in the courtyard, there came to her ears the sound of string and wood-wind instruments. At that moment Meng Ke was at his daily lesson his mother had assigned him, but as soon as he heard the music he jumped up from his seat and ran out of the courtyard gate before his mother had time to stop him.

On the main street a funeral procession was moving at a slow

pace, with trumpeters and drummers leading the way, followed by a group of mourners who were wailing and weeping without letup.

Meng Ke shuttled back and forth among the crowd of people lining both sides of the street. He was just like a little bird who has left his nest for the first time; everything in the outside world struck him as strange and intriguing. But what most stimulated his curiosity were the wind instrument players and drummers, who looked so comical as they played away on their instruments. His eyes darted from one instrument to another, as he tried to mimic all manner of expression and action on the part of the players. Presently he spotted a stick on the ground right before him; he dashed forward and picked it up. He put it to his mouth and pretended to blow it after the manner of the musicians. The procession had by now reached the cemetery on the outskirts. The coffin was lowered into the vault and a mound of earth heaped over the tomb. The ceremony over, the people got ready to leave.

All this time a curious Meng Ke had been watching from the sidelines. He was so fascinated by the proceedings that long after the last mourners had departed, he was still there playing away on his make-believe flute. He did not turn to go home until darkness fell.

Meanwhile, his mother had been waiting anxiously for him. When at last she saw him running in she was at the same time relieved and displeased. "Where have you been?" she asked him.

Instead of an answer Meng Ke put his stick to his mouth and pretended to play it in a funeral procession, humming at the same time an air which he had just learned at the funeral.

"That's no profession for you to follow, my boy!" scolded his mother, putting on a stern face. "I forbid it! Do you hear? Now come and wash and have your dinner."

Next morning, as soon as he had had breakfast, Meng Ke collected three of his young friends from the village and went for a jaunt to the graveyard on the outskirts. Once there, he lined them up.

"Let's play at funeral processions," he said to his playmates. "First, go and get a stick, each of you."

The three boys did as they were ordered, thinking it would be great fun. "Let's lay out the four sticks in the form of a square," Meng Ke said.

He climbed a cypress tree and knocked off a thicker stick, which he placed on the square to represent a coffin. This was to be the bier.

He adopted a dignified pose, and went through the motions of playing the *yu* (an ancient wind instrument) and the flute, imitating the various sounds he thought the instruments might produce. Then he issued the order: "Shoulder the bier!"

The three youngsters promptly obeyed.

"Let's move in step. Put forward your left foot first. Ready? One, two...."

At that, the kids laughed aloud.

"Stop laughing!" Meng Ke put on a serious air and tried to act like a strict disciplinarian. "A funeral is no laughing matter. You may weep or sob, but not laugh."

The three were intimidated into silence.

"Come, let's get a move on with the coffin. I'll play the music and you three start wailing." said Meng Ke.

"Wailing for whom?" one of them asked.

"Can't you wail for Dad and Mom?" retorted Meng Ke.

They marched round and round the graveyard with that symbolic bier of theirs on their shoulders, wailing and sniggering for quite a while, until they had had enough fun. Finally Meng Ke picked up bits of stone, grass stalks and what not, with which he taught his friends about the sacrificial rites performed in front of the grave, such as the laying out of sacrificial offerings, burning incense, making obeisance and kowtowing.

From that day on, almost every day Meng Ke went to the graveyard to play. Whenever there was a funeral he had the most wonderful time.

One morning mother and son, seated on the floor as was the custom in those days, were taking their simple breakfast.

"A penny for your thought!" Zhang said, knitting her brows. "Come on, eat up your breakfast."

As Meng Ke took up his bowl and was about to take his first mouthful, a boy outside the door was heard calling, "Meng Ke, are you coming out to play?"

"Yes!" Meng Ke responded eagerly, and after stuffing a handful of rice into his mouth, immediately hurried out, notwithstanding his mother's exhortation not to.

The four youngsters walked to a grave on a hillside. Meng Ke placed there little piles of stones in front of the grave. Then he stood there mumbling to himself: "This is the pork, this is the mutton and this is the beef..." Then he fetched three grass stalks and addressed his companions loftily: "Here are the joss-sticks. Come, let me teach you how to burn incense. He made a deep bow to the grave and inserted the three grass stalks in the earth in front of it. Then something suddenly occurred to him. He slapped his forehead and cried, "There's no wine! What's to be done?"

One of the boys suggested that they use water as a substitute for the wine, which they did. Then came the time for the solemn sacrificial rites.

"Watch how I go about it." Meng Ke first raised both hands breast-high with the supposed wine vessel held in them, then knelt down and sprinkled the water on the ground, telling his playmates to watch carefully. "That was what is called 'presenting the sacrificial wine'. Do you understand?" he asked as he rose to his feet.

The three boys nodded.

"Now it's your turn. Go and fetch your wine. Rehearse the things I've taught you."

They did so one after another, and in deadly earnest.

Zhang, who had been watching from afar, said to herself: "This is no place for my child. It's time I moved house."

Unhappy, she returned home. As she stood in front of the family shrine, she thought long and hard but could find no way out of her present plight. Then the idea struck her that she might consult her eastern neighbor, Fucheng. So she went over there.

On hearing her knock, Fucheng hastened to open the door. When he saw it was Zhang he expressed a warm welcome to her and asked her in. After some small talk Zhang came straight to the point.

"Uncle Fucheng, I've come to ask for your help in some petty concern of mine. Please do me a favor," she said.

"Believe me, I'll do whatever I can to help you. Tell me what it is," was the enthusiastic response of the old man.

"As you know," she said, "there are so many graves in this area. And my son..."

"Graves? Why, surely you don't have a superstitious fear of ghosts and spirits?" retorted the old man with a merry twinkle in his eyes.

"Nothing of the sort," Zhang shook her head. "My concern is about my son. His mind is full of funerals and burial rites. If he goes on like this, what chance is there for him to make a serious study of the six classical arts?* That's my worry."

"So that's how it is," said Fucheng, stroking his white beard thoughtfully. "But what do you think you ought to do about it?" he asked by way of reply.

"I'm thinking about moving away from here."

"Where to?"

"That's what I came here to ask you about. I'd like you to help find a place where the environment is wholesome for my son's education," Zhang requested tentatively. "Would you help me with this?"

"Sure, sure! By all means!" said Fu, smiling. "Young people can be influenced by close association with bad company. I'll certainly help you."

"Thank you, Uncle Fucheng," Zhang said. "Now please come with me and see for yourself how it is."

Somewhat puzzled, Fucheng followed her to the outskirts of the village.

"Look over there," she said, pointing to the four youngsters who were deeply engrossed in playing among the graves.

Fucheng strained his eyes to look in the direction she was pointing in. He uttered a long sigh before saying, "I see what you mean. Tomorrow I'll go and find a new house for you without fail."

"Thank you ever so much, Uncle," said Zhang with a deep bow.

After a moment of deep thought, Fucheng asked, "But this present house of yours is a legacy from past generations. Can you bear the thought of giving it up? 'It's hard to part with one's nest, be it ever so humble', as the saying goes."

"We may lose something here, but we can make up for it elsewhere," replied Zhang, her eyes moist with tears. "So long as I can keep my son out of harm's way and bring him up properly, with a good education, I won't care however great a loss I have to sustain."

Fucheng nodded his full appreciation. "Yes, I can understand a mother's love. Be assured, I'll do my level best to help."

Once again Zhang thanked him profusely before she took her leave.

At home she washed her hands and then burned incense, offered wine and kowtowed before the family shrine, praying to her ancestors

---

* The six classical arts were rites, music, archery, riding, writing and arithmetic.

for blessings for her son.

A few days later Fucheng dropped in to tell her that his entrusted task of finding a house for her had been accomplished.

"When would you like to go and have a look at it?" he asked.

"No need," replied Zhang. "I fully appreciate how kind you have been to us, mother and son, all this time. And you're well aware, too, why it is necessary for us to move house, so I'm sure the new house must be good, all things considered."

"The house is on the bank of a river, with a market in the neighborhood. It will be handy for you to sell the cloth you make in exchange for silk, won't it?" Fucheng said, with a self-satisfied air. "Besides, the price is reasonable."

"How much is it?" Zhang inquired.

"Five yi of fine gold,"

"I wonder how much this old house of mine can fetch," queried Zhang.

Fucheng cast a glance around the room, and went out into the courtyard for a further scrutiny of the whole building before coming back and saying confidently: "This is a high-walled house. I would say it would fetch six yi of gold at least."

"If so, I'd trouble you to sell it for me at once," responded Zhang eagerly.

"That's easily done. I'll see to it," Fucheng said.

Before three days were over a jubilant Fucheng rushed into Zhang's house to announce that a bargain had been made with Fu Ren, a man who lived nearby. Fu Ren had offered seven yi for the house, which Zhang accepted only too readily.

"There's still one more thing I'd trouble you about, Uncle," said Zhang, pointing to her loom, spinning wheel and other odds and ends, which had been bound up with ropes. "I've had all these packed up. If you're free tomorrow, I wonder if you can bring your cart to help transport them?"

"No problem. No problem!" Fucheng laughed pleasantly. "I'll come over with the cart first thing to-morrow morning. Set your mind at ease."

Early the next morning, when the rising sun had just gilded the eastern horizon, Zhang, with sacrificial offerings in one hand and holding Meng Ke's hand in the other, arrived at Mengsun's grave. She took the beef, mutton and meat out of a wicker basket and laid them out in front of the tombstone. Then she lit three incense sticks, sprinkled the wine on the grave and intoned a prayer amid sobs:

"My dear husband, here I am, praying on my knees to you. Today we're leaving our ancestral home, not because we have the heart to leave it but because we have to. If only you could understand how hard it is for us to leave it! However, I must think of our son's education." Having said this, she broke down in a flood of tears. She scooped up handfuls of earth, trying to fill up some cavities in the grave mound left by wind and rain. Then she called to Meng Ke: "Come and kowtow to your daddy!"

This was quite in the boy's line, since he had practiced it often over the previous few days with his playmates. Thus he did it in style, and in good taste, too. Even his mother had to smile through her tears.

On leaving, Zhang addressed the grave: "My husband, your son and I will come back regularly to offer sacrifices to you. May your soul rest in peace."

Back home she found that the cart had been loaded and was ready to start off. She thanked Fucheng and her other neighbors for their help, and climbed up onto the cart with her son.

At the last moment Meng Ke's three playmates hurried up to say farewell, crying out their best wishes as they ran after the retreating cart. "Remember our friendship, Meng Ke! Come back and play with us whenever you have time."

With tears in his eyes, Meng Ke could only manage to nod his head repeatedly without saying a thing.

The new house was an ordinary looking thatched cottage with three rooms. A short walk away was the river. When the cart rolled up to the gate Fucheng reined in the horse, and pointing to the padlocked door, said, "Here's your new abode."

After a brief inspection of the premises, Zhang smiled with satisfaction.

Fucheng, together will the neighbors whom he had asked in to help to fetch and carry, now came up to say good-bye to Zhang. She asked him to stay to lunch, but the old man declined graciously. "It's going to be a busy day for you," he said with a smile. "I had better hurry back. I'll come and see you soon."

Zhang saw Fucheng to the door, where she waited until he had climbed on to the seat of the cart and driven off.

When she came back she started to unpack, and was thinking of decorating her room when it occurred to her that it was time to prepare lunch. She called her son, but there was no answer. She looked here, there and everywhere, but still there was no sign of him. In her anxiety she thought nothing of her personal appearance and rushed out into the street just as she was.

The market place by the riverside was a-buzz with activity. Small traders, hawkers and pedlars of every description were doing a brisk trade. Meng Ke darted from one group of people to another, wherever heated haggling was going on. At one place he stood transfixed, watching, while two donkey dealers were busily engaged in a negotiation, talking in a language he could make no sense of, and making secret signs either by winks or by counting on their fingers. What strange people! How funny all this is, he thought.

With quick, short steps, Zhang hurried up. When she caught sight of Meng Ke among the crowd she called out, "Ke! you frightened me to death, you naughty boy!"

"Mom, just look at them," the boy said in an excited whisper, pointing at the two donkey dealers and turning a deaf ear to his mother's scolding.

Zhang snatched his hand and dragged him all the way home.

Back home Zhang gave her son a tight hug, pleading with him: "Ke, we've just moved here. The place and people are both new to us. From now on you mustn't run around, remember!"

"I'm listening. New place, yes... Not run around..." echoed Meng Ke absent-mindedly.

Zhang hastily made up the bed and put Meng Ke in it. By the time she had got dinner ready she found he had already gone to sleep. Her eyes rested on the spirit tablet to Mengsun Ji, which was yet to be placed in the shrine, and all sorts of bitterness came rushing into her mind.

It was a considerably large town where the Mengsun family had moved, some 20 *li* from the capital of the state of Zhou. Densely populated, the town enjoyed the reputation of being a commercial center, where fairs and festivals were a common occurrence. At all these events Meng Ke would go sightseeing and have great fun.

One day he was so infatuated by the killing of hogs he had witnessed in a slaughter-house that soon after he came home he made a small pig out of mud. He used a piece of wood for a knife and applied it to the neck of the model pig. Pretending that he was applying great force, he imitated the squealing of a pig being slaughtered.

At this, Zhang put down her needlework and hastened out into the courtyard to find out what the noise was. What she saw greatly upset her. The promise she made to her husband on his death-bed reverberated in her mind like a thunder: "You can rest at ease that I'll bring him up to be a respectable man without fail." She then broke down, weeping uncontrollably.

Waking up next morning, Meng Ke went straight to the window-sill to gaze at the little mud pig, which was supposed to be a dead pig drying in the sun.

On noticing this, Zhang said to herself: "This is no place for my son. We cannot afford to stay here any longer."

After breakfast Zhang took Meng Ke along the main street, her eyes darting from one house to another, until they came to a school at the western end of the street. The voices of children reading their lesson attracted Meng Ke's attention. He broke away from his mother, and ran up and peered through a crack in the door.

The schoolmaster was teaching the pupils the following text:

"The Master says, 'It is indeed a pleasure to acquire knowledge and, as you go on acquiring it, to put into practice what you have acquired. A greater pleasure still is when friends of congenial minds come from afar to seek you because of your attainments. But he is truly a wise and good man who feels no discomposure even when he is not noticed by other men.'"

Although Meng Ke had no idea what all it this meant, his memory was such that he could repeat it all afterwards without a single slip. Thus, on his way back, he recited as he went: "The Master says...."

Zhang's knitted brows smoothed out and her heart burst with joy.

From that day on, whenever there was time, she would take Meng Ke to the school neighborhood to play, and Meng Ke himself would stand outside the window of the schoolroom, listening, every time there was a reading lesson. As time went on Meng Ke was able to recite many of Confucius sayings by heart. This gladdened Zhang beyond words, and she decided to move her house to the vicinity of the school, which she did only after much effort.

The new house consisted of three rooms in a row flanked by two wings, one on the east, the other on the west. It was spring; the courtyard presented a radiant scene with the peach and apricot trees just in bud. On the first day of their moving in, Zhang started to put her plan into action of sending her son to the school. She decided on the sixth day of the third lunar month—an auspicious date to her thinking—to carry out her plan. It happened to be a fine day. The weather was mild, with a gentle spring breeze blowing and swallows flying high in the sky. Wearing brand-new clothes, one hand in his mother's, Meng Ke stood quietly outside the classroom, waiting for the moment when class was over and they could approach the teacher.

The door opened, and the schoolmaster Zeng Xun, aged 50, came out. On seeing mother and son, he asked with a puzzled air: "What's this...?"

Zhang gave him a deep bow and, pointing to Meng Ke, said, "This is my son Meng Ke. And I came here today to humbly ask that he might be admitted as a pupil to your school."

Zeng Xuan looked Meng Ke up and down. "How old is he?" he asked.

"I'm nine years old," Meng Ke cut in before his mother could answer for him.

Zeng Xun shook his head: "Too young, too young. Better wait two more years."

Zhang hastened to explain, "But his is a particular case, sir. Young as he is, he is very intelligent."

"For example...?"

"The other day we passed here. You, Sir, happened to be giving the first lesson in the Confucian Analects. What surprised me was that he learned everything he heard by heart immediately and later could repeat it straight off."

Much impressed by this, Zeng Xuan beamed broadly and encouraged Meng Ke to recite what he had learned.

Thereupon, Zhang gave an encouraging pat to Meng Ke's shoulder. "Ke, do you hear? Recite what you learned that day. What did Confucius teach us, eh?"

Meng Ke shot the teacher a timid glance, then turned to look at his mother for a moment before reciting in a clear voice the whole text which he had memorized.

Zeng Xuan nodded his head repeatedly to show his appreciation. "Nicely done! Nicely done!" he praised the boy. "But do you understand the meaning of the text?"

"Yes, I do," replied Meng Ke, very sure of himself. "It means that it is a very delightful thing to review what the teacher teaches us from time to time; a greater pleasure is to meet a friend who comes from afar; and that one might be called a gentleman in the true sense of the word if he doesn't resent the fact that his true worth is not immediately recognized by others."

Zeng Xuan was taken aback at Meng Ke's fluent paraphrasing of the text, and commented with the word "Wonderful" several times. Then, holding back a smile for a moment, he hesitated a bit in forming his words: "But I never explained the text that day, did I? How did you get to know all that?"

"Mom taught me," was the proud answer.

Zeng Xuan joined his hands together in a gesture of approbation and said heartily: "All right. I'll make an exception in your case by accepting you as my pupil."

Zhang bowed her thanks and made her son perform the obeisances such an occasion called for.

Meng Ke fell to his knees and kowtowed. "Your disciple Meng Ke here offers his thanks," he said with emotion.

"What's your literary name?" Zeng Xuan asked.

"Ziyu," replied Meng Ke.

Zeng Xuan was so pleased that he grinned from ear to ear, and said in a soft voice: "That's enough. Just get up and go to class."

Meng Ke rose to his feet and said to his mother: "Mom, you can go home. I'll study hard here. Don't worry about me."

Now that the problem of her son's schooling was settled, Zhang had never felt so happy and content before. And so she selected a fine day in the beautiful spring season to take her son along on a ride in a horse-drawn cart to pay a visit to Mengsun Ji's grave. Once there, she prayed to the deceased in the following words:

"My dear husband, I've succeeded in sending Ke to school. He is clever and quick to learn. Great things can be expected of him. May you rest in peace."

From then on she got up early and went to bed late, working hard at her loom and spinning wheel in order to earn enough to pay for her son's schooling. She felt immensely comforted at the thought that Meng Ke's education was entrusted to Zeng Xuan, and that he had been placed in safe hands.

One day, Zeng Xuan was giving a lecture on the Confucian Analects, reciting with gusto the following: "'At fifteen I set my mind upon wisdom. At thirty I stood firm.' People may differ one from another in their natural endowments; some are born intelligent, some mediocre, others dull-witted. But however intelligent a man actually is, in the final analysis it is only by hard work that he is able to achieve anything. As Confucius pointed out, even in a hamlet of ten households there must have been men as richly gifted as himself. What made the difference, however, was that none was as fond of learning as he was...."

At this juncture Meng Ke was caught in the act of whispering something to his neighbor Tao Shi.

Zeng Xuan gave a loud cough, followed by a stiffening of his face: "Meng Ke! Did you hear what I was saying just now?" he intoned.

Meng Ke dropped his head in shame and replied in a subdued voice: "I did, sir."

"Then repeat it."

Meng Ke, shifting from a squatting position to a kneeling one, started to recite loudly: "At fifteen I set my mind upon learning. At thirty I stood firm. At forty I was free from doubts. At fifty I understood the laws of Heaven. At sixty my ear was docile. At seventy I could follow the desires of my heart without transgressing the right."

Smoothing his beard with his right hand, Zeng Xuan said in a gentle voice: "All right. Now let's hear you recite the first ballad of the *Book of Songs*."

Meng Ke, in his childish ringing voice, recited the whole poem without a single pause, to the great admiration of his fellow pupils.

A smile lingering on his face, Zeng Xuan at last turned to the whole class. "So much for today's lesson. Class is over. You're dismissed."

The class broke up, and the youngsters trooped out of the room.

Zhang had long since had lunch ready; it was going cold on the table. Still there was no sign of Meng Ke. His mother was becoming anxious. She ran to the school, only to find that the school gate was locked from the inside. Fear possessed her and she hunted high and low along all the streets and lanes until she had reached into every nook and cranny of the village, but all to no avail.

Chapter Three

Meng Ke Plays Truant;
His Aggrieved Mother Teaches Him a Lesson by
Cutting Up All Her Finished Yarn

While his mother was on her wild goose chase Meng Ke had come upon a white poplar tree with his classmate Tao Shi. They saw a magpie's nest in the tree, and two magpies flying around it. Just like children always are after school, never had they felt so happy and gay.

Meng Ke challenged his companion, saying, "Let's see who can climb the tree first and steal the eggs."

Tao Shi, who was the elder by four or five years, sturdily built and coarse-featured, made a helpless gesture. "I can't climb," he said.

"I can," said Meng Ke, giving Tao a pat on the shoulder. "You wait here. I'll get the eggs for you."

The poplar stood ten meters tall. Meng Ke slipped off his shoes, spat on his hands, rubbed them, and hitched up his trousers. First he clasped the tree trunk, and then, arching his back, his four limbs clinging to the trunk, caterpillar-like, he scrambled up to the first branch in the twinkling of an eye.

The two magpies circled around his head, now and then darting at him, with shrill cries.

Tao Shi, fidgeting down below, cupped his hands to his mouth and shouted to his playmate: "Look out. Quick. Be careful!"

By this time Meng Ke had succeeded in reaching the nest, which was perched on the sunny side of a branch. He reached his hand into the nest and picked out two eggs.

"Here are two magpie eggs!" he cried in ecstasy.

Tao Shi jumped for sheer joy. "Meng Ke, take care that you don't break them, " he warned his friend.

Now a problem loomed for Meng Ke. "How am I to get down, with two eggs in my hand?" he worried.

Tao Shi saw his friend's predicament, thought for a while, then called out,"Put them in your mouth."

Meng Ke put one egg in his mouth, but found that he had no room for the second. He shook his hand and head to signify that this

wouldn't do.

Tao Shi failed to catch on, persisted in pointing to his friend's mouth.

Meng Ke absent-mindedly opened his mouth to say: "I can't," when, lo and behold, the egg rolled out of his mouth and dropped with a splash directly onto Tao Shi's head.

Meng Ke had a hard time stopping himself laughing out loud. He hastened to climb down, but not before he had put the other egg in his mouth. Once he got down he hurried to help Tao Shi wipe the yolk off his face. But just as he and Tao Shi started off on their way home Meng Ke's mother came up. Overwhelmed with a sharp sense of guilt, Meng Ke halted in front of his mother, with his head hanging down in shame. With the remaining egg cradled in his bosom, he submissively followed her home.

After he had finished his meal his mother admonished him, "Ke, now you have a school to attend it's time you settled down to study. You mustn't fritter away your time playing games. Fancy climbing a tree to get eggs! You could have fallen down and broken your neck."

Meng Ke confessed that he had been in the wrong. "I won't do it again, Mom."

By the time Meng Ke had entered the classroom and taken his seat on his first day at school Zeng Xuan had walked in and mounted the platform. The teacher gave a sweeping glance over the class before he spoke, slowly, weighing every word as he did so, "The six arts Confucius advocated are propriety, music, archery, riding, writing and arithmetic. These are required of every well-educated..."

This is nothing new to me; I can reel it off pat, thought Meng Ke. He lowered his head, suppressing a yawn, as he produced the magpie's egg from his lap and started to turn it over in his palm with keen delight.

A hand was stretched out to claim it.

It was Tao Shi's. Meng Ke put the egg into his palm ever so lightly.

Tao Shi cherished it as if it were a treasure, completely absorbed in observing it from every angle.

Some of their classmates' attention was drawn to him and the egg.

Zeng Xuan gave a dry cough, as was his habit. This rang a warning bell in Meng Ke's head. He immediately pulled himself together and put on an air of all attention. But not so with the rest of the class; all their attention was concentrated on the magpie's egg.

With an angry look on his face, Zeng Xuan gave a louder cough.

Most of the students took the warning at once. They shifted their positions to face the teacher squarely and made as if they had been listening all along.

"Tao Shi," demanded Zeng Xuan, "What are you holding in your hand, eh?"

Tao Shi rose to kneel on his seat, and stammered out. "Nothing...no-thing. There is...nothing in it..."

"Hold up your hand!" demanded Zeng Xuan, his eyes glaring.

Tao Shi raised his left hand.

"What about your right hand?"

Tao Shi could do nothing but put up his right hand, which was clenched in a fist.

"Spread your fingers!"

Tao Shi did so, but slowly.

At the sight of the egg in the boy's hand Zeng Xuan was greatly upset. "Where did you get that?" he shouted.

Tao Shi kept a guilty silence, but he cast a furtive glance at Meng Ke.

Zeng Xuan turned to Meng Ke, stern in voice and countenance. "Meng Ke, answer me: Where is the magpie's egg from?"

"I got it from a magpie's nest," Meng Ke said mechanically, rising on to his knees.

"A magpie's nest," Zeng Xuan said somewhat quizzically, "can only be found on some big tall tree. How could you reach it?"

"What's so difficult about that?" Meng Ke gesticulated with glee. "I got the egg all on my own from on top of that big poplar tree just outside the village."

The last trace of anger still lingering on his face, Zeng Xuan said, with a slow shake of his head: "In this world of ours, we must go by the principles of benevolence and righteousness. When Confucius once stayed in the state of Wei he warned Duke Ling against shooting birdes. Do you know why?"

"I don't," replied Meng Ke in an embarrassed murmur.

"The ancients said, 'Don't shoot birds in spring.' " Zeng Xuan emphasized.

"Why?"queried Meng Ke.

Zeng Xuan reverted to his normal teaching manner, which was

marked by kindness and patience. His tone softened. "Because spring is the season when birds multiply. If you kill one, you are actually killing ten or even a hundred."

Absolute silence reigned over the whole class. The youngsters were rooted to their seats, as it were, hanging on the words of the teacher.

"What's more," continued Zeng Xuan in a more affable tone, "Concentration is essential to learning." His eyes swept over the class. After a pause he said, "You can't expect to apply your minds to two things at a time, can you?"

Reactions to the question varied; some boys nodded their heads in agreement while others looked stupid, tongue-tied. Of them we will say no more.

Let us speak now of Fu Puren, who was seated in his well-appointed parlor, enjoying a cup of tea. He took a sip of it, smacked his lips and gave his full beard a smoothing-down.

Seated in the guest's place, Lang Xin pleaded in a most servile manner. "My Honored Sir, have pity on me. Please give me the benefit of your advice as to how to find my way out of this delicate situation. Otherwise, I'm afraid, I'll have to seek refuge in the Nether Regions."

"Had you followed my advice last time you could as easily have murdered a three-year-old as you would a tiny chick," Fu Puren said icily. "As it is, you have only yourself to blame for the lost opportunity. Now Meng Ke is nine years old. It will be no easy matter to do him in now. And he attends school, too. As for that widow of yours, she is no longer young. What do you want her for? There are so many women in the world who are as fair as jade and pretty as flowers. Yet you take no notice of them but go out of your way to chase a faded, withered old lady. What idiocy!"

"Your honor, you don't understand my feelings," Lang Xin defended himself hotly. "She is as beautiful as a fairy in my eyes."

Fu Puren grimaced and said peevishly: "You can only blame yourself for your loss, when all's said and done."

Lang Xin bowed twice and then prostrated himself on the ground. "Have pity on me. Show me the way please!" he said piteously.

"What is the way, " Pu replied with disdain, "except the one I suggested previously?"

"I haven't got the guts, as usual," responded Lang Xin with a tremor in his voice.

"A toad lusting after a swan's flesh, that's what you are!" Fu tried to ridicule him in order to prod him into action. "Why aspire after something that's beyond you, anyway?"

"Is there no better way than that?" queried Lang in despair.

"Since Mengsun Ji died, his wife has placed all her hopes in her son Meng Ke," said Fu. "'To induce a widow to remarry, you must cut off all her ties of affection,' as the ancient saying goes. If you don't do the same with Widow Zhang you'll have no chance of winning her at all."

"But that means taking a life!" In horror, Lang Xin clasped his head with both hands as he said this in a trembling voice.

"What about hiring someone to do it for you?" was the wicked retort.

"Things are bound to leak out. The walls have ears, you know," Lang Xin was more frightened than ever.

Fu Puren, a murderous look on his face, goaded him on: "It can be done in the greatest secrecy. Neither gods nor ghosts would know."

Let us go back to Meng Ke. That day he strolled to the edge of the village after school. There he came upon a big, tall fellow who was standing on the bank of the river, looking around as if in search of some game. He had a quiver of arrows slung over one shoulder and a powerful bow in his hand.

A large flock of wild geese in a V-formation appeared on the southern horizon. The stalwart fellow took his time drawing an arrow from the quiver and watched until the birds were overhead. Then he stretched the bow to its utmost, sending the arrow whistling toward the goose in the lead. It hit its target, and all the rest of the flock scattered pell-mell, flapping their wings frantically as they soared honking high into the air.

Meng Ke was completely fascinated by what he had seen, and it was not until the huntsman picked up his game, left and disappeared into the distance that he betook himself homeward. He had the idea of telling his mother about what he had seen on the river bank at first, but no sooner had the words come to his lips than he choked them back.

On seeing her son coming home so pleased, Zhang quickly held up a new set of clothes she had made: "Ke, try this on and see if it fits," she urged.

Meng Ke was so thrilled to have a new set of clothes of his own, he immediately put it on. He paced up and down the room, and time and again asked his mother eagerly how he looked.

His mother sized him up from every angle, felt pretty satisfied with her handiwork and finally gave her son a gentle pat on the shoulder. "Now turn around and let me put the finishing touches to it," she said.

She trimmed off all the loose ends of thread, saying, with her face wreathed in smiles: "You shall go to school in your new clothes this afternoon."

Meng Ke hurried through his meal, and without so much as wiping his mouth got up from the table and made straight for the door. "Mom, I'm going right now."

"Don't play around. Concentrate more on your lessons," his mother enjoined.

"Mom, I'll remember. Don't worry." With this, Meng Ke ran out of the door and went jogging off to school.

Lang Xin sneaked out of a by-street, and like a starved wolf frustrated in its attempts at catching a quarry, watched with baleful eyes as Meng Ke walked merrily into the school.

After clearing the dinner table, Zhang continued with her spinning in the courtyard.

Meanwhile, Lang Xin was walking to and fro outside the gate of the courtyard like a lost soul. From time to time he peered in through the chinks of the door.

At this moment, Fucheng, driving his cart, had just turned off the main street into the lane and caught sight of the prowling figure of Lang Xin. He pointed his whip at Lang Xin's back and cursed him quietly: "You low-down, wretched animal!" He waited until Lang had turned the corner and disappeared before he went up to knock at the door.

On hearing the knock, Zhang put down her work and hastened to open the door. Happily she ushered her guest in.

"How kind of you to visit my humble abode, Uncle," she said, curtsying, "during the busy spring farming season!"

"I wouldn't have come if I hadn't promised to do so," teased Fucheng with a merry twinkle in his eyes.

"Come in quickly and have a cup of tea."

The old man did so and took a seat. As he noticed that everything in the room was arranged in apple-pie order, which showed what a good homekeeper his hostess was, he smiled his appreciation.

Zhang served tea and offered it with both hands.

"Where's Meng Ke?" asked Fucheng.

"Gone to school," was the proud reply.

"At his tender age? That's extraordinary." The old man was quite impressed. "I'm surprised that the teacher accepted him," said Fucheng, sipping his tea.

"It took a great deal of talk to convince him," said Zhang.

"Just as I expected. But how are his studies going?"

"He isn't dull by any means. Only too naughty, too naughty," said Madam somewhat wistfully.

"That's nothing to worry about," Fucheng said in his booming voice, the flowing beard on his breast fluttering the while. "Only naughty boys can be expected to achieve something in the future."

Suddenly Fucheng waxed serious. "Just now I saw Lang Xin on my way here..." he said with concern.

The mere mention of the name reduced Zhang to a state of helpless rage. "That beast!" she spat out. "He's had his evil designs on me since my husband died. I used to think that he might have developed a sense of shame by this time."

"You should heighten your vigilance against such a mean fellow as that," Fucheng warned her with infinite sympathy.

"I'm much obliged for your moral support," she replied, deeply touched.

Outside, a dense cluster of willow catkins was whirling in the air. Looking out on the scene, Fucheng thought aloud with feeling: "As long as Meng Ke works hard at his studies, in ten years or so he can be expected to become something of a scholar. Let's look forward to that day."

Meanwhile, at the school, Zeng Xuan was giving a lecture on the *Book of Rites*. He discoursed in a sing-song voice: "As the *Book of Rites* puts it, the great truth in practice is to share the country with the people. To share the country with the people was once the great political belief to which Confucius dedicated his whole life, and it is also the noble ideal cherished by persons of lofty aspirations, past and present. Those of you who are out to do great things and who spurn the idea of mediocrity must never lose sight of this great and yet distant objective."

Although he was seated in the classroom, Meng Ke's thoughts had already flown out to the far and wide world. He recalled his escapade when he stole the magpie's eggs that day, and how one egg had dropped out of his mouth onto Tao Shi's pate with a loud crack—so much so that he completely forgot himself and muttered: "*Aiya! There goes my egg!*"

All his classmates cast surprised eyes in his direction.

Zeng Xuan interrupted to shout: "Meng Ke! What did you say?"

Knowing only too well that he had committed a blunder, Meng Ke nervously shifted to a kneeling position and jabbered, "I was saying...no, no,.. I didn't... I was thinking...."

"Since you didn't say anything, where did that noise come from?"

Meng Ke grew red in the face and did not know what to answer.

"Well. Granted that you didn't say anything, what were you thinking about, then?"

There was nothing he could do but tell the truth. "I was thinking about stealing bird's eggs that day."

Zeng Xuan breathed a long sigh. "Humph! Since you are so liable to outside temptations and attractions what chance is there for you to concentrate on study?"

From nowhere there sprang a cricket. First it alighted on Tao Shi's desk, then it dropped onto Meng Ke's lap. In a forgetful moment Meng Ke's entire attention was centered on catching it there and then. Even as he put his hand out to grab it, the insect leapt into the air, and Meng Ke chased after it. The whole class burst into guffaws.

"Meng Ke! What are you up to, there?" Zeng Xuan's voice was harsh with fury. "Answer me!"

Meng Ke had by now succeeded in getting the cricket into his grasp.

"I've caught a cricket," he stammered in his confusion.

Another burst of laughter rolled over the class.

Zeng Xuan's face froze. "So much for today's class. You're dismissed," he said flatly and left.

Emerging from the school gate, Meng Ke ran all the way to the river bank, the image of that big fellow shooting wild geese in his mind's eye. But he was disappointed to find there was no sign of him there. Out of idle curiosity he broke off a twig from the brambles at the water's edge, bent it crescent-shaped, secured the two ends with a willow twig for a bow-string and used another twig as an arrow. Thus he tried every way to imitate what an archer might do. But finally he had to give up with a sigh, as he found his makeshift bow and arrow wouldn't work. He flung them sulkily into the river and went home.

On entering the house he was just about to cry out, "I'm hungry, Mom," when he saw the old man Fucheng sitting there. He eagerly snuggled up to him, "How are you, Grandad?" he said.

Fucheng lifted him up. "Little naughtier, did you annoy your teacher today, eh?" he queried.

Meng Ke shook his head uncertainly.

"Can you repeat what you learned today?"

Meng Ke nodded eagerly.

"Well, good behavior and knowledge can only be acquired by hard work. Without applying yourself to study you can't hope to achieve anything. You must aim high to begin with, so as to become a pillar of society in the future. Remember that, boy." Fucheng then turned to Zhang and said, "Madam, this boy of yours looks promising; you can rest assured that he will bring glory to your family. But you must guard against that villain Lang Xin." Then he took his leave.

Time passed and it was soon summer again. On the hillock to the east of the river was a grove of pines and cypresses, dotted here and there with shrubs of plants and flowers. At the foot of the hill green pastures stretched as far as the eye could reach.

Meng Ke had a wonderful time gamboling and frolicking in and out of the bushes and playing hide-and-seek with his playmates, or hunting for squirrels and mantises. One day while he was in the midst of playing one of these games with his playmate Tao Shi his glance fell on a cluster of brambles, where there was a grasshopper chirping. Meng Ke held his breath, arched his back and moved gingerly forward.

Behind a granite boulder nearby lay Lang Xin in ambush, waiting for a chance to murder Meng Ke.

"Meng Ke!" came a cry from Tao Shi, who had been left at the foot of the hill. "I'm coming to help you to catch the grasshopper."

Like a turtle withdrawing its head at the least sound of danger, Lang Xin sneaked away immediately.

"Come here, quick," Meng Ke looked back and beckoned. But when he turned back again the grasshopper had disappeared. He slumped down on the rock, disappointed.

Somewhere in the distance another grasshopper was heard chirping. Meng Ke stood up abruptly and sprinted toward the sound. From behind him came the voice of Tao Shi: "Got it?" He was breathing hard from the climb.

Meng Ke was looking intently at a grasshopper on top of a bush. He waved his hand energetically to hush Tao Shi. The latter, taking his cue, immediately got down on his hands and knees, and inched forward on all fours to Meng Ke. When he was within some dozen paces of his friend, he whispered, "How many have you got so far?"

"Keep down and keep quiet!" Meng Ke glowered at him.

Tao Shi dared not budge.

Meng Ke took a deep breath, and in one bound he caught the insect in his fist which he raised in the air with a cheer: "I've caught it, come and look."

Tao Shi dashed up. "Let me have a look," he said eagerly.

"Take it easy!" Meng Ke knitted his brows in an effort of thought. "Now, how am I to keep it?"

"Wrap it up in my jacket, how's that?" suggested Tao Shi.

"No! It would suffocate."

"Well, what's your idea?"

"Let's weave a cage out of sticks."

"I don't know how to, though."

"Now you keep it safe. I'll do the weaving."

With the utmost care Meng Ke put the grasshopper into Tao Shi's palms.

"Hold it gently, mind you."

Tao Shi peered at the grasshopper through the gaps in his fingers. Meng Ke hurriedly put his hand on top, saying urgently: "Don't let it escape!"

He struggled with the cage for a long time before he turned out something more like a nest than a cage. But it was better than nothing, he thought. "Come on, put the grasshopper in it," he said with a smile of contentment.

The two youngsters ran frolicking up and down the hill for the rest of the day until they had caught four more crickets. Then, feeling hungry and exhausted, they plodded home.

Zhang stood in the courtyard, waiting anxiously for Meng Ke. The sun had sunk in the west and dusk was closing in, and still there was no sign of him. Fear seized her and she ran to enquire at the school, but she found nobody there. On her way back she ran into Meng Ke. She felt anger rising in her breast at the sight of him, but she managed to control herself, and she merely asked in a calm voice, "Where have you been all this time?"

Guilty-faced, Meng Ke held up his cage with the grasshoppers in it. "Look, I've been catching grasshoppers," he said.

"You played truant, didn't you?"

Meng Ke hung his head, speechless.

With maternal instinct getting the upper hand of her resentment, Zhang changed her tone to one of loving care: "Let's go home and have dinner. But don't play truant again, mind you."

With the shrilling of cicadas and myriad insects piercing the summer night air Zhang stayed awake long in her bed. She fanned Meng Ke, who was sleeping soundly by her side, lightly from time to time.

Now and then Meng Ke talked and laughed in his sleep. "Got one more here. Hurrah! Tao Shi, put it in the cage. Be quick!"

Zhang regarded him with a wan smile on her face and sighed.

The next morning, Zhang sent her son to school with the advice: "Ke, you're getting older now. You must devote more time to your studies."

In class Zeng Xuan was leading his students in reciting the *Ode to Timber*, a poem from the *Book of Songs*.

Meng Ke had been yawning since the beginning of the class. Now that his teacher was describing scenes of timber felling and birds singing he recalled how he had seen lumbermen felling huge trees one after another and how the sound of the trees falling had sent the birds off scattering with frightened cries. So wrapped up in his daydreaming was he that he broke out into a series of giggles in spite of himself.

"Meng Ke! What's so funny?" Zeng Xuan demanded severely.

Brought back to reality with a jolt, Meng Ke rubbed his eyes as he replied drowsily, "Teacher, I saw a flock of birds as well as lumbermen there."

Zeng Xuan could only shake his head, as if to say, "There's no help for him at all, what can I do?"

School was over. The sky had turned oppressively low and cloudy and the air moist and sultry. To seek some fresh air and stretch his legs Meng Ke went straight to the river bank, where he selected a less-frequented area, took off his clothes and plunged into the river up to his chest. Feeling completely refreshed, he stopped his ears with both hands, then dipped his head into the water. As he had never learned to swim all he could do was flail his limbs about to keep himself afloat. Shortly afterwards he climbed out, but not before he had succeeded in catching a small fish in the shallows off-shore. He dug a hole in the beach until he saw water oozing up in it. Then he put the fish in it and watched with great delight as the fish swam freely in the tiny pond.

Dark clouds came scudding across the sky.

A gust of wind blew over a thicket of reeds along the water's edge, revealing the furtive Lang Xin lying in wait for his prey. Having decided that there was no one else around, he stole up to the unsuspecting Meng Ke. Just as he was stretching out his hands to throttle the boy two stones flew whistling from somewhere and struck Lang's wrists almost simultaneously. Gongsun Benzheng appeared as if by magic.

"*Aiya!*" With a piercing cry of pain, Lang Xin stumbled into the river.

Frightened out of his wits Meng Ke made a dash up the bank, to grab his clothes. He looked back, to see Lang Xin swaying in the shallow waters like a wounded beast. Panic-stricken, Meng Ke scampered away without looking back once.

A squall blew up amid lightning and thunderclaps.

Lang Xin felt as if a thunderbolt had crashed down on his head, and instinctively he clasped it with both injured hands. Just as he was about to run away a thunderous voice overtook him: "Halt!"

He went all limp at this familiar and dreadful sound. Without looking up he dropped on both knees, his face down in the dust, kowtowing continuously and begging for mercy. "Heavenly hero, I beg your forgiveness..."

"The third evil deed must be punished," said Guangsun Benzheng. "I can let you off only this once. Next time, should you fall into my hands I'll be sure to kill you without mercy!" So saying, Gongsun Benzheng gave a flourish of his spear in Lang Xin's face.

"Yes, yes. I wouldn't dare...again," Lang Xin whined in the dust.

Meanwhile, Zhang was waiting restlessly at home for her son. She had gone out twice, but each time had seen no sign of him. In great agitation, she put on her rain cape of palm leaves and hurried to the school. As it happened, she encountered Zeng at the school gate. She made a curtsy to him.

"I suppose you're looking for Meng Ke, but he is not here," Zeng Xuan seemed to have anticipated what she was going to ask.

"Is he playing truant again?" asked Zhang in anguish.

"Unfortunately, yes. Clever though he is, he doesn't concentrate much on his studies in class. What a pity!" Zeng said, sighing.

Deeply grieved to hear the teacher's comments on her son, Zhang apologized and left.

Arriving home, she tossed her rain cape angrily onto the floor, and began to meditate on the best way to educate her son.

For many years work had been her escape from grief. Now, again, she sat down at her loom and started weaving. But no sooner had she done so than the shuttle jammed and the yarn snapped.

Outside, the rain was pouring down with a vengeance following closely on a deafening crash of thunder. Just at that moment Meng Ke bumped into the room, carrying his clothes in his arms, drenched to the skin.

A feeling of pleasant surprise, not unmingled with annoyance, came over her, and she went in to bring dry clothes for her son. Then she called to Meng Ke: "Ke, come over here!"

With bowed head, his hands, hanging straight down at his sides, Meng Ke stood timidly before his mother.

"Where have you been all this time?"

"To the river to bathe."

"Go get me a kitchen knife," his mother ordered.

A moment of surprise, and then, Meng Ke did as he had been told.

Zhang took the knife and with one stroke she hacked the finished yarns for a bolt of cloth on the loom into two.

Dumbfounded, Meng Ke beat a hasty retreat into a corner. It took a good while before he stammered out, "Mom, why? What for? Why did you cut your finished yarns?"

"I'd like to put that question to you. Now, if I cut all the warp asunder, can I get a bolt of cloth woven?" Madam Zhang asked in a composed manner.

"No, of course not."

"Let's compare your schooling to weaving. If you study for some time, then break off in the middle, can you hope to accomplish anything?"

The analogy prompted Meng Ke to ponder deeply, and he suddenly saw the light. "Mom, now I know that I was wrong. It was bad of me to neglect my studies and play truant." He flew into his mother's arms in a flood of tears.

Chapter Four

Meng Ke Settles Down to Serious Study; Squire Fu Gets Hoist on His Own Petard

A heavy weight was lifted from her mind when Zhang realized that her son had mended his ways by applying himself seriously to his lessons. Day and night she worked at her loom. Time flew by as her spinning wheel turned. Eight years elapsed, and Meng Ke made marked progress in his studies. A grown-up already, he stood tall, a little on the lean side, with an oval face; beneath his arched black bushy eyebrows shone a pair of large eyes which spoke of depths of thought and moral strength.

In the spring of 368 B.C. Meng Ke had reached 17 years of age. To celebrate his birthday, which fell on the second day of the fourth lunar month, his mother prepared noodles and soup, as was the local custom. After the birthday meal, Zhang asked her son what he had been writing on bamboo slips the previous night.

"I was copying a famous quotation from Confucius," was the reply.

"Show me it."

Meng Ke went to the inner room and came back with the bamboo slips, which he presented to his mother with both hands. "Here you are, Mom."

Zhang beamed with satisfaction at what her son had written and read it aloud: "The young should inspire one with respect. How do we know that their future will not equal our present?" She read and recited it alternately with relish, and ended by saying with admiration: "Learn from the ancients and then surpass them. That's the path for a man of noble ambitions. I am so glad that you have such high aspirations in you."

The next morning Meng Ke went to school as usual.

Zeng Xuan began the first lesson by saying, "For years I've been teaching you the writings of the ancient sages. But I wonder how much you've learned from their instructions." Having said this, he scanned the class for reactions.

Meng Ke cleared his throat and switched to a kneeling position on his seat.

Zeng Xuan turned to him with a nod of encouragement. "Meng Ke, give your observations," he commanded.

"I should think that of all the sages of the past, Confucius was the most outstanding," replied Meng Ke readily.

"Why do you think so?" queried Zeng Xuan eagerly, his eyebrows raised in expectation.

Meng Ke waxed eloquent: "Confucius epitomized the thoughts of all the saints and sages of the past. The six arts he advocated are required of all who aspire to achieve great things in the world. His contention that there should be no class distinctions in teaching provides an opportunity for schooling for everyone who is eager to acquire knowledge. Confucius' lofty ideals as well as his far-sighted aspirations should be the life-long objective which every noble-minded scholar must spare no effort to achieve."

Zeng Xuan smoothed down his pepper-and-salt beard and enthused, "Well said, well said!" After a pause, he questioned Meng Ke again, "What are the six arts Confucius held in highest esteem?"

"Rites, music, archery, riding, writing and arithmetic," replied Meng Ke.

Zeng Xuan stood up, walked slowly toward Meng Ke and questioned him further: "Those six arts are for scholars to master, that's true. But I hear that there is yet another category of six arts of a higher order. Do you know what they are?"

After a moment's reflection, Meng Ke replied, "I suppose you mean, Sir, the *Book of Songs, Book of Documents, Book of Rites and Ceremonies, Book of Changes, Book of Music* and the *Spring and Autumn Annals.*"

"Excellent!" Zeng Xuan could hardly contain his joy. He returned to the platform and resumed his lecture in his usual leisured manner.

"Throughout his life Confucius had three thousand disciples, to whom he taught these two categories of six arts each. If the first category trains a man in the ways of conducting himself in society, then the second trains him to learn the ways of running a country. The purpose of education, according to Confucius, is for the student to apply what he has learned in practice. According to him, if a man can't acquit himself well in the administrative task entrusted to him, if he proves unequal to a diplomatic mission, then, however fluently he may recite poetry, or however much he may have learned, it will be of no use at all."

But as soon as he perceived that he had talked over the heads of the rest of the class, he pulled himself up abruptly and switched to another topic, by asking Meng Ke: "From what I know, Meng Ke, you've laid a considerable foundation in the fields of rites, music, writing and arithmetic. How about the arts of archery and riding?"

Meng Ke modestly replied, "Your disciple has all along spent his time studying rites, music, writing and arithmetic. As for archery and riding, I'm afraid I know only their rudiments. But I'm sure I'll take them up, if there's a chance."

Zeng Xuan, his face wreathed in smiles, said, "It's spring now, the best season of the year. Let's go for an outing to the Nansha River tomorrow morning. We can practice archery there. How's that?"

All the pupils were excited at the idea, some nodding their heads, some clapping their hands, and still others shouting "Great, great!"

Zeng Xuan held up his hand for silence. He swept his gaze over the class, and it came to rest on a robust-looking young man. "Duanmu Yan, how are you getting on with your archery and riding lessons?" Zeng asked expectantly.

Promptly Duanmu rose from his seat on to his knees. "Your disciple is quite at home with those two arts," he replied.

"Good," Zeng Xuan said, "You go and have a target made this evening for tomorrow's event, will you?"

Feeling extremely flattered, Duanmu responded eagerly: "By all means, sir."

"Tomorrow morning, let's practice archery by the Nansha River. Meanwhile, don't forget to get your bows and arrows ready when you get home." Zeng Xuan reminded the boys loudly. Then he dismissed the class.

Back home, Meng Ke took down his bow and arrows from the wall, hung up a wooden board on the wall of the courtyard, and started practicing archery, which he did most conscientiously until it was time to light the lamp.

It pleased Zhang enormously to see her son so absorbed in practicing archery. She offered a prayer to her late husband: "I promised you that I would bring up Ke with my own efforts. Now you can see that I haven't let you down; you can rest content."

The next morning, when the sun had just risen over the edge of the valley, all of the students assembled by the river. Standing in front of them, Zeng Xuan announced his agenda for the archery class, emphasizing each word as he went on. "For today's archery practice, every one of you is to demonstrate what he does best, without hiding his light under a bushel."

Duanmu Yan stepped forward and produced his ready-made oxhide target, which he stuck in the sand and examined for a while before he went up to Zeng Xuan to report: "Sir, the target is set up. You can issue the order to start."

"All right," Zeng Xuan, his hands clasped behind his back, stalked to the target, then turned round to measure 50 paces back, made a groove in the sand with his foot, and addressed his students in the manner of a drill sergeant. "Bring me a bow and arrows!"

Tao Shi had by now grown up to be a sturdy young fellow. He had a swarthy round face which was set off by a pair of large bright eyes. He responded promptly to the command and handed over his bow and arrows to the teacher.

Zeng Xuan strung the bow, fitted an arrow to the string, pulled the bow to the full, aimed, and sent the feathered shaft whistling to the target. Sure enough, it hit the bull's-eye.

After a moment of stunned silence there burst out a loud cheer from among the students.

Zeng Xuan shot a second arrow, and then a third. Both hit the bull's-eye area as well.

The students jumped up and down, shouting and cheering, expressing no end of admiration for their teacher's accurate marksmanship.

Regaining his breath a little, Zeng Xuan passed his bow to Tao Shi. "Now, you have a try," he said.

Tao Shi took over, shot three arrows in quick succession, and each time hit the mark.

All his classmates crowded around to congratulate him.

Then came Duanmu's turn. He also succeeded in hitting the target.

More pleased than ever, Zeng Xuan raised his voice in high glee. "Meng Ke, now it's your turn."

Meng Ke's three arrows all missed the target, much to his embarrassment.

However, Zeng Xuan comforted him, saying, "Don't let it upset you. Skill is not something a person is born with. Since you haven't practiced archery before, how could you expect to master it in a day?

Don't lose heart. Practice makes perfect. Try again later."

Meng Ke, looking dejected, stepped aside to give way to the next boy.

As the archery practice proceeded in full swing, suddenly a dead pigeon with an arrow in it dropped to the ground in front of them.

"Whose doing is this?" demanded Zeng Xuan in a burst of anger.

In answer, there came a burst of raucous laughter from the embankment.

It came from Squire Fu Puren. Astride a sturdy iron-grey horse and followed by an entourage of some dozen vassals, he came trotting in the direction of Zeng Xuan and his group. He reined in his steed, made a cursory bow and held up his clasped hands by way of greeting. "Mr. Zeng, what made you so angry, may I ask?" he said with a sneer.

With suppressed anger still smoldering in his breast, Zeng Xuan tried hard to appear undisturbed. "Look here!" he pointed to the dead pigeon. "Was this bird killed by one of your underlings?"

"As a matter of fact, it was I who did it," said Fu with a gloating air, thrusting forward his chest in a challenging fashion.

Zeng Xuan scanned the servants, who were clustered around their master, with a withering glance, and said coldly, "I had thought that your lordship was here to practice archery. Now I realize you've come for hunting!"

Fu missed the edge of censure in what he heard, and he chattered on with his reason for outing. "You're damned right. A hunting game —that's what I'm here for. No better time than now. Being late spring as it is, when female birds are broody their legs and bones are flabby, leaving them with no strength to fly or hop, while the male ones, being preoccupied with seeking food for their mates and fledglings, have no time to be wary of arrows. So it's the best season for game, don't you think?"

"You're wrong there," countered Zeng Xuan point-blank.

"What?" Fu barked, rolling his toad-like eyes arrogantly. "Where am I wrong?"

Zeng Xuan said in as calm a voice as he could, trying his best to convince his interlocutor with reasoning: "Our ancients warned against killing birds in spring."

"Why? For what reason?" Fu glared angrily.

"Spring is the breeding season for birds. Killing one bird is tantamount to killing ten or even a hundred," added Zeng Xuan.

For an answer, Fu gave a snort of contempt.

Ignoring Fu's rudeness, Zeng further explained, "When Confucius was staying in the State of Wei he tried to dissuade Duke Ling from shooting birds."

"Confucius?" Fu retorted cynically. "What was he? Could he have been that miserable pedant who met with rebuffs wherever he went?"

This was indeed more than Zeng Xuan and his pupils could tolerate, for they had all been brought up to look up to Confucius as a great sage to whom nothing but veneration and admiration were due. Righteous indignation stirred in their breasts.

Fu held them all in contempt. With a sweep of his loose sleeves, he sneered, "Damn the obtuse pedant!"

Meng Ke rushed out from behind Zeng. "Squire Fu," said he, pointing an accusing finger at him. "What merits and virtues do you recognize in our great thinkers of the past? And what, according to you, is it that distinguishes a gentleman from a mean fellow?"

A bully notorious in the neighborhood, Fu Puren had never had anyone stand up to him like this before. For a long while he remained shame-faced and bereft of words.

The young Meng Ke, who was gifted with a glib tongue, took a great delight in deflating Fu's arrogance. "Squire Fu, why don't you answer my question?"

Driven to desperation, Fu did not so much pronounce as hiss the words out: "You pedantic Confucianists! The whole lot of you!"

"Squire Fu, what right have you to label us pedants?" Zeng Xuan queried in his restrained manner.

"Just by the right of what you said a moment ago," Fu Puren replied, poking Zeng in the face. "Mark my words, in this world of ours only the strong are fit to survive and the weak must perish. This applies to human beings as well as to birds and animals."

Zeng Xuan wanted nothing more to do with such a cur as Fu. So he turned to address his students: "Let's call it a day for our archery lesson. Duanmu Yan, go and collect your target."

Fu held up his hand. "Not so fast, all of you," he said. "Now that I know you people are capable of archery, I suggest we get up a match between our two sides. How's that?"

"We go in for archery for exercise, and for nothing else. It's never our principle to flaunt our skill in a match with anyone," said Zeng Xuan, annoyed by the challenge and keeping a severe face.

Fu Puren's underlings were all little bullies after the manner of their master, and at his order two of them pushed their way to where Duanmu Yan stood, and, each grabbing him by one shoulder, dragged him to the shooting line.

Tao Shi and some other students, who had often practiced jousting with spear and staff, looked to Zeng Xuan for instructions, determined themselves not to eat humble pie.

Fu's underlings, with their long bows slung across their shoulders were all looking belligerent, waiting for their master to issue the order.

Zeng Xuan suddenly found himself in a touch-and-go situation he had never experienced before. Having been a teacher all his life he knew nothing except to follow the precepts of the sages of old—and they had not taught him how to cope with such a situation as this. His mind was thrown into a turmoil. As a last resort, he approached Fu in an effort to appease him.

"Squire Fu," said he, "should you prefer to have the place all to yourselves for archery practice, I'm willing to oblige you. As for your request for a match between your men and my students, you must realize that my students are all greenhorns as far as archery is concerned, so please don't force them to embarrass themselves."

Fu gave Zeng Xuan a push, sending him staggering. "None of your soft soap!" he said, gnashing his teeth in hatred. "I saw just a while ago what dead shots Tao Shi and Duanmu Yan were." And pointing to Meng Ke, he added, "Only this idiot made a poor show. He missed the target every time."

His gibe enraged Meng Ke, and he darted from behind Zeng Xuan but was restrained just in time by the latter, who whispered in his ear: "Discretion is the better part of valor. Wouldn't it be an insult to your intelligence to try and reason with such a brute as he? So don't be rash."

Meng Ke tried hard to control his rage, so much so that sweat broke out in his tightly clenched fists.

To a person of Fu Puren's low mentality not to bully someone was a sign of weakness, the more so since he regarded them as a handful of frail-boned scholars and it would be a shame not to have them knuckling under. So, he unsheathed his sword and brandished it in Zeng Xuan's face. "I say a match, then a match we will have!" he roared.

Zeng Xuan, well aware that his charges were no match for Fu's bodyguards and attendants, tried to signal to Meng Ke to take the lead in refusing the challenge, which Meng Ke did.

But not Tao Shi. He was as strong as a young calf, and a young calf, as the saying goes, does not fear a tiger. He leaped from behind Zeng Xuan in one bound, crying, "Come on, I'll take up your challenge."

Fu pointed his sword at a thick-set fellow, "Xia Long, you go and have it out with him."

Without giving the pupils any time for a respite, he issued the order: "Start the contest!"

"Just a minute!" Zeng Xuan approached Fu Puren. "Some rules have to be agreed on first."

"Why bother with rules?" Fu cried, with flecks of spittle flying in all directions. "Three shots each. Whoever hits the target with the most arrows wins, that's all."

"How many are to take part in the match?"

"As many as necessary until one side wins."

Xia Long sneered at Tao Shi. "All right, kid. I'll let you start."

Tao Shi eyed his teacher as if to reassure him that he would not disgrace him by taking up the challenge.

He composed himself a little before he walked in measured steps to the line, where he stood and took aim. Lo and behold! three arrows in quick succession shot out and hit the bull's eye.

Zeng Xuan and his students let out a simultaneous sigh of relief.

Fu Puren and his men only stared at one another stupidly.

Xia Long, his initial bravado having cooled, looked somewhat off color. He knew only too well that if he succeeded, well and good, but in the event of a miss he would be in the bad books of his tyrant of a master. He stood tense at the line, and for a long while he hesitated to release his arrow, until Fu barked, "Damn you, shoot!"

Xia Long had served as a bodyguard for years for Fu Puren, and it was generally recognized that his martial skills and marksmanship were superior to those of his colleagues. He steadied his nerves and discharged three shafts, which hit the target but far from the bull's eye.

This infuriated Fu, who thrust his sword in the direction of a tall fellow among his attendants: "Jue Hu, you try!"

The man addressed as Jue Hu, whose nerves had been considerably shaken by his predecessor's unenviable performance, now started to tremble. He let fly three arrows, of which only one struck the target.

In an uncontrollable burst of anger, Fu rushed at Jue Hu and slapped him across the face over and over until the latter was left with a bleeding nose and swollen eyes. The same punishment was meted out to Xia Long, as was expected.

Zeng Xuan took advantage of this interval to signal to his students to withdraw from this trouble spot while there was still time. They took the hint quickly and made their way straight to the embankment beyond.

But the arrogant Fu was not a man to take his defeat lying down. He dashed toward the embankment and brandished his sword to stop them. "Halt! You fellows there!" he yelled as he ran. "No one is allowed to leave here, unless your side gets the upper hand!"

Zeng Xuan muttered to the boys: "We can't afford to get into a squabble with such a rogue. Let's beat a retreat to the south bank." Again, Fu Puren ordered his men to block their way.

"Squire Fu," Zeng Xuan reasoned, trying to suppress his anger, "We've already submitted to your unreasonable demand and held an archery contest with your side. Why do you prevent us from leaving?"

"Surely you don't think you're going to wriggle out of it as easily as that, do you?" Fu Puren gave a snort of contempt. "Nobody who has had any dealings with me has ever gained any extra advantage, and you least of all!"

"Squire Fu," retorted Zeng, "What are you saying? Whenever did I take advantage of you?"

"I know deep in my bones," Fu snickered, his head lifted in the air, "how you poor scholars are capable of talking one's head off with your eloquence. For the moment, I won't argue with you. I only want to point out that archery is mere trickery, nothing to speak of. When it comes to a contest, we must go for the real thing."

He sauntered away for dozen paces and called to Xia Long.

Xia Long sprang to attention. "Yes, master." he said.

"Mr. Zeng," croaked Fu Puren, his eyes fixed viciously on the teacher, "you can single out whomever you wish from among your pupils and let him compete with Xia Long. If he beats my man I'll own my defeat, and we can go our separate ways. On the other hand, if your side is defeated, then..." Blinking his toad-like eyes, Fu continued, "you shall never teach archery again."

At this, Zeng Xuan was so outraged that his hands trembled. "Squire Fu," he countered, "archery is one of the six classical arts handed down to us by the ancients. What's more, it is a form of physical training which builds up one's body, so necessary for farming and for soldiering. Why should I give it up?"

"No more idle talk! Select your man!" barked Fu.

"But what are we supposed to compete in?" queried Zeng.

"First in boxing, then fencing," replied Fu, as he stroked the handle of his sword in a cocksure manner.

All the same, Zeng wanted to avoid a confrontation, so he adopted soft tactics. "Squire Fu," he said, forcing a smile to his face, "just look at these boys. They're not strong enough to stand up against a gust of wind, so to speak. Boxing and combat with the sword are evidently not in their line. I beg for them to be excused."

Fu Puren sheathed his sword and waved his hand. "Never! Never!"

Tao Shi stepped forward and addressed Zeng Xuan: "We scholars are not to be insulted by a scoundrel! Please allow me to fight it out with his man."

"Tao Shi, boxing and fencing are more risky than an archery match," cautioned Zeng Xuan. "Any accident, and you could get seriously hurt. Think twice before taking such a risk."

"But I can't bear such a gratuitous insult!" A sense of rebellion smoldered in the boy. With a leap into the air, he landed some six or seven paces from where Xia Long stood, and confronted him in a combat-ready stance.

Eager to take his revenge for the marksmanship competition he had lost to Tao Shi, Xia Long rushed forward with an angry roar. Tao Shi, in quick response, dodged to the right and brought his left foot hard down upon the nape of Xia's neck, sending him plunging headlong in the sand.

As soon as he had scrambled to his feet Xia made another lunge at Tao Shi, his two hammer-like fists held high in the air. But Tao Shi only parried right and left, feinting with rapid blows, deliberately trying to wear down his opponent's arrogance.

Just then there came by a procession of horses and chariots, some 30 in all, with the guard of honor marching at the head and a body of retainers bringing up the rear. What pomp and circumstance! Viewed from the front, the third chariot was draped with yellow silk, its shafts inlaid with ivory, the entire vehicle glittering with innumerable precious stones. Seated in the carriage was a fair-complexioned young man in his early twenties, whose bright piercing gaze was at that moment directed at the group of people gathered on the sandy beach of the river. He was Duke Mu, ruler of the State of Zou.

When the guard in the first carriage sighted the group he immediately called the procession to a halt and hurried to report. "I beg to report to Your Excellency that there is a group of people assembled ahead for something. Your servant is going to find out and report back."

"Don't disturb them," Duke Mu enjoined gently. "I'll go and have a look myself."

The guard helped him alight.

Duke Mu further instructed that his entourage halt for a rest and that no noise should be made to give occasion for alarm.

Duke Mu walked briskly to the embankment and, concealing himself behind a willow tree, looked out upon what was going on there.

Like a lion prodded into fury, Xia charged frantically at Tao. This time Tao was not quick enough, and Xia grabbed him with both arms, lifted him high over his head and flung him quite a distance. Tao promptly rose to his feet and was about to return to the attack when Xia kicked him on the ankle, sending him sprawling to the ground. With a wild laugh of triumph, Xia Long sprang into the air and aimed with both feet at Tao Shi's chest. Quicker than it takes to say, Tao Shi rolled away from Xia's feet, and so instead of planting his feet on Tao's chest, he sank them into the sand. Thwarted, Xia grew flustered, with the result that he could only flail his arms and kick his legs in an ineffectual way. Tao Shi took advantage of this weakness of his adversary to do a mid-air somersault and plant his feet on his back, sending him face downward into the sand. It was quite some time before Xia crawled to his feet with his face all besmirched with blood.

Tao Shi stepped forward, hands clasped before him in courtesy. "Please accept my apology for the offense," he said. With that, he turned to leave.

"Hold on!" yelled Xia Long. "I grant that you've got the better of me in hand-to-hand combat. But I won't let you off until you prove that you can best me in fencing."

Although Tao Shi was never an outstanding student, he nevertheless excelled in jousting with the saber and long sword. He came from a well-to-do family with a big house. He used the backyard regularly as his drill ground. All the same, his teacher and fellow students feared for his safety if he should prove no match for Xia Long in the proposed sword combat. But what they saw was a self-possessed Tao, who said to Xia Long quite casually: "Well, I haven't got a sword with me."

Fu Puren turned to Jue Hu and said, "Hand your sword to him." Jue Hu did as bidden.

Taking the sword, Tao Shi thanked the donor. He unsheathed the sword, breathed on the blade and then started to warm up. Against the background of a willow grove, his whirling sword gleamed green and red in turn in the sunlight as he swung the sharp weapon up and down, back and forth, round and round, sometimes as slow-moving as a sailing cloud, sometimes as swift-turning as a flywheel. The bystanders stared, positively dazzled.

The contest started with Xia Long and Tao Shi positioned face to face at a distance of a dozen or more paces from each other, each holding his sword at the ready.

At this juncture Zeng Xuan intervened. "Squire Fu," he said, "let this be understood. Today's combat with swords is not of our own volition. What's more, the sword is a lethal weapon, which, once it gets out of control, may prove fatal. May I propose that instead of their fighting with the real thing, let Xia and Tao each give a round or two on his own, as an exhibition of their martial skill. That way, accidents can be avoided and their brilliant performances will be a feast for our eyes, too, don't you think?"

"Absolutely not!" Fu objected rudely. "A combat is a combat. Either you vanquish or you are vanquished. There's no other way."

"Since you insist, then let's agree on some simple rules to be observed by both parties," conceded Zeng.

"What's the point of rules here, I'd like to know? From time immemorial, killed or injured, the duelist has only himself to answer for. That's the rule, if any," was Fu's blunt reply.

Thereupon, Xia promptly lunged into the combat area with his sword leveled. Without so much as a flourish, he aimed his thrust squarely at the vulnerable part of Tao's body.

Tao Shi knew only too well what a hard case he had to cope with. For the moment he had to dodge and parry, while all the time turning over in his mind the best way to outdo Xia and yet not hurt him. This, however, deceived Xia into believing that his adversary was afraid of him, and so he pressed on with his deadly thrusts all the more relentlessly.

To and fro, up and down, for nearly 30 rounds, the two battled until Xia began to pant and gasp; finally he could only parry Tao's thrusts, right and left, with no more strength to fight back.

Then, detecting a slip in his adversary's defensive tactics, Tao lost no time in making a horizontal thrust of his sword—clash! Xia's sword was knocked out of his hand and flew into mid-air. Simultaneously Tao threw his own sword down.

It was obvious to everybody there what Tao had in mind when he did this. But not to Fu Puren. He shouted to Xia, "Pick up your sword and fight on with it!"

Xia Long's right hand was still bleeding from the impact of Tao's horizontal strike, and the excruciating pain made him knit his brows sharply. But at Fu's command he went stumbling to pick the sword up. After steadying himself for a moment he made a sudden lunge at Tao Shi. This took Tao off-guard, and he received a cut on the left upper arm.

Venomously Fu Puren urged from the sidelines: "Give it to him! One more thrust! Right into the heart!"

An angry shout burst from the embankment. "Stay your hand! Villain! How dare you stoop to such dirty tricks? Your rival acted leniently to you and yet you repay good with evil by wanting to murder him. What cowardice!" It came from Duke Mu, who had been watching all this time.

As soon as they realized who the newcomer was, the people on the spot all moved in the direction of the river bank, where they knelt down, awe-struck, expecting instructions from His Excellency.

"My good subjects, please stand up," demanded the Duke.

All rose as bidden, with Zeng Xuan and his disciples standing on the left and Fu Puren and his servants on the right.

The duke addressed Zeng Xuan: "Who are you?"

Zeng Xuan stepped forward and made a deep bow. "I am Zeng Xuan, a teacher by profession."

The duke then pointed to his students, saying, "Your pupils, I presume?"

"Yes, they are, Your Excellency," was the reply.

Smiling, the duke turned and questioned Fu Puren.

Somewhat ruffled, Fu replied in fear and trepidation: "Your humble subject is surnamed Fu. Puren is his personal name."

The duke, then, pointed to those around Fu: "Who are these people?"

"They are my attendants," Fu faltered.

"Just now I saw with my own eyes how Zeng Xuan's disciple showed mercy to your man by holding back a fatal thrust," the duke said, "and yet you didn't seem to appreciate his kindness, but even went out of your way to encourage your man to do him an injury. Don't you think that was quite ungentlemanly of you?"

Fu was rendered speechless.

"Since you're the head of an influential gentry family in this locality," continued the duke, "it is your bounden duty to set a good example yourself to the local people by obeying the law. That is a way of fulfilling your obligations to the state as well."

"Yes, yes. I'll bear Your Excellency's instructions in mind," said Fu.

Then the duke addressed Zeng Xuan again: "I often hear that you do an excellent job of teaching your pupils the six arts," he said. "I've been meaning to summon you for an interview for some time now. What a pleasant surprise to meet you here of all places! Come, come, let's go together to the city, bringing your pupils along also. There's something about which I want your opinion."

And so, Zeng Xuan and his students went to the capital in the company of the duke.

Chapter Five

Master and Servants Conspire Behind Closed Doors in a Murder Plot;
As Guests at the Court, Teacher and Students Expound Their Views on Benevolent Government

Originally named Zhu, a dependency of the State of Lu, the state was renamed Zou after Duke Mu succeeded to the throne. The capital was built on the southern slope of Mount Yishan, bordered on the south and east by a circle of hills, which formed a natural barrier for defense; to the west of the capital stretched a wide expanse of fertile plain. The duke's palace stood at the foot of Mount Yishan, with a southern exposure, commanding a view as far as the eye could see.

At the sight, Meng Ke could not hold back a sigh of admiration: "What a beautiful landscape!" As he lifted his eyes to view Mt. Yishan he saw serried rocks of strange shapes alternating with groves of lush, green pines and cypresses. Sheer cliffs rising several thousand feet looked too perilous even for monkeys to climb. "Magnificent! Magnificent!" Meng Ke murmured. "No wonder Confucius in his day was moved to a poetic mood when wandering in such hills."

All the time Zeng Xuan kept an awed silence as he followed Duke Mu on their way to the palace. When he heard Meng's voice behind him, he looked back over his shoulder and smiled.

Duke Mu led teacher and pupils straight in to the lofty, spacious palace and seated himself on the throne.

"Please be seated, everyone!" he said, smiling. Then he pointed to his left hand side: "Respected teacher Mr. Zeng, please take your seat here."

After each had taken his seat in order of seniority Duke Mu came straight to the subject he had in mind. "In today's world there is no end of trouble here and there. The great unification of the country achieved by one man, as accomplished by the several emperors of Zhou in their time has long since ceased to exist. On the contrary, the struggle among the feudal lords and princes for hegemony has become increasingly fierce, so much so that they are just like the beasts in the

forest: "The strong eat the weak, and the weak in their turn, eat the still weaker. The State of Zou, being an appendage of the State of Lu as it is, has lost more than it has gained by this situation. Now that the State of Lu is becoming weaker than ever before, we cannot of course expect their protection any longer. I have been thinking about how to build my state into a strong one and enrich my people, but so far I have not found a sound strategy. And this is why I invited you people here so that we may pool our wits. May I have the benefit of your opinions?"

In the elegant manner which was natural to him whenever he spoke, Zeng Xuan said, "When the Duke of Zhou in his day assisted King Cheng in running his government, all he did was formulate rules of courtesy and good manners, compose music and guide the people onto the path of virtue through education. Consequently, the people submitted to his rule and followed him heart and soul. The reverse is true of today's state of affairs: The feudal lords and princes reject the rites and ceremonies, and eschew benevolence and righteousness. When differences arise they choose war rather than the negotiation table. And once war breaks out it is the common people who suffer. They neglect their farming and weaving. What is worse, countless families are ruined by war. Such being the case, where can one find a strong nation and a rich people, to say nothing of a benevolent government?"

"Well said!" Greatly interested, Duke Mu further asked, "Well, to what shall I turn my hand, to begin with, if I am to guide my people onto the path of virtue through education?"

"According to Confucius, to be benevolent is to love the people," Zeng Xuan replied. "Of all things in the world, people are the most precious. While there is a world of difference between the wise and the foolish in their roles as members of society, this difference comes about only through people's actions; it is not pre-ordained. As Confucius puts it, 'By nature men are very much the same; it is through practice that they become different.' Now, my lord wishes to build our state into a strong one and make our people rich. I would say that the predominant requirement..." He broke off, casting an eye at the duke, as if he wasn't sure how the other would take his advice.

"Please go ahead!" urged the duke pleasantly.

"...the first requirement is that benevolent government be instituted," resumed Zeng Xuan. "Under a benevolent government our beautiful and fertile land will be a rallying point for people within the Four Seas. The second requirement is, let an order be issued to all town and city chiefs that irrigation canals be built, waste land reclaimed, and all those who are diligent in farming and weaving rewarded, so that the common people may be assured of having enough to eat, being warmly clothed and leading lives of contentment. The third requirement is to establish schools well staffed with competent teachers where all who are so inclined can enjoy a sound schooling without discrimination."

Duke Mu expressed appreciation for these views with many thanks. As it was getting late, he asked his guests to stay at a nearby post station for the night. "There's still something I want to hear your ideas about. Please stay," said the duke at parting.

Coming back to Squire Fu. That day, after he had suffered a defeat in the confrontation with Zeng Xuan and his pupils, followed by a severe dressing-down from Duke Mu, he felt upset for the rest of the day. On his way back home he looked like a whipped cur, as he sat astride his horse shambling sluggishly along, with his servants, looking equally dejected, shuffling along in his wake.

As it happened, Zhang came walking toward them. She was dressed in a jacket and skirt of a demure color, which enhanced her slender figure, giving it an air of natural grace. She looked serene, dignified, just as a beautiful woman of her type does look when she has reached middle age. She was carrying a basket of silken yarn.

Fu's groom was the first to notice the woman. He shook the horse's reins to alert Squie Fu. "Master, look there!" he said.

Aroused from his gloom, Squire Fu was a little irritated at first. Then, as his eyes fell on the woman in front of him, he softened his voice and asked, "Who is she?"

"She looks like the wife of the late Mengsun Ji."

"No wonder Lang Xin was so smitten with her," Fu said, slapping his thigh. "Never indeed have I seen such a pretty woman! A peerless beauty for sure!"

"Lemme grab her for you. How about it, master?" Jue Hu suggested ingratiatingly.

"Shut up!" Transfixed to the spot, Fu watched as Zhang passed by. "Wait till we get home. Then we can work out a perfectly safe plan to get her."

Now Squire Fu had a wife and two concubines. When it was announced that their husband was home, all three hurried over to make a fuss of him. However, all their efforts to win favor met with only angry rebuffs. "Get out of my sight, every one of you!" Fu yelled in an explosion of rage.

Always a party to his master's underhand dealings, Jue Hu knew only too well what the matter with Fu was. He sidled up to him and said in a whisper, "Don't get riled, master. I've got a foolproof plan. With it you can get your heart's desire, and nobody will know."

"What's your plan? Out with it, quick!" demanded Fu, impatiently.

Jue Hu whispered in Squire Fu's ear for a while.

"Brilliant! Brilliant!" repeated Fu in high glee.

Later that night Lang Xin came at the invitation of Squire Fu. The latter had already laid out a feast in the inner room for his guest.

Lang was utterly surprised at this unexpected favor the moment he arrived. He rubbed his hands uneasily. "What's this..?" he said hesitantly. "Squire Fu, I haven't done anything to deserve your gratitude. Why this feast in my honor?"

Contrary to his usual manner, Fu was full of smiles as he said, "I have requested the great honor of your presence in my humble abode simply because there's some urgent business in which I need your help..." he paused abruptly.

Lang Xin stood there, agitated, ill at ease, and yet expectant.

"Come on, take the seat of honor."

As the two settled down to the dinner table as host and guest, Fu raised his cup filled with wine, saying, "This wine has matured in my cellar for years and I never share it with anybody except as a special treat. Now here's my toast!"

Overwhelmed by his host's urging, Lang Xin downed three cupfuls in rapid succession. Still more perplexed by the way he was being treated, Lang Xin inquired, "My respected senior, what is it that you want me to do for you? I will be only too glad to be of service."

Fu ignored this and instead ordered Jue Hu: "Another cupful of wine for our guest. Three cheers for young master Lang Xin!"

Feeling that it would be ungracious not to accept the toasts, Lang Xin had to drink down three more cupfuls of wine in one gulp each. Intoxicated and bleary-eyed, he mumbled again: "What's it you want of me... Squire Fu?"

Fu tipped Jue Hu a meaningful wink, and the latter filched Lang Xin's ornamental jade pendant that was hanging from his belt.

Then deliberately Fu tried to frighten Lang Xin. "Think of what you have done!" He uttered in a tone of serious concern.

At this, Lang Xin was jarred out of his drunken torpor. His face blanched and he asked in a tremulous voice: "What have I done? Is there anything the matter? Tell me please, I beg of you."

"Meng Ke has become a scholar of great renown," said Fu. "And he has a good command of the martial arts, too. Now think of this: if he gets to know that you harbor lustful thoughts about his mother, will he stand idly by and do nothing?"

More frightened than ever, Lang Xin fidgeted in his seat, then rose abruptly and flopped down on his knees. "Do something to save my life, my respected elder, please," he begged.

"Since you have stirred up a hornets' nest, it's only right that you take the consequences," Fu drawled.

The thought of the possible consequences made Lang Xin break out in a cold sweat, and he implored in an even more pitiful manner.

"Find me some way out of my dangerous situation, would you? I am begging you on my knees!" He almost sobbed out the words.

"Listen here," Fu Puren refused to be moved. "There is a way out, but it all depends if you have the guts or not." His expression grew ruthless as he went on, "Today the duke has invited Meng Ke to the court. And so in all likelihood they will go sight-seeing on Mount Yishan tomorrow. The heights bristle with steep and rocky precipices; an ideal place to do somebody in. Tomorrow all you have to do is to watch for your chance, give him a push and your troubles are over. Though I must warn you, if you let slip this chance, then you can just wait till Meng Ke gets you for all I care!"

Like a sleep-walker Lang Xin left the house, mounted his horse, and started on his way to Mount Yishan the very same night.

Jue Hu cringed and smiled obsequiously as he stepped forward and showed the jade pendant. "Master, how do you like this little trick of mine?" he said, very pleased with himself. "If Lang Xin should succeed in killing Meng Ke, Zhang would be deprived of her only support. Then you could get her as your concubine, and willy-nilly she would give her consent. Should Lang fail in his attempt, Zeng and his students will surely kill him. That's to our advantage, too, as dead men tell no tales. And supposing Lang Xin does not have the nerve to act at the last minute, believe me, I will take my men with me and under the cover of night sneak into Meng Ke's house and kill him myself. I will leave the pendant at the scene to incriminate Lang Xin. After that I will murder Lang Xin and dump his corpse down a well, making it look as if he had committed suicide to escape punishment. So, one way or another, Zhang will be yours."

Fu Puren interrupted him by a wave of his hand and smiled his ugly smile. "I'll reward you handsomely, once she is mine," he said.

In his palace Duke Mu was having an audience with his civil and military officials.

"Yesterday I invited Zeng Xuan and his students here, and we had a discussion about state affairs. I found that many of their views were quite stimulating and helpful. Today I want this discussion to be continued, so that you all may have a chance to hear it," said the duke.

"We will be glad to, Your Majesty," they echoed in chorus.

Soon after, a palace guard rushed in to announce that Zeng Xuan and his students were waiting at the gate for an audience.

"Usher them in right away!" commanded the duke, beaming.

In response to the command in marched Zeng Xuan and his students. They kowtowed and hailed the duke.

As soon as they were seated the duke began by saying, "Your suggestions on running benevolent government yesterday I found most interesting. Today, with my ministers and counselors present, I would like you to continue to expound your views for our edification. I have read and reread Confucius' *Analects* in my spare time, and my deep impression is that the quintessence of his teaching consists in benevolent government and education through the rites. While he was serving as minister of justice in the State of Lu he practiced what he preached, with the result that during his tenure of office social order underwent a complete change, so much so that no one picked up and pocketed anything lost on the road and doors did not need to be bolted at night. But what is beyond my comprehension is that when later he and his followers went about lobbying for his political philosophy amongst the states, such as Wei, Song, Cai, Chen, Chu and Wu, none of their rulers lent an ear to him. What was the reason, may I ask?"

"His political theory was not accepted by those feudal lords, it is true," Zeng Xun replied composedly. "The reason, however, is not far to seek. It was because those rulers..."

"You don't have to be reticent," Duke Mu encouraged him. "Please go on."

"It was chiefly because those feudal lords were over-impatient for quick gains and immediate profits," Zeng Xuan explained. "Confucius lived in a time of great disorder, when the rites had disintegrated and music had deteriorated. The feudal lords all directed their attention to expanding their territories by resorting to arms and fighting amongst themselves. They knew the importance of winning a city by means of war, but they did not know how to win the hearts of their people, which was much more important. Hence they looked upon Confucius' ideals with incomprehension."

Duke Mu tried to change the subject by turning his gaze upon Zeng's students, scanning them from one to another.

"As I look over your students," he said, "I find every one of them looking bright and full of vitality. I'm sure they will be capable of great things in the future. Suppose, with your permission, I choose from among them those who have administrative ability and place them in high positions; some who are brave and combat-worthy and let them command troops, and still others who are pedagogically inclined and appoint them to teaching posts. How would you like that?"

His interest keenly aroused, Zeng Xuan smiled broadly. "I presume you are jesting, My Lord," he said. "There may be some particularly talented ones among my students, but they are still too young to be entrusted with important responsibilities."

The duke gave each of the 50 young people another close scrutiny, as a professional physiognomist would, and asked their teacher: "Which one of them would you rate as the best and brightest?"

"It is hard to say, since each has his own weak points as well as strong ones," said Zeng Xuan.

"That goes without saying," the duke nodded in assent. "Yet when all is said and done there must be some differences between one and another in their mental development. Some may be quicker and some slower, don't you agree? Well, allow me to ask: Which one amongst your 50 students do you think is the brightest?"

All eyes came to rest on Meng Ke.

The duke understood without being told. "I see," he said, and pointed to Meng Ke. "That handsome young man, of course."

Meng Ke blushed and lowered his head in embarrassment.

"What is your name, young man?" asked the duke.

"My surname is Meng, and my personal name is Ke. Ziyu is my literary name." Politely he knelt down and kowtowed. He spoke clearly, never swallowing a syllable, in the standard cultivated speech used in the official world.

Favorably impressed, the duke said pleasantly: "See how highly they all think of you. I presume you must have acquired an intimate knowledge of the *Book of Songs*, *Book of History*, *Book of Rites and Ceremonies*, *Book of Changes*, *Music*, and the *Spring and Autumn Annals*."

"I have been studying under Master Zeng since childhood, and learned the basics of poetry, writing, the rites and arithmetic. I have just begun to practice archery and riding. As for the *Book of Songs*, *Book of History*, *Book of Rites and Ceremonies*, *Book of Changes*, *Music*, and the *Spring and Autumn*, I have learned just a little of them; I can't say I have acquired an intimate knowledge," replied Meng Ke with poise and reverence.

"You are being modest," the duke returned. " Modesty benefits one, whereas conceit detracts from one. That's why great scholars of all ages are invariably modest people." Then he changed the subject by asking Meng Ke the following question: "As Master Zeng puts it, the quintessence of Confucius' teaching lies in practicing benevolent government and in educating the people in the rites. But allow me to ask: How is one to think of honor and disgrace as well as good and bad fortune in terms of his teaching?"

"Benevolent government is the basis upon which a state is to be built," said Meng Ke, showing great composure and presence of mind. "Benevolence is to honor and disgrace, and to fortune and disaster what mountains and rivers are to earth and water; they are both opposite and complementary to each other. For, without mountains and hills, rivers and lakes could not come into existence, while in the absence of water there would be nothing to irrigate the fields with. On the other hand, rivers overflowing with water bring disaster to the crops, the land and even to the mountains. Honor and disgrace are something like *yin* and *yang*, while fortune and disaster are like water and fire, with each pair mutually promoting and at the same time restraining each other, a cosmos of elements which operates in endless cycles. That is why the sage-kings of former times all practiced benevolent government. They sought honor while eliminating disgrace, creating happiness and combating disaster. Benevolent government is the cause, and honor and happiness are the effect; practice benevolent government, and honor and happiness come along of their own accord. On the other hand, if benevolent government is not practiced, then disgrace and humiliation come thick and fast, and no disaster can be averted. Nowadays there are people..." Meng Ke checked himself a moment, directing his gaze first at the duke and then looking around.

Silence reigned. All eyes were riveted on Meng Ke, whose discourse had impressed them with its sonorous tone and lofty concepts.

Intrigued, the duke urged Meng Ke on.

"Nowadays, there are people who think otherwise," continued Meng Ke. "They abhor humility and wish to win glory. Yet they do so not by proper means, but by despotic rule, using cruel tortures as punishment. They are just like certain absurd people who hate dampness and yet prefer living in low-lying land. They deserve the trouble which comes of their own seeking. What justification have they for complaining against god and man?" With that, he cast a glance over his audience and fell to thinking, head bowed.

The duke had been listening with bated breath, and now, finding that Meng Ke had ceased, he queried with a smile: "I wish to practice benevolent government and I am not a man to court trouble of my own making. At present, we have neither trouble at home nor threats from without. In such a favorable situation what should I do to begin with in the way of political reform?"

"Heroes and able ministers are produced in troubled times," resumed Meng Ke with eloquence. "The situation may be favorable, but this gives no reason for thinking that we can just sit back and relax, much less lower our guard against eventualities. In my opinion, in governing, a thing of the first importance is the appointment of able and virtuous men to key posts. If my lord is able to do this while keeping men of lesser virtue at a distance the State of Zou will not take long to become strong and prosperous. There are two categories of talented people. One possesses both talent and virtue; the other possesses talent but is lacking in virtue. If you will entrust with responsibilities those who have both talent and virtue they are bound to accomplish great things, whereas if you entrust people lacking in virtue with responsibilities it will bring no end of troubles."

"Talking about selecting virtuous and talented people, what must I do for the present?" asked the duke.

"Put those thus selected in important positions. Let them write and edit state codes and statues, and promulgate government decrees. For, without a carpenter's square or a pair of compasses one can not draw squares or circles, as the ancients put it. Government statues and decrees may be compared to the square and compasses. So it follows that only with codes and statues that are made known to the people can they be taught to abide by them and become good, obedient subjects. If this can be accomplished then the people will submit to your rule with admiration in their hearts, and consequently the neighboring states will hold you appropriately in awe. The *Book of Songs* says, "While it has not yet clouded over and rained, /I take the bark of the mulberry /And bind fast the windows. /Now none of the people below will dare treat me with insolence." Confucius once made a favorable comment on this poem, saying, 'The writer of this poem must have understood the way to rule!' Truly, if a ruler is capable of putting his state in order, who would dare treat him with insolence?"

The duke listened entranced, his face glowing all the while.

"Yet it can bode either well or ill for a state which has neither trouble at home nor threats from without. Encourage farming and run schools, and if all is done in good time the state will prosper. Indulge in pleasure and indolence, neglecting administrative affairs, and the state will weaken and its people suffer. As I see it, there is no impassable gulf between honor and disgrace, neither between happiness and disaster. Good fortune or bad, man brings it all upon himself. The *Book of History* says, "When Heaven sends down calamities/There is hope of weathering them; /When man brings them upon himself /There is no hope of escape.' This describes well what I have said."

A solemn and respectful atmosphere prevailed over the palatial hall. Both civil and military officials began to see Meng Ke with new eyes, while his teacher and fellow students kept nodding their heads in approbation.

The duke rose from his throne and approached Meng Ke in his leisured yet dignified fashion. "Today, the large states—Chin, Wei, Han, Zhao, Chu, Yan, and Qi—have set up separatist regimes by force of arms. They have long since ignored the authority of the Emperor of Zhou. A small state like Lu has to submit to them meekly, let alone our state, which is even smaller. Faced with such a situation, how is the state of Zou to get along?"

After a moment's thought, Meng Ke replied, "By sheer superiority in strength it is possible to vanquish a separate feudal lord or two, but it is hardly possible to bring their subjects around to submission."

A quizzical expression flitted across the duke's face.

"When people submit to force they do so not willingly but because they are not strong enough to resist. It is by dint of benevolent government and moral education, not by force of arms, that a state or even an empire is brought under control. Emperor Tang began with only 70 square *li* of territory, and King Wen with just a hundred. But because the two practiced benevolent government and used moral education to uplift their people they were able to win their hearts and build up an empire. Says the *Book of Songs*, 'From east, from west, /From north, from south, /There was none who did not submit.' Such was the state of affairs in those far-off days."

All of a sudden, an uproar broke out outside the palace gate.

The duke frowned. Angrily he turned to the guards. "What's that noise about? What has happened? Bring the culprit here, quick!"

Shortly thereafter, two guards escorted in a young fellow whose hair was all in disarray.

"A madman! So that's it," The duke shouted angrily, "Throw him out at once!"

But one of the guards hurried forward at the duke's feet. "I beg to report, My Lord. He isn't mad. He's Ma Fu, a man from the stables."

The man called Ma Fu wailed aloud as he sprawled on the floor, kowtowing continuously: "Spare my life, my lord! Spare my life!"

"You're a lowly groom; what wrong have you committed?" questioned the duke, in wonder.

"I beg to report, My Lord," said the guard. "He attempted to steal some of the horses' fodder today. I caught him in the act. And the evidence is right there," he pointed outside the door.

"Ma Fu, Is it true what he said?" questioned the duke.

"'Tis true, every word of it," was Ma Fu's reply.

The duke raised his voice in an outburst of anger. "What audacity, you scoundrel! While working in the palace you don't thank your luck for it but indulge in thieving. Is this the way you repay my kindness to you? Take him out and execute him."

At the command, the guards rushed up and seized upon the victim as a wolf would its prey.

"Spare my life, My Lord! Let me have my say," Ma Fu screamed amid sobs.

"What can you say, since both culprit and evidence are at hand?"

retorted the duke.

Thereupon the two guards dragged the man all the way to the door.

Zeng Xuan and Meng Ke spoke up simultaneously. "Please, My Lord, listen to what he has to say."

The duke nodded assent. "Bring him back," he shouted.

Ma Fu was dragged back.

"Well, what have you to say?" demanded the duke.

"If My Lord should think fit to sentence me to death I must deserve it, and I would die content," cried Ma Fu with a flood of tears. "What grieves my heart is the thought of my mother, who is advanced in years and in ill-health. Suppose I die, who will support her? I wish therefore, that after my death, My Lord may have pity on her by condescending to give her alms from time to time, say, the left-overs from the palace kitchen. If My Lord grants this dying wish of mine I will go to my death without regret."

This gave the duke a rude awakening, and he hastened to ask, "What made you steal the fodder?"

"It was all due to the severe drought last autumn, when we harvested nothing for all our pains. The pay I get from my service at the palace is hardly enough to keep body and soul together, what with the money spent on consulting the doctor and buying medicine. Truth to tell, My Lord, it's terribly difficult for us poor people to carry on nowadays. The fact is, for three days now mother has had nothing to eat, lying on her sick-bed. As it was, I had to steal as a last resort..."

"Surely you did not steal the fodder because you wanted to feed your mother with it?" asked the duke, utterly amazed.

"Yes, I did," was Ma Fu's reply.

"You are pardoned," said the duke, a little awkwardly.

Ma Fu kowtowed over and over again, mumbling a thousand thanks the while.

"I'll have two measures of rice plus five taels of silver given to you," said the duke, "for your mother's keep. Go and claim it without delay."

Words of praise and adulation were bandied about among those present.

The duke turned to ask Meng Ke: "Was that act of mine worthy of being called 'benevolent'?"

"Yes, I think so. Though..." responded Meng Ke.

"Well?" There was a mixed feeling of both disappointment and surprise in the duke's voice.

Without mincing his words, Meng Ke went on, "That act of yours might be called 'benevolent' in a sense, but it still falls short of what we truly mean by the word."

The duke was more puzzled than ever.

Meng Ke explained, "A ruler of a state acts as father and mother to his people. It is therefore imperative for him to see that they are well fed and warmly clothed, and lead lives of peace and contentment...."

On hearing this, the duke looked displeased, his face clouding over.

Sensing that Meng Ke had committed a *faux pas*, Zeng Xuan hastened to intervene. "It is very kind of my lord to invite us, teacher and pupils, here for an interview, for which we cannot thank you enough. But now it is time we said good-bye."

The duke said, "It is not very often that you people have the opportunity of visiting the capital. Now that you are here, why not make a trip to Mount Yishan this afternoon? It's such a beautiful mountain, you will find."

After thanking the duke profusely, Zeng Xuan and his company left the palace.

Chapter Six

Zeng Xuan Voices His Lofty Ideals
on Top of a Mountain;
Meng Ke Plays Music to Express His
Noble Sentiments

Back at the post station where they had their temporary lodging Zeng Xuan and his disciples had lunch and then started off for their trip to Mount Yishan. Coming out of the north gate of the city they began the ascent by means of innumerable steps. The mountain was famous for its abundance of grottoes and rocks of grotesque shapes; scenic spots met the eye wherever one looked. After climbing over 40 steps they came to a glade in a cypress forest. A gentle breeze carried a delicate fragrance to the nostrils. Something struck Duanmu Yan as odd, as he stood there in rapt attention. "Teacher," he said, full of wonder, "there's some strange sound coming this way. Listen!"

Zeng Xuan came up. "What sound?" he queried.

"Sounds like it's coming from a spring."

They all made their way to where the sound seemed to be coming from. As they drew nearer the sound became more distinct, sometimes as light as the tinkle of a plucked instrument, sometimes as strong as the thunderous roll of a battle drum. Presently they came to a small vale where a jumble of rocks protruded, one leaning against, and weighing down upon, another; there were caves and holes galore, but no water to be seen anywhere.

Zeng Xuan searched high and low, but to no avail. "That's odd!" he wondered aloud, twirling his beard. "We hear the sound of water, yet we can't find any spring!"

"Water! Here's a subterranean river!" came an excited cry from Meng Ke, who was just plunging into a stone cave about three feet in height. They all followed, teacher and students. Down the steep rock face trickled myriads of rivulets, which caught the sunlight filtering in through the stone crevices and reflected a riot of color. Lying at their feet was a river, the confluence of several springs, which went rippling down through many fissures. With such a wonderful sight before them,

teacher and students were struck dumb in the effort to express their wonderment.

"A stalactite!" cried Meng Ke in an excitement of sudden discovery, as he pointed to a huge block of rock overhead.

It turned out that the thing actually was composed of three gigantic rocks jammed together to form the shape of a bronze bell, hanging, as it were, in mid-air. Looking at a view like this, one could not but admire the uncanny workmanship of the creator.

Coming out of the cave, they continued their climb, Zeng Xuan in the lead. All the way beauty spots met the eye at every turn.

Though old, Zeng Xuan was still hale and hearty. He persisted in trudging uphill ahead of the young people, until half way up old age began to made itself felt and he was perspiring all over. His students then had to support him in turn. Then they stopped at an open space, where they selected an enormous boulder to sit on. From where they sat they could see the nine peaks of the mountain high up in the clouds. Zeng Xuan said, "When Confucius did mountain-climbing in his day, he set foot only on East peak but not the Middle and West ones. Why did he not try the other two peaks? Let us conquer East Peak to find out the answer, shall we?"

The youngsters each in his turn supported the old man while clambering up the steep rocky path. At long last they reached the top of East Peak. There they strained their eyes to look to the north and saw the capital of the state of Lu in the distance. And Nine-Dragon Mountain, too! It did indeed resemble a huge monster, its head raised, about to take off for a southerly flight.

Zeng Xuan looked in all directions, trying to find the answer to his question, but in vain. He then gestured to the precipice which stood facing them, and said, "Somebody in the future should have a message inscribed on this precipice here to remind coming generations of the fact that Confucius visited this place. Some among them may find the answer."

After East Peak they made their way to Middle Peak, which could be reached only by a narrow foot-path. Up they climbed, over hills and across vales, until all dripped with perspiration and gasped for breath. Middle Peak was still some way off. As they trudged laboriously on, overcoming one difficulty after another, a monolith appeared, looming up like a great wall and blocking their way.

"It looks as if no human being has ever been here since the

beginning of the world," observed Zeng Xuan. "It's too risky to go further up."

"Look here! Here's a gap we can get through," Meng Ke shouted in high glee. Sure enough, along the bottom of the block there was a crack 1/3 of a foot high and one foot wide, enough for a person to squeeze through.

Meng Ke was the first to do so. All the others followed suit, including the aged Zeng Xuan. They found themselves in a glen, surrounded on all sides by sheer cliffs, from which the lighted-hearted chatter of the 50 visitors reverberated like thunder.

The old man was so excited at this discovery that he immediately launched into a soliloquy about the pleasures of travel.

"As Confucius puts it so well: the intelligent delight in water, the virtuous in the hills; the intelligent enjoy life, the virtuous prolong life. It's absolutely true. To travel over mountains and rivers, one can achieve mental poise by identifying with Nature, and improve one's sense of beauty. And it is good physical training, too. Such a wonderful sight! It would be a great pity if I had not come here and seen it with my own eyes."

After a roll-call, teacher and students continued climbing. Presently they came to a height from which, as one looked afar, all the other mountains seemed to have dwindled in size. Meng Ke helped his teacher as they gingerly picked their way along narrow path cut into the mountain-side overlooking a yawning abyss.

Middle Peak came into view. Yet for the moment it appeared to them like some fairyland which can be seen but is beyond reach. It bristled with cliffs, bluffs and crags. Zeng Xuan seemed to have recovered his youthful vigor. "Take a look there," he urged his students, "Middle Peak on Mt. Yishan is right before our eyes, but it's no easy job to get there. Those who are determined to climb it just come along with me; those who don't can wait here. Anyway, too much care cannot be exercised in mountain climbing. By all means guard against accidents!"

Notwithstanding, all of them wanted to have a try.

"If so, lets get started. Come on!" Zeng Xuam smiled with satisfaction.

They started climbing a 50-ft-high bluff, with the old teacher leading the way. This done, they came to the east side of the peak, which turned out to be a precipitous jumble of rocks. A solitary cypress tree with a trunk about five inches in circumference jutted out from among the rocks. Thanks to this, they finally managed to arrive at a smooth ledge shaped something like a terrace. From there the peak was accessible by crawling through a one-foot-wide cave.

Now they were on a much broader terrace of rock with a breast-high protuberance in the center. Zeng Xuan climbed the latter, and after breathing a long sigh of relief, addressed his disciples: "Now I know why Confucius did not visit either Middle or West Peak."

His students below turned to him, listening.

"Confucius maintains that a king should behave in a way that befits a king, a minister in a way that befits a minister, a father in a way that befits a father, and a son in a way that befits a son. Hence there was a justification for his choice of East Peak and not the other two for climbing," he said, facing south and pointing first to the east and then the west. "At a court audience it is so ruled that the civil ministers have their places on the left and the military ministers have their places on the right. With this in mind, it is obvious that Confucius was content to function as a civil servant, and that he intended Middle Peak for a visit by a ruler of a state. Such was his way of thinking about things, alas! It is a pity that so few people appreciated his views in his day."

While enjoying the beautiful scenery, they listened to the teacher's discourse, some with good understanding but a few with only a superficial grasp of his meaning.

"In my opinion Confucius was a man of great learning and of good moral character. And he had a way of administering a state as well as conducting himself in the world. Only he seemed a little too prudent, not to say strait-laced, I think," observed Meng Ke.

"All the same, it is better to be prudent than otherwise in this world of ours," was Zeng Xuan's comment.

Atop the mountain teacher and students discussed a wide variety of topics until dusk fell, when they started on their way home.

As they walked cautiously along the edge of a precipice, at times shooting timid glances at the forest of sharp peaks below their feet, somebody behind yelled, "Meng Ke, watch out!"

Instinctively, Meng Ke clasped Zeng Xuan by the waist with both hands and dodged to one side, just as Lang Xin sprang on him. The impetus, however, sent Lang Xin plunging headlong over the precipice, while Meng Ke was left safe. At that very moment Meng Ke had caught a glimpse of a bulky figure dodging round a corner.

The figure of the man seemed familiar to him, but for the moment he could not place it.

"Who was that man?" asked Zeng Xuan with concern. "Why should he make an attempt on your life?"

Meng Ke recalled the terrible scene in his childhood when Lang Xin came at him with a murderous look in his eyes on that stormy afternoon. The more he thought about it, the more puzzled he himself felt. He shook his head. "I can't make it out," he said. "Ever since I can remember there have been just the two of us, mother and me, in the family. We have never offended anybody. Really I don't know why the man should want to do me harm."

The cheerful mood of the day much damped by the incident, teacher and disciples returned to the post station, where, after taking their supper, they spent the night.

The next morning they bade Duke Mu good-bye and returned to school.

Having made certain that Lang Xin had met his death after his unsuccessful attempt on Meng Ke's life, Xia Long hurried back through the night to report. Fu Puren was having a nap in the inner room. Aroused from his slumber, he turned upon Xia with a scowl. "What's up?" he demanded.

"Lang Xin fell over a precipice," replied Xia Long.

"You saw it with your own eyes?"

"Yes, I did."

Fu let out a guffaw. "That's good news! Bring Jue Hu here."

Xia Long did as he was told.

"Now that Lang Xin is no more," Fu Puren uttered joyfully, "Zhang is mine for a certainty. Now tell me the way to procure her to be my concubine. Be quick about it!"

"There's the rub, though," Jue Hu said with gloomy expression. "Now with Lang Xin's death things will get complicated."

"Why? Didn't you say that with his death the blame could be laid on him?" countered Fu irritably.

"That was different," said Jue Hu. "What I intended then was that all this would be contrived in a way that nobody would know; only then could the blame be laid on Lang Xin. But now the fact that Lang Xin tried to murder Meng Ke but failed is exposed in broad daylight.

His falling over the precipice was just a case of curses coming home to roost. What's worse, Gongsun Benzheng was found to have shielded Meng Ke in the background all along. Even though Zeng Xuan and his disciples were kept in the dark, Gongsun Benzheng surely knows.."

Fu was beside himself with impotent rage. He beat his head with his fists. "Is that it? No other way out?" he yelled frantically.

"As things stand now," said Jue Hu in a conciliatory tone, "all you can do, My Lord, is to bide your time, watching for a fresh opportunity."

"Get out of my sight, you good-for-nothing!" Fu dispatched his minion with a wave of his hand.

Since his excursion to Mt. Yishan with his disciples Zeng Xuan had been in an unusually euphoric frame of mind. As he watched the intent faces of his pupils from his dais, waves of warm feeling surged within him. In the past he had only known that his pupils were capable of reciting the *Book of Songs*, performing the *Rites*, discoursing on *Book of History*, and commenting on the *Music*; it had never occurred to him that among his pupils there might be such prodigies as Meng Ke, Tao Shi and Duanmu Yan, the latter of whom had acquired unusual skill in the martial arts as well. The mere thought of it sent his heart into a flutter. Nothing gives a teacher greater happiness than to see his pupils grow up healthy and strong, he thought, smiling to himself, as he picked up a *qin** and started playing. It was a piece taken from the *Book of Songs*, which had been set to music. The song sang the praises of some virtuous and wise king whose benevolent government won him the whole-hearted support of his subjects. Each stanza of the song ended with a line wishing the king long life. Zeng Xuan sang as he played. He had a good voice and he played with feeling. From time to time he would stop playing to give a few comments of his own: "He wins the love of his people who wins their hearts; he incurs the curses of his people who loses their support," and so on.

Then he began to contemplate the instrument for a while before saying, "Poetry gives expression to one's aspirations; music conveys emotion. Today I would like to make something of an investigation among you, so that I may get some idea how much you have benefitted from the lessons on the *Music* classic. He then paused for his listeners'

---

* A seven-stringed plucked instrument similar to the zither.

reactions.

Meng Ke was the first to volunteer.

"Good! Please come here and try," said Zeng, grinning with delight.

Meng Ke went to the front and made a deep bow to his teacher. "Will you assign me something to perform, or just let me make my own choice?"

"Choose whatever you like—anything you think you excel in," said Zeng, beaming with satisfaction.

Thereupon, Meng Ke seated himself, and after giving the instrument a tune-up, started to play a piece titled *King Wen Enjoys a Reputation*, an adaptation from the *Book of Songs*. All this he did with proficiency and with sensitive understanding, much to the admiration of his teacher and classmates. Following this, he sang impromptu to his own accompaniment on the *qin*.

Before the last notes had died away Zeng Xuan, all smiles, came up with favorable comments. "Excellent!" he applauded.

"You played well and sang well. I sang of a king and you lauded an emperor. That is indeed a case of 'the pupil surpassing the master'; I am immensely proud of you, young man."

Just at this moment the whole room grew dim. As the teacher and students looked out of the window, they saw that the sky was overcast with heavy dark clouds. A storm was coming on.

Zeng Xuan raised his voice above the babel of the students talking together: "It looks as if there is going to be a hailstorm. Go home now, all of you, without delay!"

No sooner had he said this than there was a deafening peal of thunder overhead, followed by a violent storm, scattering hailstones as big as eggs on the ground. The whole class was thrown into confusion.

All around, people beat drums and clashed cymbals to exorcize what they believed were the demons who were causing the disaster. Those who owned no cymbals or drums beat their bronze basins instead. The din thus raised was deafening.

Before long, the sky cleared up. A mixture of resentment and anxiety made itself felt in everybody's heart, as they looked down on the thick layer of hailstone underfoot.

Zeng Xuan mopped his brow, as he said mournfully: "It grieves my heart to think just how many people must have suffered from this hailstorm, brief as it was. Now, boys, go home, quickly!"

As they made their way home, heavy-hearted, they found strewn on the road were rushes, broken twigs and even demolished thatched houses, the aftermath of the hailstorm.

His sole concern centered on his mother's safety, Meng Ke walked homewards with rapid strides.

Zhang was at that moment mending the apricot tree, tying up some of the twigs and branches which had been torn off in the hailstorm. She was glad to see Meng Ke back, asked how the hailstorm had affected his school.

"The school's all right," said her son, "but some poor people's cabins were seriously damaged, as I saw on my way back."

"What a disaster," said Zhang with a sigh, "Who'd have expected it?"

After helping his mother sweep up the hailstones, Meng Ke went off to have a look around.

A scene of desolation struck the eye wherever he went. The banks of the Nansha River were strewn with broken twigs, stalks and branches of poplars and willows, torn off by the storm. The blighted wheat fields along the banks presented a yet more heart-breaking picture. What remained of the otherwise sturdy green plants of wheat in the milk was just a mess of broken stalks. A farmer was on his knees, wailing aloud to Heaven, beating the ground all the while with his hands. He bemoaned the bitter fate allotted to the poor people and he held Heaven at fault for allowing them to be so cruelly punished through no fault of their own.

The depressing scene and the heart-rending wails filled Meng Ke with grief and indignation. He could not bear to stand and watch a moment longer. Something must be done, he made up his mind then and there.

All that night he tossed and turned. He grieved for the common people who would be suffering from cold and hunger as a result of the natural disaster; he worried lest unscrupulous merchants take advantage of the misfortune to boost grain prices. He turned over and over in his mind what would be the best way to bring relief from the blight. Go and report to Duke Mu of Zou, he finally decided, and see whether His Highness will adopt some relief measures.

The next morning he shared his idea with his mother.

Zhang took to his suggestion with relish. "You have a heart of gold, my son," she said. "I'm so glad to hear your idea. But you must go about it with tact, mind you. Don't hurt his feelings."

"Don't worry, Mom," said Meng Ke. "I'll see what I can do."

He went further to consult with Zeng Xuan.

"You have the best of intentions in the world," Zeng said. "But," he went on after a moment of thought, "I am afraid that the duke might treat you no better than a school boy. He may not listen."

"But sir, surely you don't mean that the duke could be indifferent to the sufferings of the common people?" Meng Ke protested.

After a while Zeng Xuan suggested tentatively: "Well, inasmuch as you're quick-witted and gifted with a silver tongue, I suppose, perhaps, you could convince him. Though, I doubt it—the fact is, there have been few rulers since ancient times who have ever lent an ear to ordinary people's pleas."

"For better or worse, I'll take my chance and have a try," was Meng Ke's firm reply.

Zeng Xuan scanned his students one by one, then addressed Meng Ke: "If you insist, then let Duanmu Yan keep you company on your trip. He's bold but cautious, and can be of good help to you."

"Brother Duanmu, would you?" Meng Ke asked his classmate.

"With pleasure!" Duanmu Yan assented with alacrity.

Chapter Seven

Duke Mu Turns Down Honest Advice;
Squire Fu Clings Obstinately to His Evil Ways

The two raw youths struck out immediately on their mission to the capital. Driven by an overwhelming desire to save their people from suffering, they pushed on with their journey at top speed. Soon they arrived at a place only five *li* from their destination. Here the wheat fields and those planted with other spring crops were a lush green as far as the eye could see, quite another world as compared with where they had come from. The sharp contrast started a train of melancholy thought in both young men.

Presently, they approached the palace. A palace guard barred their way.

"We have urgent business with the duke," Meng Ke said as he bowed.

The guard ushered them in. "This way, please," he murmured.

The sounds of decadent music wafted to their ears as they entered the gate.

"It's the *Kang yue!*" remarked Duanmu Yan.

The guard led them directly to the rear of the palace. The music became louder and louder as they proceeded.

The guard went in, and soon returned with the duke's permission for them to enter.

After dusting themselves down, the two made a solemn and respectful entry.

The duke, however, befuddled and bleary-eyed, was watching a dance performed by eight bewitching beauties, exposing their necks and shoulders as they danced round and round with all manner of coquetry. Without so much as turning his eyes in their direction, the duke just motioned for his young visitors to sit down.

Meng Ke sat in a rigid posture, his eyes glued to the roof beams.

Duanmu Yan looked fidgety, as if he were sitting on needles.

The music came to a stop and Duke Mu waved his hand for the dancers to retire. He turned to the young men and queried in a listless manner: "Young fellows, what urgent business brings you here? You're

85

in the prime of life, when every second counts. Your urgent business, therefore, is to set your mind on study. The study of the *Rites and Music*... Now, tell me what is your business here?"

Meng Ke rose from his seat and dropped to his knees. "Hear my report, Your Lordship: Yesterday a hailstorm hit the area north of the capital. A large number of wheat fields were destroyed. Many houses were damaged and a lot of trees were uprooted. The hapless peasants are crying to Heaven for help. We two are here to petition Your Lordship to open the public granary to relieve the disaster victims."

The duke gestured to Meng Ke to resume his seat.

"You are no more than bookworms," he said, assuming a straight face. "What do you know about affairs of state? Zou may not be a big state, but it still owns territory of a hundred square *li*. Natural disasters such as droughts, floods and hailstorms are a common occurrence throughout the year in one area or another. If I opened the state granary for relief purposes every time there was a disaster, as you'd have me do, our state granary would have emptied itself long ago. What is more, there is the more serious problem of army provisions in the event of defense against foreign invasion. Have you thought of that?"

Meng Ke felt anything but convinced by the harangue. All the same, he braced himself to argue his case. "My lord," he stated, "'Food is next only to Heaven in importance for the people', as the saying goes. With all the farm produce destroyed by the recent hailstorm, people in the disaster-stricken areas have been driven to the brink of starvation. What are they going to rely on in the coming year? Have you thought of that, Your Lordship?"

It would seem that the duke had long been accustomed to this line of argument, as he remained impassive. "What is a farmer, anyway?" he rejoined lightly. "By definition, he is one who farms the land for a living. Now, if even farmers cannot support themselves by farming, with what shall we support ourselves who do not farm?"

Hot-blooded youth that he was, Meng Ke, on hearing this sophistry from a head of state, almost lost control of himself as righteous anger surged in his breast. Then he reminded himself that a subject must respect the dignity of his ruler. He forced down his mounting rage and put on a smile before saying, "As the proverb goes, 'In nature there are unexpected storms and in life unpredictable vicissitudes.' An unexpected hailstorm did happen in the said area, didn't it?"

Still looking unconcerned, the duke said wearily: "After all, farmers are farmers. Being farmers, they are supposed to have some surplus grain put by in every household. You people do not have to worry about them needlessly. Go back to school and stick to your lessons."

Duanmu Yan said, "Since you are the paramount leader of a state, My Lord, may I ask if you know the relationship between a ruler and his subjects?"

Superciliously the duke said, "The subjects are the water and the ruler is the boat."

Duanmu Yan came back with: "Confucius says, 'Water can both carry a boat and capsize it'..."

Having heard more than enough, his patience exhausted, the duke digressed by saying, "You're still at a tender age, and about the way of governing a country..." he faltered, and remembering Meng Ke's remarkable words that day he quickly switched to another subject. "You must study hard so that in future you may become pillars of society, the better to serve your country."

Utterly disillusioned with the duke, the two said farewell and went straight home.

The disastrous effects on the wheat fields caused by the hailstorm, on the other hand, gave Squire Fu Puren occasion for rejoicing. On the evening subsequent to the disaster he invited all the rich merchants and magnates from the neighboring villages. "Gentlemen," he announced triumphantly, "Today's hailstorm has given us a rare opportunity to make money! The affected areas extend scores of *li* around, where not a single ear of grain can be gathered. Now, we rich people here all have abundant supplies of grain in our granaries at home. Why not take advantage of the present food crisis to drive up our grain prices so that we may reap some profit out of it? It's a godsend! Why not indeed?"

The half-dozen guests all kept themselves to themselves, each making a calculation of his own. For a long while no one spoke.

Fu cast his eyes on one, then another and still another. No response. At last he got impatient, rose abruptly from his seat, and addressed one of them bluntly: "Squire Tian, what's your opinion? How do you like this idea of mine, eh?"

The man so addressed was Tian Yezi, aged 46. He looked dignified in his brown silk gown and square white cap. He spoke with deliberation, weighing each word as he did so. "Clothing, food, shelter and transportation are the four basic needs of a human being. Of the four, the first two are the most essential. Gathered here are people from the most affluent households in the state of Zou. If we should seize the opportunity to boost the price of grain, the common people would panic. This would jeopardize the stability of the whole country. Consequently, we would suffer for it ourselves. Isn't it clear enough?"

On hearing this, Fu Puren glowered at the speaker with eyes full of hatred. "In view of what you say, what should we do, then?" demanded Fu, fierce-browed.

"In my humble opinion," said Tian Yezi, unperturbed, "There's an ancient saying which goes, 'Poverty means crime.' A man who reaps profits out of others' suffering is bound to incur popular hatred. In today's world, one dispute follows another, with the result that the strong survive and the weak perish. Outwardly we rich people seem to have strong positions, but actually we are only fierce of mien, faint of heart, and can't stand up to the merest blow." Finding that nobody demurred, he continued in his serious vein: "Gentlemen, don't think that I am exaggerating things in order to create a sensation. I am not. I am merely stating a fact. Some people try put a bold front on it, and yet behind this front they take every precautionary measure possible to protect themselves, like building high walls and strengthening their doors and windows, as well as hiring bodyguards. If this isn't a sign of faint-heartedness I don't know what is. I would like to advise these people: It is better to lose an enemy than make one. That's all."

Fu Puren felt these words were directed at none other than himself. He flew into a rage and thundered at Tian: "Sheer nonsense!"

Having had his say, Tian Yezi held up his joined palms head-high in courtesy: "Good luck to everybody. Adieu!"

After Tian Yezi was gone, Fu Puren turned to the remaining guests. "Opportunity knocks but once," he reminded them. "Take heed, everybody! Don't let slip this Heaven-sent opportunity. We are not like Tian Yezi, who has only a daughter to care for. Once he gets her married off he'll be left without a care in the world. While we have many children and grand-children, and they in their turn will have theirs. To continue our family lines it is absolutely necessary to make ourselves a family fortune in good time. Otherwise our descendants will suffer."

Back at school Meng Ke and Duanmu Yan informed their teacher of what had transpired with the duke.

"That is just what I had expected," said Zeng Xuan. "Do not take it too much to heart. It is very patriotic of you to show so much concern for your country and people, and you have done your best. I feel richly rewarded too, to think that I have such high-minded and talented youths as you two among my students. A great man, however, is one who understands his times. Take walking, for example. It's no good not to make an advance while one can. Neither is it advisable to plunge ahead if there is no road. Now come along with me," He led his pupils to a place where an undersized crooked locust tree grew from under a stone slab, and pointed to the tree, saying by way of analogy: "Had this tree grown somewhere else, its trunk wouldn't have been crooked. But it is growing from beneath a stone slab, so it has to twist and turn its way for survival. The same is true of human life. Our journey through life is beset with difficulties, hardships, twists and turns. What is of vital importance to us, however, is to look these difficulties in the face and find ways and means to overcome them. At present we are visited by this natural disaster, and the local people will inevitably suffer from it. But, as the saying goes, 'Heaven never seals off all the exits—there is always a way out.' For the time being, however, there is nothing we can do but wait and see."

"But what if the people should grow desperate and take some reckless measure?" queried Meng Ke, consumed with anxiety.

"That is my fear, too," responded Zeng Xuan in a low tone.

That autumn a severe drought hit wide areas of the State of Zou. Starvation stalked the land. Famine-stricken people, holding up the old and carrying the young, abandoned their homes to seek food everywhere as hunger drove them.

One day a group of such refugees, dozens of them, gathered in front of the school gate. Soon a row broke out.

Zeng Xuan rushed out in consternation. But the moment he saw these shabbily-dressed and haggard-looking people his anger subsided a bit. He approached one of them, an elderly man who appeared all skin and bone, and asked politely: "You don't seem to be a local person, sir. How is it that you have come to this place?"

The other sized him up and said, "We are from the State of Teng. We used to live in the mountainous area in the east of Teng. This autumn's drought has devastated all our crops. There is no way we can even eke out a living there." He pointed to the others, and continued, "That's why we are here—in order to seek refuge from hunger. But we never expected that here in Zou the famine would be even more serious than ours. Sorry to have disturbed you, sir. I beg your pardon."

Zeng Xuan said, "True, here the conditions are certainly not better than where you have come from, what with the hailstorm disaster of last spring and this autumn's severe drought. Multitudes of people, too, are reduced to beggary, seeking a living in other places."

Sick at heart, he went back to the classroom.

He described to his students what he had heard from the elderly refugee and the wretched plight of his folk that he had witnessed. "Boys! Just bear this in mind: A weak nation brings impoverishment on its people. Hence, every man has a share of responsibility for the fate of his nation!"

Meng Ke said, "Teacher, the pressing need at the moment is for food and clothing for the famished people. A task of such magnitude certainly cannot be tackled by individuals such as we. It is the concern of the state when all's said and done. So, we'll have to take up the problem with His Lordship the Duke. I propose that Duanmu and I make another trip to the capital and acquaint His Lordship with the critical conditions of life of the common people. Let's urge him to take a quick decision. What do you think?"

Left with no other alternative Zeng Xuan finally agreed to the proposal. He even volunteered to go himself, as head of their three-man delegation.

Early the next morning they got their horse and trap ready and soon started off on their journey.

All along the highway to the capital people were trudging, with sorrow written all over their emaciated faces. The autumn wind blew with a vengeance, whipping up columns of yellow dust that blinded and gagged the travelers. Tufts of sere grass trembling in the wind by the roadside added to the scene of desolation.

On arrival at the city they made their way straight to the palace.

His office work done, Duke Mu had retired to his inner chamber in the palace. He was now half-reclining on his couch. "Get the music and dancing started!" he ordered his attendants.

The dancers and musicians, who had been waiting in an outer chamber, trooped in at once. The band struck up the *Kang Yue*, and the dancers glided and fluttered to the tune.

In a trice the duke was transported into his dreamland, only to be brought back to earth by a palace guard, who stepped forward to report: "Your Lordship, Zeng Xuan and his students Meng Ke and Duanmu Yan are asking for an audience."

The duke showed his displeasure with a glare. After a moment of indecision, he said with an impatient flick of one broad sleeve: "Get out, all of you!"

Flabbergasted, the dancers and musicians beat a hasty retreat.

The duke straightened his apparel before he issued the command: "Bring them in!"

Having waited for the visitors to be seated, the duke asked, "Master Zeng, what brings you to the palace this time, may I enquire?"

"Excuse your humble servant for the interruption," Zeng Xuan said, with a deep bow. "If there is anything wrong the blame is mine."

Dumbfounded for an instant, the duke guffawed. "Master Zeng, you must be joking," he gasped. "I respect you as a man of noble character and high prestige. And I admire you for being a highly competent teacher, too. Whatever is wrong with your coming? In fact, it's my pleasure to receive you again."

Zeng Xuan felt somewhat relieved at this, and so went straight to the point. "I'm coming to see you on behalf of the ordinary people of the State of Zou," he said with a candid smile.

"On behalf of the Zou people, did you say?" was the surprised query.

"Our country suffered a hailstorm last spring," explained Zeng Xuan, "and now we are faced with a severe drought. With disasters coming one after another, more and more people throughout the country have been turned into refugees. If we do not take action to relieve them soon, so that they may be fed and clothed, I am afraid,.."

Suddenly the duke's countenance changed. "There was only a brief hailstorm last spring," he interrupted, with suppressed anger, "and you had Meng Ke come here to exaggerate things to raise an alarm. Now you are here again just because we have met a none-too-serious drought. Do you mean to say that I must open my granaries to those refugees?"

"That is the only alternative, I'm afraid," was Zeng Xuan's reply.

"We have had favorable weather for crops for three years in a row," said the duke. "Surely every household must have a few piculs of grain in reserve. No, the idea of tampering with the public granaries is out of the question."

Unable to hold back, Meng Ke spoke up: "My Lord! While Confucius stayed in the state of Chu his remarks to Duke Ye about running government were, maybe you know:'To run a government is to let the common people who live nearby enjoy a life of comfort and ease, and those far off submit to its rule with admiration.' Nowadays, the people of Zou are running short of food and clothing. Increasing numbers of them are leaving their homes to seek a living. If things go on like this what will be the end of it?"

The duke grew resentful, his face getting longer and longer, till it turned a dull red.

Zeng Xuan said, "Your Lordship would do well to have people sent down to the grass-roots to make an investigation."

It seemed that Zeng's suggestion had offered him a ladder by which he could safely come down from his awkward position. The duke seized upon it and promptly responded: "That is a good idea!"

Both Meng Ke and Duanmu Yan still wanted to argue with the duke, keeping an eye on their teacher for their cue.

But Zeng Xuan knew it was a hopeless case, and he stood up and bowed farewell.

The three hurried through a simple meal at a tavern. They then took a stroll along the main street. The capital of Zou was actually a small city less than 10 *li* in circumference, with seven streets running parallel from east to west and nine avenues running from north to south. Lining both sides of the south-north avenue, which led straight to the palace and which was also the busiest thoroughfare in the city, were a succession of shop buildings with carved beams and painted rafters mixed with quite a few old, faded ones, some of which were even in a state of long neglect. Pedestrians were few and far between; most of them wore a woe-begone look. "It used to be a thriving, beautiful city," Zeng Xuan commented with a wistful sigh. "Now look at it—how depressing! And yet Our Lordship turns a blind eye to it all! This bodes no good for the State of Zou."

As the three of them wandered aimlessly about, innkeepers accosted there, taking them for travellers who were looking for a place to put up for the night.

Filled with pent-up anger as he was, Meng Ke grew more restlessly fidgety at the sight, when he said to Zeng Xuan, "Teacher, it is getting late. Time we went home."

As he looked up at the setting sun, which was shrouded in clouds of dust, the old man uttered a long sigh, his eyes filling with tears. "The destiny of Zou..." With an effort, he swallowed what he was going to say.

The sun was sinking beyond the horizon when the three emerged from the city gate. Knots of people passed them by. They had traversed a distance of some 10 *li* when Meng Ke suddenly pointed to the mountainside ahead to their right: "Look there, everyone!" he cried. As they looked toward where he was pointing they saw a pale-red ball of flame as big as a palm leaf flitting over the slope. For a long while they stood there watching, mystified. "I have often heard people say," said Zeng with a tremor in his voice, "that a certain phenomenon known as a will-o'-the-wisp sometimes appears at night in spring and autumn. This must be it. Don't be scared. It does no harm to people. Though I never saw it before myself. That we should see it today is something I can't account for. A good omen or bad—that is the question!"

"Our country has been afflicted with one disaster after another throughout the year," observed Duanmu Yan. "I think it is no accident that this will-o'-the-wisp should have appeared at this juncture. It could be an ill omen."

As a matter of fact, in his heart of hearts Zeng Xuan had thought it an occurrence of dire portent from the very first, and now, with Duanmu's affirmative remark, he sank into a more ominous mood as he sat glumly in the carriage.

Meng Ke was shrewd enough to read the old man's mind. "Teacher," he comforted Zeng Xuan, "we are now traveling in the dark of night. It is not bad to have something to illuminate our way, —be it a will-o'-the-wisp or something else—is it? Seen in this light, it must be a good omen, don't you think?"

"You clever boy, Meng Ke!" Zeng Xuan thought to himself, using a term of endearment, I did not make a mistake in my judgment of you after all. You are indeed sensible to think of a way to cheer me up!

All of a sudden there heaved into sight another ball of flame over the mountain slope, some 50 paces away from the first one. It hovered, drifted and soared eerily, an uncanny sight that made the watchers' blood run cold.

It was not until midnight that the three finally arrived home.

It was no ordinary winter that year, with little rain or snow. Countless people died of hunger and cold.

In the spring of 367 B.C. The starving were driven to eat wild herbs, grass and tree bark wherever they could find them.

An inspection of his granary told Tian Yezi the grim truth: That 10 piculs of grain were all that he had left after his relief sales over the previous few months. And yet, thronging around his front door were several hundred people who jostled each other, clamoring to buy.

A young man with a bag in his hands dropped on to his knees before Tian Yezi, kowtowing the while, as he implored him in a pitiable voice: "Squire Tian! Have pity on us poor folk. We haven't had a thing to eat for days. Do sell us some grain, please!"

Tian Yezi hastened to help the boy up. He stifled a sob before he said, addressing the crowd: "There's nothing I can do for the present, good people. I'm awfully sorry. In fact, since last summer I have been more than once selling my store of grain as best I could. But now there's very little left. Please go elsewhere for grain, do!"

A chorus arose from the crowd: "Do sell us some grain, Squire Tian! Right now, please!"

Finding himself in a quandary, Tian Yezi shouted at the top of his voice: "If you good people don't believe me, then you can send someone with me to find out all right."

Accordingly, the aforementioned young man and two elders went off with him and soon came back with the report: "What the squire said is true. There's very little grain left."

With that, the crowd dispersed.

In the meantime, Fu Puren was seated in his bed chamber. A bondmaid was massaging his legs while another was doing the same with his back.

An excited Xia Long rushed in and said breathlessly: "I...I...wish to report, sir. Tian Yezi has sold all his reserve grain."

"Bravo!" Fu slapped his thigh. He stood up. "Now it's my turn to boost the price of my grain and make a fortune. Tell them from me that my grain will be sold at five times its original price. We'll suspend the sales every third day to watch for more chances to raise the price."

The next morning, as the news spread that the grain price had risen four times, the starving people just shook their heads and sighed. Thus, for the next three days not a grain of rice was sold.

Xia Long suggested that the price be reduced a little, and Fu Puren hesitated. But Jue Hu said, "Your lordship, I think we can only afford to raise the price, not reduce it."

"Why?" asked Fu.

"First," Jue Hu explained in his usual wheedling manner, "because Your Lordship is responsible for the rise of the price. If now, for no obvious reason, you go and cut it what will people think? They will curse you for raising it in the first place, or even hold you up to ridicule. Secondly, anything that is scarce is necessarily worth a high price. During the present famine food is most of all in demand. Wait till all the others have sold out their grain, and then you can set your price as high as you like—ten times, twenty times higher—and people will still scramble for it."

"I used to think of you as all brawn and no brains," said Fu with a smile. "Never did I expect that you would be so full of wiles. Well then, I will follow your advice."

Like a lap-dog which is being fondled by its master, Jue Hu threw himself on both knees, saying, "Your slave can never fully express his gratitude to you. And he'll do everything he can to serve your interests."

At this very moment a figure flashed past the window.

"Who was that?" Fu cried, startled.

At this, Xia Long and Jue Hu rushed out, with drawn swords. Together with a gaggle of servants with lanterns and torches leading the way, they searched all around the house, but there was not a soul to be found.

"That's odd," wondered Fu Puren, full of anxious doubt, "My word! I did see it myself though—a human figure it was. Why, could the man have wings?"

In a grass-thatched hut in a pine forest Gongsun Benzheng was addressing four powerfully-built fellows: "At present, there's nobody except Fu Puren who has surplus grain in his granary. The fellow has set his mind on raising his grain price to get rich quick, without giving a thought to us poor folk who are dying of hunger. I've just been to his place and overheard that he is going to raise the grain price again. Since he's so callous I think we should..." The rest he whispered.

Having heard him out, the others agreed with one voice: "As things are now, we'll have to go through with it, come what may."

About the third watch on the following evening people from all around swarmed to Squire Fu's high-walled mansion and encircled it. At the first clamor of gongs they lit lanterns and torches, and 200-odd of them assembled before the gate. They screamed, shouted, booed and hissed in all possible ways to curse the much-hated landlord. Angry voices rent the air and the flames of their torches lit up the sky.

Fu Puren was frightened out of his wits. Trembling like a leaf, he managed to clamber to the top of the front wall by a ladder. One look at the angry mob outside took his breath away, and he had to clamber down, though his legs felt like jelly because of fear. "Xia Long, Jue Hu! Order the archers to shoot," he commanded the moment he got down. But the people outside had come prepared for this. They got out home made shields, with which they protected themselves from the hail of arrows that ensued. Hardly an hour had passed before the archers had run out of arrows, which fact, when he learned of it, sent a sudden shaft of fear into Fu's heart.

Gongsun Benzheng passed the word around in a lowered voice: "Produce your weapons, everyone!"

No sooner said than done. All sorts of weapons—spears, swords, halberds and knives—came out into the open, and simultaneously a chorus of battle-cry rang out: " Charge! Kill!"

What seemed strange was that the people just stood there, shouting their loudest, never budging a step, or making the least sign of advance.

Presently, Gongsun Benzheng led a dozen or more stalwarts and they made a rush head-on at the gate, carrying a battering ram.

Inside, Fu's servants put up a desperate struggle to hold the gate fast.

About the fifth watch, when the sky was glowing in the east, Gongsun Benzheng and his Men set up an outcry, as if they were hell-bent on breaking the gate open.

Shortly afterwards a young man ran up to Gongsun Benzheng and whispered something in his ear.

He immediately signaled to all present with a wave of his hand, and in response all the people quietly withdrew from the scene.

Fu Puren mounted his ladder again, and when he saw the retreating crowd he grew suspicious. Why are these people leaving, all of a sudden, after raising such a pandemonium? He wondered to himself. What did they come here for, after all? Then, the terrible truth dawned upon him: "My God! It's a feint of theirs; we've fallen into a trap!" In utter confusion, he yelled to his servants: "Come with me!" He led them all the way to the backyard of his house. There they found themselves gazing at a heap of ruins where the backyard wall had been. The granary had been smashed open and all its stored grain removed! "My grain! My grain!" Squire Fu wailed hysterically.

Chapter Eight

Xia Long Breaks the Law and Gets His Just Deserts; Meng Ke Turns Disaster into a Blessing

His store of grain having been pillaged and his hope of making a quick fortune having been dashed, Fu Puren gritted his teeth with hatred. "Once I nab the ring-leader of this grain raid I'll dismember him personally. I'll eat his flesh and sleep on his skin! Just see if I don't!" he swore with venom. Thereupon, he sent Xia Long and Jue Hu, each with five servants, to separately track down the leader of the grain raid.

Off they went. The search party headed by Xia Long combed through all the villages and hamlets, down to every lane, and a whole day passed but nothing came of it.

At one end of the Tian Family Village there was a grain mill, in which an old man and his daughter were engaged processing wheat flour. The former, of medium height, was attired in blue; the latter was a healthy, rosy-cheeked girl of 20 or thereabouts, with a well-proportioned figure, clad in a jacket and skirt of white. Her eyebrows were arched and in her large eyes there was a look of quick intelligence and soft refinement. The two were totally absorbed in their work, oblivious of the advent of Xia Long and his hoodlums.

As soon as he spotted them Xia Long raised his brows, and his dilated pupils flashed as he demanded menacingly: "Where did that wheat come from?"

"From my land, that's where," retorted the old man with perfect assurance.

Xia Long sneered: "In these days of famine, while everyone else has nothing to eat, how on earth can you get grain, I'd like to know? You must have stolen it!"

The old man looked daggers at Xia, his teeth set hard. "You villain! You malicious liar! How dare you slander an innocent man?"

Xia Long drew his sword and brandished it before the old man. "Slander you? I'd rather kill you!"

His indignation running high, the old man stepped forward undaunted, head held up and chest thrust out, looking furiously at the

villain. "Are you trying to bully me just because you have a powerful backer?" he yelled at Xia. "And in broad daylight, too!"

As Xia's ferret eyes shifted about they happened to fall on the young girl. With his lascivious eyes fixed upon her petty face, he smacked his lips while at the same time putting his sword back into its sheath. "May I know your name, lass?" He bowed in a disgustedly affected way.

"I don't know it," was the pert reply from the girl.

Monkey-like, Xia Long performed a pirouette and made another bow: "How old are you?" he persevered.

The girl jerked her head to one side with a defiant air.

Old Tian grabbed a broom and proceeded to sweep the half-ground wheat grains into a wicker pan. He indignantly urged his daughter Zhongqing to hurry home with him.

Tian Zhongqing took up the pan, and father and daughter were about to leave, when Xia Long, with his arms outstretched, blocked their way. "Old uncle Tian," said he, lost to all sense of shame, "you've got a peerless beauty for a daughter. Your humble servant Xia Long, aged 28, unmarried, would very much like to have her..."

Old Tian felt so insulted at this that his voice shook with rage as he spoke: "We poor folk wouldn't dare to claim ties of kinship with the high and almighty. Excuse me!"

Xia Long assumed a cringing smile, and said: "But I adore your daughter the same way that a scholar of refined cultural tastes dotes on his caged oriole."

Old Tian stamped his foot in exasperation. "Why must you pester me so when I have done nothing wrong to you?" he protested.

Xia Long struck the handle of his sword as he sneered, "You miserable dotard! Be sensible, I tell you! You don't know what's good for you. Everyone in the State of Zou knows Squire Fu's chief steward Xia Long. You should deem it a great honor to let me have your daughter as my wife. Now, yes or no?"

Old Tian, almost choking with rage, pointed an accusatory finger at Xia, and spat out, "You despicable bully! Riding roughshod over helpless people—that's all you and your kind are good for!"

"You crazy old fool!" Shamed into anger, Xia Long shouted himself hoarse, "You don't seem to appreciate favors. I could carry your daughter off this minute. How would you like that? So, submit to my terms and have done with it, and I'll gladly call you father-in-law.

Otherwise, I'll go back and tell my master that you were the leader of the grain raid last night. Squire Fu is in a towering rage right now, so he'll surely put you to death without a qualm. Then I can get your daughter easily, with you out of the way!"

"You rogue! With your day-dreams!" sneered the girl.

Xia Long threw himself upon her in one bound, knocking her pan into the air, with all the wheat and bran scattering down in a shower.

Old Tian snatched up a rake and rushed to his daughter's rescue.

Xia unsheathed his sword. One hack of it and the rake in Tian's hand was chopped in two.

Tian Zhongqing tried to persuade her father to desist. "Dad!" she said under her breath. "These are rascals, every single one of them! Let's get away from here."

"How dare you insult us!" Xia Long blurted out, and ordered his men: "Nab her for me, and off we go!"

Thereupon, the five servants rushed at the girl and carried her off.

Old Tian tried desperately to stop them, crying out in an uncontrollable passion: "Let go of her, you hooligans!"

Xia Long gave the old man a vicious punch in the chest, sending him rolling on the ground. With a snort of contempt, he stalked away.

Old Tian struggled to his feet, cried for help and ran staggering after them, until they disappeared beyond the distant horizon. He wandered back home, a lost soul. With his daughter gone, his only dear one in the world, he suddenly felt he had nothing worth living for. A terrible idea haunted his mind. He thought of committing suicide by hanging himself from a beam. But the moment he put his head into the noose of the rope his daughter's lovely image flashed into his mind's eye, and the idea suddenly deserted him. "No!" he swore, as if to heaven, "I can't leave her all on her own!"

With that, he made his way to the house of Tian Yezi. Once there, he barged in despite the door-keeper's attempt to stop him.

It happened that Squire Tian was on his way out. He inquired: "What's the matter? What makes you so upset?"

When he saw the very man that he was looking for, old Tian slumped to the ground, kowtowing.

Tian Yezi graciously helped him up with both hands, and said in a gentle tone: "Don't stand on ceremony. Just tell me what's on your mind, will you?"

After hearing old Tian's story, Tian Yezi asked his daughter's whereabouts.

"Kidnaped, that's all. I don't know where she is now," was the reply.

"That is outrageous!" Filled with sympathetic indignation, Tian Yezi announced, "I will go with you to have it out with Fu Puren and demand your daughter back!"

Meanwhile, Jue Hu and his search party had come to the gate of the school in the afternoon, where they met Meng Ke coming out, as school was just over. The encounter put Jue Hu in mind of his scheme in collusion with Fu Puren. He whispered to his underlings: "Keep a close watch on Meng Ke and wait for my signal."

On his way home Meng Ke had come to the entrance of the lane that led to his house when he found himself hemmed in by Jue Hu and his men, greatly to his chagrin. "What's this...?" he demanded.

"Meng Ke! Don't play the innocent!" said Jue Hu, putting on a great show of being in earnest. "You robbed Squire Fu's granary last night with your cronies, and now you pretend nothing happened. Stop playacting!"

"That's sheer slander!" said Meng Ke.

"Escort him to Squire Fu. He'll be dealt with there!"

And so, in spite of his strong protests, the thugs seized Meng Ke and dragged him away.

Having carried Tian Zhongqing to Fu's house, Xia Long went to report to his master first thing.

Without waiting for him to open his mouth Fu demanded, "Got your hands on the ring-leader yet?"

Xia Long scratched his head and smiled sheepishly. "I came across a suspect," he muttered.

"Have you brought him back with you?"

"No; but I've got his daughter."

"His daughter? What for?"

Xia Long stepped timidly forward and said fawningly: "She's no ordinary girl, sir. A sweet little thing for my lord!" "Indeed!" Like a cat on the scent of fish, Fu leaped from his seat and grabbed Xia's collar, asking, "Where is she?"

"In the front hall."

Xia and his men then brought Tian Zhongqing in.

Fu Puren could hardly contain himself for joy at the sight of that pretty face; he could not help extending a finger to part the stray strands of hair over her forehead. He feigned tenderness asking, "What is your name, miss?"

Tian Zhongqing jerked her head away, and, biting her lower lip grimly, kept a stubborn silence.

Xia Long supplied the answer for her: "She is called Tian Zhongqing."

Fu Puren, stirred by carnal desire, started to play the satyr with his prey. Now he pinched her cheeks, dancing attendance on her, and now he played the infatuated fool, mouthing all sorts of sweet nothings.

Xia Long, watching all this tomfoolery, before long gave a loud dry cough in order to draw his master's attention to his presence. He was waiting for the reward he thought he merited.

"You've rendered me one more outstanding service this time," Fu looked back over his shoulder to say. "Go and claim your reward at the accountant's office."

As soon as Xia was gone Fu lost no time in closing the door and fastening the latch. Then he turned back and made a leap to Tian Zhongqing.

But the girl made a quick dodge to one side, and the old lecher caught the air, lost his balance and tumbled to the ground. He got to his feet, groaning, and ran after her round and round the room, until at last he caught her in his arms from behind.

Dusk. Tian Zhongqing found herself trapped in the room. Escape? There was not the ghost of a chance!

She felt a pair of pudgy hands fondling her breasts and a burning mouth hovering over her cheeks. Suddenly she hit upon a way out of her predicament. "Squire Fu," she said, throwing the satyr an arch glance, "I'm a mere weak girl and now I have fallen into your hands. Good or bad, I have to submit to your will, you see? But look me over and you can see how dusty I am. Don't you think my proximity would only tarnish your noble person? So at least you'll allow me to have a bath and change into clean clothes before I can wait on you properly. Isn't that reasonable?"

Fu Puren stroked her cheek, saying: "My little dove, you indeed have a coaxing way with you. Well, since you take my well-being so much to heart I cannot very well refuse your request, can I? All right!"

With that, Fu let go of his victim, opened the door and called to the maids outside: "Taohong! Liulu!"

He ordered the maids to get bath-water and a change of new clothing ready. He further warned them to keep a close eye on his captive and not to let her give them the slip.

The two maids thereupon ushered Tian Zhongqing into an ante room.

When the door of the ante room was shut, Tian dropped to her knees before the two maids, pleading, "Sisters! Please help me! I have an aged father at home who was badly beaten by Xia Long. I don't know whether he is dead or alive after that awful blow!"

Taohong helped her up and said, amid sympathetic tears: "This Fu household is a hell on earth! No good-looking girl who had the ill luck of being trapped in here would expect to come away unsullied. Liulu and I, too, have been violated by the old devil."

At this, Tian Zhongqing blanched with fright and went limp all over. She prostrated herself on the ground. "Sisters, please save me," she pleaded amid stifled sobs.

"Miss Tian!" Taohong continued, "Having fallen into the clutches of this monster Fu, one can have no other way out than submit to his will and be ready to sacrifice her chastity. That's the shameful way of life we two are leading now. To try to escape untouched is to risk one's life."

"I'm not afraid of death, if by death I can keep myself pure. But if I died I would leave my poor father desolate, which I cannot bear to think of."

"Let's the three of us put our heads together to think of some better way...." at last Lulu ventured to speak up.

All this while Fu Puren hung around the courtyard, now shouting to urge them to hurry up, and now rushing into his room as if something weighed upon his mind, and back out again.

Presently Jue Hu came running up to his master, announcing excitedly: "Your Lordship, I've arrested Meng Ke."

To his bewilderment, Fu Puren queried: "What for?"

"Have you forgotten, My Lord?" Jue Hu drew nearer and said in an undertone. "You once had the intention of taking his mother as your secondary wife?"

"Well, that was one of my passing whims," said Fu, "but now I have got another delicious morsel."

The words were hardly out of his mouth when a servant rushed in to announce that Zeng Xuan and his disciples were coming.

"What do they want?" Fu inquired.

"Meng Ke," was the reply.

Fu Puren threw Jue Hu an angry glance, which made the latter wince. "A fine mess you've got me into! Now I'll have to waste a lot of breath fobbing them off."

He knew well enough from past experience that Zeng Xuan and his group were not to be trifled with. He hesitated before he sallied forth to meet them.

On meeting the teacher and his pupils, Fu held up his joined hands head high in greeting. "A pleasant surprise, indeed," he began with affected politeness, "to have you all, esteemed senior teacher and students, honor my humble abode with a visit."

As soon as they were seated Fu pretended ignorance by asking, "May I know the purpose of your visit at this time of night?"

"We are here on account of Meng Ke," Zeng Xuan came straight to the point. "We don't understand why your men have kidnaped Meng Ke. Has he broken the law? We demand an explanation."

Fu feigned surprise. "That's impossible! Kidnaped?" he protested, rolling his toad-like eyes: "Here, you!"

A servant bustled forward: "Yes, sir?"

"Fetch Jue Hu here!"

Fu kept a straight face as he asked Jue Hu, who appeared perturbed, knowing that he had been the cause of the trouble: "Mr. Zeng here says that you have arrested his pupil Meng Ke. Is that true?"

Jue Hu tried to fathom Fu's real intention by watching his facial expression by the dim light of the oil lamp, his head awry.

Fu gave a barely perceptible nod and instantly Jue Hu took the hint.

"Yes, sir, it is true," came the answer.

"Why did you do that?" Fu questioned further.

"I...I...I suspected him of having been the ringleader of the grain raid." Jue Hu faltered.

"You fool!" reprimanded Fu loudly. "He is merely a young student. How could he be capable of such a monstrous thing?"

"Yes, sir, I was too rash. I confess I was wrong."

"Well, stir yourself! Go and invite young Master Meng here!"

"Yes, sir!"

Fu turned to Zeng Xuan with an apologetic smile, saying, "The blame is mine, as I failed in my duty to discipline my man. Let me offer my deepest apologies."

Zeng Xuan dismissed this hypocrisy with a frosty smile. "You might as well explain all this to the victim himself when he comes," he said.

Now Jue Hu was afraid that his master would further take him to task, so he tried to ingratiate himself with Meng Ke. He accordingly made a fuss over him, helping him to wash, comb his hair and dust his clothes. So it was quite some time before he ushered Meng Ke out.

Self-possessed as ever, Meng Ke entered the main hall of Fu Puren's mansion. He bowed to his teacher and all the others present, saying, "I am much obliged to you for getting me out of this nasty situation. But I am afraid I have troubled you greatly."

Zeng Xuan motioned for Meng Ke to be seated next to him on a divan covered with crimson silk cushions.

Fu Puren waited till Meng Ke settled down before he said, with an embarrassed smile: "Excuse this misunderstanding young sir. All this happened because my servants, who can't tell a good man from a bad one, mistook you for...." He strode to the center of the room and raised his folded hands in a gesture of apology. "I beg your forgiveness," he said in an oily voice.

"Every injustice has its perpetrator; every debt has its debtor," remarked Meng Ke with a nonchalant air. "Since I was plotted against and humiliated by Jue Hu, he alone must atone for it. Where does an apology on your part come in?"

Fu sensed that there was more to Meng Ke's remark than met the ear, and for a moment he was rendered speechless. Then, he gestured to Jue Hu: "Stir your stumps! Make young master Meng an apology!"

Thereupon Jue Hu stepped forward and said in a deep, gruff voice: "Excuse me, a stupid, uncouth man. 'A gentleman is broadminded enough to forgive a clod's misdeeds,' as the common saying goes. I beg you to excuse me just this once." He cast a surreptitious glance at Meng Ke to see how he was reacting to his pleading, and then beat his forehead against the ground ceaselessly, saying the while: "If the young master refuses to pardon an inferior man such as I, then I will remain on my knees here until the end of the world."

"As Confucius says, 'A misdeed which is left unrectified is indeed a misdeed,'" declared Meng Ke with emphasis. "Now that you have admitted your misdeed and acknowledged that you are in the wrong, it would be ungracious of me not to forgive you, wouldn't it?"

No sooner had Jue Hu risen from the ground than he made a deep bow to Meng Ke, saying, "Just as I expected, you are a magnanimous gentleman. Woe to me that I have eyes but failed to see Mount Tai!"

Meng Ke was about to say something, when a servant rushed up to Fu and said in a low voice: "Squire Tian of the Tian Family Village is at the door, wanting to see you. There's another old man with him."

The arrival of the two men at once threw Fu off balance. He had two worries at the same time: One was that if the scandal of his kidnaping of the Tian girl should come to public knowledge his reputation would suffer; the other was that Zeng Xuan and his company would take advantage of his being caught on the wrong foot to stir up a further to-do. The mere thought of this made him restless as an ant on a hot griddle.

Meantime, Tian Yezi did not stand on ceremony but came straight in, talking and laughing as he did so. After greeting Zeng Xuan and the others, he approached Fu Puren with a brief nod, and then said in an ironic undertone: "It's highly commendable for Squire Fu to give a reception for so many distinguished guests—a sure sign of his popularity with the virtuous and the talented!"

This left-handed compliment embarrassed Fu so much that his face flushed a dull red. Disconcertedly, he held up his clasped hands in greeting: "I am much honored by your excellency," he said. "But may I inquire what prompts this visit to my humble abode?"

"I hear your men have kidnaped a girl from our Tian Family Village, I want to know if it is true," declared Tian Yezi.

Beads of sweat appeared on Fu's forehead. "How could such a thing have happened?" he countered weakly. "Impossible! I think—no, I'm sure—that my men could not commit such an outrage."

Tian's countenance grew stern and his words harsh as he said, "Be that as it may. Summon your chief steward Xia. Let's find out what he has to say."

Fu Puren felt as if a dagger had been plunged into his heart. He moaned his order: "Where's Xia Long? Bring him here and be quick about it!"

The tense atmosphere in the hall when he entered it filled Xia

Long with apprehension. He plopped down at the feet of Fu Puren, stupefied.

"Xia Long! Somebody has accused you of kidnaping a girl from Tian Family Village. Is it true?" Fu asked.

His head screwed to one side, Xia cast his eyes around the people in the hall and said haltingly: "I know nothing about it, sir."

Tian Yezi pointed to old Tian and asked, "Do you recognize him?" As Xia's glance fell on old Tian the latter's angry eyes instantly subdued Xia into guilty silence.

With all the indignation of a man scandalized, Fu Puren thundered at his steward: "You miserable wretch! How dare you spoil everything I've accomplished? How dare you commit such an outrage, which is offensive both to Heaven and common decency? Where..." He lowered his voice as he continued, "Where is she now?"

Instead of an answer, Xia Long just stared at Fu, waiting for his cue.

"Don't stare at me stupidly! Go and set her free this minute!" yelled Fu, accompanying the order with a significant wink.

"Wait!" interjected Tian Yezi. "You ought to bring the Tian girl here."

Fu Puren had no choice but do so.

Tian Zhongqing was brought in, and as soon as she saw her father she ran headlong into his outstretched arms. Father and daughter embraced each other and shed tears of joy.

Stern in voice and countenance, Tian Yezi addressed Fu Puren: "Squire Fu, surely you know the common saying which runs, 'Before beating a dog think of its master.' Now that your granary has been robbed, a misfortune which we much regret, you go and make things difficult for me, beating up and arresting people in Tian Family Village, my domain, of all places! This is indeed going too far!"

"Please calm yourself, Squire Tian," Fu Puren apologized. "I confess that I am to blame for not keeping my people under proper control. The blunder they made is all my fault. I stand corrected."

Tian Yezi then turned to Tian Zhongqing and asked with concern: "Did Xia Long harass you?"

The girl shook her head.

"What about the other people?"

"I am lucky that you came in the nick of time," she said significantly.

If such is the case, Tian Yezi thought to himself, the whole thing can be settled without much more ado. He turned and asked Fu Puren: "Are you ready to settle this affair?"

"Since it was my men who caused trouble for the Tians, father and daughter, it is only right and proper that I should compensate them in addition to my apology. I am willing, therefore, to give them two piculs of grain and five ounces of silver as compensation. How's that?"

Tian Yezi threw the father and daughter a look of inquiry. An exchange of glances between them, and they nodded agreement.

Meanwhile, Meng Ke, who had been watching the above scenes closely, now rose from his seat and spoke up in his gentle way. "A gentleman never goes back on his word," he reminded Fu. "To assure us that yours is not just a promise made only to be broken, would you please put it into execution right now before everybody here, Your Lordship? The sooner it is done, the better."

"All right," Fu Puren at once issued the order: "Xia Long, you go and get a cart ready, this minute. And let it be loaded with two piculs of flour and rice plus five ounces of silver. And you personally escort the Tian father and daughter home."

Meng Ke made a deep bow to Tian Yezi, saying, "I often hear people sing the praises of you and your virtuous deeds. It is a great honor for me to make your acquaintance here today."

Smiling, Tian Yezi replied, "The honor is mine. Your name as an extremely intelligent young man has long resounded in my ears. Seeing is believing. Truly you live up to your reputation. Well met! Well met!"

Highly pleased with what he saw, the old teacher Zeng Xuan smoothed his flowing beard with both hands. Then, holding Tian Yezi by the hand, left Squire Fu's house.

Chapter Nine

Zeng Xuan Puts His Pupil Through His Paces; Duan Ping Questions Her Spouse to Test His Aspirations

The reader has been told how Zeng Xuan, having noticed the mutual admiration Tian Yezi and Meng Ke expressed for each other, was moved to take the former by the hand and walk with him out of Squire Fu's house. Once outside, he confidentially told Tian the following:

"I would not hold back anything from you even if I could, sir. The fact is that Meng Ke is my favorite pupil. He is intelligent and fond of learning. What with his wide knowledge, coupled with a retentive memory, he far surpasses his teacher, my humble self, as far as strategic thinking is concerned. I can guarantee that there is a great future for him.

"Now, I happen to know that you have a daughter, whom you hold dear to your heart and who is both talented and virtuous. I make bold to say that she and Meng Ke would make a perfect pair, and I would like to act as the gobetween for them. Would you allow me that honor?"

Tian Yezi readily agreed, moreover with a profusion of thanks.

"The pity, however, is that, being widow and orphan as they are, they are much worse off than you may imagine," added Zeng Xuan.

"What of that?" said Tian Yezi. "Trust me to get all things ready for the wedding."

With that, the two took leave of each other, in high spirits.

Back home, Tian Yezi lost no time informing his wife of his choice of a husband for their daughter.

His wife was anxious to know who the man was.

"The son of Mengsun Ji, Meng Ke," was the answer.

She shook her head doubtfully. "I have heard of such a name," she said.

Tian Yezi gave a candid smile as he explained, "He is a descendant of the Duke of Lu. Unfortunately his father died many years ago, leaving his wife and son to fend for themselves."

"In that case, his family must be poor," she sighed, with knitted

brows.

"In a way it is," said Tian Yezi, "though his mother, Zhang, is no ordinary woman. She is such a strong character that in order to bring up her son Meng Ke properly she moved house thrice to find a congenial environment for his mental development, and worked day and night at her loom to earn enough money to pay for his schooling. So, without his mother, Meng Ke could not possibly have achieved what he has so for."

"And what about his character and appearance?" his wife asked further.

Her query pleased Tian Yezi so much that his face blossomed into smiles, and he gave a portrayal of Meng Ke in glowing terms: "He is tall and slim, with an oval face. He carries himself with dignity and talks with ease and eloquence while conversing. All in all, he is unrivaled in appearance and ability in this part of the world."

At this, his wife smiled her consent, but said that she wanted first to consult their daughter herself.

Soon their daughter Duanping was brought into the reception hall. She was of medium build, with a face as oval as a melon seed, graced by perfectly arched brows as neat as willow leaves. She was clad in a white silk coat and skirt, presenting a most graceful and charming sight in the lamplight. She approached her father with quick, short steps and inquired gently why she had been sent for.

Tian Yezi said in a doting tone, smoothing his beard as he did so: "Duanping dear, you know the ancient saying, 'A girl should get married on coming of age'. Now you are 18 years old; the right time to get married. Your mother and I have discussed this and reached the decision that you are to be betrothed to Meng Ke."

Tian Duanping blushed crimson and dropped her head in spite of herself.

"So far as personal appearance goes," continued her father, "Meng Ke is a tall, strapping fellow. As to his character, he is honest and sincere. He is an upright man who never stoops to flattery. He bears himself with confidence and dignity. As for his scholastic attainments, he is erudite and informed, and conversant with things both past and present. In this respect, I should say he is head and shoulders above his contemporaries..."

"That's enough!" his wife reproached him mildly. "Let's hear what Duanping has to say."

"Your daughter's betrothal is entirely up to her parents to decide; it is her duty to obey," was Duanping's bashful reply.

But let us now return to Zeng Xuan.

The next day, after school, he went to the Mengs and told Zhang about the purpose of his visit. His proposal was warmly welcomed.

On the second day of the fourth month of the lunar calendar in 366 B.C. when Meng Ke had just celebrated his 19th birthday, his mother summoned him. "My son," she said in a grave tone, "you are grown up now. It is time you set up a family of your own, don't you think?"

"Mother, a man is not to marry until he reaches the age of 30. That is the rule instituted by the founder of the Zhou dynasty," said Meng Ke.

"Well, it was the rule those days," said Zhang, "but times have changed. There is a time and a place for everything. Take Confucius, whom you've revered all along. He married at the age of 19. And you and the Tian girl happen to be the same age—also 19. What a happy coincidence!"

Not convinced, however, Meng Ke made as if he wanted to argue but was forestalled by his mother, who said, "My son, I might accommodate myself to you in everything you wish for but this matter which will affect your whole life. In this I won't let you have your own way. You must listen to me, and bring Duanping into the family so that I may have her to keep me company while you are out. What's more, I'm hoping that you will give me a grandson."

Meng Ke had no choice but to submit.

So it was that after much discussion between mother and son a lucky day was selected by consulting the almanac, and in due course Tian Duanping joined the family as Meng Ke's wife. From then on the three formed a well-knit new family, in which each member loved and respected the others, and their happiness knew no bounds.

At the *Qing Ming** Festival, Zhang, having prepared beforehand the sacrificial offerings of wine, meat, incense and the like, took Meng Ke and his new wife with her to visit Mengsun Ji's grave. Arriving there, Meng Ke performed all the rites such an occasion demanded, including the "three obeisances and nine kowtows" before the grave.

---

* *Qing Ming*—"Clear and Bright"—is a festival which falls in the middle of the spring. On this day people pay visits to their ancestral tombs in the countryside.

After that, Zhang proposed a visit to their erstwhile friend, the kind-hearted old Fucheng, from whom they hadn't heard for years. But when they got to Wild Duck Village they learnt to their great sorrow that he had died seven days previously. Cherishing the memory of the dear old man in their hearts, they paid a visit to his grave with tears of grief and sacrificial offerings.

Now that he was a married man, Meng Ke was relieved of all domestic cares, thanks to Duauping's loving attention. Thus he was able to concentrate on his studies. Being gifted, he made tremendous progress in learning, and extended his interest to every field of knowledge. Having decided that this young man had a promising future in store for him, Zeng Xuan was more than willing to impart to him his rich store of knowledge, the fruit of a whole lifetime's scholarly labor.

One day, while a class was in progress, he halted midway to glance around at the pupils, his eye finally resting on Meng Ke.

"Meng Ke, how far have you reached in your study of the *Book of Songs, Book of History, Book of Rites, Book of Changes, Book of Music*, and *Spring and Autumn Annals*?" he asked. "Would you mind telling me and the class?"

After a moment's reflection Meng Ke replied modestly: "In my humble opinion these six classics are extremely profound—so much so that even if I gave my whole life to the study of them, I'm afraid I would not be able to master them. So far, I have only attained some rudimentary knowledge of them."

It was clear that Zeng Xuan fully agreed with this, though he refrained from comment. He simply paced up and down in his slow, measured fashion. Presently he posed another question: "Would you give us the gist of the *Book of Rites* as you understand it?"

This fired Meng Ke with enthusiasm, and he promptly launched into the following explanation:

"The *Rites* is a work collected and collated by Confucius and his disciples. It is a most dependable document for textual research into the origins and development of ancient society and Confucianism, as well as the cultural relics handed down from those times. Particularly noteworthy is the fact that this book, for the first time in human history, postulates the idea of 'The ultimate truth is the sharing of the world with the people'. It further points out that the way to bring this about is, as the first step, to run the world as one would a well-to-do family, a formulation which I think is of practical significance for posterity."

"Well done!" commented Zeng Xuan, all smiles. "You have a thorough understanding of the *Book of Rites*, I must say." After a short pause he continued, "Now let us proceed to the *Book of Changes*. Would you say something about this classic too?"

Encouraged by his teacher's praise, Meng Ke waxed even more eloquent this time: "The *Book of Changes* is composed of two main parts: One deals with the two symbols *gua* and *yao*; the other with the texts of *gua* and *yao*. Altogether, there are 64 *gua* and 384 *yao*. A theory then emerges which may be summed up in the sentence: When all means are exhausted changes become necessary; once changed, a solution emerges. Accordingly, I think, the present-day discussions about the five elements must have their origin in this book."

"By the way, explain the five elements theory, will you?" said Zeng Xuan in a highly pleased tone of voice.

"The Five Elements," explained Meng Ke, "metal, wood, water, fire and earth, both reinforce and neutralize one another. Wood reinforces fire, fire reinforces earth, earth reinforces metal, metal reinforces water, water reinforces wood—hence mutual reinforcement. At the same time, water neutralizes fire, fire neutralizes metal, metal neutralizes wood, wood neutralizes earth, and earth neutralizes water —hence mutual neutralization."

Zeng Xuan went on to question Meng Ke on a miscellany of subjects, and his student answered flawlessly.

"Excellent!" said Zeng Xuan, raising his hand over his head in a gesture of congratulation. "You are fully qualified to be a teacher now!"

All his classmates threw Meng Ke glances of admiration and envy.

Next, Zeng Xuan sounded Meng Ke out on his political views.

"Since the beginning of the Spring and Autumn period," the teacher began, "the feudal lords have continuously set up separatist regimes by force of arms, fighting each other, each trying to do the other down. Do you think there were just wars among them?"

"None at all," was Meng Ke's prompt answer. "The Spring and Autumn period knew no just war, as the saying goes. When Emperor Wu of Zhou enfeoffed his feudal lord he did so from the good intention that each of his princes might do a good job of running his state well in a concerted effort to bring prosperity to the whole of the empire of the Zhou Dynasty. But, contrary to his pious wishes, these princes—there being no lack of rapacious ones among them—gave themselves up to mutual slaughter. They seized cities and took territory, all to the detriment of the common people. Things often change into their opposites; the more one wants to subjugate others, the more isolated one becomes and the more disastrous the defeat one brings upon oneself."

"But there were so many feudal princes during the Spring and Autumn period; could it be that there was not a single good one among them?" Zeng Xuan queried.

"Nothing is good or bad except by comparison," said Meng Ke. "Some princes may have been better than others. But the truth is that none of them took the interests of the empire into account, and instead of fighting each other treated each other with respect and worked jointly to make the empire prosperous and strong. The only thing they were all proud of was their ability to wage war. This was deplorable."

At this, Zeng Xuan could not refrain from asking, "Why, indeed?"

"If the ruler of a state practices benevolent government and conducts state affairs in accordance with the rites his subjects will submit to him with heartfelt admiration, and they will vie with one another in offering their services for the common cause, thereby making it possible for the state to become rich and strong. And once the state has become rich and strong it will stand unrivaled in the world. When Lord Tang of the Shang Dynasty practiced benevolent government he gained the whole-hearted support of his people. When he marched on the south the northern barbarians complained, and when he marched on the east the western barbarians complained. They all said, 'Why does he not come to us first?' Similarly, when King Wu of Zhou marched on Yin he had only 300 war chariots and 3,000 brave warriors. But these were the words he addressed to the people wherever hextended his rule: 'Do not be afraid. I come to bring you peace, not to wage war on you.' Hence the people submitted to him most willingly, so much so that they knocked their heads on the ground by way of welcome. Such were the kingly ways of the afore-mentioned rulers that they conquered for no other purpose than that of winning peace and happiness for the people. Theirs were truly deeds of benevolence practiced in a big way."

"Should His Lordship appoint you to high office," suggested Zeng Xuan, "what would you undertake to do then?"

"In running a government it is important to appoint the good and able to office. Provided that His Lordship had the good grace to adopt my advice or warnings, I would certainly do my level best to recommend to him the best and ablest people in our state. And once these people were installed, the five basic virtues of kindness, justice, good manners, wisdom and honesty will prosper and weapons will be rendered useless. Only then will people live in peace and prosperity. Thus our example will certainly be followed by other feudal princes, and consequently peace and stability will be established throughout the empire."

Meng Ke's discourse so exhilarated his teacher that he gave a long sigh of admiration, his head thrown back and his eyebrows dancing with glee: "You have the makings of a great statesman, I am sure that if His Lordship employs you the State of Zou can be made strong. And if the Zhou emperor employs you, you can bring peace and order to the empire. How lucky I am to be able to count you among my students! Ah, I have not lived in vain!"

"The credit must go to you, sir, that I have been able to become what I am," was Meng Ke's modest reply.

"I am enormously proud of you, all the same," said Zeng Xuan. "But talking about the present, do you not think it time that you entered service so that you can give full play to what you have learned? I place great hope in you."

Back at home Zeng Xuan's words kept ringing in Meng Ke's ears. Yes, why not? he said to himself, when one studies something it can be for no other purpose than that of applying it. If one does not apply one's acquired knowledge to real life, does that not defeat its purpose?

At dinner time he joined his mother and wife at the table. His abstracted expression rather puzzled the two women. When questioned he answered only in monosyllables, and the two women could do nothing but leave him to himself.

It was growing dark when they finished their supper, which had been taken in silence. After she had washed the dishes Duanping came to the west room, where Meng Ke was, and lit the oil-lamp for him.

Rummaging about among his library of bamboo slips, Meng Ke finally hunted out the *Book of Rites*. His eyes fell upon the first sentence of the chapter *Li Yun* which ran: "THE GREAT TRUTH TO BE PRACTISED IS TO SHARE THE WORLD WITH THE PEOPLE."

He took up a writing brush, dipped it in ink, and copied the Chinese characters on a long and wide piece of bamboo. He viewed his effort from different angles and, satisfied at last, put it to one side of his desk. Then, another bamboo slip came into his view which bore the words, "The young should inspire one with respect. How do we know that their future will not equal our present?" in his own handwriting. He took it up, blew the dust off it, and, reading it over for some time, put it alongside the first one. He turned to find Duanping standing behind him, an understanding smile on her face.

To be understood by someone you love for something you have done is indeed a great consolation which can be transformed into an inexhaustible source of strength. Such was the case with Meng Ke at that moment, as he impulsively held up the bamboo slip with the *Li Yun* chapter on it so that the lamp-light could shine on it, and drew his wife close to him, pointing to the text as he commented, "Just imagine what a far-sighted and noble undertaking for mankind to strive for, this 'To share the world with the people'!"

To this, Duanping seemed to have some reservations of her own, as she said after a moment's hesitation: "I should think that it is something for the emperor and his princes to consider. It is far beyond your reach."

"Definitely not!" retorted Meng Ke in deadly earnest. "Every man has a share of responsibility for the fate of his country. It is true that one man is distinguished from another by his natural gifts and acquired abilities. But if everybody regarded the world as one family in which every member did his duty and contributed his bit, and in which the emperor loved the princes, the princes respected the emperor, the princes loved their subjects and the subjects respected their princes there would be no slaughter, no war. And, in the absence of fear of war and enslavement, the broad masses of the common people would concern themselves solely with their own jobs, till their land and weave on their looms. Peace and order would then come about of their own accord!"

"But the present condition of things, alas, is a chaos of strife among the feudal princes, while the common people are left hungry and dying by the wayside! To talk about 'one world—one family', isn't it futile?" queried Duanping in a tone of sheer helplessness.

"The trouble with the present-day world is that few people in it - whether rulers, or ruled - give any serious thought to learning.

Ignorant and stupid people, in most cases, are those who refuse to learn. It is not for nothing, I think, that the ancient sage Confucius compared a man who doesn't learn to something of a brute."

Meng Ke's remark intrigued his wife, who now asked tentatively: "Can it be that you're going to follow Confucius's example by setting up a school?"

"Not for the present, perhaps," said Meng Ke. "But I can have a try once I think I am qualified for it."

"Judging by your talent and political insight, don't you think you could put them to good use by engaging in politics?"

Meng Ke gave a long sigh before he said, "I've been to the court more than once and I know only too well what kind of a man that Duke Mu is. He is young and has little to recommend him. What's worse, all day long he wallows in sensual pleasures, losing himself in such decadent music as the *Kang Yue*, unable to extricate himself. The year before last, when this area was hit by a hailstorm, my father-in-law was generous enough to empty his granary to sell grain to the poor people, whereas Duke Mu remained unmoved, never lifting a finger to help them. That's the ruler of Zou for you! How could we trust the running of the state to such a man?"

The couple stayed awake all that night, laden as they were with the major cares of the day.

Next morning they had just got out of bed when they heard a flurry of knocking on the gate. Meng Ke opened it to find a flustered-looking Duanmu Yan announcing between gasps that their teacher Zeng Xuan was seriously ill.

After informing his mother and wife of the bad news, Meng Ke immediately rushed to Zeng Xuan's home together with Duanmu Yan.

The old teacher was lying in bed, pale and haggard, and groaning incessantly, surrounded by his pupils, who all looked anxious and yet helpless.

At the sight, Meng Ke lost all control and fell down on his knees before the bed. With one hand he gently moved the invalid's hand away from his pained breast and massaged it with the other, whispering words of comfort the while. "Bear it for a moment, sir. I'll send for a doctor straightaway."

Slowly Zeng Xuan opened his eyes and shook his head, saying, "No need. There's no help for it whatsoever."

The words pierced Meng Ke's heart like a thousand arrows. Tears welled up in his eyes, and his voice became hoarse as he asked, "What's the malady you are suffering from, sir? Why so sudden, without any warning?"

Zeng Xuan slowly raised his hand and stroked his breast with it without saying a word.

A heart attack! Meng Ke was at a loss what to do to ease his teacher's pain.

"I think I am dying," Zeng Xuan began. "I am approaching 70, so I think I have lived long enough. Only, I cannot bear the thought of leaving you all." As he said this the tears gushed from his eyes.

"I may call myself lucky," he continued, "to have been able to follow in the footsteps of Confucius' by adopting teaching as my profession. I am glad to know that I have turned out such a number of promising young men like you, who are praiseworthy both in character and scholarship. Much to my regret, however, I shall not live to see you accomplish great deeds."

Some students began to shed silent tears, while others broke into sobs.

"Do not weep, boys!" admonished Zeng Xuan, smiling weakly, but with tears still in his eyes. "You must bear in mind that for a man to make his way in this world it is most important for him to keep his moral integrity wherever he goes. When you are in office you must help the emperor and princes to overcome difficulties, and cast your lot in with the common people, come weal or woe. When teaching, try following Confucius example and impart to your students all the solid knowledge that may prove beneficial to society. Even if you end up as a commoner you must not do anything beyond the pale of the law, and you must be content with your lot. Furthermore, do not forget that life is never all plain sailing. When things go well with you, do not become conceited and throw your weight about; when in difficulties, do not lose heart and succumb to defeatism."

At this point, Meng Ke tried to quieten him for fear that too much talking might prove fatal to the patient.

With a wan smile on his face Zeng Xuan twitched his bluish lips, saying, "Meng Ke, my dear boy, you are intelligent and hardworking, and I'm sure that there is a great future in store for you. After my death, be sure to pass on to others what you are called upon to do, that is, to open a school to enroll all those who are amenable to learning, to teach them the six arts and educate them in moral excellence. If you get the opportunity of a political career try to persuade your prince to practice benevolent government and conduct state affairs according to the rites... But then, there is a weakness in your character, which I..." His voice grew weaker and weaker until abruptly it stopped.

A chorus of desperate cries broke out from the students, who came pressing around the sick-bed: "Teacher! Teacher!"

Zeng Xuan, summoning up the little strength that remained to him, moved his hand from his chest, and finally managed to grasp Meng Ke's hand with it until he breathed his last, when it slowly relaxed.

It is extraordinary the way things are in this human world of ours; when some people wail bitterly over a loss there are yet others who gloat over their gain from it.

And so it was that when the news came to him that Zeng Xuan had died Fu Puren was overcome with joy. He roared with laughter, shouting triumphantly: "Good riddance! Good riddance! One more stumbling-block removed from my way."

"My Lord, I hear people say that the old fogey praised Meng Ke to the skies," said Jue Hu. "And his dying instruction was for Meng Ke to take over his school and carry on with his teaching work. In my opinion, it is this Meng Ke you'll have to reckon with in the days to come."

"What's so remarkable about the kid that I should fear him?"

"True, you don't have to consider him for the present. But what about the future?"

"The future? What then?"

"By the time he has set up his school and enrolled students, he will have become something to be reckoned with."

"Well, what am I supposed to do?"

"The best defense is offence, you know."

"How?"

"I've learned that Tian Yezi's birthday falls on the fifth day of the fifth month. On that day Meng Ke is sure to take his wife along to congratulate his father-in-law. We can take the opportunity..."

"That will be killing two birds with one stone! How clever you are!" Fu Puren laughed boisterously.

Chapter Ten

Jue Hu Is Punished for Committing Arson; Xia Long Attempts Murder Only to Be Hoist on His Own Petard

Our narrative has progressed to the point where Fu Puren was being convinced by Jue Hu's argument that Meng Ke would in time become somebody influential enough to settle accounts with him. Now Jue Hu came out with his plan of action.

"On his father-in-law's birthday," said Jue Hu, "it is expected that Meng Ke will take his wife along to congratulate him. Let me take my men and set fire to his house. That way, both Tian Yezi and Meng Ke, both enemies of yours, can be killed off, and you will be avenged."

His plan was immediately taken up, and the necessary arrangements were made there and then.

It was wheat-harvesting time, and the local villagers were busy getting in the harvest in the cool of the evening. All along the highway that connected one village with another and on the crisscross footpaths between the fields the harvesters shuttled back and forth.

Tian Zhongqing's house was situated at the east end of Tian Family Village. Her father was now working in the field while she herself carried sheaves of wheat back home. On one of these trips two bulky fellows, brushed by her. She stopped short, thinking to herself: "Strange! Two wayfarers at this late hour! And when everybody is so busy, too!" She looked fixedly at them, as it seemed to her that one of them was familiar. She searched her memory and soon got it: Xia Long! She all but uttered the name aloud. What mischief is he up to this time? So thinking, she hastened after them at a safe distance all the way to her own house. She was about to lay down her load before continuing, when caution told her that this would incur their suspicion. So she kept on following as if she had further to go with the wheat sheaf.

Xia Long and Jue Hu went straight to Tian Yezi's house, which stood at the west end of the village. Under the cover of darkness, and taking advantage of the occasion when everybody else was preoccupied

with the harvest, they took their time looking around the exterior of the house, and presently skulked away.

All this while Tian Zhongqing had been on the watch. Now she was left wondering to herself: "What are they up to? Murder, burglary or what?" She then put down her load by the wayside and hurried to Tian's house.

The Tian couple had just put out the light ready for bed when they heard the knock. Tian Yezi hastened to opened the door, and to his surprise found Tian Zhongqing standing there.

After a brief bow the girl said, "Squire Tian, I've something urgent to tell you."

She was invited into the reception hall, where she bowed to the mistress of the house and took a seat. Then she proceeded to describe about her seeing Fu's chief steward and another man, their suspicious activities and her misgivings.

"I've come at this time of night to warn you. By all means be on your guard, please!" she stressed anxiously before taking her leave.

The spring of that year saw a spell of glorious weather on the land of Zou. On the fifth day of the fifth month, a felicitous time for husking and sunning grain for the villagers, Meng Ke and his wife Tian Duanping, birthday gifts in hand, were on their way to Tian Family Village. At the entrance they came across Tian Zhongqing and her father at the village mill.

On seeing the couple, without so much as a brief greeting, the Tian girl plunged head-long into a narration of her recent sighting of Fu's chief steward and his henchman, which she had told Squire Tian. "Take care!" she warned.

Tian Zhongqing's nocturnal visit and her warning had left Tian Yezi in a disturbed state of mind. Why should they harm me? he puzzled. He was, therefore, immensely relieved to see his son-in-law and daughter, with whom, he thought, he might take counsel.

"You have come at the right time," he said with a smile of welcome. "There is something worrying me about which I need your advice."

"Some unpleasantness on the evening before last, do you mean?" responded Meng Ke with the promptness of a sharp-witted, outspoken man.

"So you have learned about it!"

"The Tian girl told me just a while ago."

"What are they up to, anyway?"

"In dealing with a cruel and evil fellow of Fu Puren's type," said Meng Ke, "one cannot be too careful."

While stroking his beard with both hands, the old man fell to thinking. "Spying out the layout of my house at night—this can only mean that a sinister robbery plot is being hatched," he muttered.

"I think otherwise," disagreed Meng Ke. "Fu Puren has more of a design on your life than on your money."

"But he's a money-grubber after all," Tian Yezi wrinkled his brow in deep thought. "Besides, I have never wronged him in the past, nor have I wronged him lately. Why should he want to harm me?"

"My dear sir," Meng Ke said emphatically, "you know how Confucius put it: 'A superior man is calm and serene, whereas an inferior man is constantly worried and anxious.' It is therefore easier to recognize a superior man than to see through an inferior man. You've more than once trod on his corns. You did so rightly and out of a sense of righteousness, I'm sure—but for his part, being nasty-minded as he is, he is sure to take it much to heart, thinking that you deliberately discredited him, hurt his pride. Hence he sees you as an enemy."

"But I do not remember having ever hurt him, let alone deliberately."

"If I remember correctly, on two occasions you hurt him, though unbeknown to yourself: one was when you sold grain to the refugees the year before last, and the other was when last year you went to his place to claim back the Tian girl kidnaped by his men. The noble way you behaved put him to shame, and accumulated shame gives rise to hatred. That is how it is."

"You may be right. But why is it that for over a year he has not tried to take his revenge? Why now?"

"For four reasons," continued Meng Ke, counting upon his fingers, "First, last year Fu Puren sent his men to arrest me, which incident was obviously an act of wilful provocation on his part but for which the trouble-maker must have had some ulterior motive of his own; second, thanks to your timely rescue, I was able to come out unscathed, and consequently he stands convicted of the crime of wanton arrest; third, he failed in his attempt to harm me only to find that his evil scheme ensured that I had the good luck to become related to you by marriage; and fourth, Master Zeng Xuan entrusted me on his death-bed with the task of running his school after him. It is chiefly because of these four counts that Fu Puren hates me and he will be content with nothing less than my destruction."

This made Tian Yezi realize the dangerous situation he was involved in, and he hastened to ask, "What method do you think they would use to kill us, then? And in what way can we defend ourselves, pray?"

Meng Ke meditated for quite a while before he said, "If he wants to destroy the whole of us at one go it must be done in the daytime when Duanping and I are still here. In that case he wouldn't dare conduct his evil activities openly but would resort to some sinister method."

"There are all sorts of sinister methods," his mother-in-law chipped in, "which would it be, I wonder?"

"In my judgment," Meng Ke said, "it would be either poison or arson."

The atmosphere was heavy with consternation.

"Right now during the wheat harvesting," Meng Ke went on, "large amounts of wheat stubble are left around the walls of people's houses. So it would be easy enough for them to hit upon the idea of setting fire to a house."

"It is easy to dodge a spear thrown in the open, but hard to guard against an arrow shot from hiding," said Tian Yezi. "We must work out a fair counterfoil measure."

Meng Ke took his time in presenting his idea as to how to cope with the situation.

"Fu Puren is utterly devoid of conscience," said Meng Ke. "He has done enough evil to get himself caught in the long run. So let's get a dozen or more stalwart fellows, and when the time comes we'll catch them red-handed."

Everyone agreed that this was an excellent plan. Tian Yezi and his daughter set out to ask the neighbors for help while Meng Ke and his mother-in-law started upon their task of preparing to douse the fire if the villains tried to set to burn the house down.

The sun had climbed to its zenith, and people who had been working in the fields were coming home for their mid-day meal.

Tian Yezi, Meng Ke and their wives, their minds clouded with worries, paced up and down the courtyard waiting for the critical moment. Eight powerfully built fellows, armed with clubs and pitch-forks, were hidden behind the house wall or perched on ladders.

After a while there emerged from the thickets by the river three furtive figures, who, having made up their minds that there was not a living soul around, began to slink toward the rear courtyard wall of the Tians' house. The first one turned out to be none other than Jue Hu himself. He and the other two snatched up armfuls of wheat stubble, piled it at the foot of the wall, and were about to ignite it when a sharp whistle came from among watchers hidden in wheat stacks some distance away. At the signal, the eight hefty fellows within the wall clambered over it, and joined those outside who had first discovered the incendiarist. They all set up the cry: "Thieves! Fire!" and soon the evil-doers were surrounded by angry people. Jue Hu successfully made his escape thanks to his martial skills, but he left his two accomplices white-faced and crumpled on the ground, kowtowing ceaselessly and whining for mercy.

Disregarding their piteous entreaties, the angry people trussed the two men up and were about to subject them to further punishment when Meng Ke and Tian Yezi issued forth to stop them.

"Please, good people, don't use physical violence upon them," Tian Yezi held up his clasped hands in greeting. "You have saved my family and property in the nick of time, for which I owe you an immense debt of gratitude. But for the moment I beg of you not to beat them."

"The villains! Death is what they deserve! Why spare them?" the villagers replied in chorus.

"They've been put up to it by Fu Puren," said Tian Yezi. "We ought to keep them alive as evidence to incriminate Fu, don't you think?"

"Right! Then let's go for the real criminal!" the crowd yelled.

Tian Yezi glanced at Meng Ke, and the latter nodded his assent.

Tian Yezi thanked the people again for their cooperation, where-upon several strong fellows came forward to seize the two men and drag them toward Fu's house, with Tian Yezi walking ahead and nearly 100 villagers following.

Now let us come back to Fu Puren. After he had sent Jue Hu on his sabotage mission he sat back looking forward to hearing good news. But just as he was building castles in the air there barged in Jue Hu, pale-faced and trembling all over, altogether a sorry-looking figure. Jue Hu sank to his knees and reported in a stutter: "Your Lordship! We were forestalled. They had a lot of people lying in ambush around the house ready for us..."

This threw Fu Puren into a towering rage. Blue veins stood out on his forehead as he yelled at his slave: "Where the devil are the other two men?"

"We were outnumbered and the other two were caught."

Fu kicked Jue Hu in the forehead, cursing as he did so: "You good-for-nothing! Now that they've got our men in their hands there'll be the devil to pay!"

The vicious kick pained Jue Hu into contortions, and he clasped his head with both hands as he pleaded with his master: "My Lord! Please pardon me this once. I swear I'll perform one more creditable service to atone for my crime."

His eyes dilated with fury, Fu Puren stamped his foot and cursed venomously: "I've a good mind to have you put to death!"

A servant rushed in to report: "Tian Yezi and a group of men are at the door."

Fu Puren felt a cold shiver running down his spine. He turned to Jue Hu: "Get out of sight! Get out!"

Like a rabbit escaping from a butcher's knife, Jue Hu scrambled to his feet and in one bound scurried into the inner chamber.

Making an effort to buoy himself up, Fu Puren stalked out, but when he saw a crowd of people thronging the hall, each one looking daggers at him, he felt his legs suddenly give way with fright. With one hand he shielded his breast and with the other protected his forehead as he sidled up to Tian Yezi and bowed deeply, saying humbly: "Much obliged for your presence here. Welcome! Welcome!"

Tian Yezi, almost bursting with indignation, fixed Fu Puren with a burning stare and asked pointedly: "Squire Fu, you are well aware what your steward has been up to, I presume."

Fu Puren stuttered, "No...er, no...er...What has he been up to?"

Tian Yezi pointed to two men who were huddled in a corner and demanded, "Tell me who they are."

Fu Puren made a show of looking the two men over before he flatly denied, saying,"Wherever did these two brigands come from? Sorry, I don't know them."

"Since you don't know them, well, I'll have to take them away and dispose of them at my own discretion," said Tian Yezi.

At this, the two men threw themselves at the feet of Fu Puren, crying desperately for help from their master: "My Lord! Save us please!"

Fu Puren gave a sweep of his sleeve disdainfully, shouting as he did so: "You ruffians from nowhere! How dare you claim that I'm your master? Here, somebody! Take them out and flog them to death!"

"Not so fast!" Tian Yezi cut in, stern in both voice and countenance. "You are trying to remove two of your accomplices so that you can wriggle out of your responsibility as the main culprit, aren't you?"

"That's preposterous!" yelled Fu Puren, loud in voice but weak at heart.

"If that's the way it is, then there's nothing else I can do but take them away with me," said Tian Yezi.

"Please yourself!" was Fu Puren's reply.

Thereupon, Tian Yezi turned round to face the crowd, holding up his folded hands head-high in greeting, and said, "Dear neighbors! You have all heard Squire Fu's assertion that these two men don't belong to his household. So, all that is left for me to do is take them away to be dealt with properly."

The two men scurried on hands and knees to Fu Puren, crying for mercy: "My Lord, we risked our lives for you. You can't abandon us like this!"

Fu Puren kicked them away, roaring like a maniac: "Get away from me, you blackguards!"

At a signal from Tian Yezi several people seized the two men and carried them off.

Back home, Meng Ke addressed Tian Yezi: "Sir, we must take some precautions against the possibility that Fu Puren may charge us with the crime of libel."

"What should we do, then?" asked Tian Yezi.

"Let me report this affair to the duke in the capital and see what his lordship will do about it."

It was at the time when spring was changing into summer and when a south wind was always blowing at this time of year. Meng Ke was riding in a carriage on the main road which linked the State of Lu to the State of Zou. A multitude of thoughts flashed across his mind as he went. The internal strife of the feudal princes, deception and cheating between man and man, each trying to do the other down —gloomy thoughts generated by what he had seen or heard of in late years weighed on his mind like lead. "What a strange world!" he thought aloud. "On the one hand people are prattling about the merits of practicing benevolence and justice, and on the other no small number of people cling to doing the contrary. While everybody knows by instinct the necessity of food and clothing, there are others who give no thought whatsoever to people suffering from hunger and cold..."

The south wind was growing in intensity. Ensconced in his carriage, Meng Ke pursued his train of thought of how to approach the reigning prince of Zou and of what argument to use to prevail on him to condemn Fu Puren. His thoughts were thus engaged when suddenly he saw a cloud of dust flying up over the mountain-side to his left, and in no time at all a piebald thoroughbred with a rider came galloping toward him. It was none other than Xia Long himself. Meng Ke understood in a flash: The man had been sent by Fu Puren to assassinate him.

Xia Long pulled up right in front of the carriage, and, without stirring from his saddle, addressed Meng Ke after a cursory bow: "Young Master Meng, how are you? Allow me to ask, where you are bound."

Meng Ke returned his greeting and said, "For the capital."

"For what purpose, eh?" cross-questioned Xia Long aggressively.

"To purchase some birthday presents in honor of my father-in-law."

Xia Long laughed boisterously and scornfully. "Your father-in-law had his birthday only yesterday. You're telling a bare-faced lie! Going to lodge a complaint against someone with the court, aren't you?"

"Well, what if I am?"

"Then, woe betide you!"

Meng Ke immediately took up the sword he had prepared and whipped it out in a self-defense stance.

"Since I'm on Squire Fu's payroll I must do his bidding. Young Master Meng, let me tell you the unpleasant truth: My special mission here today is to intercept and kill you."

Meng Ke held him up to mockery by questioning him ironically: "Because you eat out of somebody else's rice-bowl, must you go out of your way to murder people?"

"Young Master Meng," said Xia Long, "if you were in my position you would do the same."

"Never!" said Meng Ke indignantly and with curt finality.

" Under no circumstances would I!"

Meanwhile their confrontation had drawn a crowd of curious people, and Xia Long glanced right and left uneasily. "I won't waste my time wagging tongues with you," he said. "This is my ultimatum: If you take your own life with your sword it would spare us both a certain amount of unpleasantness."

"I dare you to have the courage to commit murder for all to see!" Meng Ke declared solemnly.

With that, Meng Ke lifted his long whip with a vigorous jerk and came down with it neatly on the ear of Xia Long's horse. Frightened, the horse reared up, gave a long whinny and dashed away up the mountain slope, rider and all. Seizing the opportunity, Meng Ke urged his horse on with another crack of his whip and sped on to the capital without more ado.

Xia Long brought his horse back on to the main road and chased after Meng Ke. With his sword handle he lashed the horse all the way and the beast raced ahead as swiftly as an arrow shot from a bow. In the twinkling of an eye he had caught up with Meng Ke's carriage, and when at last he was abreast of where Meng Ke was seated he gave a deadly thrust with his sword....

A ghastly cry pierced the air.

Looking back, Meng Ke saw Xia Long kneeling on the road, with a tall strong fellow standing over him. With a bow in his left hand and a sword in his right, the latter glared down at the terrified Xia Long. Who should the stranger be but his good friend Tao Shi himself! Overjoyed, Meng Ke immediately got down from his carriage and hastened forward. Seeing an arrow stuck in Xia Long's arm, he knew at once what had happened. He turned to his friend and made a deep bow: "Dear Tao Shi, you have saved my life in the nick of time. Thanks, many thanks, indeed!"

Tao Shi returned the courtesy after he had replaced his sword and bow, and said, "That's all right. Don't stand on ceremony."

"How did you know that I was here?"

"Your father-in-law was afraid that you might fall prey to a plot on this journey of yours, so I was sent to protect you all the way without your knowing it. Just as we expected, Fu Puren had indeed hatched a vile plot, sending his man to murder you. The viper!"

"Had it not been for your timely rescue I would have fallen victm to his sharp sword. What a close shave!" sighed Meng Ke.

Tao Shi pulled out his sword, handed it to Meng Ke, saying: "Brother, take this sword, kill this scoundrel with it and be avenged."

On hearing this, Xia Long knocked his head on the ground continuously: "Fu Puren is the cause of it all—he's the real criminal. I'm a mere tool in his hands. Please forgive me!"

His anger still unabated, Tao Shi brandished his sword over the terrified Xia Long's head, saying, "We definitely cannot forgive you. You're more of a willing tool than anything else; once you are set free you will go on doing evil if there's the chance."

"No! No! I won't That I swear!" screamed Xia Long in desperation.

"Stand up!" was Meng Ke's stern demand.

Like a whipped cur, Xia Long scrambled up from the ground while gripping in his left hand the dangling arrow that was still bedded deep in his right arm.

Meng Ke helped pull the arrow out for him. The process caused Xia Long to groan and moan, his face contorted with pain.

"To let a wicked man like this go free," demurred Tao Shi, "is tantamount to letting a tiger return to the mountain. Rather than that, I would prefer to kill him right now."

"True, he deserves that," explained Meng Ke. "But what I'm going to do now is to take him along so that I may present him before the court as to incriminate Fu Puren."

Tao Shi volunteered to be his escort, and Meng Ke accepted his friendly help with many thanks.

In due course they came to the gate of the palace. A palace guard went in with Meng Ke's request for an audience with the duke, but after a long time he reappeared with the order: Meng Ke is to wait until the afternoon.

Chapter Eleven

**Abiding by His Principle of Tolerance,
Tian Yezi Lets Xia Long Go Free;
Acting on His Promise, Duke Mu Presents
Meng Ke with Gifts Galore**

The duke's dilatory response to his request for an interview struck Meng Ke as insulting, but for the time being he had no choice but to go elsewhere until the duke should deign to see him. First he went to the main street to find a pharmacy, where he had Xia Long's arrow wound dressed. Then he had lunch at a restaurant before making his way back to the palace.

The Duke had just finished his morning audience with his ministers and officials, and was now being entertained with music and dance, together with his duchess and concubines in the rear palace.

A guard tiptoed in and reported in a low voice: "Meng Ke is at the gate, sire, requesting an interview."

Duke Mu slowly opened his eyes and, stretching himself languorously, barked, "Let him in!"

The guard walked out and announced, "By His Highness' order: Let Meng Ke in!"

After going through the necessary forms of ceremonial greeting, Meng Ke took the seat he was assigned to.

The duke asked coldly: "Meng Ke, what are you here for this time, eh?"

Meng Ke spoke up without any preamble: "I am here to bring an accusation against Fu Puren. The man is a notorious scofflaw, doing every evil imaginable under the sun. He has committed robbery, arson and kidnaping in our area, thinking that he can get away with anything simply because he is rich and powerful."

"Is your accusation based on evidence?" questioned the duke, straight faced and glowering.

"Last spring," Meng Ke began, "for no rhyme or reason, he had a girl from the Tian Family Village kidnaped and dragged off to his house. On the same day his men snatched me off the street and

dragged me to his house also. Yesterday, while I was at my father-in-law's, celebrating his birthday, he sent his men to set fire to the house in an attempt to murder us. Today, on my way here, his chief steward tried to murder me. I was only saved by my friend Tao Shi's intervention."

"Who can prove all this?" said the Duke.

"Xia Long who attempted to murder me, is now at your palace gate under escort. Two of the would-be arsonists were caught on the spot, while the principal escaped no one knows where."

"It seems that since you yourself have been involved in all these incidents there must be some kind of feud existing between you two," the duke said.

"No, there isn't," said Meng Ke. "I only know that there did occur some dispute between my father-in-law and Fu Puren over the sale of grain the year before last."

"So that's it!" the duke said brightly, "I knew there must be some cause for it. But when all's said and done, as the supreme ruler of a state, surely I'm not expected to judge such petty quarrels among you common people, am I?"

Overwhelmed with despair, Meng Ke bowed his farewell to the duke with the words: "Excuse my interruption, My Lord!"

Meanwhile, Fu Puren was waiting for the good news that Xia Long would bring him. Time passed and evening came. Still Xia Long did not show up. Fu grew impatient, and impatience soon developed into annoyance. He felt that he must find somebody to vent his spleen on. The 'somebody' was of course none other than Jue Hu, the man responsible for the aborted arson attempt.

"All my trouble is because you, you miserable good-for-nothing, allowed two of my men be caught. Now they can use them as evidence against me, what chance is there for me to ward off the charge? I'm finished!"

"I deserve to die! I deserve to die!" Jue Hu moaned.

"The only way out for both of us at the moment is to remove those two blunderers, so that they can have no chance to speak up," said Fu Puren.

"I see what you mean," said Jue Hu. "This evening I will slip into Tian Yezi's house and finish them off."

"Tian Yezi has got no extra men to stand guard. In all probability the two are being held in custody somewhere else."

"Where could they be, then?"

"Most likely they're at Tian Zhongqing's, I reckon."

Sure enough, the two were indeed being held in the west room in Tian Zhongqing's house. A group of young men from Tian Family Village was taking turns to watch over them. It happened to be the busy farming season, and the local people had their supper late as a rule. Thus when the young farmer on watch went home for his supper it was already dark. Jue Hu, in hiding, watched for his chance, and when nobody was looking he emerged from the shadows and crept round the earthen wall of the house until he came to the west room, where his two men were imprisoned. In one bound he leaped onto the thatched roof and tore a hole in it, through which he let himself down. His sudden appearance gave the two prisoners a scare, but before they had time to cry out Jue Hu stopped them by saying in an urgent whisper: "I'm here to rescue you. Don't make a sound!"

Completely taken in, the two men uttered no end of thanks. As they did so, Jue Hu, taking them off guard, tapped a finger at the acupoints of the two men's larynges, and at once they were rendered mute. Jue Hu set to work and in no time at all he was gone, leaving the two men lying in a pool of blood.

Let's pick up the story at the point at which we left Meng Ke on his unsuccessful mission to the capital. He and Tao Shi returned to Tian Family Village with Xia Long under escort. After hearing Meng Ke relate his bitter experience at the palace Tian Yezi looked up at the sky and gave a long sigh of profound sorrow, saying at the same time: "Our state of Zou is going to the dogs!"

When Tao Shi was introduced Tian Yezi expressed both his gratitude and admiration for the heroic deed he had performed in defense of his son-in-law.

After supper that evening the three settled down under the lamplight to a discussion about the way to dispose of Xia Long.

"Since the duke refuses to incriminate Fu Puren and punish him we would do better to let that sleeping dog lie," Tian Yezi began. "If we rush matters and drive him to desperation he will commit more atrocities."

"But if we don't get rid of such a villain as he is," said Tao Shi, "the local people are bound to suffer. If I had my way, I'd sooner have him die under my sword than leave him alone."

"Oh no," admonished Tian Yezi. "That is not the proper way a gentleman in the true sense of the word should conduct himself. As gentlemen we're called upon to be tolerant and return good for evil."

At this juncture, Tian Zhongqing burst in looking flustered, with the news that the two men in her detention had been murdered.

"It must have been done by men dispatched by Fu Puren, who wanted to silence the culprits," Tian Yezi surmised.

"What if Fu Puren should come and demand we turn over his men to him?" asked Tao Shi.

"I should say it is absolutely impossible that he would, after he has denied in public that they were his men," said Tian Yezi. "For the present, bury the two corpses quietly in the wilderness, and that should be the end of the matter. The ticklish problem, though, is this man Xian Long...."

"Since things have come to such a pass," said Meng Ke, "it is unwise to further enrage Fu Puren by punishing his lackey. What my father-in-law said is right: We don't have to wake a sleeping dog. And there is no harm, either, in having Xia Long in our keeping, as we can do some work to bring him round to see the light; after all he's a mere tool in Fu Puren's hands."

"Well said, my boy!" said Tian Yezi with a smile. "Please do as you think fit to straighten him out."

Meng Ke soon went to fetch some food which he served Xia Long in person, saying pleasantly: "Here's some food for you—I suppose you must be hungry by now."

The man fell upon the food like a ravenous wolf and soon it was finished, after which he said hoarsely: "Thanks a lot! Now I can go to my death on a full stomach, I am content. Come now, I'm ready!" So saying, he stretched his head out.

"Xia Long, " said Meng Ke. "It was not our intention to send you to your death on a full belly. Our intention was to feed you so that you may go home!"

"Really?" said Xia Long incredulously.

Meng Ke nodded as he said with assurance: "I mean what I say. A gentleman never goes back on his word."

At this Xia Long fell on his knees and knocked his forehead on the ground, saying, "You are a real gentleman, sir. A magnanimous-hearted gentleman. I swear to Heaven that from now on I'll never be an enemy to you!"

"From now on don't molest good people. Do good by them," advised Meng Ke.

Xia Long swore again and again that he would take Meng Ke's advice and turn over a new leaf. Meng Ke saw him to the gate, and there, pointing to the road that stretched before them, he further advised: "Benevolence and righteousness are like this road. Follow it unswervingly and you will ultimately attain your desired object."

"Woe is me!" wailed Xia Long as he shed tears of repentance. "Now I know that I was unable in the past to tell good people from bad, and consequently I sought the wrong patron in Fu Puren and did so many things that trespassed against the way of benevolence and righteousness."

"Men are not saints; how can they be free from faults?" Meng Ke said earnestly. "You did go astray but there is still time to mend your ways, and better late than never."

"Thank you! Good-bye till we meet again!" With that Xia Long left for home.

After Xia Long had gone Tao Shi was left wondering, "Could he really be a case of 'A butcher becomes a Buddha the moment he lays down his knife'? —I give him the benefit of the doubt!"

"I cannot guarantee that he is certain to become a good man, but somehow I have a feeling that he is not a hopeless case," said Meng Ke.

"Brother," conceded Tao Shi, "you *do* have a heart of gold, may God bless you!"

Now back to Fu Puren. He had been waiting for Xia Long with trepidation, and when his henchman returned Fu asked anxiously: "Why so late? Is Meng Ke dead or not?"

"Fool that I was!" Xia Long put on a show of self-accusation by beating his breast and stamping his feet, saying, "He shot an arrow at me before I could overcome him."

"Surely Meng Ke's martial skills can't be superior to yours, can it?" queried Fu Puren, his blood-shot toad's eyes popping out threateningly.

"My martial skill is by no means inferior to his," Xia Long explained humbly. "But the fact is that when I reached a slope where I could command a view of Meng Ke and his gig, that cursed horse of mine suddenly started to neigh, thus betraying my presence. Meng Ke must have guessed what I was up to, and so let fly with an arrow, which hit my arm before I knew what had happened."

Not convinced, however, Fu Puren shot another question at him: "Where have you been all day, eh?"

"I was afraid that the bad shape that I was in might arouse suspicion, so I had my wound dressed at a pharmacy first, then I hid in the mountains till it was dark, when I slipped back. That's why I have been so late, you see."

"Well, that sounds sensible," Fu Puren emitted a sigh of relief. "We might as well consider ourselves lucky that no one knows we were involved, even though we didn't succeed in killing Meng Ke."

After these repeated setbacks to his sinister operations, Fu Puren dared not take any more reckless steps and, like a tortoise, he withdrew into his shell for the time being. It will be some time before we hear of him again.

Now let's come back to Meng Ke.

By the year 363 B.C. our hero had reached the age of 22, and it was three years since he had got married. Time passed quickly and soon it was spring again, a glorious season of red peach blossoms and green willow leaves. One day, Meng Ke's mother was standing in her courtyard before the apricot and peach trees, completely lost in thought. The trees in their full bloom touched a chord in her heart. These plants have weathered many a frost and snow, she thought to herself, and now they are happily bathing themselves in the spring breeze. Yearly they blossom and bear fruits, her train of thought continued, but how is it that my daughter-in-law Duanping gives no sign of pregnancy, though it has been nearly three years since she married my son? Obsessed with this thought, she summoned Meng Ke to her presence and asked him the reason why. The question stunned him for a moment before he blurted out, with a naive grin: "I don't know, either."

"People say that the god of Mount Nishan answers one's prayers readily," Zhang went on, "and lots of people go there to pray. Confucius's mother, Yan Zhengzai, too, went there to pray for a son, and sure enough, scarcely a year had passed before a son was born to her—That was Confucius. Mount Nishan isn't far from here, no more than 60 *li*. You should take Duanping along there to pray. And may the god bless you with good luck."

"Mother, you are too obsessed by the idea of a grandson, aren't you?" retorted Meng Ke. "Anyway, I won't go, Mount Nishan god or no Mount Nishan god!"

But Zhang remonstrated further: "Your father died in the prime of life. You are his only son. To continue the family lines is your filial duty—how can you ignore it?"

"We are still young, Duanping and I. Don't worry, Mother," said Meng Ke.

Zhang could find no way to further remonstrate with her son, and tears of helplessness gushed out of her eyes in a steady stream.

Neither could Meng Ke see his way to convincing his mother. All he could do was to wipe her tears away and comfort her as best he could. "Listen to me, Mother," he said. "In order to fulfill Master Zeng's dying wish, I have been thinking of running a school to admit promising youths to be trained in the six arts and be instilled with moral excellence, so that, once they have the chance, they may serve their people with credit."

Zhang smiled through her tears upon hearing this. "This is a noble ambition for you, my son!" she said with fervor. "For a man to follow his true path in this world, nothing is worth more than to win a good name for himself by doing something beneficial for his fellow men, and the vocation of teaching is indeed one of the noblest. It takes ten years to grow a tree, but a hundred to rear a person, as the proverb goes. I just want to ask, how soon will you take on this task?"

"Of course, it brooks no delay. I will start as soon as I can," was Meng Ke's resolute reply.

The following day he collected his friends Tao Shi and Duanmu Yan, and shared his idea of running a school with them. They took to his plan with glad hearts.

"You're more than equal to this calling of teaching, I'm sure," said Duanmu Yan, "since you are so erudite after so many years of hard study."

"My son Tao Yin is now five years old—Some day soon you'll admit him as a pupil, I hope," said Tao Shi jokingly.

"My school will be open to all who are keen to receive an education," said Meng Ke in a mock-serious tone. "Why should I make an exception of your son?"

There and then they reached the decision that Tao Shi would be responsible for the renovation of the school premises previously used by Zeng Xuan. Duanmu Yan was to post bills and write a memorial to the Zou court with regard to the opening of the school. In the meantime Meng Ke was engrossed in preparing for the Opening Day.

Five days passed, and over 50 youngsters had applied for admission to the school.

The day at last came for Meng Ke to assume his role as a teacher instead of a student. He taught the six arts in the prescribed order and propagated his doctrine of benevolence and righteousness more by example than by precept. Because his knowledge—which he had acquired through sheer hard work—was both far-reaching and solid, and, what is more, he was oratorically gifted, his eloquent lectures made what seemed dead things on bamboo slips come to life. A year's teaching work gained him great fame and high prestige, and educated people throughout the land vied with each other in calling him Master. As time went on, he came to be known to the world as Meng-Zi or Mencius.

When his fame came to the duke of Zou's ears, the duke entrusted his senior minister Xiahou Yi with 50 yi of gold to give to Mencius at his school as mark of his high esteem. This happened in the autumn of 362 B.C.

As Xiahou Yi approached the school gate Mencius was in the middle of a lecture on the *Yan Yuan*, a chapter in the *Analects of Confucius*. The minister stopped outside the lecture room door and stood there listening with bated breath. It was not until he knew that Mencius had finished his lecture that he ventured to knock at the door.

Hearing the knock, Mencius immediately opened the door, and, on seeing that the visitor was Xiahou, hurriedly made a bow, apologizing as he did so: "Your visit took me by surprise, sir. The blame is mine that I failed to welcome you in time."

Xiahou Yi, in his early thirties and delicately featured, was a man of stately and prepossessing appearance. As he politely returned Mencius' greeting, he said with a pleasant smile: "Since I came barging in unannounced, I should say the blame is mine!"

Thereupon, Mencius ushered the minister into the lecture room. After exchanging further civilities they took their seats as host and guest on the teacher's platform, from where Mencius now addressed his students: "Boys, you see I am entertaining a distinguished guest, so you can all go home now."

Standing in awe of their teacher's honored guest, each of the students politely excused himself and quietly left the room.

Deeply impressed by what he had seen, Xiahou Yi commented with admiration: "The Master has been running the school only a little more than a year—but what courteous, likeable boys His Excellency has turned out in so short a time!"

"You flatter me, Your Excellency," said Mencius.

"His Highness the Duke has noted how well you run your school," said Xiahou Yi, "He places great hopes in you. I was sent by His Highness today expressly to present you with this 50 *yi* of gold to help you meet daily expenses."

Mencius accepted the gold from an attendant and expressed his thanks to the duke for his good wishes, as well as to his envoy for the visit.

His mission fulfilled, the minister stood up to say good-bye.

After seeing off Xiahou Yi, Mencius immediately fetched Duanmu Yan and Tao Shi for a consultation. "His Lordship the Duke had the grace to have his minister present me with 50 *yi* of gold," said Mencius as he showed them the gift. "I wish to put it to good use. Well, how about erecting a larger building for our school at the west end of the village? What do you think?"

"Excellent!" His friends jumped with joy at the idea and volunteered their help, full of praise at the same time for Mencius' enterprising spirit and farsighted planning. It was decided then that Tao Shi was to take charge of the construction project.

Barely two months had elapsed when a new school building came into being, thanks to Tao Shi's energetic and swift work. He did not wait long to invite Mencius and Duanmu Yan to make a tour of inspection.

The new school campus consisted of spacious courtyards, classrooms and other accommodation, high-roofed, roomy and well-lit, with a seating capacity of 500 people. The layout quite impressed Mencius, who began to regard Tao Shi as a budding architect. But then a doubt arose in his mind when he thought: The ancients were very particular about social rank when building houses. For a common dwelling a building with five rooms only was allowed, and a nine-room building was reserved exclusively for top-ranking people.

He consulted Tao Shi on this, and the latter said, "It is true that the ancients were strict when it came to dwellings, but a school is a different matter. A school is an institution of learning, which even the children and grandchildren of princes and emperors have to attend at one time or another. In their day our own Duke Zhao and Duke Ding, and Duke Ai of the State of Lu, as well as Duke Jing of the State of Qi and Duke Ling of the State of Wei—all of them sought advice from Confucius, and so they might be considered students of the Master. Why should an institution of learning not be shaped to fit the highest rank?"

"But the floor space for the courtyards seems a bit too large, for all that," said Mencius.

"I took into account the fact that the students will have to practice the rites and ceremonies."

"How thoughtful of you!" interposed Duanmu Yan. "Now I know you are anything but a coarse-grained sort of person, as you're in the habit of calling yourself."

"Next spring let's plant cypresses and junipers around the court-yards," Tao Shi suggested. "When they grow they will shelter us from the wind in winter and provide us with cool shade in summer."

Soon, Mencius' school moved to the new site. The following spring they had cypresses and junipers planted all around the court-yards. With a sense of carefree ease, Mencius devoted all his time to his teaching work.

In the summer of 360 B.C. the rainy season set in in the State of Zou. One day when school was over and the sky had cleared up, Mencius set out on his way home. The air felt invigorating after a shower of rain, and he walked at a leisurely pace, his heart filled with contentment. But the moment he entered the door, he was shocked to see his wife retching heavily, her hands clasping her belly.

Chapter Twelve

**Duanping Gives Birth to a Son, to the Joy
of the Whole Family;
Mencius Pours out His Grievances Against a Corrupt
Government at the Graveside of His Worthy Teacher**

We were told in the last chapter how Mencius, on arriving home, got a terrible fright at the sight of his wife in the grip of illness. Hurriedly he rushed over and gently pounded her back, inquiring anxiously the while: "Is it anything serious? Shall I send for a doctor?" He turned to look for his mother, only to find her beaming, a damp towel in hand, and eyeing him significantly. Presently, Duanping left off retching, and she turned to him with a smile. There was joy, warmth and pride in her glance. The reason suddenly dawned on him as he queried in a flutter of excitement: "How long is it since you...?"

For an answer Duanping bashfully lowered her head, smiling to herself.

Zhang chided her son with loving care: "Silly boy, how careless of you! It's two months and more and yet you had no idea of it!"

She started to make a fuss over her daughter-in-law, now dabbing her forehead with the damp towel and now smoothing down her hair.

The scene filled Mencius with a sense of domestic bliss, and presently he was moved to say, "Mother, from now on, you and Duanping don't have to work so hard day and night in order to earn a living. The income I get from running the school doesn't amount to much, it is true, but it is sufficient to pay our daily expenses. You're getting on for 50, and Duanping is in the family way, so you must make sure you don't overwork yourselves."

"I've been working at my loom for scores of years and I've got used to it," said his mother. "I find in physical activity a good antidote to illness; it strengthens the physique, gives me a good appetite and helps me to sleep."

"Be that as it may," said Mencius, "one's health cannot be overlooked."

"I know how to take care of myself," said his mother. With that,

she settled down to her spinning.

But just before she started to work, she became aware that Duanping was washing her hands preparatory to going to the kitchen. She immediately stopped her, as she said, "Duanping dear, go back to your bedroom and get a bit of rest. Leave the kitchen work to me, will you? I was chattering away so, that I clean forgot it's time to prepare the dinner!"

"I'm all right now," Duanping said with a wry smile. "Don't let it trouble you."

"No trouble at all. You are pregnant, so let me do it for you, there's a dear." So saying, she made Duanping abandon the job she was doing in spite of her energetic protests. "Go to your bedroom, now."

On the 15th day of the third month of the lunar calendar in 359 B.C. Tian Duanping gave birth to a boy. He was named Zhongzi. The birth of a male member into this simple family was really a big and joyful event, which was duly celebrated.

With the passage of time, as Mencius' renown as an educator grew more and more students from neighboring states came to apply for admission to his school. By the year 351 B.C. the school had attained an enrollment of 600 students.

One day Mencius had just finished teaching a class on the *Book of Changes* and was going out into the courtyard when through the school gate walked in a man in his early twenties, attractive in manner and deportment. He was of medium height and was wearing a scholar's gown. A pair of bright, piercing eyes looked out from a swarthy round face. He was altogether a heroic-looking young man, Mencius decided.

The stranger bowed to Mencius before introducing himself. His name was Yue Zhengke, he said, and he had come from the State of Lu for purpose of seeking knowledge from the master.

"Have you studied the six arts?" questioned Mencius.

"Yes, I've studied them, but not thoroughly enough," was the reply.

"Studying is like scaling a height," said Mencius with a smile, "it must be accomplished step by step, and each step counts. It is in the nature of things that a learner can reach no depth of knowledge in the initial stage. But just keep on learning assiduously and you can achieve something in the end."

Yue Zengke interposed with his thanks, after which Mencius continued, "Confucius was a great scholar for whom I have boundless respect and admiration. I have long since cherished the hope that one day I can visit the temple and the Forest of Steles dedicated to his memory. Since you come from the State of Lu, I take it that you have first-hand knowledge of his monuments?"

"Of course, sir," said Yue, "I was born and bred in the capital of Lu and have been to the temple and Forest of Steles many times."

"Wonderful!" said Mencius, beaming with pleasure. "tomorrow would you guide me there?"

Taking this request as if it were a conferred favor, Yue agreed readily. "I will be only too glad to be your guide," he said.

And so it was that the next morning a carriage stood ready at the school gate, with volunteer driver Yue Zhengke waiting beside it.

Soon they were on the road. Yue proved to be an expert driver, and horse and carriage sped on like the wind. Half a day had hardly passed when the South Gate of the capital of Lu came in sight. They had covered 50 *li*.

The city gate was flanked on both sides by towering walls built of massive blocks of stone, which extended east and west as far as the eye could see. As he observed the majestic sight, Mencius thought to himself: "What a big city it is! Eloquent proof of its one-time mighty and prosperity and a witness to the height of civilization the State of Lu once reached." He pointed to an earthen mound on the eastern side of the road and asked Yue what it was."

"Dancing Rainbow Terrace," was the reply.

"So that's the rostrum where the official Prayer to Heaven was performed. I believe Confucius used to frequent this place with his disciples," said Mencius.

When they reached the gate they had to wait while soldiers stopped every comer and goer for a close and often ill-mannered questioning and body search. Annoyed, Mencius, who had first intended to alight and go straight into the city on foot, now thought better of it and preferred to stay in his carriage.

The streets in the city ran straight and wide, with rows of shops lining both sides, all doing a brisk trade. Here and there were buildings with carved beams and painted rafters, whose architectural style was so consistent that they seemed to be the works of one and the same artist. Most of the streets were bustling with pedestrians and vehicles.

As Mencius viewed all this from his carriage he thought to himself: "Although the State of Lu is on the decline, it is still in better shape than the State of Zou."

Presently the carriage brought them to an intersection. Yue Zhengke asked Mencius which place he wished to visit to begin with.

"Let us go and buy some incense sticks first," Mencius said, "and go and pay homage to the Duke of Zhou at the Royal Ancestral Temple."

They went straight to the temple with the incense sticks, but some hundred paces from it Mencius asked Yue to halt the carriage and stepped down. Having adjusted his garb and flicked the dust from his hat, he proceeded.

The temple caretaker, impressed by the stately and prepossessing air of the visitor, hastened forward with a courteous bow and inquired politely: "Whence do you come, sir?"

Mencius returned his bow and answered, "I am from the State of Zou."

"May I ask your name, sir?"

"Meng is my family name and Ke is my given name."

The caretaker was astonished. Finally he blurted out, "I have long heard your name, sir. Seeing you in person, now I realize that you indeed live up to your fame!"

"You are too kind," said Mencius.

"Your Excellency is here to offer a sacrifice to the Duke of Zhou, I presume?" asked the caretaker.

"Right," replied Mencius. "I have only just arrived in Lu."

"May I make so bold as to ask why you chose here prior to visiting the Confucius Temple?"

"Let me tell you why," said Mencius. "There is not the least doubt about Confucius being a great philosopher, whose merits will be remembered throughout the ages. But do not forget the fact that while Confucius—as he admitted himself—had no regular teachers all his life, he was most influenced by the Duke of Zhou's thought. Although he was born five centuries later than the duke—hence the impossibility of his learning directly from him—yet his thought was chiefly based on the latter's, that is, the theory of benevolent government and rule by observing what is right and proper. In this sense Duke Zhou might be considered his teacher, don't you think? It is natural, therefore, that I give priority to Duke Zhou in today's itinerary."

"That sounds reasonable." said the caretaker. "Now sir, please come this way."

Thereupon, Mencius was ushered into the Royal Ancestral Temple, with Yue Zhengke following in his wake.

The temple consisted of three groups of buildings complete with both front and rear courtyards, all canopied by a dense foliage of tall cypresses and junipers. The grounds were carpeted with sere grass and chrysanthemums. A solemn silence reigned over the whole place.

The caretaker led his visitors straight to the main hall in the rear group. Facing them as they entered was a statue of the Duke of Zhou. Two other statues, one of Bo Qin, the first reigning prince of Lu, and one of the Golden Man, stood on each side.

Mencius first lit his incense sticks, then, with these in his clasped hands, he made obeisance most reverentially and finally stuck the sticks in the bronze incense burner in front of the statue of the Duke of Zhou. Only after he had completed these initial rituals did he enter upon the sacrificial ceremony, which consisted of a short eulogy of the deceased and the "three obeisance and nine kowtows". To the other two statues he made each a deep bow only. The Golden Man, life-sized, plainly clothed and shod in black cloth shoes, had an animated expression in his eyes. Conspicuous were the three strips of white cloth which were pasted vertically over his mouth. This was taken to mean that one must guard against one's speech and actions. In addition, a message to this effect was inscribed on his back. Mencius uttered a sigh after reading it and commented, "The Duke of Zhou purposely wrote this on the robe of the Golden Man as a caution for Bo Qin that he must be discreet in word and deed. And in order that this caution might serve as a constant reminder to him, the duke further had the Golden Man follow him all the way from Hao, the capital of the Zhou Dynasty, to the State of Lu. This shows what a wise and prudent statesman he was!" Then an idea suddenly occurred to him, and he asked, "But I know for a fact that the inscription on the Golden Man was originally found in the Hou Ji Temple in the eastern capital of Luo. How comes it to be here?"

"This inscription was actually added by the people of Lu as a token of their admiration for the Duke of Zhou, as well as memento of Confucius' subsequent visit to the Hou Ji Temple," the caretaker explained. "It was put there as a warning to the people of Lu to spur them to work hard to rebuild their state."

"Diseases enter by way of the mouth," said Mencius. "And so do disasters. If it is possible, though not probable, that the former can be prevented, then it is possible that the latter can be prevented, all depending on whether one listens to warnings."

"Good medicine tastes bitter," Yue Zhengke chipped in, "and good advice pains the ear. What can you do with someone who rejects good advice and refuses to listen to warnings?"

"The phoenix chooses nothing but the *wutong* tree to perch on," said Mencius, "and a wise man offers his services only to a virtuous king."

"Can a minister possibly turn a benighted ruler into an enlightened one?" said Yue Zhengke.

"He can," Mencius replied without hesitation, but then added, "But he will find much difficulty in doing so if his prince is obdurate, or his colleagues do not cooperate, or there are crafty sycophants and arch-careerist stirring up trouble at court."

Yue Zhengke pointed to the inscription as he quoted, "Do not talk too much as too much talking can give the talker away. Do not over-reach yourself or you will find trouble. Now, if everybody abides by this warning, is there any room for advice that jars on the ear? And without this ear-grating advice, how can a given prince or emperor be guided onto the right path?"

"I think the words you quoted," said Mencius with an indulgent smile, "are applicable only in some extreme cases. The intention is to fight shy of irresponsible idle talk, far from being a taboo on talking itself."

Emerging from the main hall, Mencius proceeded to the *youzuo*. A vessel for containing water, the *youzuo* was large at the top and narrow toward the bottom. It was fixed to a wooden frame in such a way that when a moderate amount of water was poured into it the vessel hung vertically in the air but if too much water was added it tilted and the water poured out. "And this must be what they call the *youzuo*, I suppose?" Mencius inquired of the caretaker.

"Exactly," said the latter.

"It seems to warn us that pride comes before a fall, doesn't it?" Mencius said to Yue Zhengke.

Presently they came back to the temple gate, and, on stepping out, Mencius turned to take leave of the caretaker, holding his folded hands up in courtesy as he did so. He was no sooner seated in the carriage than he felt his stomach rumbling with hunger and found that he was thirsty too. By then the sun was already dipping toward the west, so he instructed Yue to find a restaurant where they could have supper. "After that, we can visit the Confucius Temple," he told Yue.

It took them a little while to find a suitable restaurant. There they ordered vegetarian noodles and soup. After eating, they drove straight to the Confucius Temple.

Situated on Jueli Street, the temple had been Confucius' former residence, but it had been renovated by Duke Ai of Lu in 478 B.C. The whole structure struck one as simple and crude; a melancholy affair, indeed, for a monument to the memory of such a great man as Confucius, thought Mencius as he followed the temple warden in. All the things once used by Confucius were there: a carriage, bows and arrows, bamboo slips and the like. The relics evoked in Mencius' mind's eye a picture of the world in which the great sage had moved, and he fell into a nostalgic mood as he lingered there. He made offerings at the shrine and performed the ceremony of kneelings and prostrations, the burning of incense and the libation, and it was not until it grew late that he departed.

The next day they went sightseeing at the Forest of Steles as scheduled.

The Forest sprawled over a hillock on the south bank of the Sihe River outside the north gate of the city. Emerging from the gate as he urged his horse and carriage on, Yue Zhengke pointed his whip at the distant prospect: "Look there, sir! The Confucius Forest!"

"Halt!" ordered Mencius.

Somewhat baffled by this command, Yue Zhengke glanced at Mencius over his shoulder and reined in the horses, and the carriage slowed to a stop.

Mencius jumped down, and after he had adjusted and dusted off his clothing he said, "Let's get the carriage parked somewhere, then we may go there on foot."

Accordingly, Yue drove the carriage to an inn and entrusted it to the proprietor to take care of. This done, he bought some incense and followed Mencius to the Forest where Confucius' tomb lay.

As the two proceeded in solemn fashion to the tomb, they saw a young man completely absorbed in going through the ceremony of burning incense, pouring wine and kowtowing before it.

Mencius made a sign to Yue that he was not to interrupt, and, waiting until the young man had done, stepped forward to address him, with a bow: "Excuse me, may I ask you where you are from?" he enquired.

"I'm from the state of Wei," replied the young man, using the standard speech. "My name is Peng Geng."

He was of stocky build and had a pleasant honest face. Mencius, interested, asked again: "Have you come from Wei specially for the purpose of making a sacrifice to Confucius?"

"Yes, that's what I've come here for," said Peng Geng. "I've been studying the classics and practicing the six arts since childhood. The pity is that I haven't had the chance to study under a famous teacher. I hear there is a teacher called Mencius in the State of Zou who venerates Confucius as his teacher. He is said to be proficient in the six arts and erudite and well-informed. So, after Lu, I shall be going to Zou to seek instruction from Mencius."

"What a coincidence," Yue Zhengke interjected with unrestrained glee. "Here is the very Mencius you are looking for!"

"Indeed!" Awe-struck, Peng Geng hurriedly made kowtows to Mencius. "I am too stupid to recognize your esteemed presence. I beg your pardon, sir."

Mencius hurried over to help him up, saying as he did so: "Don't be so polite, please."

Peng Geng rose to his feet as bidden and stood to one side meekly. Then Mencius introduced Yue Zhengke to him, and the two exchanged ceremonial greetings.

"Since it is on account of me that you made this trip here," said Mencius, "you may join us on our return journey to Zou after we have completed our sacrificial ceremony to Confucius. How's that?" To this Peng Geng agreed with alacrity.

Meanwhile, Yue Zhengke had set up a temporary altar before the tomb. He now lit three joss sticks and handed them to Mencius. Holding the joss sticks in both hands, Mencius bowed before the tomb, then stuck them in the incense burner on the altar. Again Yue presented Mencius with a bronze goblet filled with wine, with which the latter went through the motions of the libation. This completed, the three of them took up the requisite positions and performed the three kneelings and nine prostrations. After this, they made a round of the grave, observing as they went the luxuriant growth of the cypresses and junipers all round which had been planted by Confucius and his disciples themselves. Presently, Yue stopped in his tracks and pointed to a juniper on the roadside. "This was planted by Yan Hui*". Further on, he pointed out another: "This was planted by Zeng Shen**," He continued identifying objects of interest, much to Mencius' amusement. Intrigued by his companion's example, Peng Geng did the same by directing Mencius' attention to a tree some hundred paces away: "That pistachio tree was planted by Duanmu Ci."

Now Duanmu Ci, better known as Zi Gong, one of Confucius' favorite disciples, was also from the State of Wei, and the fact that Peng Geng had singled him out for mention was of course no accident. With a knowing smile, Mencius questioned Peng Geng: "When Confucius died and the three-year mourning period had come to an end, all his disciples left for home, one after another. Only Zi Gong stayed on for another three years before going home. Why did he do that?"

After a moment's thought during which he blinked his large, intelligent eyes frequently, Peng Geng said with deliberation: "I suppose there were three reasons for his doing so. First, when the aged sage fell seriously ill all his disciples came at one time or another to look after him, with the exception of Zi Gong, who happened to be doing business away from home at that time. When at long last he hurried to the sick-bed, Confucius only managed to say 'Dear Ci! Too late! Too late!' before he died. It seemed as though Zi Gong could never forgive himself for this lapse of his; he had to prolong his mourning to six years as a way to ease his stricken conscience. Second, I reckon there must have been many other disciples like Zi Gong who would gladly have done the same to demonstrate their affection and respect for the memory of their dear departed master. But most of them had the problem of earning a livelihood and supporting their families; they could not afford to stay away from him for long. Unlike them, Zi Gong came from an affluent family, and so he did not need to worry about his daily bread. Third, Yan Hui, Zeng Shen, Zhong Zi and Duanmu Zi were Confucius' favorite students, and his devoted followers. Confucius regarded them almost as his sons, and they reciprocated with equal intensity of natural affection. Yan Hui and Zhong Zi both died

---

* Yan Hui—the most brilliant of Confucius' disciples, who died at the early age of 29.

** Zeng Shen—another disciple of Confucius, well-known for his emphasis on filial piety.

long before Confucius. As for Zeng Shen, though he was young, he was the only one to take over the mantle of teaching from the master. At the time he was preoccupied with his school work. That left Zi Gong, who had the advantage of being without trouble at home, and thus he was able to observe his mourning for Confucius at the graveside for six long years."

"You know Zi Gong so intimately," praised Mencius. "You are indeed worthy of being called his countryman."

Presently Mencius enquired of Yue Zhengke: "Just now you said that a tree had been planted by Yan Hui. But how could it have been, since he died before Confucius?"

Yue Zhengke replied: "Sorry, that was a slip of the tongue. As a matter of fact, it was planted by Yan Lu by proxy for his son."

The three talked as they went until they left the Confucius Forest, and came to the inn outside the north gate of the city, where their carriage had been parked. When it was ready the two young people vied with each other for the privilege of driving their teacher.

"Brother," said Yue Zhengke, "do let me drive. Your long trip here from the State of Wei must have exhausted you. Come now, just get on and make yourself comfortable by sitting back with our teacher."

Peng Geng had no choice but to submit and so took his seat by the side Mencius.

Soon they were on the highway. But just as they were approaching the city gate, out stalked a big fellow, blocking their way.

Chapter Thirteen

Mencius Accepts Gongdu Zi as His Disciple in the Capital of Lu; The Master Heads off a Disaster Thanks to the Disciple's Intervention

Taken aback, Mencius made a closer survey of the oncoming fellow, narrowing his eyes. Of a stocky and imposing build, the stranger was dressed in a warrior's apparel and had an impressive sword hanging at his side. He had a sun-tanned face and prominent eyes beneath bushy eyebrows. He planted himself right in the carriage's path with all the air of a pugnacious gamecock. He then began to berate the occupants of the carriage. Now Yue Zhengke knew a thing or two about martial arts and, being a full-blooded youth, he was anything but a weakling. Such gratuitous insults were more than he could tolerate. "You oaf! None of your insolence!" he yelled in a burst of anger. "What on earth have we done to upset you?"

"Ask yourselves!" said the fellow with a disdainful smile. "I hate people like you who stuff themselves with food the livelong day and never do a stroke of work. Look at this fine carriage. It you're not some of the idle rich I don't know what you are. Humph! Woe betide you, now that you have come up against me!" So saying, he advanced threateningly on Yue Zhengke.

"Listen to what I have to say," said Yue Zhengke.

"There's no reasoning with you stinking parasites," rejoined the man. "Save your breath as well as mine! Come on, have a taste of my iron fist. Then I'll make short work of you with this sword."

Yue Zehngke knew he had got a foolhardy fellow to deal with. Still he wanted to make a last effort to save the situation from getting worse. Accordingly, he forced a smile and said, "My gallant fellow, just listen to me for a moment, will you?"

"No!" The fellow remained as hostile as ever. "One doesn't expect ivory from a dog's mouth!" he sneered.

"You are going too far!" said Yue Zhengke.

"Let me give you a piece of my mind," said the fellow, "Gongdu

Zi—that's me—I tell you, knows what to love and what to hate. His code of conduct is to curb the violent and assist the weak. There's only one man in today's world who merits his respect and admiration."

"Who?" asked Yue Zhengke.

"Mencius!" Gongdu Zi pronounced the name syllable by syllable and with feeling.

"Do you know him personally?" queried Yue Zhengke.

"No, I haven't had that honor yet," said Gongdu Zi, "though I've cherished his name in my heart for a long time."

"What makes you worship him so?" asked Yue again.

"I think he is remarkably intelligent," said Gongdu Zi with fervor, "and erudite. He enjoys a wide reputation as a great scholar. I have long been meaning to seek him out and acknowledge him as my teacher, but so far I haven't had the opportunity of seeing him in person, more's the pity!"

On hearing this, Mencius, who had been all this time sitting silently in his carriage, now interrogated the stranger from where he sat: "Look here, young man," he said. "Since you wish to have Mencius as your teacher, surely you must know what he upholds and what he disdains?"

Without paying the least heed to the etiquette called for on such an occasion, Gongdu Zi flounced over and stuck his head in at the carriage window, demanding of Mencius: " Who are you anyway?"

"Never mind who I am; just tell me what you know about Mencius, that's all."

"He esteems Confucius, looking up to him as his teacher. He is versed in the six arts, conversant with things past and present, and he upholds the principle of benevolence and righteousness. Moreover, he urges men to practice benevolent government and conduct administrative affairs according to the rites. And he condemns wanton aggression among the feudal lords."

Mencius jumped down from the carriage and, after looking the man up and down, was about to introduce himself when Peng Geng, who could no longer restrain himself, cut in: "This is Mencius himself! Get down and kowtow in apology right now!"

Stunned, Gongdu Zi stammered, "What? Is that true?"

He turned to look at Mencius, who smiled as he nodded his head continually.

Shamefaced, Gongdu Zi flopped to the ground. "I beg your

pardon, Master," he groaned.

"Gongdu Zi!" commanded Mencius with a stern countenance. "Stand up!"

Thereupon, Gongdu Zi rose to his feet and took his place on one side, with both his hands hanging at his sides, looking for all the world like a penitent sinner. "You've got a bold and uninhibited character," observed Mencius, "Which is a good quality in itself. However, there is a limit to everything. Once you go beyond the limit you will end up exposing yourself as a churlish ignoramus. Think back on the way you behaved just now, making wild guesses about our social status, calling us bad names, and even going to the length of threatening us with violence—all this you did without any discrimination at all! As it is, how am I to accept you as my disciple?"

Mortified, Gongdu Zi stamped his foot violently, fell to his knees before Mencius once more and kept knocking his head on the ground while tears were trickling down his cheeks.

"How old are you?" Mencius asked.

"Nineteen."

"Where from?"

"The State of Lu."

"Stand up!"

"Admit me, sir, I beg, as your disciple," pleaded Gongdu Zi, "or else I should have no courage to continue to live in the world."

Their little drama had by now drawn quite a crowd of curious onlookers. Yue Zhengke seized this opportunity to put in a good word for Gongdu Zi. "Master, I think Gongdu Zi may have drunk a little more than was good for him, and that may explain his driveling and raving. Now he has sobered up and is himself again. Perhaps you can forgive him and have the good grace to accept him as your disciple?"

Peng Geng also interceded for Gongdu Zi, construing his misdemeanors the after-effects of a besotted mind.

But Gongdu Zi jerked his head up to glare at Peng Geng and protested, "No, I haven't drunk anything."

Peng Geng tipped him a wink, and Gongdu Zi caught the hint. So he responded promptly: "Yes, yes, that's the honest truth, sir! Just now I had a drop too much. In my befuddled state, I did things that I shouldn't. Please forgive me, sir."

The naive manner in which this was said goaded the bystanders to laughter.

Consequently, Mencius bade Gongdu Zi to stand up, and graciously agreed to accept him as one of his disciples. Mencius introduced Yue Zhengke and Peng Geng to him, and the three young men exchanged civilities among themselves.

At noon they drove to the Jueli Inn in the city. Mencius and Yue Zhengke being no strangers there, the attendant ushered the party into four first-class rooms.

After lunch Mencius started on a lecture on the *Book of Songs* with the three young people as his main audience. When he came to the line concerning self-restraint: "A flaw in jade can be erased by mere polishing; a falsehood in a word cannot be recalled," he commented, "Confucius used to judge by this line whether or not a man was wise and good. He was fully justified in doing so. For if everybody used it as his touchstone there would not be a single sordid or mean thing happening in all the world!"

The words were hardly out of his mouth when a hubbub was heard from downstairs.

Mencius put down the bamboo slips of the classic and went to the veranda and looked down: a burly fellow was grappling physically with the attendant and berating him roundly. "Clear ten of your best rooms for me this minute!" he threatened, brandishing his fist in his victim's face. "I won't take 'no' for an answer! Or I'll bash your head in!"

Still trying his hardest to please, the attendant said in a wheedling tone, a forced grin on his face: "My honored patron, you know it is our practice to treat any client of ours with honor. 'What a pleasure it is to have friends come from afar!'—that is what Confucius said and the way we receive our clients as well. But I am sorry to say that all our rooms are booked today."

Notwithstanding, the burly fellow punched the attendant in the chest, sending him staggering to the ground. "Give me your ten best rooms now or you are a dead man." he shouted.

On seeing this, Gongdu Zi ran down and grabbed the fellow by the collar, demanding sternly: "Stop playing the tyrant, I warn you!"

The bully struggled desperately, trying to free himself from the iron grip of his opponent, but in vain. Finally he managed to say: "My quarrel is with the attendant; what has it got to do with you?"

"Quarrel, you say?" retorted Gongdu Zi. "Then why knock him to the ground?"

Meanwhile, Mencius too had come downstairs, and he tried to intervene before the situation got out of hand. "Don't rush!" he remonstrated with Gongdu Zi. "Try to make him listen to reason. No more violence!"

Gongdu Zi gave the fellow a vigorous push: "Get out of here!" he gnarled.

This sent his victim head foremost into a wall. He turned his battered face round to Gongdu Zi, only to swear impotently: "You'll pay for that, you swine!" and was gone, pursued by hoots of laughter from the bystanders. But enough of this. Let's come back to Mencius and company. At the suggestion of Mencius, the four of them made a trip to the Sishui River, or Four Springs River, a scenic spot no more than 5 li from their temporary lodging.

It was spring, and the glorious weather as well as the beautiful landscape disposed them for walking rather than riding. Thus they strolled along in a leisurely fashion, talking and joking all the way, and before they knew it they had reached the riverside.

The river rises at the western foot of Mount Peiwei. Four springs spout from fissures in a rock face to converge and become a river, hence the name. As it was the dry season a narrow strip of water rippled between snow-white sandy beaches. Pale-grey storks, white egrets, wild ducks and gulls were everywhere in evidence.

Presently Gongdu Zi stooped to pick up a pebble. Just as he was about to throw it at one of the birds Mencius stopped him.

"Don't frighten them!" said Mencius. "Look, how they are enjoying themselves! Birds feed on insects and are therefore mankind's friends. They have too many natural enemies to defend themselves against as it is; how can we harm them? We should protect them instead."

Convinced, Gongdu Zi gently laid the pebble back on the ground.

Afterwards the four paced to and fro for a while on the embankment before they settled down to rest on the sandy beach. Soon, they were talking freely concerning various topics as the occasion prompted them.

"In the old days," Gongdu Zi began, "Confucius often took his disciples off on country excursions. Come to think of it, though, the old sage was definitely a man of serious disposition who treasured every bit of his time. I wonder, being what he was, how he could possibly spare himself for those pleasure trips?"

"Confucius was truly that sort of man, as you say," remarked Mencius. "Ever since his childhood he had been working hard. So absorbed and occupied he was in his pursuit of knowledge that he often neglected food and sleep. 'Live and learn' was more than a precept to him. He lived up to it, so much so that even old age came upon him unawares. But on the other hand he knew only too well the salutary influence that traveling over mountains and rivers can have in forming a man's character. He said, 'The clever delight in water, the virtuous in the hills. The clever are restless, the virtuous calm; the clever enjoy life, the virtuous prolong life.' He made excursions and climbed mountains all for the purpose of cultivating his character and tempering his will. But the object of cultivating one's character and tempering one's will is not limited to self-perfection only; in the final analysis, it is to build up strength of character and mind the better to serve society and the people."

Just then, a goshawk shot out of the blue, swooping down on a water bird. In no time at all Gongdu Zi whipped out his sword and threw it at the goshawk. The lethal shaft, swift as an arrow, whistled through the air and hit the bird, piercing right through its body while it was circling some three feet above the river's surface. The bird fell splashing into the river, sword and all.

Amazed at this extraordinary feat of marksmanship, Mencius and the other two were unstinting in their praise of Gongdu Zi.

When the sword was retrieved from the river bed and presented to Mencius for inspection, the latter, while fondling it in his hands in admiration, asked its owner affably: "My dear fellow, do you happen to know the background of this extraordinary sword?"

"It was handed down from my ancestors," replied Gongdu Zi. "When my father gave it to me, he said that everything else we might part with, but we mustn't give up this sword."

"So it is a family heirloom, then!" Mencius continued to contemplate the sword. "But what do you call it—say, a dubbed name given by its forger?"

"It is a family heirloom, as a matter of fact," said Gongdu Zi. "We call it 'Hanguang'."

"Hanguang?" Mencius echoed in happy astonishment. "Tradition says that a certain Kong Zhou of the State of Wei owned three swords named respectively Hanguang, Chengyin and Xiaolian, which had been handed down from the Yin Dynasty. Of the three, Hanguang was most famous for its cutting edge. So sharp was it that it was said to be able to cut iron as if it were mere clay."

"I was born and bred in Wei," said Peng Geng. "Never have I ever heard of a person by the name of Kong Zhou, nor have I heard about the three swords."

"A rare treasure is more often than not most jealously guarded by its owner," said Mencius. "He would not breathe a word of it if he could help it, would he?"

"Then how did it fall into the hands of Gongdu Zi?" Peng Geng pursued.

"It may have been that the original owner had fallen on had times and eventually he had to sell it, or some unexpected disaster happened to him so that its ownership changed hands." Having said this, Mencius started to brandish the Hanguang sword on the spur of the moment. His movements were at once brisk, precise and steady, and won loud applause from the spectators.

He continued his sword exercise a while longer before he concluded with a request that Gongdu Zi should favor them with a performance of his own, with which Gongdu Zi complied readily.

Taking the sword, Gongdu Zi held up his clasped hands together in courtesy, saying, "Since you insist, I'll make an exhibition of myself, good or bad."

So saying, he began by running around in a circle once, in short, quick steps, the sword held firmly in his hands, his body slightly leaning to one side. The introductory display was soon followed up by a series of movements executed in advance or retreat. Sometimes he leaped into the air as lightly as a squirrel; sometimes he twisted his frame around or bent low with the natural grace of a monkey. When he attacked, he did so with an impetus that was irresistible; when he put up a defense, he stood his ground invulnerably. He appeared, as it were, in a circle of cold light, while he brandished his sword this way and that with lightning speed.

The other three were full of praise for him as he sheathed his sword and came up to accept their congratulations.

"Sir," Peng Geng asked Mencius, "just now you said something about the Hanguang sword having the miraculous qualities of being invisible and insubstantial, didn't you? But we see it here so clearly. How is that?"

"That's just a manner of speaking," said Mencius with a smile. "A hyperbole used by people to describe its excellence. Surely, there cannot possibly be a sword in the world which is invisible and insubstantial, can there?"

"Now I understand!" said Peng Geng.

Mencius picked up the dead goshawk from the sand. "This bird came here to hunt for food, only to meet its death, " he said with a sigh. "If we had not come to this place today, or if Gongdu Zi had not joined us, would it have been killed? So you see, it all depends on chance or what is called 'fate', after all!"

Thus they chatted and cracked jokes all the way back to the inn, where they stayed the night.

Now let's take up Fu Puren where we left him sometime previously. As the fame of Mencius grew the mere mention of the name sent chills down Fu's spine. Good and evil are never reconcilable. The more he thought of Mencius and of the disputes he had with the man over the previous years the more Fu's fear of him grew, and so did his hatred. All this time he had been sending his men to spy on Mencius, and so he naturally found out that Mencius had gone to Lu, this time with one of his students, a certain Yue Zhengke. It transpired that the fellow who had got into a row with the attendant at the Jueli Inn had been one of Fu's hired thugs. By picking a quarrel with the attendant he had got to know that Mencius was staying in the inn, after which he hurried back to inform Fu.

"Well done!" Fu exclaimed, springing to his feet. "Bring Jue Hu here! But don't let Xia Long know."

Why—you may ask, gentle reader—should Fu prefer not to let Xia Long in on the matter? This is because he had become suspicious of Xia Long lately, as every time he plotted against Mencius' life, the latter, unlike his usual self, showed little interest.

Presently Jue Hu was ushered in. "Mencius is staying at the Jueli Inn in the capital of Lu," said Fu Puren. "Take eight of your men with you on horseback, and get there as quickly as you can. As soon as the thing is done, set fire on the inn to destroy any evidence that may compromise us."

"Yes sir!" responded Jue Hu obediently.

"This time, if you come a cropper again," added Fu with a malevolent expression on his face, "I'll have you put to death immediately."

When the drum tower sounded the third watch of the night Jue Hu and his men changed into their night garments and approached the rear wall of the Jueli Inn. "Bear in mind," Jue Hu warned the others, "it's succeed or die! Under no circumstances whatever shall we leave a man alive behind."

"Up we go!" With that, Jue Hu led the way over the wall and into the courtyard, the others following hard upon him. They soon found the room where Mencius was. The big fellow who had been the first to track down Mencius this time prized open the door with a dagger and made his way gingerly to the bed where he thought his would-be victim must be sleeping. As he plunged his sword with a vigorous thrust into the bed he let out a piercing cry of pain and dropped down in a pool of blood. A shiny bright sword was sticking in his own breast!

Gongdu Zi originally came of a scholar's family in the State of Lu. From his early childhood his father had cherished him as the apple of his eye and wanted to teach him all the knowledge he had acquired himself. But the boy seemed more inclined to the martial arts. Being skilled in the martial arts himself, his father was only too glad to share his know-how with his beloved son. Father and son made it a daily routine to practice boxing, and jousting with the spear, saber and sword, besides reading and writing. At the age of 15 Gongdu Zi was already a fully-developed and tall lad who was skilled in all sorts of weapons. One day his father summoned him to his presence. "My boy," lectured his father, "The aim of the martial arts, according to our ancient wise men, is a two-fold one: to keep fit and to defend oneself in times of war. Provided that you adhere to this two-fold aim, I'll allow you to continue. Otherwise I forbid you to practice the martial arts, for it will do you more harm than good."

Gongdu Zi at once dropped to his knees, swore an oath to his father: "I swear that I'll abide by the two-fold principle."

Thereupon the old man fetched a sword down from the beam and dusted it off before saying solemnly: "This sword is named 'Hanguang'. It is a time-honored sword, said to be a relic from the Yin Dynasty. It has been three generations since it came into our keeping, you know —a family heirloom. But it has never been used to harm a single person. Here I hand it down to you. With it you can perfect your swordsmanship, safeguard yourself, and, if occasion demands, do away with the enemies of the people. Under no circumstances must you use it to harm innocent people, though."

Taking the sword, Gongdu Zi said, "I will for ever bear your instructions in mind; I will do nothing that may disgrace your honored name."

His father addressed him again: "I was told that a certain Mencius in the State of Zou is a remarkable man of virtue and talent. Now that you are 19 years of age, an adult already, it is high time you had a teacher of his caliber to advance your learning. Why not pay him a visit?"

Surprised that his father had anticipated him, Gongdu Zi rejoined excitedly: "That's the very thing I've been longing to do!"

And that is how we last found Gongdu Zi in the capital of Lu and his happy, though somewhat histrionic, encounter with Mencius on the road.

So much for the digression; let's come back to our story. That day when Mencius and his three disciples returned to the inn from their trip to the Sishui River they had supper and then retired for the night. For Gongdu Zi it had been a day of unusual happenings, what with his wrangle with the big fellow at the inn and his delightful outing in the company of Mencius. So excited was he as he reviewed the varying scenes before his mind's eye that for a long while he could not get to sleep. Suddenly the ugly face of the big fellow reappeared in his imagination and a terrible idea crossed his mind: "What if that guy should come for me tonight to avenge himself?" Perturbed, he immediately put on his clothes and went to Mencius' room.

"What is the matter?" asked Mencius as he let him in.

"I was anxious lest that fellow I had the tussle with come to take his revenge," said Gongdu Zi, full of apprehension. "With a blackguard like that we cannot be too careful."

"Yes, you are right," said Mencius. "But what precautions can we take at this time of night?"

"I've already thought of a counter-measure, just in case," said Gongdu Zi. "You can join Yue and Peng in their room for tonight and I'll move to your room. If he gets into this room he will be playing right into my hands, and woe betide him then! And if he should go to the other room where you're going to spend the night with Peng and Yue, they can well protect you. And at the least sound I'll come to your rescue."

Accordingly they made the change, and the four of them slept with their clothes on.

Anxiety-ridden, Gongdu Zi tossed and turned in his bed. When the third watch had just been sounded his sensitive ear caught a click at the door. Promptly he snatched up his sword and hid himself by the bed. He watched with bated breath till the assassin neared the bed and made his thrust and at the same moment stabbed him through the heart.

Seeing that his murderous plot had fallen through and one of his men had been killed, Jue Hu knew that any further attempt would spell his doom. So he made his escape by jumping down from the landing of the stairs and was gone.

Gongdu Zi pulled his sword from the body of the big fellow, stopped the rest of Jue Hu's men from running out by the door, and killed three of them there and then. Those who were still left upstairs struggled desperately to find a way out, but in vain. Two were killed by Yue and Peng, and one who found no way of escape finally committed suicide by slashing his throat with his own sword. Much to his annoyance, Gongdu Zi realized that Jue Hu was nowhere to be found.

The proprietor of the inn roused from his sleep by the pandemonium, rushed upon the scene. Lantern in hand, he inspected the premises and ended up pointing an accusing finger at Mencius. "These were all murdered by your men! " he gasped. "Don't leave, any one of you! You will come with me to the magistrate's tomorrow to see justice done!" He was trembling all over.

Chapter Fourteen

Loyal to an Evil Master as Ever, Jue Hu
Clings to His Evil Ways;
Turning Over a New Leaf, a Reformed Xia
Long Performs a Good Deed

When the inn proprietor saw to his horror that Mencius and his company had turned his place into a veritable shambles by perpetrating mass slaughter, his fear of being implicated in the crime sent him into fits of wailing. He kicked up a row with Mencius, during which he grabbed the latter by the collar, clamoring for justice.

The man appeared to be in his late forties, as Mencius judged by the light the lantern shed upon him. Dressed in a loose gown with wide sleeves, he had a pair of shiny black eyes in a smooth-skinned face. A wispy beard hung from his chin. Presently Mencius addressed him with courtesy: "Please don't get into a panic, sir. Since every injustice has its perpetrator, every debt has its debtor, as they say. And since they were a handful of dubious characters breaking in here for no other purpose than that of killing me, it stands to reason that the whole thing has nothing to do with you and your inn. They were killed by my disciples, a fact we'll not deny. And so, if and when the local authorities want to make an inquiry into it, naturally we are obliged to cooperate. But allow me to ask you, though, these gangsters, all in dark night garments, their faces masked, identities unrevealed, and one of them committing suicide—isn't this sufficient proof that they were just riff-raff employed by somebody to murder me? Now that this somebody's attempt has been defeated, will he have the nerve to raise a hue and cry, thereby exposing himself?"

At this, the proprietor calmed down a little, but queried timidly: "That's the end of it all? Is it what you mean?"

"Yes, it is," said Mencius. "Since I am the one who was responsible for this confrontation, I will have these eight men encoffined and buried at my own expense, and that's all there is to it."

The man was rather puzzled by this strange offer of Mencius', and

he further asked, "They were sent to assassinate you, and they were your enemies, weren't they? How is it that you should go out of your way to be so generous to them?"

"Well, I think that they were not really my enemies," said Mencius. "But they were put up to this dastardly deed by someone who is my enemy.""You're truly an open-minded and magnanimous sort of person, sir!" the man said, with an appreciatory smile. "May I ask your name, please?"

"Mencius."

The proprietor began to regard his interlocutor with increased respect. Presently he dropped to his knees, saying, "Sir, you are a present-day sage, with Confucius as your predecessor and conducting yourself on the principle of benevolence and righteousness. What a fool I am that all this time I have been unaware of your illustrious presence!"

Mencius hastened to pull him to his feet. "Please do not stand on ceremony. I am merely a student of Confucius, in no sense worthy of so pompous a form of courtesy from you."

As he stood up, the man began to introduce himself: "I'm Sima Zhong. This inn I inherited from my father. Running it does not bring me in that much money. Still I can say I've earned enough and to spare. Since these people met their deaths at my place, it is only right that I should pay for their burial."

"Not at all," Mencius insisted. "I would rather that you didn't. I brought you all this trouble, so I have to pay for the loss thus incurred."

After some polite skirmishing between the two, each protesting that the other shouldn't be charged, at last Mencius had to give in. And in due course, the eight corpses were properly disposed of in the way the innkeeper arranged. Because not a single soul was found to prosecute on behalf of the dead men, and nor did the local authorities register the case for investigation, the whole thing was hushed up and no more was heard of it. Alas!--so runs the commentary of the local people--Such is the ignominious end of the eight fellows who tried to help a villain do evil.

After breakfast Yue Zhengke asked of his teacher: "Shall we go for an outing to Mount Nishan today as originally planned, sir?"

With Mencius's prompt consent, Gongdu Zi quickly got his carriage ready before the inn.

While checking out at the desk, the innkeeper at first refused to take their money but relented on Yue's insistence.

The four said farewell to Sima Zhong: "Good-bye till we meet again!"

Soon they were out of the east city gate on their way to Mount Nishan and in less than two hours' time arrived at the foot of the mountain. Gongdu Zi pulled the horse to a halt. On looking back, he found his passengers covered with dust, and, with an apologetic smile, said, "Perhaps I drove a little bit too fast?"

They trudged upwards along the steps leading to the Nishan Deity Temple, which perched on an overhanging cliff, the mere sight of which took one's breath away. As they drew near they saw a young couple kneeling at the entrance, their heads bent in prayer, evidently for a son to be given to them. "People say," said Mencius laughing, as he remembered the words his mother had once said to him, "That the Nishan Deity answers one's prayers miraculously. You pray for a son, and a son is given to you. How funny!" The four talked and joked as they went. Soon they found themselves by the Yishui River. The river meandered its way from north to south. With the sunlight reflected on its rippling surface it resembled a huge white dragon in flight. "That is the river about which Confucius once made his famous remark: 'All things in nature are passing away even like this—ceasing neither day nor night!'" said Mencius. "The Sage was hardworking and he treasured his time like gold. He set us an example that will take us a whole lifetime to emulate."

Just then, from the dam on the upper reaches of the river a man came running up. Instantly a suspicion crossed their minds that this might be somebody sent by the innkeeper after them.

The stranger was about 20 years old, tall and slender, with a fair-complexioned face which had a distinguished air about it. He bowed low when he approached Mencius, introducing himself as he did so: "My name is Xianqiu Meng. Allow me to pay me respects to the Master."

"Xianqiu?" The name sounded familiar to Mencius, who muttered in wonder: "But that is the name of a town in the State of Lu, isn't it?"

"Just so, sir," Xianqiu Meng explained. "Because I live in Xianqiu I named myself after it."

"But how could you recognize me on sight?" asked Mencius.

"Yesterday I heard that Your Excellency had come to stay at the Jueli Inn in the capital," said Xianqiu Meng, "and so this morning I hurried there, only to find that you had set off for this place. I recognized you easily since there're few people hereabouts, and, what's more, you are so distinguished-looking."

"You are welcome to join us," said Mencius, "if that is what you are here for." "I've come here in too much of a hurry to present you with my First-Meeting gifts," said Xianqiu. "Excuse this lapse of mine. To make up for it, I will go back to the capital to buy them before I join you."

"Oh, please do not trouble yourself," said Mencius. "I endeavor to run a school and enroll students all for the purpose of training talented people so that they may benefit their fellow men in the future. As long as they can fulfill that purpose I shall feel content."

Thus Xianqiu Meng was persuaded to stay, and that evening the five of them returned to Mencius' school in Zou. Our narrative leaves them there for the moment and takes up the story of a character called Wan Zhang. This young man had his home in the capital of the State of Jin. Bereft of his mother early in life, he had spent a very unhappy childhood at the hands of a cruel stepmother. For him, however, this hard life turned out to be a blessing in disguise, for it eventually helped to toughen his nature and make good his deficiencies. He grew up to be a man of great determination and with a singleness of purpose. Richly gifted and by dint of hard work, he acquitted himself pretty well in the study of the two categories of six arts*. By 350 B.C. Wan Zhang had reached the age of 18. The renown of Mencius as a great scholar of the day drew his attention and he longed very much to meet him. And so in the spring of the same year he took leave of his parents and set out on a pilgrimage to seek out the man he so much admired. It took him a good 12 days to reach the frontiers of Zou, because of the many hardships and difficulties which the inclement climate of the loess plateau imposed on him. Once in the State of Zou he made inquiries as to how to find Mencius as he pressed on.

Twilight was falling when Wan Zhang came to a crossroads. He

---

* The first category of six arts refers to the rites, music, archery, riding, writing and arithmetic; the second category refers to the *Book of Songs, the Book of History*, the *Book of Rites*, the *Book of Changes*, the *Music* and the *Spring and Autumn Annals*.

halted, casting his eyes about as he did so. There was not a single soul around. He sat down by the roadside, thinking that he might ask his way of some passer-by. Soon fatigue came over him and he dozed off, his head resting on his knees and with both arms clasped around them.

Suddenly a stentorian voice sounded in his ears: "Hi! What a queer fish—sleeping in broad daylight by a roadside!"

Wan Zhang awoke with a start. What he saw was a tall strongly-built fellow towering over him. He had a square face, with a pair of large eyes beneath bushy eyebrows. He wore a long pale-blue gown and a brand-new sword dangled from his waist. Wan Zhang hastily rose to his feet, rubbing his sleep-heavy eyes as he did so. "Good day, sir!" said Wan Zhang. "Excuse me, but may I know your name and where you are from?" he asked. The man introduced himself as Xu Bi and said that he hailed from the State of Xue. It turned out that both men had the same purpose, that of seeking to study under Mencius, and so they traveled together.

Striking out eastwards, they soon came to a village. Presently a middle-aged man came their way, and Wan Zhang hastened forward to ask if he happened to know where Mencius' school was.

"You've asked the right man, bless your soul," said the man, smiling somewhat artful. "I happen to know him personally. Come this way, please."

The man led Wan Zhang and Xu Bi direct to Fu Puren's house, and he turned out to be none other than Jue Hu, Fu's second steward!

Since his failure to assassinate Mencius at the Jueli Inn the previous spring, Fu Puren had been living in constant fear of the former's reprisal, the more so as he learned that more and more young people were being admitted to his school, among whom not a few were skilled in the martial arts. He trembled at the thought that these people would soon come for him to seek revenge and that his life would be in danger. Consequently, he had conferred with Jue Hu in his sanctum, out of which had come two counter-measures: 1) He had offered high wages to hire able-bodied youths, skillful with weapons, to enlarge and strengthen his domestic staff, so that when the time came he could fight it out with Mencius; 2) He had his trusted men planted at the entrance-way to Mencius' school to intercept those who sought to study there.

That was how Wan Zhang and Xu Bi came to be ushered into Fu

Puren's house. But to continue our story:

Jue Hu led the young men to the outer reception room and asked them to wait.

They did not wait as asked but sauntered out into the courtyard on their own. A mere glance at their surroundings told them that this obviously was not a school but some rich man's mansion. A sudden fear seized Wan Zhang, and a muffled cry escaped him: "Damn it! We're in a trap! Let's run for it!"

Before they had moved a few steps they heard the outer gate banged shut, and footfalls sounded behind them. Jue Hu ushered Fu Puren in.

"Welcome! Welcome!" effused Fu, an artificial smile on his otherwise brutal face. "Welcome to our honored guests from afar."

Wan Zhang stepped forward and made a bow and queried. "I beg to ask, sir, what's all this about?"

Regarding them as his prisoners having no chance of escape, Fu said brazenly: "This is my house, if you want to know! You are being treated by Fu Puren, whose great reputation must be nothing new to you, I presume?"

His notoriety was of course nothing new to Xu Bi, since Xu's hometown in the State of Xue was only some 100 li away. So at the mention of the name Xu Bi flared up, demanding severely of Fu: "We've come to apply for admission to Mencius' school. Why did you have us brought to this place?"

"Since you are here," said Fu, "you may as well stay and make the best of it. You have no cause to fly off the handle, though."

"Squire," said Wan Zhang placatingly, "it's getting late, kindly let us go."

"I've already had a dinner prepared in honor of you gentlemen. Please stay," said Fu Puren.

"Do stay please," chimed in Jue Hu.

"I'm but an obscure scholar," responded Wan Zhang impassively. "What have I done to deserve this honored treatment, I should like to know?"

"Let's go!" said Xu Bi in his deep, gruff voice.

"No, you don't!" said Fu. "All people within the four seas are brothers, as your Confucius put it, and we are all one family. Come now, dinner is ready."

Xu Bi now questioned him bluntly: "What's all this importuning us to stay to dinner for? Would you tell me the reason why?"

Jue Hu said, "Listen to my advice, young men. Mencius is nothing but a petty schoolteacher. All that he is capable of is spouting some quotations from Confucius and wagging his glib tongue to hoodwink people. It doesn't pay for you to dance attendance on him, young and talented people as you are. On the other hand, Squire Fu comes of an eminent family and a respected clan, and is himself a man of property. He treats people with sincerity, too. Come to him for shelter and there will be a bright future for you."

"You're talking rot!" shouted Xu Bi angrily. He was beside himself with injured pride. "Who do you think we are, you dirty lackey! Do you suppose we would stoop so low as to wallow in the mire with you? You are daydreaming!"

Stung, Fu yelled at Jue Hu to "teach them a lesson".

At a nod from their master, all Fu's servants rushed up and clustered threateningly around Xu Bi and Wan Zhang.

Jue Hu unbuckled his sword belt and handed it to one of his men. This done, he went swaggering up to Xu Bi and threw a punch at him.

Xu Bi, undaunted, countered the blow with his right hand, at the same time throwing his sword to his companion with his left.

Jue Hu, who had thought that his opponent was a mere youngster to begin with, now came to realize that he had a real adversary to tackle. So he mustered up all the physical strength he was capable of in preparation for a fresh attack.

For Xu Bi, however, this was the first time he had ever come to blows with an antagonist, much as he had practiced the martial arts for many years. Hence he dared not treat his opponent lightly, the more so since he guessed that he was a most sinister and crafty character.

And so it was that the two glared at each other with hatred. With his master watching on the sidelines, and a troop of servants as the cheering squad, Jue Hu launched an assault at Xu Bi for the second time. The latter dodged sideways, leaving Jue Hu to strike thin air, much to his mortification. Shame-faced, he went for Xu for the third time, but before he knew what had happened the latter had leaped over his head, and he missed his target again. He was too embarrassed even to glance to Fu Puren and his men, who now watched him with mocking contempt. Time and again Xu eluded his crushing blows by precipitate leaps and bounds. His repeated failures to floor his adversary had by now deprived Jue Hu of much of his initial dash, and he realized that these was no way that he could match Xu as far as unarmed combat was concerned. No sooner had he reached this conclusion than he sprang to one side and snatched his sword from the hand of his man. He grimly resolved that he would fight to the death in this combat with Xu Bi. With the weapon in hand, he challenged his rival to a sword fight. Xu Bi knew better than to take up this new challenge, so he beckened to Wan Zhang to join him in fighting a way through Fu's hirelings. They had little opposition until they reached the outer gate, where another group of people armed with spears and halberds this time, blocked their way. The only way they could get out was by jumping over the courtyard wall, which they did, much to the exasperation of Fu Puren. "Blockheads, all of you! After them! Don't let them escape!" he ranted.

Recovering from their initial confusion, his men threw their weapons in the direction of the two runaways. But it was no use; the pair were already at a safe distance. Then Jue Hu ordered, "Let fly the arrows!" Before Xu Bi had time to take action to shelter himself and his companion an arrow lodged in his left arm, and both were taken prisoner.

Trussed up, the two were dragged before Fu Puren. The old squire crowed over his prisoners in malicious triumph: "Young men, learned a lesson, have you? I'll teach you a yet more bitter lesson to make you know what it is to oppose Squire Fu." He told Jue Hu to put his victims in the dungeon. "No water and no food until I hear them sing another tune!" was his vicious injunction.

Xu Bi and Wan Zhang were thus pushed into a windowless cell. The damp air felt chilly and an overwhelming stench assailed the nostrils.

Suddenly they heard two thuds outside. Wan Zhang and Xu Bi stared at the door, wondering what had happened. The door opened and a figure slipped in, gently pushing the door closed behind him.

"Who is it?" demanded Xu Bi.

"Hush!" warned the figure. "I am here to help you." In the dark, he used a dagger to cut the ropes that bound Xu Bi and Wan Zhang. Then he whispered, "Come with me!" He opened the door again and asked Xu and Wan to help him carry the corpses of the two guards into the cell. This done, he closed the door and locked it again. Then he led Wan Zhang and Xu Bi over the garden wall at the back of the house.

Once at the edge of the village the stranger asked, "Where were you making for when Fu seized you?"

"Our original plan was to study under Mencius," said Wan Zhang. "Now that you've saved us, perhaps you can help us find his school."

"The master could be at his home right now," said their rescuer. "I may as well take you there."

They were just starting off when they heard a deep voice behind them: "Xia Long! Wait a moment!"

Instinctively Xia pulled out his sword, turning round simultaneously: "Who are you?" he demanded.

"There's no need for me to conceal my true identity from you, or from anybody for that matter. Gongsun Benzheng—that's my full name," said the man.

Somewhat relieved at hearing the name, Xia Long said, smiling: "Glad to make your acquaintance, sir."

"There's one thing on which I wish to be enlightened," said Gongsun. "What caused you to help two men who must be strangers to you?"

"I owe my life to Mencius, and he is my benefactor," said Xia. "And these two gentlemen have come to pay him a visit. Naturally I should help them."

"Don't you fear that Fu Puren might wreak vengeance on you?"

"I used to be a fool who could not tell a good man from a bad one. For a long time in the past I did lots of evil things because I served a devil of a master. Even death would not expiate all the crimes I committed for his sake. Then Mencius came along. He helped me to see myself in a true light, and I started trying to do some good deeds in order to make amends for my crimes. Mr. Gongsun, I can tell you that Fu Puren has long since kept a close watch on my movements, and it is only because I have one thing left undone that I choose to stay for the time being. But as soon as I get it done I'll make myself scarce. You have come in good time. I'll leave these two gentleman in your care. Please be kind enough to take them to Mencius house."

"Don't worry, I will," said Gongsun.

Xia Long made as if he were going to say something more, but then thought better of it and was gone.

Thereupon, Gongsun took Wan Zhang and Xu Bi to Mencius.

Mencius wondered at his nightly visitors: "What makes you three people drop in at my humble abode at this time of night?" he inquired kindly.

Wan Zhang and Xu Bi hurriedly went down on their knees, speaking at the same time: "Excuse me, sir, for this presumption..."

Mencius said, "Please stand up."

Gongsun Benzheng cut in, "These two young men got acquainted with each other on their journey here with the common desire to study under you. Unfortunately they were lured into Fu Puren's house by his man Jue Hu. Fu tried to keep them there by force but they refused to submit. That's how they ended up being imprisoned."

"But how did you manage to escape?" Mencius asked Wan Zhang and Xu Bi.

"It was Xia Long who rescued them," Gongsun Benzheng informed him.

"Xia Long!" exclaimed Mencius in pleased surprise. "I am glad to hear of it. So he has turned over a new leaf after all!"

"I have kept an eye on him throughout," said Gongsun. "It's true that these two young men were saved by him."

Mencius turned to look Gongsun in the face for a moment before he asked, "You look familiar to me somehow, my good fellow. May I ask your name?"

After Gongsun had given his name, Mencius suddenly remembered. "Was it you, sir, who saved me in the river? Yes, it was you, too, who shielded me at Mt. Yishan. And the hero who brought down a wild goose with a single arrow..."

At this moment Mencius' mother emerged from her room. She stared at Gongsun for quite a while, and, having made certain that this was unmistakably the man who had saved herself and her son, immediately went down on her knees: "You're our benefactor, sir!" she cried. "For all the kindness you've done us we owe you an immense debt of gratitude!"

The deep feelings with which the old lady offered her thanks quite disconcerted Gongsun, so much so that for a moment he did not know how to respond. Utterly confused, he returned her thanks by kneeling down himself, saying as he did so: "Madam, as a matter of fact, you Mengs are my benefactors and not the other way round."

Surprised, Zhang queried, "Why do you say that?"

"It was His Excellency Mr. Mengsun who delivered me from the clutches of Fu Puren, you know. He bought my liberty, nay, my life with money out of his own pocket."

"I see," was all Zhang managed to say at last.

All of a sudden, a frantic beating of gongs assailed their ears, accompanied by a babble of voices, warning that a fire had broken out.

Chapter Fifteen

An Arrogant Youth Learns a Bitter Lesson;
A Wise Schoolmaster Imparts His Wisdom
to His Pupils

To continue our story. On hearing the fire alarm, Mencius led his students to the edge of the village. There they saw clouds of dense smoke and flames lighting up the sky. Mencius immediately ordered his students to fight the fire.

At their teacher's summons, the students turned out in full strength, some shouldering shovels, others carrying pails, and hurried to the scene. It transpired that it was Fu Puren's mansion which had caught fire. His fellow villagers were all there, looking on unconcerned, none lifting a finger to help. Thus they watched, their hands tucked in their sleeves, while the hated squire's property was being reduced to ashes. They muttered to each other: "Good is rewarded and evil punished," "God's will be done", or "That's the retribution he deserved!"

The conflagration, it so happened, had killed 18 members, covering three generations, of the Fu family. Most of the squire's bodyguards and servants were burnt to death, too, except for a few lucky ones who happened to have stayed for the night in the lodge, and had managed to make their escape. When the time came to clean up the rubble the villagers did not find the bodies of Xia Long or Jue Hu, burnt or otherwise.

Mencius led his students back to the school and asked the cooks to get dinner ready. It was already daybreak when Wan Zhang, Xu Bi and Gongsun Benzheng had finished their meal. Mencius saw that Xu's wounds were properly attended to, then had the three lodged in the students dormitory.

That afternoon Zhang took her daughter-in-law Duanping and grandson Zhongzi to the school to see Gongsun Benzheng, and once more offered a profusion of thanks for the gallant deeds he had performed for their family over the past 30 years.

"Mr. Gongsun," she added with concern, "where do you live? How

is your family?"

"I'm all on my own," replied Gongsun, after some hesitation. "I live in a cabin on the southern slope of Nine-Dragon Mountain."

"Since you are alone, would you like the idea of working with me, then?" inquired Mencius with interest.

"You took the words right out of my mouth, my son!" said Zhang.

"I'm just a numskull," responded Gongsun with a smile. "I don't even know how to read or write. How could I be of any use in a school?"

"Those enrolled in my school are young people of great promise hailing from the various states throughout the land. They are all decent people, very easy to get along with, you can be sure of that. Well, you will come as an asset to us, what with your expertise in the martial arts and practical experience of actual fighting. When war breaks out talents like yours will be much needed by the state. I, too, will recommend you to His Lordship most strongly. How does that strike you?"

"Well, obedience is the best obeisance, as they say," said Gongsun excitedly. "If you have so much confidence in my abilities, I can only obey."

"In running a state, neither civil nor military talents can be dispensed with," continued Mencius. "Now that you have joined us, we can pool our efforts to train my 600-odd students to be all-round fine fellows who are versed in both the military and civil arts. If and when we succeed in so doing, they will certainly contribute a great deal to the well-being of the state."

Enthralled by the prospect, Gongsun wanted very much to set to work at once. He asked leave of Mencius to go back for the weapons he had left in his cabin. Thereupon Mencius gave orders for Gongdu to take him there in the school.

"Mr Gongsun is eminently skillful with his weapons," Mencius told Gongdu. "From now on you should learn from and help each other, to make up each other's deficiencies."

Mencius' words annoyed Gongdu somewhat, and it was sometime before he sullenly muttered, "Yes sir."

Zhang cast a sly eye at her daughter-in-law with an ill-concealed smile on her face, as if to say: "Looks as if he doesn't think so highly of Gongsun Benzheng as all that, doesn't it?"

"An arrogant young man, indeed," said Duanping, "but he'll suffer for it, sooner or later he will suffer for it, I'm afraid."

Presently the two women took up Zhongzi between them and were going to leave for home, when the boy kicked his legs in the air, protesting coyly: "Grannie! Mommy! I want to go to school!"

Duanping shook her head, saying, "You're still too young. You cannot go to school yet."

Zhongzi pouted and piped, "I'm not too young. I'm nine years old. Grandma often tells me my father went to school when he was nine."

Zhang said, "It's true, though. Confucius said of himself that he stood firm at 30. Counting from now, it will take 21 years for little Zhongzi to be 30. Come to think of it, what a huge amount of knowledge he will have acquired by that time!" She turned round to address her son: "How would you like to have Zhongzi at school?"

But Mencius said, "That won't do. Better wait till later. The youngest student is 15 years old. Zhongzi would be out of place here."

Zhang threw a glance over the students in the courtyard before she said helplessly: "All right, if that's the way you look at it."

After sending off his mother, wife and son, Mencius went straight to the classroom to lecture on the *Book of Rites*.

Back to Gongdu and Gongsun Benzheng on their way to the latter's home on Nine-Dragon Mountain.

Gongdu, who had an unduly high opinion of himself as regards his skill with weapons, considered it beneath his dignity to drive for Gongsun and his injured pride kept rankling as he maintained a sullen silence all the way. He got more impatient when they entered a pine wood and the driving became more difficult. Once they reached the cabin and when Gongsun had brought out his weapons into the open, Gongdu could hardly stop laughing aloud at the sight of them. "You call these your weapons, dear sir? I bet you, even if you left them by the roadside no passer-by would give them more than a glance, let alone pick them up. And yet I've come all the way to fetch them. What a waste of labor!"

To these taunts Gongsun turned a deaf ear for the time being and kept himself fully occupied with collecting his weapons and things which were scattered all over the ground and which he now gathered up by the armful and deposited onto the cart one by one with all the patience of a saint.

This further irritated Gongdu, so much so that he impulsively pulled out from the weaponry a rusty spear and threw it 30 paces away, saying disdainfully as he did so: "What use can you have for such junk?"

Again Gongsun in his unruffled manner went and picked it up, wiped off the dust with his sleeve and put it back on the cart.

Again Gongdu picked it up and threw it away, this time it flew 40 paces.

Still unperturbed, Gongsun went and picked it up, and, just as before, gave it a dust-off and replaced it on the cart.

Gongdu mustered up all his strength to throw the rusty spear away for the third time, and it flew high into the air until it came spinning down and finally got caught in the branches of a tall cypress tree.

Driven beyond forbearance, Gongsun demanded in a severe tone: "Churlish fellow!! You and I got acquainted only a short while ago, and I did nothing wrong to you in the past nor have I hurt you in any way right now—why do you insist on humbling me in such a provoking manner? Do you want to humiliate me till I eat dust or what?"

"What if I do, then?" said Gongdu with a contemptuous sneer. "But I do like to say what I mean. I challenge you to an archery contest to see if you're really as terrific as the Master claims you to be. See here, there's not a single soul about, except you and me. There's nobody here to see you eat humble pie, and I won't tell anyone, do you agree?"

"What if the result is the other way? What will you have to say then?" asked Gongsun, unmoved.

"You think you can beat me—at your age? What a joke!" said Gongdu, thumping his chest as he did so.

"Well, if that's your opinion of yourself, come and try—no more nonsense!" Gongsun snapped.

After getting his bow and arrows from the cart Gongdu pointed to a small cypress tree on top of a hill opposite and said, "Let the trunk of that tree be our target. The upper half is for me and the lower half for you. Three shots each."

Gongsun agreed readily.

Gongdu discharged three arrows in quick succession. They stuck in the upper half of the tree in a vertical line at equal distances, apart, just like three joss-sticks in an incense-burner. He turned triumphantly to his rival, a broad grin on his face. "Mr. Gongsun, your turn now," he said.

Gongsun matched the other's marksmanship with three arrows neatly planted in the lower part of the tree.

Surprised, Gongdu thought to himself: "What a sly old fellow! He has some tricks up his sleeve. I must be careful around him."

Gongsun put his bow in the cart before he turned round to ask, "Are you satisfied now? Or shall we try something else, eh?"

"It's up to you," responded Gongdu.

Gongsun pointed to the spear which was dangling in a tree some way off: "Try to get that spear down."

"How?" Gongdu said, puzzled.

"Come along!" With that he led the young man to the foot of the cypress tree and said, "See if you can get it with a single leap from the ground."

Gongdu could see all too clearly that he could not make it unless he grew wings. Disheartened, he muttered, "Who can jump that high?"

"Surely you can," said Gongsun.

"So high?—No, I can't!" Gongdu shook his head as he said this.

"If you don't, then you are the loser."

There was nothing Gongdu could do but try. He unbuckled his sword belt and laid it on the ground. He walked back several paces, turned around, looked up at the spear and then down for a considerable while before taking a run at the tree. He jumped as high as he could but fell for short of the spear. He retraced his steps and tried once more, and failed again. Exhausted and depressed, he had to lean upon the trunk of the tree for a respite.

"Well, now let me try," said Gongsun. Likewise, he walked a few paces back, dashed to the foot of the tree and executed a sudden leap into the air. In the twinkling of an eye he was back on the solid earth, the spear in his grasp.

Gongdu was very impressed but he refused to show it. Instead, he talked big in an effort to cover up his embarrassment. "Leaping and jumping are mere ostentatious display—pleasant to the eye but not of much practical use. What really counts is combat with real weapons." He scooped up his sword from the ground with a flick of his toes as he said by way of a challenge: "Let's try swordplay."

Feigning an air of timidity, Gongsun protested, "My word! Swordplay is no joke; the least slip and you're done for. Better you use your sword while I use a staff. Will that suit you, lad?"

"Nonsense!" said Gongdu. "Think you can take on my sword with one of these wretched staves of yours? What idiocy!"

"Say what you like. You stick to your precious sword and I to my wretched staff—That's fair enough, isn't it? Come on!"

Obsessed with the single idea of redeeming his lost honor, Gongdu was only too eager to throw himself into the fray. Thereupon he lost no time in launching an attack on Gongsun, sword at the ready.

At first Gongsun just parried his thrusts without hitting back. Gongdu was deceived into thinking that his fearsome onslaughts had overwhelmed his adversary, and therefore he pressed on with added ferocity.

By then Gongsun had retreated to the foot of a cliff, when all of a sudden, by thrusting his feet against the cliff surface, he bounced in a somersault right over Gongdu's head and landed some 30 feet away. Gongdu, as soon as he had recovered from his shock, turned round and attacked again.

Thus one who persisted in attacking and the other who put up a defense by dodging, back and forth, round and round, went on with their tussle. But the cocky young man was too anxious for an immediate victory and consequently he neglected his defense. Thus, as the fighting dragged on, his weak spots gradually became exposed to his rival. And that was how eventually he sustained a thrust in the belly in an unguarded moment from the staff of Gongsun. But just as he doubled up with the pain in his stomach he received a blow on the back wrist. "Ouch!"—the sword flew out of his grasp. As it circled in the air Gongsun bounded forward, catching it as it fell. He turned round to look at Gongdu, whose left hand was clutching his right and his face contorted with pain.

At this moment a rabbit scuttled into sight, followed by a fox in hot pursuit. Gongsun kicked a stone, which struck one of the forelegs of the fox, sending it limping and yelping away.

His masterly feat struck Gongdu dumb with admiration; he at once fell to his knees and declared, "I am conquered, wholly and entirely. I submit to you as my master."

Gongsun helped him up with both hands, which gesture of magnanimity made Gongdu feel all the more ashamed of himself as he said, "I am no better than if I were a miserable frog in a well who sees not the great wide world. Now that I know what superb martial skills you command, the truth dawns on me that a man puffed up with pride is bound to lose."

With earnest wishes couched in sincere words, Gongsun counseled him: "Speaking of martial skills, I should say you have quite a few strong points. For one thing, you're strong, supple and quick-witted; for another, you've had a solid basic training; third, you have a precious sword that has no equal in the world; and fourth, you're outspoken, kind-hearted and by no means given to wanton killing. On the other hand, though, there is a fatal weakness in your character, and that is, you are headstrong and conceited. Virtues are more often than not double-edged. For instance, for a man to be outspoken is not bad at all, but when it comes to dealing with people of a calculating type he can easily be duped. And your *Hanguang* sword is doubtless a most powerful weapon, but once some scoundrel hears of it he may try all means to procure it, even to the extent of doing you harm."

Gongdu was profoundly stirred by these words so sincerely delivered, and once more he made a kowtow to express his heartfelt thanks.

Presently, as they got ready to return, Gongdu urged the other to make himself at ease in the cart while he did the driving.

But Gongsun insisted on doing the driving.

Gongdu could do nothing but obey, and he climbed on to the cart first. With a swing of his long whip, Gongsun drove the cart skillfully out of the forest onto the highway. By the time they reached the school gate, the sun had sunk beyond the horizon.

That evening Gongsun called in Gongdu, had his wrist wound dressed and, giving him an avuncular pat on the shoulder, said with assurance: "Go to bed now, lad. Tomorrow you'll find your wrist as sound as if nothing had happened to it. Good night!"

From that time on, a friendship grew up between the two in which the difference in years was completely forgotten. And there our narrative, for the moment, leaves them.

Let us pick up instead the thread of our story that leads to the court of the State of Zou. During an audience given by His Highness Duke Mu one morning, Xiahou Yi memorialized the former by saying, "Your Lordship, since Mencius set up a school of his own after the manner of Confucius, to whom he looks up as his Preceptor, intellectually-oriented young people throughout the land have been beating a path to his door seeking his instruction. People respect him as a modern sage. Your humble servant hereby requests Your Lordship to condescend to bestow on him bountiful largesse with the hope that he may be still more dedicated to his teaching task and train more talented youths to serve our state and even the empire."

The duke granted his request with smiling approval.

But the crafty Dongye Sixiao had other ideas. A jade tablet* held in both hands, he stepped out of the ranks of ministers and after casting his ferret eyes over those present, began thus: "This Mencius has gathered about him quite a number of students, perhaps as many as 600. It is true that many of them are out of the common run —learned, knowledgeable and skilled in the martial arts. And they could certainly become pillars of society if they were loyal to their state. But if, on the other hand, they should go and hatch a sinister plot or have some political ax to grind, the consequence would be..."

Xiahou Yi reacted in nervous agitation, accompanied by hasty speech and angry looks: "A sinister plot indeed! What right has His Excellency to suspect Mencius' loyalty to the state—a man who conducts himself on the principle of benevolence and righteousness? And his disciples are reputed to be learned, well-behaved scholars. Such suspicion is entirely groundless!"

"All the same, where is there a man who truly knows the inner workings of another? With certain people one can't be too careful," said Dongye cynically.

"Unwarranted suspicion is sure to stir up trouble, which can only serve to complicate things, don't you know?" countered Xiahou.

"If a man takes no thought for the morrow, he will be sorry before today is out," was Dongye's retort.

"Those whose ways are different do not make plans together," said Xiahou with finality.

The two men looked daggers at one another, neither yielding an inch to the other.

Presently Dongye said, "This Mencius of yours is nothing but a pedantic Confucian scholar. By rights he should occupy himself with phrase-mongering and pen-pushing only, why must he go for the martial arts and all that?"

"The six arts, which constitute the basic curriculum for every scholar, include archery and riding. What's so inexplicable about their going in for the martial arts? Besides, they are also a form of physical

---

* This was an elongated pointed piece of jade held in both hands during an audience with a ruler, sometimes containing a "prompt".

training, good for building up the health, aren't they? A sound mind lies in a sound body. Those are just the sort of people Mencius undertakes to train for the state, people who are developed in an all-round way—morally, intellectually and physically," expounded Xiahou.

The debate went on until the duke intervened, a wry smile on his face: "I know both of you mean well for the stability and prosperity of the state. So there's no need to bandy words any more. My mind is made up. I hereby decree that Minister Xiahou Yi be sent as my envoy to present Mencius with 50 yi of pure gold. Tell Mencius from me that this is bestowed in recognition of his merits in running his school and training useful persons for the state, and that he is to redouble his efforts hereafter to turn out more and better graduates whom the state needs in times of both peace and war."

Xiahou Yi set off on his mission as decreed, and there we leave him for the present. Now let us return to Gongsun Benzheng, who was from an impoverished family but who nevertheless had long entertained the noble ambition of performing patriotic deeds. He had remained in obscurity until he found a patron in Mencius, who appreciated him for his noble character as well as his martial accomplishments. With Mencius' support, he had bought five acres of land west of the school as the site for his drill ground. There he trained his 600 students daily, beginning with running, through hand-to-hand combat and down to battle formation. This continued for six months, and he was pleased to see that his students had made remarkable progress and his efforts had not been expended in vain.

One day, it being Archery Day by the calendar of the State of Zou, Mencius said to Gongsun: "It is already half a year since you took up your present job of martial training. Today is Archery Day, a proper occasion for a review of what the students have accomplished through their archery lessons. What do you think?"

"That's just what I was going to suggest, sir," responded Gongsun, and he at once ordered Gongdu to have the students assemble on the drill ground.

The review started with the less-advanced trainees, and as it proceeded brilliant performances were displayed, each performer surpassing the last, much to the satisfaction of coach Gongsun. The apex of his joy was reached when the time came for the last 100 to give their performance. Each of them shot three times and every arrow hit the bull's-eye. Mencius was greatly impressed.

"Your performances have indeed attained the acme of perfection," Mencius praised the performers in glowing terms. "You young people are really capable of great things in the world, for which I cannot praise you enough. One thing, however, you must bear in mind. The purposes for which we go in for martial training are first of all to keep fit and secondly, to defend the state against enemy aggression. The greater combat ability you have, the more prudently you should behave yourselves and the less you should flaunt your combat ability. Remember what Confucius taught us: When wrong and improper, do not look; when wrong and improper, do not listen; when wrong and improper, do not speak; when wrong and improper, do not move. Blessed are those who have some talent to help them carry on in this world, but under no circumstances must they swell with pride and lord it over others. There is the sentence in the inscription on the Golden Man which runs, 'Those who seek to do others down will eventually suffer defeat at the hands of a superior enemy.' This caution you young people must bear in mind."

Gongdu, Xu Bi and the others all responded with a chorus of "Yes sir!"

Mencius then turned to speak to Gongsun Benzheng: "Mr. Gongsun, I must thank you for your invaluable help in making the students what they are today. I am certain these young men can be of great service to the state in the future if the authorities recognize their potential and employ them. And that will be to your credit too."

"But I am nobody. How dare I hope for such recognition?" was Gongsun's humble reply.

Mencius seized the moment of general enthusiasm to put forward a novel proposal: "Would Mr. Gongsun oblige us with a performance of his unique martial skills? That would be a feast for our eyes!"

His proposal met with loud cheers.

Thereupon, Gongsun stepped forward and asked Gongdu and Xu Bi to join him in a "Single Spear Vs Pair of Swords" display.

As Gongsun adopted a stance and called out "Begin!" the other two, swords at the ready, made a dash at him. Sometimes, Gongdu and Xu Bi launched frontal attacks, sometimes they attacked pincer-like, while Gongsun met their onslaughts with all the steadiness of a veteran. The weapons clashed as the one-against-two match continued until 30 rounds were recorded without either side coming out the victor. But just at this point the spear suddenly fell from Gongsun's hand—intentionally—to ground, and thus he was exposed to the sword-thrusts of his attackers. But, quick as lightning, Gongsun shied away adroitly and in turning around he succeeded in catching their hands with the swords in them. While holding their hands aloft, Gongsun shot out his legs fan-wise and the two were sent sprawling right and left to the ground. But before the audience had time to applaud a solitary "Bravo" sounded from behind.

Chapter Sixteen

Three Students of Mencius Impress
the Duke with Their Martial Skill;
Teacher and Students Ascend Mount Tai
to Watch the Sunrise

We related in our last chapter how the "single spear *versus* double swords" combat display by Gongsun and his two opponents enraptured the spectators and how, just before they had time to applaud a solitary "Bravo!" burst forth. Mencius looked around to find that the cheerer was Tao Shi! Delighted, he asked, "When did you come, brother?"

"Only this minute," said Tao Shi. "I've come to watch the fun, seeing that it is the locals' Archery Day. I have long heard about these bright pupils of yours, who are versed in both polite letters and martial arts. Seeing is believing all right—theirs is a well-earned reputation, for sure. And Mr Gongsun's skill with the spear is most impressive. I must congratulate you, dear brother, that you have the good luck to have his co-operation in running your school."

Mencius said, "Since you are here, brother, why not entertain us with a match against Mr Gongsun?"

To this, Tao Shi at first politely declined. But then Mencius, taking him by the hand, led him up to Gongsun, saying, "Mr Gongsun, let me introduce you to my erstwhile schoolmate Tao Shi. He has an excellent command of various weapons. To watch you two perform, each showing his own accomplishments, would be a rare treat for us."

Gongsun and Tao Si exchanged courtesies, and for a moment or two they just stood there, sizing each other up.

Tao Shi was the first to break the ice, saying, "Mr Gongsun, allow me to attempt a trifling feat." So saying, he strode to the weapons rack and took a bow and arrows from it. Then he took aim at the target and shot three arrows one after the other. The arrows all hit the bull's-eye, forming a perfect triangle.

A storm of applause broke from the crowd.

Gongsun said, "Let me try the broadsword exercise." There was more applause.

Gongsun picked two broadswords from the rack and did warm-up exercises before launching into his performance proper. Soon he was whirling his two swords so rapidly that they looked like two streaks of lightning encircling him, as he turned somersaults or leaped into the air. His swords formed such a shield of light as to seemingly defy the penetration of a needle.

His brilliant display called forth one round of applause after another.

Tao Shi followed up with another sword technique, which thrilled the watchers just as much as his marksmanship had done.

"Wonderful!" cheered a different voice from all the rest.

Mencius turned round to look and found that the praise had come from none other than His Excellency Minister Xiahou Yi. "I beg your pardon, sir," said Mencius apologetically, "but you have come unannounced, which fact deprived me of the privilege of welcoming you at the door."

"Let us eschew ceremony, teacher," said Xiahou, beaming. "I have brought good news for you."

"What news?" Mencius asked in surprise.

"His Lordship the Duke sent me here to present you with 50 *yi* of gold in recognition of your merit in running your school."

After thanking him, Mencius offered to take Xiahou inside for a cup of tea, but the latter wanted to stay and watch the students exercising.

As if his good wishes had been anticipated, the students already had a chair kept vacant for him.

As soon as he was seated, Mencius gave orders for Gongsun to lead the students in paired-off wrestling. They all participated with furious energy and in style, which filled Xiahou with admiration. After that, Mencius took him to a tour of inspection of the school premises before he left.

The goodwill with which Duke Mu of Zou had twice bestowed largesse on Mencius in time tipped the balance of his feelings in favor of the duke, but here we anticipate.

It was spring in the year 349 B.C., a favorable year for the State of Zou as regards crops. The *Grain Rain* phase of the lunar calendar had just passed when the farmers started sowing the five grains.

One morning, Mencius summoned Wan Zhang, Gongdu and Xu

Bi to his presence and said, "Confucius used to have free talks with his disciples, in which he often encouraged them to talk about their ambitions. Now spring is in the air; everything looks fresh and gay. At a time like this nothing would please me more than to hear each of you talk about his ambition. How do you like this idea?"

For a while the three young men just stood there looking at each other in blank dismay.

"What is ambition," continued Mencius, "but an earnest desire for some type of achievement? There is no harm in talking about that, is there? Please speak your minds."

Wan Zhang was the first to speak:"In today's world the feudal princes are involved in a chaotic struggle for power, with the result that no state enjoys a day of stability and no people are assured of their means of livelihood. The root cause of all this is that Confucius' theories of li (propriety) and yue (music) have been neglected. I came all the way here from the State of Jin to learn benevolence and righteousness from you. If in future I can work my way up to a position in His Highness' government I will certainly try my hardest to win his trust and thereby prevail on him to listen to advice, employ the virtuous and the talented, and practice benevolence."

Mencius commented, "Excellent! Yours is indeed a noble ambition."

Xu Bi said, "I have been fond of jousting with spear and staff since childhood. And I am interested in the art of war. If an opportunity presents itself, in answer to a call from His Highness I would command an army to defend the state."

Mencius said, "A worthy ambition, too."

Gongdu then piped up, "I have a hasty temper; I'm afraid I'm not made to be a minister or a general. Therefore, I'd like to follow my master in learning righteousness and benevolence all my life."

"Wherever is there a disciple who follows his master all his life?" Mencius asked, smiling indulgently.

Gongdu replied, "But Confucius had dozens of disciples who followed him for 14 years on his lecture tours of the states."

At this point Yuezheng Ke brought a youth in to see Mencius. "This is Teng Geng," he said, "younger brother of the ruler of Teng. He seeks admission to your school."

The young man had a tall and slender figure, was fair complexioned and delicate-featured and amiable-looking. He was simply dressed.

Teng Geng went down on his knees before Mencius, saying, "Teng Geng pays his respects to the master."

"Come to think of it, since you have the distinction of being a younger brother of the reigning prince of Teng, do you not think it beneath your dignity to seek me as a teacher?" said Mencius after he had introduced Wan Zhang, Xu Bi, and Gongdu to the newcomer.

Blushing a little, Teng Geng replied, "But, sir, everybody knows that you follow the example of Confucius, and advocate benevolence and righteousness. Young men who want to achieve anything at all strive to be the first to seek your help. I am ignorant and have no claim to distinction. I am only afraid that my humble self may not prove worthy of your instruction."

Thereupon, Mencius graciously accepted Teng Geng as his student, and asked Yuezheng Ke to take him to see Gongsun Zheng.

After they had departed Mencius proposed to Wan Zhang, Xu Bi and Gongdu that the next day the four of them go to the capital for an audience with the duke. "To express our thanks for the largesse he has bestowed," explained Mencius.

When the next day they arrived at the court they were promptly received by the duke.

"I have achieved nothing remarkable in running a school," began Mencius, "and I could not but feel extremely flattered by the fact that Your Lordship has twice presented me with presents for what little I have accomplished. Today I have brought my disciples along to offer our heartfelt thanks to you in person."

"It is my sincere hope," said the duke with a genial smile, "that you will continue to train useful people for the State of Zou." Having said this, he cast an appraising look over Wan Zhang, Xu Bi and Gongdu, and then asked Mencius with interest:"Sir, I hear that you have admitted over 600 students to your school. They are from various states of the empire. And they are virtuous and talented—some are conversant with the six arts, others skilled in martial arts. Am I right? I wonder what about these three young men of yours. What is each of them good at?"

"Wan Zhang is good at the six arts. And Xu Bi and Gongdu are skilled in the martial arts," Mencius replied.

"Well," said the duke with a broad grin, "since these students of yours are good at the martial arts, I presume that they must have a good deal of skill. Let us watch them show their prowess, shall we?"

Mencius said, "Excuse me for saying so, but they are both young and rash. It would be no laughing matter if by a slip somebody here should get hurt. So, I make bold to suggest that Your Lordship allow them to perform in some open place."

"As you wish," agreed the duke with alacrity. "Let us move out to the courtyard." So saying, he made his way to the porch of the palace, where he seated himself on a crimson couch kept ready for him. To his left was Xiahou Yi, and Dongye Sixiao was on his right. The rest of the officials took their seats according to rank.

In the meantime, the palace guards had brought in a variety of weapons.

"Which of the weapons would Your Highness like to see demonstrated?" Mencius asked.

"Whichever they are best at," was the answer.

At that, the two students held up their clasped hands in a gesture of greeting, first to the spectators and then to each other. They started with archery and then went on using all the different weapons available. Every form of the martial arts they did to perfection, and to no end of applause from their audience. "What superb performances! An eye-opener for me indeed!" was the duke's enthralled comment at the end.

But Dongye Sixiao's long wizened face waxed yet longer. "Your Lordship," he said cryptically, "beware of these young men of his! Should they stir up trouble one of these days, it could mean our doom."

"Your Lordship," said Xiahou, "these disciples of Mencius will prove a great asset to our state. If Your Lordship appoint them to important positions they are sure to accomplish great things for you."

The duke now turned to face left and now to face right, knowing not which of them he should answer first.

Mencius asked, "Would Your Lordship like to see more?"

The duke said pleasantly: "No. That's more than enough for one day's enjoyment, isn't it? Thank you, dear sir! You have done praiseworthy work in turning out such martial talents as they. To mark my appreciation I would like to present you with a horse and carriage."

The duke further addressed himself to Wan Zhang: "The master brought you here to see me because you are his top student, if I'm not mistaken? I now present you with a volume of the *Analects of Confucius*. I wish you to make more efforts to delve into the essence of Confucianism, so as to be better equipped intellectually for future service to the state."

Finally the duke presented Xu Bi and Gongdu each with a precious sword, praising them at the same time for their extraordinary accomplishments in the martial arts.

Time flowed on, and soon it was autumn again. On the 13th day of the eighth month of that year Mencius took his students on a journey to Mount Tai.

Mid-autumn presented Mount Tai in a splendor of colors; yellow grass, red maple leaves, golden chrysanthemums and dark-green pine and cypress trees. Springs, brooks and waterfalls produced tinkling music.

Mencius and his students made their arduous way up the sacred mountain; the narrow zigzag trail led them from one scenic spot to another, and climbing became more and more difficult with the stiff rise of the incline. Xu Bi and Gongdu followed Mencius closely every inch of the way. It was not until noon that they reached the very top of the mountain. There they strained their eyes to look afar and they felt as if they were on top of the world; all the mountains around seemed to dwindle in size beneath their gaze. "No wonder Confucius had the same feeling when he came here and saw this scene," commented Mencius wistfully.

After looking round for a while, he raised a question: "Where do you think is the best vantage point for a full view of a sunrise or moonrise?"

"To watch a sunrise," said Yuezheng Ke, "the best way is to catch the fleeting moment when the sun just appears leaping above the sea's horizon. Hence, your high vantage point must be complemented with a good viewing platform."

Mencius stroked his beard, nodding his head slightly.

Presently, Wan Zhang, pointing to a monolith on the top of a hill beneath them which projected into a valley, said, "That rock is to my mind the best vantage point from which to view a sunrise or moon-rise."

Mencius said: "Let us go and have a look."

When they got there, sure enough, it commanded a good view of the sea in the distance. And it was decided then that they would watch the sunrise from that spot the next morning.

At the first cockcrow the next morning they went there as scheduled. The sky was turning bright in the east. The eastern skyline appeared like an artist's palette on which shimmered a riot of color. In a trice, a fiery red sun had leaped out with a seeming tremor above the sea and slowly ascended, sending out a myriad shafts of light. The majestic sight threw all the observers into an ecstasy of joy. Mencius was just as excited as his students, as it was the first time he had ever set eyes on the sea.

Presently Yuezheng Ke said, "Sir, it's time for breakfast; shall we go back?"

Aroused from his meditation, Mencius said smiling: "How spellbinding is the beauty of nature! It so absorbs us that we even forget our hunger!"

But just as Mencius and company set off on their way back, a young stranger approached them.

Chapter Seventeen

Yezi Performs One More Charitable Deed for the Famine-Stricken; Dongye Tries to Mislead an Addle-headed Prince

To continue our story. The young man went straight up to Mencius and hurriedly dropped to his knees, saying in standard speech: "Sir! Gongsun Chou pays his respects to Your Excellency."

Mencius hastened to pull him to his feet, then took the measure of him before asking about his birthplace and his age.

The young man, aged 18, was from the State of Qi. He was immaculately dressed and had an aristocratic air about him, which impressed Mencius favorably from the start.

Mencius then introduced him to his students and shortly afterwards took them down the mountain and back to their temporary lodgings.

From the 17th day of the eighth month, Mencius began giving lectures in the pine wood at the foot of Mount Tai, which drew listeners from near and far, most of them young people who wanted very much to get on in the world. The forum lasted five days.

One day, on the way home Mencius and his students came to a place between the rivers Sishui and Zhushui which somehow seemed to strike him as familiar. Mencius commanded his driver, Gongdu, to halt. "The two rivers fertilize the land of Lu, which gave birth to the sage of old ages, Confucius. Immortal are his contributions to the coming generations, and his honored name will be cherished for ever. Here we are on the very spot where the sage was buried, why not go and pay homage to his grave?"

Soon his message was passed to the others, and they all jumped down from their carriages and went on foot after him to the Confucius Forest. Having made their offerings at the tomb, they resumed their ride to the city, where they put up at the Jueli Inn as of old.

On learning of his old patron's arrival, the inn-keeper, Sima Zhong, hurried out to welcome him. "It's indeed a pleasure to see you again after so long, sir!" he exclaimed. "Things have changed a lot with you too. Spic-and-span carriages and a bigger following—a world of

difference from last time. Yours is really a case of 'A scholar who has been away three days must be looked at with new eyes.'"

"You are joking, my host," Mencius answered in the same bantering vein. "With so many people patronizing your inn, it must be a paying proposition, I am sure."

"I'm afraid this small inn of mine cannot accommodate such a host..." said Sima Zhong. Mencius interrupted him by saying, "Oh, just check in as many as you can; we shall find other places for the rest."

In the evening Sima Zhong hosted a dinner in honor of Mencius and company.

On the second day of his stay in the capital of Lu Mencius began a series of activities of sightseeing inside and outside the city and giving lectures. One day, as he was giving a lecture on the *Book of Rites*, a man came forward and kowtowed to him, introducing himself as Wulu Zi from the State of Ren. Mencius had to stop his lecture and raise him up with both hands. As the man stood to one side, Mencius subjected him to close scrutiny before he asked, "How old are you?"

"Twenty-five," replied Wulu Zi.

"Ren is not very far from Zou," said Mencius. "How is it that you did not come to study under me at a younger age? Do you not remember Confucius' remark about his starting to learn at 15?"

"How could I forget the Master's teaching," Wulu Zi protested, "But the fact is, I had a bitter childhood: At three years old I lost my mother, and at five my father died. I survived my childhood only by the kind help of my uncle, who adopted me as his son. The family wasn't so well off then, so I had to do one odd job or another to eke out a living. Only in recent years have things begun to improve as my three cousins have grown up. Uncle expects a lot of me and has sent me here to seek your instruction."

His recital of his unhappy childhood touched a sympathetic chord in Mencius as he recalled his own, which was in no way different except that he had a good mother to shelter him. "How lucky that you had such a kind-hearted uncle to take you under his protection!" exclaimed Mencius with a sincere sigh of admiration.

"It is true," Wulu Zi went on, "that he cares more for me than he does for his own sons. At present, my three cousins are doing farm work at home, as my uncle selected me for schooling."

"Only a man with a benevolent heart is capable of that!" commented Mencius with deep feeling. "Now just imagine what a brotherhood we would achieve throughout the world, if every last one of us acted like your uncle. And what a peaceful world we would have then!"

Presently Wan Zhang suggested to Mencius: "Sir! The State of Lu was founded in the early years of the Zhou Dynasty, and already has a long history. There are many historic sites and scenic spots worth seeing. It's still early; will you take us to have a look round?"

Mencius replied, "That is just what I want to do. Let us first view Longevity Mound, said to be the birthplace of the Yellow Emperor, outside the east gate of the city."

Accordingly they started off in an easterly direction, Mencius walking at the head. After traveling about one and a half miles they saw an earthen mound looming ahead on the plain.

Gongdu pointed it out and said, "That's Longevity Mound."

The mound turned out to be in a state of long neglect, overrun with seared yellow grass and brambles, altogether a picture of desolation. Only a few cypresses and junipers nearby seemed to show any sign of life. Mencius could hardly contain a feeling of sadness at a sight like this, and he commented in a sentimental vein: "The Yellow Emperor was a sagacious sovereign, revered as the remotest ancestor common to all the nationalities of Central China. Legend tells us that he vanquished the chieftain Emperor Yan, conquered Chiyou and finally established his empire. As a result, all the tribes submitted to his supreme authority and dubbed him the Yellow Emperor. After his empire was consolidated he took measures to educate his subjects in husbandry and weaving. Sericulture, pottery, wheeled vehicles, written symbols, music, medicine and arithmetic are all said to be inventions of his time. The *Classic of Internal Medicine* is attributed to him, which, tradition holds, is a research work on medicine he produced in co-operation with Qi Bo, Lei Gong and others. Hence its alternative title, *The Yellow Emperor's Classic of internal Medicine*. To this day no one has taken the trouble to erect a monument to honor the memory of such a great historical figure. What has happened to the manners and morals of the time?"

Xianqiu Meng objected, "But they say this is actually Shao Hao's grave."

"Is it? Then, the greater is the shame!" replied Mencius.

During the period of 348-346 B.C. three consecutive bumper harvests were celebrated in the State of Zou. Mencius seized the propitious occasion to seek an interview with the duke, during which he offered felicitations and counsel.

"My lord," Mencius said, "This succession of bumper harvests has brought peace and prosperity to our people, a happy event well worth celebrating. But under no circumstances must we slacken our vigilance amid rejoicing. As you know, natural phenomena are unpredictable. However, since the introduction of the lunar calendar, the 24 Solar Terms of the year* can be calculated, and the waxing and waning of the moon can be forecast. The *Jiazi* system means a complete cycle of 60 years. Within every cycle of 60 years lesser to serious droughts will inevitably occur, with a duration of four or five years or even longer. After droughts will come bumper years of like duration, that is, four or five years or even longer. But after this, though, the years will tend to be waterlogging ones, which will also endure for four or five years or even longer at the worst. Such a process will repeat itself in a never-ending cycle. So, My Lord, it is advisable to bear in mind that one must prepare against want in times of affluence."

His interest fully aroused, the duke asked, "Granted that what you say is true, what am I supposed to do to ensure that my subjects may always live lives of plenty, rain or shine?"

Mencius replied, "Man proposes, heaven disposes. There is no way to change the law of Nature. All you can do is adapt yourself to it."

"But how?" asked the duke.

Mencius explained, "The eastern part of Zou is mostly mountainous. There, because of the poor soil, crops are most vulnerable to drought. The local people should, therefore, pay attention to building irrigation works and planting drought-resistant grain. Let all the mountain sides be planted with fruit trees. Let people on the plain also dig irrigation canals, renovate field banks, and dig wells, so that in favorable weather bumper harvests can be guaranteed, and even when drought of waterlogging strike, their effects can be reduced to the minimum."

"What must be done for the present then?" pursued the duke.

Mencius said, "We have enjoyed bumper harvests for three years running. We ought to build more granaries and storehouses to ensure more reserve grain. Food is next to God for the people, for what drives them to banditry if not hunger? Given enough grain, people don't have to abandon their homes and wander as beggars, and social order can be maintained."

The duke gave the sage an appreciative smile, and commented,

"Thank you for your good counsel. Very helpful!" Then he gave orders to the two ministers Xiahou Yi and Dongye Sixiao: "You both have heard Mencius' words. Now you are to take 100 *yi* of gold each from the public accounts, and go and supervise the building of more granaries. Let us be prepared against times of shortage."

The duke asked yet more questions, to all of which Mencius gave ready and fluent answers. The latter's quick wits and wide knowledge filled the duke with admiration. He finally said, "Were I to have your assistance in governing the State of Zou, the day would not be far off when it would grow strong and prosperous."

At this, Dongye suddenly frowned and protested, "My Lord! Your order to build granaries will be obeyed at once—but are they intended for permanent or temporary use?"

The duke said, "State granaries can only be permanent; that goes without saying."

The way Dongye cut in while the Duke was talking (it seemed to Mencius) was evidently an attempt to prevent him from giving a promise of a high position to Mencius. And so, much put out, Mencius bade the duke a hasty farewell and stalked out of the palace.

On his way home Mencius thought to himself: I have the best intentions in the world to help run an efficient government but this Dongye fellow rushed in to interfere. To think that His Lordship should allow such a mean person to hold a high position at his court! What chance is there for virtuous and able men to work for him? The State of Zou is bound to suffer for it! So Mencius returned home, embittered and disappointed.

During the summer of 345 B.C. a disastrous rainstorm struck Zou. Floods inundated the western plain, wide areas of farmland were destroyed and farmsteads were demolished. Homeless farmers were driven to beggary in a desperate quest for food. Large parts of the state presented scenes of utter devastation and hunger stalked the land.

Anxiety-ridden, Mencius went to see his father-in-law Tian Yezi.

Tian was now well past 60, with a head of hoary hair. He had expected his son-in-law's visit, and shared his anxiety about the state of affairs.

"It breaks my heart to see the common people suffering from this natural disaster," Tian said, "and yet I can think of no effective way for their salvation. The little I can possibly do for them is perhaps to have the whole of my reserve grain delivered to them as an emergency relief measure. Of course this would be just like trying to put out a burning cartload of faggots with a cup of water—completely useless! But that is the most that I, a mere individual, can offer in the way of material aid, isn't it?"

Mencius said, "How kind of you, dear sir! I'll certainly get my disciples to help you with the distribution of the grain."

On the day of his relief grain delivery, Wan Zhang and Yuezheng Ke came to help, and famished people from all directions flocked to Tian's house, praising his humanity to the skies.

Our narrative now switches to Duke Mu of Zou. Continuous reports about the serious effects caused by the recent rainstorm quite unsettled the duke, and it was in such a disturbed state of mind that he summoned Dongye Sixiao.

Making a great show of being serious, Dongye began, "Your Highness, I have come on purpose to tell you some bad news: Mencius is a sorcerer!"

Somewhat stunned, the duke asked, "What makes you say so?"

Dongye cast his ferret eyes right and left to intimate that this was going to be highly confidential, not to be overheard by any outsider.

The duke accordingly waved to the guards: "You may retire."

Dongye continued, "When Mencius was here last time he said something about there being no way of knowing Nature's ways. If what he said is true, how is it that he said again that after so many years there comes drought and after some years again there will be waterlogging. Isn't this proof enough that he is a sorcerer practicing the black arts?"

Consternation written all over his face, the duke wondered aloud: "Can it be that such people really exist—people who can summon the wind and bring the rain?"

"Such a man is to be met with only once in a century," said Dongye, his eyes gleaming with a cunning light. "Come to think of it, if he wasn't a sorcerer, how could he possess such power as to forecast a change of weather? And how is it possible for him to enlist so many brilliant young people in his camp without casting a spell upon them?"

The more he listened, the more disturbed the duke became, and he asked in a trembling voice: "How can I deal with a sorcerer, if Mencius really is one?"

Dongye assured him: "Do not worry, My Lord. But be careful not to play into his hands, that is all. The next time you see him, just cold-shoulder him, and he will be too timid to try to harm you."

Misfortunes never come singly, as the popular saying goes. Only two years after Zou had barely recovered from the rainstorm disaster of the summer of 345 B.C., another rainstorm, more serious, battered the land again. The wide expanse of the western part of the state was turned into a huge swamp. Countless numbers of the common people perished in the deluge.

Faced with a situation like this, Mencius had no alternative but to go and seek help from the duke. In spite of the driving rain, he and his disciples drove post-haste to the Zou court.

The duke had the fright of his life the instant he saw Mencius in person. He made an effort to steady himself by ordering his guard to offer a seat for the unexpected guest.

"For what am I honored by this visit of yours, sir?" he asked tentatively.

"I have come to report to Your Highness about the grave situation our state is plunged in at this moment," Mencius replied. "Thousands upon thousands of people have been rendered homeless by this flood. Your Highness is urged to adopt radical measures to succor the masses of refugees."

"What do you propose, sir?" asked the duke.

"Your Highness, the situation is becoming desperate with the continuing downpour," Mencius explained. "The number of victims is increasing all the time. I would therefore suggest that, first, let more people be organized and despatched to the affected areas to help with drainage and fighting the flood; second, let detachments of soldiers be sent to the River of Four and the White Horse River to build and consolidate embankments; and third, open up the state granaries to the refugees. These things must be done without delay."

The duke appeared at a loss, giving no response.

Mencius urged him again: "My Lord, the common people all look up to Your Highness and the ministers and counselors of the court as their parents. Are there parents who would see their children suffer and not lift a finger to help?"

At this juncture, Dongye Sixiao rushed in and said airily: "What a thing to say! You don't think you're the only one to feel for the suffering of the common people, do you? But what about His Lordship, our reigning prince? The capital is likewise threatened by the torrential rain. The common people ought to protect their supreme ruler and his ministers and officials before everything else, oughtn't they? By the same token, are there children who would disregard their parents' lives being threatened?"

Outside, lightning accompanied by peals of thunder flashed unendingly and rain poured down with a vengeance. Mencius had to force down his rising spleen in order to talk the duke into accepting his plea for the common people. For the moment he just ignored Dongye's fallacious reasoning. "The common people are the lifeblood of a nation," he continued. "Without these ordinary people to fall back upon, do you think you could carry on for even a minute longer? Do you think you could live on air?"

"Shut up!" yelled Dongye, utterly discomfited. "No more of your tongue-wagging! Don't think you can mislead people by fabricating rumors! His Highness the Duke's sanctity is not to be violated by a mere pedant. Never!"

Overwhelmed with righteous indignation, Mencius stood up to his full height: "Take care! Take care! The people are of supreme importance; the altars to the gods of earth and grain come next; last comes the ruler!"

Like a dog who has his master's backing, Dongye yapped furiously with flecks of spittle flying in all directions: "This is sheer rebellion! How dare you go challenging the supreme authority of His Highness the Duke!"

Undaunted, Mencius went on in an even tone: "You Excellency, please calm yourself. Surely you are not unaware of the everyday truth that water can float a boat, but it also can capsize it?" After a pause, he added, "I beg to ask: if the people are forced to leave the territory of Zou because of the intolerable living conditions here, could the state possibly become strong? And could a weakened Zou possibly have the strength to resist foreign aggression?"

These words fell on the duke's ear like a peal of thunder, and he was rendered speechless for a long while.

Chapter Eighteen

Mencius Settles a Poser for Wulu Zi;
Zhongzi Learns Martial Arts from Gongsun

Mencius made no further attempt to remonstrate with the duke, knowing full well that he would only be flogging a dead horse, so he gestured to his students, saying as he did so: "Back to school we go!"

It was still raining hard, and driving on the slippery muddy road was made yet more difficult by a stiff head wind. Gongdu Zi all the time brandished his whip, urging the horse on.

Presently he said resentfully: "How I hate that old scoundrel Dongye! The mere sight of his ugly mug makes my blood boil. How I wish I could slip in his house tonight and make short work of him with one thrust of my sword! Let one such bad sort survive in the world, and people are doomed to suffer and the state is in for trouble."

Mencius rebuked him severely, saying, "Gongdu, don't talk rubbish! We are all law-abiding folk, open and above-board—how could we stoop to such a crime? I forbid you to speak so. Above all, curb your actions!"

Immediately Gongdu realized that he had been in the wrong and set to criticizing himself with all sincerity. As a matter of fact, Mencius rather liked this student of his for his simple-minded, straightforward way; thus he changed his severe tone to one of gentle persuasion and said,"You'd better think twice before speaking or acting. Do you still remember what Confucius says in this connection?"

"Yes, I do," replied Gongdu promptly. "When wrong and improper, do not look; when wrong and improper, do not listen; when wrong and improper, do not speak; when wrong and improper, do not move."

Mencius: "Henceforward you must act upon it!"

"I will, sir," came the obedient reply.

The five of them had covered some dozen *li* when the rain subsided little by little, but the wind gained momentum. Gongdu shook the raindrops off his sleeves, and presently asked his master: "May I ask your excellency a question: since men are very much the

same, how comes it that one ends up a gentleman and another, a commoner?"

After a moment's reflection, Mencius replied: "The human organs of hearing, sight, taste and smell are unable to think and can easily be misled by external things, and so it requires such thinking organs as the heart or brain to command and monitor them. That which we often refer to as moral excellence, be it benevolence or righteousness, can only be attained through the functioning of the thinking organ, the heart. If a man succeeds in establishing goodness in his heart first and foremost, then he can attain benevolence and righteousness, and the lesser organs of the senses can do nothing to despoil it. One who succeeds in doing this is a gentleman, whereas one who fails to do so is a common man."

It was getting dusk when they arrived back at school. Mencius gave orders for Gongdu and Yuezheng Ke to fetch Xianqiu Meng, Peng Geng and Wulu Zi.

Soon the five young people were gathered in Mencius' room. The latter addressed them as follows:

"I want you all to go back to your hometowns to have a look and see if the neighboring states of Lu, Teng and Ren are also affected by the present disaster. You can also have the convenience of seeing your relatives there."

Gongdu said, "Those states must be affected as well, since they are so close to Zou."

"You cannot be too sure, though," said Mencius. "All the same I want first-hand knowledge to set my mind at ease."

Gongdu interjected, "'When one is not in office one makes no enquiry about office work.' This is Confucius' teaching, isn't it? Now your excellency does not serve the duke of Zou, nor are you a minister of Lu or any of the other states. So why bother about their business?"

Mencius replied sternly: "'A benevolent man retains a loving heart'. Could you have forgotten this remark Confucius made? The common people are the lifeblood of a nation. If you have their welfare in mind at all you must find every means to make them rich and then let them have access to a good education. Such is Confucius' theory of a rich people and a strong nation'."

He continued, "Confucius' loving heart embraced the whole of mankind. Now, the territories of Zou, Lu, Teng and Ren are under the jurisdiction of the Zhou emperor; should we not treat them equally, without any discrimination?"

Gongdu stood to one side, silent.

Mencius dismissed them: "It's getting late. Good night, everyone!"

Early the next morning the five students went their separate ways home. It turned out that—strange as it would seem—though it had rained cats and dogs in Lu, Teng and Ren on more than one occasion, and in some cases there had even been rainstorms, as yet there had been no disaster. Thus they all heaved sighs of relief and returned in a happy frame of mind, of which for the time being no more.

Our scene flashes back to Wulu Zi. What had happened to him on this homecoming trip to Ren?

His uncle was overjoyed to see him back, and after the young man had told him what he had come home for, his uncle was pleased to say, "See, I did absolutely right after all when I sent you to Mencius for schooling, didn't I? The Master is truly a paragon of virtue, mark my words!"

Uncle and nephew immediately entered upon an intimate conversation in which they exchanged news about events since their last separation. Presently they heard a knock at the door, and when Wulu opened it there stood his neighbor Wen Li. As they had been good friends since childhood, each had a soft spot in his heart for the other. After exchanging a few words of greeting, Wen Li said, "There's one thing I've been wanting to ask you about, something which has been puzzling me for a long time. I hope you can help out."

"Please don't hesitate," said Wulu with a smile.

Wen Li explained, "Everybody says that food is next to God for the people. That explains the importance of food, doesn't it? But then Confucius emphasized the importance of the rites in one of his talks with his disciple Yan Hui. Now my question is: which is more important, the rites or food?"

"The rites, of course", replied Wulu with finality.

"Which is more important, the rites or sex?" Wen Li asked again.

"The rites, of course," replied Wulu.

"Suppose you would starve to death if you insisted on the observance of the rites, but would manage to get something to eat if you did not. Would you still insist on their observance? Again, suppose you would not get a wife if you insisted on the observance of the rites, but would get one if you did not. Would you still insist on their observance?"

Wulu thought hard for quite a while but was unable to answer. He gave a candid smile before saying, "Sorry, I cannot answer your question; I am out of my depth, really. But I think I can take it up with my teacher and find a solution. Wait till then, all right?"

"Much obliged, brother," said Wen Li.

The next day Wulu returned to school and gave a full account of the discussion to Mencius.

Mencius saw no problem there. "What difficulty is there in answering this?" he asked. "There is a rule or standard in everything. If you bring the tips to the same level without measuring the difference in the bases, you can put an inch-long piece of wood on top of Mount Tai, and it will reach a greater height than the tallest building. In saying that gold is heavier than feathers, surely one is not referring to the amount of gold in a clasp and a whole cartload of feathers? If you compare a case in which food is important with a case in which the rites are inconsequential, then the greater importance of food is not the only absurd conclusion you can draw. Similarly with sex. Go and reply to the questioner in this way: 'Suppose you would manage to get something to eat if you took the food from your elder brother by twisting his arm, but would not get it if you did not. Would you twist his arm? Again, suppose you would get a wife if you climbed over the wall of your neighbor on the east side and dragged away the daughter of the house by force, but would not if you did not. Would you drag her away by force?'"

It seemed as though the scales had suddenly fallen from his eyes, and Wulu retraced his way back to Ren and recounted the answer to Wen Li.

"What an erudite and talented teacher you have got!" emthused Wen Li. "He is quick-witted and persuasive. It is not for nothing that the world recognizes him as a sage! I can only regret that I cannot possibly have the good luck of studying under him, as I've got a family to look after and a living to earn."

Wulu secretly congratulated himself on his good fortune in having a helpful uncle, and his gratitude to him knew no bounds. After giving his friend a few words of comfort, he bade him goodbye and returned to Zou.

Back to Mencius again. Since his repeated attempts to offer services to the Zou court had been rebuffed, he had to content himself by placing all his hopes on bringing up the younger generation in the proper way. In learning from Confucius he adopted the heuristic method of teaching and constantly made improvements to his curricula. Thanks to his eloquence and his skillful use of analogy, his lectures on the *Book of Songs*, *Book of History*, *Book of Rites*, *Book of Changes*, the *Music* and *Spring and Autumn Annals* were most welcome to his students, and they made tremendous progress in their lessons.

One day, as he came home after school he found to his surprise that his mother, wife and son were all looking at him eagerly as if expecting something. "What is the matter, Mother?" he wondered aloud.

Zhang patted Zhongzi's shoulder and said to Mencius: "Look here! Your son is even taller than you are!"

Mencius turned his gaze on Zhongzi and was delighted to see that his son was already fully-grown. "Yes, indeed!" he said with pleasant surprise, as if the idea had first occurred to him. "It is time he went to school."

"Good," Zhang responded quickly. "Let him go to school tomorrow."

Mencius addressed Zhongzi: "Those who are allowed to attend my school are mostly young men from the states of the empire who want to carve careers for themselves. Now, what is your ambition, my boy?"

Zhongzi lowered his head, a sheepish grin on his face.

His grandmother tugged at his sleeve to prompt him:"Your dad is questioning you. Answer him quickly."

At this, Zhongzi plucked up his courage and answered: Restore order and bring peace to the empire, develop the Great Way and bring about the ideal of One World."

"What do you mean by the Great Way?" asked Mencius.

"The lofty ideal, father," said Zhongzi.

"Do you know the standard speech?"

"Yes, father, I do."

"Say 'lofty ideal' in the standard speech this time."

Zhong-zi did as he was told.

In the evening, while enjoying the cool air under the apricot tree in his courtyard, Mencius called his son to him. "It's good that you entertain a noble ambition at a tender age," he began, "but such an ideal can hardly be realized without generations of people taking part, people who are single-minded and who are dedicated to their ideals. Now I want to know what your plan is for the immediate future?"

Zhongzi answered readily: "To follow you in running a school and teaching."

"It takes ten years to grow a tree, but 100 years to train a person properly, as the saying goes," Mencius reminded him. "To be a teacher, one must have a strong sense of responsibility toward the students. The least lapse on the part of the teacher and harm is done to the younger generation. By the way, what is required of a teacher, if you are going to be one?"

Zhongzi said, "It is the teacher's duty to educate people, to impart knowledge, and above all, to teach them how to be a gentleman."

Mencius was delighted to see his son so mature in his judgment, thinking to himself: Indeed, it is high time he went to school.

Meanwhile, Zhang and Tian Duanping had been listening in on the conversation between father and son, satisfied smiles on their faces.

Presently, a sudden thought occurred to Zhongzi to put a question or two to his father. This way, I can collect a bit of knowledge, too, he thought and he started on a series of questions which Mencius answered readily:

"What is your ambition, Father?"

"I cherish benevolence in my heart and let righteousness guide me. I carry out moral education among the people in order that all men from emperor down to the common people may become useful and virtuous members of society."

"What is your approach to study?"

"Study diligently and think hard."

"Your opinion of book knowledge?"

"Reading is always profitable. The more you read, the better. It is essential to acquire knowledge through reading, but one must ruminate over what one has read and be good at drawing inferences."

"Do you believe everything books say?"

"If one believes everything books say, it would be better for books not to exist."

"How is one to get on with a friend?"

"Good friendship is based on sincerity and loyalty."

"Does making friends have anything to do with moral excellence?"

"As Confucius put it, a man of moral excellence enjoys good

neighbors. A man of moral excellence has friends wherever he goes."

"Does an amoral man have friends of his own?"

"Yes, he does. But he only has friends of his own ilk. Things of a kind come together; people of a mind fall into the same group, as the proverb puts it."

"How do you view wealth and honor?"

"Wealth and honor—everybody is after them. I am no exception. But unless they are obtained in the proper way, I will not accept them."

"How do you view poverty?"

"Everybody abhors poverty and wants to avoid it. I am no exception either. But unless I can avoid it in the proper way, I will just accept it."

'How do you approach a gentleman?"

"I hold him in deep respect and want to make friends with him."

"How do you look upon a moral duty?"

"When that duty devolves upon me, I will certainly not give way to others."

"How do you look upon evils and their perpetrators?"

"I abhor evils as deadly foes, and nothing pleases me more than to see the end of them."

"How do you use your time?"

"I treasure my time like gold."

"For whom do you have the greatest admiration?"

"The duke of Zhou and Confucius."

"Whom do you hate most?"

"Those people who wantonly trample on the rites and music as upheld by the duke of Zhou and Confucius."

"What world of order do you anticipate most?"

"A peaceful world in which people of all nations lead prosperous lives."

"What do you fear most?"

"A war-torn world in which the common people are the only ones to suffer."

"Of all the remarks made by Confucius which one do you like best?"

"The one that goes, 'The young should inspire one with respect; how do we know that their future will not equal our present?'"

This answer perplexed Zhongzi somewhat, and he hesitated a bit before he queried: "Excuse me, but Confucius had so many wise sayings to his credit and his *Analects* alone contains a host of aphorisms, why do you single out this one?"

Mencius explained, "Since the Central Kingdoms were established over the breadth and length of the Central Plains, a human society has come into shape and made constant progress. The motive force that propels this society forward emanates from wise kings and sages like Fu Xi, the Yellow Emperor, Yao, Shun, Yu, Tang, King Wen and King Wu, and Confucius, all of whom made their contributions in their time. Society can never remain in a static state, neither can it retrogress. The progress of society comes from rising generations of wise kings and sages. Such is the message my favorite quotation conveys to me."

"I see what you mean," said Zhongzi.

Zhang took the opportunity of a pause in their conversation to remind Zhongzi of the topic of his schooling. Promptly he questioned his father: "What about my entering school, Father? Do you agree?"

Mencius said, "All right, I will accept you as my student. But you must be modest and prudent in front of your senior schoolmates. And be sure to learn from them."

Zhang said with a smile: "I've been waiting to see this day for oh! so long! Now I see my expectations fulfilled!"

Mencius saw by the moonlight the silver-grey head of his mother and all sorts of feelings welled up in his mind: From the first day he began to think on his own, he knew there were only the two of them in the family, mother and son, depending on each other for warmth and comfort. Days and nights, he saw her working away at her loom or spinning-wheel. In what little time she could spare she had to prepare meals, and sew and mend. "What a great woman!" Mencius said to himself. "What a noble character! It is she who over the long years worked her fingers to the bone to keep the family going. It is she who denied herself everything in order to bring me up. Without her I could not have become what I am today: a schoolmaster who boasts a following of nearly 1,000 pupils. And it is she, too, who has taken pains to help bring up my son." So thinking, his eyes moistened.

The following morning Zhongzi followed his father to the school. As father and son crossed the school courtyard friendly glances were thrown in their direction.

Mencius took his son direct to Gongsun Benzheng and said, "Mr. Gongsun, I am bringing my son Zhongzi to you. He knows nothing about archery or riding. I want you to give him a course of training. Please be strict with him."

"Be assured, sir," said Gongsun, winking at Zhongzi with a roguish smile, "I'll take him in hand firmly, as you say. If he doesn't behave himself, see if I don't give him a good flogging!"

It was all Zhongzi could do not to laugh out aloud, seeing that his future teacher was just putting on an act to humor his father.

From that day on, Gongsun treated his charge as if he were his own grandson. His unsophisticated, honest character and his good-natured face acted upon the boy like a balm. Whenever free, they would indulge in idle chat. Wherever the master went, the young apprentice followed like his shadow.

One day Gongsun was teaching Zhongzi archery. As the boy fitted an arrow to his bow his posture in doing so quite impressed the teacher. But when it came to shooting, his three shafts all missed the target, to his intense disappointment. Gongsun comforted him, saying, "Don't lose heart, my lad. In practicing archery, as in everything, perseverance wins the day. You don't expect to leap ever Mount Tai in one jump, do you? You've had a good beginning and your pre-shooting stance is not bad either. Just keep on practicing, and you will succeed sooner than you expect."

After he had said this, he had Zhongzi take off gown and step into a knee-deep trench, from which he was made to jump out. In and out and in and out, thus he went on until he had done the required 100 standing jumps. By that time, he was sweating all over, his head was swimming and his eyes could not focus. After that he did muscular strength drill for the arms, and then abdominal muscle drill, and it was not until he was completely exhausted that he could call it a day.

In 346 B.C., Meng Zhongzi was 15 years old. He took Confucius as his model (who began to study with a will at the age of 15) and managed to master five of the six arts, much to the satisfaction of Mencius and Gongsun.

One day Gongsun suggested to Mencius that he take Zhongzi along for a trip to the capital. On the way he could conveniently teach the boy the art of carriage driving, he said.

Mencius agreed, and as the carriage rolled along, Zhongzi was as happy as a fledgling who sees the great wide world for the first time. Everything seemed strange and new to him. His eyes, big with wonder, darted here, there and everywhere, and questions one after another rose to his mind.

"Grandad," he began, "who invented the carriage?"

This took Gongsun by surprise, and, pretending to be annoyed, he replied, "Today I'm taking you out in order that you may learn how to handle a horse. I don't want you to keep on prattling all the time."

"But I happen to know that Confucius asked about everything he saw when he visited the Royal Ancestral Temple," protested Zhongzi.

Overawed by the mention of the Sage's name, Gongsun had no alternative but to answer, "It was probably Fu Xi or Nü Wa who invented the carriage. No, I think it was the Yellow Emperor."

Zhongzi went on, "Who invented the spear, sword, halberd and...?"

"I've handled every type of weapon since I was a mere child and mastered most of them, but it never occurred to me to ask about their inventors," Gongsun answered, puzzled.

"Weren't they criminals?"

"What a question! Why?"

"They use weapons to slaughter people," the boy said. "Weren't they criminals who invented these lethal weapons?"

"No. You can't lay the blame on them. Let me ask: Was the man who invented the belt a criminal too?"

Zhongzi looked at Gongsun with dilated eyes. "That's a ridiculous question to ask!" he said.

"But answer it," Gongsun insisted.

Zhongzi replied in a self-assertive manner: "He deserves only credit and no blame."

"Some people hang themselves with their belts," Gongsun explained. "Now, according to your logic, what's the difference between the two: the man who invented the belt and the man who invented a weapon, since both inventions cause death to people?"

Zhongzi was stumped by the question, and remained tongue-tied for a good while.

"The ancients invented weapons," Gongsun continued, "in order to fight wild beasts to obtain food. As time went on, they turned into instruments of crime in the hands of bad people. So the blame must be laid on the bad people, not on the inventors of the weapons." He pointed to a well by the side of the road, adding: "Suppose someone committed suicide by throwing himself into the well, would you blame the well digger?"

Zhongzi looked satisfied at this explanation.

By then they could see the city gate of the capital in the distance. Eager to find out what it looked like (since it was the first time he had ever been to the capital), Zhongzi stood up in the carriage and craned his neck. Suddenly they saw a great commotion among the pedestrians ahead of them. Gongsun pulled up short as he saw a procession of horse riders and carriages emerging from the city gate.

Chapter Nineteen

A Princess Falls Victim to Love at First Sight; Two Childhood Friends Are Further Bound to an Engagement

Leading the way were 25 standard-bearers, each holding a colored pennon. There followed eight mounted soldiers. Then came a long line of carriages. In the first open carriage were seated Xiahou Yi and Dongye Sixiao. Immediately after this came a gorgeously decorated coach, inlaid with gold and jade, and fronted with a pearl and kingfisher screen, in which were Duke Mu of Zou and Duchess Jiang. There were 30 more carriages which were occupied by civil and military officials.

Young Zhongzi was full of curiosity. He jumped down from the carriage and hurried near to the luxurious coach.

Duke Mu and his wife from time to time parted the window curtains and peered out. Their daughter Yan-Yan, a girl of 16, was seated between. A frivolous little thing, and also in her pubescent years, she grew fidgety the moment she set eyes on Zhongzi, who was now standing by the roadside across from them. She was struck with admiration at the sight of this fine young man. Even as the coach moved away, she cold not bear to take her eyes off him.

All this did not escape her mother's experienced eye. She nudged her husband, pouting her lips and rolling her eyes significantly.

Duke Mu, puzzled, asked, "What has come over her?"

The duchess said, "Oh, dear! You are slow!"

"Who's that young man?" the duke asked.

Duchess Jiang called out the driver to halt and sent her personal guard to make the enquiry.

Soon the guard came back and said, "Your Lordship! That young man is the son of Mencius. Zhongzi is his name."

The name of Mencius almost made the duke jump out of his skin, and it was a good while before he uttered a sigh and said, "Mencius is truly a man of remarkable intelligence. It is regrettable..."

The duchess interrupted with: "What's wrong with him? Can't you tell me? There's no one else here, just the three of us?"

"I'm well aware what's coming over Yan-Yan," said the duke gloomily. "But the terrible thing is, Mencius is a socerer."

"What?" cried the duchess. "But you used to respect and admire him so. It can't be true!"

The duke told her in timid voice: "He's capable of the black art, you know."

"Who told you that?"

"Dongye Sixiao."

Thereupon, the duchess exploded with "Damn the fellow! He's at his dirty tricks again!"

The duke hurriedly clapped his hand over her mouth.

Because of the sudden halt, Xiahou and Dongye came over to ask the reason, and so the duke immediately gave orders to his driver to resume their journey to Mt Yishan.

Back from the excursion to Mt. Yishan, Yan-yan was no longer herself. She lost interest in everything, staying all day long cooped up in her boudoir, refusing to see anybody, even her parents. Zhongzi's image haunted her all the time. Three days passed, and on the fourth, when she got up in the morning and looked in the bronze mirror she could hardly believe her eyes when she saw her sallow face, and dull, lackluster eyes. She swooned.

Her maid hastened to call the duke and duchess. When he saw the pitiable state their daughter was in the duke glanced meaningfully at his wife and led her to the rear apartment.

"What on earth is the matter with her?" the duke asked.

"Why ask when you know the answer yourself?" his wife replied.

The duke heaved a sigh and said. "I'm the one to blame for not taking her in hand strictly from the first. I've spoilt her in fact. Yet for all that, how can she fall for that son of Mencius at the mere sight of him? She's being flighty!"

The duchess asked, "What's wrong with Mencius, anyway? He may not be one of the high-ups, but he is recognized as a present-day sage. We could lose nothing by marrying Yan-yan to his son, could we?"

The mention of Mencius' name sent a shiver through the duke. "Didn't I tell you that he is a sorcerer?"

"That Dongye is a narrow-minded, shifty sort of fellow," the duchess protested. "You mustn't believe anything he tells you."

She had no sooner finished when a palace guard came in to announce that His Excellency Minister Dongye was at the door.

"Show him in!" commanded the duke in an unpleasant mood. The duchess retreated to the inner chamber.

Dongye came in with his son. After making their ceremonial kowtows to the duke, Dongye introduced the boy: "This is my son Zhi. Today I take the liberty of presenting him to Your Highness so that he may profit by your instruction."

The duke studied the boy's face for a minute, and, favorably impressed, asked with interest: "How old is he?"

"Your humble servant is 18 years old," said Zhi.

"Are you married yet?"

Dongye jumped at the opportunity of putting in a word for his son: "He isn't married yet, Your Lordship."

"Betrothed?"

"Not yet, either."

"I have it in my mind to..." began the duke.

The duchess, who had been eavesdropping next door, picked up an oil-lamp and knocked it loudly against a table.

The noise made the duke swallow back what he was going to say. It also gave Dongye a warning that the sly fellow was too cunning to miss, and without more ado he beat a hasty retreat, together with his son.

Thereupon, the duchess emerged from behind the partition and pleaded with her husband: "If Yan-yan is so taken with Meng Zhongzi, why not help her to fulfill her heart's desire?"

With fear still lingering on him, the duke said, "I can't get over the suspicion that Mencius is a sorcerer after all."

"It can't be true!" pleaded the duchess. "Dongye is talking rot. He simply wants to sling mud at a gentleman."

"All the same, I can't say for sure that he isn't a sorcerer," the duke replied.

"What's so terrible about that, anyway?" said Duchess Jiang with determination. "Even a ferocious beast like the tiger never eats its own cub. Granted that Mencius is a sorcerer, would he possibly do any harm to his son and future daughter-in-law?"

"What's your idea, then?"

"Let Yan-yan be betrothed to Meng Zhongzi."

"Who is going to be the matchmaker?"

"Minister Xiahou Yi. He is a loyal servant of yours."

The duke was convinced. When Xiahou was brought the duke told him: "Dear sir, I've a favor to ask of you. Since that outing to Mt Yishan my daughter Yan-yan has been head over heels in love with Meng Zhongzi, and this one-sided love of hers—giddy thing that she is!—has made her seriously ill. To cure this trouble of her heart, one must seek the help of the man of her heart. So I'm planning to have her betrothed to that boy. Would you consent to be the go-between?"

Xiahou agreed readily and immediately set off on his happy mission. But of this no more for the moment.

Our narrative now returns to where we left Gongsun and Meng Zhongzi on their ride to the capital and their brief encounter with the duke's carriage and his retinue at the city gate. Having had their fill of sightseeing, they started on their way home. Zhongzi talked from nineteen to the dozen and Gongsun tried to answer his questions to the best of his knowledge. Before they knew it, they were back at school.

Zhongzi helped to unharness the horse, led it into the stable and tied it up, all of which he did dexterously under the watchful eye of a smiling Gongsun. They were on their way to their living quarters, when Tao Shi, leading his son Tao Ying by the hand, came in by the school gate. He and Mencius had been friends since childhood and their children in their turn had become good friends too. Tao Ying had a sister who was the same age as Zhongzi and was his playmate in childhood. Later on, as they grew older, the taboo that a boy and a girl were not allowed to touch hands in giving and receiving prevented them from becoming more intimate, and they had to keep their distance from each other, however reluctantly. But this only added to their admiration for each other. Whenever they met, on rare occasions, their expressive eyes spoke volumes. Zhongzi loved Tao Qin for her gentle manners and her obvious kindness, and Qin, for her part, adored Zhongzi for his intelligence and his honest and manly character. All this, meanwhile, did not escape their parents' eyes. Inwardly they were pleased and bided their time.

Thus on seeing the Taos, Zhongzi was elated. He hastened forward, making a deep bow as he inquired eagerly: "Are you here on a formal visit or for something of importance?"

"To settle accounts with your father," said Tao Shi jocularly.

Seeing Zhongzi's surprised expression, Tao Shi hastened to add, "My son Tao Ying is older than you by two years, and yet you entered school last year, didn't you? Why is it that Tao Ying wasn't admitted, then?"

As soon as Zhongzi ushered the Taos into his father's study Tao Shi, without so much as a greeting, plunged headlong into an accusation: "You're being unfair to your old friend, brother, aren't you!"

Blank-faced, Mencius retorted, "What has happened? Why this accusation, my friend?"

Tao Shi said, pointing to Tao Ying and Zhongzi: "Since Tao Ying is two years older than Zhongzi, why have you already let Zhongzi enter your school and not Tao Ying?"

Having got to the root of the matter, Mencius smiled indulgently and said, "So that's how it is! Well, you can set your heart at ease. If Tao Ying so wishes, he can enter this minute."

Tao Shi responded with a broad smile and hastened to make his son to kowtow to his future teacher, which he did obediently.

Tao Shi further said, "There's another thing I want to have your help for. It's like this..."

Mencius told Zhongzi to take Tao Ying to see Gongsun before he turned to Tao Shi: "Well, what is it about? Please go on."

Tao Shi blushed a little before he faltered, "How old is Zhongzi, may I ask?"

Mencius, surprised, said, "What has happened to your memory? Surely you know he is the same age as your daughter Tao Qin. But why?"

Tao Shi admitted, "Right. Both are 15 now. Today I have come to see you for two reasons: The first is about Tao Ying's schooling and the second is to discuss with you about Tao Qin and Zhongzi. Would you agree to their marriage?"

Mencius was nonplussed, and said, "Our two children have grown up together and know each other so well...."

Tao Shi interrupted in a burst of delight: "So you have agreed?"

"But they are still too young for marriage, I think."

"No matter. I only want to obtain your consent to their betrothal, the marriage can wait."

"Who is to be the matchmaker?" asked Mencius.

"There is Duanmu Yan for one," suggested the other.

Mencius was delighted: "You could not have made a better choice,

I would say. Well, I will see him first thing tomorrow about it."

"There is no need. He is coming now," said Tao Shi.

In came the ebullient Duanmu like an echo: "I'm coming! To offer my heartiest congratulations—the match is as good as made without the matchmaker!" he cried.

The three faced each other, then all laughed aloud together.

That evening Mencius went home and informed his family about the matter. They all expressed approval, with Zhang wanting to see the betrothal ceremony held in the shortest time possible. She gave her reason: "I'm well over sixty and I'm looking forward to the day when I can have the joy of dandling my grandchild on my lap and seeing the domestic scene of four generations living under one roof."

The next day they sought out a soothsayer to help them determine an auspicious date for the betrothal ceremony, and in due course Zhongzi and Tao Qin were formally engaged.

One day Mencius was in the middle of a lecture on the *Book of Changes* when Gongsun Benzheng broke in to announce that "His Excellency Minister Xiahou is here on some particular mission."

When the two met, Xiahou came straight to the point without bothering with the standard words of greeting: "Esteemed Sir, I have come expressly to offer my congratulations."

Mencius was quite taken aback. "I beg your pardon," he queried.

With his face wreathed in smiles, Xiahou said, "His Lordship and the duchess have condescended to give their daughter to your son in marriage." As he said this, he produced a red wrapper from within his wide sleeves, which he offered with both hands, adding, "Here's the card with the Eight Characters for Yan-yan's horoscope written on it."

Mencius said apologetically: "But my son was engaged only recently; his betrothed is the daughter of my good friend Tao Shi."

Chapter Twenty

Duke Mu Falls into a Trap Set
by a Wily Minister;
The Lovesick Princess Grabs the First Man
Who Comes to Hand

On hearing the news that Zhongzi was already engaged, Yan-yan collapsed on her bed in a dead swoon. The duke's house was at once thrown into great confusion. There was a terrible to-do, as the duke, the duchess and a gaggle of maids made a lot of fuss over her, raising shrill cries of anguish, trying to bring her back to consciousness. But all in vain. Finally the palace physician was called in.

He eyed the patient for some time before saying, "The princess' illness was caused by some emotional shock."

The duke protested, "How can you diagnose without even taking her pulse, but just by a mere glance?"

The physician replied, "The way she behaved indicated symptoms of melancholia caused by depression of the spirits. She cried and laughed by turns without rhyme or reason—which tells us that she wanted very much to unbosom herself and yet she could find nobody to unbosom herself to. That's how, Your Lordship."

The duchess chimed in, "Is there any wonder-working cure for her trouble?"

"Your Grace," said the physician, "where is there such a panacea in the world, I wonder? All a good doctor can do is to suit the remedy to the case."

The duchess then snapped, "Well, make out your prescription and be quick about it!"

The physician replied, "Even the best doctor in the world can be good only at curing some diseases, but never all. Your humble servant is no exception."

"Do you mean to say hers is an incurable disease?"

"Nothing of the sort."

"Then what did you mean?"

"Here is a case in which the popular saying may apply: The best

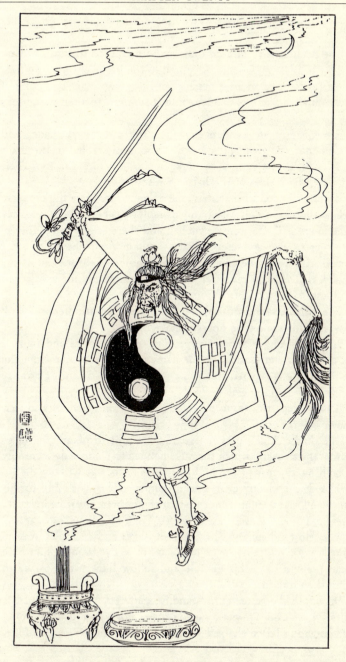

cure for a trouble of the heart is to find out the object the heart pines for."

The duchess gave him an understanding nod and tipped a wink to her husband, with whom she retired to the inner chamber. Where they reached a decision after much discussion that a court meeting of ministers and officials be held to find a solution to their daughter's problem.

Subsequently an announcement to the effect was made, and ministers and officials in their hundreds soon assembled in the main hall. They wished long life to the duke in chorus before they took their positions on both sides of the hall according to rank.

His face clouded with anxiety, the duke declared in a husky voice: "Since our last trip to Mt Yishan my daughter has been taken seriously ill. She looks as if she were bewitched and there seems to be no way to cure her trouble at present. Today I summon you here because I reckon that there my be one among you who can help me out of my difficulty, that is, who can offer an efficacious remedy for my daughter's illness."

The ministers and officials all looked at one another in blank dismay, and for some time nobody spoke up.

Presently Dongye Sixiao stepped out of their ranks and said, "I know a sorcerer-cum-doctor, by the name of Yin Ce, a man from the State of Lu. He is reputed to have a magic power for curing strange maladies and expelling evil spirits."

"If so, I deputize you to pay him a visit, taking rich gifts so that he may come the sooner."

One of the duke's personal guards was sent to obtain five yi of gold from the treasury, which the duke handed to Dongye deferentially with both hands, instructing him to speed on his way without delay.

Back home, Dongye at once summoned his son Zhi to his presence and said to him: "I'm sure that the princess must be lovesick, and yet her father has asked me to get Mr Yin Ce to exercise evil spirits from her. How ridiculous! Yin Ce is an old friend of mine. You go and prepare for yourself a black robe, and once I've brought him here you can pretend to be his disciple and follow him to the palace to perform the exorcism."

Zhi was flabbergasted at this, and he stuttered, "F-f-a-a-ther! I-I-I-I'm afraid I can't do. I'm not a necromancer, nor a wizard. If anything should go wrong I'd be charged with the crime of deceiving the duke, and that would mean death for me."

Dongye gave a light-hearted smirk, saying, "Calm down! That Duke Mu of ours is a worthless ruler, easily duped. When the time comes all you have to do is play-act, muttering incantations and taking your cue from Yin Ce in whatever he does, that's all. If the princess can be cured thus, you both can claim the credit. If you should fail, well, the entire blame will be on Yin Ce and not on you."

Zhi asked, "Father, why must you make me take risks?"

Dongye broke into a loud guffaw before saying, "How naive you are, my son! Remember what I just said: "The trouble with the princess is that she is lovesick. Now, suppose you can get in her good graces, what then would you expect? She will be restored to her normal self and she will become my daughter-in-law as well. A girl from the royal house—to be my daughter-in-law! Think of that! In this world who is there that does not crave glory and wealth? It would be a great stroke of luck to have her join our Dongye family, don't you think?"

But Zhi said, looking doubtful: "Still, I'm not so sure about it."

"My son, being lovelorn, she is sure to be smitten by such a handsome young man as you," Dongye wheedled.

Zhi was somewhat put off balance by this flattery and queried uncertainly: "I'm good-looking, did you say?"

"Yes, you are," Dongye assured him, and, picking up a bronze mirror from the table, he handed it to his son. "If you don't believe me, just have a close look at yourself," he urged.

Holding the mirror in both hands, Zhi looked at his reflected image from every angle imaginable until he was satisfied that he was indeed good-looking, as his father had said he was. "Well, I will have a try, if you wish," he finally consented.

Dongye, all smiles, said, "Once you are at the palace be sure that you carry yourself with grace. In front of the princess see that you exhibit all the best there is in you. Handsome is as handsome does, you know. What takes a woman's fancy in a man is his gallantry and devotion. So, exert your utmost to win her heart, and if you do as I say she will be yours."

Intoxicated with the prospect, Zhi hung on his father's words, nodding his head all the while.

With this matter settled, Dongye at once took his departure for Lu and returned the next morning with the sorcerer-cum-doctor Yin Ce.

Duke Mu went far out of the palace gate to meet his guest. He was impressed to find that the visitor was dressed in a robe patterned with the Eight Diagrams, shod in cloth shoes with wavy cloud patterns, and with a sword (its hilt made of peach wood) hanging from his side and a horse-tail whisk in his hand. He wore his hair long and dishevelled, and he had a broad square face and protuberant eyes. Altogether, he looked like a demon come down to earth.

He held up his clasped hands in courtesy to the duke: "Please accept the greetings of a humble priest," he intoned.

The duke replied, "I am much obliged for your honored visit, Venerable Priest. A feast is already laid out in your honor. Come this way please."

The three went into the reception hall and the instant they settled down in their seats Yin Ce cast an eye at Dongye before he bowed to his host and said, "I beg to inform Your Highness that Dongye Zhi happens to be a disciple of mine. If you don't mind, I would like to have his help for my exorcism."

The duke inquired of Dongye: "Isn't this Dongye Zhi your son?"

"Yes, he is, Your Lordship," said the other.

The duke immediately had Dongye Zhi fetched and the latter prostrated himself on the ground in courtesy to the duke.

"My daughter has had the ill-luck of contracting a strange disease, much to my grief," explained the duke. "If you, master and disciple, can cure her. I will reward you handsomely."

"Please rest assured, Your Highness. We'll do everything we can to expel the evil spirits that are now dwelling in her body," said Yin Ce.

As soon as they had finished feasting the duke asked when they intended to hold the exorcism.

Yin Ce said, "This midnight will do." He further explained that daylight constitutes the greatest menace to demons and evil spirits, and that in the daytime they take shelter in the victim's body and refuse to leave until the dead of night. So, he concluded, the best time would be around midnight, when the evil spirits detached themselves from the human body, which could then undergo the operation without being hurt.

In his anxiety for a quick cure for his daughter, the duke swallowed the soothsayer's nonsense hook, line and sinker.

When the time came for his esoteric operations Yin Ce led his supposed disciple to Yan-yan's door, placed four pieces of peach wood and two basins of pig's blood across the threshold, and went into the room, muttering incantations as he did so.

The two maids had the fright of their lives when they saw the sinister figure of the exorcist and they shrank back in dither. Thereupon Yin Ce commanded them in a deep booming voice to withdraw.

With the whisk in his left hand and the sword in his right, the priest now began his devil-expelling operations. He flourished his sword and waved his whisk alternatively, all in a make-believe manner as if he knew what he was doing, while all this time he never ceased gibbering his incantations. Presently he put his mouth to Zhi's ear and whispered, "Look here, there's only the two of us. Do as you see fit. Right now!"

"But I'm scared stiff," said Zhi.

"Don't forget that you are Dongye Sixiao's son!" said Yin Ce fiercely. "Like father, like son. You should prove worthy of him!"

Meanwhile, a hundred palace guards had stationed themselves outside the door, their swords unsheathed and arrows fitted to their bowstrings as if ready for a formidable enemy.

Yin Ce shouted from within: "Please Your Highness, give orders that nobody must be allowed in without my consent!"

The duke did as requested and added, "Those who disobey will be punished by summary execution!"

Yin Ce let the door stand ajar, produced a mask from inside his robe, which he stealthily put over his face, then made his way to Yan-yan's bedroom.

The lovelorn girl was now a mere shadow of her former self. In her distracted state of mind she thought she heard somebody talking in the outer room, and she struggled to sit up in bed. Oh, my! Good gracious! In the dim light a hideous monster was approaching her. She broke into pitiful cries of "Help!" and then fainted.

Yin Ce now urged Zhi to go and play the guardian angel: "Protect and comfort her, quick!"

Zhi responded promptly by rushing to the bedside. He gesticulated with sweeps of his sleeve, crying as he did so: "Get away demon! Make thyself scarce or perish!" This done, he turned with a smile to Yan-yan.

The girl rose from her bed and threw herself into Zhi's arms, trembling and crying ceaselessly: "Help me! Help me, my guardian angel!"

Seeing this, Yin Ce doffed his mask, put it back in his bosom, returned to the outer room and once again flourished and waved his whisk and sword in the same way as he previously had done, with only the difference being that his incantations were by now rendered intelligible and loud enough for everybody outside to hear: "Demon, begone! Flee to whence thou came! I'll spare thee this once out of mercy. Don't let me set eyes upon thee again! To damnation with thee! Begone!"

When the people outside heard this, they stood stock-still, their hearts beating wildly in their breasts.

This farce having come to an end, Yin Ce tiptoed to push the door to Yanyan's room slightly ajar. Peeping in, he saw the princess nestled against Dongye Zhi's breast, sobbing. Satisfied, he immediately stalked out into the corridor.

"Good news!" he announced, "The demon has taken flight. The princess is well again."

But when the duke went in and saw what he saw, he flew into a rage: "Shameless wretch! How dare you! Guards, arrest this fellow!" he roared.

At this, Dongye Sixiao, who had been hovering behind the palace guards, felt his heart sinking, knowing that his son must have done something wrong. He was about to go in to see what the problem was when Yin Ce came out with his peach-wood sword held lengthwise, blocking the way. "Nobody is permitted to go in except the duke and the duchess!" he commanded.

In an uncontrollable rage the duke stalked across the room to the bed, and Dongye Zhi had to free himself from the embrace of Yan-yan and retreat rapidly to one corner of the room. In her half-dazed state of mind Yan-yan refused to let him go and padded on bare feet closely behind him, muttering incessantly: "Help me, my guardian angel!" Dongye Zhi was left no way to retreat and had to give himself up wholly and entirely to her out-stretched arms, much to the horror of the duke, who stamped his foot with a muffled cry of resentment: "Disgraceful!"

The duchess, however, reacted to the scene differently. A winsome smile came to her face and she dragged her husband away by the sleeve.

Chapter Twenty-One

Duke Mu Tries to Train His Intractable Heir;
A Loyal Minister Escorts the Heir to School

As she saw clearly the way Yan-yan demonstrated her love for Zhi, the duchess was moved to drag her husband to the outer room, where she whispered the following:

"Evidently Yan-yan has got her eye on this son of your minister's, the way she snuggled up to him just now. And you saw it all for yourself, didn't you? But it is prescribed by the rites that, in giving and receiving, a man and a woman should not touch each other. If this scandal gets about what will public opinion say? And how is Yan-yan to take the consequences? Think of that."

The duke scratched his head helplessly. "What is to be done then?" he asked plaintively.

The duchess continued, "Even if it's a trap set by Dongye, we'll have to fall for it, for better or for worse."

"A trap?"

The duchess explained, "Now that things have come to such a pass our only alternative is to accept the accomplished fact and let Yan-yan marry Dongye Zhi, that's all. After all, we can't afford to see Yan-yan pining away because of frustrated love again, can we?"

"Well, I suppose not," the duke admitted. "Very well, my love, we will do as you say."

It was decided there and then that husband and wife were to talk respectively to Dongye Zhi and Yan-yan.

When Dongye Zi was summoned and saw the duke's face, now no longer angry, he knew that the danger was past, and he stood at his ease in front of the duke, waiting for his instructions.

Yan-yan immediately followed as soon as Zhi was called, but before she had time to reach the door, her mother stopped her. "Yan-yan dear, don't go. I want to have a word with you. What do you think of Dongye Zhi?"

Bashfully Yan-yan lowered her head.

The duchess went on, "Marriage is for a lifetime, and a lifetime affair is not to be trifled with, mind you. Think carefully, my child."

Yan-yan replied almost inaudibly: "I do think he is very nice to me."

"Have you made up your mind what you're going to do next?"

Yan-yan nodded slightly.

"Well, I suppose the thing is as good as settled," said the duchess. With that, she joined her husband in the outer room.

"Mr. Dongye," she said, "you and Mr Yin Ce have done a good job, having brought about a complete cure for my daughter's illness, for which we cannot thank you enough. I have a mind to give my daughter to you as your bride. How would you like that?"

Dongye Zhi threw the duke a glance and lowered his head in silence.

The duke asked with a smile: "Why don't you speak, Mr Dongye? Do you agree?"

His words provoked Dongye Zhi to such a pitch of excitement that he was ready to burst, and he was soon on his knees, kowtowing: "Thank you for your condescension. Your slightest wish is my command; how would I dare disobey? But marriage is no small matter, and I wouldn't dare to decide myself without the consent of my parents."

"That's as it should be," agreed the duke with appreciation, and he at once gave orders for Dongye Sixiao to be summoned.

The minister had been cooling his heels outside the gate in a state of suspense, and on hearing the summons he came running in. Once there, he dropped to his knees at the feet of the duke and duchess: "Reverence to Your Highness the Duke and Your Grace the Duchess from your humble servant!" he gasped.

Duke Mu said, "In token of my gratitude to you for your good counsel, which has effected a cure for my daughter's illness, I would like to betroth her to your son. What is your opinion?"

Dongye Sixiao, of course, accepted the duke's proposal with no end of thanks.

The duke further rewarded Yin Ce with 20 *yi* of gold, but at this point our story turns to the duke's son Gu Tu.

He was 18 years old but he behaved as if he were five or six, for he cared for nothing but play and study was his pet aversion.

One day, while he was engrossed in flying a kite, he suddenly heard his father calling him. In his fright, he let the string out of his grasp and the silk kite drifted high into the air. He bit his lips in a fit of annoyance and turned to run away.

The duchess eyed her husband reproachfully, saying, "Spare the rod and spoil the child. We parents are to blame for what he is. We are being over-indulgent to him."

Duke Mu glowered at her and strode off in a huff.

He went straight to Gu Tu's quarters, in a courtyard west of the palace buildings. The earthen wall and thatched roof of the young man's quarters could be glimpsed through the dense foliage of locust trees as you looked from afar. What a nice, secluded spot for concentrated study and research! Thought the duke as he walked along. And yet this worthless son of mine thinks naught of all this, giving himself up to childish pranks. Unruly offspring! So this is how you repay your parents for their painstaking efforts in bringing you up! Thus thinking, he angrily pushed open the unlatched red-painted door of the courtyard. But even as he stepped inside he heard his son's private tutor's voice, and he stopped short and listened.

Gu Tu was sitting cross-legged on the ground by the side of a low table, toying with some bamboo slips in an absent-minded way, while Ding Yuben, the private tutor, knelt on both knees in front of his charge, remonstrating vehemently: "Young master, listen to me. I beseech you. Time and tide wait for no man. The good and wise men of antiquity were invariably those who treasured their time like gold. You are 18 now. It is high time you studied hard and with a will. Apart from anything else, if only for the sake of your parents who have placed high hopes on you, do you not think that you should bestir yourself and work hard?" (Gu Tu stopped his ears with both hands, his head uplifted and his eyes fixed on the ceiling.) Ding continued with emphasis: "You must not disappoint your parents, who expect great things of you!" (Gu Tu remained as unmoved as ever.) Now the tutor started to knock his head against the ground in a self-abnegating way of remonstration: "Young master, if you dislike me because you think I am shallow in knowledge and incompetent as a tutor you can report this to the duke and the duchess and employ a better one, and I will not complain. But all the same, there is no reason for you to neglect your lessons!" He propounded his theme relentlessly. Gu Tu first got vexed, then turned a deaf ear and finally dozed off. Notwithstanding, the tutor continued to have his say: "Young master, it is no small matter if your future career should be affected just because I have failed in my duty as a teacher. I would then stand condemned through the ages. Oh, young master, I am imploring you now on my knees!"

Having heard enough, the duke barged in without announcement, and when he saw the unseemly posture of his son he flew into a rage. "For all the grand tutor's earnest remonstrations, you refuse to listen but have the audacity to fall asleep. Confounded scamp! Do you want to drive me to distraction?"

Gu Tu scrambled hurriedly to his knees, rubbing his sleepy eyes as he did so and at a loss for an answer.

"You have sinned against your ancestors, your parents and the grand tutor," added the duke.

Ding Yuben made a kowtow before he said, "I am incompetent as a tutor. I am ashamed to face your lordship. And I beg for punishment."

By now the duke had calmed down a little, and he comforted the tutor as follows: "My dear sir, I overheard your good advice to my son just now. You have done absolutely right by my unfilial son. Wherein do you deserve blame? No, I must praise you for the patient way you have dealt with him. Please stand up."

A man of well over sixty, Ding Yuben struggled to his feet slowly and painfully. He thanked the duke for his "big-hearted magnanimity in putting up with an insignificant and humble tutor."

The duke addressed Gu Tu, who had meanwhile risen to his feet at his father's order: "From now on you must study hard. The next time I catch you at your tomfoolery I'll relegate you to the status of a commoner and send you packing." With this, he went back to his palace proper, where he related to the duchess all that had passed.

The duchess commented, "It's really hard on the tutor to have such an urchin as his pupil; I do feel sorry for him. But I hear that Mencius has a reputation as a rigorous disciplinarian and educator. How about sending our boy to him for training?"

Reclining listlessly on his couch, his eyes closed, the duke replied in a tired voice: "I've just given him what-for. Let's keep a close eye on him for a while and see if he mends his ways. Then I'll decide what to do."

Three days elapsed. With her son's problem weighing on her mind, the duchess thought she might as well see for herself how Gu Tu was doing in his studies. So she went to his quarters. Reaching there, she took her position quietly by the window through which she could see clearly all the goings-on in the studio.

Ding Yuben was saying, "Young master, today we continue with

Chapter One, Verse 14, of the *Analects*. Be sure that you listen with all due attention and commit everything to memory. Don't let your mind wander."

Gu Tu retorted impatiently: "You harp on the same stuff every time you begin a lesson. Don't you know a story gets stale when it's twice told? It really gets on my nerves to hear you repeat yourself all day long."

Ding replied, "That is because my young master does not concentrate on his studies. So I have to repeat the same thing over and over again to attract his attention. This also explains why we make so little progress in our lessons."

"My fault, is it?" grumbled Gu Tu. "The more you complain about me, the less interest I'll have in my lessons."

The tutor now went down on his knees, pleading piteously: "Young master, time flies like an arrow and youth's a stuff will not endure. Bestir yourself and work hard."

The boy then surprised his teacher by saying, "Well, get on with it. What am I supposed to learn, eh?"

In quick response, Ding Yuben got up from the ground and said, "Good! Then read after me, sentence by sentence. Let's begin:'Confucius says, A gentleman never seeks after rich food nor comfortable living. He acts promptly and weighs his words thoughtfully. He sets a man of morality as his model, by whose standard he rectifies himself. Such a gentleman can be called a good scholar too.'"

"You read too fast," Gu Tu complained. "I can't follow you, much less remember the next. I give up!"

Ding Yuben pointed to the bamboo slips in front of him: "Read your text and do not stare at me."

"I don't want to, that's all there is to it!"

"Well, let us take up the *Book of Rites* for a change, shall we?"

"No."

"How about the *Book of Songs*, then?"

"Nor that, either."

"The *Spring and Autumn Annals*?"

"Never! Never! Today I'm in no mood for anything, that's all." He sprawled over his desk and the moment his head fell on his folded arms, he was asleep.

By this time Duchess Jiang had brought the duke along, and when they saw this they stormed in and, without addressing a word to the tutor, they dragged their son away.

It was only then that Duke Mu of Zou came to the painful realization that there was no way of educating his only heir except by sending him to Mencius for strict training, as his wife had suggested. Contrary to his expectations, his decision made his son jump with joy.

"Bravo!" the boy cheered. "Mencius has a hundred pupils in his school. I shall have a wonderful time with them."

The duke rebuked him harshly: "All you know about is play! What about study—that's what I'm sending you there for?"

The duchess put in mildly: "Darling, you are a prince. And a prince must be aware of his elevated position. Do behave yourself in a way worthy of your title. Besides, you are to be sent there mainly for study. You must study diligently the six classic arts of rites, music, archery, riding, writing and arithmetic until you master them."

Gu Tu said, "I'm the son of the Number One man in this state; there are plenty of people who would love to drive me in my chariot. Why should I learn to ride?"

The duke explained, "The six arts are the required courses for every gentleman-scholar nowadays. Study them you must!"

The duke immediately had his guard send for Xiahou Yi. When the minister came, he commissioned him to take Gu Tu to see Mencius. He was to take 50 yi of gold for the master as an introductory gift, he further instructed. And so that very day the minister took Gu Tu to Mencius' school.

Born and bred in the palace from childhood, Gu Tu had seldom had a chance to see the outside world. The thought that he was going to have a ride with his father's minister made him thrilled. From the moment he climbed into the carriage, sitting as he did beside the minister, his eyes darted, full of wonder, now at this, now at that. Presently a river in the distance attracted his attention. "What are those people doing?" he said as he nudged the minister, who was sitting with closed eyes. The latter gave a start and strained his eyes to look. About 50 people were gathered on the river bank, cheers bursting out from among them from time to time. He counted on his fingers awhile before saying to Gu Tu: "Today is Archery Day, as it happens. Probably there is a tournament going on there."

At the word "tournament" the young man grew restless. Complaining of the driver "not knowing his business", in an excess of impatience he reached over and snatched the whip from the man and gave one of the horses two vicious cuts. The sharp pain made the horse first rear up with a wild neigh, then prance forward furiously, bringing the other horse along with it willy-nilly until they reached a stone bridge over the river. Now it so happened that at this critical juncture a horse-and-cart was coming from the opposite direction. When the carter saw the situation, he immediately pulled up his horse as it reached the bridge, and in one bound leaped right in front of the oncoming carriage. He seized the bridles of both horses, averting a disaster in the nick of time.

The breath-taking sight held all the onlookers spell-bound, including those practicing archery on the beach. They stopped what they were doing for the moment and came crowding around the sturdy cater with admiration written all over their faces.

A cold shiver ran down Xiahou Yi's spine when he got down from his carriage and surveyed the scene before him: The left wheel of the vehicle was just an inch short of the edge of the bridge! He turned round and thanked the carter with clasped hands held head-high, saying, "We owe our lives to you, my man. Many, many thanks!"

The carter, the minister saw, was tall and of a stocky and imposing build, with bulging eyes in a sun-tannned face. He returned the thanks and said, "It was nothing, sir, I assure you."

Xiahou continued admiringly: "I saw with my own eyes just now the feat of strength you displayed. It was amazing! Extraordinary! We are proud of you. Indeed, the State of Zou is proud of you."

The driver said humbly: "You praise me more than I deserve, sir. Thank you all the same. As a matter of fact, I'm just a coarse-grained fellow who has brawn but no brain. Although I have a certain amount of physical strength I have little culture."

Xiahou smiled candidly as he queried, "May I know your name, my hero.?"

The driver replied, "Hao Zhi. And may I know yours, sir?"

"Xiahou Yi."

"So you are the distinguished minister!" Hao Zhi slumped to his knees in awe "Your humble servant has long heard your honored name. An upright and honest official! It's indeed my good fortune to meet you in person today."

Hao Zhi pointed to Gu Tu, asking the minister: "This gentleman is...?"

Xiahou Yi hastened to introduce Gu Tu to the carter, but in doing so he mentioned only his name but made no reference to his provenance.

Gu Tu, who had scarcely got over his recent fright, managed only a hasty, haphazed gesture of greeting with a single flick of a sleeve, saying, "Thank you for your rescue, my man," As he did so, he produced an ingot of gold from inside his robe. "Here are 12 ounces of gold as a token of my gratitude," he said. "Please accept it."

Looking somewhat put out, Hao Zhi replied flatly: "When I saw that three people's lives were endangered, I knew that it was only right to lend a helping hand. It would be churlish to claim a reward."

Gu Tu flushed scarlet at this flat refusal.

But Xiahou Yi took the gold, thrust it into Hao Zhi's hand and gave him a friendly pat on his shoulder: "Please accept it. He meant well. Do accept it with thanks. Please do!"

Gu Tu only said with a nonchalant air, his eyes resting on the carriage: "Don't bother. Move the carriage on to its right track, that's all I'm asking now."

Thereupon, Hao Zhi and the carriage's driver by sheer physical force lifted up the carriage and carried it to the middle of the bridge. This proceeding made Gu Tu gape with wonder.

Xiahou then said to the carter: "Please tell me where you live."

Hao Zhi answered, "Over there beyond Mt Yishan, sir, in the backwoods." So saying, he backed out his cart to give way to Xiahou's carriage and then continued on his way.

For a long time Gu Tu kept an awkward silence in his carriage.

Xiahou Yi sought to draw him out of his shell. "Practice makes perfect," he began. "What you saw just now quite impressed you, did it not? Such a perfection of skill must have taken that carter 15 years of rigorous training and constant practice, to say the least, I can assure you. Hao Zhi risked his life to rescue us—what made him do so? It was because he has a kind heart, it's true, but also because he can rely upon his superb skill. Confucius became a sage because he never tired of learning and never felt ashamed to ask and learn from his subordinates. Mencius has become what he is today—a contemporary sage —also because he studies hard and never tires of learning either."

Gu Tu stared at Xiahou strangely: "Now I understand!" he blurted out. "This lecture of yours is an attempt to bring a lost sheep back to its pen. Am I right, sir?"

Xiahou merely smiled and gave an acquiescent nod.

"I know," Gu Tu said with a heavy sigh, "there is truth in what you said. But the pity is, alas! the Lord of Heaven is being grossly unfair to me: I am not gifted with brains."

Greatly amused, Xiahou retorted, "You are wrong there, young master!"

"What do you mean?"

"In my humble opinion," said Xiahou Yi, trying his best to be convincing, "the young master is far from stupid. The reverse is true: He is enormously clever; he has every quality in him to make him a good scholar. Take kite-flying for example. He is skillful at it and got the hang of it at the first try. Apart from the sons of the common people, who are not a patch on you at kite-flying, even sons of the civil and military officials of the court cannot compare with you at all. And in cock-fights, too, you always come out the winner. All this shows that you are incomparably clever."

Gu Tu grinned from ear to ear: "You certainly know how to flatter people, sir!"

Xiahou Yi protested, "I was simply stating facts."

"Tell me then: Why is it that every time I set eyes on a book I feel sleepy?" asked Gu Tu naively.

However much he tried, Xiahou could not think of a convincing and diplomatic reason.

Gu Tu persisted,"Speak up, sir. Why and whatever for?"

Knowing full well that he could not talk for long before his listener got out of his depth, and that he could not afford to tell the naked truth, which would hurt the boy's vanity, Xiahou hesitated a long while before saying jokingly: "Perhaps it is because the part of your brains that activates learning still lies dormant, I am afraid."

"Brains?" asked the mystified Gu Tu. "How many brains have I?"

Xiaohou pointed to a building in the distance: "There, you see, is the school of Mencius!"

Soon their carriage stopped at the school gate. There was not a soul about, but sounds of cheerful shouting could be heard from the training ground. "I suppose Mencius and his students are now on the training ground, practicing archery and riding," Xiaohou remarked. "Let us go and have a look."

There in the open space Gongsun Benzheng was giving a class in archery. He put each of his trainees through his paces, three shots each. So far so good, but when it came to the turn of Shen Qiang, a youth of 20, the lad appeared nervous, glancing timidly at the coach.

Gongsun encouraged him kindly: "Have no fear, lad. Stand up to the test and you can pass."

Shen Qiang let fly three arrows one after another, but all missed the target, some quite wide of the mark. He was overwhelmed with embarrassment. For a time he just stood rooted to the spot, not knowing what to do next, much to the amusement of Gu Tu, who scoffed, "What a duffer!"

Shen Qiang was stung and raged at Gu Tu, with pointed finger, demanding menacingly: "Who are you growling abuse at, fellow?"

"If the cap fits, wear it!" was the sneering reply.

Shen Qiang lunged forward, grabbing at Gu Tu's collar with one hand and striking him with the other.

Chapter Twenty-Two

Duke Mu's Spoilt Heir Becomes a Serious Student at Mencius' School;
A Marshal's Delinquent Son Undergoes Hard Training

"Shen Qiang, behave yourself!" shouted the coach. He rushed up and separated the two students.

"Stupid ass!" Gu Tu yelled at Shen Qiang, seeing that he was safe from the other. "That is what you really are. I have a right to say what I think."

Xiahou Yi tried to restrain him by putting a hand on the shoulder of his charge: "Young master, you must not behave as if you were in the palace."

His chin tilted up and his eyebrows raised, Gu Tu swept a haughty glance across the crowd and became silent.

Meanwhile Mencius had come up. When he saw Xiahou, he hastened forward: "How do you do, Minister?"

"How do you do, master?" said Xiahou.

Mencius, as soon as he set eyes on Gu Tu, understood the purpose of the minister's visit. "And this gentleman...." he asked out of mere politeness.

Xiahou called Gu Tu over: "Please young master, come here and pay your compliments to your teacher Mencius."

Mencius said, "Let us not stand on ceremony. I want you to make Mr Gongsun's acquaintance. He excels in the martial arts."

Gu Tu was about to perform a kowtow when Gongsun stopped him, saying, "The young master need not extend such a grand form of homage, I'm not worthy of it."

Mencius invited both Xiahou Yi and Gu Tu to his study, where the three took their seats as host and guests.

Xiahou Yi broached the subject of his call: "Master. The duke and the duchess have entrusted me to bring their son to your school so that he may receive a sound education both morally and intellectually. I offer thanks on their behalf in advance."

Mencius replied, "I have always held up benevolence as the principle and righteousness as the way, and the ideal of the state being

a family community is what I seek. Now that His Highness the Duke has the pleasure of sending his son to my school, I am duty-bound to give all that there is in me to help him."

Xiahou Yi said, "It is very kind of you to say so. You live up to your name as a great scholar. Since I first made your acquaintance I have come to realize more and more that you are not only a great scholar but also a great patriot. The duke and I have not mistaken your character."

"Life is short," said Mencius. "We are granted three score and ten years, but the prime of life, during which we can serve our state and people best, is fleeting. Who is there that does not hanker after a life of comfort and ease? Yet there are so many people who just spend their days and nights in idle talk or doing nothing at all, as if happiness could come of its own accord. They have no ideals of their own, nothing to strive for. A mere vegetable existence—that is what they endure. No! Anyone who is out to achieve great things at all must treasure his time as a miser treasures his gold, and he must work hard at the same time, too."

All this time Gu Tu had sat there listening, unconcerned, but Mencius' remark about time being like gold seemed to touch a chord within him.

Xiahou had been watching for his charge's reaction, and presently he rose to his feet, making a half bow to Mencius: "Master, the young master has been listening to your instructions with great interest, as you see. He is unusually intelligent; if only you can expend a little time and effort on him I am perfectly confident that he will turn into a prominent figure to the glory of our people and state."

Mencius echoed his praise: "As I observe, the young master's physiognomy—he has a square face and big ears—promises that he has a great future in store for him."

All this was meat and drink to Gu Tu, who could not keep back a self-satisfied smile.

Xiahou called to the driver, who was waiting in the courtyard: "Bring the parcel here!"

A yellow silk parcel was at once brought to him.

Xiahou stood up and presented it with both hands to Mencius: "Here is 50 yi of gold which His Lordship bestows on you. Please accept it."

As can be expected, there was a profusion of thanks on the part of the recipient, as well as a warm send-off for the minister now that his mission had been successfully fulfilled, the details of which our narrative omits.

Let's come back to Mencius and his recently admitted student. After seeing Xiahou off he interviewed Gu Tu in his study.

The latter was sitting cross-legged on the ground, ill at ease. The elegant and debonair air with which Mencius deported himself filled him with awe. For the first time in his life he began to experience a feeling of inferiority.

Mencius perceived this all, he hastened to put his new student at his ease by asking in a gentle voice: "Which books have you read, young master?"

"I...er...I.. the *Book of Songs*, *Book of History*, *Book of Rites*, *Book of Changes*, the *Music*, and *Spring and Autumn Annals*... and so on and so forth."

Mencius chuckled to himself. "If so, would you please tell me what are the compositions of the *Book of Songs*?" he queried good-humouredly.

Go Tu fidgeted, and remained tongue-tied.

Mencius urged, "Answer me, please!"

Sweat breaking out on his forehead, Gu Tu finally stammered out an answer which was so preposterous that Mencius simply did not know whether to laugh or to cry. Abruptly he stood up and taking a bundle of bamboo slips* from the bookshelf, he spread it before the young man: "Read aloud the first song from the *Book of Songs* for me."

His face covered in sweat, Gu Tu strained his eyes to focus on the text. But before he had read very far, Mencius stopped him. "You don't have to go on. By the way, who was your tutor?"

"Dingyu Ben," was the answer.

"How long did he teach you?"

"Six years."

"Where is he now?"

"Still in the palace."

Mencius called in Yuezheng Ke. He told the latter to arrange a room for Gu Tu and added, "Starting tomorrow, you teach the young master how to read and write."

---

* In ancient China books were written on narrow bamboo strips which were bound together by leather thongs or cords so that they could be rolled up when not in use.

"Me? Teach the young master?" said Yuezheng, in surprise.

"Correct," said Mencius.

"You aren't joking, Master, are you?" queried Yuezheng incredulously.

"I am not," said Mencius without a trace of flippancy.

"But why?"

"You will find out why as soon as you start to teach him."

Yuezheng made a hesitant retreat from the room, but not before he had made Mencius aware that a room had been made ready for the newcomer.

Mencius then turned to speak to Gu Tu, growing severe both in tone and countenance: "From now on you are to be tutored by Mr Yuezheng. See that you respect him and learn from him. Start reading the *Analects of Confucius*. Memorize as you read and memorize as you copy. The book contains a total of 16,590 characters. Copying it once only takes three days. Nothing difficult in that, is there? So I want you to copy it 10 times within a month. And memorize the whole text so thoroughly that before three months are out you will be able to recite it from memory. Lastly, within six months make sure that you have a thorough grasp of its meaning."

Meek as a lamb—a great contrast to his former arrogant self—Gu Tu acquiesced, however reluctantly.

Mencius further told Yuezheng Ke that if Gu Tu should make no progress his tutor was to answer for it.

And so, under a task master, the duke's heir was subjected to a rigorous course of daily reading, rote-learning and calligraphy. A month passed, and sure enough this tutor found that he had made perceptible progress.

One day Yuezheng Ke took him out for an excursion in the wilds. They came to a river. It was late spring, when willow floss drifted in the air like snowflakes and grey storks were busy hunting food in the river. Gu Tu felt as happy as a prisoner newly released. He was enraptured by what he saw. A flock of storks were frightened at his approach and disappeared into the air, much to his disappointment. Yuezheng Ke commented, "The storks have flown away, but soon they will come back. Not so with the river waters. Once they are gone, they are gone for ever. You cannot step into the same river twice."

Gu Tu suddenly realized the truth of this, as he said, "The same holds true for time."

Yuezheng Ke was pleasantly surprised to hear his pupil talk so intelligently, and at once urged him to go back to do his daily stint.

When they reached the school gate the sound of Gongsun commending somebody loudly reached their ears.

Gu Tu dashed to the drill ground, eager to find out what was going on. It turned out that the martial arts coach was teaching Shen Qiang how to shoot an arrow. Gu Tu felt keenly the wrong he had done to Shen Qiang the previous time, and a desire arose in him to offer an apology when he had the chance. Presently Yuezheng Ke called to him, urging him to go back to the classroom. Catching sight of Gu Tu, Shen Qiang, whose humiliation at the hands of the man a month before still rankled in his breast, called to Gu Tu: "I suppose you've come to teach me how to use a bow and arrow now."

By this time Shen Qiang had got to know everything about the influential background of Gu Tu. But then, he himself was no small fry either. He was the son of Marshal Shen Zicheng of the State of Lu, who had rendered meritorious services in battle and thereby enjoyed the special favor of the Lu ruler. He had no cause to eat humble pie in front of Gu Tu, son of the ruler of a mere appendage to Lu.

Now Gu Tu, repentant as he was of what he had done when he had first met the other, had to force down his rising anger and turn to leave, ignoring the challenge.

"Are you going to scuttle off as if nothing had happened since you insulted me last time?" Shen Qiang had meantime planted himself right in front of Gu Tu, all out for a wrangle.

"I should think we are quits, now that you've insulted me," said Gu Tu.

"You insulted me in public, with hundreds of people looking on," retorted Shen Qiang. "Now I'm only insulting you with no other people present. This is not the way to settle accounts, is it?"

"What do you suggest, then?"

"A martial arts contest."

"Done!" Gu Tu, who had been practicing martial arts since childhood, took up the challenge at once. He drew his bow and let fly three arrows in succession. All three hit the target, with one hitting the middle of the bull's eye. Not such luck for Shen Qiang, however. Of his three arrows, only one hit the target, much to his mortification and shame.

His vanity deeply hurt, the descendant of the marshal of Lu

flourished a tightly clenched fist vigorously: "Come on, I challenge you to a boxing match!"

Out of this match Shen Qiang came the winner, but only narrowly because he had the advantage of greater physical strength.

Gongsun Benzheng, seeing the dust-smeared faces of the two combatants, called a halt.

But Shen Qiang wanted to further crush his rival's morale and wouldn't hear of it. He challenged Gu Tu to sword combat.

Gongsun knew well enough Shen Qiang's skill with the sword but not Gu Tu's, and this was the opportunity for him to find out, so he agreed promptly.

Gu Tu was not one to take defeat lying down, and throwing out his chest said proudly: "I'm ready when you are."

Meanwhile his tutor grew anxious lest a serious injury be caused to either party, as Mencius would hold him responsible. So he interrupted, saying, "Swordplay is risky. Let's play safe, all right?"

"Let them have their way," said Gongsun with assurance. He wanted to ascertain just how far Gu Tu had progressed in martial skills.

"Remember, swordplay is not mortal combat. You are on the drill ground, not on the battlefield. Enough is as good as a feast," said the coach as he handed a sword to each of them from the weaponry rack.

"Ready! Go!" Gongsun issued the order.

Each with his sword at the ready, Shen Qiang and Gu Tu stared at one another, fierce-eyed.

Shen Qiang launched an attack immediately, but his movements at critical junctures were often ineffectual and out of joint, which made him vulnerable to sudden and unexpected counter-attacks. Gu Tu realized this quickly and took his time while pretending that he was no match for the other and that all he could do was parry and dodge. Shen Qiang, growing overconfident, persisted in his frontal thrusts all the more vigorously, but all missed momentum as Gu Tu nimbly warded them off right and left, much to the annoyance of the attacker.

Then the momentum of one of his vicious thrusts overbalanced Shen Qiang and he only stopped himself falling headlong by planting his sword in the ground. Vexation and resentment throbbed in his breast. He threw dust into Gu Tu's eyes with the point of his sword, and taking advantage of the split second when the latter was rubbing his eyes, he gripped his sword with both hands and aimed it at his opponent's breast.

At this critical moment Gongsun picked up a pebble the size of a walnut from the ground and shied it at one of Shen's wrists. The latter let out a yelp of pain, and his sword dropped to the ground. With one hand on his stinging wrist, Shen Qiang looked about him, wondering where the missile had come from.

Gongsun said calmly, playing the innocent: "Enough is enough. That's all for today. Go back to your classrooms, both of you."

Shen Qiang asked, "But who was the winner?"

Gongsun replied with good humor: "Neither of you, since each lost a point or two. Wait till next time."

Gu Tu protested, "He threw dust in my eyes. That's a foul. He's the loser for sure."

"You resorted to a dirty trick!" countered Shen Qiang.

Gu Tu retorted, with a perplexed expression: "When did I play a dirty trick?"

Shen pointed to the pebble on the ground: "Look at that! Who else did it?"

Gu Tu realized that it was his tutor who had helped him out of danger, and he therefore threw him a glance of gratitude.

Gongsun said, "There's no sense in taking these things too seriously."

Yuezheng Ke relieved his charge of his sword and put it back where it belonged. "Let's go back and review your lessons," he said to Gu Tu.

Once they were on their own, Gu Tu, still resenting the pebble incident, asked Yuezheng: "Who is this Shen Qiang after all? What a rude and unreasonable fellow!'

"He is the son of Marshal Shen Zicheng of Lu," answered Yuezheng Ke.

"I see," said Gu Tu. "Well, I suppose that explains it." Yuezheng Ke remonstrated with his pupil: "Young master, His Highness your father wants you to acquire knowledge of the rites and the skills of archery and riding. Don't let such trivial personalities affect your studies. Take my advice."

Meanwhile Gongsun Benzheng was also teaching a worldly wise lesson to his vengeful trainee. He did so while applying medicine to the injured wrist of the latter. "Young master, although the fault was Go Tu's when he held you up to ridicule last time, you are to blame for what happened today. One more friend promises one more chance, whereas one more enemy spells an additional block in your way. So it's better to lose an enemy than make one. Now, you sprinkled dust in his eyes; that was one foul. Then you tried to plunge your sword into his breast; that was another foul. If he hadn't skillfully thrown that pebble in the nick of time your sword would have done its work. How would Mencius then have answered His Highness the Duke and your father? And what would happen if this incident should cause a dispute between Zôu and Lu? The consequences would be serious. Think of that. So take my advice and from now on don't act rashly out of personal feelings, for in doing so you can only play into other's hands and harm yourself. I would therefore advise you to make up to Gu Tu and bury the hatchet between you two. Such a friendship would prove advantageous to both states and their peoples."

Shen Qiang thought that there was sense in this, and he agreed to act upon his advice.

Consequently the two young people, Gu Tu and Shen Qiang, became reconciled and clasped hands in amity.

One day Mencius called in Gu Tu to check the latter's studies.

"How have you been getting on with your lessons on the *Analects of Confucius*?" asked Mencius with a solemn air.

"I have been working hard on it without a moment's relaxation, sir," said Gu Tu.

"Well, recite the full text of the first chapter from memory," said Mencius.

Gu Tu had learned the whole thing by heart from beginning to end, and his recitation was marked by both fluency and accuracy.

Mencius was just about to praise his pupil when Gongdu Zi burst in, in a flurry of excitement.

Chapter Twenty-Three

Xiahou Recommends a Good and Wise Man to the Duke of Zou;
Dongye Harbours Malicious Intent Against His Political Rival

As we learned in the last chapter, Mencius was about to say something in praise of his new student Gu Tu when Gongdu barged in to announce that His Excellency Minister Xiahou was at the school gate.

Mencius went out to usher the minister in. After they had exchanged greetings Xiahou asked about Go Tu's studies.

Mencius said, "You have come at the right moment, sir. I had just tested him when you were announced."

In the meantime, Gu Tu had appeared from the study to welcome Xiahou.

Xiahou asked about his progress in his lessons, but the boy merely smiled, holding off an answer.

Mencius spoke up, "You do not have to ask; just test him here and now, and you will know."

As soon as they had settled down in the study Mencius began, "Young master, His Highness the Duke has sent His Excellency the Minister here to check up on your studies. Now you can recite the second chapter, 'On Government', from the *Analects of Confucius* without consulting the text, can't you?"

With a ready "Yes, sir", accompanied by a clearing of his throat, Gu Tu launched into a resonant recital of the 24 verses of the chapter without the slightest pause. His rendition was both rhythmical and full of feeling.

"A scholar," commented Xiahou with delight, "who has been away three days must be looked at with fresh eyes, as they say. I am glad to find that you have made so much progress in your lessons. So will His Highness the duke be when he finds out, I am sure. But I wonder if you have mastered the rest of the *Analects* with equal facility?"

"The *Analects* runs to a total of 20 chapters, all of which I can

repeat from memory," was the reply.

"Wonderful!" Xiahou could hardly contain himself with excitement as he turned to Mencius and said, pressing his palms together at the same time: "You are a marvel, Master! A matter of thirty-some days and you have wrought a metamorphosis in the young master's character; he is so far removed from his former self! No wonder the intelligent and the capable throughout the empire are attracted to you! You have the talent of a minister. You could help run a state or even an empire."

Mencius said with a smile: "You praise me in exaggerated terms. The fact that the young master has made such marked progress must be attributed to Yuezheng Ke. For the past month he has spent day and night with the young master, helping him with his lessons and teaching him how to be a gentleman."

Upon this, Xiahou smiled his gratitude at Yuezheng, then asked Mencius tentatively: "Master, since you have the makings of a statesman, why not take office?"

Mencius murmured, "I have been working hard at my studies since childhood for no other purpose than that one day I may serve the people with competence."

Xiahou started to stroke his beard in token of his appreciation: "Suppose I recommend you to His Highness? How would you like that?" he suggested.

Gu Tu chimed in: "I could press my father to employ you as a senior minister the next time I see him."

Mencius responded with a cool smile: "Thank you for your good will. The pity is that I'm not of such stuff as officials are made of. By nature I am upright and never stoop to flattery. For people like me the road to officialdom is beset with difficulties. I would rather dedicate myself to the cause of education."

Xiahou reminded him: "Confucius did teaching work while in office. You can do the same, can you not? You can set an example for your students to follow. If you make signal achievements in office the rulers of the various states will compete with one another to seek your pupils out to employ them in their service."

Mencius seemed to be convinced by this argument.

Xiahou further assured Mencius: "Now I am going back to report to the duke. Wait to hear good tidings."

On taking leave of Gu Tu, he urged him to do still better at his studies.

In their private quarters in the palace of the State of Zou, Duke Mu and the duchess were awaiting with anxiety their emissary Xiahou, who was to bring them news about their son.

A guard announced the arrival of the minister.

Soon a smiling Xiahou bustled in and reported that he had come back with good news about the young master.

"Since the young master was admitted to Mencius' school, every day he has stayed in his room, reading and writing. He has memorized the *Analects* so thoroughly that now he can recite the whole thing straight off."

This sounded too good to be true, and both duke and duchess wore expressions of doubt.

"But your humble servant actually tested him on the spot. His recitation was most admirable," Xiahou reassured them.

"Heaven be thanked! My son has turned over a new leaf after all!" uttered the duchess with a sigh of relief. She held her folded hands high in the air in a gesture of gratitude to Heaven.

But the duke was still incredulous. "Could Mencius have so miraculous an influence over my son?" he asked.

"Indeed he has," reaffirmed Xiahou, all smiles. "What is more, more of his pupils are no ordinary people either," he added.

The duchess said, "Such being the case, why not have him summoned to the palace and appoint him Grand Tutor, so that on the one hand he can teach our son poetry and good manners and on the other give Your Highness counsel in affairs of state?"

Seeing that the duke was in two minds about this, Xiahou hastened to say, "Mencius is a sage worth his weight in gold. He possesses unusual abilities of statesmanship. And his pupils are the best and brightest of their generation. If Your Highness had him to assist in running the State of Zou, it would take no more than five years to make her strong and prosperous. By that time, we would have nothing to fear from the states of Qin and Wei, however strong they might be, not to mention such lesser states as Lu."

It would seem that Duke Mu had something on his mind which it would be awkward to disclose, for he just sat there, looking down at his beard, silent.

Presently a guard came to report that His Excellency Mr. Dongye was requesting an audience.

What made Dongye want to see the duke at this time of night? It was because he knew that Xiahou Yi, back from his visit to Mencius, would necessarily talk about the sage's merits in glowing terms to the duke. He was afraid lest the duke should be talked into accepting Mencius as his counselor, and he had come in the devil's own hurry in order to divert the duke from such a course.

When questioned by the duke about the purpose of this untimely visit, Dongye said sheepishly, after casting a glance at the duchess and Xiahou: "Your humble servant has been much concerned about His Excellency Mr Xiahou's visit to the young master at Mencius' school. I will have no peace of mind unless I know that everything is well with the young master there."

Duke Mu breathed a long sigh of relief before saying, "Your loyalty to me is much appreciated. I thank you."

Dongye pursued, "But allow me to inquire after the young master. How is...?"

Duke Mu said with a smile: "Your young master has made tremendous progress."

Dongye faked a smile as he said, "May the Lord of Heaven bless him!"

Xiahou was reluctant to talk about Mencius with his political rival present, and so he begged to take leave of the duke.

The duke motioned him to stay, saying, "One moment! While Mr. Dongye is here, let us resume our discussion on how to make proper use of Mencius, shall we?"

Dongye gave an involuntary gasp of dismay at this mention of Mencius, and he rolled his eyes slyly, saying to himself: "Just as I had expected!"

The duke turned to him: "My dear Dongye, how would you estimate Mencius the man, eh?"

The blunt way the question was posed took the other aback, and for a moment he was rendered speechless. But he quickly regained his presence of mind and said loudly: "Mencius is a latter-day sage. He is supremely intelligent."

It was Xiahou's turn to feel nonplussed: Surely this is not Dongye speaking? He asked himself.

Equally puzzled by what he had heard, the duke stared at his minister stupidly, unable to fathom him.

Dongye went on: "Mencius follows the ways of the good and wise men of old by establishing a school and taking a personal interest in teaching; he has proved worthy of his reputation as a latter-day sage. His school is said to have an enrollment of some 700 students, which fact alone bespeaks the outstanding achievements he has made as a teacher."

The duke came straight to the point: "I have a mind to ask him to take office. Then, what position do you suggest would be suitable for him, my dear sir?"

Dongye cast a sly glance at the duke, the duchess and Xiahou in turn, before he spoke snidely: "Mencius is a Confucian scholar, nothing more. It would be detrimental to the state if a mere academic should be charged with affairs of state."

The duke stared at him in utter confusion. "Just now you spoke highly of him as a supremely intelligent man; how is it that you now deprecate him as a dry pedant?"

"Those Confucian scholars," Dongye wagged his glib tongue, "are a handful of empty talkers. When it comes to running a state they prove to be more of a hindrance than a help. The sort of knowledge they prattle on about is just so much moonshine—nice to look at but no use at all."

The duchess said, perturbed: "If what you say is true, we've done wrong in sending the young master to Mencius' school, is that not so?"

Dongye replied, playing the sycophant: "There are so many schools of thought in the world, Madame—Confucianism is just one of them. Mencius has taken over the mantle of Confucius, but their theory of government is of no practical use, in my humble opinion."

"But I find Confucius' principle of the relationship between monarch and minister and so forth very useful in establishing my authority as a ruler," said the duke. "How can you say it is useless?"

Dongye quibbled, "Your humble servant was only saying...Confucianism counts as only one of many theories. It sets out to teach people to acquire knowledge about the rites, to learn to read and write, and so on. It is useful in that it imparts rudimentary knowledge to beginners. But if you intend to train the young master to be a man of administrative ability who is capable of holding the reins of government we must learn from other schools of thought as well."

Xiahou Yi butted in: "My esteemed sir, you prattle about Confucius' and Mencius' philosophy being of no practical use in running a state, but I want to ask you one question: When Confucius was serving as Police Commissioner in Lu, he produced a transformation of social order so impressive that a thing dropped on the road lay there till its owner returned, and doors did not need to be locked at night. How could he possibly have done that if his theories were of no practical use, as you say?"

Duchess Jiang chimed in, "Mr Dongye, didn't you say that Confucius' learning was just moonshine? But how was he able to rule his state so well if that was so?"

Dongye said after a long and awkward silence: "But I hear the disciples of Mencius come from all over the empire. Some are the sons of reigning princes of states, while some are the pampered offspring of rich and powerful households. They think nothing of traveling long distances to Mencius' school. But what for? Just because they want to learn the rites and culture, do you imagine?"

The innuendo of the question made Duke Mu sit up. "Can there be any ulterior motive behind all this?" he asked with alarm.

"The world is full of black hearts; one cannot be too careful," warned Dongye in an ominous voice.

"Your Lordship," said Xiahou, springing to the defense of Mencius, "I know for certain that all of Mencius' disciples are upright and honest. They are open and above board. They look up to Mencius as their teacher because they want to learn the six arts from him and to increase their abilities. There can be no ulterior motive, I'm sure."

Dongye rounded on him: "The human heart is unfathomable. How are you to get to the bottom of the hearts of several hundred people, dear sir?"

Xiahou countered with: "A gentleman wears his heart on his sleeve. Observe and you know what he is; listen and you know his heart."

Dongye leered and was going to further defend his position, when the duke intervened, saying, "No more exchange of words between you two. My mind is made up. Leave this Mencius problem for now. It's getting late. Go home and have a good rest. Good night!"

And so Xiahou Yi went home disconsolate. He spent a sleepless night, tortured by the painful thought that he had failed dishonorably in his promise to his friend Mencius.

Let's come back to Mencius. When he got to know that Gu Tu

had been doing well in his lessons and that he was in no way stupid, he let him attend his classes in the company of Yuezheng Ke. One day, as he was lecturing on the *Analects*, suddenly Xiahou's promise came to his mind as he read aloud with feeling the following passage from the text: "The Master said, 'A man may be able to recite the three hundred odes from the *Book of Songs*, but if, when given a post in the administration, he proves to be without practical ability, or when sent anywhere on a mission, he is unable to answer a question, although his knowledge is extensive, of what use is it?'"

Yuezheng Ke asked, "May I make bold to ask, does a man of promise necessarily seek a post in government?"

After musing a while, Mencius answered with a smile: "There is no doubt that the ultimate aim of study is to apply the knowledge one has acquired to practice. Those who have great ambition bid fair to achieve great things; those who have small ambition are doomed to accomplish only small things; those who have no ambition will achieve nothing at all."

Wan Zhang asked, "I have no ambition to become a public servant, so does this mean that I shall not amount to much in future?"

Mencius explained, "There are all kinds of professions in the world, and intellectual faculty and ability vary from man to man. Whatever profession one is engaged in, great things can be achieved in it. Formerly, when Shi Xiang-zi* was music preceptor at the court of Jin, Confucius traveled long distances in order to learn music from him. He did the same with Chang Hong, who was music master to the Zhou emperor. Hence every profession can produce talents and experts. It all depends on whether one has the aptitude and will power. Every man has his own choice. There can be no forcing it. But in no circumstances whatsoever can one dispense with lofty aspirations and high ideals."

He then went on to dismiss the class. "So much for today," he said, as he rolled up the bamboo strips before him.

Back in his study Mencius stood before the bookshelves on which were rolls of bamboo strips, the books of his time. He blew the dust off their surfaces, thinking to himself: "Mean and dirty fellows in the world are just so much dust and dirt. If you don't sweep them away, they will multiply." All of a sudden, the sly face of Dongye Sixiao

---

* Shi Xiang-zi, otherwise known as Shi Kuang, was a famous musician in ancient China.

flitted across his mind. He felt his heart sinking, and in low spirits he made his way to the drill-ground, where the students were practicing archery, or boxing, or jousting with some type of weapon or other. He stood watching for quite a while and the sight buoyed him up so that he went straight to the stack of weapons and took a sword from it. He began to do fencing exercises on his own as a way to banish his gloomy thoughts. Then he called Gu Tu and Shen Qiang over and expressed his wish to see them perform.

Gu Tu blushed and stammered, "I beg to be excused, Master. I am not yet ready to give a public display."

Mencius turned to Shen Qiang: "Well, how about you?"

Contrary to his usual self, Shen Qiang said, with lowered head: "It is true that I come from a general's family in Lu. But I loitered away my time in childhood and never learned to read or write. However, since coming to your school I have learned much, but it doesn't count as compared with the time I lost. I don't want to make a poor exhibition of myself. Therefore, I beg your pardon."

Mencius was most pleased to hear the two young men talk so modestly, and encouraged them to make still further progress.

He then changed the subject by asking, "I hear that from the first day you entered school, you bore each other a grudge: Why was that?"

Gu Tu blushed violently for shame and hung his head.

Shen Qiang's voice faltered: "It was because of...hmn...because of... Oh, it was nothing at all."

"Good!" said Mencius. "I'm glad it's over and done with. From now on, you will get along with each other even better, will you not?"

Both young men jerked up their heads and smiled at one another knowingly, as if to say: "We are good friends already!"

Mencius impressed on them fervently: "From now on you must show concern for each other, help each other and work even harder, so that on graduation you will win glory for your parents."

Gu Tu and Shen Qiang replied with one voice: "Yes, sir."

Mencius was about to say something more to the two young men, when he heard someone calling to him from behind.

Chapter Twenty-Four

Mencius Suffers One More Setback
in His Quest for a Political Career;
Zhang Comforts Her Son and Urges Him
to Forge Ahead

As mentioned in the preceding chapter, Mencius was thrown into a most pleasant frame of mind on learning that Gu Tu and Shen Qiang had become good friends, and he was moved to want to say more in the way of encouragement when someone accosted him on a matter of urgency.

He turned to find a sturdy fellow attired as a man-at-arms leading a roan horse and holding a whip in his right hand.

The man made a deep bow to Mencius before saying: "Master. His Excellency Mr Xiahou is seriously ill. I'm sent here to inform you."

Mencius was shocked to hear the news. He lost no time having his carriage got ready and was soon on his way to see Xiahou Yi himself.

All the way Gongdu drove the vehicle like the wind, urging his horse on with both the bridle and the whip. When they arrived at Xiahou's house Mencius did not wait but rushed straight in. He heard Xiahou's voice repeating over and over again: "Master! I have grievously let you down—what a worthless fellow I am!"

Mencius went in quietly and approached the sick-bed, saying, "Dear sir, it grieves my heart to find you so seriously ill. What is the cause, may I ask?"

Xiahou Yi forced open his tired eyes and said weakly: "I am worthless. I have found no way to talk the duke into recognizing your true worth and thereby appoint you to an important position. I'm a complete failure!"

Mencius tried to comfort him by saying, "Do not torment yourself needlessly. We can do nothing if His Lordship has a prejudice in favor of Dongye Sixiao. Just forget them. Let us talk about your health now. From what I observe, your indisposition originates from a depressed mind."

Xiahou answered, "You have hit the nail on the head! Since that day I failed to bring His Lordship around to accepting you I have been feeling stifled."

Mencius said with a smile: "Do not be hard on yourself. You will only be playing into Dongye's hands if you go on tormenting yourself like this. Who else at court can hold out against Dongye if not you? So preserve yourself by all means."

Xiahou Yi breathed a long sigh, saying, "But I really deeply feel regretful that such a brilliant talent as you are should be totally neglected, alas!"

Mencius replied, "From antiquity until the present day countless people of talent and capability have been neglected or even wasted. Think of Confucius in his day. Though he lived to a ripe old age and traveled in many states, the princes saw in him little, and one after another turned their backs on him. Who am I as compared with the Sage? I am thankful that I am still young and strong. The world is wide and there is room enough to exercise my poor abilities."

Xiahou thought that there was more in this remark than met the ear, and he at once shook Mencius' hand vigorously, pleading, "Venerable Master, listen to me. You are a citizen of Zou, and it is to Zou that you owe your allegiance, first and foremost. On no account must you go and serve any other state, even if His Lordship ignores you for the time being!"

Mencius said: "There is no territory under Heaven which is not the Zhou emperor's. In future, wherever I may find myself, I will go in for nothing but educating youth. To train talent for the benefit of the people—nothing gives me greater pleasure than that."

Xiahou, deeply moved, said, "To hear you talk but once, dear sir, is worth more than reading ponderous tomes of enlightenment. Placed in a high position though I am, I confess that I have accomplished nothing in comparison with you, much to my shame."

But Mencius said: "You enjoy high prestige and command universal respect. How can I be compared with you? Please don't tax yourself with unavailing thoughts. For the time being just take a good rest and get a speedy recovery."

Mencius was about to take his leave, when Yuezheng Ke and Gu Tu appeared at the door, downcast.

"What is the matter?" Mencius asked anxiously.

Gu Tu replied, on his knees: "Master! I have just been to see my father. I tried to prevail on him to employ you in office, but he would not listen to me, all because of that Dongxiao fellow's intervention...."

"Please stand up, young master," was Mencins' reaction.

As if the sense of injustice had overwhelmed him, Gu Tu could not restrain his tears of bitterness! "I simply cannot make out why my father would not listen to my advice. Instead, he must needs listen to Dongye's nonsense."

Mencius soothed him with "It cannot be helped. Thank you for your goodwill all the same."

Xiahou Yi, who had in the meantime got out of bed, stamped his foot and swore, "Woe is me that I was born under an ill star, to have the bad luck to have to serve the court alongside a villainous minister!"

Mencius said, with a candid smile: "Your Excellency, there is no forcing the development of human affairs. Since His Lordship does not think much of me, there is little help for it. Say no more about it."

Xiahou Yi continued, notwithstanding: "Unless I succeed in bringing the duke round to employing you, I cannot die content."

Mencius comforted him as much as he could before he took his leave.

When Mencius and his two pupils reached home it was already dusk.

Zhang and Tian Duanping had prepared a sumptuous dinner in honor of their return, during which Mencius and his students repeatedly exchanged toasts late into the night.

Gu Tu knew what was perturbing the mind of his teacher, and subsequently on more than one occasion tried to persuade his father the duke to employ Mencius, but all to no avail.

From that time on, Mencius set his mind exclusively on his teaching work, and ten years had soon passed, during which time his parents-in-law had died.

One day in the autumn of 335 B.C., when Mencius was 50 years of age, as he returned home after school his eyes lighted on the yellowing leaves of the peach and apricot trees in the courtyard, which started a train of melancholy thoughts in him. He went quickly into his room and peered into the bronze mirror. To his dismay, he saw there an old man with a wrinkled forehead and greying temples. "Could that be me?" he wondered aloud.

Duanping happened to drop in at this moment, bringing a bowl of gruel. "Who else is it, if not you yourself?" she teased.

"I am getting old without my noticing it," Mencius said wistfully as he smiled at his wife, and he discovered for the first time that there were a few wrinkles on her forehead too. He grew thoughtful.

Mencius said, "Since I began to run a school, I have admitted close on a thousand students. They were the best and brightest of their generations. But so far, not one of them has ever been appointed to an important position by the Emperor of the Zhou Dynasty or the rulers of the various states. What a waste of talent! The pity of it! The pity of it!"

Tian Duanping set down the bowl and expostulated with her husband: "The present Emperor of Zhou exists in name only; actually he has no power to control his empire. The local princes under him are locked in an endless contention among themselves for hegemony. All they are good for is warfare and intrigue, and they let benevolent government and rule in accordance with rites go hang. In a troubled time like this, how can you have the heart to want your students to go into service for those warlords? If they did, they would come to no good end. Better bide your time, don't you think?"

Mencius remarked in a bitter vein: "Time and tide wait for no man. And I have reached fifty, an age when a man should know his limitations and be resigned to his fate, as Confucius put it. Most of my students are now past thirty or even forty. They are like pearls cast before swine, Where is there any justice in the world I should like to know?"

Zhang emerged from her room, saying affectionately: "It's noble of you to keep at heart the interests of your students and hate to see the common people suffer because of the disputes between the feudal princes. Now I come to think of it, Confucius traveled round the various states with his disciples, trying to persuade the local princes to practice benevolent government and rule according to the rites; you can do the same."

Looking at his mother, with her hoary head and wrinkled face, Mencius felt apologetic and tears rose to his eyes. "Dear mother," he said, "I have been an undutiful son to you, as all these years I have been preoccupied with my teaching work so that I have had little time left to attend to your wants. You are over 70 now; how can I bear the thought of leaving you and traveling far away?"

"I feel richly rewarded by just hearing you say so, my son," said Zhang, deeply moved. "Of the four cardinal virtues of loyalty, filial piety, honor and fidelity, loyalty comes first of all, and is therefore predominantly important. One must serve one's home country with loyalty before one can afford to care for one's home, because if one is deprived of one's homeland, one's home is lost too; then what is the use of talking about one's duty to one's parents? So it is my earnest hope that you will be able to talk those princes or even the Zhou Emperor himself into accepting your political philosophy about benevolence and the rites, so that peace can be restored to the whole of the empire and the common people can lead decent lives, with no lack of food or clothing. As for myself, I'm still hale and hearty. So don't worry about me; you just go and do what is best."

Her exhortation at last got the better of his anxious doubt, and Mencius assented with tears of joy and words of thanks.

His wife too urged him: "I can take good care of mother. You can trust the family to me and Tao Qin. Since she married Zhongzi and became one of us she has been a great help. She is indeed an intelligent and kind-hearted girl."

After meditating a long while, Mencius called his son to his presence, and said, "Zhongzi! You are now 25 and a family man to boot. You stay at school and help Mr Gongsun run the school and look after Grandma for me."

Zhongzi replied, "But I want very much to go out into the world with you to broaden my mind and also learn about state affairs. Would you agree to my going with you?"

Mencius abstained from giving 'yes' for an answer but merely smiled.

Zhongzi eyed his father appealingly.

Zhang sniggered presently, saying, "Silly boy, don't stare at your dad stupidly. He has already agreed; can't you see?"

The next morning Mencius went to the school and addressed his students: "You have acquired a good command of the two categories of the Six Classic Arts and the *Analects of Confucius*. It is now time for you to put your knowledge to the test in real life. In the present-day world the powerful princes of the states throughout the empire are fighting among themselves for hegemony. An otherwise unified empire is being torn apart by endless internal strife. The common people are cast into an abyss of suffering. Confronted with a situation like this, who can be expected to come to their rescue and carry out reform by promoting a policy of benevolent government and rule by the rites, if not we ourselves? Therefore I am thinking of taking you all along on a trip to the various states to try to persuade their rulers to abandon their warlike ways and practice benevolent government. How do you like my idea? Are you willing to go with me?"

The students all agreed at once.

Overjoyed, Mencius scrutinized the faces of the students who were seated in the front row, and then said with emphasis: "But the journey may be hard, I must warn you beforehand, as it involves traversing long distances and surmounting all kinds of hardships or even perils. Confucius said,'While his parents are alive a son should not travel far. If he does, he must have a stated destination.' So those who have problems at home, should remain behind."

Wan Zhang knelt up where he squatted and said, "Allow me to ask, Master: which of the states are we going to stop off at as the first leg of our trip?"

"I was thinking of the State of Qi first of all," was Mencius' prompt reply.

"That's my birthplace! May I have the pleasure of driving the carriage for you this time, sir?" asked Gongsun Chou with expectancy.

"You may. We shall all have to take conveyances, so everybody will have a good chance of practicing the art of driving. Let us start three days from now. Now go back and make necessary preparations for the journey, everyone." Mencius dismissed them.

So the class broke up, each student going his own way to prepare for departure.

Mencius made his way to Gongsun Benzheng's quarters. "Mr Gongsun," said he on seeing the latter, "Since the first day you came to my school the students have profited a lot from your martial training. They have learned not only the martial skill of defending themselves against enemies but they have built up strong physiques as well. All the good you've done us I will remember as long as I live. In three days' time, we shall begin our long journey to all the states throughout the empire. I will leave the school to your care, if you are willing to undertake such a responsibility.

Gongsun said, gravely: "Master, you helped me out of straitened circumstances. I owe you a debt of gratitude which I do not know how to repay. As you are preparing to journey abroad, I think I should go with you, for though I'm getting old, I'm still alive and kicking, and besides, with so large a following, perhaps you will need extra help once in a while, don't you think? And last but not least, I really cannot bear the thought of parting from you all. Do let me go with you, please do!"

Mencius was only too glad to comply. He bowed his thanks, saying, "You are most welcome to join us, dear sir!"

Gongsun Benzheng, all smiles, said, "Thank you very much, sir."

Mencius was turning to go, when Yuezheng Ke hurried in and whispered in his ear: "Sir, Gu Tu has gone to the capital without leaving word."

Chapter Twenty-Five

Gu Tu Pleads in Vain with His Father to Employ Mencius; Mencius Stops at Qi in His Tour of the Empire

When Mencius learned that Gu Tu had gone home without giving notice, he remarked sadly: "Oh, the boy is indeed changed! Who would have thought it? But I am certain nothing will come of it, for all his good wishes."

Now let's see why Gu Tu suddenly took his departure and whether Mencius' prediction came true after all.

When Gu Tu got back to the palace he was perspiring all over, and to the surprised duke, who was engrossed in watching a music and dance performance by his harem, he gasped apropos of nothing: "My master is going...and...on...on a journey."

After recovering from his initial surprise, the duke responded nonchalantly: "Well, what's so remarkable about that? Since he is so conceited and boastful, it will do him a lot of good to meet with some rebuffs from those arrogant princes. It will teach him a lesson or two."

His face contorted with rage and blue veins standing out on his temples, Gu Tu angrily waved his hand to call off the performance. The dancing girls scattered in fright.

Gu Tu made an effort to control his temper, then went down on his knees. "Father! Mother! Please heed my words. Zou is a small state. Now, with all the bigger ones struggling for supremacy we are bound to lose to one of them in the end if we do not find ways to enrich the people and make the state strong."

"Rich and strong indeed!" retorted Duke Mu resentfully. "It is easy enough to talk." He jumped up from his seat impulsively and pointed at his wife: "See how your son behaves to me! He adopts the very same tone Mencius used in lecturing me."

The duchess said in self-defense: "Mencius is a brilliant scholar. What's wrong if our son sets him up as his model? Don't you see how learned the boy has become?"

Gu Tu said in support of his mother: "What mother said is true. Since I entered Mencius' school I have learned not only a great amount

272

of book knowledge but also his noble character."

Stubbornly, the duke demanded of his son: "You give me an account of his character then!"

"He is noble", Gu Tu began. "He adheres to principles, not yielding to pressure; he learns with indefatigable zeal and never tires of teaching people; he has a breadth of mind large enough to embrace the whole world. Moreover, he is deeply concerned with the fate of his country and people; he is strict with himself but tolerant towards others; and...."

"That's enough!" yelled the duke in anger. "I sent you to study under him in order that you could learn good manners and proper conduct. I never expected that you would go and pick up his self-glorification and exaggerations wholesale. If you go on like this how are things going to end?"

The duchess intervened to pacify her husband by saying, "Calm yourself, my dear. Have patience to hear what he has to say, can't you?"

"Go on then," said the Duke darkly.

The duchess signaled to her husband by patting her knee, and thereupon he grunted, "Stand up and speak!"

Headstrong as ever, Gu Tu did not budge from where he knelt, but went on, "I beg your pardon, sir. There is one more thing I wish to say. I am grateful to both of you that you had the good grace to allow your son to study under Mencius. For I have thus come to know that he really is no ordinary mortal...."

"How so?" As if he had been touched on a raw spot, the duke bridled.

"He is erudite, being well versed in ancient and modern learning. Indeed he cherishes lofty aspirations, and is entirely dedicated to the idea of benefiting the world and humanity. I wish, therefore, that I could follow him all my life as his disciple. And I hope you will grant my wish."

The duke stamped and roared with anger: "You are talking through your hat! You are my sole heir; if you don't stay with me and learn the ways of government, who is to succeed to my throne?"

"Please don't be angry with me, I beseech you," Gu Tu pleaded calmly. "It should not be difficult for you to keep me here. All you have to do is appoint Mencius to the position of Senior Minister."

"Impossible!" was the duke's petulant reply.

"Father dear," Gu Tu appealed again, "think of this: A man like

Mencius—so brilliant, so high-aspiring, so far-sighted and with the courage of his convictions—such a man you can come across only once in a lifetime. Invite him to work for you, please do. Now is the time. In three days he will leave Zou on his tour of the various states to campaign for his doctrines with those princes. You'll only have yourself to blame if he is employed by any of them. Take action now before it is too late!"

"What blame am I supposed to take, eh?" asked the duke.

"There are two counts," blurted out Gu Tu in his outspoken way. "One, you take no recognition of real talent when it is before your very eyes; two, you are jealous and cold-shoulder the good and the capable."

"What Dongye said is true after all," said the duke with a cynical smile. "Those Confucian scholars are no better than a bunch of glib-tongued idle talkers. They can persuade you that white is black and would have us believe that the dead are alive. I admit that you have learned something of the rites from Mencius, but at the same time you have acquired his art of sophistry too. You do disappoint me!"

Gu Tu rejoined, "If Father should choose to belittle Mencius I cannot help it. There's little I can do now but follow him wherever he goes."

"None of your impudence!" shouted the duke. "I forbid you to have anything more to do with Mencius from now on."

Gu Tu impulsively rose from his knees and turned to go.

"Where are you going?" inquired the duke.

"To school," said his son.

"This is high treason! Come, men!"

Two palace guards rushed up and carried Gu Tu off to the dungeons.

The duchess was left begging on her knees in tears that Gu Tu might be pardoned if only because he was their only son.

The duke sighed helplessly as he hastened to help his wife up, saying as he did so: "You are being stupid, my dear! Didn't you hear Gu Tu say just now that Mencius was leaving Zou in three days with his followers? This is just a little ruse of mine to stop him deserting us. Set your mind at rest; I'll see to it that he is all right."

The truth dawned on her at once and she melted into smiles.

Mencius, meanwhile, knew why Gu Tu had rushed back and guessed that his attempt to influence his father would come to nothing. Still, he hoped against hope that the duke might change his mind and keep him in Zou so that he could give full play to his talents in the service of his homeland. But three days elapsed and there was no sign of Gu Tu coming back.

And so, on the morning of the fourth day Mencius mounted his carriage after bidding his mother farewell. He was just starting off, when he saw another carriage racing toward him in a cloud of dust. He decided that it must be Gu Tu with a message from his father, so he jumped down from his own carriage in a hurry.

But the newcomer was not Gu Tu but his old friend Xiahou Yi. He had come to inform Mencius how Gu Tu had infuriated the duke by his championing Mencius' cause and thereby got himself thrown into prison.

On learning this, Mencius could do nothing but bemoan his fate and the ill star under which he had been born.

After an exchange of farewells the two friends parted.

As mentioned previously, it was Gongsun Chou who drove the carriage for Mencius, and he did so with meticulous care. They were closely followed by Gongdu Zi, Xu Bi, Wan Zhang and Teng Geng in another carriage, and aboard a third carriage were Yuezheng Ke, Peng Geng, Xianqiu Meng and Wulu Zi. There were yet 80 more carriages in the convoy, which was composed of 688 people in all, presenting an impressive sight as it rolled all the way to the State of Qi.

They started early and halted late, and by the evening of the sixth day they had come to the southern main gate of the capital of Qi. The garrison soldiers were startled at the sight of so large a troop of people. So much so that they dared not open the gate but raised the drawbridge, and the archers all had their bows drawn to the full ready to shoot, as if they had been confronted by a formidable enemy.

Gongsun Chou turned to Mencius and said, "It looks as if they don't know what we are here for."

As he looked back over his shoulder at the long procession of carriages, Mencius said smiling: "I cannot blame them for that, though. I suppose they take us to be invaders."

Gongsun Chou advanced as far as the moat, whence he called aloud to the soldiers, cupping this mouth with both hands as he did so: "Hear me, guards! The present-day sage Meng Fu-zi (Mencius) on a visit to the State of Qi."

A lieutenant emerged from the gate-house. He shaded his eyes with his hand and peered down for a good while before he asked,

"Which one of you is His Excellency Meng Fu-zi?"

Mencius stepped down from his carriage and went forward, presenting himself: "I am that humble person."

The man held up his clasped hands in greeting: "The people of Qi are greatly honored by Your Excellency's visit. Please wait while I go and open the gate for you." So saying, he sent a messenger to inform King Wei of Qi before he came down to have the drawbridge lowered and hastened forward to meet Mencius.

The lieutenant apologized for the delay and offered his services in finding a lodging house for his guests, for which Mencius expressed his thanks.

On Gongsun Chou's recommendation, they put up at the Metropolis Inn, one of the best hostels in the capital.

As Mencius and his retinue drew up before the inn a large crowd immediately gathered. Among the onlookers was one who seemed to be in his thirties, of medium height and particularly noteworthy for his looks and dress. He never ceased casting glances here and there, as if he had some purpose. It turned out that this man had been sent by King Wei for reconnaissance. He was Deputy Minister Zhuang Bao. What he saw disturbed him. He therefore hurried back to the court of Qi and informed his master.

When the duke heard that Mencius had come with such a great number of people and carriages, he gave an involuntary gasp of alarm.

"Is there any native of Qi in his following?" he asked Zhuang Bao.

"Yes, there is—a certain Gongsun Chou, who has been driving for Mencius on their way here," replied Zhuang Bao.

Now King Wei of Qi, who was in his fifties, had by this time been reigning over his state for 22 years. Decades of court life with its intrigues and struggles were beginning to tell on him: He looked worn-out and shriveled and what remained of his goatee beard was completely white. He remained thoughtful for a while, uncertain of the purpose for which Mencius had come to Qi. He stood up from his cushioned divan and paced to and fro, muttering to himself: "What's the purpose, anyway—of this sudden visit of his?"

Presently Zhuang Bao said, "Would Your Lordship summon Prime Minister Zou Ji, General Tian Ji and Military Counselor Sun Bin for a consultation?"

This suggestion was accepted, and the three courtiers soon presented themselves to the king.

"Mencius has come to Qi with such a pompous following. What do you think he intends to do, sirs?" King Wei asked.

Zou Ji was the first to speak: "So far as I know, Mencius is a man of remarkable intelligence and great learning; he has the gift of the gab and always outwits his rival in argument. He worships the Sage Rulers of old as well as Confucius, setting his mind on realizing his dream of a government run on the principles of benevolence and righteousness. He has come to Qi for two objectives, namely, to show off his 600-odd disciples so that the princes of the states may recognize their worth, and to talk them into employing both himself and his disciples."

Now that his doubt had been removed King Wei broke into a smile, saying, "So that's all. I was alarmed for nothing, then."

"Your Highness can set his mind at ease," said Tian Ji. "Mencius frequently cites the authority of Yao and Shun and models himself on Confucius. So he is unlikely to do anything underhanded."

King Wei then asked, "In that case, shall I grant him an audience?"

"You are obliged to, My Lord," urged Zou Ji without a moment of hesitation.

"What time do you think proper?"

"Tomorrow," was Zou Ji's prompt response.

"Why this hurry?" asked the king, a surprised look in his eyes.

"These Confucian scholars," said Zou Ji, "are highly principled, basing themselves on benevolence and righteousness. If you do not receive them promptly they will think you apathetic to benevolence and righteousness, which of course is not the case. So it would be better to receive them at your earliest convenience and treat them with due respect. This way, the world will say you are a good and wise king who is courteous to the virtuous and condescending to the scholarly. Besides, in an audience with them, you can sound them out as to the purpose of their visit to Qi. More, if you happen to find a talented person or two among them, you can enlist him in your government. With these advantages in view, the sooner you receive them the better, do you not think, My Lord?"

The other two voiced their support at the same time, whereupon the king detailed Zhuang Bao to invite Mencius to an audience the following day.

The next morning Mencius took Gongsun Chou, Wan Zhang,

Yuezheng Ke and Gongdu Zi along in response to the king's invitation. They rode with all speed to the palace, and when they reached there, welcoming music greeted their ears. Mencius had never felt so happy as he was now, expecting that his talent might be worthily evaluated by King Wei of Qi, and consequently that he and his disciples would have the possibility of fulfilling their ambition of public service. So thinking, he straightened his cap and gown as he led his disciples sedately into the reception hall of the palace.

The music came to an abrupt halt at their approach. Mencius bowed to the king, saying, "Greetings to Your Majesty from Meng Ke and his disciples Gongsun Chou, Wan Zhang, Yuezheng Ke and Gongdu Zi."

Beaming with pleasure, the king signaled for Mencius and company to be seated.

Mencius swept gaze across the ministers and officials present before taking his seat.

The king commented with admiration: "I often hear people say that Mencius is as fine as the jade ornament on a cap. Now I see with my own eyes that description is no exaggeration."

"You flatter me, My Lord," Mencius muttered, making a slight bow where he sat.

"People say that you have opened a school and enrolled a large number of students. I suppose your graduates are legion?" the king added.

"That is true. Thank you for the compliment," replied Mencius matter-of-factly.

The king asked, "Who was your own teacher, may I ask?"

Mencius replied, "His surname was Zeng. Xuan was his personal name."

The king further asked, "What subjects do you teach in your school?"

This being a favorite topic of his, Mencius fell on it with relish, saying with enthusiasm: "All the subjects Confucius used to teach and which he himself practiced by example. They are the rites, music, writing and arithmetic—which are taught in class—and archery and riding, which are taught in the open air."

The king gave a contemptuous smile as if he had caught Mencius off guard, as he said, "They say Your Honor advocates benevolent government, professes rule by the rites and opposes war. Is this really the case?"

"So it is," replied Mencius.

"In that case," pursued the king, "since Your Honor opposes war, and indeed you once professed that in the *Spring and Autumn Annals* there were no just wars. Well then, why do you need to teach your students archery and riding?"

Mencius replied, "There, you misunderstand me, My Lord. I do not oppose war in general. There is just war and there is unjust war. I only oppose unjust war. Far from opposing a war that is just, I uphold it."

"But why," asked the king, "do you maintain that there were no just wars in the Spring and Autumn period?"

Mencius explained, "There is a line from the *Book of Songs* which runs: 'There is no territory under Heaven which is not the king's.' If all territory under Heaven belongs to the Zhou Emperor, then the ceaseless wars between the states under the sovereignty of the empire can be only internal strife. How can internal strife be called just?"

Turning these remarks over in his mind, King Wei of Qi exulted, saying, "An inference can be drawn from your remark that the emperor is the supreme ruler of the empire and the reigning prince the supreme ruler of a state, is that not so?"

"No!" Mencius said firmly. "I would rather say that the people are of supreme importance and a ruler is only secondary."

The king was stunned, and a profound hush came over the assembled ministers and officials. They looked at one another blankly. Those who were sympathetic to Mencius were filled with anxiety for him.

Chapter Twenty-Six

Mencius Excoriates the Ills of the Times to King Wei's Face; He Eulogizes the Good and Wise of Antiquity

The awkward silence consequent on his remark about the secondary role of a ruler left Mencius undisturbed; however, he just sat there staring into space, a merry twinkle in his eyes.

It was all the king could do not to appear angry but to comb his scant goatee with his fingers as he was wont to do in moments of stress. He asked of Mencius in a sarcastic tone: "What justification have you to say so, my dear sir?"

"The people may be compared to river waters," Mencius responded readily, "and the ruler to a boat. The former can sink the latter as well as float it. Now, of the two, which do you think is the more important, Your Majesty?"

The king was rendered speechless.

Mencius wanted to test the king's capacity for tolerance, and so he pursued his argument relentlessly saying, "You have people before you have a state, and you have a state before you have its ruler. There is a common expression: 'The Empire, the state and the family'. The empire has its basis in the state, the state in the family and the family in one's own self. If you do without people, where do families come from? And by the same token, where do the states and their rulers come from?"

Seeing that his master had been put at a disadvantage by Mencius' rhetoric, Zou Ji, the prime minister, hastened to his rescue. He faced Mencius, saying, "How can the common people and a king, as the supreme ruler, be mentioned in the same breath? The supreme ruler upon whom the fate of a whole people depends!"

Mencius replied, "It is difficult to be a gentleman but not so difficult to be an official."

Looking perplexed, Zou Ji asked Mencius to explain this conundrum.

Mencius did so: "There are gentlemen and there are common fellows. The two categories of people are as far removed from one

another as white is from black. A gentleman is highly principled and never given to flattery. He befriends the virtuous and distances himself from flatterers, whereas the common fellow is merely a political acrobat whose mind is bent on evil and who stops at nothing to achieve his treacherous purposes. Everybody knows that it is better to be a gentleman than a common fellow. But knowing is one thing and doing is quite another. There are plenty of people, though, who choose to be common fellows rather than gentlemen. There are still others who support common fellows and not gentlemen. Therefore I say it is difficult to be a gentleman."

Zuo Ji's face turned red as he questioned loudly: "Then what cause have you to say that to be an official is not so difficult?"

Mencius replied, "It would cost one very little to be an official so long as one did not offend good and wise ministers and counselors, that's all."

Zou Ji asked, "Why is that?"

"Because what they respect and admire, the people of their state, the people of their empire will respect and admire as well," came the answer. "Hence the influence of virtue will spread far and wide like a spring breeze giving life to everything it caresses."

The remark seemed to touch a sympathetic chord in Tian Ji, for he hastened to ask, "But suppose I would wish to love somebody and be friends with him, and yet he wouldn't reciprocate, what then?"

Zou Ji raised his eyebrows and threw an angry glare at his colleague.

This did not escape Mencius' notice, and he decided that there must exist some feud between the two men. He therefore remarked, with an air of unconcern: "In that case, one must examine oneself to see if one cherishes love and friendship enough to move the other's heart. In whatever one does, one must first examine oneself if one fails to achieve the desired result, and not blame Heaven or man for one's failure. Hence, the *Book of Songs* says, 'There is neither good nor bad fortune which man does not bring upon himself.'"

Now Sun Bin, the military strategist who was interested in the history of the three dynasties of Xia, Shang and Zhou, raised a question as to the root cause of the rise and fall of these dynasties.

Mencius waxed eloquent as he continued, "In my view, the reason why Xia, Shang and Zhou succeeded in winning the empire is that they based themselves on benevolence, which accounts for their rise.

And they lost the empire solely because they stopped practicing benevolence. Practice benevolence, and you win; fail to do so, and you lose. This applies to individuals as well as the body politic. It is therefore a matter of vital importance, involving life or death, survival or doom. The pity is that nowadays there are still a lot of people who do not practice benevolence and justice. On the one hand they are afraid lest they lose their empire, state or fief, and on the other they are bent on doing things contrary to benevolence. These people may be compared to a sick man who hates to see a doctor or a light drinker who takes to copious amounts of intoxicating drink."

Nervous and uneasy, King Wei wriggled in his seat as he said in a cold tone: "I have been planning to make my state strong enough to repulse any invader and maintain internal order so that my subjects may enjoy a happy and peaceful life. Please inform me how I can achieve this?"

Mencius explained, "One cannot draw squares or circles without a carpenter's square or a pair of compasses. The carpenter's square and compasses are the measures for squares and circles, as the Sages are the examples by which a man is to be measured. As a ruling prince he should fulfill his obligations as such; as a minister he should fulfill his obligations as such too. In both cases, just follow the examples of Yao and Shun*. If, in serving one's ruler, one fails to behave as Shun did toward Yao, that spells malfeasance on one's part; if one fails to use Yao's method and attitude to rule, one is doing harm to one's subjects."

A ghost of a smile flitted across the king's face as he asked mildly: "Would you please explain in more detail, sir?"

"Confucius explained this explicitly enough," said Mencius. "There are two ways to rule: One is to practice benevolent government; the other is to exercise tyranny over the ruled. If benevolent government obtains, a state will prosper and its people will live happy lives. Consequently the people will give wholehearted support to the ruler. Conversely, if tyranny is practiced, the people will groan under the tyrannical rule. Consequently the state will be jeopardized. In which case, where will the ruler be then? Such a ruler will be posthumously dubbed 'You' or 'Li'.** The name will stick and even his descendants,

---

* Yao was the embodiment of kingly virtue, and Shun, besides being a sage king, was also the embodiment of filial virtue.

** King You, the tyrant under whose rule the Zhou Dynasty came to its end. King Li, another tyrant previous to the above-mentioned.

however remote, will be able to do nothing about it. The *Book of Songs* says, 'The lesson for the Yin Dynasty was not far to seek: It lay with the age of the Xia Dynasty.' The proverb 'Take warning from the upturned cart ahead' describes well what I have said."

King Wei asked, "How is one to tell a wise ruler from an obtuse one?"

Mencius said, "Under a wise ruler men of small virtue serve men of great virtue, and men of small ability serve men of great ability. But under an obtuse ruler the small serve the big, and the weak serve the strong. Both types of ruler are subject to the dictates of Heaven. Those who are obedient to Heaven are preserved; those who go against Heaven are annihilated. Duke Jing of Qi said, 'Since, on the one hand, we are not in a position to dictate, and on the other, we refuse to be dictated to, we are destined to be exterminated.' With tears he gave his daughter to the ruler of Wu as a bride. Now the small states emulate the big states, yet feel ashamed of being dictated to by them. This is like disciples feeling ashamed of obeying their masters. If one is ashamed, the best thing is to take King Wen as one's model. He who models himself on King Wen will prevail over the whole Empire—in five years if he starts with a big state, and in seven if he starts with a small state. The *Book of Songs* says, 'The descendants of Shang exceed a hundred thousand in number. But because God so decreed, they submit to Zhou.' Confucius also pointed this out for us when he said, 'Against benevolence there can be no superiority in numbers. If the ruler of a state is drawn to benevolence he will be matchless in the Empire.' Now to wish to be matchless in the Empire by any means but benevolence is like holding something hot and refusing to cool one's hand with water. The *Book of Songs* says, "Who can hold something hot and not cool his hand with water?'"

Somehow King Wei felt there must be some innuendo in Mencius' discourse, but however hard he tried he could not catch the real drift of it; he therefore asked no more questions but remained silent.

Realizing that King Wei was not the type of ruler he was seeking, Mencius abruptly stood up and took his leave without more ado. "I came to seek an audience with Your Majesty chiefly to present my views but not tribute. I beg your pardon if there was anything wrong in my remarks. Now I wish to take my leave."

Aroused from his unpleasant thoughts, the king, after a moment's hesitation, said somewhat hypocritically: "Your remarks have benefitted me a great deal. Indeed I find them most helpful."

Head high, Mencius stalked out, with his disciples following upon his heels. They arrived at the Metropolis Inn in low spirits.

Mencius hurried through his midday meal, then settled down to read in his room. But his mind was upset by his experience of the morning and he could not bring himself to concentrate on his reading. Presently Gongsun Chou, Wan Zhang, Yuezheng Ke and Gongdu Zi dropped in.

Wan Zhang asked, "You don't look your normal self, sir. There's nothing the matter, I hope?"

"No". Mencius responded. "I am perfectly all right."

Wan Zhang persisted, "But it looks as if you are in low spirits."

"There is something grieving me," Mencius admitted.

"What is it?" asked Wan Zhang.

"The times," said Mencius. "These dark times."

Wan Zhang was puzzled: "Your worthless disciple does not understand what you mean. Please enlighten him."

Mencius breathed a long sigh before he went on to explain:

"In the present-day world men of little or no virtue are lauded, while men of virtue are devalued. Just now I only said what I sincerely thought at the court, and you saw what happened! Those ministers and officials got as frightened as if I had been a monster. But if a minister dares not rebuke his superior to his face, he is as good as being disloyal to him. And a ruler of a state who does not heed advice that jars on the ear is letting himself grope in the dark."

Wan Zhang made as if he was going to speak, but then stopped.

Mencius perceived this and he looked displeased, saying, "Wan Zhang! Surely you don't think that I would dread hearing good advice like King Wei of Qi, do you? Why don't you speak up, eh?"

Shame-faced and ill at ease, Wan Zhang finally found his tongue, and said, "I was going to say that your remarks were out of place."

"You think that my mentioning the secondary role of a ruler was out of place, perhaps?" asked Mencius.

Wan Zhang nodded, still ill at ease.

A sudden change came over Mencius as he broke into a broad smile, saying, "Such is my character that I never prevaricate; I say what I mean. In Confucius' words, a noble man should be square and above board. A noble man has nothing to conceal from his fellow men. However, as I think back now, what I said at the court needs be reworded. The sentence should be like this: The people are of supreme importance; the altars to the gods of earth and grain* come next; last comes the ruler."

Yuezheng Ke beseeched, "Could I hear more about this, sir?"

Mencius explained with added verve: "That is why he who gains the confidence of the masses of the people will be emperor; he who gains the confidence of the emperor will be a feudal lord; he who gains the confidence of a feudal lord will be a counselor. When a feudal lord endangers the altars to the gods of earth and grain he should be replaced. When the sacrificial animals are sleek, the offerings are clean and the sacrifices are observed at due times, and yet floods and droughts come, the altars should be replaced."

Mencius' last words sounded like an open declaration of rebellion, which struck terror into the hearts of his listeners. Involuntarily they cast furtive glances outside.

Mencius laughed aloud, with all the frankness of a man with a clear conscience, as he assured them, "There is no cause for fear. I am no trouble-maker nor a demagogue. Whatever I say, no matter where —be it at the Qi court or here in your presence now—I do so straight from my heart. A ruler of a state, if he is good and wise at all, should consider carefully whether my remark is true or not. A counselor, if he is good and wise at all, should examine himself and ask whether he is a loyal courtier who dares to tell the truth that hurts or a mere sycophant whose only thought is that of self-preservation. Think of this: If a state has good and wise leader, assisted by good and wise ministers and counselors, a state where the virtuous and capable are employed in office and where freedom of speech is encouraged—could such a state not become strong and prosperous? If the reverse is true, the road to free speech is blocked and flatterers and mediocrities are placed in office—could such a state not fall into a decline?"

Wan Zhang remarked, "Good medicine cures disease, it is true, but it tastes bitter. Good advice may save a man from committing an error, but it jars on his ears. I am afraid that King Wei did not take your advice with good grace."

"I thought so too," said Mencius. "And that is what disappointed me so. I had expected King Wei to be a good and wise ruler, since he has the sagacity and courage to have such capable men as Zou Ji, Tian

---

* "The altars to the gods of earth and grain" is the symbol of independence of the state.

Ji and Sun Bin in his government. It is because he has this trio to help him in running the state that Qi has become as strong as it is now. By winning the campaign at Changling, Qi saved the State of Han, thereby acquiring the status of a big power. Much to my regret, however, King Wei is not the good and wise ruler I had imagined. It is truly said that knowing a person by repute is not as good as seeing him in the flesh. His is a case in point."

Gongdu Zi said, "Since he is not a good and wise ruler, as you say, why not leave Qi here and now?"

"He may not be a good and wise ruler," Mencius said. "But he is nevertheless an able politician, having made some accomplishments of his own. Were the Duke of Lu as well as the Duke of Zou nearly so able as he, the two states would not have come to such a miserable pass as they are in now. Since we are here already, why not make the most of it by staying a little longer, doing some research into the local conditions and customs?"

"That's a good idea!" cried Gongsun Chou, trying to distract his teacher from his gloomy thoughts. He proposed that they go and visit the Academy at Jixia, a center of scholarly activities founded by a former duke of Qi. Scholars from all over the empire were invited to give lectures there.

Mencius took to the proposal readily, and soon they started off, with Gongsun Chou acting as the driver and guide.

Jixia lay at the foot of Mount Ji on the western outskirts of Linzi, capital of Qi. The Academy was built in a style that quite impressed Mencius. In the courtyard were planted roses of many different varieties, and cypresses lined both sides of the path that led to the main building. As Mencius and his party walked past six rows of buildings they saw a man standing on an earthen platform addressing a group of people. The speaker was about 24 or 25 years old. He was of medium height, fair-complexioned and dressed in a style that was typical of a Confucian scholar. He spoke fluently, using the standard speech.

"....In this world of ours," he was saying, "it is imperative for us to base ourselves on the principles of benevolence and righteousness, and to take loyalty and filial piety as our first considerations." He went on to explain the meanings of the words benevolence, righteousness and gave illustrations to show their denotations and connotations.

His speech was from time to time interrupted by warm applause. Each time he would raise his folded hands and shake them up and down repeatedly to express his hearty thanks. Presently his glance came to rest on Mencius, and he gave a start in spite of himself. Instantly he came down from the platform and approached Mencius, making a deep bow: "Your Honor, please accept a greeting from a junior," he said.

Taken aback, Mencius wondered aloud: "We don't know each other, why this...?"

The man explained in all sincerity: "Your appearance tells me that you are anything but an ordinary listener."

Mencius chuckled, saying, "But why?"

The other explained, "You are distinguished-looking, like a sage. I presume you are most likely the very man in whom I can find my worthy teacher, sir."

Gongdu Zi put in hastily: "Absolutely true. He is the present-day Sage Men-...." The man did not wait for him to finish but hastened to step forward and make a deep bow once more to Mencius, introducing himself as "Gao Zi".

"Glad to make your acquaintance," Mencius said with a smile. "You were delivering a wonderful speech just now," he commented. "And in explaining 'benevolence' and 'righteousness', you indeed pinpointed the very essence of those two virtues. Please accept my congratulations."

The listeners crowded round to congratulate Gao Zi.

A voice called out from among the crowd, requesting Mencius to take the floor, and the request was immediately echoed by all present.

This warm response presented a sharp contrast to the cold reception he had experienced at the Qi court. Stirred to the depths of his being, Mencius said in a trembling voice: "The language of virtue does not move the heart nor stir the soul so penetratingly as the language of music. Your profound sentiments of friendship have overwhelmed me; I think I had better play some music to repay you."

Mencius took the ancient *qin* which Gao Zi fetched for him, made himself comfortable by sitting cross-legged on the ground, and after tuning the strings a little began to play the *Ode to King Wen* from the *Book of Songs*. The *Ode* sings the praises of King Wen's political and military achievements. Apart from playing, Mencius also gave a vocal rendition of the texts of the ensuing six odes, which won him prolonged applause from the audience. Smiling graciously, he waited until the applause died down before he said, "Good government goes deep into and wins the hearts of the people, but never does it do so as effectively as good education."

"Good government only wins wealth for the people, but good education wins their hearts," Mencius went on emphatically. "King Wen attached equal importance to running benevolent government and good education. That is why he came to be known as the Sage King throughout the ages. Similarly, the Duke of Zhou, because he assisted King Cheng in running a benevolent government, formulating rites and music, and introducing education, has also come down to us as a time-honored sage."

Gongdu Zi asked, "Which of them should be held up as the First Sage since man came into the world?"

"A good question, indeed!" said Mencius with zeal. "Since man came into the world, it is none other than the Duke of Zhou who should be respected as the First Sage."

Wan Zhang chimed in, "Would you kindly favor us with a recital of the exploits of the sages of old, esteemed sir?"

"A sage is one," continued Mencius, warming to his favorite topic, "whose example and precept inspire a hundred generations of people. Bo Yi would not look at what was wrong or improper, nor would he listen to what was wrong or improper. He would only serve the right prince and rule over the right people. He took office when order prevailed and relinquished it when there was disorder. He would not take his place at the court of evil men, nor would he associate with them; for him to have done so would have been like sitting in mud and pitch. He fled from the tyrannical rule of King Zhou of the Yin Dynasty and settled on the edge of the North Sea, waiting for the troubled waters of the empire to return to limpidity. Hence, hearing of the way of Bo Yi, a covetous man will be purged of his covetousness and a weak man will become resolute."

Wan Zhang asked, "What kind of sage was Bo Yi, when all is said and done?"

Mencius replied, "He was a sage who kept his reputation unsullied."

Wan Zhang again asked, "And what about Yi Yin?"

"He was a sage," replied Mencius, "with a keen sense of responsibility. He would serve any prince and rule over any people, would take office whether order prevailed or not. He said, 'Heaven, in producing the people, has given to those who first attain understanding the duty of awakening those who are slow to understand, and to those who are the first to awaken the duty of awakening those who are slow to awaken. I am among the first of Heaven's people to awaken. I shall awaken this people by means of the Way of Yao and Shun.' When he saw a common man or woman who did not enjoy the benefit of the rule of Yao and Shun he felt as if he had pushed him or her into the gutter. Such was the extent to which he considered the empire his responsibility."

Wan Zhang asked yet again: "What kind of sage was Liu Xiahui?"

Mencius replied, "Liu Xiahui was a sage who accommodated himself to circumstances. He was not ashamed of a prince with a tarnished reputation, neither did he disdain a modest post. When in office he did not conceal his talent, and always acted in accordance with the way. When he was passed over he harbored no grudge, nor was he distressed even in straitened circumstances. When he was with a fellow villager he simply could not tear himself away. 'You are you and I am I. Even if you were to be stark naked by my side, how could you defile me?' Hence hearing of the way of Liu Xiahui, a narrow-minded man will become tolerant and a mean man generous."

Wan Zhang asked further: "What kind of a sage was Confucius?"

Beaming, Mencius replied, growing animated both in voice and countenance: "He was of all the sages the one who best knew his times. When he left Qi, Confucius started only after emptying the rice from the steamer, but later when he left Lu he said, 'I proceed as slowly as possible. This is the way to leave the state of one's father and mother.' Such was the man who would hasten his departure or delay it, would remain in a state or would take office, all according to circumstances. Confucius was the one who gathered together all that was good. To do this is to open with bells and conclude with jade tubes.* To open with bells is to begin in an orderly fashion; to conclude with jade tubes is to end in an orderly fashion. To begin in an orderly fashion is the concern of a wise man, while to end in an orderly fashion is the concern of a sage.

---

* This refers to the proper order of musical performance.

Wisdom is like skill, shall I say, while sagacity is like strength. It is like shooting from beyond a hundred paces. It is due to your strength that the arrow reaches the target, but it is not due to your strength that it hits the mark."

"Well said! Well said!" someone praised loudly from the back of the crowd.

Chapter Twenty-Seven

At the Metropolis Inn Mencius Sets Forth
His Views on Current Events;
In the Wilds Gongdu Zi Encounters
His Long-Sought Enemy

Mencius turned to look, and he found the man was quite familiar but for the moment he could hardly place him somehow. On inquiry he learned that he was Chunyu Kun, a counselor of the Qi court, who had been present at Duke Wei's audience with Mencius that morning. A man of humble origin who had risen to high position by his wits, Chunyu Kun used to be a prominent member of the group of thinkers gathered at the Jixia Academy and later married into the family of Housheng Buhai, a celebrated Confucian scholar of Qi, who appreciated his talent. As a courtier he had achieved notable merits by his strategic thinking and diplomatic skill, and in fact had saved his country from many a dangerous situation. Hence he was one of Duke Wei's favorites.

Mencius had long heard about the man's fame, and so he hastened to meet with the necessary courtesies and invited him to the Metropolis Inn to have a talk.

As soon as he was settled in his seat, Chunyu Kun broached the subject which he had come to discuss: "Have you come to Qi with the purpose of trying to talk the king into accepting your political theories of benevolent government and the rites? Or do you propose to take office in Qi?"

Mencius replied, "Neither. It is my humble wish to follow Confucius' example in touring the various states. He was a sage who understood his times best."

Chunyu Kun rejoined, "As I see it, you are also a sage who is wise enough to size up the present situation by abandoning Zou and Lu in favor of Qi."

"You have misunderstood me, I'm afraid," said Mencius.

Chunyu Kun said with assurance: "I think I am justified in saying so. You pronounced at the court this morning that if the king would

take King Wen as his example, he would prevail over the empire, in five years if he started with a big state, and in seven if he started with a small state. From this I presume that you must have failed in your efforts to sway the dukes of Zou and Lu in favor of your argument. Secondly, in the empire today King Xian of Zhou acts merely as a figurehead. The seven major states—Qin, Wei, Han, Zhao, Chu, Yan and Qi—are now fighting for hegemony. Qi, as the dominant state in the east of the empire, boasts rich natural resources and vast territory. If you wish to put down the internal strife amongst the feudal lords, restore order to the empire and rescue the people from their misery, who else can you rely on if not the ruler of Qi? Lastly, surely you are well aware of the fact that King Wei is a good and wise ruler who casts his net wide for the virtuous and talented?"

Mencius appraised his interlocutor with fresh eyes but kept silent.

Chunyu Kun continued, "You quoted from the classics in your speech at the court and expounded on benevolence and righteousness. You did so because you had lost faith in King Wei, thinking that he was no longer the ruler you took him for."

Mencius began to realize that Chunyu Kun was indeed perspicacious. "No wonder he enjoys the trust of his ruler," he thought.

"Since your mind is set on great accomplishments," added Chunyu Kun, "and making a name for yourself, you must do something to win the king's favor so that he may feel obliged to enlist your services, don't you think?"

This suggestion made Mencius anything but pleased. On the contrary, he took it as if it were a personal affront, as he promptly retorted resentfully: "Sorry to say, but Meng Ke has never bowed his head to anyone in his life, least of all stooped to ask a favor of King Wei."

Chunyu Kun tried to explain things away by saying with an ingenuous smile: "You take me wrong, sir. What I mean is that in order to gain one's end, however noble, sometimes one has to make some concessions or compromises. I did not mean that you should play up to people of power and influence."

Overcome by some sense of regret over his *faux pas*, Mencius recovered his composure and fell to thinking.

After a moment of awkward silence, Chunyu suddenly asked, "How would you appraise the five Leaders of the feudal lords, sir?"

Mencius asked in reply: "Does Your Excellency mean Duke Huan of Qi, Duke Wen of Jin, Duke Mu of Qin, Duke Xiang of Song and Duke Zhuang of Chu?"

"Precisely," admitted Chunyu Kun. Mencius then expounded: "The five leaders of the Spring and Autumn period all had some merits each in their own right there is no gainsaying that. But there is no denying the fact that the five leaders were offenders against the three kings. By the same token, the feudal lords of today are offenders against the five leaders of the feudal lords, and the counselors of today are offenders against the feudal lords of today."

Chunyu Kun protested, "Excuse my dull wits, but I don't quite understand the whys and wherefores of all this. Do enlighten me, please."

Mencius grew eloquent as he went on, "When the emperor goes to the feudal lords, this is known as a 'tour of inspection'. When the feudal lords go to pay homage to the emperor, this is known as a 'report on duties'. The emperor makes his tour twice a year. In spring the purpose is to inspect the plowing, so that those who have not enough for sowing may be given help; in autumn the purpose is to inspect the harvesting, so that those who are in need may be given aid. When the emperor enters the domain of a feudal lord, if the land is opened up and the fields are well cultivated, the old are cared for and the good and wise honored, and men of distinction are in positions of authority, then that feudal lord is rewarded—the reward taking the form of land. On the other hand, on entering the domain of a feudal lord, if the emperor finds the land neglected, the old forgotten and the good and wise overlooked, and grasping men in positions of power, then he delivers a reprimand. If a feudal lord fails to attend court, he suffers a loss in rank for a first offence, and is deprived of part of his territory for a second offence. For a third offence the emperor's troops will move into his state. Hence the emperor punishes but does not attack, while a feudal lord attacks but does not punish. The five leaders of the feudal lords intimidated feudal lords into joining them in their attacks on other feudal lords. That is why I said, 'The five leaders of the feudal lords were offenders against the three kings.' Of the five leaders, Duke Huan of Qi was the most influential. At the meeting at Kuiqiu the feudal lords bound the animals, placed the text of the pledge on record, but did not sip the blood of the animals. The first item of the pledge was, 'Sons who are not dutiful are to be punished; heirs should not be put aside; concubines should not be elevated to the status of wives.'

The second was, 'Honor good and wise men and train the talented so as to make known the virtuous.' The third was, 'Respect the aged and be kind to the young; do not forget the guest and the traveler.' The fourth was, 'Gentlemen should not hold office by heredity; different offices should not be held concurrently by the same man; the selection of gentlemen should be appropriate; a feudal lord should not exercise sole authority in the execution of a counselor.' The fifth was, 'Dykes should not be diverted; the sale of rice to other states should not be prohibited; any gift of a fief should be reported.' The last was, 'All those who have taken part in this pledge should, after the event, come to a proper understanding on the former basis.' The feudal lords of today all violate these five injunctions. That is why I said that the feudal lords of today are offenders against the five leaders. The crime of encouraging a ruler in his evil deeds is small compared to that of pandering to his unspoken evil desires. The counselors of today all want to do wrong in order to please their princes. That is why I said that the counselors of today are offenders against the feudal lords of today."

Chunyu Kun showed his complete acquiescence and appreciation by nodding his head.

Their talk continued over the dinner table.

Presently Chunyu Kun asked Mencius about his erstwhile teacher Zeng Xuan.

Mencius said, "Though obscure, Mr Zeng had a solid foundation in learning. He was a man of excellent caliber, and I have always had a profound respect for him."

Chunyu Kun commented, "In life a man may count himself lucky in the true sense of the word if he has good parents, a good initiatory teacher and good friends at the same time."

"I am one of those lucky men then!" cried Mencius. "I remember in childhood how I used to play truant often, and Mother had to move house three times in order to choose a suitable neighborhood. Once she even cut the web of her loom to teach me a lesson. I remember too that on his death-bed, Mr. Zeng pointed out my fatal weakness. But I did not catch clearly what he said before he died. How I wish I had! As for good friends, I may claim Minister Xiahou Yi of Zou for one. And now here I have the good luck to find a true friend in you. So you see, I have the complete three types of luck. How fortunate I am!"

Both laughed aloud in a congenial atmosphere of friendship.

After dinner, Chunyu Kun followed Mencius into the latter's room, where their conversation continued.

"As I judge it," he began, "the man who is to carry on the Way of Confucius and develop it can be none other but yourself, sir."

"I have done no more than take over his doctrine, I have far from developed it."

"Your doctrine can be traced to Confucius," returned Chunyu Kun. "But strange to say, your temperament is so different from the Master's."

Mencius remained silent.

Thinking that his remark must have hurt the other, Chunyu Kun hastened to apologize: "Forgive me if I said anything improper. It was innocently meant, sir."

"Not at all," said Mencius with a placating smile. "You judged me all too correctly. I see that you have an insight into character. I have long known about this trait of mine, which up until now even I have not been able to name. Perhaps that is just what my old teacher Mr Zeng Xuan wanted to say but failed to do so clearly in his last gasps."

At this moment, Shen Qiang came in to announce that a certain Mr Haosheng wanted to see Mencius.

Under the lamplight, Mencius found the visitor to be a white-haired and fair-complexioned old man. Chunyu Kun introduced Mencius to his father-in-law, saying, "This is the present-day sage Mencius."

"Much honored to meet you," said the old man with great delight, and he went on to invite Mencius to his home some day in the future. Shortly after that he left with Chunyu Kun.

After seeing his guests off, Mencius retired to his room. The events of the day had stirred him and for a long time sleep would not come. He stood before the window, meditating, until he heard the bell-tower strike five watches, when he went to bed.

The next day Wan Zhang, finding his teacher in low spirits, suggested that they go for an outing to the outskirts of the city, to which Mencius agreed with alacrity.

After breakfast they started off, Gongsun Chou acting as the driver as before and Gongsun Benzheng and Mencius seated shoulder to shoulder in his carriage. All the rest of the students followed in their carriages. The splendid procession made the passers-by pause and sigh with admiration.

They came to a wooded area where red leaves met the eye at every turn. A northerly wind arose, now whirling the fallen leaves into the air and now chasing them along the ground. Mencius was just about to call a halt, when a hare leaped out from the roadside ditch.

Gongdu Zi and Xu Bi instantly jumped down from their carriage and gave chase. The hare streaked away and soon disappeared, but the two wouldn't give up and pursued it up hill and down dale until they found themselves on a mountain ridge where they could see their quarry scampering beyond their reach. Suddenly a woman's cry broke the stillness. They stopped in their tracks and listened. "Let's go and find out what's happening," said Gongdu. They clambered over the ridge into the valley beyond. There they saw a man lying in a pool of blood and hard by another man sprawling over a woman. The sordid sight outraged Gongdu so much that he roared like an injured lion and rushed on the man, followed closely by Xu Bi. At the sound, the man jumped up from his victim and started to run.

Gongdu recognized him as Jue Hu, Fu Puren's steward, who had escaped during the fire we described previously.

When two foes meet their eyes flash with anger, as the saying goes. "Get the devil!" yelled Gongdu. "No escape for him this time." They started the pursuit with a vengeance, as Jue Hu, like a hunted animal, tried to hide himself in every nook and cranny that came to hand. It took them a good two hours before they finally spotted him hidden in a crevice. But a cornered beast will fight back, and Jue Hu was certainly not one to surrender himself easily since he was inordinately vain about his martial skill. Thus he extricated himself from his predicament by one single spring with his powerful legs while warding off with the sword in his hand the thrusts of his attackers. Then he ran for his life. And so the chase began afresh, until at last they came to a densely wooded spot. Jue Hu took advantage of the tree trunks and branches to shield himself from direct thrusts from his attackers and between whiles he counter-thrust. This continued for some time, until suddenly Xu Bi, who was too eager for victory, made a home-thrust at Jue Hu's breast. But the latter was quick enough to dodge, and Xu Bi's sword ended up buried deeply in a tree trunk. Taking advantage of Xu Bi's struggle to pull his sword out, Jue Hu aimed a savage cut at Xu Bi's right arm.

Chapter Twenty-Eight

Gongsun Conducts an Exercise in Battle Formation; Haoshen Throws a Dinner Party in Honor of Mencius

Our last chapter related how Jue Hu struck with his sword at Xu Bi's right arm when the latter tried to pull out his own sword from the tree trunk. But just at this critical juncture there flashed a cold light, followed by a piercing cry of pain from Jue Hu, and his severed arm, together with the sword, fell at Xu Bi's feet.

Jue Hu knew that his fate was sealed, and so he threw himself upon the two swords that Gongdu and Xu Bi pointed menacingly at him. The two blades penetrated his breast at the same time and it was all over with him.

"Serve him right, the wretch!" said Gongdu, as he pulled out his sword.

"How shall we dispose of his corpse?" asked Xu Bi.

"Let it be. Let's hurry and see about his two victims!" With that, they sped down the slope to the gully, where the hapless woman was found weeping over the body of her father, who had been murdered by Jue Hu.

Gongdu Zi asked, "How did it happen that Jue Hu was involved here?"

The girl told her story between sobs, as follows: "Five years ago, the scoundrel suddenly made his appearance in the locality, from God knows where, and because he had acquired martial skills and what not he came the tyrant over the local people, and did all sorts of evil things. Many a woman of good family background fell a victim to his bestial lust. Since he saw me this autumn, he had his wicked design on me. He offered to take me for his concubine but was flatly turned down by my father. Today my father brought me for hunting (he was a hunter by profession), and Jue Hu saw his chance for...."

"Well, we have put an end to this dastard," Gongdu Zi assured her.

The girl thanked them profusely, saying that they had removed a scourge.

Gongdu and Xu Bi helped the woman with the burial of her

father, the details of which we omit.

In the meantime, while waiting for Gongdu and Xu Bi, Mencius proposed that Gongsun make use of the recess to conduct an exercise in battle formation with all his students taking part.

Though over 70 years old, Gongsun Benzheng was still hale and hearty. He responded to Mencius' proposal with avidity and immediately commanded Peng Geng, Hanqiu Meng, Shen Qiang and Teng Geng to perform the "snake alignment", for, according to him, this was a comparatively simple maneuver. Then the four leaders each commanded a detachment of soldiers marching in four directions to about 100 paces away, where they halted to begin "operations".

Mencius was asked to mount his carriage to review them, which he did, and when asked for his comments he responded with a delighted "Well done!"

After this they proceeded to perform the "eight-diagram formation". Just then Gongsun Chou called their attention and pointed toward the southern hills. From the forest at the foot of the hills came three people. "Looks like Gongdu and Xu Bi. But who is the person with them?" they all wondered.

Immediately Gongsun Chou drove his carriage to meet them and soon came back with Gongdu, Xu Bi and the woman. On hearing the latter's sad story, Mencius presented her with one *yi* of gold and had his disciples escort her home.

The episode quite dampened everyone's enthusiasm, so Mencius gave orders for going back.

When they returned to the inn they saw Chunyu Kun waiting in the courtyard.

He had come to invite Mencius and his disciples to a banquet hosted by Haosheng Buhai. "My father-in-law wants to honor you with a banquet because he holds you in high esteem. Please favor us with your presence," he requested politely.

Mencius accepted the invitation with alacrity, and in due course started off for the banquet, taking along Wan Zhang, Yuezheng Ke, Gongsun Chou, Gao Zi and Teng Geng.

Haosheng, all smiles, met them at the gate, and taking Mencius by the hand led them through a zigzag colonnade into a well-appointed parlor where a sumptuous feast was all prepared for them.

After three toasts, during which rare delicacies such as bird's-nest and sharks'-fin soup, and bear paws were offered one course after another, the host suggested, "Let us have some music and dancing to celebrate the occasion."

At his signal, eight musicians and four dancing girls stepped forth. The dancers sang as they glided and waltzed to the accompaniment of light music:

"How gaily call the deer
While grazing in the shade.
I have welcome guests here,
Let lute and pipe be played;
Let offerings appear
And lute and strings vibrate.
If you love me, friends dear,
Help me to rule the state."

As Mencius watched the dancing and listened to the music he found, much to his delight, a picture on the wall, an illustration of the theme of *The Deer Call* from *The Book of Songs*, come to life before his very eyes!

Again the lines came to his ears:

"How gaily call the deer
While nibbling southern fare.
I have welcome guests here
With advice beyond compare.
My people are benign;
My lords will learn from you.
I have delicious wine;
You may enjoy my brew."

Presently Haosheng Buhai raised his bronze goblet with both hands and addressed Mencius: "Dear sir, do you hear that? 'I have delicious wine; you may enjoy my brew.' Come on, let's drink to our hearts' content!"

Mencius graciously did as requested and offered a toast to the host yet again.

The dancers went on with the following lines:

"How gaily call the deer
Eating grass in the shade.
I have welcome guests here,
Let lute and flute be played.
Play chimes and zither fine;
We may enjoy the best.

I have delicious wine
To delight the heart of my guest."

By now Haosheng Buhai was already in a state of cheerful inebriation as he downed another gobletful of wine, saying, "The author of the poem had a full understanding of a drinker's heart for sure! And the composer of the song, too, was no less a poet himself! Confucius once said that the *Shao Music* had attained the perfection of beauty; I think the *Deer Call* is equally perfect and beautiful!"

Mencius nodded his full agreement. The music affected him like a balm, and he had not enjoyed such peace of mind for a long time. Will the same concord and harmony as expressed in the music descend on the empire under the reign of the Zhou Emperor one day? He asked himself wistfully.

Haosheng Buhai continued to ply Mencius with wine and importuned him to name a song for the entertainers to perform.

"Since you insist," Mencius said after a moment's reflection, "let it be *Ode to King Cheng*. How about that?"

"Bravo!" Haosheng smiled agreeably. "A better choice could not be made by a man who upholds the rites and morals of the Zhou Dynasty such as you are, sir. Now let's hear how King Cheng's virtuous conduct and exploits were praised in a song."

Accordingly, to the soft notes of the music, the dancers sang as they danced:

"By great Heaven's decrees
Two kings with power were blessed.
King Cheng dare not live at ease
But day and night does his best
To rule the State in peace
And pacify east and west."

The instant the strains of the song had died away, Haosheng Buhai said to Mencius: "I can feel how your heart was beating to the rhythm of the song, my dear sir."

Mencius returned him an understanding smile. He raised his cup to the host, toasted him and emptied the bumper at a drought.

Presently Haosheng Buhai changed the subject by asking Mencius: "What sort of a man is Yuezheng Ke?"

Mencius was surprised at this question from his host. He took full stock of the patriarch, as he ruminated for a while. Then he replied, "A good man. A true man."

Haosheng Buhai thereupon asked, "What do you mean by 'good' and 'true'?"

Mencius explained, "The desirable is called 'good'. To have it in oneself is called 'true'. To possess it fully in oneself is called 'beautiful', but to shine forth with this full possession is called 'great'. To be great and transformed by this greatness is called 'divine'. Yuezheng Ke has something of the first two qualities but has not quite attained the last four."

Haosheng Buhai, having cast his eyes at Mencius and his four disciples in turn, said, "Each of these disciples of yours impresses me as stately and prepossessing. I can guarantee that they will achieve something great in future. Whichever head of state employs them in important positions will certainly bring order and peace to the empire."

Mencius made a slight bow before he replied modestly: "You flatter them too much, I am afraid."

"Confucius set up a school on his own," Haosheng Buhai went on. "Of his 3,000 disciples, 72 graduated as experts in the six arts. By doing this, he set a shining example for later generations. Now, you have been doing exactly what the Old Sage did in his day. So I presume the coming generations will hold you up as a counterpart of Confucius."

Mencius was made ill at ease by all this, and he hastened to disown any pretensions: "What are you saying, sir? No. Ever since man came into this world there has only been one Confucius. His achievements are as glorious as the sun and the moon, and will endure as long as Heaven and Earth endure, whereas I, Meng Ke, am but a student of the Sage. Who am I to be mentioned in the same breath with Confucius!"

"Well, let posterity decide on its own unbiased verdict," Haosheng said with an apologetic smile, and after a pause asked further: "What should an upright and benevolent man hold dear to his heart?"

His normal self again, Mencius said with enthusiasm: "An upright and benevolent man should set store by benevolence and righteousness. Benevolence is the heart of man, and righteousness his road. If a man be without the virtues proper to humanity, what has he to do with the rites of propriety? If a man be without the virtues proper to humanity, what has he to do with music? said Confucius. He also said, 'The determined scholar and the man of virtue will not seek to live at the expense of injuring their virtue. They will even sacrifice their lives to preserve their virtue complete."

Haosheng Buhai nodded and commented, "Well said" before further asking, "What should a feudal prince regard as his precious possessions?"

Mencius intoned, "The precious things of a prince are three: the territory, the people and the government. Those who treasure only pearls and jade are bound to suffer as a consequence."

Chunyu Kun interposed, "Sir, you always have 'benevolence' and 'righteousness' on your lips and make it your business to practice them yourself. I confess I know them but little. So would you kindly explain them in detail for my benefit?"

Mencius said with a grin: "If I remember correctly, when you had just arrived at the Jixia Academy in Linzi from your birthplace in the east how you gave lectures that held your audience spellbound. And that is how your King came to recognize your talent and hence use you in important positions. Such being the case, how is it possible that you do not know about benevolence and righteousness? Is it that you want to test me, or what?"

"Oh, no, no!" Chunyu Kun hurriedly denied the suggestions. "When I said I did not know, I really and truly meant it. That is why I asked, and I am asking now."

Mencius said, "'Benevolence' means 'man'.* When these two are conjoined, the result is the Way. The *Book of Rites* says, "'Righteousness' means 'right'." To practice what is right is righteousness. If an individual does not act in accordance with the Way but does things contrary to benevolence and righteousness, then the Way will not go with his wife, much less with other people. If, in commanding others, one deviates from the Way and runs counter to benevolence and righteousness, then it is even impossible to command one's wife; how would it then be possible to command others?"

Just then Peng Geng appeared at the door with the announcement that Mencius was wanted at the inn. Mencius forthwith stood up and took his leave.

---

* The Chinese characters for "benevolence" and "man" are identical in pronunciation, and they are in fact cognate.

Chapter Twenty-Nine

Kuang Zhang Asks About Self-Denying Purity by Quoting a Local Example; Mencius Stresses Filial Piety as a Must for Self-Cultivation

When informed that somebody wanted to see him at the inn, Mencius took leave of Haosheng Buhai and Chunyu Kun, and returned to his temporary lodging. On entering the courtyard he was met by Zhongren accompanied by a simply dressed man with a square face upon which bristled a prickly moustache. He looked to be in his late fifties.

The stranger introduced himself as Kuang Zhang. Mencius politely bowed him into the reception hall, and as soon as he was seated had a servant bring him tea and refreshments.

Kuang Zhang spoke without preamble: "From what I hear, sir, you have followed in the steps of Confucius by taking up teaching as a profession. Your disciples are found in countless numbers throughout the Empire, they said."

Mencius chuckled and said, "You sir. Is there a teacher in the world who can lose count of his students?"

Kuang Zhang ignored the retort and continued, "My dear sir, the world knows that you impart the six arts to your students and deliver lectures on benevolence and righteousness. But why do you not stay in your native place instead of coming to Qi to seek an audience with King Wei, trying to influence His Majesty with your theories? Could you give me the reason?"

Mencius maintained a dignified silence.

"Is it because you think that Zou and Lu are not as powerful as Qi, or what?" Kuang Zhang added.

Mencius gave a sigh before saying, "You do not understand, sir. Man goes upwards and water flows downwards, as the proverb goes. What man is there who does not aspire to something higher, I should like to know?"

Kuang Zhang said, "Judging by your talents and moral worth, you

are more than qualified for premiership. So how is that you have never occupied any government post, big or small?"

Mencius replied, "A good and wise man helps others to understand clearly by his own clear understanding. The Sage is a teacher to a hundred generations. Bo Yi and Liu Xiahui are such people. Hence, hearing of the way of Bo Yi, a covetous man will be purged of his covetousness and a weak man will become resolute. And hearing of the way of Liu Xiahui, a narrow-minded man will become tolerant and a mean man generous. Nowadays, people are otherwise; they try to help others understand by their own benighted ignorance. How can they succeed?"

Kuang Zhang asked once more: "Of the three princes of Qi, Lu and Zou, which one do you think is best and wisest?"

For an answer, Mencius offered a contemptuous smile.

Kuang Zhang went on, "In my humble opinion, there are many unwise and immoral persons in authority today. Why is that?"

Mencius replied, "From antiquity until the present there have been cases of rulers who do not take the way of benevolence but who retain their rule notwithstanding. But there has never been a case of a ruler who does not take the way of benevolence and yet wins an empire."

"I know very well," said Kuang Zhang, "that Your Honor advocates benevolence and righteousness as the fundamentals. But, I presume to ask, in what sense do you consider them fundamental?"

Mencius then launched on a lengthy explanation: "'Benevolence' means 'man'. Therefore, a man should be benevolence personified. Though I myself have not yet attained such an ideal state, I am trying hard to do so. 'Righteousness' means 'right'. In doing anything one should do just what is right, no more and no less. Though I myself have not yet managed this, I am trying hard to do so. Fish is what I want; bear's paw is also what I want. If I cannot have both, I would rather take bear's paw than fish. Life is what I want; dutifulness is also what I want. If I cannot have both, I would rather take dutifulness than life. On the one hand, though life is what I want, there is something I want more than life. That is why I do not cling to life at all costs. On the other hand, though death is what I loathe, there is something I loathe more than death. That is why there are troubles I do not avoid. If there is nothing a man wants more than life, then why should he have scruples about any means so long as it will serve to keep him alive? If there is nothing a man loathes more than death, then why should he have scruples about any means so long as it helps him to avoid trouble? Yet there are ways of remaining alive and ways of avoiding death to which a man will not resort. In other words, there are things a man wants more than life and there are also things he loathes more than death. This is an attitude not confined to the moral man but common to all men; the moral man simply never loses it. Here is a basketful of rice and a bowlful of soup. Getting them will mean life; not getting them will mean death. When these are given with abuse, even a wayfarer will not accept them. And when they are given after being trampled upon, even a beggar will not accept them."

"Now I understand," said Kuang Zhang with a broad grin. "Your Honor takes an aversion to those mean fellows who bow and scrape before the powerful!"

"I abhor evils as deadly foes, that's all," replied Mencius.

Kuang Zhang said, "I thought as much. That explains why you have been wary of taking office. You hate those mean officials too much for that."

"'Those whose courses are different cannot lay plans for one another,' as Confucius put it," was Mencius' reply.

"In what way does a gentleman differ from other men?" asked Kuang Zhang.

"A gentleman differs from other men in that he retains his heart," remarked Mencius.

"Would you please expound further for me," the other begged.

"A gentleman retains his heart by means of benevolence and the rites. The benevolent man loves others, and the courteous man respects others. He who loves others is always loved by them; he who respects others is always respected by them. The Book of Rites says, 'Courtesy demands reciprocity.' Suppose a man treats you in an outrageous manner. Faced with this, a gentleman will say to himself: 'I must be lacking in benevolence and courtesy, or how could such a thing happen to me?' When, on looking into himself, he finds that he has been benevolent and courteous, and yet this outrageous treatment continues, then the gentleman will say to himself: 'I must have failed to do my best for him.' When, on looking into himself, he finds that he has done his best and yet this outrageous treatment continues, then the gentleman will say, 'This man does not know what he is doing. Such a person is no different from an animal. One cannot expect an animal to know any better.' Hence, while a gentleman has perennial worries, he has no unexpected vexations."

Kuang Zhang asked, "What worries has a gentleman?"

Mencius said, "His worries are of this kind: Shun was a man; I am also a man. Shun set an example for the empire worthy of being handed down to posterity, yet here am I, just an ordinary man. That is something to worry about."

Kuang Zhang asked: "But if one worries about it, what should one do?"

Mencius answered, "One should strive to become like Shun. That is all."

Kuang Zhang then asked, "Does a gentleman have any other worry?"

"He has no worry other than that," Mencius assured him.

"What does it take to make a gentleman?" Kuang Zhang persisted.

Mencius was, of course, equal to this challenge too: "He never does anything that is not benevolent; he does not act except in accordance with the rites. That is a gentleman for you."

"When something unexpected happens to him, how should he behave?"

"Look not at what is contrary to propriety; listen not to what is contrary to propriety; speak not what is contrary to propriety; make no movement which is contrary to propriety—This way, even when unexpected disaster comes his way, a gentleman remains unperturbed."

It was getting dusk by now. Kuang Zhang got up to say, "It is getting late. Thank you for your instructions, which I have found very edifying." He made an appointment with Mencius to go sightseeing on Ox Mountain the next day, and the guest took his leave.

On their way out they came across Gongdu Zi, Xu Bi and Yuezheng Ke. Mencius introduced Kuang Zhang to them. Gongdu Zi at once pulled a long face and cast a hostile glance at the latter, who did not notice in the falling twilight. However this did not escape Mencius' sharp eyes.

After breakfast the next morning Mencius summoned Gongdu Zi, Wan Zhang and Gongsun Chou to his presence and told them of his appointment with Kuang Zhang. "I want you three to join us," he said.

Gongdu looked unhappy, as he stood on one side, head bowed, without uttering a word.

Mencius took this all in but did not show it. Instead, he asked with an unconcerned air: "Who is going to drive the carriage?"

Gongsun Chou and Wan Zhang both responded quickly before Gongdu Zi mumbled his half-hearted offer: "Sir, let it be me."

"Good", said Mencius. "Get it ready, then."

By the time they got their carriage and horses ready Kuang Zhang had driven up in his own carriage. After an exchange of greetings, Mencius and Kuang Zhang shared one carriage, with Gongdu Zi acting as the driver. Gongsun Chou and Wan Zhang rode in the other, leading the way.

The capital of Qi presented a brisk scene even at this early hour of the morning. The main street was bustling with traffic and pedestrians. As Mencius watched all this from his carriage a host of thoughts and feelings came crowding into his mind. My native state of Zou, as compared with Qi, pales into insignificance, he thought with a sigh. Nor was Lu superior by comparison, either. Lu was once strong, too, he thought, as it resisted the might of Qi in the east and challenged the aggressive Wu and Chu in the south. He deplored the fact that Duke Ding of Lu had been so foolish as to accept 80 beauties and 120 thoroughbred horses as gifts from Duke Jing of Qi, to the neglect of his affairs of state. Consequently Confucius had to leave his own state of Lu, where, thanks to his able administration, no one picked up anything lost on the road and doors did not need to be shut at night. If Confucius had stayed on in Lu and if Duke Ding had continued to use him, would Lu have come to such a pitiable pass as it was in now? Mencius wondered bitterly.

He was so wrapped up in his own thoughts that he sat there completely oblivious of the presence of his companion, who in the meanwhile was giving a lively description of the local historical sights and scenic spots.

Mencius' reticence intrigued Gongdu Zi and he turned back to look, only to find his teacher in a brown study, leaving Kuang Zhang in the cold. He chuckled to himself: "Serve you right! (meaning Kuang Zhang) Unfilial son that you are, how dare you try rubbing shoulders with the present-day sage!"

Now the mother of Kuang Zhang, because she had failed in her duty toward her parents-in-law, had offended his father, who had killed her and had her buried beneath the stables. When his father died, someone advised Kuang Zhang to have his mother re-buried in their ancestral graveyard together with his father, but he would not agree. Hence the local people condemned him as an unfilial son. Later, when, as marshal of King Wei of Qi, he had repelled invading forces from Qin, people advised him again to rebury his mother, and again he had refused. The people of Qi despised him all the more for that. And that accounted for Gongdu's hostility to him also.

Soon their carriages left the city behind and entered the open countryside. Overhead was a crystal-clear blue sky that stretched as far as the eye could see, and the charming autumn scenery gave Gongdu thrills of delight. He breathed in hard and long, then let out a shrill whistle for sheer joy. Whack! He lashed out his whip as if he wanted to punish the undutiful son who was now seated in his carriage.

Over the wide expanse of the plain patches of lush-green wheat met the eye one after another. Dewdrops on the leaves glistened in the morning light. A whiff of the northerly wind, and they were gone, much to the disappointment of Mencius. "Beautiful things," he mused sadly, "are after all short-lived. What more can one expect of a dewdrop?"

Meanwhile Kuang Zhang, wondering why his companion remained silent for so long, tried to make himself pleasant by putting a question to Mencius: "They say that a sage knows about everything under the sun, even though he keeps himself indoors. I presume, sir, that you know a good deal about the State of Qi?"

"I know very little," was the rejoinder.

"Then what do you think of men of scrupulous integrity?" Kuang Zhang changed tack. "Are there any of them in Qi in your view?"

Mencius replied, "The proverb says, 'As distance tests a horse's strength, so time reveals a person's heart.' As I have been here only a couple of days how am I to know who is a man of scrupulous integrity and who is not? Besides, I know few people here."

"But I suppose you know a man by the name of Chen Zhongzi?"

"Yes, I do."

Kuang Zhang continued, "When he was in Yuling he went without food for three days, till he could neither hear nor see. A plum which had been more than half-eaten by worms was lying beside a well. He crept up, took it in his hand and ate it. Only after this, did he regain his hearing and sight. Now there was an abundance of fruit growing all over the hills at Yuling, but he would sooner go hungry than pick one for himself. Is not Chen Zhongzi a man of scrupulous integrity in the true sense of the epithet?"

"Among the people of Qi," said Mencius emphatically, "I must give Zhongzi the credit of being a supreme gentleman. Even so, how can he pass for a man of scrupulous integrity?"

Kuang Zhang queried in bewilderment: "But why not?"

Mencius replied, "Because it is impossible! Unless one becomes an earthworm, for only so can it be done; an earthworm eats the dry earth above and drinks from the Yellow Springs below."

Kuang Zhang was even more bewildered.

Mencius went on, "An earthworm is a beneficial insect. It burrows in the soil and helps to loosen it by its burrowing, which is advantageous for farming. It has an integral character of its own indeed. How could Chen Zhongzi bear comparison to it?"

Kuang Zhang, not convinced in the least, retorted, "Chen Zhongzi is honest and upright. He never does wrong to anyone, nor does he damage anything. Why cannot one compare him even to an earthworm?"

Mencius asked, "Was the house where Zhongzi lived built by a Bo Yi? Or was it built by a robber like Zhi*? Was the millet he ate grown by a Bo Yi? Or was it grown by a robber like Zhi? I am afraid that even he himself does not know the answer."

Kuang Zhang said with disapproval: "What does it matter? He himself made sandals and his wife made hemp and silk thread to barter for those things."

Mencius explained, "Chen Zhongzi belongs to an ancient and noble family of Qi. His elder brother Dai had an income of ten thousand bushels, but Zhongzi considered his brother's income ill-gotten and refused to benefit from it, and he considered his brother's house ill-gotten and refused to live in it. He lived with his wife in Yuling apart from his brother and mother. One day when Chen Zhongzi went home for a visit and found that his brother had been given a present of a live goose, he knitted his brows and said, 'What would one want this honking creature for?' Another day, his mother killed the goose unbeknown to him and gave it to him to eat. Just then his brother came home and said, 'That is the meat of that honking creature.' Chen Zhongzi went out and vomited it all up. He ate what his wife prepared but not what his mother prepared. He chose to live in Yuling, a remote hilly region, rather than in his brother's house. Is

---

* Robber Zhi was the most notorious bandit in ancient China.

that the way of a man of scrupulous integrity? With such principles as Chen Zhongzi holds, his way of life, if pushed to its utmost limits, would only be possible if he were an earthworm."

Kuang Zhang savored Mencius' words and was silent for a long while. The only sound that came to their ears was the creaking of the carriage wheels rolling onwards.

They were about six *li* away from the city, when Kuang Zhang raised a question again. "There are quite a few people in the world," said he, "who at one time or other longed to accomplish some good deeds but who in the end got nothing accomplished. Why is that?"

Mencius said, "Today we are going to Ox Mountain. Well, I would like to take the mountain as an example to illustrate my point. There was a time when the trees were luxuriant on Ox Mountain. As it is on the outskirts of a great metropolis, the trees were constantly being hacked with axes. Is it any wonder that they are no longer there? During the respite they get in the day and in the night, and moistening by the rain and dew, there is certainly no lack of new shoots coming out, but then the cattle and sheep come to graze upon the mountain. That is why it is as bald as it is. People, seeing only its baldness, cannot imagine that it ever had fine trees, and that this is the nature of the mountain."

Kuang Zhang was inwardly surprised and he gave an involuntary gasp. "You've been here before, sir?"

"No, I haven't."

"You are simply amazing, sir!" Kuang uttered a sigh of intense admiration. "It seems that there is nothing under the sun that you do not know."

Mencius demurred, "You flatter me, sir." And after a little pause, he continued, "Do you remember the famous saying by Confucius: 'By nature, men are nearly alike; by practice, they get to be wide apart?' Can what is in man be completely lacking in moral inclinations? A man's letting go of his true heart is like the case of the trees and the axes. When the trees are lopped day after day, is it any wonder that they are no longer fine? If, in spite of the respite a man gets in the day and in the night and of the effect of the morning air on him, scarcely any of his likes and dislikes resemble those of other men, it is because what he does in the course of the day once again dissipates what he has gained. If this dissipation happens repeatedly, then the influence of air in the night will no longer be able to preserve what was originally in him. And when that happens the man is not far removed from an animal. Others, seeing that he resembles an animal, will be led to think that he never had any native endowment. But can that be what a man is genuinely like? Hence, given the right nourishment there is nothing that will not grow, and deprived of it there is nothing that will not wither away. Confucius said, 'Hold on to it and it will remain; let go of it and it will disappear. One never knows the time when it comes or goes, neither does one know the direction.' It is perhaps to the heart that this refers."

It took them less than two hours to reach the foot of Ox Mountain. Sure enough, it was bare of trees. All they saw were clumps of thorns and thistles here and there with a herd of mountain goats nibbling at the blades of grass among them.

Kuang Zhang, who had jumped down from the carriage, gave a long sigh, with his hand on his breast, observing, "How true is the saying, 'Evil communications corrupt good manners.' Thanks to your instructions, I have come to realize what an enormous influence circumstances can exert upon everything on earth. I had thought that there had never grown any tree on the mountain right from the beginning, now I can draw the inference from this that it is important to cultivate one's virtue as a man."

Mencius said, "Since we are here, let us climb to the top and look to the capital of Qi from on high. The view must be wonderful, don't you think?"

Thereupon, Gongdu and Gongsun Chou parked their carriages, and then joined Mencius and the others on the ascent of the mountain. As they stood on summit they could see the city in the distance enveloped in the red, yellow and green foliage of trees. On the plains around were dotted hamlets and villages, sunk, as it were, in a deep slumber. In the south were rolling hills, inscrutable and mysterious.

Mencius sank into a reverie as he stood there, looking far into the distance. The scenery before him seemed to have deprived him of his power of speech.

Now, Wan Zhang, who had been standing behind his teacher all this time, tried to distract him from melancholy thoughts by calling his attention to the passage of time.

Mencius, awakened from his reverie, uttered an involuntary "Aiya!" and said, "How time does fly! It is really getting late. I suppose we should start down."

And so they started off, chatting and laghing all the way home.

From that day on, Kuang Zhang often made appointments with Mencius for sightseeing. Finally Gongdu was unable to hold himself back any longer, and he questioned Mencius with suppressed anger one day when there was nobody around: "It is true that Kuang Zhang ranks high as a general at the court of Qi, but he is dubbed an undutiful son by the whole country. Why do you, Master, not only associate with him but even go out with him for pleasure trips? Please can you tell me why, sir?"

Mencius placated his hasty-tempered disciple by having him installed in a seat first, then started to explain himself:

"As I see it, filial piety is a major virtue. It is impossible for a man to be loyal if he is unfilial to his parents. Similarly, if a man is disloyal, he can not be expected to be benevolent and righteous. What the world commonly calls undutiful in a son falls under five heads. First, the neglect of one's parents through laziness of limbs. Second, the neglect of one's parents through indulgence in playing games and chess and fondness for drink. Third, the neglect of one's parents through miserliness in money matters and partiality toward one's wife. Fourth, indulgence in sensual pleasures to the shame of one's parents. Fifth, a quarrelsome and truculent disposition that jeopardizes the safety of one's parents. Has Kuang Zhang a single one of these failings?"

Gongdu Zi rejoined, "Qi, the mother of Kuang Zhang, because of her undutiful conduct toward her parents-in-law, offended his father. The latter killed her in a fit of anger and had her buried beneath the stables. Well, granted that she deserved death for what she had done, all the same it was going too far to have her buried beneath the stables as a punishment. Though he be a general today, he was born of his mother's womb; he owes his being to her, doesn't he? Now, the people of Qi urged Kuang Zhang to have his mother reburied in his ancestral burial-ground. If he had done that it would have been a deed of filial piety. But he did not. Can you still say he is a dutiful son?"

Mencius argued. "His father died without leaving instructions. If Kuang Zhang should rebury his mother in spite of the fact that his father left no instructions, that would be taking advantage of his father because he is dead. Would you then dub him filial?"

Just then, Wan Zhang came to the door with his teacher's washing, but on hearing the conversation he halted for a moment before going in. He laid down the washing and was just about to leave, when Mencius stopped him.

"Wan Zhang, wait a minute, will you? We are discussing the problem of filial piety. You are welcome to join us."

Accordingly, Wan Zhang took a seat.

Mencius asked him: "How does your step-mother treat you?"

Taken off guard, Wan Zhang faltered, "Though she is my step-mother, she treats both my brother and father well. I respect her and I am obedient to her."

Mencius commented, "You are a man who can exercise self-restraint."

Wan Zhang became nervous lest more awkward questions should be put to him, so he forestalled Mencius by asking, "Sir, in making friends with others what are the essential things which one should keep in mind?"

Mencius replied: "In making friends with others, it is important to seek out men of kindred spirits, those of a sterling and integral character. Not an easy job that, though."

"Why is that?" queried Gongdu Zi.

Mencius explained, "It is easy to recognize a gentleman, but not so easy to see through a mean fellow. There are a lot of people we daily come into contact with—some good, some bad and some nondescript. You benefit a good deal by making friends with a gentleman, but you will get yourself into no end of trouble by consorting with a mean fellow."

Wan Zhang asked him to continue.

Mencius did so: "In friendship, what counts most is one's moral character. A genuine friendship allows of no self-interest or personal considerations. To cultivate a friendship one doesn't rely on the advantage of age, position or influential connections; in making friends with someone you do so because of his virtue, and you must not rely on any advantages you may possess, such as age, position or wealth. There was once a marshal in Lu by the name of Mengsun Mie, who was a contemporary of Confucius' father, Shuliang He. He had five friends, including Yuezheng Qiu and Mu Zhong—the names of the other three I have forgotten. Mengsun Mie was a noble with a hundred chariots and held a high position too. He had these five as friends because they lacked his position. If these five had his position, they would not have accepted him as a friend. Not only does this apply to rulers of small states, but sometimes also to rulers of large states.

Take Duke Ping of Jin for instance. He had quite a few men of virtue serving him as ministers and counselors, such as Qi Xi, Zhao Wu, Shi Kuang and Shu Xiang. These were all famous men whose illustrious exploits awed the feudal princes. Now there was a man called Hai Tang who lived in obscurity in a poor lane, reluctant to take office. Duke Ping, knowing him to be a wise and virtuous scholar, often paid him a visit and treated him with the respect due to a teacher, asking his advice about governing the country. In time they became bosom friends. But every time Duke Ping came for a visit, he would wait outside the door until he was summoned. He entered when Hai Tang said 'Enter', sat down when Hai Tang said 'Sit down', and ate when Hai Tang said 'Eat'. And he ate his fill even when the fare was unpolished rice and vegetable broth, because he did not dare do otherwise. But Duke Ping went no further than this. He did not share with Hai Tang his position, his duties, or his revenue. He only paid respect where it was due. This is the honoring of good and wise men by a gentleman, not the honoring of good and wise men by kings and dukes. Shun went to see emperor Yao, who placed his son-in-law* in a mansion elsewhere. He entertained Shun but also allowed himself to be entertained in return. This is an example of an emperor making friends with a commoner. For an inferior to show deference to a superior is known as 'honoring the honored'; for a superior to show deference to an inferior is known as 'honoring the good and wise'. These two derive, in fact, from the same principle."

There suddenly arose the sound of weeping and wailing from the street, and Mencius immediately sent Gongdu and Wan Zhang to find out the cause.

.* After 70 years as Emperor, Yao wanted a successor, and Shun was recommended to him. Yao gave Shun his two daughters as wives. Though Shun was still a commoner at the time, Yao treated him as an equal.

Chapter Thirty

King Wei Goes Hunting on a Snowy Day in the Company of His Ministers; Gongsun Executes a Feat of Stone-Throwing to Rescue a Beast of Good Omen

Gongdu Zi and Wan Zhang further got Gongsun Chou and Gao Zi to go with them to find out the cause of the street disturbance. Arriving on the scene, they found two middle-aged women involved in a heated argument with a man, who looked about the same age. The two women were lamenting in a flood of tears while the man bowed and scraped apologetically to them without let-up, trying desperately to hush them up as best he could. Some of the onlookers tried to intervene but most just shook their heads and sighed helplessly.

Gongsun Chou went over to the women and raised his clasped hands in salute: "Ladies, excuse my intervention but may I inquire the cause of your distress?"

One of the women answered after dashing away her tears: "It's too scandalous to tell."

The other woman sobbed, "He's our husband. All day long he ignores his proper occupation and loafs away his time. All that he is good at is fooling around and cheating people."

The man hurriedly threw her a glance to stop her from going on, afraid that more about himself would be exposed.

The woman, however, turned on him defiantly, stamping her feet and denouncing him vociferously: "Every time he goes out, he comes back, stuffed to the eyeballs with food and drink. When questioned where he has been, he always says that some rich and influential person has treated him. It's a bare-faced lie! We haven't seen any rich or influential person honor us with a visit. Never have I seen one! This morning, as always, he put on an act with me as if he were going to a feast given by some rich friend of his, which I doubted very much. I followed him without his knowing it. He went the whole length of a street and yet there was not a single person to say 'hello' to him. I followed until he disappeared into the graveyard on the eastern

outskirts. There I found to my horror that he was begging food from the people who had come to offer sacrifices to their dear departed. So that's the way he fills himself up each time he comes swaggering back home! Oh, what a confounded shame to have such a villain for a husband! My God!"

Gongsun Chou took the man to one side and admonished him in an undertone: "Listen to a piece of advice from a stranger, sir. You wronged your family by doing the abominable thing. To get along in this world a man must be honest and fair, square and above board. Think of the shameful thing you've debased yourself to do. How can they not feel deeply hurt and humiliated? Hurry up, now! Take them home and don't wash your dirty linen in public again."

Gao Zi also came up and joined in with his admonitions. Thereupon, the man tried his hardest to get reconciled with his wives, after which they went home.

Mencius, left alone in his room, picked up a book at his elbow and was about to start reading it, when Yuezheng Ke announced the arrival of His Excellency Mr Chunyu.

Chunyu Kun hurried in and said, "Excuse my interruption, sir. You have been for more than three months. I hope everything goes well with you?"

"Yes, thank you," said Mencius cordially.

Chunyu Kun said, "The local weather has been undergoing a sudden change, from which His Majesty the King predicts that it is going to snow heavily one of these days. It is one of his customary practices that after a heavy snow every year he has his ministers and generals go hunting with him on the outskirts of the city. Preparations for such an excursion are now under way. I have come with his message that you are welcome to join us when the time comes."

Mencius was only too pleased to hear this, and he accepted the invitation with alacrity.

After the visitor was gone there came in Peng Geng, who asked of Mencius: "There is a problem which baffles me. Would you kindly give me an answer, sir?"

Mencius asked him to be seated, and queried with an encouraging smile: "Well, what is it?"

Peng Keng said: "I make bold to ask, does a gentleman pass judgments on others behind their backs?"

Mencius replied without hesitation: "Everybody talks about everybody else and is always being talked about by somebody else, as the saying goes. The difference is that when a gentleman judges others he adopts an attitude of seeking truth from facts. For him, right is right, and wrong is wrong. He does not conceal faults. Neither does he gloss over them. He goes by the golden mean. An inferior man, however, does otherwise, he picks up things by hearsay and bandies them about. Sometimes he even adds inflammatory details to a story in order to vilify his victim. Here is a quotation from Confucius: 'To tell, as we go along, what we have heard on the way, is to cast away our virtue.'"

Peng Geng hesitated for quite a while before he brought himself to continue with: "I hear people criticize Zhuang Bao as a despicable self-seeker and a shameless flatterer who dances attendance upon the prime minister and who stops at nothing to curry favor with those in authority. Every two or three days he will throw a party in his home, sometimes with a bevy of beauties, to entertain his superiors."

Mencius remarked with a sigh: "Alas, men of Zhuang Bao's type —there are, there are. They can be found not only in Qi but also in other states. Since man came into this world people of every description have played their parts. Since emperors, kings, and feudal princes made their appearance on earth there have existed loyal ministers and crafty ministers. Those who were loyal to their sovereigns and states spared no effort in the performance of their duties, even at the cost of their lives, while the crafty ones shamelessly sought personal gain by practicing favoritism, chasing out dissidents and making false charges against their political rivals...."

Before he had finished in came Gongdu and Wan Zhang to report on their peacemaking mission.

Mencius commended their noble act, and he further pointed out that the two women had done right in exposing their husband for what he was. "They knew what they were doing," commented Mencius, "for they had a strong sense of shame. Not so, though, with some wives and concubines whose husbands will stoop to any shamelessness in order to win promotion and gain riches."

But Gongdu Zi protested, "Surely it was preposterous for the two women to expose their husband's shabby doings to the public gaze."

"You must make allowances for their injured pride," explained Mencius. "They only wanted to wake their husband up to the error of his ways, that's all."

The sky suddenly became overcast with dark clouds, a harbinger of a big snowfall in the offing.

Mencius thereupon informed his disciples of King Wei's invitation to go hunting after the first snowfall and ordered them to get their bows and arrows ready for the event.

There was a heavy snowfall that night. On opening the door the next morning they found the courtyard already knee-deep in snow. Snowflakes as big as goose feathers were falling with a vengeance. By evening it had stopped snowing, but a strong northerly wind blew up, with a sharp drop in temperature. Mencius read awhile the *Book of Rites* under the lamp but soon the freezing cold air sent him shivering into bed.

The next morning he awoke to the chirping of sparrows under the eaves. When he went outside he was delighted to find that the sky had cleared up. Most of the students were up and about and were scattered here and there around the courtyard, reading, practicing martial arts or throwing snowballs. It did his heart a lot of good to find every one of them so full of vim and vigor. "Some already carry themselves like scholars!" He smiled at his own thoughts. He tried, after the manner of Confucius, to classify his students into types, each according to his aptitude. "Wan Zhang ranks first in virtuous conduct," he murmured to himself, "and Gongsun Chou and Wulu Zi come next. For administrative talent, it should be first Yuezheng Ke, then Peng Geng and Teng Geng; for military affairs, first comes Gongdu Zi, then Xu Bi and Xianqiu Meng; for knowledge of documents,..."

"Master!" came a loud greeting from Gongsun Benzheng. "I happen to know that King Wei invited you to go and join his hunting party on the outskirts. May I have the pleasure of going along with you, sir?"

"You are most welcome," said Mencius, smiling amiably. "You are a good hand at hunting as everybody knows."

Very flattered by this, Gongsun Benzheng said, "You truly understand my mind, dear sir!"

Shortly thereafter, Chunyu Kun was announced.

He stalked up in a light-hearted way, giving Mencius to know that a hunting party was to be formed that day and that the King was waiting for Mencius and his disciples to honor the occasion.

In due course, they came to the Qi palace in their long train of carriages. The Royal equipage was already there. Decorated with gold and pearls, and carved with dragons and phoenixes, it presented a sharp contrast to all the other conveyances lining the road in front of the palace.

Alighting from his carriage, Mencius followed Chunyu Kun through the palace gate. All the ministers and generals in their hundreds had already assembled before the dais in a solemn hush, waiting for the King. Mencius went forward to exchange greetings with Zou Ji, Tian Ji, Sun Bin, Kuang Zhang and others. This done, he took his position in line and then stood there, waiting at his ease and gazing at the magnificent buildings all around.

Suddenly, Zhuang Bao emerged from the eastern entrance passage leading to the inner palace, and announced in stentorian tones: "His Majesty the King!"

More awe-struck than ever, all the officials straightened up, chanting in one voice: "Good health to the King!"

King Wei of Qi entered and announced, "Today I will have you all go with me for an outing. Our pastimes will be hunting and viewing the snow scenery. I hope you will enjoy them."

He then walked to where Mencius stood and smilingly addressed the latter, saying, "Master, may I have the honor of your company in my carriage on this trip?"

Mencius said, with a profound bow: "The honor is mine, Your Majesty."

And so Mencius mounted the royal equipage after the king, and the whole procession moved off.

After a while the King asked Mencius: "Did the ancient kings have the same fondness for enjoyment of snow scenery and hunting?"

Mencius replied: "Snow is a symbol of purity and saintly beauty. It can inspire one with a longing for something pure and perfect. Hence sage kings of old enjoyed and admired snow. As for hunting, the ancients had to hunt in order to live, so it goes without saying that it behooved their kings to set them an example in advocating it."

The King then asked, "Is it permissible to kill any wild animal?"

"No!" replied Mencius in a decided manner. "Everything on earth has its advantages and disadvantages. There are injurious animals and there are beneficial animals. Injurious animals such as jackals, wolves, tigers and leopards are harmful to human beings, and therefore should be hunted and killed; whereas animals of good omen and beneficial animals like deer should be protected."

At this King Wei summoned Zhuang Bao to whom he issued the

order that nobody was to kill deer, roe-buck or musk deer in the forthcoming hunting.

Mencius went on to say, "There are also harmful birds and beneficial birds."

"I know that storks and phoenixes are beneficial birds," said the King. "Should I order that they not be killed, either?"

Mencius gave a start of surprise.

The King promptly corrected himself by saying, "Storks are birds of passage—yes, that's right—and so they have migrated to the south by now... Well, as to phoenixes, so far I haven't yet had the good fortune to see one."

Mencius remarked significantly: "A phoenix perches nowhere except on a *wutong* tree. If Your Majesty has a mind to invite a phoenix, all you have to do is plant more *wutong* trees, that's all."

King Wei seemed to miss the meaning implied, since he smiled vacantly as he said, "Well, what would you say of human relationships in general, sir?"

After a thoughtful silence, Mencius beamed at the idea coming up in his mind as he presently said, "Mankind roughly falls into two categories: good and bad. Among ministers, too, there are loyal ones and crafty ones."

"How is one to distinguish between good and bad, as well as between the loyal and the crafty?" asked the King.

Mencius explained, "Check what a man says against what he does. A loyal minister invariably behaves like a gentleman—He is open-hearted, square and aboveboard. His first consideration is the interests of his country and people. He tells the truth, only the truth and nothing but the truth. To do so, sometimes he goes so far as to rebuke his superior to his face at the risk of his own life. How apt is the ancient saying that home truths grate on the ears! Hence, loyal ministers as likely as not come to a bad end simply because they have the best intentions in the world! Crafty ministers, on the other hand, use blandishments to win others' confidence, playing the wolf in sheep's clothing. Is it any wonder that they get themselves in the good books of some benighted, incompetent ...." Mencius swallowed back what he was going to say as he cast a sidelong glance at his companion and found, much to his amusement, that his face was changing color!

The snow on the road made the going difficult. The horses were sweating profusely and the soldiers, who held colored pennons aloft, panted and puffed at every step as they trudged along. This continued for quite some time until they passed Ox Mountain and reached the foot of another mountain, when a forester came running up to report: "Forester Song Lin is here awaiting Your Majesty's commands."

King Wei told him: "We are here for hunting and enjoying the snow scenery. Just take us to whichever scenic spot you think best."

The forester climbed to his feet and pointed to a hill-top on the left, saying, "Over there, Your Majesty, one can see the capital to the north and command a view of the many gullies in the south. From there, sire, you can both enjoy the snow scenery and watch the hunting."

"Good!" said the king. "Let's go straight away."

Thereupon, two bodyguards rushed up to help the king dismount and thence walk to the hill-top. Other guards offered to help Mencius also.

Zou Ji, Tian Ji, Chunyu Kun, Kuang Zhang, Wan Zhang, Gongsun Chou, Gongdu Zi, Peng Geng, Teng Geng, Xu Bi and others arrived on the summit one after another.

Mencius asked, "Where is Mr Gongsun Benzheng?"

"Here I am, sir!" was the old veteran's quick reply, as he stepped forward from behind Mencius. His face was wreathed in smiles.

Seeing that his old friend was so full of energy, Mencius remarked, pleased: "You indeed have an iron constitution. How I envy you, sir!"

Gongsun Benzheng replied only with a candid smile before he resumed his position behind Mencius.

After his ascent of Ox Mountain on his previous outing, Mencius found the panoramic view of the capital entirely different. On a fine day after snow the whole city gleamed red in a vast sheet of white. It looked so pure, so grand, so far removed from all that was called evil. Mencius felt his soul so uplifted that he offered a prayer to Heaven: Would that a good and wise Ruler of Man be given to the world to teach his people to live as purely and as sublimely body and soul as snow transforms the good earth; and would that peace and order be restored to the human world as soon as possible. Presently he looked down on the paths along which he had come, full of twists and turns. And then, as he swept a glance over the snow-capped mountain ridges to the south he noted their jigsaw-like unevenness! "Will the unevenness between man and man one day be smoothed out? And how?" he wondered wistfully.

Zhuang Bao came up to tell King Wei that preparations for hunting had been made and it was now for His Majesty to issue the order, which he did immediately.

Zhuang Bao mounted a boulder, from which vantage point he flourished a green pennant, calling out "Start!"

Six groups of hunters took part in the 'encircle and hunt' maneuver. They climbed along four slopes separately, heading for the tops, one group to each of the two side slopes and two groups to each of the middle slopes. Bows and arrows in hand, they kept on climbing upwards, and every so often a man was left stationed on the spot, and so on until, on reaching the top, there was only one man left.

Mencius could see for himself that all along the slopes the hunters were posted at roughly equal distances and three long nets had been set up, blocking each of the outlets of the three gullies. Mencius could not help uttering a cry of admiration; never before had he seen hunting conducted on so grand a scale.

Presently Zhuang Bao waved his green pennant three times, and all the hunters along the mountain slopes as well as those on the tops set up a hue and cry. This was followed by a bedlam of noise from the blocked gullies, as the hounded beasts and fowls tried desperately to find a way out.

Zhuang Bao waved his banner again, and all the hunters sprinted downhill with wild cries. Jackals, wolves, foxes and wild boars in their dozens stampeded in a panic, leaving themselves easy prey for the hunters' arrows.

Mencius spotted two deer dashing far ahead of all the rest, and his heart went all out to them, hoping against hope that the two lovely things might escape harm. But lo and behold! They halted at the foot of the mountain and looked about them. But wherever they looked, there were archers! They made their way toward the mountain top, where stood the King and his party. Halfway up they saw the people there and turned back to run again.

Zou Ji seized his bow, fitted an arrow to it and drew it to its full extent. But just as he aimed at one of the deer and was about to shoot Tian Ji stopped him, saying, "Didn't you hear His Majesty's decree? We are not allowed to shoot any deer today."

Zou Ji turned upon his colleague with a glower and took aim once more.

King Wei saw this with an inward groan, but could do nothing about it.

Now Zou Ji was originally an itinerant politician, a good hand at the zither, and by a ready tongue and a quick wit he had worked his way to the position of prime minister under King Wei. At that time the king was young, without much experience in the ways of government, and Zou Ji did much to help him to administer affairs of state, such as revising the laws and introducing effective measures to supervise his officials at all levels. He insisted that all people, whether officials or commoners, should be encouraged to criticize the government and even rewarded for doing so. He recommended able and prestigious ministers for garrison duty in border regions. All these efforts of his had in due time borne fruit: Qi had grown from a weak to a strong state. And consequently Zou Ji took to claiming credit for this for himself and becoming arrogant.

Thus he set his master's decree at defiance and let his shaft fly in spite of Tian Ji's intervention, which had been well-meant. He was just gloating over his triumph, when a sharp crack was heard and his arrow veered to the right and hit a pine tree. The startled Zou Ji strode up to the tree, but not before he had darted Tian Ji a withering glance. He pulled out the arrow and detected scratches on the shaft, manifestly left by a stone.

Meanwhile King Wei and his other officials were thunderstruck. Whence came the stone? They wondered aloud.

As Mencius and his disciples turned to look about them, they spied Gongsun Benzheng lurking behind a pine, a mischievous smile on his face. The truth dawned on them all. Gongdu Zi took the occasion to stick up a thumb for Gongsun Benzheng to see before Mencius had time to stop him with a meaningful wink. All this was not lost on Zou Ji, who thereupon stalked up to Gongsun Benzheng in a rage. "Mr What's-your-name!" demanded he, shaking the arrow in his hand. "So you did this, eh?"

Gongsun Benzheng held up his clasped hands in greeting and replied: "Yes, I did. Please excuse my clumsy interruption. I go by the name of Gongsun Benzheng, if you would like to know, sir."

Zou Ji ignored his greeting but asked in a drawling voice: "How long have you been working for Mencius, may I ask?"

"Twenty years or so," was the reply.

Zou Ji went up to King Wei and made the following proposal:

Since Mencius had so large a following of disciples among whom there was no lack of highly-skilled martial combatants, would His Majesty have the pleasure to watch them perform. "It would be a rare opportunity for them to show their skills," he reasoned.

King Wei asked, "But in what way?"

Zou Ji pointed to the beasts blocked by the nets in the gullies and said, "Let us watch how they kill those animals."

The king consulted Mencius, who in his turn asked Gongsun Benzheng his opinion.

"Your humble servant is more than willing to please His Majesty the King and His Excellency the Minister," said Gongsun Benzheng.

"Good!" Zou Ji addressed Zhuang Bao: "Let the hunters halt for a while!"

Accordingly Zhuang Bao raised a yellow pennant and waved it three times.

All the hunters at once stopped in their tracks.

Meanwhile Gongsun Benzheng made Gongdu Zi and Xu Bi follow him, making straight for the gully where they halted some hundred paces away from their targets. Presently Xianqiu Meng, Wulu Zi and Shen Qiang joined them. They were all eager to show off their skills to impress the king.

Gongsun Benzheng was the first to raise his bow: Twang! Twang! Twang!—three wolves dropped dead as soon as the sounds were heard.

A chorus of cheers broke out from the surrounding hunters.

Then came Gongdu Zi's turn. He killed three jackals in a row...

All of a sudden, a hoarse cry escaped from Zou Ji, and he collapsed in the snow.

Chapter Thirty-One

In Collusion with His Superior, Zhuang Bao Devises a Sinister Scheme to Incriminate a Court Rival; Out of a Humane and Righteous Heart, Tian Ji Urges His Majesty to Assist a Neighboring State

The reader may wonder how was it that Zou Ji should collapse to the ground when Gongsun Benzheng and Gongdu Zi had just killed their quarry with remarkable accuracy? The reason is that a sudden fear had given him a heart attack. What was this fear, the reader may further ask? To answer the question we must begin at the beginning.

For Zou Ji was an ambitious man to begin with, and his ambition grew as the king aged and became more fatuous and self-indulgent. As time went on, he conceived a plan to usurp power. He therefore tried by hook or by crook to win covert supporters and to exclude outsiders. In this way, he thought, when the opportunity arose, he could take over and declare himself king. His open defiance of the king's order not to shoot harmless animals was intended to monitor the king's reactions as well as a blustering gesture to awe his colleagues. He never expected that his smug calculation would fall through because Gongsun Benzheng cut in to thwart his attempt to shoot a stag. Then the unusual marksmanship of Mencius' disciples was too much for him.

The incident caused the king to lose his enthusiasm for hunting, and he immediately put an end to the day's outing by issuing the order: "Back to the palace!"

After a couple of days' recuperation at home Zou Ji was his normal self again. In the meantime, a new plan was brewing in his tortuous mind. In order to seize power from King Wei he had to first of all isolate him by removing all the officials who were loyal and obedient to him. After this was done, other courses of action would follow and his ultimate objective would be realized in due course, he thought.

Thus every night whenever his active mind robbed him of sleep he would assess every official of the court in turn, judging the pros and cons of each, and finally he reached his conclusion that Tian Ji was his Number One enemy. Then came Chunyu Kun, Sun Bin and Kuang

Zhang. In his daily dealings with these men he would let none of the inner workings of his mind reveal his real intentions as he bided his time for the coup.

Zhuang Bao was his willing instrument and henchman. Day and night Zhuang had his men follow the tracks of Tian Ji, Chunyu Kun, Sun Bin and Kuang Zhang.

In the spring of 333 B.C., Qin gathered massive forces on the borders of Yan preparatory to an invasion. Duke Wen of Yan sent Ji Shan as an envoy to seek help from the State of Qi. Ji Shan first went to visit Tian Ji, as the two were previously acquainted.

"Damn the king of Qin!" said Tian Ji hotly after hearing the envoy's pathetic appeal. "It seems he draws no lesson from his disastrous defeat at our hands last time. Now he is out to invade your state again. This is really outrageous! No! I can't just stand by and watch him do it."

Ji Shan produced a blackish-green jade from his bosom, which he offered to his host with the utmost deference, saying, "Please accept this little gift as a token of regard from Duke Wen of Yan."

At this, Tian Ji stiffened and retorted with an air of solemnity: "No, sir! I cannot accept this. What would the world say?"

Ji Shan wheedled, "But the duke means well. This is a mere token of goodwill and friendship, nothing else."

"It is honorable and righteous to curb the violent and assist the weak," Tian Ji said. "Who ever heard that an honorable and righteous deed could be bought with jade or pearls? Tomorrow morning I will certainly report to our king on the critical situation facing Yan and urge him to send troops to your assistance. As for the jade, please take it back."

With that, he had Ji Shan put up at the government hostel.

It is truly said that walls have ears: The above conversation had already been noted by one of Zhuang Bao's spies.

Soon Zhuang Bao brought his news to Zou Ji. He put his mouth to the latter's ear and whispered, "The envoy from Yan has presented a piece of jade to His Excellency Tian."

"Has he accepted it?" demanded Zou Ji anxiously.

"No, he hasn't," was the reply.

"Where is it at the moment?" asked Zou Ji, his eyes gleaming with greed.

"In Ji Shan's keeping still."

His whole mind riveted on the thought of getting the jade for himself, Zou Ji looked lost for a moment, but Zhuang Bao was quick on the uptake.

"I think..." He began to share his ideas with his patron, who kept nodding his head to show his appreciation. "Brilliant! Brilliant!" commented the latter at last.

Directly after he arrived home, Zhuang Bao summoned one of his servants, to whom he whispered for a moment or so and then spoke aloud: "Be sure that you get it without fail!"

In the still of the night Ji Shan was sound asleep in his room in the hostel, his jade lying on the bed-side table. A man camouflaged and muffed in a black garment lifted the door latch with the blade of a knife and slipped in. He tiptoed to the table, picked up the jade and turned to go. As he did so he found a sword held at his throat. Frightened out of his wits, he gasped, "Who are you?"

The other man, who was also in black garment, demanded in a menacing tone: "Surrender the jade or you die!"

The jade-pilferer suddenly uttered a stifled gasp: "Here comes another one!"

As the second man turned back to look, the other seized the moment to run. The second man chased him as far as a high wall, where the pilferer turned round to defend himself with his own blade. He got a cut in his right arm from the sword of his pursuer, uttered a loud cry of pain and dropped his sword. The other man picked up the blade by a single swing of his foot and dragged the jade-pilferer to Tian Ji's house.

Threatened with torture, the jade-pilferer finally confessed as follows:

"It was the man sent by Zhuang Bao to spy on Your excellency who divulged the whole thing. Zhuang Bao thereupon dispatched me to steal the jade for him. Once he got it he was going to accuse you of taking a bribe from Ji Shan."

Tian Ji gave a sardonic laugh and said, "That's ridiculous! Ji Shan offered the jade to me but I turned it down outright. How can that be called taking a bribe?"

The burglar explained, "The fact is that when Ji Shan offered it to you there was nobody there but yourselves. Now that Ji Shan finds his jade stolen, he is bound to suspect you to be a hypocrite. Back home he will spread rumor about you to his duke, and the people of Yan will call you a hypocrite too. Even people here would regard you with suspicion."

Tian Ji breathed a long sigh before saying, "I was only afraid that some burglar would harass His Excellency Ji in his sleep, so I had a man sent to protect him without his knowing about it. Little did I expect that a high-ranking official would have stooped to such dirty tricks. How unpredictably vicious the human heart is!" He paced up and down the room for a moment, and then asked the man: "Now, you were caught in the act; how are you going to defend yourself?"

The man plopped down on his knees, pleading for mercy.

"I can show you mercy," said Tian Ji, "but your master will certainly not; as soon as he gets to know that you have fallen into my hands. Well, I will keep you here for the time being to see how things turn out."

The man thanked him, with tears of gratitude.

It suddenly occurred to Tian Ji that it had been an extraordinarily long time since he had sent a messenger to Ji Shan. "Why hasn't he come back yet?" he asked the servants. They all shook their heads, looking lost.

It so happened that Zhuang Bao, having sent his man to steal the jade, had sent another to find out if his mission had been successful. Now this man got to the hostel just in time to overhear the conversation between Tian Ji's messenger and Ji Shan. He waited till the messenger stepped out, when he pounced on him from behind and, with one arm round his throat, dragged him all the way to Zhuang Bao's house. He reported to Zhuang Bao what he had heard. The latter was alarmed and broke into curses: "The damned blockhead! He has let me down!"

Just then, a servant from Zou Ji rushed in to report that Zhuang Bao was wanted by the prime minister.

When the prime minister learned from Zhuang Bao that he not only had not procured the much coveted jade, but, what was worse, the man sent to get it had also disappeared, he flew into a passion. "Be quick to find his whereabouts and report back!" he commanded the cowed Zhuang Bao.

Meanwhile, Tian Ji had been waiting for his messenger, but in vain. He asked himself with misgivings: "Can it be that Zhuang Bao has got his hands on him? If so, then as soon as the knowledge comes to him that both the man and the jade are now in my hands, he will try every means to save his man or even murder him to cover his tracks." Presently he thought of the envoy from Yan and his safety. Immediately he sent four of his servants to guard him. "Tomorrow morning, see that you escort His Excellency Ji to the palace," he enjoined.

The next morning King Wei of Qi had his usual audience with his civil and military officials. The civil officials, headed by Prime Minister Zou Ji, ranged themselves on the left side; the military officials, headed by Grand Marshal Tian Ji, ranged themselves on the right side. Thus, Zou and Tian stood face to face.

Tian cast a glance at his counterpart, but the other was stony-faced. Thereupon, he stepped forward, the jade in both hands, and reported, "I beg to inform Your Majesty that an envoy from the State of Yan is at the gate, requesting an audience."

"Usher the envoy in!" King Wei commanded.

"I hear," King Wei began as Ji Shan took the seat offered, "that Qin resorts to arms against your state—for what cause, I wonder?"

"For no reason whatsoever," replied Ji Shan, "except that they have blind faith in military strength and want to subjugate Yan and make it one of their vassal states. It is our ardent wish that Your Majesty dispatch troops to the assistance of Yan as quickly as you can."

The king turned to his ministers for their opinions.

Tian Ji spoke first: "Unjust war is something hated and opposed by all the world's peoples. Now, as Qin is launching aggression against Yan without any justification, Qi as a neighbor of Yan in the north, is also imperiled. In my humble opinion, if only for the sake of our own safety we are bound to send picked troops to fight shoulder to shoulder with Yan in resisting Qin."

Then Zou Ji stepped out of the ranks and said, "I think not. In the past, when Qin made war on Qi, Yan just watched in safety while we fought. What help did we ever get from our northern neighbor? None! Hence, we owe them nothing. Besides, Qi is not strong enough to stand all the attritions of a war. So, in my opinion, we would do better not to send help to Yan."

Next Tian Ji spoke up: "Qin's ambition to conquer the whole of the empire is plain for all to see. How can we afford to relax our vigilance?"

"Aren't you exaggerating, my dear sir?" protested Zou Ji.

Tian Ji rejoined, "Think of Confucius' warning, sir—If a man takes no thought for the morrow, he will be sorry before today is out."

Zou Ji was having none of this: "Since our borders are strongly guarded by able and combat-worthy generals, what can the men of Qin do to us? Didn't our General Tian win many a battle over Qin in his day and return home with flying colors?"

Tian Ji retorted, "It would be so much better to resist the Qin invaders outside our borders before they plunge in to sack our cities and plunder our property."

Zou Ji said, "What grounds have you for saying that Qin must necessarily invade Qi after it has conquered Yan, I should like to know?"

"Recall what it did in the past, observe what it is doing at present, and one can predict its future actions," was Tian Ji's riposte.

The King turned to Chunyu Kun and asked him his opinion.

"I think that Qi can only be strong and its people prosperous as long as a situation of peace and stability persists around it," said Chunyu Kun. "But if an enemy state invades our borders, a growing feeling of insecurity will cause the citizens to neglect their farming and weaving. And if the enemy troops should march into the heart of our state we would be too weak to resist them."

The King turned to Sun Bin, who said, "There indeed are signs that Qin cherishes the ambition to lord it over the rest of the states. If we do not check it in good time, sooner or later we shall suffer for it."

Zou Ji looked meaningfully at Zhuang Bao, intimating that he should speak up.

The latter, who was only too willing to make amends for the disservice he had done the prime minister, now went all out to defend his master's position. "Your Majesty," he argued, "It is enough if we simply refrain from attacking Yan while it is being invaded by Qin. It will not pay to offend Qin by sending troops to aid Yan. For, after all, war is a matter of vital importance to a state, involving life or death, survival or doom, so we must exercise great caution. Besides, if we should dispatch our crack forces to assist Yan, some other state may take the opportunity of attacking us from behind. What would we do then?"

Zou Ji, very pleased with Zhuang's argument, chimed in with: "Your Majesty, it is no trifling matter to talk about sending troops to help Yan. Please think carefully before doing anything rash."

As if a weight had been lifted off his mind, King Wei rejoined with a sigh of relief: "The Prime Minister is talking sense. I'm fully agreed."

All in a fluster, Ji Shan bowed and scraped, pleading: "Your Majesty, please hear me out. Yan and Qi are neighboring countries, as closely related as the lips and the teeth; if one falls the other is in danger too. Please listen to reason!"

But the king's mind was made up: "I have no more to say. The audience is adjourned."

Tian Ji was about to protest, when the king stopped him with a wave of his hand.

He returned home in deep gloom, and his mood was not alleviated one bit when a servant came up to report that Zhuang Bao's man—the burglar, that is—had escaped.

"When?" Tian Ji demanded.

"We only discovered the fact just now, sir," whined the servant.

Tian Ji yelled, "You idiots! How could you let that damned burglar give you the slip?"

The servant replied, "He said he needed to answer a call of nature. We had to let him go, but the rascal made a fool of us and escaped."

"What happened to the jade?" demanded Tian Ji.

"It's still in the house, sir."

Tian Ji emitted a deep groan at this, and observed bitterly: "If he had taken it with him I might have had some alibi. But now, with the thing in my house, I am in a proper fix." He ordered his servant to have his horse saddled. "I'm going to hand over this jade to His Excellency Mr Ji this minute. It is a trap which the evil-minded Zhuang Bao has set for me. But I won't play into his hands!" With this, he hastened to the hostel.

Seeing the agitated state in which he had come, Ji Shan was surprised and asked: "What brings you here, Mr Tian? Is anything the matter?"

Tian Ji explained, "Sir, you do not realize it, but your jade has stirred up quite a to-do. Don't blame me if I hold your duke responsible for this. Surely he must know that this is no ordinary jade. In fact it is a national treasure, worth several cities. Why must he go and try to make a present of it to others, I'd like to know?"

Ji Shan explained, "It is all because of our national crisis. My duke has to part with what he most treasures, though reluctantly. He is left with no alternative."

Then Tian Ji had an idea: "Now I come to think of it, if you were to offer the jade as a gift to King Wei of Qi, perhaps you can move him."

"I would like to try." said Ji Shan, "Shall I go right now?"

"That won't do." Tian Ji found himself in a dilemma. "If you had done so during the audience this morning the king would have been pleased to accept it as a first-meeting gift. But after what happened this morning, you can be sure that he will not accept it..."

Ji Shan said, "I see what you mean. But how am I to dispose of the jade?"

Tian Ji said, "Keep it for yourself for the time being. In the meantime, I'll try my utmost to persuade the King to send troops to help Yan."

Chapter Thirty-Two

A Thief Cries "Stop Thief!" a Malevolent Courtier Cooks up a False Charge Against His Innocent Colleague; Mencius' Worthy Disciples Explain in Simple Terms the Essence of the Rules of Propriety

The conversation between Tian Ji and Ji Shan was suddenly interrupted by a servant who barged in to inform them that Tian's house was being raided by a group of hooligans.

Tian Ji rushed back, only to see four bulky fellows standing in the courtyard. He could hardly contain his anger as he demanded sharply: "By whose order are you intruding into my house like this?"

One of them made a curt bow, saying, "Your Excellency Mr Tian, we beg your pardon for our lack of manners. We have been sent here by His Excellency Mr Zhuang in quest of a piece of jade, which, according to him, has something to do with Your Excellency."

Tian Ji said: "The jade was brought here by Mr Ji, the envoy from Yan. What concern is it of Mr Zhuang's?"

The man replied : "Ours is not to reason why; ours is but to do or die. Please allow us retrieve the jade."

Tian Ji shouted harshly: "I forbid you! Mr Ji is an envoy from the state of Yan. None of your insolence!"

The man, who had seen Ji Shan hurriedly trying to hide the jade, tipped a wink to the other three, saying aloud, "Let's go and get the booty with no more delay!"

"Booty?" retorted Tian Ji, bridling up. "What do you mean?"

"The jade, that's what I mean," was the reply.

"This is outrageous!" Tian Ji yelled, stamping his foot in a towering passion. "The jade is his own possession, he has the right to carry it with him, hasn't he?"

The man made another bow to Tian Ji, saying, "Your Excellency! We only do what our master tells us to. If you have any objections, you can have it out with him."

Tian Ji couldn't make head or tail of what was happening to him.

In despair he sent one of his servants to fetch Zhuang Bao to clear up the enigma himself.

But soon word was brought back that Zhuang Bo had been summoned to the king's presence.

It so transpired that Zhuang Bao had learned from the servant who had made good his escape from custody in Tian Ji's house that the jade was still in Tian's place. So he had immediately sent another of his men there to reconnoiter Tian's movements. When he learned that Tian had gone to the hostel to meet Ji Shan he inferred that the two must be plotting something involving the jade. Consequently he had the four burly fellows sent to raid Tian's house, while he himself hurried to the prime minister's.

Zou Ji, on hearing his lieutenant's report, said gloatingly: "Let us go to the palace right now and denounce Tian Ji for taking bribes."

At the palace, King Wei was languishing in the company of his favorite concubines, and so was anything but pleased by this interruption.

He inquired woodenly: "What brings you two here—nothing serious, I hope?"

"We have come on account of a piece of jade, Your Highness," said Zou Ji.

The King, wide-eyed with wonderment, queried, "A piece of jade?"

Zou Ji replied, stressing every syllable as he went, "Yes, the jade! The one which the envoy from Yan, Ji Shan, brought along with him here yesterday. A rare treasure it is, worth several cities. He originally intended to present it to Your Majesty as a gift, but then it came to the notice of His Excellency Mr Tian..."

"You mean Tian Ji, I suppose," said the king.

"No other," continued Zou Ji. "He saw it and his avarice got the better of him. Remember his performance this morning during the audience?—How he repeatedly urged Your Majesty to aid Yan in resisting Qin's aggression? That was only a futile attempt to cover up his clandestine dealings with the Yan envoy."

"Are you sure that you have not made a mistake?" asked the king.

Zhuang Bao chimed in with "He returned the jade to Mr Ji directly after his secret dealings came to light. If Your Majesty has any doubt about it, he can make an on-the-spot investigation at the hostel."

"All right! Off we go, then," cried the king. The king's carriage was made ready and he was driven to the hostel, followed by the two court officials in their own carriages.

Meanwhile at Tian Ji's house the wrangle about the jade continued, neither side willing to yield to the other. This dragged on for nearly two hours until Ji Shan, feeling apologetic about the whole thing, came out with his jade in his hand to intervene. "No more squabbling about a mere stone, sir," he said to Tian Ji. "Since they have come particularly for this jade, I'll gladly hand it over to them. That's all there's to it."

"But that is one of your national treasures, isn't it? How could you let it fall into common fellows' hands?"

Just then the approach of the king was loudly announced, and king Wei himself and Zou Ji, with a troop of palace guards, appeared on the scene.

Tian Ji at once fell to his knees in an attitude of apprehensive respect, saying, "My homage to Your Majesty."

"What are you doing here?" the king demanded.

Tian Ji was stuck for an answer, then faltered out, "I...I...."

"I suppose you are not here about some jade, eh?" rasped the king.

Tian Ji knew that there was nothing for it but to tell the truth, so he said straight out: "Yes, sire. I am here to see if the jade is in safe hands."

"In safe hands?" sneered King Wei. "Need a grand marshal of Qi take so much trouble over a petty piece of jade? Well, why don't you speak up?" Out of the corner of his eye, Tian Ji watched how pleased with himself his political rival was at that moment, and resentment rankled in his breast. He bit his lip and said firmly: "I beg to inform Your Majesty, that the truth of the matter is..."

Zou Ji cut in by saying, "Mr Tian, listen to me. His Majesty has no time to listen to cock-and-bull stories. Just confess to him what you have been doing behind the scenes."

"That's right," cried the king. "Out with it! Now!"

So Tian Ji explained, "Yesterday the envoy from Yan, His Excellency Mr Ji, arrived in Qi. He brought a piece of jade with him..."

Before he had finished his sentence King Wei queried eagerly, "Where is the jade now?"

At this, Ji Shan emerged from his room, fell to his knees, and offered the exquisite green jade in both hands: "Here is the jade. Please deign to look it over, Your Majesty."

Covetousness written all over his face, the king took the jade and fondled it for a good while as if he could not bear to part with it.

Zou Ji said, "Mr Ji. You came to Qi to seek assistance for Yan. Why did you bring this jade ornament with you?"

King Wei repeated the question.

Ji cast a glance at Tian Ji, who remained impassive, then replied, "I was preparing to present it to you, sire."

King Wei, beaming all over his face, said, "Were you? Good. I'll take it as a gift from King Wen of Yan. Please convey my thanks to him on your return."

Thereupon Ji Shan cried, "My Lord! Does that mean that you are going to send troops to aid Yan?"

"Well,..." King Wei turned to Zou Ji, who shook his head vigorously.

"This can wait", the king said hastily. "Let us discuss it later, all right?"

Tian Ji protested, "My Lord! Life is a give-and-take business. It is not the way of Confucius to take without giving something in return."

This put King Wei in a quandary as he muttered in a confused way: "Well, what is to be done, after all?"

Zou Ji seized the occasion to cross-examine Ji Shan: "Why is it, sir, that you did not present the jade to His Majesty during the morning audience?"

Ji Shan was hard put to find an excuse, and before he could think of one, Zhuang Bao cut in overbearingly: "Your Excellency, may I ask, has anybody else have seen this jade of yours?"

"All the court officials of Yan have seen it," was the reply.

"How about people here?"

Ji Shan was rendered speechless.

"I have seen it," said Tian Ji

"When?" asked Zou Ji.

"Last night."

"Where?"

"At my house."

King Wei was visibly stung as he angrily reprimanded Tian Ji: "What impudence! How dare you have the priority over me to look at a rare treasure like this!"

Zhuang Bao said by way of a hint to the King: "This is lese-majesty, I'm sure."

"Exactly", said King Wei. "You are cheating me."

Ji Shan made a bow to the king, explaining, "Sire, I am to blame for all this. Mr Tian is innocent."

The king, however, ignored the envoy's intercession, and went on reproving Tian Ji, accusing him of insubordination.

Tian Ji defended himself by retorting, "I think I'm straightforward and honest. And I serve my sovereign lord with all my heart and soul. I feel no qualms about anything I have done. What crime is there for somebody to charge me with, I should like to ask?"

His retort stung the king to anger and he exploded: "Is this the way you talk to your sovereign lord, whom you claim to serve with all your heart and soul?"

Zou Ji spoke unctuously in an effort to humor the king: "Calm yourself, Your Highness. Mr Tian committed an error only in a moment of aberration. Considering that he is a grand marshal who has performed meritorious deeds for Qi, you should graciously pardon him this once, I pray you."

His anger still unabated, the king impulsively gave one of his wide sleeves a contemptuous fling, saying, "It's just because he thinks he is somebody that he behaves so arrogantly toward me." With that, he departed in a huff, followed by his retinue.

Ji Shan said apologetically to Tian Ji: "It is all due to my incompetence that you are implicated."

Tian Ji said with a heavy sigh: "A fall in the pit; a gain in your wit. Well, this jade affair can serve as a bitter lesson!"

Ji Shan asked, "Is there any hope of your country sending forces to assist Yan, sir?"

"No hope at all, I'm afraid," was the gloomy reply.

Ji Shan wailed, "Oh, woe is me! When I left Yan I gave some pretty big assurances to my sovereign lord, and now I have to go home empty-handed. Even the jade was given away for nothing. This is sure to earn me the mockery of my countrymen. Oh, Heaven! how am I to face my master?"

Tian Ji said by way of comfort: "Don't take it too hard, Your Excellency. When Duke Wen knows what problems you faced, he will certainly forgive you."

Abruptly Ji Shan made a deep bow to Tian Ji, saying, "Please take good care of yourself, sir. I am finished!" And before Tian Ji could prevent it, he had cut his throat with his own sword, and died on the spot.

Tian Ji knelt by the corpse and shed tears of bitterness. He bemoaned the tragic death of his friend and he cursed his own impotence which had made such a disastrous end possible.

He had the corpse properly encoffined and had his servants escort the hearse to the State of Yan. He swore that if the least chance came his way he would command an army to aid the homeland of his dead friend.

News that Ji Shan had committed suicide soon reached Zhuang Bao and Zou Ji, and the two immediately held a conference on how to cope with the situation.

Zou Ji maintained, "The envoy's death suits our purpose. The king has already accused Tian Ji of insubordination today. So, on the occasion of tomorrow's morning audience we shall be able to impeach him for murder, as nobody else witnessed the death except himself. He couldn't clear himself of the stigma even if he had a hundred mouths in his head. The king will be scandalized and make him pay the penalty."

Zhuang Bao cried in his most sycophantic tone: "Yours is indeed a masterly-minded contrivance; I cannot admire you enough for it!"

But of their scheme to frame Tian Ji, for the time being, no more. Let us take up another thread of our story.

As recounted previously, Tian Ji had a messenger sent to Ji Shan's house. But unfortunately this man was intercepted and was placed in custody by Zhuang Bao. Now this man was one of Tian Ji's many devoted servants who were well trained in the martial arts. By sheer skill, he managed to struggle free of the ropes that bound him. This done, he slipped into Zhuang Bao's living quarters but found he was not there. The thought of revenge uppermost in his mind, he went further to the prime minister's residence, where, under the cover of night, hiding himself under the window of the room in which Zou Ji and Zhuang Bao were having their conference, he overheard all there was to hear. He lost no time in hurrying back to report to his master.

On hearing of his enemy's wicked plot against him, Tian Ji shook with mounting fury as he bellowed, "For so many years I have shed my heart's blood to work for the welfare of my country and my people, only to have their treacherous trap sprung on me. Is there any justice in this world? If this can be tolerated, what cannot be tolerated? I swear: "This world is not big enough for me and them—either they die or I do!"

His servant comforted him, saying, "Never say die, my lord. Keep the hill green, and you'll never lack fuel for winter again—think of the truth in the proverb. The best thing to do now is to flee."

"Where could I go?"

"To Yan."

"Impossible." said Tian Ji with a frown. "How could I explain this affair to Duke Wen?"

"There's no time to lose, sir," exhorted the anxious servant. "Your life hangs in the balance! Flee the capital first thing and let the rest take care of itself."

Tian Ji had no alternative but nod his assent.

Meanwhile, Mencius had been busy with his lectures. He had found that there was little chance for him to help run state affairs in Qi, with a decrepit and muddle-headed king like Wei ruling it and a fierce power struggle being waged between Zou Ji and Tian Ji.

We see him with his disciples gathered around him on a warm spring day in the backyard of the Metropolis Inn, his temporary lodging at Qi. *Yue ji* roses in their different varieties, peony and *shaoyao* are in full bloom, contending in beauty and fascination with one another. A delicate fragrance of scent caresses the nostrils as a gentle breeze wafts across the faces of the scholars.

Presently Mencius turned to Gao Zi and said: "The other day, while we were at the Academy at Jixia, you gave a good lecture on benevolence and righteousness. I would like you to give one on propriety, knowledge, and sincerity. We would enjoy it so much on a fine day like this. Would you be so kind?"

Gao Zi at first declined with humility, and then, after much encouragement from Mencius and his fellow students, started to say, "Propriety is the first essential for the management of a state, as well as human conduct. It is as important to a state as weights and measures, squares and circles are to objects."

Mencius interrupted at this point, saying, "I happen to remember that there is a story about how Confucius taught his son Li to study the *odes** and the *Rites*." Do you know what he said."

Gao Zi answered readily: "Confucius said: 'If you do not learn the rules of propriety your character cannot be established. If you do not

* The *Book of Songs*, also known as *the Book of Odes*.

learn the *Odes* you will not be fit to converse with.' This stresses the importance of propriety as regards human conduct."

Mencius smiled his complete agreement.

Gao Zi continued: "Propriety is the code of conduct for all gentlemen in all situations. The philosopher You said:'In practicing the rules of propriety natural ease is to be prized.' What is natural must be proper also. Hence, in the ways prescribed by the ancient kings this is the utmost quality, and in things small and great pay attention to it. Yet it is not to be observed in all cases. If one, knowing how such appropriateness should be prized, manifests it without regulating it by the rules of propriety, this likewise is not to be done."

Tao Yin, thereupon, asked, "If that is the case, then your rules of propriety can only be restraints on human conduct, can they not?"

"Right," replied Gao Zi, unhurriedly. "It says in the *Rites*: "Benevolence, righteousness and other moral qualities, if devoid of the rules of propriety, will become impracticable. Without them, social custom and practice cannot be rectified; disputes and litigations cannot be settled; proper relationships between ruler and subject, superior and subordinate, father and son, and between siblings cannot be established; student and teacher cannot become on intimate terms; court attendance and military training cannot be carried out with dignity and prestige; and sacrificial offerings cannot be conducted with solemnity and piety. In a word, propriety plays a decisive role in establishing relationships, clearing up doubts, defining similarities and differences, and distinguishing right from wrong."

Once again Mencius nodded his agreement.

Gao Zi then said, "Esteemed sir, there are so many learned ones among my fellow students—why not let them air their views too?"

"A good suggestion," agreed Mencius. "But who would you suggest?"

"Wan Zhang,"was the prompt reply.

Mencius thereupon invited Wan to say something about knowledge.

"With pleasure!" Wan Zhang rose and began to speak slowly: "The *Rites* says: 'A love of learning approaches a love of wisdom.' Some people may be clever, others stupid. But, however clever one may be one still has to learn. Only by learning constantly and constantly reviewing what one has learned can a person proceed from one thing to another and draw inferences. Confucius said, 'In a hamlet of ten families there may be found one as honorable and sincere as I am, but not so fond of learning.' Such was the attitude of Confucius toward learning, the attitude of a wise man celebrated in history. How can we lesser mortals have a different attitude?"

Meng Zhongzi (Mencius' son) asked, "What distinguishes a wise man?"

Wan Zhang replied, "There are four characteristic features by which a wise man is to be known: 1) a wise man is free from perplexities; 2) he has a keen insight into a person's character and knows how to assign jobs to his subordinates commensurate with their abilities; 3) he enjoys life; and 4) he has a clear idea about what is right and what is wrong, including a due regard for precedence in position."

On Mencius' prompting, he went on to the subject of "sincerity".

"Sincerity is the guide to action for a man of noble ambition and humanity. And because he abides by it he lives his life open-heartedly and does everything squarely and above-board. In addition, sincerity is the prerequisite for cultivating a friendship. Say what you mean, and friends will flock to you. On the other hand, if you say one thing but mean another, making promises only to be broken, then your friends will desert you in no time. Third, sincerity is the basic virtue for a man to go into politics. If the reigning prince be sincere and open-minded his officials will show allegiance to him, with the result that each and everyone of them will hold himself responsible for the task with which he is entrusted. And by the same token, if the officials be sincere and open-minded, this will make the common people rejoice and they will be content with farming and weaving. People from far will be drawn to them like magnets, too. Fourth, sincerity constitutes one of the qualities embodied in a subject's loyalty to his ruler. It necessitates observance of the rites and allows of no disobedience to one's ruler. This was the way the ancient wise kings won the confidence of their ministers and which made their illustrious achievements possible. Their ministers reciprocated. Thus, given that the ruler and his ministers enjoy mutual trust, and that civil and military officials co-operate in common endeavors for the state, a stable situation will surely emerge where administration operates smoothly and people live in harmony together. Otherwise, popular unrest sets in and a crisis breaks out. Hence, the ancient sage kings advocated benevolence, righteousness, propriety, knowledge and sincerity."

"Well said!" uttered a familiar voice. It was the inn-keeper Zhong Ren, coming up to Mencius, all smiles, with his thumb up in the air: "What a brilliant speech I have just heard from your disciple! My heartiest congratulations, sir." He had come to fetch them to supper, and their lectures were wound up for the day.

Mencius was just going to bed, when he heard somebody knocking at his door. He opened it only to find it was his son Zhongzi. It was oh! so long since he had an intimate chat with his darling son, and his heart went all out to him as he inquired, "Are you all right, my boy?"

Zhongzi replied; "Yes, rather. But somehow I feel very sad at the mere thought of my old granny. I can't get to sleep for thinking of her, and so I have come to seek your advice."

"What's your problem, then?" asked Mencius.

"Of duties which is the most important?"

"One's duty towards one's parents."

"What is the most important thing to watch over personally?"

"One's own character."

Zhongzi shook his head, saying, "Sorry, but I don't quite understand why."

Mencius explained, "To watch over one's own character is to keep oneself to one's duties and not allow oneself to get morally lost. I have heard of a man who, not having allowed his character to be morally lost, is able to discharge his duties towards his parents. But I have not heard of one morally lost who is able to do so."

Zhongzi asked again: "Apart from the duties towards one's parents, are there other duties one should discharge?"

Mencius explained, "There are many duties one should discharge, but the fulfilment of one's duty towards one's parents is the most basic. Zengzi, in looking after his father Zeng Dian, saw to it that he always had meat and drink, and, on clearing away the food, always asked to whom the leftovers should be given. When asked whether there was any food left, he always replied in the affirmative. After Zeng Dian's death, when Zeng Yuan looked after Zengzi, he, too, saw to it that he always had meat and drink, but, on clearing away the food, never asked to whom it should be given. When asked whether there was any food left, he always replied in the negative. He did this so that the leftover food could be served up again. This can only be described as looking after the mouth and the belly. Someone like Zeng Zi can truly be said to be solicitous of the wishes of his parents. One does well if one can emulate the way Zeng Zi treated his parents."

Zhongzi remarked, "I spent my childhood and boyhood under the tender care of Granny. I can never forget her loving kindness. Since I came to Qi I have often thought of her. I want very much to go back and see her. Would you agree?"

Mencius was hugely pleased to hear his son say this, and readily gave his assent, saying, "Good! Let Tao Yin accompany you. You can leave tomorrow."

At this point, sounds of wheels rolling and horses galloping struck the ear. On opening the door and looking out, Mencius saw a group of chariots thundering westward.

Chapter Thirty-Three

In Setting Forth His Views on Good Government, Mencius Defines a "Heaven-Appointed Officer"; His Doctrines Making No Headway, the Master Makes an Abrupt Departure for Home

As Mencius saw the chariots he experienced a sinking of the heart, knowing that something untoward must have happened. He had Gongsun Chou and Gao Zi, both of them being locals, sent to gather information.

Our story reverts to Tian Ji. After he had been informed that Zou Ji and Zhuang Bao had been working hand in glove to incriminate him and that his life was in danger, he had taken his servant's advice to flee from Qi. At the moment he is addressing his servants.

"I don't know," he began, "how I offended His Excellency the Prime Minister so that he threatens my life. For the time being, I have to flee and find a refuge somewhere for myself and my family. Here is some money for traveling expenses. Make your escapes as best you can!" Having said this, he ordered his steward to give each of the servants a packet of silver.

All the servants importuned their master to let them stay with him and it was not until after much reasoning on the part of Tian Ji that they desisted.

"As soon as the dust settles and the king sees me in my true light, I'll call you all back," Tian Ji promised.

After dispatching his servants, Tian Ji and his family members, young and old, mounted a carriage and hastened to the south city gate.

The soldier on duty, on being told that it was Minister Tian's traveling party, let them pass without more ado.

Once outside the metropolis, they sped on in the direction of the State of Yan and soon disappeared into the dark of night.

When Zhuang Bao arrived with troops to arrest Tian Ji he was an hour too late.

That was the information Gongsun Chou and Gao Zi brought back to Mencius from their errand.

"These are the contemporary rulers for you!" Mencius gave out a long sigh. "They cannot tell right from wrong, good from evil. Alas!"

Gongsun Chou tried to divert Mencius from his depressing thoughts by making conversation, and so he asked, "What should a wise and good ruler do so that his officials and military officers may serve his country with steadfast devotion?"

Mencius replied, "If a ruler gives honor to men of talent and virtue, and employs the able, so that outstanding men are in high position, then scholars throughout the empire will be only too pleased to serve at his court. If in the market-place goods are exempted when premises are taxed, and premises exempted when the ground is taxed, then the traders throughout the empire will be only too pleased to store their goods in his marketplace. If there is inspection but no duty at the border stations, then the travelers throughout the empire will be only too pleased to go by way of his roads. If tillers help in the public fields but pay no tax on the land, then farmers throughout the empire will be only too pleased to till the land in his realm. If he abolishes the levy in lieu of corvee and the levy in lieu of the planting of mulberry trees, then all the people of the Empire will be only too pleased to come and settle in his state. If he can truly execute these five measures, the people of the neighboring states will look up to him as to their father and mother —since man came into this world no one has succeeded in inciting children against their parents. In this way he will have no match in the empire. He who has no match in the empire is a Heaven-appointed official, and it has never happened that such a man has failed to become a true ruler."

"But what if a ruler acts improperly?" Gao Zi asked.

Mencius replied, "Then his counselors must find ways to correct him. A red flower is set off by its green leaves; a ruler is supported by his good and wise ministers. The pity is, in real life, the opposite is often the case. A ruler is more often than not surrounded by flatterers who envy the good and able and discriminate against those who hold different views. They resort to slander and stir up trouble. Think of Mr Ji Shan of Yan. What had he done to deserve such a tragic death? And Mr Tian Ji, too. He did nothing wrong and yet he needs must leave Qi in order to avoid political persecution."

Deeply moved by Mencius' remarks, Gao Zi commented bitterly:

"Everybody has a good word to say for the loyal and the virtuous and everybody abhors crafty sycophants, whereas in reality it is only the loyal and virtuous who suffer and the crafty sycophants who win favors. This is proof enough that there are too many benighted rulers in the empire."

"So it is!" said Mencius with feeling. "If the ruler is just, then nobody under him can be unjust. Put the reigning prince to rights, and there is stability in the state. Put the emperor to rights, and there is stability in the empire."

Gongsun Chou said, "Master, if you were to hold the reins of government in Qi could a repetition of the success of Guan Zhong and Yan Zi be predicted?"

Smiling, Mencius said: "You are very much a native of Qi! You know only of Guan Zhong and Yan Zi. By the way..." he continued after a pause, "do you know who Zeng Si was?"

"Yes," replied Gongsun Chou, after a slight bow. "He was the younger son of Zeng Zi."

"Right," Mencius went on. "Someone once asked Zeng Si: 'Sir, how do you compare with Zi Lu? Zeng Si answered with an air of embarrassment: 'Even my late father held him in awe—How dare I compare myself to him?' When asked again: 'In that case, how do you compare with Guan Zhong?' Zeng Si looked offended this time. 'Why do you compare me with such a man as Guan Zhong?' he retorted. 'Guan Zhong enjoyed the confidence of Duke Huan of Qi so exclusively and managed all his affairs for so long, and yet his achievements were so insignificant. Why do you compare me with such a man?' Now, if it was beneath even Zeng Si to become a Guan Zhong, are you saying that I aspire to be one?"

Gongsun did not look so convinced, as he argued, "Guan Zhong made Duke Huan leader of the feudal lords, and Yan Zi made him illustrious. Are they not good enough for you to emulate?"

Mencius replied, "For me to make the King of Qi a true King is as easy as turning over one's hand."

Gongsun Chou queried, "If that is as you say, then I am more perplexed than ever. Virtuous as King Wen was, he did not succeed in extending his influence over the whole of the empire when he died at the age of one hundred. It was only after his work was carried on by King Wu and the Duke of Zhou that his influence prevailed. Now you talk as if becoming a true ruler were an easy matter. In that case, do you find King Wen an unworthy example?"

"How can I stand comparison with King Wen?" said Mencius after a moment's reflection. "From King Tang to King Wu, there appeared six or seven wise and sage kings, and the empire was for long content to be ruled by the Yin Dynasty. What has gone on for long is difficult to change. Wu commanded the homage of the feudal lords and maintained the possession of the empire as easily as rolling it on his palm. King Zhou was not far removed in time from King Wu. There still persisted traditions of ancient families and fine government measures handed down from earlier times. Furthermore, there were the Viscount of Wei Zi, Wei Zhong, Prince Bi Gan, the Viscount of Ji and Jiao Ge, all fine men, who assisted King Zhou. That is why it took him such a long time to lose the empire. There was not one foot of land which was not his territory, nor a single person who was not his subject. On the other hand, King Wen started with a territory of only one hundred square *li*. That is why it was so difficult. The people of Qi have a saying: 'You may be clever, but it is better to make use of circumstances; you may have a hoe, but it is better to wait for the right season.' To my mind, the present is a comparatively easy time to practice royal government. Even at the height of their power, the Xia, Yin and Zhou dynasties never exceeded a thousand square *li* in area, yet Qi has the requisite territory. Moreover, the sound of cocks crowing and dogs barking can be heard all the way to the four borders. Thus Qi has the requisite population. For Qi no further extension of its territory or increase of its population is necessary. The king of Qi can become a true ruler just by practicing benevolent government, and no one will be able to stop him."

Gongsun Chou remarked, "Apart from Qi, there are Qin, Wei, Han, Zhao, Chu and Yan in the present-day empire. These six states also have vast areas of territory and large populations. Yet not one of their rulers can bring his influence to bear upon the whole realm. Why is that?"

Mencius replied, "Simply because none of them practices benevolent government. Never has the appearance of a true ruler been longer overdue than it is today; never have the people suffered more under tyrannical government than they do today. It is easy to provide food for the hungry and drink for the thirsty. Confucius said, 'The influence of virtue spreads faster than an order transmitted through posting stations.' At the present time, if a state of ten thousand chariots were to practice benevolent government, the people would rejoice as if they had been released from hanging by the heels. Now is the time when one can, with half the effort, achieve twice as much as the ancients did.

A cock crowed, and a new day dawned.

Mencius opened the door of his room and inhaled a mouthful of invigorating fresh air. He looked up at the sky. The spring rain was still pattering without let-up, as if a special providence meant to clean up all the filth and mire in the human world and lay a smooth path for Tian Ji's forced journey.

Presently Meng Zhongzi and Yin Tao came up with their luggage to say goodbye to Mencius.

"There's no need to say goodbye," said Mencius. "I have changed my mind. I am going back, too, with all my disciples."

Zhongzi exclaimed in surprise: "But why this sudden change of plan, Father? Yesterday you did not mention anything about this."

Mencius replied, "Qi is a major state in the east of the empire. I came here with the hope that I might help the king practice benevolent government. How was I to know that he would turn out to be so muddle-headed? He trusts only the crafty and fawning, and take a dislike to the loyal and virtuous. This time the ill luck has fallen to Tian Ji to make his escape; to whom will it fall next, I wonder? We are going back to Zou."

Word soon reached Chunyu Kun that Mencius was soon to leave Qi for Zou, and so he made a flying visit to the latter.

"My dear sir, are you going back to Zou?" he asked Mencius the moment he set eyes on him.

"Yes, I am," was the reply.

Chunyu Kun said, "But, Venerable Master, everybody knows that you are a staunch advocate of benevolence and righteousness both in theory and in practice. I shall be much obliged if you can benefit me with a detailed explication of these two virtues."

Mencius said with a smile: "Everybody knows, too, that Your Excellency is an erudite scholar. There is nothing beyond your ken. Do you mean to test me, or what?"

"No, no, no," said Chunyu Kun. "Honestly, I know very little about it, so please have the kindness to enlighten me."

Mencius thereupon explained, "'Benevolence' means 'man'. When these two are conjoined, the result is 'the Way'. In the *Book of Rites*,

"'Right' means 'proper'." To do what is proper—that is righteousness. If one does not act according to the Way, thereby running counter to benevolence and righteousness, then the Way will not work on one's own wife, much less on other people. If in transactions with other people one does not pursue the Way but runs counter to benevolence and righteousness, then one will not be able to command even one's wife, much less other people."

Chunyu Kun said, "Nowadays people uphold the taboo that, in giving and receiving, man and woman should not touch each other—is this prescribed by the rites?"

"It is," replied Mencius.

Chunyu Kun said after a moment's meditation: "If one's sister-in-law were drowning, should one stretch out a hand to help her?"

Mencius replied, "Not to help a sister-in-law who is drowning is to be a brute. It is prescribed by the rites that, in giving and receiving, man and woman should not touch each other, but in stretching out a helping hand to a drowning sister-in-law one uses one's discretion."

Chunyu Kun then put on a holier-than-thou air, saying, "Now that the empire is drowning, why do you not help it—you and your disciples, who are versed in the six arts?"

Mencius replied, "When the empire is drowning one helps it with the Way; when a sister-in-law is drowning, one helps her with one's hand. Would you have me help the empire with my hand?"

Chunyu Kun said, "My dear sir, your abrupt departure from Qi is something to do with the Tian Ji affair, I presume?"

Mencius gave a sigh and said, "That a loyal and righteous man like Mr Tian should come up against such a misfortune, after all the good he did for Qi, alas! So would you expect any other virtuous and capable man to stay here? With such a benighted king as Wei on the throne, what hope is there for the future of Qi?"

After seeing off Chunyu Kun, Mencius had Yuezheng Ke settle accounts with the inn cashier, himself getting ready to leave. But at this juncture it was announced that the king was coming in person to say farewell.

Mencius was anything but pleased to hear this, but went out listlessly to meet King Wei.

Said the king as he alighted: "I was informed only recently that you are leaving for Zou. Here is a small gift to see you off. Please accept it."

A guard came forward with a wooden box, which he laid at Mencius' feet.

"In the box is a hundred *yi* of gold," said the duke. "Please have a look."

Mencius looked gloomy, as if he had been humiliated. "I have done nothing for Qi," he said in an injured tone, "to be worthy of such a rich reward. Far be it from me to accept it as a gift."

King Wei protested, "What are you saying? You have done a lot for us by giving lectures that was a good service for Qi. One good turn deserves another, can't you see?"

"I can appreciate your kindness," said Mencius impassively, "but this gold I definitely cannot accept."

Embarrassed, the king muttered, "So you will not do me the courtesy of accepting my gift?"

"My Lord, are you not forgetting the maxim?" asked Mencius.

"What is that?"

"A gentleman's friendship is above material interests."

King Wei flushed with anger. Wheeling round, he fumed at his guards: "Take it away!"

That day Mencius and his disciples traveled 80 *li* and then stopped at a large town for the night. But before they had finally settled down to rest, there suddenly appeared Kuang Zhang at the inn door. He had been apprised of Mencius' departure too late, so he had to come in the devil's own hurry on horseback in the hope of overtaking him, he explained apologetically.

"Your sudden departure from Qi," added Kuang Zhang, "took me by surprise, Venerable Master. I heard about it from Mr Chunyu only a short while ago. I am lucky to have caught up with you here."

"Much obliged," said Mencius somewhat uneasily, "to have you come all this way to see me off. But let's go in and talk."

Their talk lasted the whole night, the topics constantly changing from the politics of the Qi court to those of the empire, and it was not until the next morning that the two parted company, when Kuang Zhang started back to the capital of Qi and Mencius continued his homeward journey with his retinue of disciples.

Now back to Mencius and his homebound party. On the noon of the third day they found themselves on a mountain slope looking out over a spacious valley. From there they spotted two men in the valley crossing swords with each other. Intrigued, Mencius asked Gongdu Zi to pass on the word "Halt!" "Let's take a rest and watch them," he suggested.

Mencius and Gongsun Benzheng stepped down from their carriage and found themselves a shady spot from which they could watch at their leisure.

The two duelists, one bulky and the other thin as a nail, were well-matched and the game was hotly contested in the first fifty bouts. Presently the thin one pretended to leave his chest vulnerable to a frontal attack. Rising to the bait, the bulky one thrust at him, but before he had reached his target, the thin one as quickly as lightning had dodged away. Just as quickly he turned round and made a slash with his sword, which clashed with his opponent's. The sword flew out of the hand of the latter and dropped to the ground. To the amazement of all who watched, the bulky fellow, far from showing any hostility, picked up his tunic from the ground, put it on and went down on his knees before the thin man. All this he did with a most solemn and reverential air. The thin man helped him up with both hands, helped him gird himself with his sword, and hand in hand they both walked northwards 30 paces and bowed, and back to the south, and bowed again.

Much puzzled by what he saw, Mencius said to himself: "What kind of a ceremony is this, I wonder?"

Gongsun Benzheng said, "Probably they are swearing an oath of fraternity."

"They have chosen the right spot for that, I bet!" interjected Yuezheng Ke.

Gongdu Zi asked, "What is the name of this locality?"

Yuezheng Ke answered, "This valley is known as Jia Gu. When Confucius was prime minister to Duke Ding of Lu and Yan Yin was prime minister to Duke Jing of Qi they held a meeting here." He indicated the two men in the valley, casting a glance at Mencius as he added, "That's the very spot where the two states joined hands in an oath of friendship."

Thereupon, Mencius said, "Let's press on with our journey."

The caravan started to move again. They were climbing down towards the bottom of the valley, when the two duelists came running up to meet them. They bowed to Mencius, asking, "Is it Master Meng we have the honor of addressing?"

Gongdu Zi pulled up his horse, and demanded in return: "Who are you?"

The thin fellow introduced himself as Chong Yu from the State of Song, and his partner as Chen Zhen from the State of Chu.

As Mencius alighted from his carriage, he said to them: "Just now we watched you matching each other in swordsmanship. What was the occasion for that?"

Chen Zhen kept silent, his head bowed.

But Chong Yu pronounced in his stentorian voice: "We got acquainted at the foot of Mount Tai. And as we both happened to have the same idea of seeking your instruction, we became traveling companions. We talked very congenially as we went along, and then the idea occurred to us to swear the oath of brotherhood. The trouble, though, is that we only know that we are the same age, but we know not our birth dates. So it was hard to say which of us is senior, and which junior, you see. Consequently we hit upon the expedient of a match of swordsmanship as the solution: He who won would be the senior and he who lost, the junior."

Greatly amused, Mencius asked: "Were you both born in the same year?"

"Yes, we were," Chen Zhen and Chong Yu replied at the same time. "We were both born in the 12th year of the reign of King Xian of the Zhou Dynasty. We are 25 in the current year."

"So the upshot was that Chong Yu should be the senior, wasn't it?" Mencius said.

Chen Zhen nodded.

"Do you acknowledge your defeat?" Mencius asked him.

Chen Zhen spoke up in an open-minded manner: "Of course! When a man of honor gives his word, there's no going back on it. Since I lost to him, I own up to it. You saw how I kowtowed to him as a junior should, didn't you?"

Mencius replied, "Well, you are scholars, are you not? And you said that you wanted to study under me, right? Now my question is, why did you choose to fight it out with swords rather than hold a competition in the liberal arts?"

"We did, as a matter of fact," said Chong Yu.

"How?" asked Mencius.

"I asked him ten questions from the Six Arts and he did the same to me, and we came out even," was Chong Yu's explanation.

Mencius rejoined, "That is to say that you both scored the correct answers. But that was no way of testing your abilities in real life." Having said this, he made these two new recruits mount one of the carriages in his retinue, and their journey continued.

Chapter Thirty-Four

Mencius Goes to Song to Preach Benevolent Government But Meets with a Cold Reception; The Crown Prince of Teng Asks the Master to Clarify Some Moral and Intellectual Problems

It had been over six months since Mencius had left home, thus his joy at reunion with his family after such a long separation can be imagined. Three generations, young and old, happily gathered under one roof, and celebrations for the occasion went on for several days on end, the details of which can be omitted for the convenience of our narrative.

In the year 327 B.C. the State of Qin launched fresh attacks against Yan, Chu, Han and Zhao. Incursions into its neighboring states were daily reported. Mencius, always concerned over the fate of his state, people and empire, watched these developments with growing anxiety.

One day while he was sorting out his library, one of his disciples, Chong Yu, dropped in to inform him that the ruler of the State of Song had recently been changed.

"Who is the new one?"

"He is called Yan, brother of the former duke."

"What do you think of him?"

"He is trying to practice benevolent government. With such a virtuous man on the throne there would you go and lend a helping hand?"

"Well, I would like to," said Mencius, full of interest.

Their talk was interrupted by Wan Zhang, who suggested, full of misgivings: "Sir, you would do better not to go. As I see it, the new duke may allege that he is going to practice benevolent government but this could incur the displeasure of King Wei of Qi and King Huai of Chu. If these two big states should attack small Song, what can you do about it?"

"No matter," said Mencius in full possession of himself. "Former-

ly, when Tang was in Bo his territory adjoined the State of Ge. The Earl of Ge was a wilful man who neglected his sacrificial duties. Tang sent someone to ask, 'Why do you not offer sacrifices?' 'We have no suitable animals,' was the reply. Tang sent gifts of oxen and sheep to the Earl of Ge, but he used them for food and continued to neglect his sacrificial duties. Tang once again sent someone to ask, 'Why do you not offer sacrifices?' 'We have no suitable grain,' was the reply this time. Tang sent the people of Bo to help Ge with the plowing and also sent the aged and young gifts of food. But the Earl of Ge requited kindness with enmity and he led his people out and waylaid those who were bringing the gifts. Those who resisted were killed. The *Book of History* says, 'The Earl of Ge treated those who brought food as enemies.' That is the incident to which this refers. When an army was sent to punish Ge the whole empire said, 'This is not coveting the empire but avenging common men and common women.' From then on, in 11 campaigns, Tang became matchless in the empire. When he marched to the east, the western barbarians complained. They all said, 'Why does he not come to us first?' And when he marched to the south, the northern barbarians complained in the same vein. The people longed for his coming as they longed for rain in time of severe drought. Those who were going to market did not stop; those who were weeding went on weeding. He punished the rulers and comforted the people, like a fall of timely rain, and the people rejoiced greatly. The *Book of History* says, 'We await our Lord. When he comes we will suffer no more.' The state of You did not submit. Tang went east to punish it, bringing peace to men and women. They put bundles of black and yellow silk into baskets as gifts, seeking the honor of an audience with the king, and declared themselves subjects of the great State of Zhou. This proves that his punitive acts were only meant to rescue the people from water and fire and punish their cruel rulers. Hence, the *Great Declaration* says, 'We show our military might and attack the territory of Yu, taking captive their cruel rulers. Our punitive acts are glorious. In this we surpass even Tang.' So it is all a matter of whether or not kingly government is practiced. If it is, all within the Four Seas will raise their heads to watch for your coming, desiring you for their ruler. Qi and Chu may be big states, but what is there to be afraid of?"

Wan Zhang then said, "Yan ousted Sicheng Zihan and set himself up as king. He usurped his elder brother's throne, forsooth. Would you say he is benevolent?"

Mencius replied, "It all depends on what sort of man that Sicheng Zihan actually was. If he had been a good and wise duke it would have been malevolent of Yan to have ousted him. But the fact is, Sicheng Zihan is a very wicked man, cruel and debauched. As a ruler, he treated people like dirt and put them to death out of mere whim. The people of Song hate him like poison. Yan did well to have his brother expelled from Song. Nay, it would have been better to have had him killed!"

Wan Zhang added after some hesitation: "Duke Yan of Song merely professed his willingness to practice benevolent government; it's hard to say if he will abide by his promise."

"That is true," observed Mencius. "To judge a man one must not just listen to what he vows to do. What is more important, one must watch to see if he is as good as his word. A man is judged not by what he says, but by what he does. A gentleman must think and act in one and the same way."

Wan Zhang continued, "What sort of a man is this Duke Yan, after all, I wonder?"

Mencius said, "Listen to his words and observe his actions, and you can sum him up. We can never pass judgement on a man unless we can observe him at close quarters."

That summer Mencius went to Song with his disciples.

Though a small state, Song enjoyed a reputation for having a long history, and ancient sites and places of historical interest were everywhere in evidence. The capital, Pengcheng, appeared antique and exquisite.

As soon as they had checked in at an inn, Mencius took his disciples on a sightseeing tour of the city proper. Very soon his presence had become known to the citizens, but no sign of an invitation was shown on the part of the sovereign of Song even after five days had elapsed. A disappointed Mencius had to content himself with giving lectures at the inn.

Knowing pretty well the mental attitude of Mencius, Gongsun Chou asked the latter outspokenly: "What is the significance of your not trying to see the sovereign of Song, sir, since we have been here for so long?"

"In ancient times," Mencius said after heaving a long sigh, "one did not try to see a feudal lord unless one held office under him. Once Duanmu Gan climbed over a wall to avoid a meeting with Lord Wen of Wei; Xie Liu bolted his door and refused admittance to Duke Mu of Lu. Both went too far. When forced, one may see them. I suppose you know the story of Yang Hu presenting Confucius with a steamed piglet? Well, Yang Hu wanted to see Confucius, but disliked acting in a manner contrary to the rites. It was so prescribed at that time that when a Counselor made a gift to a Gentleman, and the Gentleman was not at home to receive it, the Gentleman had to go to the Counselor's home to offer his thanks. Yang Hu waited until Confucius was out before presenting him with a steamed piglet. But Confucius also waited until Yang Hu went out before going to offer his thanks. At that time if Yang Hu had taken the initiative in showing courtesy to Confucius, how could Confucius have refused to see him? Zeng Zi said, 'Sycophants work harder than peasants in the fields in summer.' Zi Lu said, 'To concur while not in agreement and to show this by blushing is quite beyond my understanding.' From this it is not difficult to see what it is a gentleman cultivates in himself."

Gongsun Chou then said, "You have come to Song from Zou with the particular purpose of helping its ruler practice benevolent government, haven't you?"

Mencius replied, "Do not tell me that the sovereign of Song knows not what I have come here for. He knows all right, but he does not want to receive me. What bad manners! We cannot expect benevolent government from such people."

"Then why not leave, seeing that the ruler of Song acts so arrogantly?"

Mencius said with a forced smile: "Not for a few more days yet. Meanwhile, I will just watch how things develop."

And so Mencius stayed in Song, sometimes giving lessons to his disciples, other times going on excursions into the suburbs.

One day, while he was on one of these outings, he came across a big fellow standing all alone on a dyke. The man, with his hands clasped behind his back, was reciting something to himself as he contemplated the bubbling river. Mencius motioned to his students to be quiet before he approached the stranger. The man was reciting a line from Confucius: "All things in nature are passing away even like this—ceasing neither day nor night!"

At the sound of somebody approaching, the stranger wheeled round to meet the friendly glance of Mencius. Raising his clasped hands in salute, he inquired politely: "You look out of the common run—so stately, so prepossessing. Could it be Mencius I am speaking to?"

Mencius smiled his acknowledgment.

The stranger introduced himself as Chen Dai from the State of Chu. And he further explained that he had come to Qi on purpose to seek the Master's teaching. "Heaven grants me the luck to meet you here of all places!" He added, his eyes dancing with genuine delight. Exhilarated, Mencius admitted him as his disciple there and then.

Another day, Yuezheng Ke ushered in a guest to Mencius. He was the crown prince of the State of Teng. This man was aged 30, of medium height, elegantly dressed and sedately behaved.

"I have been sent by my father, the Marquis of Teng, as envoy to the State of Chu," the prince began. "While passing through Song on my way there, I happened to get to know you were here, so I make this visit in the hope of hearing your instructions. May I receive your favor, Venerable Master?"

With due ceremony, Mencius requested the Prince to be seated, and a conversation between host and guest ensued.

The prince opened with, "Since the Spring and Autumn period the feudal lords of the states have been involved in ceaseless strife for supremacy and the empire has never had a moment of peace and order. Why is that?"

Mencius explained, "It all originates from a lust for power. In the early years of the Zhou Dynasty, King Wu, in his efforts to bring the empire under better rule, divided the Central Kingdoms into several states and enfeoffed the feudal lords so that they might rule their territories separately. However, these rulers; due to their private desire for expansion, started to wage aggressive wars against one another. That is why I said, 'In the Spring and Autumn period there were no just wars!' Now the same chaotic condition of things is facing the empire!" He forced down the righteous indignation that was rising in him and continued, "But think back to the times of Yao, Shun, Yu, Tang, Wen and Wu. Those were good old days indeed! What a contrast to the present!"

The prince said, "I know well enough that you strive, as did Confucius in his time, for the goal of an empire of states shared by the common people. But allow me to ask you another question: Is human nature inclined to be good, or is it inclined to be bad? In other words, is it inborn or cultivated?"

Mencius explained, "Confucius made a brilliant exposition of this problem when he said, 'By nature, men are nearly alike; it is through practice that they drift wide apart.' From this it can be seen that human nature, good or bad, is a matter of self-cultivation. The adage 'Evil communications corrupt good manners' points to the same conclusion."

The prince said, "I wish to nurture my good nature. What can I do about that?"

Mencius replied, "For a man to give full realization to his heart is for him to understand his own nature, and a man who knows his own nature will know Heaven. By retaining his heart and nurturing his nature he is serving Heaven. Whether he is going to die young or to live to a ripe old age makes no difference to his steadfastness of purpose. It is through awaiting whatever is to befall him with a perfected character that he stands firm in his proper destiny."

"Do you believe in destiny, sir?" enquired the other.

"Yes, I do," said Mencius. "Nothing happens that is not due to destiny. However, one accepts willingly only what is one's proper destiny. That is why he who understands destiny does not stand under a wall which is on the verge of collapse. He who dies after having done his best in following the Way dies according to his proper destiny. It is never anyone's proper destiny to die in fetters."

The prince rejoined, "I am a crown prince, heir to the throne. As such, what I say or do has a great bearing upon my country and people. I must therefore nurture my nature to the best of my ability. How can I do that?"

Mencius explained, "No man is devoid of a heart sensitive to the sufferings of others. So try your best to nurture such a sensitive heart in yourself. Such a sensitive heart was possessed by the sage kings of old like Yao and Shun, and this manifested itself in their compassionate government. With such a sensitive heart behind compassionate government, it was as easy to rule the empire as rolling it on your palm."

The prince listened, entranced, his eyes fixed on Mencius all the while.

Mencius continued eloquently: "My reason for saying that no man is devoid of a heart sensitive to the sufferings of others is this: Suppose a man were all of a sudden to see a small child on the verge of falling into a well, he would certainly be moved to compassion, not because he wanted to get in the good graces of the parents, nor because he wished to win the praise of his fellow villagers or friends, nor yet because he disliked the crying of the child. It is simply because he had a heart sensitive to the sufferings of others, the same as everybody else has. From this it can be seen that whoever is devoid of compassion is not human, whoever is devoid of shame is not human, whoever is devoid of courtesy and modesty is not human, and whoever is devoid of the sense of right and wrong is not human. Compassion is the germ of benevolence; the sense of shame, of dutifulness; courtesy and modesty, of observance of the rites; the sense of right and wrong, of wisdom. Man has these four germs just as he has his four limbs. For a man possessing these four germs to deny his own potentialities is for him to cripple himself; for him to deny the potentialities of his prince is for him to cripple his prince. If a man is able to develop all these four germs that he possesses, it will be like a fire starting up or a spring coming through." He cast his listener a penetrating glance, then changed his tone to one of resoluteness, saying, "When these are fully developed, he can take under his protection the whole realm within the Four Seas. But if he fails to develop them, he will not be able even to serve his parents."

All smiles, the prince remarked with hearty appreciation: "Well spoken! Well-spoken! Never have I heard a talk so edifying to my mind. Thank you ever so much, my dear sir."

He stood up to take his leave, saying, "I have to hurry on my journey to the State of Chu. I'll come to you again for more instructions, if ever there's a chance. Good-bye till then."

Mencius wished him a pleasant journey, and they parted.

Another day a counselor from the State of Song came to visit Mencius. The man looked to be in his fifties, tall and slender, and who deported himself with dignity. He introduced himself as Dai Yingzhi.

"You have been here for quite some time, sir," he began, "but what with one thing and another, I have not been able to pay my respects to you until now. I must beg your pardon."

"Not at all," said Mencius. "It is fully understood that a man moving in official circles cannot be the master of himself."

Dai Yingzhi thanked him for his understanding. "Now there is one thing for which I would wish to hear your enlightened instructions," he continued.

"Please go on."

Dai Yingzhi said, "I am an excise officer at the Song court, responsible for both treasury and granary. We are unable in the present year to change over to a tax of one in ten or to abolish customs and market duties. What would you think if we were to make some reductions and wait till next year before putting the change fully into effect?"

Mencius replied with the following analogy: "There is a man who appropriates one of his neighbor's chickens every day. Someone tells him:'This is not how a gentleman behaves.' He answers, 'May I reduce it to one chicken every month and wait until the following year to stop altogether? I put it to you, sir: Is this the proper way to go about one's business?"

Dai Yingzhi said, "No, it is wrong."

"When one realizes that something is morally wrong," continued Mencius, "one should stop it as soon as possible. Why wait for next year? What's more, the levying of a tithe is too much for the common people as it is. It should be abolished."

"You are absolutely right," Dai Yingzhi agreed. "As soon as I secure an audience with His Majesty a tax reduction will be put into effect at once."

Peng Geng then appeared at the door to announce the arrival of another "Mr Dai", to the surprise of Mencius, who immediately hurried out to receive this unexpected visitor.

He was Dai Busheng, about 40 years of age and with an easy grace of manner about him. After civilities had been exchanged between the three, the conversation turned to the current situation in Song.

Dai Busheng said, "I venture to ask, sir: Song is a famous state with a long history. But in recent years it has steadily deteriorated. Please enlighten me with your shrewd judgment—in what way can we make the state strong and prosperous?"

Mencius replied, "To govern means to guide aright. If you lead the people with correctness, people high and low will follow you on the correct path. If the ruler of a state is benevolent his subjects will be benevolent also. If the ruler of a state is righteous, his subjects will be righteous also."

Dai Busheng asked, "How is one to make one's sovereign observe the rites and become benevolent and righteous?"

Mencius challenged him: "Do you wish your sovereign to be

good?" (Dai Busheng nodded in the affirmative) "Well, I shall speak to you plainly. Suppose a counselor of Chu wished his son to speak the language of Qi. Would he have a man from Qi tutor his son? Or would he have a man from Chu?"

"A man from Qi, of course," was the prompt reply.

Mencius said, "Good. With one man from Qi tutoring the boy and a host of Chu men chattering around him, even though you caned him every day to make him speak the Qi tongue you would not succeed. Take him away to some district like Zhuang or Yue for a few years, then even if you caned him every day to make him speak the Chu language you would not succeed."

The meaning implied in Mencius' figure of speech suddenly dawned on Dai Busheng, and he queried, "Do you mean to say that there is a lack of men of virtue around the duke of Song?"

For an answer, Mencius merely smiled.

Feeling that he was personally involved, Dai Busheng retorted somewhat vehemently: "His Excellency Mr Yingzhi and my humble self may not be what you are pleased to call 'men of virtue', but we do wish the best of everything for the empire and the state. And speaking of men of virtue, there is still a Mr Xue in our midst..." He halted, watching expectantly to see how Mencius would react to the name.

"Do you mean Xue Juzhou?" asked Mencius.

Dai Busheng replied, all too pleased with himself: "Yes, that is the man."

Mencius said, "I have heard Mr Xue spoken of as a man of virtue since I came to Song. He is said to be living in the palace too, and so you think him a man of virtue. But my question is, if everyone around the duke, old or young, high or low, is a Xue Juzhou, then who will help the duke to do evil? On the other hand, if no one around the duke is a Xue Juzhou, then who will help him to do good? What difference can one Xue Juzhou make to the duke of Song?"

Dai Busheng protested, "But our sovereign lord has said that he is going to practice benevolent government."

"Can you judge whether a man is good or bad simply by what he says? Or by what he does?" Mencius challenged him.

Dai Busheng said, "Mostly by what he does." Then, after a pause, he rejoined, "You sound as if you doubt that our sovereign lord is sincere about practicing benevolent government."

"No," said Mencius. "What I mean is that when the ruler of a state promises to practice benevolent government, he must follow it up with concrete measures necessary for its implementation. When Yao and Shun practiced benevolent government they did so in the natural course of things, being benevolent men themselves. Tang and King Wu of Zhou emulated their find example and made experiments of their own. When it came to the Five Leaders of the feudal lords in the Spring and Autumn period, they just used benevolent government as a means to attain their private ends. But as time went on, what was make-believe has become a historical fact—who would deny it? Now look at your sovereign lord—all promises but no deeds. How can the world acknowledge him as a good and wise ruler?"

After Dai Yingzhi and Dai Busheng had left, Chen Dai asked of Mencius, "Sir, it seems that you hold it against the ruler of Song for not granting you an interview, am I right?"

"What can I say of a man who knows not what good manners are?" responded Mencius resentfully.

Chen Dai then said, "But sir, I am outspoken and straightforward. Please don't take to heart what I'm going to say."

Mencius smiled ruefully. "Not at all. Please have your say."

Chen Dai continued, "All this time you are here in Song, the duke takes no initiative to summon you, neither will you take the initiative to meet him. This is just sticking to mere form. You are a man of noble ambition. There is no need for you to be bogged down by these inhibitions. Why not stoop to conquer, so long as you can achieve your noble end?—the noble end of helping the ruler of Song to practice benevolent government. Moreover, it says in the *Records*, 'Bend the foot in order to straighten the yard.' That seems worth doing."

Mencius retorted, "Young man, you see only one side of the coin. There are certain major issues on which one cannot compromise. Let me cite you an instance. Once Duke Jing of Qi went hunting and he summoned his game keeper by having someone wave a pennon. The game keeper did not come, and the duke almost had him put to death. 'A man whose mind is set on high ideals never forgets that he may end up in a ditch; a man of valor never forgets that he may forfeit his head.' What did Confucius find praiseworthy in the game keeper? His refusal to answer to a form of summons to which he was not entitled. What can one do about those who go without even being summoned? Moreover, the saying 'Bend the foot in order to straighten the yard' refers to profit. If it is for profit, I suppose one might just as well bend the yard to straighten the foot."

Chen Dai listened with great attention as Mencius continued, "Once, the officer Zhao Jian sent Wang Liang to drive the chariot for his favorite, Xi on a bird hunt. In the course of a whole day they failed to catch one single bird. Xi reported to his master: 'He is the worst charioteer in the world.' Someone told Wang Liang of this. Liang asked, 'May I have another chance?' It was with difficulty that Xi was persuaded, but in one morning they caught ten birds. Xi reported to his master: 'He is the best charioteer in the world.' 'I shall let him drive for you,' said Zhao Jian. He asked Wang Liang, but the latter refused. 'I drove him according to the proper rules,' said he, 'and we did not catch a single bird all day. Then I used underhand methods, and we caught ten birds in one morning. The *Book of Songs* says, 'He never failed to drive correctly, and his arrows went straight for the target.' I am not used to driving for common fellows. May I be excused?' Even a charioteer is ashamed to be in league with an archer. Even when doing so means catching a mountain of birds, he would still rather not do it. What can one do about those who bend the Way in order to please others? You are mistaken in making light of the offensive behavior of the Song ruler and his ignorance of the rites. There has never been a man who could straighten others by bending himself."

Chapter Thirty-Five

In Fawning on His Superior, the Crafty Minister Courts Disaster;
Nobody's Enemy But His Own, a Benighted Duke Bemoans His Sudden Bereavements

While Mencius was going out to the courtyard the crown prince of Teng appeared at the gate, coming in to meet him. He was just back from his diplomatic mission to Chu.

As soon as he was seated, the prince began: "This journey of mine has helped me a lot in understanding the world. It is truly said that traveling ten thousand *li* is worth more than reading ten thousand books."

"I'm glad to hear that, sir," said Mencius. "But what was your impression of Chu?"

The crown prince gave a long sigh before he remarked, "After my visit there, I began to realize how much smaller and weaker the state of Teng is in comparison."

"You are wrong there, my prince," Mencius said with an indulgent smile. "Once, Cheng Jian said to Duke Jing of Qi: 'He is a man and I am a man. Why should I be in awe of him?' Similarly, Yan Hui said, 'What sort of a man was Shun? And what sort of a man am I? Anyone who can make anything of himself will be like that.' Gongming Yi said, 'When he said that he modeled himself on King Wen, the Duke of Zhou was only telling the truth.' Now if you reduce Teng to a regular shape, it would have a territory almost 50 *li* square. It is big enough for you to accomplish great things. The *Book of History* says, 'If the medicine does not make the head swim, the illness will not be cured.'"

"Your words are pregnant with meaning," said the prince as he stood up and made a bow. "Thank you for your good advice." Soon afterwards he left for Teng.

A severe drought hit the State of Zou in the summer of 326 B.C.

An emergency session was called at the court, at which Xiahou Yi proposed to Duke Mu that the state granaries be opened for the

relief of the countless victims of the widespread famine. The common people were the lifeline of a nation, he reasoned. Now hunger drove them from pillar to post, and few people were left for farming and weaving. If such a condition of things persisted, the state power would be imperilled. So, opening the public granaries to relieve the famished people was the only remedy, Xiahou Yi concluded.

Duke Mu, however, was unmoved: "Impossible! Public grain is appropriated from the peasants bit by bit, no easy job. How could we give it away? What is more, I myself need it, and you officials can't do without it either. Nor the army. No, no! Perish the thought!"

Xiahou Yi continued to try to persuade him: "Take my advice, My Lord. The important thing at the moment is to win the hearts of the people. Win them and you have all; lose them and you lose all. There may be a limit to the store of grain, yet once you hand it out to them to meet their desperate needs, you will win their hearts and they will look up to you as their parents. Consequently, in the event of domestic trouble or foreign invasion they will go through fire and water to stand by you."

But Duke Mu was dismissive: "No need to worry on that score. With me ruling over Zou, the state is rock-firm. What chance is there of domestic trouble or foreign invasion."

"Father," interrupted Gu Tu, "Mr Xiahou is talking sense. Confucius warned us: 'If a man takes no thought about what is distant, he will find sorrow near at hand.' It is advisable to take a long-term point of view."

Duke Mu laughed out loud, saying: "You need not be overanxious, my son."

Gu Tu was about to dispute the issue further, when a guard came in to announce that the envoy Zang Cang from Lu was waiting for an audience.

Granted admittance, Zang Cang strode in, head held high. He was tall and rather portly. He cast an glance of great disdain at the assembled officials and then made a perfunctory bow to Duke Mu before saying in an affected tone: "My homage to your lordship."

Though hardly pleased with the haughty manner of the envoy, the duke had to let him take a seat before he inquired about his purpose of his visit.

Zang Cang spoke curtly: "This is the seventh month already, and yet we have not received the tribute you promised. Why?"

"But we sent it to your court, I am sure," said the duke

"When was that?"

"In the fourth month."

"Who sent it?"

"Dongye Sixiao."

Zang Cang demanded aggressively; "Why didn't we get it, then?"

"You didn't?" Beads of sweat broke out on his brow as Duke Mu looked at Dongye Sixiao with puzzlement. "What happened, Mr Dongye?" he demanded.

"My lord," said Dongye. "it is true that I did not deliver the tribute. It was because ...well, I thought it was terribly unfair that we should pay this tribute to Lu every year for no other reason than that they are big and rich and we are small and poor. And so I took it upon myself to have the pigs, sheep and cattle kept in the imperial gardens for the time being, without having them sent to Lu."

"What impudence!" Sudden fury seized the duke as he gasped at his favorite minister: "You...you...must apologize to His Excellency Mr Zang this minute!"

Dongye Sixiao said: "My Sovereign Lord, we have our pride to think of. Since Lu for many years has not done us the least favor, why should we humble ourselves by paying them tribute. It is disgraceful!"

Zang Cang, deeply stung, exploded: "Do you mean to say that Zou is going to revoke its tribute owing to Lu?"

Dongye Sixiao, not to be intimidated, answered back: "That is right."

Zang Cang stood up abruptly, "You must eat your words. Or you'll suffer for it. Don't say I didn't warn you!" With that, he walked out in a huff.

He hurried back to Lu and reported to Duke Ping: "My Lord, Duke Mu showed no respect for your authority at all. When I demanded the tribute from him, he flung insulting words in my face. He even stigmatized you as muddle-headed, incompetent and what not, and said it was far beneath their dignity to offer you tribute. He swore that he would one day lead an army to smash the palace of Lu and have you dismembered to avenge their long years of humiliation at the hands of Lu."

At this, Duke Ping stamped with fury and immediately summoned General Shen Zicheng to the palace. That very evening a host with 500 chariots commanded by General Shen marched on the State of

Zou.

It happened to be a moonless night and rain clouds hung low. An appendage to Lu, Zou had insufficient garrison soldiers on its borders as a rule. Thus the invading troops met little resistance all the way to the capital of Zou, which was a mere 70 *li* away.

The capital was surrounded on three sides by mountains, with only the west gate leading to the plains. The sudden roll of battle drums threw the whole city into a great panic. Duke Mu was almost paralyzed with fear, but when he summoned his ministers only the loyal Xiahou Yi made his appearance.

The duke stood up, glaring. His voice cut like a knife: "Where is Dongye Sixiao? He is the man who has brought on all this trouble; now he gives us the slip. Damn him!"

Xiahou Yi offered to take command of the defense of the city but was turned down on grounds of his old age. Finally it was Gu Tu, the duke's heir, who volunteered to take the command.

Too late! By this time the invaders had already stormed in. Before Gu Tu had emerged from the outer gate the palace was besieged and Gu Tu was killed by enemy arrows.

A search was made by the enemy soldiers for Duke Mu, but he was nowhere to be found. General Shen, though puzzled, had to let it rest, and instead ordered one of his lieutenants to find Dongye Sixiao. "Go and get hold of the old villain and make short work of him!"

Scarcely had an hour passed before the man returned to report that Dongye Sixiao and all his family had been slaughtered.

"Well done!" said Shen Zicheng. "He deserved it. Let that be a lesson to Duke Mu, who used such mean fellow to court trouble. We are avenged. Let's go back to report to our masters."

The lieutenant asked, "What about Duke Mu? He has not been caught yet."

Shen Zicheng replied, "He must have escaped from the palace and hidden himself somewhere. Just let him be. He will have learned his bitter lesson from this debacle, I'm certain. Sooner than you expect he will submit to us, with his tribute."

Let's come back to Duke Mu and Xiahou Yi. It turned out that the two had managed their escape at the first sign of the crisis. When they learned that the Lu invaders had stormed the city they made their way across the rear courtyard of the palace, slipped out by a back door and found themselves on a path that led to the depths of the Yishan

Mountains. On the way they ran into a stalwart fellow who turned out to be the hero who had once saved Xiahou Yi's life. Hao Zhi was his name. The man installed the duke and the minister in a rocky cave, and he himself kept watch outside. As soon as he saw that the Lu troops had withdrawn, Hao Zhi escorted them back to the palace.

The sudden raid from Lu had deprived Duke Mu of both his son and daughter, not to mention 30 or so of his officials, including his favorite Dongye Sixiao.

Coming back to Mencius. It soon came to his knowledge that Zou —his birthplace—had been raided and that over 30 officials had been killed in the disaster. His injured patriotic feelings allowed him to stay in Song no longer, and so, after a hasty farewell to the local duke and his friend Dai Busheng, he made his way home overnight.

The very day he arrived in Zou he requested an interview with Duke Mu, taking Gongsun Chou and Wan Zhang along.

Duke Mu told him: "In this catastrophe most of my officials died, and both my son and daughter were killed also. Yet none of my people would risk their lives to defend them. There are too many to punish, but if I do not punish them they will continue to look on with hostility at the death of their superiors without going to their aid. What do you think is the best thing for me to do?"

Mencius asked, "Do you wish me to tell you the truth? Or would you prefer to hear a pretty lie?"

"The truth, of course," exclaimed the duke.

Mencius, growing grave, replied pointedly: "It was all a disaster of your own seeking. You and your ministers must take the blame."

The duke's mouth dropped open; the blood drained from his face.

"In years of bad harvest and famine," Mencius went on relentlessly, "close on a thousand of your people suffered, the old and the young being abandoned in the gutter, the able-bodied scattering in all directions. Yet your granaries were full and there was failure on the part of your officials to inform you of what was happening. This shows how callous those in authority were and how cruelly they treated the people. Zeng Zi said, 'Take heed! Take heed! What you mete out will be paid back to you.' It is only now that the people have had an opportunity of paying back what they received."

The duke shook with suppressed anger, his face flushed crimson.

Undaunted, Mencius raised his voice, as if to give his listener a warning: "But beware! You should not bear them any grudge. Practice benevolent government and the people will be sure to love their superiors and die for them. Otherwise they will regard them as their enemies."

The duke could no longer control himself. He jumped up from his throne and pointed an accusing finger at Mencius: "Meng Ke! How dare you talk to me in such an insolent manner! Do you still consider me your sovereign lord or not."

Mencius stood up and said proudly: "In my view, the people are of supreme importance; the altars to the gods of earth and grain come next; last comes the sovereign."

The duke demanded threateningly: "What did you say?"

Mencius repeated what he had said.

The duke stamped his foot. "Listen to this, everybody. From now on, stop granting Meng Ke any bounties or rewards. Nobody is allowed to consort with him!"

Mencius threw out his wide sleeves in a gesture of protest, then held up both hands to smooth down his greying beard before he said aloud: "I, Meng Ke, make my way through this world as a straight and honest man. Above, I am not ashamed to face Heaven; below, I am not ashamed to face man. I cherish benevolence and justice as my companions, loyalty and faith as my friends. Hence, wherever I go I lack nothing in the way of financial help. What do I care for this denial from Zou?" With that, he went off in a huff with his two disciples.

Back at his living quarters, Mencius declared to all his disciples that he would fast for three days, much to their astonishment.

Gongdu Zi asked Wan Zhang and Gongsun Chou about it, and was told what had happened during the morning interview.

Gongdu Zi said, "Why not leave this state altogether and have done with it? There's no need to torment himself by fasting."

Gongsun Chou replied, "Maybe he wants in this way to give the duke a rude awakening so that he may come to realize his error."

Wan Zhang chimed in, "Or to express his deep sympathy for those who are now suffering for hunger and cold?"

Who knows indeed? The three of them were reduced to conjecture."

Chapter Thirty-Six

Home Again, Mencius Resumes His Time-Honored Job of Teaching;
His Favorite Disciple Questions Him on the Rites

Mencius went on fasting until finally his disciples turned out in full force to remonstrate with him. This was when Gongdu Zi, Yuezheng Ke, Xianqiu Meng, Shen Qiang and others, who were natives of Lu, came kneeling before him with their pathetic appeal: "Master! Don't torture yourself, for pity's sake! If you must do so in order to shame the ruler of Lu, punish us instead. Please do!"

Mencius was moved to say, "Please stand up, all of you. What wrong have any of you done to be punished for?"

All stood up as requested, except Shen Qiang.

"Why are you still kneeling, Shen Qiang?"

Shen Qiang said, "My father commanded the invasion of Zou. As a result, many officials of Zou were killed and my crony Gu Tu met his death too. I feel ashamed of what my father has done to Zou. So please punish me, teacher."

Mencius observed with cold reason: "There exists an unequal peace treaty between Lu and Zou, a troublesome matter left over by the former rulers of the two states. The truth of the matter cannot be explained clearly in a word or two. Nor can it be tackled in a haphazard way. However, Dongye Sixiao, as a senior minister should have good understanding of it. He chose to do what he did because he wanted to exasperate the Lu ruler and stir up trouble. Though he never expected that Lu would launch an attack so soon."

Shen Qiang replied, "Let us say that Dongye Sixiao deserved his death. But what of the deaths of the other officials? Was not that a senseless waste of human lives!"

Mencius explained, "The fact that the Lu troops could so easily have intruded into our state only shows just how stupid and weak Duke Mu is, and what a bad lot his ministers and officials are. That also accounts for the callous indifference of the local people. Not a single soul offered resistance to the invaders. None except, perhaps, one Hao Zhi, who went only to the rescue of Mr Xiahou Yi. From this you can

see that the common people's eyes are discerning and they are clear about what to hate and what to love." After a pause, he bent forward to ask, "Why don't you stand up yet, Shen Qiang?"

"Let me be punished for my father's crime," insisted the other.

Mencius said, "No, your father committed no crime. For he could not but obey an order from his sovereign lord. He let his soldiers kill only those bad elements like Dongye Sixiao, but did not allow them to harm the common people. Such a commander is creditable. Far be it from me to blame him."

"But his soldiers killed my good friend Gu Tu," cried Shen Qiang.

"That is a different case", said Mencius. "Gu Tu died a heroic death in defense of his state and people. His death was a glorious one. We will forever remember him."

Shen Qiang felt as if a great weight had been lifted from his mind as he clambered up slowly from the ground.

Mencius stood in the courtyard of his temporary lodging in the capital of Zou, from time to time looking out to see if there was any messenger from Duke Mu to summon him. There was none! His hopes for a change of heart in the duke evaporated, and he decided there and then to go home to resume his teaching job.

Three months elapsed. One day, while he was in his study reviewing his boyhood scribbling on bamboo slips, his son came in to announce that the crown prince of Teng had sent his grand tutor Ran You to visit him.

Mencius responded with great delight: "Invite him in, please!"

Ran You, in his mid-50s, tall and with a longish face, approached Mencius with a debonair air. He conveyed his Master's regards to Mencius and then informed the latter of the recent death of the ruler of Teng.

"The crown prince told me that he had never been able to forget your profound instructions in Song", said the visitor. "He sent me here to ask your advice before making funeral arrangements."

"Please accept my condolences," said Mencius. "The funeral of a parent is an occasion for the giving of one's utmost. Zeng Zi said, 'Serve your parents in accordance with the rites during their lifetime; bury them in accordance with the rites when they die; offer sacrifices to them in accordance with the rites; and you deserve to be called a good son.' I am afraid I am not conversant with the rites observed by the feudal lords. Still, I have heard something about funeral rites."

Ran You earnestly requested to hear more about this, and Mencius continued, "Three years as the mourning period, mourning dress made of rough hemp with a hem, the eating of nothing but rice gruel —these stipulations were observed in the three dynasties of Xia, Shang and Zhou by men of all conditions alike, from emperor to commoner."

Before Ran You left Mencius had Teng Geng brought in and told him of his elder brother's death. He then sent him along with Ran back to Teng for the funeral.

Ran You's visit left Mencius favorably impressed with the crown prince of Teng as being a modest and sensible man.

One day while Mencius was engaged in gardening in his school orchard, Gongdu Zi came up to ask: "When Teng Geng was studying under you he appeared to deserve your courtesy. Yet you never answered his questions. Why was that?"

Mencius said: "It is my way to treat all my disciples on an equal footing. I could not possibly regard him with special respect just because he is the younger brother of the reigning prince of Teng."

Gongdu Zi enquired again: "I found sometimes that when Teng Geng asked you questions, you didn't seem to show patience enough. Why was that?"

Mencius said, "I never answer any questioner who relies on the advantage he possesses of position, capability, age, merit or status as an old friend. A gentleman teaches in five ways. The first is by a transforming influence like that of timely rain. The second is by helping the student to realize his virtue to the full. The third is by helping to develop his talent. The fourth is by answering his questions in every way you can. And the fifth is by setting an example that others not in contact with him can emulate."

"How is it that the selfsame teacher can turn out students who are wide apart?"

Mencius patted a Chinese juniper as he replied: "A carpenter or a carriage-maker may give a man his tools, but he cannot make him skillful in the use of them."

His son Zhong Zi slipped quietly to his side and told him that the grand tutor of Teng had turned up again.

The two met like old friends after a long separation and hand in hand went into the study.

Ran You opened the conversation with, "When I went back and reported your instructions to the crown prince, it was proposed to observe the three-year mourning period. But all the officials were opposed to this. The crown prince could not make up his mind, so he sent me here again for your advice."

"I see", said Mencius. "Confucius said, 'When the ruler dies the heir entrusts his affairs to the prime minister and sips rice gruel, with a somber face. He then takes his place and weeps, and none of his numerous officials dare show a lack of grief. This is because he sets the example. When someone above shows a preference for anything, there is certain to be someone who will outdo him. The gentleman's virtue is like the wind; the virtue of the common people is like the grass. Let the wind sweep over the grass, and the grass is sure to bend.' The solution to this matter rests with the crown prince and no other."

When later Ran You reported on his mission to the crown prince, the latter said, "That is so. It does, indeed, rest with me."

And so, for five months the crown prince stayed in his mourning hut, issuing no orders or prohibitions. The officials and his kinsmen approved of his conduct and thought him well-versed in the rites. When it was time for the burial ceremony, people came from all over the state. The crown prince displayed such a grief-stricken countenance and wept so bitterly that the mourners were greatly delighted. From then on the crown prince began to regard Mencius with keen admiration and often sent to ask advice from him.

One day in the early spring of 325 B.C., when warm sunshine from an unbroken azure sky shone on the verdure of Mount Yishan, Mencius was standing in the school courtyard, a look of ineffable sadness on his face. Now he contemplated the new shoots of the trees, now he fondled the beard hanging down to his breast. Every springtime brings a new lease of life to grass and plants, but we human beings can be young only once, he reflected sadly. He felt more sad at the thought that he could find no way to practice benevolent government and bring peace and order to the empire.

Suddenly his disciple Shen Qiang ran up to report: "Master, good news for you! I've just heard that Duke Ping of Lu has offered Yuezheng Ke a post in his government. In fact I got the news from my father."

This so elated Mencius that he could not sleep all that night.

The next morning Gongsun Chou came over for confirmation of the news.

"This is true. I was so excited I didn't get to sleep the whole night."

Gongsun Chou asked, "Has Yuezheng Ke great strength of character?"

"Not particularly."

"Is he a man of thought and foresight?"

"No."

"Is he widely informed?"

"Nor that, either."

"Then why were you so happy that you could not sleep?"

"He is a man who is drawn to the good."

"But is that enough to cope with affairs of state?"

Mencius explained, "To be drawn to the good is more than enough to cope with the empire, let alone the State of Lu. If a man is truly drawn to the good, then, within the Four Seas men will come, thinking nothing of the distance of a thousand *li*, to bring to his notice what is good. On the other hand, if he is not drawn to the good, then men will say of him: 'He seems to say "I know it all".' The way one says 'I know it all' with its accompanying look of complacency will repel men a thousand *li*. If gentlemen stay a thousand *li* away, then the flatterers will arrive. Can one succeed in one's wish to govern a state properly when one is surrounded by flatterers?"

Sure enough, three days later, Duke Ping of Lu had Yuezheng Ke appointed vice-minister.

Delighted at the appointment, Mencius led his disciples to Lu, staying, as ever, at the Jueli Inn. As a matter of course, he went to the Royal Ancestral Temple and Confucius Temple to offer sacrifices. He anticipated that Duke Ping would summon him.

On learning of Mencius' arrival, the duke had intended to invited him for an audience, as he said to his favorite Zang Cang one day: "Meng Ke is widely recognized as the present-day sage. I would like to meet with him and employ him as a high counselor to help me run state affairs. What do you think?"

Zang Cang rolled his beady eyes cunningly and said, "My Lord, would you say that Meng Ke knows anything about the rites?"

The duke answered, "I am amazed at you! How could a world-renowned sage not know the rites?"

Zang Cang smiled cryptically, then said, "If he knew the rites, why did he not stay in Zou, his homeland, to help Duke Mu of Zou with his administration?" As the duke made no reply, he went on, "Think of this, My Lord, a man who refuses to serve his country to which his father and mother belong—what can you expect of him? I'm only afraid, though, that he must harbor some evil design of his own."

Stunned, Duke Ping demanded: "What evil design? Out with it!"

Zang Cang rejoined, "Every effect has its cause. Does it not occur to you, My Lord, that over the past few years Mencius has been to Qi and Song? But never has he been to Lu for a special purpose. Now he has come here with a host of disciples. I fear it must be for the debts we owe him."

More bewildered than ever, Duke Ping queried stupidly: "The debts? You say I owe him debts?"

Zang Cang said, "Last summer, when General Shen launched that expedition of ours against Zou, our men killed 33 of its officials and officers. Mencius must have come to settle scores with us, I'm sure."

Shen Qiang informed Mencius of the above conversation.

At this, Mencius uttered a long sigh, saying, "When a man goes forward, there is something which urges him on. When he halts, there is something which holds him back. It is not in his power either to go forward or to halt. It is due to Heaven that I failed to meet the Duke of Lu. What can a mean fellow like Zang Cang do about it?"

Consequently Mencius abandoned his intention to see Duke Ping of Lu. Thereupon Sheng Qiang suggested, "Master, I hear that the crown Prince of Teng has succeeded to the throne. Why not go to Teng?"

Mencius' eyes lit up at this, and he decided to go to Teng the next day.

When Mencius and his disciples arrived, Teng Geng put them up at the Shang Gong guest-house, the best of its kind in Teng.

While waiting for a summon to an audience from Duke Wen of Teng, Mencius often joined his disciples in their forums on the Six Classic Arts. At one point, Wan Zhang raised the following theoretical problem:

"When you stayed in Song the year before last, Master, you thought fit not to take the initiative to see its reigning prince because he showed no initiative himself. But on the present occasion, considering that you and Duke Wen are already old friends, would it not be more polite on your part to take the initiative and pay him a visit?"

"No, it would not," replied Mencius.

"On what grounds may I ask?"

Mencius explained, "Those who live in the capital are known as 'subjects of the marketplace', while those who live on the outskirts are known as 'subjects in the wilds'. In both cases the reference is to commoners. According to the rites, a commoner does not dare present himself to a feudal lord unless he has handed in his token of allegiance."

Wan Zhang said, "When a commoner is summoned to perform corvee labor he goes to serve. Why then should he refuse to go when he is summened to an audience?"

Mencius replied, "It is right for him to go and serve, but it is not right for him to present himself. Moreover, for what reason does the prince wish to see him?"

Wan Zhang said, "Probably for the reason that he is well-informed or that he is good and wise."

"If it is for the reason that he is well-informed", countered Mencius, "even the emperor does not summon his teacher, let alone a feudal lord. If it is for the reason that he is a good and wise man, then I have never heard of summoning such a man when one wishes to see him. Duke Miao frequently went to see Zisi. 'How did kings of states with a thousand chariots in antiquity make friends with gentlemen?' he asked. Zisi was displeased. 'What the ancients talked about,' said he, 'was serving them, not making friends with them.'"

Wan Zhang then asked, "Is a prince ill-advised to make friends with gentlemen?"

"No", said Mencius. "It is advisable for a prince to be courteous and friendly toward good and wise people. The reason for Zisi's displeasure was this:'In point of position, you are the prince and I am your subject. How dare I be friends with you? In point of virtue, it is you who ought to serve me. How can you presume to be friends with me?' If the ruler of a state with a thousand chariots cannot even hope to be friends with him, how much less can he hope to summon such a man."

Wan Zhang again asked, "Confucius, when summoned by a prince, did not wait for the carriage to be harnessed. In that case was Confucius wrong in what he did?"

"Again, no," said Mencius. "Confucius was in office at that time, and he had specific duties to do, and he was summoned in his official capacity."

His disciple continued his queries: "As things stand, it is rather difficult for a prince to want to meet with a man of virtue, isn't it?"

"Not so difficult as you think", was Mencius' reply. "Just by clinging to the rites and set rules he will have managed it." After a pause, he added, "To wish to meet a good and wise man while not following the proper way is like wishing him to enter while shutting the door against him. Rightness is the road and the rites are the door. Only a gentleman can follow this road and go in and out through this door. The *Book of Songs* says, 'The highway is like a grindstone. Its straightness is like an arrow. It is walked on by the gentleman and looked up to by the small man.'"

Wan Zhang gave a light cough, then made as if he was going to speak up, but stopped abruptly.

Mencius gave him a brief glance. "If you have anything to say, say it," he encouraged the young man.

Wan Zhang still hesitated.

"Well, if you have something on your mind which it would be awkward to disclose, you are welcome to keep it to yourself," said Mencius.

At last Wan Zhang stammered, "Sir, somehow I find you are a little too proud in your approach to any prince you meet, if I may say so."

Mencius said, looking unusually grave: "When giving counsel to the high and mighty it is necessary to look upon them with contempt and not to be awed by their pomp and circumstance. Their halls are lofty, with eaves projecting several feet. Were I to meet with success, I would not indulge in such things. Their tables, laden with food, measure ten feet across, and their female attendants are counted in the hundreds. Were I to meet with success, I would not indulge in such things. They spend their time drinking, driving and hunting, with a retinue of a thousand chariots. Were I to meet with success, I would not indulge in such things. All the things the present rulers do I would not do, and everything I do is in accordance with ancient institutions. Why, then, should I cower before them?"

Wan Zhang said: "With your talents and virtue, sir, you ought to have occupied some important position in the government with abundant emoluments, to the benefit both of your family and state. The reason for your failure to achieve that, I am afraid, is just that you tend to despise the rulers, and so they fight shy of you. Is not this something to be regretted?"

Mencius said with a sigh: "All men share the same desire to be exalted. But, as a matter of fact, every man has in him that which is exalted. The fact rarely dawns on him. What man exalts is not truly exalted. Those Zhao Meng exalts Zhao Meng can also humble. The *Book of Songs* says, 'He has filled us with wine, he has satiated us with his goodness.' The point is that, being filled with moral virtue, one does not envy other people's enjoyment of fine food. And, enjoying a fine and extensive reputation, one does not envy other people's fineries."

Wan Zhang said, "To my mind, sir, if you were appointed a high minister you would be placed in a position of strength to promote your cause of humanity and justice."

"What more do I want for? All the ten thousand things are there in me!" Mencius said with confidence. "There is no greater joy for me than to find, on self-examination, that I am true to myself. Do your best to treat others as you would wish to be treated yourself, and you will find that this is the shortest way to benevolence."

"But sir, if you hold yourself so aloof from worldly considerations, who is there in the world to seek your friendship?"

"Things of a kind come together, people of a mind fall into the same group. The best gentleman of a village is in a position to make friends with the best gentlemen in other villages; the best gentleman in a state, with the best gentlemen in other states; and the best gentleman in the empire, with the other leading gentlemen in the empire. And not content with making friends with them, he goes back in time and communes with the ancients. When one reads the poems and writings of the ancients, can it be right not to know something about them as men? Hence one tries to understand the age in which they lived. This can be described as 'looking for friends in history'. As a matter of fact, there are a lot of people I can call my friends. What do I care if a handful of feudal lords do not grant me audiences?"

Chapter Thirty-Seven

Duke Wen of Teng Pays Mencius a Visit and
Asks About Ways of Government;
Bi Zhan Consults the Master About the Nine-Squares
System of Dividing the Land

As Mencius was busily engaged in a conversation with his disciple Wan Zhang in the Shanggong guesthouse a brilliant equipage halted at the gate, and Duke Wen of Teng himself, the very man Mencius had eagerly been expecting, stepped out. As can be imagined, the mere sight of his old friend exhilarated Mencius so much that he went across the yard at a run to welcome him.

The greetings over, Duke Wen expressed his thanks for Mencius' former instructions about the funeral arrangements for the late duke. "The funeral," said he, "turned out to be a great success, to the contentment of all. Had it not been for your help, we would not have achieved such satisfactory results."

Mencius demurred, "The credit must go to you, my lord. Not me."

The duke's face registered mild surprise as he queried, "Why do you say that, sir? It was only according to your instructions that I performed the funeral rites as I did."

Mencius said, "The subject proposes and the ruler disposes."

As Duke Wen listened with rapt attention, Mencius went on expounding, "One could not produce planes and straight lines without the level and the plumb-line; nor could one draw squares or circles without a carpenter's square or a pair of compasses. Everybody knows that. However, when it comes to the question of benevolence and righteousness, some people ignore the general rule. These two virtues are just like the carpenter's square or compasses. If one applies them, the empire can be made to go round in one's palm. The fact that My Lord made the funeral a success simply shows that he not only knows the rites but also applies them."

The duke mused a while, with a furrowed brow, and then enquired again: "As you know, sir, Teng is a small state, wedged between Qi and Chu, both of which are mighty powers. Should I be

subservient to Qi or should I be subservient to Chu?"

Mencius shook his head before saying, "This is a question that is beyond me, I am afraid. But if you insist, I would say that there is only one course of action I can suggest and that is, dig deeper moats and build higher walls, and defend them shoulder to shoulder with the people. If they would rather die than desert you, then all is not lost."

"I find your discourse clear and logical. I will do my best to adopt your ideas."

With that, he rose and left.

After seeing the duke off, Mencius went back to his room, and just as he was about to pick up something to read there rushed in his son Zhongzi with the bad news that his grandfather Gongsun had been taken seriously ill. By the time Mencius reached the sick-bed, Gongsun Benzheng had lapsed into a coma and Mencius had to call loud and long before he slowly opened his eyes. On seeing Mencius he smiled weakly, and summoning the last iota of strength that remained to him, he mumbled, "After my death, please bury me at the foot of Nine-Dragon Mountain..." He then passed away.

Gongsun Benzheng's remains were later interred on the south side of Nine-Dragon Mountain in accordance with his dying wish.

Another day, Duke Wen of Teng made a second visit to Mencius. He told Mencius that the state of Qi was going to fortify Xue, evidently with a design on the territory of Teng. "I am greatly disturbed," said Duke Wen. "What is the best thing for me to do?"

Mencius said, "Draw your lesson from the past. In antiquity when Tai Wang was in Bin, the Di tribes invaded. He tried to buy them off with hides and silks; he tried to buy them off with horses and hounds; he tried to buy them off with pearls and jade; but all to no avail. Then he assembled the elders and announced to them:'What the Di tribes want is our land. I have heard that a man in authority never turns what is meant for the benefit of men into a source of harm to them. It will not be difficult for you, my friends, to find another lord. I am leaving.' And he left Bin, crossed the Liang Mountains, built a city at the foot of Mount Ji and settled there. The men of Bin said, 'This is a benevolent man. We must not lose him.' Then they flocked after him as if to market."

Duke Wen shook his head, looking dubious.

Mencius went on, "Yet there were others who rejected the idea of leaving their homeland. They said, 'Why must we leave the land which our ancestors handed down to us from one generation to another. No! We cannot. We would sooner die than leave.'"

Duke Wen said, "They did right. I share their sentiments."

Mencius commented, "Tai Wang did that, not out of choice but because he had no alternative. If a man does good deeds, then amongst his descendants there will rise one who will become a true ruler. All a gentleman can do in starting an enterprise is to leave behind a tradition which can be carried on."

Duke Wen's expression softened.

Mencius added, "As for whether or not one can succeed in the end after all, it depends on Heaven's will."

Duke Wen asked, "How am I to cope with Qi?"

Mencius replied, "There is no other way but by practicing benevolent government in Teng."

From then on Duke Wen, acting on Mencius' advice, applied himself to governing his state in the spirit of benevolence. He encouraged agriculture and weaving, and lessened corvee. It took him little time to restore peace and order to the whole state. He was immensely happy, and in gratitude he would often made Mencius rich gifts of gold and silver.

The summer of 324 B.C. bid fair for a bumper harvest for Teng, with its long spells of fine weather. All over the mountains and plains was an endless stretch of green plantation. There was hope in everybody's heart. And it was in such a cheery state of mind that Duke Wen presented himself to Mencius one day.

"Esteemed sir," began the duke as soon as he was seated, "Heaven has been good to me since I began to practice benevolent government on your advice. Today I would wish you to talk more about the way of government. May I have the pleasure?"

"Splendid!" Mencius could hardly contain himself for joy.

Duke Wen asked, "What is the best way to govern a state?"

Mencius said, "For a ruler of a state, there are a thousand and one things to be done. Work should be done in order of importance and urgency."

"But as far as Teng is concerned, what is the most important and urgent task for me to tackle?" asked the duke.

Mencius replied, "The business of the people must be attended to without delay." He picked up a bundle of bamboo strips on which was inscribed the *Book of Songs*, unrolled them and, indicating the characters on them, said, "Here is the poem I have in mind which may explain my meaning: 'In the day time they go for grass; /At night they make it into ropes. /They hasten to repair the roof; /Then they begin sowing the crops.' This is the way of the common people. Those with constant means of support will have constant hearts, while those without constant means of support will not have constant hearts. Lacking constant hearts, they will go astray and plunge into excess, stopping at nothing."

The duke winced at the picture and his countenance registered disquiet.

Mencius looked at his listener steadily, then continued, "To punish them after they have fallen foul of the law is to set a trap for the people. How can a benevolent man in authority allow himself to set a trap for his people?"

The duke breathed a sigh of relief and relaxed into a posture of ease.

"Hence," Mencius went on, "a good ruler is always respectful and thrifty, courteous and humble, and takes from the people no more than is prescribed. And what is most important, the levying of taxes must be carried out strictly according to prescribed rates. Tax rates should not be too high and are not to be subjected to erratic changes."

Duke Wen asked, "What should be the proper rates of tax, do you think?"

Mencius replied, "In the Xia Dynasty each family was given 50 *mu* of land, and the '*gong*' method of taxation was used; in the Yin Dynasty each family was given 70 *mu* and the '*zu*' method was used; in the Zhou Dynasty each family was given 100 *mu* and the '*che*' method was used. In fact, all three amounted to a taxation of one in ten. '*Che*' means 'commonly practiced'; '*zhu*' means 'to lend help'. A good and wise man of old by the name of Long Zi said, 'In regulating land, there is no better method than the *zhu* one, and no worse than the *gong* method. With the *gong* method, the payment due is calculated on the average yield over a number of years. In good years, when rice is so plentiful that it goes to waste, the people are no more heavily taxed, though this would mean no hardship. But in bad years, when there is not enough to spare for fertilizing the fields, the full quota is insisted upon. If he who is father and mother to the people makes it necessary for them to borrow because they do not get enough to minister to the needs of their parents, in spite of having toiled incessantly all the year round, he causes the old and young to be abandoned in the gutter, wherein is he father and mother to the people? The *Book of Songs* says, 'May the rain come down on our public field, and then upon our private field.' It is only in the *zhu* method that there is a public field. From this we see that even the Zhou Dynasty practiced the *zhu* method. So Teng should do the same."

Duke Wen asked, "If I practice benevolent government by treating the common people as my children and consequently the common people regard me as their parent, what remains to be done then?"

Mencius explained, "When the common people are able to lead a life of plenty it is necessary to provide them with an opportunity for good education. Here schools like *xiang, xu, xue*, and *xiao* come in useful. *Xiang* means rearing, *xiao* means teaching and *xu* means archery. In the Xia Dynasty, it was called *xiao*, in the Yin *xu* and in the Zhou *xiang*, while *xue* was a name common to all three dynasties. They all serve to make the people understand human relationships. When it is clear that those in authority understand human relationships, the people will be affectionate. The *Book of Songs* says, 'Although Zhou was an old country, it took on a new lease of life.' This refers to King Wen." He let his eyes rest on the duke's face for a moment, then added, "Should a true ruler arise, he is certain to take this as his model. Thus he who practices this will be a tutor to a true ruler."

The autumn of that year saw a bumper harvest in Teng, and people vied with one another in paying their land tax. To celebrate the occasion, Duke Wen of Teng sponsored an excursion to the countryside to enjoy the autumn scenery, to which Mencius was especially invited.

That day Mencius was made to share a carriage with the duke, and they were driven to a scenic spot planted with pear trees. As they strolled around and looked near and far Duke Wen's eyes were caught by a solitary pear which peeped out from under a cluster of leaves. He could hardly resist the temptation of picking it. He weighed it in his right hand, then in his left, saying to Mencius as he did so: "When a thing is scarce, it is precious. In what way would you like me to dispose of this lovely pear, sir?"

Mencius replied, "Whichever way you think fit, my sovereign lord."

The duke then asked one of his attendants to cut the fruit into several pieces, of which he took one for himself, offered another to

Mencius and let the rest be shared among his attendants.

As Mencius received into his proffered hands the tiny bit of pear, he piously voiced his thanks. All the others followed suit.

After eating his portion, Mencius said to the duke: "I feel hopeful about the future of Teng." When the latter asked why, Mencius replied, "Your sharing of the small pear with others may be a trifle in itself but for me it was a gesture symbolic of a benevolent heart beating in your breast. With such a benevolent man as ruler, Teng bids fair to prosper." At this, the duke laughed out loud.

On their way back Duke Wen asked Mencius about the possibility of the nine-squares system of dividing the land being introduced in Teng. But before Mencius had time to say all he had to say, their carriage pulled up at the palace gate. At parting, Duke Wen told Mencius that he would send his official Bi Zhan over the following day to hear his opinion.

True to his word, the duke sent Bi Zhan over to the Shang Gong guesthouse the next morning.

Bi Zhan said to Mencius: "My sovereign lord wishes to promote his project of benevolent government. He has sent me here to seek your instructions about the nine-squares land-division system. I hope you will have the kindness to enlighten me, sir."

"Splendid!" Mencius began with verve. "Benevolent government must begin with land demarcation. When boundaries are not properly drawn the division of land into squares and the yield of grain used for paying officials cannot be equitable. For this reason, despotic rulers and corrupt officials always neglect boundaries. But once boundaries are correctly fixed there will be no difficulty in settling the distribution of land and the determination of emolument."

Bi Zhan asked, "How is land demarcation to be done?"

Mencius explained, "Teng is limited in territory. Nevertheless, there will be men in authority and there will be the common people. Without the former, there would be none to rule over the latter; without the latter, there would be none to support the former. As for rates of taxation, I would suggest that in the country the tax should be one in nine, using the *zhu* method, but in the city it should be one in ten, using the *gong* method. From ministers downwards, every official should have 50 *mu* of land for sacrificial purposes. In ordinary households every extra man is to be given another 25 *mu*. Neither in burying the dead nor in changing his abode does a man go beyond the confines of his village. If those who own land within each prescribed lot befriend one another both at home and abroad, help each other to keep watch, and succor each other in illness, they will live in love and harmony. A square *li* covers nine squares of land and each nine squares of land consists of 900 *mu*. Of these, the central plot of 100 *mu* belongs to the state, while the other eight plots of 100 *mu* each are held by eight families who share the duty of caring for the plot owned by the state. Only when they have done this duty dare they turn to their own affairs. This is what sets the common people apart. This is only a rough outline. As for embellishments, I leave them to your prince and yourself."

"Worthless as I am, I will certainly do as you say, sir," promised Bi Zhan.

He went back to report all this to the duke, who immediately appointed him to take charge of the land demarcation according to the nine-squares system. Bi Zhan summoned all the heads of the districts and told them about the advantages of the system and the specific measures of implementation, and after six months of busy work a new land division system had been completed throughout the country.

With the arrival of the Qingming Festival in the spring of 323 B.C., the common people of Teng were found working on their newly allotted squares of land. Then came the Grain Rain, the time for sowing the five grains.

Mencius took Teng Geng, Wan Zhang and Gongsun Chou with him on a tour of the countryside, wanting to see for himself how the new land system worked. As they drove along the country roads, blocks of fields marked off with boundary stones flitted past. The farmers were all working away in their fields.

Presently Mencius called "Halt!" to his driver, and he got down from his carriage and betook himself to a field where rice seedlings had been lately planted. As he gazed on them he suddenly broke into a hearty sigh of admiration, saying, "Admirable indeed is this ruler of Teng!"

Peng Geng said, "His new land reform indeed has won the hearts of the common people. From the way they work in their fields, I can realize their happiness."

Mencius commented, "Thanks to this new land system, the farmers will be saved from being exploited by corrupted officials, and the land tax will be levied on an equitable basis. And where there is equitable taxation, there is benevolent government."

It began to drizzle. Mencius looked up to the sky, which hung low and grey. "It look as if even the Lord of Heaven has been moved by the duke's good deed; we are in for a shower of spring rain which is timely for the growth of the spring crops," said he with good humor.

Back home that evening, Mencius was too excited to get to sleep. He envisioned to himself how much good Duke Wen's benevolent government might bring to his people and what an important part he himself was to play in the days to come....

But at daybreak the next morning he felt dizzy and weak. He was forced to stay in bed.

Chapter Thirty-Eight

Convinced by Mencius' Arguments, Chen Xiang
Abandons His Original Belief;
With the Courage of His Convictions, Mencius
Leads the Fight Against Foreign Invasion

On learning that Mencius was ill, Duke Wen of Teng came to see him, bringing his personal physician along. After feeling his pulse, the doctor diagnosed the illness as a slight cold. "It is nothing serious," he comforted Mencius. "Take the medicine I have prescribed and you will get well soon. You have got a sound constitution, sir, and believe me, you will live to a ripe old age." Mencius thanked him for his good wishes. And above all he thanked the duke for the trouble he had taken to see him despite the many claims on his time.

Sure enough, Mencius made a speedy recovery after taking the medicine and under the meticulous care of his disciples. However, this bout of illness also cast a deep shadow on his mind, as he looked into a mirror to find that oh, old age was already upon him—he was on the wrong side of seventy now! It was only then that he fully realized why Confucius remarked on the insidious creeping up of old age. It was books that had made him what he was, his temperament, his character and his idiosyncrasies.

Now that he was well his daily routine continued: reading and teaching. Almost with each passing day a new student came to him. The majority of his earlier graduates had for one reason or another left for home. He felt deeply hurt at the thought that no other student of his had obtained a position in government than Yuezheng Ke. Can this be Heaven's will? he asked himself bitterly.

One day Wan Zhang came to call, and when he found his teacher in low spirits he tried to engage him in conversation by raising a question: "What are the things that a gentleman delights in, sir?"

Mencius said, "A gentleman has three things in which he delights, and to be ruler over the empire is not among them."

"What is the first delight?"

"That his parents are alive and his brothers are well."

"What is the second delight?"

"That when looking up, he has no occasion for shame before Heaven, and below, he has no occasion to blush before men."

"And the third delight?"

"That he has the good fortune of having the most talented pupils in the empire."

Wan Zhang further asked, "Why do you say that to be ruler over the empire is not amongst the three delights?"

Mencius answered, "An extensive territory and a vast population are things a gentleman desires, but what he delights in lies elsewhere. To stand in the center of the Empire and bring peace to the people within the Four Seas is what a gentleman delights in, but that which he follows as his nature lies elsewhere. That which a gentleman follows as his nature is not added to when he holds sway over the empire, nor is it detracted from when he is reduced to straitened circumstances. This is because he knows his allotted station. That which a gentleman follows as his nature, that is to say, benevolence, righteousness, the rites and wisdom, is rooted in his heart and manifests itself in his face, giving it a sleek appearance. It also shows in his back and extends to his limbs, rendering their message intelligible without words."

Let us come back to Duke Wen of Teng. As a result of his land reform, that is, his introduction of the nine-squares system of dividing the land, the people of Teng looked up to him as their Sage King. His fame as a good and wise reigning prince spread far and wide. Many people from the adjoining states came to him for shelter.

There was a man by the name of Xu Xing who preached the teachings of Shen Nong*. His followers, numbering several score, all wore unwoven hemp, and lived by making sandals and mats. He came to Teng from Chu, had an audience with Duke Wen and told him: "I, a man from distant parts, have heard that you, My Lord, practice benevolent government. I wish to be given a place to live and become one of your subjects." The duke thereupon gave him a house and provided him with food.

There were also Chen Xiang and his brother Xin, both followers of Chen Liang. They came to Teng from Song, carrying plows on their backs. "We have heard," said they to Duke Wen, "that you, My Lord,

* A legendary emperor credited with the invention of agriculture.

practice the government of the sages. In that case you must yourself be a sage. We wish to be the subjects of a sage." Duke Wen granted their request and supplied them with board and lodging. Thence the brothers settled down in Teng. One day they paid a visit to Xu Xing, a man of character whom they regarded with respect. The three felt like old friends after an exchange of views, and both brothers venerated Xu Xing as their mentor. Then Chen Xiang asked, "Esteemed sir! Do you think Duke Wen of Teng a truly good and wise ruler?"

"I think so," replied Xu Xing. "Though he has never been taught the Way."

"Why do you say so, sir?" questioned Chen Xiang, not without some surprise.

Xu Xing took his time as he answered the question. "To earn his keep a good and wise ruler shares the work of tilling the land with his people. He rules while cooking his own meals. Now Teng has granaries and treasuries. This means the prince inflicts hardship on the people in order to keep himself in comfort. How can he be a good and wise prince?"

When later he managed a meeting with Mencius, Chen Xiang repeated Xu's words to the latter, who put on an indulgent smile, saying, "Seeking no help whatsoever from others—this may be Xu Xing's credo, I suppose."

Chen Xiang replied, "That's it, I think."

"But it won't do!" said Mencius with a resolute air. "Then why did he think it necessary to seek lodging from the duke?"

Chen Xiang was at a loss for words.

Mencius asked, "Does Xu Xing only eat grain he has grown himself?"

"Yes," said Chen Xiang.

"Does Xu Xing only wear cloth he has woven himself?"

"No, He wears unwoven hemp."

"Does Xu Xing wear a cap?"

"Yes."

"What kind of cap does he wear?"

"One of plain raw silk."

"Does he weave it himself?"

"No. He trades grain for it."

"Why does Xu Xing not weave it himself?"

"Because that would interfere with his work in the fields."

"Does Xu Xing use an iron pot and an earthenware steamer for cooking rice and iron implements for ploughing the fields?"

"Yes."

"Does he make them himself?"

"No. He trades grain for them."

Mencius pursued with insistency: "To trade grain for implements is not to inflict hardship on the potter and the blacksmith. The potter and the blacksmith, for their part, also trade their wares for grain. In doing this, surely they are not inflicting hardship on the farmer either. Why does Xu Xing not be a potter and a blacksmith as well, so that he can get everything he needs from his own house? Why does he indulge in such multifarious trading with men who practice the hundred crafts? Why does Xu Xing put up with so much bother?"

Chen Xiang replied, "But surely it would be impossible to combine the work of tilling the land with that of the hundred crafts!"

Mencius took him up on this with: "Now, is ruling the empire such an exception that it can be combined with the work of tilling the land?" (Chen Xiang listened quietly.) "So, you see, there is the necessity of division of labor. There are affairs of great men, and there are affairs of small men. Moreover, it is necessary for each man to use the products of all the hundred crafts. If everyone had to make everything he used the empire would be led along the path of incessant toil. Hence it is said, 'There are those who use their minds and there are those who use their muscles. The former rule; the latter are ruled. Those who rule are supported by those who are ruled.' This is a principle accepted by the whole empire."

Chen Xiang appeared somewhat self-conscious.

Mencius continued eloquently: "In the time of Yao the empire was not settled. The Flood still raged unchecked, inundating the land. Plants grew rank; birds and beasts multiplied; the five grains did not ripen; birds and beasts encroached upon men, and their trails crisscrossed even the Middle Kingdom. The lot fell on Yao to worry about this situation. He raised Shun to a position of authority to deal with it. Shun put Bo Yi in charge of fire. Bo Yi set the mountains and valleys alight and scorched them, and the birds and beasts went into hiding. Yu dredged the Nine Rivers, cleared the courses of the Ji and the Ta to channel the water into the sea, deepened the beds of the Ru and the Han, and raised the dykes of the Huai and the Si to empty them into the Yellow River. Only then were the people of the Middle

Kingdom able to find food for themselves. During this time Yu spent eight years away from home and passed the door of his house three times without entering. Even if he had wished to plow the fields, could he have done it?"

Chen Xiang began to feel uneasy.

Mencius continued, "Hou Ji taught the people how to cultivate land and grow the five kinds of grain. When these ripened, the people multiplied. This is the way of the common people: Once they have full bellies and warm clothes on their backs they degenerate to the level of animals if they are allowed to lead idle lives without education and discipline. This gave the Sage King further cause for concern, and so he appointed Xie as the minister of education, whose duty was to teach the people human relationships: love between father and son, duty between ruler and subject, distinction between husband and wife, precedence of the old over the young and faith between friends. Yao, therefore, said, 'Encourage them in their toil, put them on the right path, aid them and help them, make them happy in their stations, and by bountiful acts further relieve them of hardship. As the Sage King worried to this extent about the affairs of the people, how could he have leisure to plow the fields?"

Chen Xiang became more uneasy.

Mencius had not finished his exposition yet. "Yao's only worry was that he should fail to find someone like Shun, and Shun's only worry was that he should fail to find someone like Yu and Gao Yao. He who worries about his plot of 100 *mu* not being well cultivated is a mere farmer. To share one's wealth with others is generosity. To teach others to be good is conscientiousness. To find the right man for the empire is benevolence. Hence it is easier to give the empire away than to find the right man to rule it. Confucius said, 'Great indeed was Yao as a ruler! Heaven alone is great, and it was Yao who modeled himself on Heaven. So great was he that the people could not find a name for him. What a ruler Shun was! He was so lofty that while in possession of the empire he held aloof from it.' It is not true that Yao and Shun did not have to use their minds to rule the empire. Only they did not use their minds to plow the fields."

By this time Chen Xiang was looking greatly agitated.

Mencius continued,"I have heard of the Chinese converting barbarians to their ways, but not of their being converted to barbarian ways. Chen Liang was a native of Chu. Being delighted with the way of the Duke of Zhou and Confucius, he came north to study in the Middle Kingdom. Even the scholars in the north could not surpass him in any way. He was what one would call an outstanding scholar. You and your brother studied under him for scores of years, and now that your teacher is dead you turn your back on him. When Confucius died and the three-year mourning period had come to an end his disciples packed their bags and prepared to go home. They went in and bowed to Zigong and then, facing one another, they wept until they lost their voices before setting out for home. Zigong went back to build a hut in the cemetery and remained there on his own for another three years before going home. One day, Zixia, Zizhang and Ziyou wanted to serve You-ruo as they had served Confucius because of his resemblance to the Sage. They tried to force Zeng Zi to join them, but Zeng Zi said, 'That will not do. Washed by the Yellow and Han rivers, bleached by the autumn sun, so immaculate was he that his whiteness could not be surpassed. Now you turn your back on the way of your teacher in order to follow the southern barbarian with the twittering tongue, who condemns the way of the former kings. You are indeed different from Zeng Zi. I have heard of coming out of the dark ravine to settle on a tall tree, but not of forsaking the tall tree to descend into the dark ravine. The *Odes of Lu* says, 'It was the barbarians that he attacked; it was Jing and Su that he punished.' It is these people the Duke of Zhou was going to punish and you want to learn from. That is not a change for the better, is it?"

Chen said, trying to defend his position: "If we follow the way of Xu Xing there will only be one price in the market, and dishonesty will disappear from it. Even if you send a mere boy to the market, no one will take advantage of him. For equal lengths of cloth or silk, for equal weights of hemp, flax or raw silk, and for equal measures of the five grains, the price will be the same; for shoes of the same size, the price will also be the same."

"But you are forgetting one basic fact," said Mencius, "and that is that things are unequal in value. And different values entail different prices, a fact which is universally recognized. Some are worth twice or five times, even a thousand and ten thousand times, more than others. If you reduce them to the same level it will only bring confusion to the empire. If a roughly finished shoe sells at the same price as a finely finished one, who would make the latter? If we follow the way of Xu Xing, we will be showing one another the way to being dishonest. How can one govern a state in this way?"

Chen Xiang was left without an argument and finally took his leave in discomfiture.

Going out, Mencius found Gongdu Zi standing quietly by the door. When he enquired the reason, Gongdu Zi said, "Excuse me, sir. I was just going to ask you a question when I saw you had a guest. So I had to wait."

"Now, what is your question?" asked Mencius.

Gongdu Zi said, "Outsiders all say that you, sir, are fond of disputation. May I ask why?"

"It is not that I am fond of disputation", said Mencius, "but that I have no alternative. In other words, I am forced into it. I will tell you why. The world has existed for a long time, now in peace, now in disorder. In the time of Yao the water reversed its natural course, flooding the central regions, and the reptiles made their homes there, depriving the people of a settled life. In low-lying regions people lived in nests; in high regions, they lived in caves. The *Book of History* says, 'The Great Flood was a warning to us.' Yu was entrusted with the task of controlling the Flood. He led the flood water into the seas by cutting channels for it in the ground, and drove the reptiles into grassy marshes. The water, flowing through the channels, formed the Yangtze, Huai, Yellow and Han rivers. Obstacles receded and the birds and beasts harmful to men were annihilated. Only then were the people able to level the ground and live on it.

"After the deaths of Yao and Shun, the way of the Sages declined and tyrants arose one after another. They pulled down houses in order to make ponds, and the people had nowhere to rest. They turned fields into parks, depriving the people of their livelihood. Moreover, heresies and violence arose. With the multiplication of parks, ponds and lakes, arrived birds and beasts. By the time of the tyrant Zhou, the Empire was again in great disorder. The Duke of Zhou helped King Wu to punish the tyrant Zhou. He waged war on Yan for three years and punished its ruler; he drove Feilian to a corner by the sea and slew him. He annexed 50 states. He drove tigers, leopards, rhinoceroses and elephants to the distant wilds, and the empire rejoiced. The *Book of History* says, 'Lofty indeed were the plans of King Wen! Great indeed were the achievements of King Wu! Bless us and enlighten us, your descendants, so that we may act correctly and not fall into error." Mencius sighed and went on, "But good times did not last long and soon heresies and violence broke loose again when the world declined and the Way fell into obscurity. There were instances of regicides and parricides. Confucius was apprehensive and he..."

Gongdu Zi cut in: "He composed the *Spring and Autumn Annals*."

Mencius said, "Yes, he composed the *Spring and Autumn Annals*. Strictly speaking, this is the Emperor's prerogative. That is why Confucius said, 'Those who understand me will do so through the *Annals*; those who condemn me will also do so because of the *Annals*.'"

"Why should people condemn a sage like Confucius?" asked Gongdu Zi.

Mencius explained, "Ever since human society came into existence there have been two types of people: those who are loyal and virtuous, and those who are crafty and adulatory. The former are open-minded, with a clear idea of right and wrong, while the latter are given to caballing, excluding all who hold different views from themselves. Confucius painted a truthful picture of his times in his book. He praised what should be praised and condemned what should be condemned in no ambiguous terms."

Gongdu Zi said, "What he wrote in his *Annals* all belongs to history. Why should his descendants condemn him?"

Mencius replied, "Although the events and persons he wrote about are things of the past, yet they can hold, as it were, a mirror up to the present, to show some people their ugly features. People of that ilk naturally resent it."

"In that case, how should a gentleman look upon the *Annals*?" queried the other.

"One should write history in the same manner," Mencius said with passion, "to record what actually happened. That is all."

"The pity is," he grew pensive as he went on, "the world is falling into decay, and principles make no appeal. And no sage kings have appeared since then. Feudal lords do as they please; people with no official position are uninhibited in the expression of their views, and the words of Yang Zhu and Mo Di fill the empire. The teachings current in the empire are those of either the school of Yang or the school of Mo. Yang advocates everyone for himself, which amounts to a denial of one's prince; Mo advocates love without discrimination, which amounts to a denial of one's father. To ignore one's father on the one hand and one's prince on the other is to be no different from the beasts. Gongming Yi said, 'There is fat meat in your kitchen and there are well-fed horses in your stables, yet the people look hungry and in the outskirts of cities men drop dead from starvation. This is to show animals the way to devour men.' If the way of Yang and Mo does not subside and the way of Confucius is not proclaimed, the people will be deceived by heresies and the path of morality will be blocked. When the path of morality is blocked, then we show animals the way to devour men, and sooner or later it will come to men devouring men. Therefore, I am apprehensive."

"Now I understand," said Gongdu Zi. "You take up the cudgels to safeguard the way of the former sages against the onslaughts of Yang and Mo and to banish excessive views so that the public may not be led astray. Am I right?"

"Right!" said Mencius. "I, too, wish to follow in the footsteps of the three sages in rectifying the hearts of men, laying heresies to rest, opposing extreme action and banishing excessive views. I am not fond of disputation. I have no alternative."

The son of King Wei of Chu, Xiong Huai by name, succeeded his father in the year 328 B.C. Violent by nature, he is notorious in history for his pugnacity. From the day he ascended the throne, King Huai —for that is what he was called—came under the influence of his fawning subordinates, believing everything he was told and persecuting those who were truly loyal and good to him. As a result, his court was plunged into decline and he himself became increasingly isolated.

Tian Ji, the one-time high minister and grand marshal of Qi, had been enfeoffed in Jiangnan some time after he had escaped to Chu to seek political asylum with King Wei. Now with King Huai on the throne, he found his position precarious as he knew the latter had long been plotting against him, so he returned to Qi as soon as he learned of the death of Zou Ji.

As already mentioned, King Huai was a belligerent ruler. Now that he saw that his neighbor, Teng, was growing strong and prosperous through the practice of benevolent government, he wanted to pull out this thorn in his side.

In the winter of 321 B.C., he had his commander-in-chief, Wu Xiao, lead an attack on Teng. The aggressive forces, with 300 chariots, broke through one pass after another, smashing all resistance as they advanced until they approached the capital of Teng.

Duke Wen was alarmed and he at once sought Mencius out for consultation.

Mencius asked, "Just how many chariots are there in the capital?"

"No more than 100," came the reply.

"That is enough for my purpose," said Mencius.

Duke Wen was puzzled: "But that is only one third the number Chu's" he protested. Mencius advised, "Let each gate of the city be guarded by 25 chariots. Raise all the draw bridges and shut the gates tight. I will go and negotiate with them in person. I will try and talk them into reason. If this fails, I will lead my students to fight shoulder to shoulder with the Teng soldiers and civilians against the invaders. The city will stay secure."

The duke lost no time ordering Bi Zhan to see to the defenses. Meanwhile Mencius had all his students gathered together, and addressed them thus: "Chu has sent its troops without justification. This is a downright invasion. We cannot just stand by. We must join the Teng people to repulse the invaders. Victory is the due of the Teng people!"

The students, filled with righteous indignation, cried as one man: "Victory is the due of the Teng people!"

Then Mencius assigned combat duties to each of his students. Xu Bi was to guard the south gate, Xianqiu Meng, the north gate, Chong Yu, the east gate, and so on. He entrusted Shen Qiang with the particular task of safeguarding Duke Teng. All the rest, he further instructed, were to join the common people of Teng and help defend the city. He himself made his way straight to the west city gate, taking Chen Zhen and Chen Dai with him.

At this time, the tops of the walls which surrounded the city were already crowded with angry people, some with bows and arrows, others with swords and spears, all in full battle array, standing ready for the approaching invaders.

As the city gate opened and the drawbridge was lowered at his order, Mencius followed by Gongdu Zi, sallied forth. They walked straight to the Chu army, which had halted about 400 paces away.

Chapter Thirty-Nine

Helping a Tyrant to Do Evil, Wu Xiao Fights for a Lost Cause; Counting on Three Favorable Conditions, Mencius Helps the Weak Against the Strong

As was related in the previous chapter, Mencius, with Gongdu Zi, strode forward fearlessly toward the Chu army. A standard fluttering in the wind with the big character "Wu" on it first met his eyes. The Chu soldiers stared aghast at the two strangers as they drew nearer and nearer. When they reached within 50 paces of the lead chariot, the commander, Wu Xiao, sprang up abruptly, brandishing his sword to them as he shouted, "Who are you?"

Mencius looked him over and found him to be a man of medium height, broad shouldered, and solidly built. He had bushy eyebrows, prominent eyes and on both cheeks bristled thick whiskers. He had a thick-lipped mouth, too. All this bespoke a combat-worthy general.

"Halt right there!" He made a savage cut in the air with his sword, describing an arc. "If you don't I'll order my archers to shoot."

"Ha, ha,..." Mencius guffawed. "My dear general, what's the meaning of all this swashbuckling? Why, there are only two of us, I and my disciple here, while you have the full strength of 300 chariots and 900 troops at your command. Are we so terrible as to strike terror into your heart?"

Mencius added contemptuously: "This only shows that you are outwardly strong and inwardly weak."

Shamed-faced, Wu Xiao gave the order for his soldiers to lower their bows and arrows.

Mencius stepped forward and raised his clasped hands in greeting: "I suppose you are General Wu Xiao? May I ask why you have come all this way with this formidable host?"

Wu Xiao pointed his sword to the city, saying: "I have orders from my sovereign lord to subjugate Teng."

"Upon what pretext?" Mencius demanded.

Wu Xiao stammered, "I'm a soldier. My only duty is to obey.

Whichever state my sovereign lord orders me to attack, I attack. That's all."

Mencius said, "Duke Wen of Teng practices benevolent government; that's how he turns his state into a prosperous one. And now you want to subdue it through force of arms! You are fighting for a lost cause. How can you hope to win?"

Wu Xiao broke into a boisterous laugh, and said, "Since I became a general, I have never lost a battle. How can a small state like Teng, with no more than 100 chariots, hold out against my well-trained and powerful army?" He seemed puzzled for a moment, and then demanded suddenly: "Who the devil are you?"

"Meng Ke from Zou."

"A-ha-!" Wu Xiao crowed, screwing up his face into a foxy glare. "So you are the sage who follows in the steps of Confucius, preaching 'benevolence' and 'righteousness'!"

"I am."

"What, may I ask, did Confucius end up with, after all?" challenged Wu Xiao.

"He did a lot of good." Mencius replied with perfect assurance. "All his life Confucius preached benevolence and practiced it. When in office, he made Lu into a well-governed state, where people would not even pick up objects that had been dropped in the road and where doors did not need to be bolted at night. His students, most of them talented and learned, were scattered all over the empire. When he toured the various states he taught the feudal princes the way of the former sage kings. He did an excellent job in editing the *Book of Songs*, *Book of Rites*, *Book of Changes* and the *Music*. And he wrote..."

"Enough!" Wu Xiao broke in. "A perfect devotee of Confucius, that's what you are, for sure! All praise and no censure. But what about his failures, eh?"

"Failures indeed!" Mencius retorted robustly. "The whole empire knows that he was noble-minded, open and above board. It is completely futile to throw mud at him!"

"What about his predicament in Kuang—and then in Chen and Cai? Weren't those his failures?" retorted Wu Xiao.

"They were no failures of his," Mencius said disdainfully. "They were simply traps laid by rogues who hated him."

"You Confucians are a handful of sophists," scoffed Wu Xiao. "I won't argue with you. But I want to know what you are here for."

Mencius replied, "To help you see your way to withdrawing your troops."

Wu Xiao sneered, "You are talking nonsense. Why should I withdraw when the capital of Teng is well-nigh falling into my hands? Besides, there's my sovereign lord's decree, which I have to obey."

Mencius retorted, "I suppose you are sure of victory?"

Wu Xiao, arrogant and imperious, replied, "It's a foregone conclusion."

"May I inquire why?"

"My forces are invincible. It's as simple as that!"

"You are wrong, general."

"Where am I wrong?"

"Do you know how to forecast the outcome of a war?"

"By assessing the relative strengths of the belligerents."

"That constitutes only one of several factors."

"What are the others?"

"Weather conditions, terrain and human unity. As far as these three factors are concerned, your army is at a disadvantage. And what is more, favorable weather is less important than advantageous terrain, and advantageous terrain is less important than human unity."

By then dark clouds were massing in the sky. Mencius indicated the sun which was being clouded over, and continued, "Now, Chu lies in the south and Teng lies in the north, and you southerners come north to fight; that is your first disadvantage. Your troops are fatigued by long-distance travel and you do not know much about the local terrain; that is your second disadvantage. Duke Wen practices benevolent government and his people are united as one man; that is your third disadvantage. So you see, you have no chance to win. No chance at all."

"You are talking through your hat!" Wu Xiao laughed aloud.

Mencius ignored this ridicule and went on, "Suppose you laid siege to a city which was smaller even than Teng's capital, with inner walls measuring, on each side, three *li* and outer walls measuring seven *li*, and you failed to take it. Now in the course of the siege there must have been, at one time or another, favorable weather, and in spite of that you failed to take the city. This shows that favorable weather is less important than advantageous terrain. Sometimes a city has to be abandoned, in spite of the height of its walls and depth of its moat, the quality of arms and abundance of food and supplies. This shows that advantageous terrain is less important than human unity. Hence it is said that it is not by boundaries that the people are confined, it is not by difficult terrain that a state is rendered secure, and it is not by superiority of arms that the empire is kept in awe. He who has justice on his side will have many to support him; he who has not justice on his side will have few to support him. In extreme cases, the latter will find even his own flesh and blood turning against him, while the former will have the whole empire at his behest. Hence, either a gentleman does not go to war or else he is sure of victory, for he will have the whole empire at his behest, while his opponent will have even his own flesh and blood turning against him. Now that the prince of Teng practices benevolent government the whole empire regards him with admiration. So much so that even a fastidiously honest man like Xu Xing prefers to make his home in Teng—and he is a native of Chu! Look at your King Huai, showing partiality for the crafty and the fawning while excluding the good and wise, wantonly engaging in military aggression against his neighboring states, only to set others against himself. If you want to fight for such a ruler are you not helping a villain do evil?"

This enraged Wu Xiao so much that he jumped up with an angry howl: "How dare you vilify my sovereign lord!"

Mencius continued unperturbed: "Calm yourself, general. I am only telling the truth, however ugly it may be. If you do not listen but insist on your way by fighting it out with the people of Teng your army will be put to rout in no time. Heed my warning, if only for the sake of your honored name."

"For me, Wu Xiao, in this life," said the other, with a self-important air, "there is only advance, no retreat; only victory, no defeat. Don't waste your breath spouting nonsense any more. Get yourself out of here right now, you and your lackey. Why make a senseless sacrifice of yourself here of all places?"

Mencius said gravely: "I, Meng Ke, will never submit to pressure, much less knuckle under to evil. Now that you stubbornly want to invade Teng in spite of my advice, well, I have no choice but to join them and fight back. Justice is on our side; we are sure to win."

But Wu Xiao and his men all laughed Mencius to scorn.

Wu Xiao dashed away the tears of laughter and waved his hand at Mencius, saying, "You Confucian scholars may be good at wagging your tongues, but when it comes to warfare, you are no better than simpletons. Clear off now, be quick!"

"So you are determined to go to war with Teng?" Mencius enquired gravely.

"Yes, we are!" said Wu Xiao. "Unless Teng submits as subject to us and pays us tribute, I'll fight to the death, mark my words."

Gongdu Zi remarked with suppressed fury: "There's no reasoning with a brute!"

"Whom do you mean?" asked Wu Xiao.

"I mean you," retorted Gongdu Zi.

Wu Xiao hissed through his clenched teeth: "If I don't teach you a lesson, perhaps you will not know who I am!"

Gongdu Zi sneered, "I know you are no small fry. But what then?"

"Good!" Wu Xiao took a bow and arrows from one of his men, and assuming the air of a world conqueror, said, "Let me teach you what's what! Take that!" With that, he aimed at Gongdu Zi and let fly the arrow.

Gongdu Zi jerked his head aside for the fraction of a second and the arrow flew over his shoulder.

Angered and abashed, Wu Xiao discharged another arrow direct at Gongdu Zi's heart. Again Gongdu Zi outmaneuvered him by an adroit dodging of his frame and the arrow disappeared nowhere.

Utterly put out, Wu Xiao roared at his soldiers: "Let fly your arrows!"

As the soldiers proceeded to fit their arrows to their bows, Mencius intervened, saying, "Aren't you ashamed of yourself, General Wu? We are only two individuals, teacher and disciple, while you boast a powerful host, 300 chariots and 900 soldiers strong. And now you order your soldiers to shoot us two. Do you call this a match of strength or what? No! This is sheer murder! Shame on you!"

Hearing this, Wu Xiao stamped his foot with impotent rage. Finally he had to countermand his order.

When Mencius and Gongdu Zi went back to report on their unsuccessful mission, Duke Wen grew apprehensive.

Mencius tried to comfort him, saying, "Don't be afraid, my lord. Here's the severe winter and there is a piercing wind blowing. I am certain that the Chu soldiers cannot stand up to such inclement weather. And so long as we can hold our ground, however fiercely the enemy fights, he has no chance of entering the city." He pointed to the Teng soldiers, who were now putting up a heroic fight against the invaders, saying, "Unity is strength. See how brave these people are! Stick it out and we will win."

"It is snowing." Someone cried.

Sure enough, big flakes of snow were swirling down. Mencius said in an elated voice: "A big snowfall will make it more difficult for the Chu invaders to take the city."

Duke Wen made a deep bow to Heaven, murmuring his thanks for this divine help.

Mencius said, "The present situation is that Chu's force is strong and ours is weak. So we can only assume the defensive. My lord should order the arrow smiths to make more bows and arrows."

The duke immediately gave the order. As an encouragement, he offered rewards for those who produced more arrows in the shortest possible time. Penalties would be given to slackers, he further instructed.

The sudden change of weather, on the other hand, had a dampening effect on the Chu soldiers' ardor. But in spite of that, Wu Xiao dispatched 50 chariots to each of the east, south and north gates in order to tie down Teng's defensive forces. He himself commanded 150 chariots to attack the west main gate.

He halted at a spot some 100 paces away from the gate. All the rest of his chariots behind him fanned out.

Proudly he stood on his commander's chariot and, cupping his hands to his mouth, shouted to the officers and men of Teng on the wall: "Listen! All of you! I have come at the command of my sovereign lord King Huai to lead this expedition against Teng. If you surrender, well and good; if you resist, you will die to the last man. This is my ultimatum. Come now, no more shilly-shallying!"

Gongdu Zi could hardly control his anger, and he was on the point of charging out to fight when Mencius stopped him. "Be not impetuous," he warned sternly. "Self-defense is our only way of survival."

Hearing no response, Wu Xiao ordered his soldiers to shout their challenges in groups and in turns. To provoke the other side into action, they used the most foul terms in their battle cries.

In an uncontrollable fury, however, Gongdu Zi tusked as far as the battlements where, as he leaned out, he shouted back in a mocking tone: "So you troopers of Chu are here not to battle but to swear, are you?"

Wu Xiao at once gave the order to shoot.

A shower of arrows rained on the battlements but not one hit Gongdu Zi, since he had already dodged behind a merlon. "Wu Xiao has made us a nice present of so many arrows," he was pleased at the idea that he had played a trick on the enemy. So he then took every chance to trick the enemy soldiers into shooting, and in no time there were a multitude of spent arrows scattered all over the wall tops, much to the amusement of Mencius, who, however, watched his disciple's act of daring with his heart in his mouth all this time.

Wu Xiao saw through this trick only when it was too late, as he found to his intense mortification that Gongdu Zi exposed himself only between intervals in shooting. He called a stop to the shooting at once. Presently he brightened up at an idea that occurred to him. "Now all take aim at the ropes holding the drawbridge and shoot!" he ordered.

At the order, a swarm of arrows flew toward the drawbridge. The ropes were hit in close succession and the strands became loosened. The drawbridge started to sag.

Mencius, alarmed, began thinking hard as to how to cope with this dangerous situation.

The drawbridge went down with a clatter as the last strands of the ropes parted. A loud cheer of triumph broke out among the Chu soldiers, and simultaneously they started their frontal assault upon the city gate. To force the massive gate open, the Chu soldiers used hefty battering rams specially made for the purpose. In the process, seven of the Chu soldiers were shot dead but yet more rushed to help. The gate at last started to yield to the heavy pounding, to the joy of General Wu Xiao and his soldiers but much to the horror of the Teng defenders.

At this critical juncture, Gongdu Zi snatched up one end of a long rope, sprang from the wall and landed on the drawbridge. In the twinkling of an eye he fastened the rope to a belaying ring on the drawbridge and then called out, "Hoist away, you there!" Soon the bridge was raised high up in the air again.

His feat of daring stupefied Wu Xiao for a moment before he yelled at his soldiers: "Shoot him! Shoot him!" But it was no use. Gongdu Zi wielded his *Hanguang* sword, hacking right and left as he went, and by the time he reached the gate 13 enemy soldiers had fallen under his sharp weapon.

He regained the top of the wall again in a single bound. All came up to congratulate him, including Duke Wen and Mencius, praising him for his death-defying courage and extraordinary skill in the martial arts.

The frustrated Wu Xiao now decided on a plan to seize the city by using scaling ladders. But this again failed because most of his soldiers were hit by the arrows that rained down on them before they could reach the foot of the wall. Finally a particularly wicked plan formed in his mind.

At midnight a fire broke out in the Chu camp. Subsequently heart-rending cries and loud curses of hatred could be heard from the pandemonium.

At first the Teng defenders were mystified and perturbed. What was happening in the Chu camp? They asked one another anxiously.

A terrible thought occurred to Mencius as he said to himself with a sinking heart: "Lord of Heaven! Can this mean that the villain is going to sacrifice the innocent people of Teng? The beast!"

All turned to him, surprised.

Mencius went on in an aggrieved tone: "They could possibly use the Teng people as so many shields against our arrows to cover their attack."

Enraged at this possible act of brutality, Gongdu Zi and Shen Qiang both agitated for a foray against the enemy camp. "To save our people, we should launch a sudden attack on them, even at the cost of our lives. Master, we beg you to give the order!"

Mencius, however, shook his head, saying in all gravity: "You must not! Brash physical courage will not help in this situation. Have you forgotten the lesson of Zi Lu?"

Gongdu Zi assured him: "Set your mind at ease, Master. What we are going to do is by no means foolhardy." He then whispered in Mencius' ear, and Mencius finally gave his consent.

And so Gongdu Zi and Shen Qiang led 50 soldiers under the cover of night and the falling snow out of the main gate of the city. They first lowered the drawbridge, and, having crossed it, lay in ambush by the side of the moat.

An hour later hundreds of Chu soldiers holding torches came along herding about a 100 Teng people on the way to the gate.

Wu Xiao shouted to the defenders on the wall: "Listen to what I have to say. Look here! These are your people. Open your gates and let our troops in, and we will guarantee their safety. Otherwise, we will kill every last one of them before your very eyes."

It broke Duke Wen's heart to see his people like so many lambs on the point of being butchered. He turned to Mencius, saying with deep remorse: "What have I ever done to bring such a calamity down on my people? Oh! Oh —"

Mencius comforted him: "Don't grieve, My Lord, they will be saved very soon."

Wu Xiao shouted again, this time in a sneering way: "Prince of Teng, why don't you speak up? Are you afraid? Surrender now, and your people will live." He then made his soldiers drive the Teng captives forward until they neared the moat.

A sudden war cry broke out from the 50 Teng soldiers lying in ambush by the moat. They broke cover and charged into the ranks of the Chu troops, wielding their spears and swords. Taken by surprise, the enemy soldiers scattered in all directions like a flock of sheep, many falling killed or wounded as they ran.

Mencius saw all this, and he at once told Duke Wen that it was time to launch a counterattack.

Soon battle drums sounded from all the four gates of the city as infantry and mounted soldiers rushed out. Soon the Chu troops were surrounded on all sides. Realizing that he was incapable of saving such a desperate situation, General Wu Xiao committed suicide. The siege of Teng by Chu was lifted.

Chapter Forty

Duke Wen Rewards Mencius with Gold for Services Rendered; Mencius Continues His Tour of the States Propagating His Gospel of Benevolence

To celebrate their victory over the Chu invaders, Duke Wen of Teng laid out a sumptuous feast in honor of those who had won merits during the siege. Then he went to Shanggong to present Mencius and his disciples with 100 yi of gold. "That we have been able to repulse the Chu invaders," he told Mencius gratefully, "is all because we had your all-out support. Indeed, without your help, the consequences for Teng would have been dreadful."

Mencius said, "Not at all, my lord. I should say that it was all because you have practiced benevolent government, and consequently you have the wholehearted support of your people. King Huai of Chu started a war of aggression against Teng. That was acting against Heaven's will, and so he was punished. Even if we, master and disciples, hadn't come to your help, in the long run Teng would have won, because justice is on your side and the people are on your side."

Duke Wen said in all sincerity: "All the same, I cannot but present you with something as a token of my gratitude. Here is 100 yi of gold. Please have the kindness to accept it."

Mencius answered, "My lord, if only you can persist in practicing benevolent government and guiding your people in line with the rites so that Teng may become strong and its people rich, shall I feel satisfied. As for your reward, I definitely cannot accept it."

Duke Wen had no alternative but to take back his gold, and then he left.

In the spring of 320 B.C. Mencius took his disciples on an excursion to the suburbs of the Teng capital. The idyllic rural scene soothed his heart, but his active mind always brought him back to the empire, which was in the throes of internecine wars.

Wan Zhuang, who was with him then, ventured to make conversation by asking, "Is Duke Wen of Teng a benevolent ruler, would you

think, sir?"

"He is," was the ready reply.

"Is he benevolent enough to be ruler of the empire?"

"He may have ability enough to rule over a state with a territory of 100 square *li* but not enough to rule over the empire."

"Why is that?"

"To rule over the empire, the ruler must possess high-minded ambitions and an all-embracing heart; and he must have a lofty vision and have energy enough to give effect to this vision in whatever manner best suits his talents. But Duke Wen has none of these."

Wan Zhang asked, "What is your plan for the present, sir?"

Mencius answered with a resolute air: "We shall go to the State of Wei."

Duke Wen hurried to the Shanggong as soon as he heard of this, and tried to persuade Mencius to stay, but in vain.

Duke Wen said, "Teng is a small state, and this causes Chu to want to annex it. Thanks to your wise instructions and your disciples' prowess, we were able to defeat Chu's invasion last winter. Should Chu come again to avenge its disgrace, from whom could I seek help? That is my fear."

Mencius gave a candid smile, saying, "Do not fear, my lord. Heaven helps those who help themselves. As I said last time, so long as you practice benevolence you will have your people's full support. Unity is strength. What can Chu alone do to you? Besides, it is only a year since King Huai suffered his defeat, he will not forget his bitter lesson so easily."

Still uncertain, however, Duke Wen remained silent for some time. Then he made his attendant present a wooden casket to Mencius. "Reverend sir, herein is a hundred *yi* of gold. Kindly accept it," he said humbly. This time Mencius accepted his present cheerfully and with many thanks.

After the duke had left, Gongdu Zi asked Mencius: "Are you sure that Chu will not invade Teng again, sir?"

"Yes," said Mencius with complete assurance. "If King Huai of Chu should launch an aggression again, he would choose a stronger state as his target."

"Why?"

Mencius explained, "King Huai has set his mind on the conquest of the empire. He thinks he will not fulfill his ambition unless first of all he is able to subjugate some bigger states."

Just as Mencius had expected, several years later, King Huai of Chu took advantage of domestic unrest in the State of Yue and swallowed that state up, transforming it into a prefecture, renamed Jiangdong. In 299 B.C. King Huai went to the State of Qin in person, thinking wishfully that he might claim the land back which he had lost to Qin. Ironically he was held as a hostage by King Zhao of Qin until he died in 296 B.C. But this is anticipating the events of the story. In the meantime, let us return to Mencius.

Soon after he saw Duke Wen off, he and his disciples left Teng for Wei. They spent their first night in the city of Xue, which had been a state but later fell to Qi. When the mayor of the city heard of Mencius' arrival, he gave him a warm reception and presented him with 50 yi of gold, which Mencius accepted with thanks.

Chen Zhen found this beyond his comprehension, and so he enquired, "Master, I happen to know that once when you left Qi, King Wei offered you a present of gold, which you declined. Last winter, when Duke Wen of Teng offered you gold, you refused again. Then once when we were in Song, the Prince of Song offered you 70 yi of gold, and you accepted it gladly. Yesterday Duke Wen of Teng offered you 100 yi and you accepted too. Today, again, you accepted 50 yi from the mayor of Xue." Watching to see how Mencius would react, he summoned enough courage to speak out: "In my judgment, if your refusal in the first instance was right then your acceptance on subsequent occasions must have been wrong. On the other hand, if your acceptance was right, then your refusal must have been wrong. You cannot escape one or the other of these two alternatives."

Mencius replied with conviction: "Both refusal and acceptance were right. When I was in Song I was about to go on a long journey, and for a traveler there is always a parting gift. Since it was intended as a parting gift, why should I have refused? Such was the way I behaved in Teng yesterday and in Xue today. But in the case of Qi, I had no justification for accepting a gift. To accept a gift without justification is tantamount to being bought. Surely a gentleman should never allow himself to be bought. Last year we helped Teng defeat the Chu invaders, and yet I refused to take the gold which Duke Wen offered to me as a reward. I did so because I had no plan for a long journey then, and therefore there was no point in accepting a gift. If it was meant as a reward for what we had done in defending Teng against the invaders, more was the reason for our refusal, as we fought in the name of justice. Can justice be bought with money?"

Peng Geng commented, "In my opinion, sir, it is absolutely right for you to open a school and enrol students. But is it not excessive to travel with a retinue of hundreds of them in scores of carriages, and to live off one feudal lord after another?"

Mencius explained, "If it is not in accordance with benevolence and righteousness, one should not accept even one basketful of rice from another person. If it is, there is no basis for your accusation. Shun accepted the empire from Yao without considering it excessive, when it was in accordance with benevolence and righterousness. I guide you people on to the path of morality and the rites. Even if I should travel with more followers and more carriages there should be no reason to call that excessive."

Peng Geng protested, "But it is not right for a man not to earn his keep."

Mencius replied, "If people cannot trade the surplus of the fruits of their labors to satisfy one another's needs, then the farmer will be left with surplus grain and the women with surplus cloth. If things are exchanged, you can feed the carpenter and the carriage maker. Here is a man. He is obedient to his parents at home and respectful to his elders abroad, and acts as custodian of the way of the ancient sage kings for the benefit of posterity. In spite of that, you say he ought not to be fed. Why do you place more value on the carpenter and the carriage maker than on a man who practices morality?"

Peng Geng objected, "It is the intention of the carpenter and the carriage maker to make a living. When a gentleman pursues the way of the ancient sages, is it also his intention to make a living?"

Mencius said, "What has intention got to do with it? If he does good work for you, then you ought to feed him whenever possible. Moreover, do you feed people on account of their intentions or on account of their work?"

"On account of their intentions," said Peng Geng.

Mencius said, "Now here is a man who makes wild movements with a trowel, making a mess of the wall he is working on. Would you feed him because his intention is to make a living?"

"No, of course not," came the reply.

Mencius pronounced, "Then you feed people on account of their work, not on account of their intentions." Abruptly he rose to his feet and, as if he were making a proclamation to the whole world, intoned, "All my life I have been traveling here and there despite wind and rain for no other purpose but to urge the feudal lords to practice benevolent government and to act upon the rites, so that my ideal of the people may ultimately be realized. Being bound to such a heavy duty as I am, is there any justification to say that I do not earn my keep?"

Wulu Zi, who was habitually taciturn, now ventured to ask, "In what way can good intentions be turned into distinguished merit as far as a feudal lord is concerned?"

"Without a carpenter's square or a pair of compasses, squares or circles cannot be drawn; without the six pipes, the pitch of the five note cannot be correctly adjusted," said Mencius, his bright, piercing eyes scanning his listeners. "Even if you had the keen eyes of Li Lou and the skill of Gongshu Ban you could not draw squares or circles without those instruments. Even if you had the acute ears of Shi Kuang you could not adjust pitches correctly without the six pipes. Even if you knew the way of Yao and Shun you could not rule the empire equitably except through benevolent government. Now there are some who, despite their benevolent hearts and reputations, succeed neither in benefiting the people by their benevolence nor in setting an example for posterity. This is because they do not practice the way of the Former Kings. Hence, goodness alone is not sufficient for government, and the law unaided cannot make itself effective. The *Book of Songs* says, 'Do not swerve to one side, do not overlook anything; / Follow established rules in everything you do.' No one ever erred through following the example of the Former Kings.

"The sage, having taxed his eyes to their utmost capacity, went on to invent the compasses and the square, the level and the plum-line, which can be used endlessly for the production of squares and circles, planes and straight lines, and, having taxed his ears to their utmost capacity, he went on to invent the six pipes, which can be used endlessly for setting the pitch of the five notes, and, having taxed his heart to its utmost capacity, he went on to practice government that tolerated no suffering, thus putting the whole empire under the shelter of his benevolence. Hence, to build high, one should always take advantage of hills, and to dig deep, one should always take advantage of rivers and marshes."

Wulu Zi said, "But society is developing. Can the Way of the Former Kings hold true for all times. Is it not subject to change?"

"Yes, the Way of the Former King leads us to the beautiful ideal of an empire for the people," said Mencius in a determined manner. "It is not subject to change. Nevertheless, in the course of running benevolent government and applying education in the rites, different measures may be adopted. Can one be deemed wise if, in governing the people, one fails to take advantage of the way of the Former Kings?"

Wulu Zi asked, "What kind of people are fit to be in high position?"

Mencius replied, "Only the benevolent man is fit to be in high position. If a cruel man is in high position he will be able to disseminate his wickedness among the people. When those above have no principles and those below have no laws, when courtiers have no faith in the Way and craftsmen have no faith in measures, when gentlemen offend against the right and common people risk punishment, then it is good fortune indeed if a state survives. Hence it is no disaster for a state when its city walls are not impregnable and its arms are not abundant. Nor is it a disaster when waste land is not brought under cultivation and wealth not accumulated. The recent victory of Teng, which is small and weak, over Chu, which is big and strong, bears out the truth of this. But when those above ignore the rites, those below ignore learning, and lawless people arise, then the end of the state is at hand. The *Book of Songs* says, "Heaven is about to stir, /Do not chatter so.' To chatter is to talk too much. To ignore dutifulness in serving one's ruler, to disregard the rites in accepting and relinquishing office, and to make calumnious attacks on the Way of the Former Kings is what is meant by 'talking too much'. Hence it is said, 'To take one's prince to task is respect; to discourse on the good and keep out heresies is reverence.'"

The next morning Mencius and his party continued their journey, and after several days they arrived at the east city gate of Daliang, capital of the State of Wei. When the guards learned that it was the distinguished sage Mencius and his disciples they immediately bowed them in without more ado.

The streets of the city appeared broad and neat. Conspicuous to the eye were the many weaponry shops, where spears, swords and halberds of every description were put on sale.

Mencius and company had just settled down at a post house when a familiar face appeared. It was none other but his old friend Chunyu

Kun!

"How is it you are here?" asked Mencius, pleasantly surprised.

"Oh, it's a long story," replied the other. "But this is no time to go into detail. In short, I met with the same fate as Tian Ji. He fled to Chu and I came to Wei for refuge, that's all. Now I am here with a summons from King Hui for you."

So pleased was Mencius at this that he eagerly asked, "What time am I to attend court?"

"Right now, if it suits you."

Mencius took Wan Zhang and Gongsun Chu along. Chen Zhen was to drive the carriage, and on the point of starting off he turned back to ask Mencius: "Excuse me, sir! Isn't he the reigning prince of the state of Wei? Then he must be King Hui of Wei. Why do you call him King Hui of Liang instead?"

Mencius explained, "When Marquis Wu died 49 years ago, his son —that is, the present king—succeeded him as marquis of Wei. Later he moved his capital to Da Liang. It is for this reason that Wei is also known as Liang. This is how I come to call him 'King Hui of Liang'."

In the carriage, Mencius asked Chunyu Kun, who shared the carriage with him, how his father-in-law was. He learned, much to his sorrow, that the old man had died three years before. Then he asked about his impressions of King Hui, but the latter merely smiled and said nothing.

Before long they came to a straight thoroughfare, at the furthest end of which loomed a grand palace within high walls.

The carriage came to a stop in front of the gate. Chunyu first stepped down and helped Mencius to dismount. Then he led the way to the inner palace.

King Hui, about 70 years old, was already waiting at the entrance, all smiles.

A band struck up some gay music of welcome. The king said cheerfully: "Venerable sir, this way, please."

"Thank you very much, Your Majesty." With that, Mencius entered, followed by the king.

The necessary ceremonial greetings done, each took his seat.

"Venerable sir," King Hui began. "You have come all this distance, thinking nothing of a journey of 1,000 *li*. You must surely have some way of profiting my state?"

Though a grey-haired and decrepit old man, King Hui appeared far from senile, thought Mencius as he made the following retort:

"Your Majesty, what is the point of mentioning the word 'profit'? All that matters is that there should be benevolence and righteousness. If Your Majesty says, 'How can I profit my state?' and the ministers and counselors say, 'How can I profit my family?' and the inferior officials and commoners say, 'How can I profit my person?' then those above and those below will be trying to profit at the expense of one another and the state will be imperiled."

King Hui's countenance suddenly changed, but Mencius ignored this and went on: "When regicide is committed in a state of ten thousand chariots, it is certain to be by a vassal with a thousand chariots, and when it is committed in a state of a thousand chariots, it is certain to be by a vassal with a hundred chariots."

King Hui grew tense and rigid.

In spite of that, Mencius pursued with his deductive reasoning, adding, "A share of a thousand in ten thousand or a hundred in a thousand is by no means insignificant. Yet if profit is put before righteousness, there is no satisfaction short of usurpation."

King Hui demanded, with raised eye-brows: "What is to be done in that case, sir?"

"All that matters is that there should be benevolence and righteousness!" said Mencius decidedly. "No benevolent man ever abandons his parents, and no dutiful man ever puts his prince last. It is only benevolence and righteousness that count. What is the point of mentioning the word 'profit'?"

King Hui became his normal self, as he said in a mild tone: "I have been wanting to practice benevolence and righteousness all my life, and for this, I think, I have done my best. Yet I have achieved little so far. Why is that?"

Mencius said, "Example is better than precept, Your Majesty. By practicing it yourself, you first set an example for your people. Then they will spontaneously come under your influence."

King Hui wished to change the subject, and so he asked, "I hear, sir, that you helped the Prince of Teng to practice benevolent government, and that in doing so you achieved something. How did you go about it?"

Mencius replied in understatement: "In fact I did just one thing for him, if you would like to call it 'help'."

King Hui asked eagerly: "What was it?"

Mencius continued, "The land reform—known as the nine-squares system of dividing the land. Its great merit is that it ensures a reduction of tax rates. With taxes reduced, the common people submit to their ruler heart and soul, and consequently they rest content with their farming and weaving. And once farming and weaving are unhindered the people will be well-fed and warmly clothed and consequently the state will become prosperous and strong."

King Hui murmured skeptically: "Could a mere tax reduction have achieved so tremendous an effect?"

Mencius explained, "To run a benevolent government, the most important thing is to make its people rich, thereby winning their trust. In the empire of today, the taxation system, as well as tax rates, varies from state to state. There are taxes on cloth, taxes on grain, and there are also taxes on manpower. As regards tax rates, there is the levying of two tenths, a ten to even a twentieth of the produce. A good and wise prince will do everything possible to reduce tax rates, adopting at the same time only one single taxation rate. If two different taxes are adopted at once, the ordinary tax-payers are bound to suffer from hunger; if three taxes are adopted, then a terrible situation will arise in which a father is driven to abandon his son, and vice versa."

Beads of sweat broke out on King Hui's forehead. He felt Mencius' words like a ton of bricks threatening to crash down on him. He instinctively flinched back.

Just then a palace guard came up and reported that the banquet was ready.

Chapter Forty-One

King Hui of Liang Regales Mencius with a Musical Performance at a Dinner Party; The Master Preaches Benevolent Government to the King, But His Words Fall on Deaf Ears

The reader was told in our last chapter how, in remonstrating with King Hui, Mencius dwelt on the necessity of reducing tax rates to relieve the distress of the common people, and how the king felt the sting of it. Then, greatly to his relief, a palace guard came in to report that the banquet was ready. The king then turned to Mencius, and said, "Esteemed Master, I have had a banquet specially prepared to honor your visit. Come on in, and let us continue our talk over a cup of wine, shall we?"

Accordingly Mencius followed the king into the banquet hall, where a magnificent spread was already prepared. A bevy of ladies-in-waiting shuttled back and forth, and music, gay, vivacious, and high-toned, resounded in the air.

King Hui raised his golden goblet in a toast, and Mencius toasted back with all politeness. A change of mood came over the king as soon as he had downed one cup of wine: He became exuberant and talkative as he commented with gusto on this and that delicacy, showing himself to be a regular gourmet.

When the wine had gone round three times the king, by now quite tipsy, shouted, "Let the musicians play!"

At the order, the musicians began to play To Guests, a piece from the Book of Songs, and at the same time, eight gossamer-clad dancing girls glided forth and danced as they sang:

"How gaily call the deer
While grazing in the shade!
I have welcome guests here.
Let lute and pipe be played.
Let offerings appear
And lute and strings vibrate.
If you love me, friends dear,

Help me to rule the state."

This was originally a festal ode which had been sung at entertainments for King Wen's guests from the feudal states, but the present performance with its perverted ways of dancing and singing style scandalized Mencius and his disciples as a complete distortion of the original theme. Wan Zhang, Gongsun Chou and Chen Zhen felt insulted, while Mencius glowered and glared at the king, who at the time was totally lost in his sensual pleasures, appearing oblivious to everything else.

Chunyu Kun quickly sensed what was wrong and he at once suggested to the king that the program be changed.

"What?" He said, jolted, as if awakened from a beautiful dream. "Why is that necessary?" he demanded in an unpleasant voice.

Chunyu Kun gave Mencius an uneasy glance by way of an answer.

It was not until then did the king realize what was the matter, and he gave a curt wave of his hand in the direction of the dancers. "That is enough!" he commanded.

The music came to a sudden stop and the dancers made their exit in silence.

The king then turned to Mencius with an embarrassed smile on his face, and said, "Please help yourself to more food, sir," and began to ply him with wine.

Reluctantly Mencius raised his goblet and responded to the king's toast.

Presently Chunyu Kun proposed a toast first to the king, then to Mencius and his disciples. This done, he suggested pleasantly that another piece from the *Songs* be presented, which, according to him, "carries overtones of good luck and has sweet melodies". It was the *Longevity*. King Hui gave his consent. Soon another batch of young maidens appeared, this time dressed fully and in good taste. They danced and sang to the accompaniment of solemn and melodious music:

"Plants grow on the southern hill
And on the northern one grows grass.
Enjoy your fill,
Men of first class.
May you live long
Among the throng!"

This time both Mencius and his three disciples smiled their

appreciation.

"In the south grow mulberries
And in the north poplars straight.
Enjoy if you please,
The glory of the state.
May you live long
Among the throng!
Plums grow on the southern hill
On the northern one, medlar trees.
Enjoy your fill,
Lord, as you please.
You're the people's friend;
Your fame's no end.
...."

Mencius grew more pleased and excited as he listened, so much so that he held up his golden goblet in both hands, saying aloud: "Your Majesty! I wish you...."

He held off in the middle of his sentence as he found much to his chagrin, that the king had gone to sleep! On hearing himself addressed, however, the king awoke with a start, and, all of a fluster, he rubbed his eyes and picked up his ivory chopsticks, mumbling as he did so: "Master, please help yourself...oh, no, no, no...please drink. Every one, now, please." Confronted with such a ridiculous situation, Mencius knew not whether to laugh or to cry. He permitted himself to take a sip of his wine and then put the goblet down.

Wide awake now, the king knew that he had committed a faux pas, and so he irritably called a stop to the performance.

He addressed Mencius: "Master, it is now the height of spring. I would like to get up a spring excursion tomorrow. May I have the pleasure of your company?"

Mencius replied, "The pleasure will be mine, and much more so, I should say, since we have just arrived here. It will be such a treat for us to go sightseeing in your country."

"Very well. Let's make it tomorrow," said the king.

Accordingly Mencius led his disciples to the palace the next morning. Chunyu Kun introduced all the Wei officials to him. Before long, King Hui came out and insisted on Mencius sharing his carriage.

The excursion party traveled 20 li and came to a densely-wooded marshy area, abounding in birds and beasts.

King Hui and Mencius climbed down from the carriage and approached a pond, looking around at the wild geese and deer. Mencius, who was standing by the king's side, watched for his chance to air his philosophical views. Presently the king asked, "Are such things enjoyed even by a good and wise man?"

Mencius replied in a frank and open way: "Only if a man is good and wise is he able to enjoy them. Otherwise he would not, even if he had them."

King Hui said nothing. There was perplexity in his eyes.

"Take King Wen and King Jie as examples from history," said Mencius. "The *Book of Songs* says about King Wen:'He surveyed and began the Sacred Terrace. /He surveyed it and measured it; /The people worked at it; /In less than no time they finished it. /He surveyed and began without haste; /The people came in ever-increasing numbers. /The king was in the Sacred Park. /The doe lay down; /The doe were sleek; /The white birds glistened. /The king was at the Sacred Pond. /Oh! how full it was of leaping fish!' It was with the labor of the people that King Wen built his terrace and pond, yet so pleased and delighted were they that they named his terrace the 'Sacred Terrace' and his pond the 'Sacred Pond', and rejoiced in his possession of deer, fish and turtles. It was by sharing their enjoyments with the people that men of antiquity were able to enjoy themselves. But what of King Jie? He behaved just the other way round. While his people hated him to the very marrow of their bones, he nevertheless glorified himself by saying, 'My possession of the empire is like there being a sun in Heaven. Is there a time when the sun will perish? If the sun perishes, then I shall perish.' The *Tang Shi* records the burning hatred his people bore for him when they swore, 'O Sun, when wilt thou perish? We care not if we have to die with thee!' Now, when the people were prepared to 'die with' him, even if the tyrant had a terrace and pond, birds and beasts, could he have enjoyed them all by himself?"

King Hui mounted a hill and looked to the north, where, through the floating clouds one could catch glimpses of the great wall which had been built 27 years before under the auspices of the king himself.

"I had that wall built," the king declared proudly to Mencius, "to defend against aggression from the State of Qin. See how grand and imposing it is. If you are interested, I will show you around there some day."

Mencius: "At your pleasure, Your Majesty."

And so, one day shortly after the events we have described, King Hui took Mencius on a trip to the great wall on the northern frontiers of Wei, several hundred *li* from the capital. With the king's consent, Mencius took along with him his disciples Wan Zhang, Gongsun Chou, Peng Geng, Gongdu Zi, Xianqiu Meng, Wulu Zi, Xu Bi, Chong Yu, Chen Zhen, Chen Dai, Shen Qiang and Tao Ying, and his son Zhongzi.

It took several days before they reached their destination. The wall stretched its meandering way along the mountain ridges. Beyond was the State of Qin.

The travelers were now at the foot of a mountain. King Hui, in high spirits, asked if Mencius had enough vigor to go mountain climbing. The former assured him that though he was old and lean on the look of it, yet he was strong enough to have a try. And he did, though not without the support of his personal bodyguards fussing around him. Mencius followed suit, with the help of his disciples.

They climbed up along the footpath. On and on. The masson pines gave off a delicate fragrance and the red azaleas bloomed in full glory. Spring has no speech, thought Mencius, nothing but rustling and whispering. Would that the human world were like this, he longed wistfully. That there be no conflicts, no struggles among men so that everybody may live a carefree life, happy and content with his lot...

Suddenly there arose the howling of wolves from a ravine. From where they were, they could see four wolves hunting two deer. They chased their victims round and round without let-up.

"Abominable beasts!" King Hui burst out with anger. "Deer are lovely animals. Why, I myself even refrain from killing them as a rule when hunting. I will not allow those beasts to touch my pets. Here, men!"

"Yes, sir?" responded his guards in one voice.

King Hui ordered them: "Go and kill those wolves!"

Gongdu Zi rushed up, saying: "Your Majesty, would it not be more convenient if we shot them from this distance?"

The king surveyed him awhile before he said assuredly: "This shooting of yours may be convenient, but you could easily kill the deer by mistake."

Gongdu Zi said, "Never fear, Your Majesty. We will shoot only the wolves. There is no possibility of killing the deer, you have my word."

King Hui nodded his assent.

Thereupon Gongdu Zi, Xu Bi, Shen Qiang and Chong Yu fitted arrows to their bows, running several paces forward as they did so, then hid themselves behind a nearby bush. In no time the four wolves had been shot dead. The two deer craned their necks to look around a bit, then trotted away into the forest beyond.

King Hui and his guards were struck dumb by the sight for a moment, before they broke into loud cries of ovation: 'Bravo! Superb marksmanship!"

Chunyu Kun turned to Mencius and said, "All the credit goes to you, dear sir, for having trained so many dead shots!"

Mencius demurred, "It is nothing, since 'Archery' is one of our required courses for graduation."

Chunyu Kun rejoined, "All the same, it must have taken them much hard work to achieve that level of skill."

"That is true," admitted Mencius. "The proverb 'Practice makes perfect' explains that."

Presently they reached the top. Beneath their eyes was a section of the great wall which at that moment was being built. On close inspection, they found that most of the builders were thin, with hair disheveled and faces begrimed. To their horror, quite a number of them were even in chains while working in teams of threes or fours. This sight pained Mencius so, that he turned upon the king with suppressed anger: "What is the matter, Your Majesty? Why these...?"

"The matter?" returned King Hui with an air of unconcern. "What do you mean?"

"Your Majesty!" Mencius indicated the people who were chained together. "They are doing such back-breaking work; why put them in chains?"

The king gave a guffaw, and explained, "They are prisoners-of-war, if you want to know. They were committing murder, arson and all sorts of evil in the last war, when we nabbed them. They might count themselves lucky that I didn't kill them. Now I let them build this great wall for me. What's the harm, eh?"

Mencius remonstrated, looking most severe: "It is only the truly virtuous man who can love. All good and wise kings have a loving heart. High or low, all are human beings made of flesh and blood, after all—Why treat them like this, Your Majesty?"

The king retorted in an effort to defend himself: "They are our prisoners of war, and so they are our slaves, aren't they? I couldn't very well treat them like honored guests, could I? After all, this treatment of prisoners is that which I learnt from the ancients."

"There have been good ancients and bad ancients," said Mencius. "Yao, Shun, Yu, King Wen, King Wu, the Duke of Zhou and Confucius—Those were paragons of virtue. They all owned a loving heart. King Jie of the Xia Dynasty, King Zhou of the Shang Dynasty and others of the same cruel type were the common enemies of the people. I beg Your Majesty not to doubt what I say."

King Hui replied, "Our Wei soldiers meet the same fate at the hands of our enemy states when captured, you know. In some cases, they suffered a great deal more, even."

Mencius, whose heart went all out to the poor creatures, made one more effort to remonstrate with the king. "Benevolence is man's mind and righteousness is man's path," said he in a more persuasive tone. "Benevolence wins honor and malevolence brings disgrace; justice gains and injustice loses. One who upholds justice shall not be alone. My Lord, you must not pay back evil with evil."

King Hui asked, "What do you expect me to do in the present case, allow me to ask?"

"Set them free," urged Mencius, "So that they may go home and be united with their dear ones."

King Hui shook his head. "If I did that, the world would regard me as a laughing-stock," he protested.

"Nothing of the sort!" said Mencius. "If you did that, people would sing your praises in chorus."

The king massaged his temples with both hands for a while, and then he said, "Should I be so tender-hearted as that, how could you expect me to rule a state? And to hold sway over the empire?"

Mencius said, "You are wrong there, My Lord."

"Where am I wrong?" asked King Hui.

Mencius said, "He wins a state who wins the support of his people. He wins the empire who wins the hearts of his subjects."

"Please go on," King Hui urged.

Mencius quoted from history: "Time was when the empire was under the tyrannical rule of King Zhou of Shang. Bo Yi fled from his misrule and settled on the edge of the North Sea. Later, when he heard of the rise of King Wen he stirred and said, 'Why not go back? I hear that the present king takes good care of the aged.' There was another man of virtue by the name of Jiang Taigong, who fled from Zhou and settled on the edge of the East Sea. When he heard of the rise of King Wen he stirred and said 'Why not go back? I hear the present king takes good care of the aged.' These two were the grand old men of the empire, and they turned to King Wen. In other words, the fathers of the empire turned to him. When the fathers of the empire turned to him, where could the sons go? If you practice benevolent government like King Wen did, you will certainly be ruling over Wei or even the Empire within seven years."

"Oh, the ups and downs of my life—You never know!" remarked King Hui with feeling. "There was a time, though, when Wei was mighty and strong equaled by no other state in the whole of the empire. But now I have fallen on bad days, as you may well know that I was worsted in a battle with Qi in the east and my eldest son, Shen, was taken captive and died forth with. Moreover, I lost a battle to Qin in the west, together with territory of 700 *li* square west of the River. Then I ceded eight cities to Chu as a result of my submission to it." He walked around quite agitated and then hissed through his clenched teeth: "This is really galling and humiliating! How can I endure it without venting my wrath on those prisoners?"

Mencius exhorted him further: "My Lord! As you know, 'Every injustice has its perpetrator, every debt has its debtor.' It was the rulers of those states who made you eat humble pie. What have these poor fellows to do with it? Are they not victims of tyranny themselves, in the final analysis?"

King Hui queried, "So you would have me release those fellows after all, do you mean?"

Mencius replied, "Yes, I do, and all for your benefit."

"For my benefit?"

"Yes, and for the benefit of Wei as a whole."

"Very well, I am ready to listen to what you have to say."

Mencius continued, "Any state, be it small or big, is able to bring the empire under its influence so long as it practices benevolent government. This is more so with such a big state as Wei. If you practice benevolent government in good faith, and if you reduce tax rates and exempt the wretched from punishment, then husbandry and handicrafts will flourish and your people will be well fed and warmly clothed. Then you should open schools on a wide scale, teaching your people how to read and write, and how to behave at home and abroad.

Once you have accomplished all this, your state will be strong enough to repulse any invader."

"Truth to tell," sighed King Hui, knitting his brows, "I have done my best for my state. When crops failed in Henei I moved the population to Hedong and the grain to Henei, and reversed the action when crops failed in Hedong. I have not noticed any of my neighbors taking as much pains over his government. Yet how is it that the population of the neighboring states has not decreased and mine has not increased?"

Mencius bowed his head in thought for a moment. Then, raising it brusquely, said, "Your Majesty is fond of war; may I use an analogy from it? After weapons are crossed to the rolling of drums, some soldiers fled, abandoning their armor and trailing their weapons. One stops after 100 paces; another stops after 50 paces. What would you think if the latter, as one who ran only 50 paces, were to laugh at the former, who ran 100?"

"He has no right to," said the king. "He did not quite run 100 paces, that is all. But all the same, he ran."

"If you can see that," said Mencius, "you will not expect your own state to be more populous than neighboring states.

"If you do not interfere with the busy seasons in the fields, then there will be more grain than the people can eat. If you do not allow nets with too fine a mesh to be used in large ponds, then there will be more fish and shrimps than they can eat. If hatchets and axes are permitted in the forests on the hills only in the proper seasons, then there will be more timber than they can use. When the people have more grain and more fish and shrimps than they can eat, and more timber than they can use, then their livelihood can be safely maintained. When they are well fed and warmly clothed, then benevolent government begins.

"If the mulberry is planted in every household with five *mu* of land, then those who are 50 years old can wear silk. If chickens, pigs and dogs do not miss their breeding seasons, then those who are 70 years old can eat meat. If each lot of 100 *mu* is not deprived of labor during the busy seasons, then families with several mouths to feed will not go hungry. Exercise due care over the education provided by the village schools, and discipline the people by teaching them the duties proper to sons and younger brothers, and those whose heads have turned grey will not be carrying loads on the roads. When a situation arises in which the aged are taken good care of, the young are given a good education, and people in general enjoy a life of plenty, then the empire will duly submit to your rule."

At this point Mencius swept a withering glance over the officials present, saying, "Now, when food meant for human beings is so plentiful as to be thrown to dogs and pigs, you fail to realize that it is time for garnering. When men drop dead from starvation by the wayside, you fail to realize that it is time for distribution. When people die, you simply say, 'It is none of my doing. It is the fault of the harvest.' In what way is that different from killing a man by running him through, while saying all the time: 'It was none of my doing. It was the fault of the weapon.'" After a long pause, he added with emphasis: "Stop putting the blame on others, Your Majesty. Devote yourself to practicing benevolent government, and the people of the whole empire will flock to you."

Chapter Forty-Two

On Witnessing Brutalities Done to the Penal Laborers, Gongdu Zi Strikes a Blow for the Weak; Satiated with Food and Pleasure, One of King Hui's Concubines Seeks Love Elsewhere

As the conversation between Mencius and King Hui proceeded it was suddenly interrupted by an angry roar from Gongdu Zi. They turned to look only to see the stout fellow rushing at a Wei soldier who was lashing a group of prisoners with a leather whip. The latter were at the moment carrying blocks of stone. Gongdu's enraged look and his precipitous approach quite frightened the soldier, and he shied away, throwing down his whip as he did so.

Mencius shouted, "Gongdu Zi, control yourself!"

His disciple pointed to the prisoners, whose bodies were covered with weals. "Look at that, sir!" he cried.

Pairs of sad eyes turned up to Mencius as he came down from where he stood. Drawing nearer, he found that all the prisoners wore fetters and shackles, their ankles smeared with blood. The sight made Mencius boil with rage, but on second thoughts he suppressed his rising anger and questioned King Hui in an impassive tone: "From which of the states are these prisoners of war, Your Majesty?"

"From Qin and Qi," said the king.

"How many from each?"

The king was quite stumped by this question and for a moment remained tongue-tied. Then he turned to the officials about him but they all shook their heads.

One of the soldiers, however, offered an answer, and it was: 800 or so from Qin and 600 or so from Qi.

The king's jaw dropped as he questioned again: "Are there as many as that?"

The soldier replied with a timid stutter: "Beg to report, Your Majesty...those were the original numbers."

King Hui asked: "What is the current number?"

The soldier replied, "Today there are only 600 Qin soldiers and

200 Qi soldiers remaining."

"What about the others?" was Mencius' sharp query.

The soldier replied in subdued voice: "They are dead, sir."

Chunyu Kun asked bluntly: "How is it that so many prisoners have died?"

"They came from the east," said the soldier; "and were not accustomed to the local climate."

Presently Mencius asked King Hui: "Would you not wish to make Wei prosperous and strong?"

The king replied, "Yes, I would. It is my lifelong wish, too."

Mencius said, "The Way lies at hand, yet it is sought afar; the thing lies in the easy yet it is sought in the difficult."

"What do you mean?" asked the king.

Mencius said, "If only everyone loved his parents and treated his elders with deference, the empire would be at peace."

The king asked: "What is so difficult about it? I think everybody can do that."

Mencius pointed to the prisoners at the work-site: "Do they not also have parents and brothers? Now, being reduced to such a wretched state as they are, could they be expected to love their parents or respect their elders?"

Left without an argument, the king just stared stupidly.

Mencius drove his point home, speaking heatedly: "A respectful man will not be insulting to others; a man who practices frugality will not rob others. Yet today's feudal lords—some of them, I mean—make it their business to insult and rob others. They go all out to conquer...."

The king's face turned incandescent with suppressed anger.

Mencius took no notice of this, but went on, "It was through losing the people that kings Jie and Zhou lost the empire, and through losing the people's hearts that they lost the people."

The mention of something far away and long ago restored his peace of mind somewhat, and so the king asked eagerly: "What do you think is the way to win the empire, sir?"

Mencius explained, "There is a way to win the empire; win the people and you will win the empire. There is a way to win the people; win their hearts and you will win the people. There is a way to win their hearts; amass what they want for them and do not impose what they dislike on them."

"I am willing to hear more about that," said the king.

Mencius gave a sigh, and said, "The people turn to the benevolent as water flows downwards or as animals head for the wilds. Thus the otter drives the fish to the deep; thus the hawk drives birds to the bushes; and thus kings Jie and Zhou drove the people to Shang Tang and King Wu. Now if Your Majesty is drawn to benevolence, then all the feudal lords will drive the people to you. You cannot but win the empire."

The king felt as if the empire was already within easy reach, so intoxicated with the idea was he.

"At the present day, though," Mencius added gravely, "those who want to be king are like a man with an illness that has lasted seven years seeking the *ai* herb that has been stored for three years. If one has not the foresight to put by such a thing, one will not be able to find it when the need arises."

The king lowered his head in disappointment.

Mencius continued, "If one does not aim steadfastly at benevolence, one will suffer worry and disgrace all one's life and end in the snare of death. The *Book of Songs* says, 'How can they be good? They only lead one another to death by drowning.' This describes well what I have said."

The king grew restive, his feet shifting uneasily as he said with a sheepish air: "Then what on the earth is the way out?"

Mencius said, "Before everything else, set these prisoners free. Let them go home to rejoin their people."

The king turned to his officials for their opinions, and they all expressed approval, saying that it would be the most sagacious and kindest act His Majesty could think of.

And so it was that the king gave his decree on the spot: Let the Qin and Qi prisoners go free!

As can be imagined, the emancipated prisoners of war could not sing the praises of King Hui loudly enough, the details of which may be omitted in our narrative.

For the first time King Hui realized the genuine joy to be got from a benevolent act, and he felt as if he were on the top of the world. Presently he asked Mencius: "What must I do next, sir?"

"Stop building the great wall at once," was the reply.

"Why?" asked the puzzled King Hui.

Mencius explained, "A benevolent ruler has no match in the world. If you practice benevolent government in Wei, who would dare invade you?"

But King Hui protested, "The great wall is almost completed. It would be a great pity to leave it unfinished. No! It won't do."

Mencius said, "As I see it, it is a crushing burden on the people which wastes money and manpower. Leave it now, and you will be none the worse for it."

King Hui sighed: "I know very well that I fall short of both virtue and talent to build Wei into a strong state. Besides, I am getting old."

Mencius said with a smile: "When Shun lived in the depths of the mountains, he lived amongst trees and stones, and had as friends deer and pigs. The difference between him and the uncultivated man of the mountains then was slight. But when he heard a single good word, witnessed a single good deed, it was like water causing a breach in the dykes of the Yangzi or the Yellow River. Nothing could withstand it."

Now our story turns to King Hui's second son Si. From childhood, Prince Si had a natural aversion to scholarship, and spent most of his time training with spear and staff. Since Wei suffered the defeat in the campaign against Qi at Maling, during which time Wei's commanding general Pang Juan committed suicide and Crown Prince Shen died as a prisoner in Qi, Prince Si had sworn that he would wreak vengeance on his enemy. So day and night he worked hard at training himself in the art of warfare. He got his father the king's consent to have a space of five acres set aside for him. There he had high walls built, enclosing a drill ground, 20 solidly built dungeons and other facilities. He got his father to grant him 20 Qin and Qi prisoners-of-war, whom he put in his dungeons pending use. Then he offered high prices to hire men who were skilled in martial arts as coaches of foils. Whenever he found it dull in his daily exercise, he would bring the prisoners out to amuse himself with. Sometimes he let them fight one another in pairs—Qin versus Qi—while he and his attendants watched the fun. At other times he had a piece of fruit placed on each of the prisoners' heads to make them living targets for shooting practice. As a result, the number of his prisoners dwindled until there were 16 left. His domain was a forbidden area and few people knew of its existence.

On the day we are describing, the sun blazed down like fire and the earth felt scorching to the touch. Prince Si and his attendants were lounging about under poplar trees, sipping tea while each wagged a palm-leaf fan.

Prince Si, aged 40, had a tall, slim figure, and was clad in the garb of a knight. Presently he called out in his bully-like manner: "Here, man!"

In answer to the call, a bulky menial stepped forth: "Yes, sir!"

"Fetch me a Qin and another Qi slave here!" was the order.

Soon two slaves were brought. Both were in shackles. Their clothes were merely rags and their faces ashen-grey.

The servant freed them from the shackles. This done, he asked the prince: "What is your pleasure, sir?"

"Let them fight a round of hand-to-hand combat!"

The two started to fight, back and forth. Round and round. Sweat streamed down their emaciated chests while hatred smoldered within their breasts. An hour had elapsed when all of a sudden they both fell to the ground exhausted.

"Playing tricks, are you?" yelled the prince. "Beat them!"

At this four fiendish-looking fellows rushed up, whips in hand, and set on them savagely, like bloodhounds. They kept on flogging until their victims fainted away, their bodies bruised and lacerated.

"Bring another!" ordered Prince Si again.

Another victim was brought, a Qin prisoner.

To satisfy the prince's mere whim, this time the poor creature was used as a living target. A musk melon was set on top of his head.

The "living target" trembled like a leaf.

An archer stood 50 paces away. He took aim and let fly an arrow. It split the melon with a crack, splattering the pulp all over the head of the "living target". The tormentors cheered, whistled and laughed.

Another melon was placed on the man's head and a second archer came up to shoot, then a third and so on till the victim was so frightened that he wet his pants and finally he collapsed in a dead swoon.

Prince Si stood up, stretching himself with a languid air, and told his attendants to carry the man back to his cell.

Presently he hit upon a novel idea of amusing himself: to display one's marksmanship in the moonlight. "There is nothing remarkable about shooting accurately in broad daylight, is there?" he observed to the others. "Today is the 15th day of the seventh month. Let's do it under a full moon tonight."

"Wonderful!" chorused all the others, playing up to him.

Prince Si had a wife and two concubines. They lived in a courtyard compound alongside the west wall of the rear palace. Lady Zheng, the wife, occupied the center rooms, and Lady Bian and Lady Mei, the concubines, had their rooms in the east and west wings, respectively. Prince Si, in his preoccupation with his ambitious plan to vanquish Qin, Qi and Chu, and his daily exercises in the martial arts, spent little time in their company as a rule. Left to themselves, unhappy as they were, the three ladies whiled away their time playing chess or guessing games.

That day, the ladies were playing their usual games under an old locust tree in the courtyard when their husband made a sudden appearance. He had just returned from his forbidden domain. All at once they came crowding around him, plied him with food and drink and whisked a fan over him. To all their importunate attentions, however, Prince Si only responded with an impatient shrug of his shoulders, and without so much as a "Hello' went straight to his room. There he lay down on his bed, turning over in his mind his ingenious idea of "shooting practice in the moonlight". The three ladies, deeply hurt, repaired to their separate quarters.

At nightfall a full moon climbed over the roof of the east-wing building. The three ladies, bored stiff, got together again. They shed silent tears over their loneliness. Then Lady Zheng, who was the oldest of the three, stopped crying and said, "Let's stop pitying ourselves, sisters. A fool is one who bows to grief. Why not find some pleasure on our own somewhere, eh?"

"Yes, why not?" Lady Bian smiled through her tears. "Do let us go somewhere and try to find some fun for ourselves!"

Lady Mei said, "Don't be rash! We belong to a royal household and it is absolutely impermissible for us womenfolk to go anywhere out of bounds."

Lady Zheng explained, "I simply meant that we could take a turn in the back garden on such a fine night."

And so to the Imperial Garden they went, each taking a fan in hand.

The Imperial Garden was built on a grand scale, with a lotus pond in the center surrounded on all sides by a variety of pavilions and other buildings. A zigzag bridge arched across the pond. An artificial hill built of strange-shaped rocks loomed due north. In the moonlight everything here appeared mysterious and dream-like.

Suddenly Lady Zheng made a furtive gesture to her companions and pulled them with her behind a tree, where she whispered, "Look! There's a woman on the other side of the pond, don't you see?"

As Lady Bian and Lady Mei strained their eyes to look, they discerned that there really was a young woman there. She was pacing back and forth, now lifting her head to look at the moon, now looking about, as if she was waiting for somebody.

Lady Mei whispered back: "Who is she?"

Lady Bian said, "From her figure and manner, she looks like Lady Jian."

"What is she doing there, all alone?"

"Waiting for her lover, I suppose."

Lady Zheng scolded her: "Don't talk rubbish! This is the sacred ground of the palace; No such behavior is allowed!"

Lady Bian wondered aloud: "Can it be that she is contemplating suicide because somebody wronged her??"

"Not likely," said Lady Zheng. "Anyway, it's no concern of ours. But let's wait and see how things turn out."

Accordingly, they stayed behind the tree, watching with bated breath what move Lady Jian would make next. All was quiet except for the chirping of insects.

All of a sudden, two light hand-claps broke the silence. Immediately after, the woman was seen moving quickly to the nearby wall. Then, another two hand-claps, made ever so slightly, and the woman, overjoyed, clapped her hands in answer. In a trice, a bulky man masked in black clambered over the wall, and the moment he touched ground held the woman closely to his breast, kissing her passionately. Then they dodged behind the artificial hill.

The three ladies gasped in mock horror, and after a moment of embarrassed silence Lady Bian suggested, "Let me call people to catch them in the act."

"You mustn't!" said Lady Zheng. "Think of the consequences once the scandal gets about. Lady Jian shall die for it. And if we should be the cause of her death we would have committed a sin, too."

Lady Bian whispered, "How can such a thing be tolerated in the palace? Shouldn't we do something to punish her?"

Lady Zheng said, "Heaven sees everything. He will punish her, you can be sure about that."

After about an hour Lady Jian emerged from behind the artificial hill. She looked right and left to make sure there was nobody around before she turned back to beckon.

Out came the bulky fellow, this time without his mask.

"He Chang!" the three ladies stifled cries in unison.

Our story flashes three years back to a morning audience presided over by King Hui of Liang. It happened to be the 15th of the eighth month of the year. As the audience came to an end, the king proclaimed to his subordinates that he would hold an evening party to enjoy the moon and that he hoped they would be kind enough to attend.

It was at that party that Lady Zheng first saw He Chang. The man had started his career as an officer, later rising to vice-minister. He was handsome and had a reputation for having an eye for the ladies. And it was at this party too that Lady Zheng got to know that Lady Jian had an affair with this He Chang.

It so happened that as the evening party was progressing in full swing, Lady Jian, who had been snuggling up to the king with her charms and graces all this while, suddenly excused herself and made off. Quietly she climbed down the hill and there she had her rendezvous with her lover.

Lady Zheng happened to be present at the party that night, and she was just wondering at the odd behavior of Lady Jian when she heard the latter's waiting maid call in the courtyard: "Mistress, His Majesty is looking for you."

"I'm coming right now," was the answer. Shortly Lady Zheng saw Lady Jian reappear in the company of her waiting maid. At the same time, as she turned to look, she found He Chang was also back at his original place. Involuntarily she muttered to herself: "Can there be an affair between those two?"

Chapter Forty-Three

Inconstant in Her Love, Lady Jian Abandons the Old for the Young; Casting off His Old Self, a Remolded Xia Long Performs a Good Deed for His Erstwhile Foe

Lady Zheng's suspicion that there was an affair between Lady Jian and He Chang had turned out to be true after all. The fact is that since the night they had their first tryst in the imperial garden, for three years now the clandestine lovers had kept their dates, come rain or shine.

Back to Prince Si and his "moonlight shooting" escapade. That night, when he arrived at the drill ground the moon was already high in the sky. He immediately ordered one of his underlings to bring out a prisoner.

"Of which state, sir?" asked the man, jingling a bunch of keys.

"A Qi prisoner," Prince Si rasped, gnashing his teeth. He was thinking of his brother, who had died a prisoner in the State of Qi.

Thereupon a Qi captive was made to stand with a musk melon on his head.

A line of archers, each in his turn, started to shoot.

One, two, three...six—six melons were smashed by the arrows.

A "Hurrah!" broke out from the watchers.

But just as the seventh archer took his stand and drew his bow, a piercing cry rent the air. For a brief moment the people present showed no surprise, thinking that this must be from the "living target". Then, to their terror, they found the victim was the archer himself. As they looked up, they caught a glimpse of a man camouflaged in black on the wall. The archers discharged a shower of arrows. But too late! The man had disappeared. They searched high and low but no trace of him could be found.

Dejected and crestfallen, Prince Si went home earlier than usual that night. He went straight to Lady Bian's room. In bed the latter told her husband what she had seen in the garden that night. This aroused

his suspicions. The matter kept haunting his mind; he could not get to sleep...

Meanwhile, Lady Jian was in her room, musing over her recent meeting with her lover. She felt so happy that she burst into song:

"To gather vines goes she.
When her I do not see,
One day seems as long as months three.
To gather reeds goes she.
When her I do not see,
One day seems as long as seasons three.
To gather herbs goes she.
When her I do not see,
One day seems as long as years three."

Suddenly Prince Si barged in, sword in hand. "Shameless harlot!" he demanded sternly. "Who are you yearning for at this late hour? Confess!"

Lady Jian received such a shock that, clasping her head with both hands, she stumbled into a corner, petrified. It was quite some time before she found her tongue, saying breathlessly: "Prince, sir! I'm a well-behaved wench. I've done nothing to disgrace His Majesty and deserve this."

Prince Si yelled, "Dare you deny it?"

Lady Jian protested, "I am innocent. I beg you not to listen to slanderous talk."

"Slanderous talk indeed!" Prince Si placed the point of his sword against her breast. "There is always some reason for a rumor. No smoke without fire!"

The word "rumor" relieved Lady Jian somewhat. Now that she knew where she stood, she flew into a tantrum, turning the tables on her inquisitor, saying, "You fool! So that's how you find me guilty, do you? On no more evidence than a mere rumor! I'll impeach you for libel, just see if I don't!"

Now it was the prince's turn to be surprised. "Why do you say that?" he questioned inanely.

Seeing that her bluff had taken effect, she began to use her old coquettish tricks.

"Give a dog a bad name! All out of jealousy—those mud-slingers! Bah!"

"Jealousy?" inquired Prince Si.

"Yes," Lady Jian twisted her slender waist about, hitching up her skirt as she did so, and then she added coyly: "They think I am pretty and sweet-tempered, and that I enjoy exclusive favors with His Majesty and all that. So they have grown jealous and hate me."

Prince Si suddenly found her to be such a ravishing beauty as she stood there in the candlelight, playing the coquette, that for a moment he completely forgot himself, his sword dropping to the ground of its own accord.

Seizing the moment, Lady Jian took his hand in hers and put it to her breasts, then drew her mouth to his ear, whispering in the most bewitching manner: "There is no time like the present, darling. Come on now..."

While in bed, the two had the following conversation:

"You must promise to keep me company from time to time," said Lady Jian.

"How about once a month? Let's make it the fifth, all right?"

"That's too long an interval."

"Then let's meet on the tenth, twentieth and thirtieth of every month. How about it?"

"Don't break faith with me, though."

"Oh, my angel! Your crown prince wouldn't dare."

"My crown prince, did you say? Then you regard me as the queen consort?"

"Why not? Surely you're my queen consort."

"Do you regard me as the present queen consort or a queen consort to be?"

"I don't understand."

"If you regard me as the present queen consort, then you have committed the crime of incest against your father the king, not to say offending public decency. Have you thought of that?"

Prince Si was awed into silence.

Lady Jian gave him a winsome smile, saying gleefully: "If you treat me as your prospective queen consort, I will gladly serve you as bed-companion all my life. But you must set me up as such with due form once you ascend the throne."

Prince Si was nonplussed: "But you are just one of my father's concubines; how can you become my queen consort?"

"You are afraid that would be illegal, right?"

The prince nodded.

"You are wrong," said Lady Jian forcefully.

"Why?" asked Prince Si.

Lady Jian then spoke plausibly and at length, saying, "Your father the king is approaching 70 years old, he has not long to live. When he dies you will be the monarch of Wei. Succession to the throne means ownership of everything here. Wei's boundless territory belongs to you. The palace belongs to you. All your father's concubines will come into your possession also. Those you want, you can keep for yourself, those you don't you can let go..."

"No," the Prince hastened to interrupt, "I would rather have you alone."

This was more than she had expected of him, and Lady Jian questioned eagerly: "Do you mean that, really?"

Prince Si said, "Nothing that a sovereign says can be treated as a joke; you must be aware of that."

Lady Jian stared at him in awe.

"Now, look at you!" said Prince Si cajolingly. "Just because I mentioned 'sovereign', you get such a scare! How faint-hearted! But when all is said and done, is it really so far off—the day when I become that 'something'?"

Just then loud cries from outside struck their ears. Prince Si hurriedly slipped on his clothes and, snatching up his sword, went out. His underlings informed him that all the prisoners had escaped from his drill ground.

"How about the wardens?" asked Prince Si.

"All killed," was the reply.

The cells all stood open, and not a single prisoner remained. As Prince Si inspected the scene, he discovered that most of the locks had been cut through by some sharp weapon. He was just trying to use his sword to cut a lock in order to test out its sharpness when somebody spoke behind him. He faced about to find that it was General Wu Fa. He had come with orders from the king to fetch the prince, "Last night a soldier guarding the East City Gate was killed by somebody, and a group of horsemen were let out."

Prince Si exploded, "So my prisoners were spirited away on horseback? Damn it all!"

Wu Fa said, "Your Highness, I think this could have been done by Mencius' disciples."

"They are mere bookworms", retorted the prince. "They wouldn't have the guts to. Besides, how would they know that I kept prisoners here?"

Wu Fa said, "Maybe you don't know that there are quite a few of them who are skillful with weapons. The other day when we were at the building site of the great wall on our northern frontier four of Mencius' disciples shot four wolves dead on the spot all at the same time, what a marvelous feat of marksmanship! I wouldn't have believed it if I hadn't seen it with my own eyes."

Prince Si queried, "But how could they possibly find out that I kept prisoners here?"

Wu Fa made a great show of being in earnest, saying: "Most probably Mr Chunyu let out the secret, if I'm not mistaken. Originally he was a high minister of Qi, but he later came to Wei for refuge. Who knows what his real purpose was?"

Prince Si shook his head. "No, it could not have been him. He had no idea that there were prisoners of war here."

Wu Fa said, "There is no telling, though. Things do leak out."

Prince Si grew thoughtful.

Wu Fa continued, "Mr Chunyu is in close association with Mencius. He must have divulged the secret to him."

Prince Si remained dubious.

Wu Fa drew nearer to the prince and said secretively: "I hear that one of Mencius' disciples—Gongdu Zi his name—is highly skilled in the martial arts. He owns a precious ancient sword that cuts iron like clay and becomes invisible when wielded by his hand...."

His avarice aroused, Prince Si hastened to ask, "What is it called?"

"It is called 'Hanguang'," replied Wu Fu.

"In that case," said the prince, pointing to the damaged lock, "this must have been done by him."

Wu Fa suggested, "Why not go to Mencius' lodgings and confront Gongdu Zi with the charge?"

Accordingly, he took the prince with him to the post station where Mencius and his disciples had their temporary lodgings while staying in the capital of Wei. Once there, Prince Si, after the conventional greeting, went straight to the point, saying to Mencius: "I hear, Venerable Master, that your favorite disciple Gongdu Zi has a precious sword called 'Hanguang', Would you please call him out so that I may have a look?"

Menciu said, "I am afraid that he is not here. He went home a fortnight ago. When he comes back, I will send him to you without fail."

Disappointed, Prince Si bade Mencius a hasty "Good-bye" and was gone.

Mencius was left puzzled. One question after another arose in his mind: Why had Prince Si made this sudden visit? Was it possible that he should suspect Gongdu Zi to be responsible for the prison breakout? Or had he paid this visit for the sole purpose of inspecting the 'Hanguang' sword? And who, after all, was at the bottom of the incident? He felt terribly uneasy. To divert his mind, he went out to check on his students at their lessons. He found those ranked uppermost in martial skills, such as Xu Bi, Xianqiu Meng, Shen Qiang, Chong Yu and Chen Zhen, were all there.

Gongsun Chou came up to ask Mencius: "Sir, I thought that you would be happy to learn that those prisoners had been rescued by someone, but now I find you so pensive about it, why?"

"Let me tell you why," said Mencius. "The mere fact that the prisoners of war are saved from perdition is a good thing in itself. But in present case, this was done at the cost of lives, which is most deplorable! For the prison wardens and the soldier on duty were killed through no fault of their own. They were innocent; they should have had the right to live. Unless one is driven to the last extremity, it is inadvisable to save people by using such a drastic method."

Gongsun Chou said, "The other day, when we came back from our trip to the wall that Wei is building, you asserted with conviction that there must be some prisoners of war still remaining somewhere else in Wei. Facts bear out that your judgment was entirely true. But how did you form your judgment, sir?"

Mencius replied, "King Hui of Liang told me so."

Surprised, Gongsun Chou queried: "When did he do that?"

Mencius said, "His eyes told me."

Gongsun Chou shook his head, saying: "Sorry, I don't quite understand, sir."

Mencius explained, "There is in man nothing more ingenuous than the pupils of his eyes; they cannot conceal his wickedness. When he is upright, a man's pupils are clear and bright; when he is not, they are clouded and murky. How can a man conceal his true character if, as you listen to his words, you observe the pupils of his eyes?"

"What you say is true," Gongsun Chou admitted with a puzzled frown. "But how does this concern King Hui of Liang, sir?"

Mencius said, "That day we were at the building site, when I inquired whether or not in other places there were Qin and Qi prisoners of war, the king looked not his normal self, but with uncertainty in his eyes; he wavered a good deal before he faltered out a 'no'. From this I concluded that there were yet prisoners of war from Qin and Qi in Wei."

Gongsun Chou asked, "What kind of a man is King Hui in your opinion?"

"The man is far from benevolent!" was the indignant response.

"Why do you say so, sir?" further asked Gongsun Chou.

"Because," said Mencius, "a benevolent man extends his love from those he loves to those he does not love. A ruthless man extends his ruthlessness from those he does not love to those he loves."

"What do you mean?" asked his disciple.

Mencius became even more indignant, and replied, "In order to gain further territory, King Hui of Liang sent the people whom he does not love to war, bringing about their destruction. He suffered a grave defeat, and when he wanted to go to war a second time he was afraid he would not be able to win, so he herded the young men—among them his own son—he loved to their deaths as well. This is what I meant when I said a ruthless man extends his ruthlessness from those he does not love to those he loves."

After Gongsun Chou was gone Mencius remembered some thing which had occurred some 20 days previously. He had been standing in the courtyard when Gongdu Zi approached him showing great respect and saying that he wished to go home to see his parents, and that he hoped that Mencius would grant him permission. Mencius gave his permission outright and further supplied him with five yi of gold for traveling expenses.

Now this minor incident prompted Mencius into anxious thoughts. He associated it with the recent happenings: the prison broken into by somebody with a sharp sword, a troop of horse riders bursting through the East City Gate, and the prison wardens and the soldier at the gate killed off in summary fashion. All this could have been done by Gongdu Zi, impetuous and chivalrous as he was, he thought. "But where can he be now?" Fear for his safety suddenly seized Mencius.

To answer Mencius' question, let's come back to Gongdu Zi. That day, coming back from their trip to the great wall, he had heard from Chunyu Kun that there existed a drill ground supervised by King Hui's second son Prince Si, where he used human beings as targets for shooting practice. He had set his mind on finding out for himself about this. Thus, without Mencius's knowledge, he set to work one day. His reconnaissance led him to a place west of the rear palace, where a considerable space of ground enclosed by strongly built high walls could be seen. Gongdu Zi decided that it must be the drill ground in question. As he walked on, musing over his plan of action, he found himself pausing before a tavern at the mouth of a lane. Suddenly he heard himself called and he recognized the person with a start. It was none other than his old enemy Xia Long, the one-time steward of Fu Puren.

"What are you doing here?" inquired Gongdu Zi in surprise.

"Well, it's a long story," Xia Long began. "That year, you remember? I set fire to Fu Puren's house, and that angered Jue Hu, who wanted to kill me. I defeated him in a fight, but he fled I know not whither."

"He fled to Qi," Gongdu Zi informed him.

"Did he change his evil ways?"

"No, he was as bad as ever."

"What then?"

"Xu Bi and I did him in eventually."

"No more than he deserved," Xia Long sighed.

Gongdu Zi then enquired, "How are you getting on, Steward Xia?"

"Please spare me that title, sir, it makes me feel ashamed of myself." Xia Long went on to give an account of his wanderings in the previous few years. He had finally settled down in Wei and opened the tavern. He was married and now had a son and a daughter. He was just going to call them out, when Gongdu Zi stopped him.

"Don't trouble yourself, Mr Xia," he said. "There's enough time for that. For the moment, is there any quiet corner where we can talk things over?"

Thereupon Xia Long ushered him into a small room inside the tavern. Gongdu Zi began, "There is something I want to ask you. Do you know anything about a drill ground round here where Prince Zi of Wei uses human beings as shooting targets?"

Instinctively Xia Long shot a stealthy glance at the door before he said in a subdued voice: "Indeed, there is. There is no need to conceal anything from you, sir. The drill ground lies beyond the high wall alongside the east of the road. If you want to have a good look at it, better wait until it is midnight. Then I'll act as your guide there."

"Don't you fear the consequences if we're caught?" Gongdu Zi asked.

Xia Long said: "Your teacher Mencius once saved my life, for which I owe him a debt of gratitude I can never repay. I'm obliged to do everything for him, even at the risk of my life. What fearful consequence is there to daunt me?"

Gongdu Zi said, "You're a good fellow. I thank you in advance. But this is nothing to do with Mencius, for my teacher has no knowledge of what I'm attempting to do. So promise me not to tell anybody about this, all right?"

Xia Long nodded his consent with alacrity.

That very night the two donned night garb, and slipping into the drill ground they made a reconnaissance of the physical features of the place, particularly the prison cells. Back at the tavern they decided on a course of action to be taken as follows: Gongdu Zi was to procure money to buy horses and Xia Long to collect the wherewithal for emergency needs. In the daytime Gongdu would stay indoors at the tavern, and in the dead of the night he would continue spying out the conditions of the drill ground. Thus ten days passed, until on the moonlit night of the 15th, the date with which the reader is already acquainted, Gongdu Zi saw with his own eyes how Prince Si made his underlings practise shooting at a prisoner of war. The shocking scene roused his indignation, and before he knew it, he had released his arrow, killing an archer on the spot. That same night, he and Xia Long rescued the Qin and Qi prisoners and saw them safely out of the city gate before they returned. There in the tavern. Gongdu Zi remained in hiding another eight days until he had made sure there was no suspicion about him, when he made his way out of the city. He purchased a horse and carriage, and then came back in proper style, to the great joy of Mencius and company. He made as if he had really been to his home, his story being so plausible that nobody suspected him.

Chapter Forty-Four

Bai Gui Talks Big About His Merits
in Curbing the Flood;
Gao Zi Debates with Mencius on
the Question of Human Nature

No sooner had Gongdu Zi returned than Prince Si paid Mencius another visit.

Has he come expressly for the Hanguang sword? Mencius thought to himself. Or has he some ulterior motive? So thinking, he introduced Gongdu Zi forthwith.

"My dear Gongdu Zi," said Mencius, "Our guest has long heard about your precious Hanguang sword, which he thinks is a rare treasure in the world. Would you please show it to him?"

Gongdu Zi, far from being flattered, hesitated for a moment before handing over his sword with both hands to the prince.

Taking the sword, the prince inspected the scabbard for a while, then slowly unsheathed the blade.

His face showed disappointment as he put it back into its sheath again. Then he remembered what Wu Fa had told him about the sword. "Fetch me a piece of iron, man!" he ordered his attendant. A kitchen knife was brought.

The prince turned to Gongdu Zi. "This sword is said to have the power of cutting iron like clay. Has it really? May I test it out, sir?"

"As you please!" was the curt reply.

Thereupon, the prince raised the sword. Down it went—and the knife was cleft into two pieces, neat and clean, to the loud applause of the onlookers.

A light of rapacious greed shone forth from the prince's eyes, as he uttered words of praise, saying, "Wonderful sword! Wonderful sword!"

Fondling the sword as if he could not part with it, the prince finally put it back in its scabbard, then offered it with both hands to Gongdu, saying respectfully: "Much obliged for the favor, sir." With that he left.

For some time King Hui of Liang had been lying in bed, brought down by giddiness and tinnitus. As soon as he felt a little better he summoned his prime minister Bai Gui to his presence and asked about the harvest that year. When he was informed that it was the best his country had ever seen, he was so happy that he wanted his minister to accompany him to see Mencius at once. "I have not seen him for a long time," he declared. "Let us go to his place and see what he is doing."

Mencius met them at the gate. The necessary etiquette performed, Mencius inquired after the king's health.

King Hui said, "I have felt slightly indisposed over the past few days, it is true. But I am well now. The good news of a bumper harvest makes me particularly happy. I am ready to listen to what you have to say."

Mencius expressed his congratulations on the bumper crop as well as his best wishes for the king's well-being. Then he let his eyes rest on the king's face for a moment before he ventured to say, "Your Majesty! May I have your permission to..."

King Hui remarked, "Why, this is so unlike you! You used to be so outspoken and straightforward."

Mencius then asked bluntly: "Is there any difference between killing a man with a staff and killing him with a knife?"

"There is no difference."

"Is there any difference between killing him with a knife and killing him with misrule?"

"There is no difference there, either."

Mencius pursued his argument tenaciously: "You have just said that this is a year of bumper harvest in Wei, have you not? But why is it that your people do not fare any the better for it? They look hungry, and on the outskirts of cities men drop dead from starvation while in your kitchen there is fat meat, and in your stables there are well-fed horses. This is to show animals the way to devour men. Even the devouring of animals by animals is repugnant to men. If, then, one who is father and mother to the people cannot, in ruling over them, avoid showing animals the way to devour men, wherein is he father and mother to the people? When Confucius said, 'The inventor of burial figure in human form deserves to have no progeny,' he was condemning him for the use of something modeled after the human form. How, then, can the starving of the very people be countenanced?"

King Hui began to wriggle in his seat, displeasure written all over his face.

"What would you have me do, sir?" he demanded with resentment.

"Encourage your people to engage in farming and weaving, rewarding those who are active in their work, reduce tax rates, absolve them from corvee labor, set up schools, and put an end to saber-rattling."

Bai Gui said, "I should like to fix the rate of taxation at one in 20. What do you think of that, sir?"

Mencius replied, "Your way is that of the northern barbarians. In a city of 10,000 households, would it be enough to have a single potter?"

"No. There would be a shortage of earthenware."

"Well, it is good for you to understand this much."

"But I am afraid that I still don't understand what you mean, sir."

Mencius explained, "In the land of the northern barbarians the five grains do not grow; millet is their only crop. They are without city walls, houses, ancestral temples or the sacrificial rites. They do not have diplomacy, with its attendant gifts and banquets, nor have they the numerous offices and officials. That is why they can manage on a tax of one in 20. Now here in Wei, or anywhere else in Central China for that matter, how can human relationships and men in authority be abolished? The affairs of a city cannot be conducted when there is a shortage even of potters. How much more so if the shortage is of men in authority? Those who wish to reduce taxation to below the level laid down by Yao and Shun are all, to a greater or lesser degree, barbarians, while those who wish to increase it are all, to a greater or lesser degree, Jies."

Bai Gui now proceeded to blow his own trumpet, as he said with a self-complacent air: "Since I assumed my present position as prime minister to his majesty, I have had a great wall built in the north, thereby keeping out the Qin aggressors, and I have had a big dam erected in the south to control flooding." He looked Mencius in the face, adding proudly: "In dealing with water problems I am better than Yu the Great."

"You are mistaken," said Mencius. "In dealing with water, Yu followed the natural tendency of water. Hence he emptied the water into the seas. Now you empty water into the neighboring states. When water goes counter to its course, it is described as a 'deluge', in other words, a 'flood', and floods are detested by the benevolent man. You are mistaken, my good sir."

Disgruntled, the king and his minister took their leave.

Wan Zhang asked his teacher: "I hear that this Prime Minister Bai Gui is an incorruptible official. Does not that make him a good one?"

"You oversimplify things, though," said Mencius. "The prime minister may be counted as a good sort. But considering his high position in such a big state as Wei, what he has done is far from enough. In other words, he is little different from many other ministers we know nowadays."

Wan Zhang waited eagerly for Mencius to expound upon this theme.

Mencius continued, "Those who are in the service of princes today all say, 'I am able to extend the territory of my prince, and fill his coffers for him.' The good subject of today would have been looked upon in antiquity as a pest. To enrich a prince who is neither attracted to the Way nor bent upon benevolence is to enrich a Jie. Again, they say, 'I am able to gain allies and ensure victory in war for my prince.' Such a good subject of today would have been looked upon in antiquity as a pest. To try to make a prince who is neither attracted to the Way nor bent upon benevolence strong in war is to aid a Jie. Following the practice of the present day, unless there is a change in the ways of the people, a man could not hold the empire for the duration of one morning, even if it were given to him."

Chen Zhen interrupted, "Under what conditions would a gentleman in antiquity take office?"

Mencius replied, "There are three conditions under each of which he would take office. Equally, there are three conditions under each of which he would relinquish it. First, when he was sent for with the greatest respect and in accordance with the proper rites, and told that his advice would be put into practice, he would go. But when his advice was not put into practice, he would leave, even though the courtesies were still observed. Second, when he was sent for with the greatest respect and in accordance with the proper rites, he would go, though his advice was not put into practice. But he would leave when the courtesies were no longer meticulously observed. Third, when he could no longer afford to eat either in the morning or in the evening, and was so weak from hunger that he could no longer go out of doors, then he could accept charity from the prince who, hearing of his plight, gave to him out of kindness, saying, 'As I have failed, in the first instance, to put into practice the way he taught, and then failed to listen to his advice, it will be to my shame if he dies of hunger in my domain.' But the purpose of this acceptance would be merely to ward off starvation."

Chen Zhen said, "Sir, you are a man of extraordinary ability and profound wisdom; yet for so long no prince of any state has come to recognize your true worth and make good use of you. Why is that, sir?"

Chen Zhen's words weighed like lead upon Mencius' mind. What his teacher Zeng Xuan had said on his deathbed sounded in his ears again. He fell to thinking hard, then gave a long sigh, and said, "The times! Destiny! It is due to Heaven that I have become what I am. Though I cannot but think of those of our ancients: Shun rose from the fields; Fu Yue was raised to office from amongst the builders; Jiao Ge from amidst the fish and salt; Guan Zhong from the hands of the jailers; Sun Shu'ao from the sea and Bai Lixi from the market. They all began their lives in obscurity, but in due course each of them accomplished something for himself once he had won the trust of his superiors. That is why Heaven, when it is about to place a great burden on a man, always first tests his resolution, exhausts his frame and makes him suffer starvation and hardship, frustrates his efforts so as to shake him from his mental lassitude, toughen his nature and made good his deficiencies. As a rule, a man can mend his ways only after he has made mistakes. It is only when a man is frustrated in mind and in his deliberations that he is able to innovate. It is only when his intentions become visible on his countenance and audible in his tone of voice that others can understand him. As a rule, a state without law-abiding families and reliable counselors on the one hand, and, on the other, without the threat of foreign invasion, will perish. Only then do we learn the lesson that we survive in adversity and perish in ease and comfort. Those who refuse to employ me know not the lesson. What could they expect but the fate of self-destruction!"

Chong Yu said, "Sir, I am afraid that the root cause of this neglect of you is that you set your ideals too high for those petty-minded princes to grasp. Do you not agree?"

These words touched Mencius to the quick as he reflected, asking himself: "What is the fatal weakness in my character, after all? Am I too critical in my efforts to rectify others even though I have the best intentions for their own good? Or is it because I see things clearly that other people fail to see, hence their jealousy?"

Chong Yu went on, "As I observe, where there are loyal ministers and men of worthy virtue in a government, there inevitably appear their antipodes: the villains. Out of the conflicts between the two, the latter inevitably triumph. Why must it be so, sir?"

After musing awhile, Mencius replied, "Good and wise ministers in general are those who are open-minded and square and above-board. Being as they are, they can easily be duped. On the other hand, villains are full of machinations. They can stoop to all sorts of monstrous tricks to gain their private ends. To make things worse, there emerges a muddle-headed ruler who listens only to the sycophants. The outcome can only be the tragic end of the good and wise ministers."

Chong Yu exclaimed, "I can hardly imagine a human being capable of such knavery!"

Mencius said, "Terrible indeed is the subtle influence which circumstances can exert on a man's thinking. In a sense, disaster is a blessing in disguise. It is often through adversity that men acquire virtue, wisdom, skill and cleverness. The estranged subject or the son of a concubine, because he conducts himself with the greatest of caution and is constantly on the watch for possible disaster, succeeds where others would have failed. There are men whose purpose is to serve a prince; they will try to please whatever prince they are serving. There are men whose aim is to bring peace to the state; they achieve satisfaction through bringing this about. There are the subjects of Heaven; they practice only what can be extended to the whole empire. There are the great men; they can rectify others by rectifying themselves."

Chong Yu then said. "For any man, it is only right to be kind and righteous towards his fellows. Why should so many people choose to do the opposite, and help a tyrant to do evil?"

Mencius replied with a sigh: "Benevolence is the heart of man, and righteousness his road. The people you are referring to are those who reject the heart as well as the road." He paced around among his students, who formed a circle about him. "Even with a *tong* or a *zi* tree, anyone wishing to keep it alive will know how it should be tended. Yet when it comes to one's own person, one does not know how to tend it. Surely one does not love one's own person any less than the *tong* or the *zi* tree. This is unthinking to the highest degree. Or rather I would call such a person utterly shameless. A man must not be without shame, for the shame of being without shame is shamelessness indeed!"

Chen Zhen asked, "Does the sense of shame mean so much to a man, I venture to ask?"

Mencius replied, "Great is the use of shame to man. He who indulges in craftiness has no use for shame. If a man is not ashamed of being inferior to other men, how will he ever become their equal?"

Chen Zhen raised another moral problem for Mencius when he asked: "What is the way to cultivate one's mind?"

"The cultivation of one's mind or heart," said Mencius, "is as necessary as cultivation of one's body. A man loves all parts of his person without discrimination. As he loves them all without discrimination, he nurtures them all without discrimination. If there is not one foot or one inch of his skin that he does not love, then there is not one foot or one inch that he does not nurture. Is there any other way of telling whether what a man does is good or bad than by the choice he makes? The parts of the person differ in value and importance. Never harm the parts of greater importance for the sake of those of smaller importance, or the more valuable for the sake of the less valuable. He who nurtures the parts of smaller importance is a small man; he who nurtures the parts of greater importance is a great man. Now consider a gardener. If he tends the common trees while neglecting the valuable ones, then he is a bad gardener. A man who takes care of one finger to the detriment of his shoulder and back without realizing his mistake is a muddle-headed man. Confucius advocated practicing virtues of greater importance rather than otherwise. Anyone who is able to practice benevolence and righteousness in a big way will be able to handle the empire in the palm of his hand. Hence, there is no other way of cultivating one's heart except by practicing benevolence and righteousness."

Wan Zhang interrupted with a suggestion that Mencius should take them out on a trip to the countryside, as it was such a fine autumn day, to which all agreed with a loud cheer.

And so they went. The countryside was bustling with activity, as the farmers were busy with harvesting and planting at the same time.

Presently Mencius saw a man approaching. Of medium height, he wore coarse clothes made of hemp. As he drew nearer, Mencius found him to be a grey-headed old man. He halted a few paces away, then raised his clasped hands in greeting, saying, "Can this be the Venerable Master Mencius I'm addressing?"

Mencius returned his greeting. "Yes, it is I. May I know your name, sir?"

"My surname is Gao," said the old man. "I am commonly known as Gao Zi."

Mencius gave a start at the name, then began to survey the man more closely before he remarked in a disdainful tone: "You have made quite a reputation for yourself, sir. I suppose you are being modest?"

Gao Zi: "Upon my word, I don't live up to my reputation. I'm straightforward and outspoken and I have got a propensity for discussing things with others, that's all."

Mencius enquired: "Is there any particular thing you want to discuss with me? Please speak up, sir."

Gao Zi: "It seems that our views on human nature differ widely."

Mencius countered with: "I know your views only by hearsay. Now that we have this chance meeting here, I suppose I may have the benefit of your opinions."

Gao Zi launched his attack: "Your theory is that human nature is good, am I right?"

"Yes, it is," said Mencius in a decided tone. "Well, do you have any doubts about that?"

Gao Zi said, "In my view, human nature is like the *qi* willow, and righteousness is like cups and bowls. To make morality out of human nature is like making cups and bowls out of the willow."

Mencius assumed a grave air: "I put it to you: Can you make cups and bowls by following the nature of the willow? Or must you mutilate the willow before you can make it into cups and bowls? If you have to mutilate the willow to make it into cups and bowls, must you, then, also mutilate a man to make him moral?"

Stumped by the question, Gao Zi remained silent.

Mencius went on, "Surely it will be these words of yours that men in the world will follow to bring disaster upon morality."

Having racked his brains for a while, Gao Zi threw back his head, and said, "Human nature is like swirling water: Give it an outlet in the east and it will flow east; give it an outlet in the west and it will flow west. Human nature does not show any preference for either good or bad, just as water does not show any preference for either east or west."

"That certainly is the case," said Mencius. "Water does not show any preference for either east or west."—he grew stern in countenance, demanding of his opponent, "But does it show the same indifference to high and low?"

Again Gao Zi was at a loss for an answer.

Mencius continued, "Human nature seeks the good, just as water seeks low ground. There is no man who is not good; there is no water that does not flow downwards. Now in the case of water, by splashing it one can make it shoot up higher than one's forehead, and by forcing it one can make it stay on a hill. But how can that be the nature of water?"

Gao Zi gave no response.

"It is the circumstances that make it so," continued Mencius. "That man can be made bad shows that his nature is no different from that of water in this respect."

Gao Zi said, "The inborn is what is meant by 'nature',"

"Is that the same as 'white is what is meant by 'white'?" asked Mencius.

Gao Zi nodded his agreement.

Mencius regarded him with contempt and queried, "Is the whiteness of white feathers the same as the whiteness of white snow, and the whiteness of white snow the same as the whiteness of white jade?"

Gao Zi nodded vigorously, saying: "Exactly so."

"In that case," demanded Mencius sarcastically, "is the nature of a hound the same as the nature of an ox and the nature of an ox the same as the nature of a man?"

Gao Zi blushed to the roots of his ears and was tongue-tied. He looked over to the farmers out in the fields, bending over their harvesting, and suddenly he got an idea: "Appetite for food and sex is nature. Benevolence is internal, not external. Righteousness is external, not internal."

"Why do you say that benevolence is internal and righteousness is external?" Mencius asked.

Gao Zi explained, "That man there is old, and I treat him as an elder. He owes nothing of his elderliness to me, just as in treating him as white because he is white I only do so because of his whiteness, which is external to me. That is why I call it external."

"There may be no difference between our pronouncing of a white horse to be white and our pronouncing a white man to be white," Mencius said, with a piercing glance at Gao Zi. "But is there no difference between the regard with which we acknowledge the age of an old horse and that with which we acknowledge the age of an old man? And what is it which is called righteousness? The fact of a man's being old? or the fact of our giving honor to his age?"

Gao Zi replied, "My brother I love, but the brother of a man from Qin I do not love. This means that the explanation lies in me. Hence I call it internal. Treating an elder from Chu as an elder is no different from treating an elder of my own family as an elder. This means that the explanation lies in their elderliness. Hence I call it external."

"Our enjoyment of a roast," said Mencius with a contemptuous smile, "provided by a man from Qin is no different from my enjoyment of my own roast. Even with inanimate things we can find cases similar to the one under discussion. Are we, then, to say that there is something external even in the enjoyment of a roast?"

Gao Zi made a surly departure there and then.

Back at their lodgings that day, Gongdu Zi asked Mencius the following question:

"According to Gao Zi, there is neither good nor bad in human nature. But others say that 'Human nature can become good or it can become bad, and that is why, with the rise of King Wen and King Wu, the people were given to goodness, while with the rise of King You and King Li, they were given to cruelty.' Then there are others who say, 'There are those who are good by nature, and there are those who are bad by nature. For this reason, Xiang could have Yao as prince, and Shun could have the Blind Man as father, and Qi, Viscount of Wei and Prince Bi Gan could have Zhou as nephew as well as sovereign.' Now you say human nature is good. Does this mean that all the others are mistaken?"

"As far as what is genuinely in him is concerned, a man is capable of becoming good," replied Mencius. "That is what I mean by good. As for his becoming bad, that is not the fault of his native endowment. The heart of compassion is possessed by all men alike; likewise the heart of shame, the heart of respect and the heart of right and wrong. The heart of compassion pertains to benevolence, the heart of shame to dutifulness, the heart of respect to the observance of the rites, and the heart of right and wrong to wisdom. Benevolence, dutifulness, observance of the rites, and wisdom are not welded on to me from the outside; they are in me originally. Only this has never dawned on me. That is why it is said, 'Seek and you will find it; let go and you will lose it.' There are cases where one man is twice, five times or countless times better than another man, but this is only because there are people who fail to make the best of their native endowments. The *Book of Songs* says, 'Heaven produces the teeming masses, /And where there is a thing there is a norm. /If the people held on to their constant nature, /They would be drawn to superior virtue.' Confucius commented, 'The author of this poem must have had knowledge of the Way.' Thus where there is a thing there is a norm, and because the people hold on to their constant nature they are drawn to superior virtue."

Just then Wan Zhang came in, looking rather nervous. He whispered something in Mencius' ear and the latter blanched at once.

Chapter Forty-Five

Mencius Explains the Rank System of the Zhou House to One of His Admirers;
King Hui of Liang Dies, Nursing a Deep Grievance Against His Incestuous Son

When Mencius heard from Wan Zhang that his childhood friend Tao Shi had died, he at once sent for Tao Ying and Zhongzi, enjoining the young men to go home without delay.

He said to them: "Gentlemen in antiquity never took on the teaching of their own sons. Therefore, after the funeral you should not come back to me but stay at home to serve your grandmother and mother. Do you understand?"

Tao Ying and Zhongzi replied, "We will comply with your wish, Father."

Gongsun Chou, who happened to be there, presently asked: "Why does a gentleman not take on the teaching of his own son?"

"Because in the nature of things," said Mencius, "it will not work. A teacher necessarily resorts to correction, and if correction produces no effect, he will end up losing his temper. When this happens, father and son will offend each other. The son will say, 'You teach me by correcting me, but you yourself are not correct.' So father and son fall out, and it is bad that such a thing should happen. In antiquity people taught one another's sons. Father and son should not demand goodness from each other. To do so estranges them, and there is nothing more unfortunate than estrangement between father and son."

Gongsun Chou said, "But Confucius used to teach his son Li himself, didn't he? And you have been teaching Zhongzi all along, sir. Is there not some contradiction here?"

Mencius explained, "Confucius' and my teaching methods are entirely different from those of others. Ours is to guide, to help our pupils to find their way themselves. This way of teaching gives full play to initiative in learning. No estrangement between teacher and pupil or between father and son can possibly occur therefrom. Do you remember the story of Confucius teaching his son the *Book of Songs* and

Book of Rites?" (Gongsun Chou nodded his head.) "He could in no way hurt his son by using the method he did, could he? In my case, I kept Zhongzi by my side for two reasons: One was to let him learn martial arts from Mr Gongsun Benzheng for the purpose of self-defense and physical strength, and the other reason was to let him keep the old bachelor company. Now that Mr Gongsun is no more, there is no occasion for him to stay with me."

At daybreak the next morning Zhongzi and Tao Ying had their carriage readied and were going to say goodbye to Mencius, when the latter said with feeling: "Back home, you two must serve your mothers with devotion proper to a dutiful son. And you, Zhongzi, should take particular care of your grandmother in my stead, mind you."

His eyes filled with tears, Zhongzi replied, "Please don't worry, Father. I'll do everything as you wish."

No sooner had he gone out than he came back, looking anxious, and said in undertone: "Father, you must watch out for that Princeling of Wei. He is said to be cruel and heavy-handed in dealing with his subordinates. And he is full of sinister motives, too. You must be on your guard against him!"

Mencius acquiesced with a nod.

Tao Ying, who was waiting for his companion to one side, now asked Mencius: "When Shun was Emperor and Gao Yao was Chief Justice, if the Blind Man killed an innocent person, what was to be done?"

"Arrest him and put him in prison," said Mencius with curt finality. "He would not get away with it just because he was Shun's father, would he?"

Tao Ying said, "But would Shun not try to stop his father being imprisoned?"

"Not, indeed," said Mencius. "How could Shun stop it? Gao Yao had his authority from the law."

"Then what would Shun have done?" Tao Ying wondered aloud.

Mencius said with assurance: "Shun looked upon casting aside the empire as no more than discarding a worn shoe. He would have secretly carried the old man on his back and fled to the shore of the sea and lived there happily, never giving a thought to the empire."

With that, Zhongzi and Tao Ying bade goodbye to Mencius and their fellow students, and set out on their journey home.

Just then Wan Zhang ushered a man in to Mencius, introducing him as Beigong Qi.

The man had a haggard face. He was about 55 years old and carried himself like a gentleman. He was tall and dressed like a scholar.

He made a deep bow to Mencius, took a seat as invited and then sat upright with his loose sleeves hanging down at his sides.

After making a slight bow in return, Mencius enquired, "I am much honored by your presence at my humble abode, but may I know in what way I can benefit by your instructions?"

"Not at all, not at all," Beigong Qi responded with an air of self-abasement, protesting, "Who am I to impart instructions, shallow in learning as I am? In fact, I can hardly claim to be a Confucian disciple at all. You are the Sage of today who carries on the sacred traditions of the past and clears a path for the future. Your name is on everybody's lips. The honor is mine to have the privilege of seeing you in person, sir."

Mencius changed his countenance to one of severity, saying, "Have you come here just to praise me? Or what?"

"No. There is a problem for which I want your help," Beigong said with humility, "and that is, what was the system of rank and income like under the House of Zhou?"

Mencius gave a long sigh before saying, "This cannot be known in detail, for the feudal lords destroyed the records."

"Why did they do that?" asked the other.

Mencius said: "Because they thought that the knowledge of that system would put themselves at a disadvantage."

"Is there any hope of its recovery, sir?" asked Beigong Qi.

Mencius said, "Though I have heard only a brief outline of it, here it is; The emperor, the duke, the marquis and the earl each constituted one rank, while the viscount and the baron shared the same rank, thus totaling five grades. The ruler, the minister, the counselor, the gentlemen of the first, second and third grades each constituted one rank, totaling six grades.

"The territory under the direct jurisdiction of the Emperor was 1,000 square *li* under a duke or a marquis 100 square li, under an earl 70 sqaure li, while under a viscount or a baron it was 50 square li, totaling four grades. Those wo held territories under 50 square *li* had no direct access to the emperor. They had to affiliate themselves to a feudal lord and their territories were known as 'dependencies'. That is why even today small states like Zou and Teng are still Lu's vassals.

"The minister of the emperor enjoyed a territory comparable to that of a marquis; the senior gentleman of the emperor enjoyed a territory comparable to that of viscount of a baron.

"The territory of a large state was 100 square li, and its ruler enjoyed an income ten times that of a minister, a minister four times that of a counselor, a counselor twice that of a gentleman of the first grade, a gentleman of the first grade twice that of a gentleman of the second grade, a gentleman of the second grade twice that of a gentleman of the third grade, and a gentleman of the third grade the same as a commoner who was in public service, in other words, in every case an income in place of what he would get from cultivating the land.

"The territory of a medium-sized state was 70 square li, and its ruler enjoyed an income ten times that of a minister, a minister three times that of a counselor, a counselor twice that of a gentleman of the first grade, a gentleman of the first grade twice that of a gentleman of the second grade, a gentleman of the second grade twice that of a gentleman of the third grade, and a gentleman of the third grade the same as a commoner who was in public service, in other words, in every case an income in place of what he would get from cultivating the land.

"The territory of a small state was 50 square li, and its ruler enjoyed an income ten times that of a minister, a minister twice that of a counselor, a counselor twice that of a gentleman of the first grade, a gentleman of the first grade twice that of a gentleman of the second grade, a gentleman of the second grade twice that of a gentleman of the third grade, and a gentleman of the third grade the same as a commoner who was in public service, in other words, in every case an income in place of what he would get from cultivating the land.

"What a farmer got was what he reaped from 100 mu of land, the allocation of each man. With an allocation of 100 mu, a farmer could feed nine persons, eight persons, seven persons, six persons, or five persons, according to his grading as a farmer. The salary of a commoner who was in public service was also graded accordingly."

Beigong Qi broke into a broad smile at the end of this explanation, saying, "I find your discourse most elucidating, sir, for which I cannot thank you enough." With that, he left.

Our story reverts to King Hui of Liang. As the saying goes, ill news spreads apace. In the course of time rumors about his son's carryings-on with his favorite concubine Lady Jian reached his ears. He felt abjectly betrayed by his son and his concubine, and it was not long before he died from a sudden heart attack.

In the spring of 319 B.C. his son Si, known to history as King Xiang, ascended the throne.

The king had two infatuations: Lady Jian and the Hanguang sword.

So, one morning to his ministers and officials he declared his intentions in the following vein:

"From childhood I developed a passion for weapons. But even today I have not got a sharp one to my liking. I want the best sword maker in the world to forge me a sword as sharp and as powerful as the Hanguang. What is your opinion, everyone? Once I get a sword of that kind I will use it to defend my kingdom, kill our enemies and ensure our safety."

The officials looked at each other in blank dismay. For a long while, no one spoke up.

King Xiang then addressed General Wu Fa: "I would have you find a master sword maker for me, and I will reward you handsomely when this is done."

"At your service, Your Majesty," said Wu Fa.

King Xiang then changed the subject: "It is only a couple of days since I ascended the throne, and I have not yet appointed the Queen Consort formally. Who do you think is the best choice?"

Bai Gui said,"Your Majesty, in my opinion, Lady Zheng should be the only choice since she is your legal wife."

The king wagged his head in annoyance, so much so that the stringed beads on his crown tinkled loudly.

The officials were frightened into silence, heads lowered. Years of officialdom had taught them that silence is golden when a sovereign gets incensed.

King Xiang put on a straight face and, sweeping his angry eyes across his intimidated officials, pronounced aloud: "I name Lady Jian as the Queen Consort, and that is that."

After an awkward moment Bai Gui ventured to ask cautiously: "My Sovereign Lord, you mean the Lady Jian who..."

The king, unabashed, took the words out of his mouth: "...who was no other than the late king's favorite concubine."

"But I think..." Bai Gui broke off as soon as he saw the king's sullen countenance.

Now He Chang, who had all along been thinking of taking Lady Jian as his second wife after the death of King Hui, groaned in despair: "There goes my love!" on hearing the king's bare-faced pronouncement. But after recovering from his first shock of disappointment, he summoned up enough courage to say, though timorously: "Your Majesty, Lady Jian was the deceased king's favorite. I am afraid that it would not be right for you to make her the Queen Consort. And then there is a moral problem to be considered."

"How dare you!" The king flew into a towering rage. "I am the supreme authority in this kingdom of mine. What I say goes. What moral problem is there? Death to him who defies my will!"

He Chang had no choice but to hold his tongue in complete submission.

Bai Gui, however, said, "This is a matter of prime importance. Please think twice before acting, Your Majesty."

The king had a sudden feeling of regal isolation when he found there was no warm response even among his trusted followers. "Well, this can wait. You may retire." He concluded the morning audience with an impatient wave of his hand and made his way straight to Lady Jian's residence.

One day when he was dallying with Lady Jian General Wu Fa suddenly requested an interview. Annoyed, the king demanded angrily: "What emergency has arisen to get you into such a state, General?"

"I beg to report, Your Majesty," Wu Fa said, "that I have just received word that hostilities have broken out afresh between Qin and Chu!"

"What should we do, wedged as we are between them?" asked the king anxiously.

Wu Fa's reply was a cunning one: "When the egret and the clam are locked in a fight, the fisherman has all the gain. We can watch from the sidelines till they fight to the finish, then we can easily defeat them both. We can recover our lost territories too."

King Xiang said, "Not a bad idea. But for the moment you can leave."

Wu Fa was just turning to go when he caught a glimpse of Lady Jian through the parted curtain, who gave him a wink. Consumed with lust, the man had a momentary impulse to seize his desired object in his arms but the presence of the king sobered him.

After Wu Fa was gone King Xiang sent Bai Gui to summon Mencius.

Arriving at the palace, Mencius found the new king to be a man of wretched appearance and flighty of manner. He was anything but pleased.

After greeting the sage, King Xiang asked brusquely: "How can the empire be settled, Venerable Master?"

Mencius said, "The empire can be settled through unity."

"In your view," asked King Xiang, "of all the feudal lords today, who is the one to unite it?"

"One who is not fond of killing can unite it," was the reply.

"Could people follow such a ruler?"

"No one in the empire will refuse to follow him," said Mencius. "Does Your Majesty not know about young rice plants?"

The king smiled wryly: "Of course I know about young rice plants."

Mencius went on, "Should there be a drought in the seventh or eighth month, these plants will wilt. If clouds begin to gather in the sky and rain comes pouring down, then the plants will spring up again. This being the case, who can stop it? Now, in the empire amongst the shepherds of men there is not one who is not fond of killing. If there is one who is not, then the people in the empire will crane their necks to watch for his coming. This being truly the case, the people will turn to him like water flowing downwards with a tremendous force. Who can stop it?"

The king had a hangdog look.

The more Mencius looked at the king the more he found him to his distaste, and the less he was willing to continue the conversation. Finally, he stood up and took his leave.

Back at his lodgings, his disciples crowded round him, plying him with questions.

Chen Dai asked, "What was your impression of King Xiang of Liang, sir?"

Mencius said, "When I saw him at a distance he did not look like a ruler of men. When I went close to him I did not see anything that commanded respect. Alas! This is no place for us! Let us prepare to leave now."

But Chen Dai objected, "Can't you, sir, take him in hand and educate him, considering your talent and learning, to be a ruler of moral worth?"

Mencius replied with indignation: "There are any number of ways to educate people and my disdaining to do so with him is one of them."

It happened to be the 15th night of the second month. A full, bright moon rose high in the sky. King Xiang of Liang was testing the many swords which General Wu Fa had his men make for him. He tried one and then another, and yet another...

Meanwhile, Wu Fa, his thoughts centered on Lady Jian, stealthily approached the rear palace. As he drew near to where he thought the woman's boudoir was he suddenly heard light footsteps approaching. He hurriedly dodged into a corner. It was Lady Jian herself, all alone. Wu Fa watched until he saw her going out by the courtyard gate and making her way to the rear garden. Then he followed her with bated breath. Presently they reached the artificial hill. All of a sudden, Wu Fa made a lunge at the woman, and she was in his arms wholly and entirely. At first she thought it was her sweetheart He Chang as she lisped coyly: "This is not your usual way of courtship, my love!"

"What way is that?" asked Wu Fa.

Lady Jian gave a start of recognition, and she whirled round, demanding angrily: "You scoundrel! What are you doing? What do you take me for?"

Wu Fa said, "Aren't you the late king's concubine? Who else, eh?"

Lady Jian retorted, "I shall soon be the Queen Consort—so beware!"

Wu Fa was stunned for a moment before he said slyly: "Now, I ask you, my Queen Consort, what are you here for at this time of night? A tryst with some lover, I suppose?"

Stung to the quick, Lady Jian flared up and cried shrilly: "You dirty sycophant! How dare you to insult me, a chaste woman! I'll inform against you to His Majesty. You just wait!" Her cursing grew louder and louder.

Suddenly the sound of a single handclap was heard from beyond the wall.

Before Lady Jian could cry "Help!", Wu Fa clapped one hand over her mouth and with the other strangled her. The poor woman kicked her feet a little, and then was no more!

Another handclap. Wu Fa dragged the corpse to the back of the artificial hill. This done, he drew his sword, sidled up to the foot of the wall and looked up. A bulky fellow leaped down from the top of the wall and stood before him. Wu Fa thrust his sword right through the heart of the black-clad stranger. Tearing off the black mask, he recognized his victim to be He Chang. In a flash everything dawned upon him.

He went back to King Xiang and found him still preoccupied with his sword testing.

Acting as if nothing had happened, he quietly approached the king and said in an undertone: "Shall we call it a day, Your Majesty?"

Just then a night watchman, panic-stricken, came up to announce: "Murder! Murder!"

"What?" cried King Xiang.

"Two corpses in the imperial garden, Your Majesty" the night watchman croaked.

Chapter Forty-Six

The Murderer Wu Fa Tries to Shift the Blame
Onto Gongdu Zi;
Righteousness Personified, Mencius Adheres
to His Righteous Way

When King Xiang saw the corpse of Lady Jian he immediately commanded Wu Fa to arrest the murderer.

Wu Fa did not budge but shifted his cunning eyes, saying, "Your Majesty, in my humble opinion, it is better not to let this bad news get about." He indicated the corpses of He Chang and Lady Jian.

"Why?" asked the king.

Wu Fa cast his eyes to the attendants present.

Taking the hint, King Xiang immediately ordered his attendants to leave.

Wu Fa said, "My Lord, under no circumstances must you let this news be spread around. You see, here is one who was an imperial concubine and the other a vice-minister, murdered in the middle of the night..."

"You mean there was something between them?"

"It's as clear as day, Your Majesty, isn't it?"

"Well, who could be the murderer? And why?"

"I can say for certain that the man must be one who is loyal to Your Majesty."

"Why do you say so?"

"He wouldn't have His Majesty so disgraced."

"Right. But something must be done about this whatever you say."

Wu Fa said in subdued voice: "Don't you covet the Hanguang sword, Your Majesty?"

"I do indeed," said King Xiang. "Not a day passes but I long for the possession of it."

"There is a way to procure the sword if only you try," hinted the other.

"But how?" asked King Xiang.

Wu Fa explained, "You can send a man to invite Mencius to the

palace. Just tell him that somebody saw his disciple Gongdu Zi slipping into the rear palace at midnight; and that his disciple first committed rape and then murder. You can this way get Gongdu Zi convicted and put him to death. Ultimately his Hanguang sword will come into your possession."

"What if he should deny the accusation?"

"Put him through torture."

"If even that should fail, what then?"

"Impossible. The flesh is weak, you know."

"All right," said the king. "Let me summon Prime Minister Bai."

But when Bai Gui came he told the king that Mencius and his disciples had left Wei only the day before.

"I saw them go with my own eyes," said Bai Gui. "Gongdu Zi was driving the carriage for Mencius at the time and no mistake about it! By now the party must have covered well over 30 li. How could Gongdu Zi have done such a thing? He can't be in two places at the same time, can he?"

Wu Fa tried to justify himself by saying, "Maybe somebody disguised himself as Gongdu Zi and did it, who knows? Anyway, we need to get Gongdu Zi back to get to the bottom of this business."

Impassioned with the idea of securing the Hanguang sword for himself, the king agreed readily, saying, "Take 50 chariots and bring back Gongdu Zi without fail!"

Bai Gui tried to dissuade the king from this course, but in vain.

So Wu Fa started on the pursuit with the 50 chariots. They overtook Mencius' party at a poplar wood.

Taken by surprise, Mencius asked, "General, what is your purpose here with these troops and chariots?"

Standing up in his chariot, Wu Fa made a slight bow before he replied, "Venerable Master, I beg your pardon. Last night Lady Jian was found murdered. And the finger of accusation has been pointed at your disciple Gongdu Zi."

"Ridiculous!" snorted Mencius. "Gongdu Zi has been with me all this time; how could he have done it? Sheer nonsense!"

"You'll have to excuse me, sir," Wu Fa made another bow. "I can do nothing but obey my orders. So please surrender Gongdu Zi to us."

Mencius spoke with the force of justice: "My disciples all believe in benevolence and righteousness and act on them. Gongdu Zi is no exception. You have no cause to accuse him of murder. If you must find the real murderer, that is your business, but I forbid you to lay hands on an innocent person!"

Wu Fa retorted, "His Majesty ordered me to arrest Gongdu Zi, and so arrest him I must! I have no choice."

At this, Gongdu Zi whipped out his Hanguang sword and came with it at Wu Fa: "Here I am. If you dare touch me, you'll have a taste of my sword!" As he said this he gave a horizontal sweep of his powerful weapon and, at the mere sound of the swish, six poplar trees were cut down. "That could be your end, I warn you," he said to Wu Fa.

The other turned ashen. He knew he was no match for Gongdu Zi, and he had to watch, paralyzed with fear, as Mencius and his party disappeared into the distance.

Back again to Mencius and his disciples. After the event we've just described, they had traversed another 20 *li* when they reached a crossroads. There stood a carriage with a man standing by it. He looked to be in his mid-50s, square-faced, clad in a coarse hemp robe and with a yellow kerchief of the same material wound round his head. "A recluse, I suppose?" thought Mencius.

The stranger came forward, beaming with delight. "This must be Venerable Master Meng, if I'm not mistaken?" asked he, after a deep bow.

Gongdu Zi pulled up the horse, and Mencius stepped down from the carriage and returned the greeting. "Yes, I am Meng Ke from the state of Zou. And you?"

The stranger replied, "I am Jing Chun."

"I have long heard about you as an itinerant rhetorician," Mencius said. "You are famed for your diplomatic talent. What can I do for you, sir?"

Jing Chun said, "There is something I am not so clear about. May I have the benefit of your instruction?"

"Certainly," said Mencius.

Jing Chun continued, "Can itinerant politicians such as I, who make a living by traveling from one feudal court to another expounding their political theories on 'vertical' and 'horizontal' alliances be looked upon as great men?"

Mencius gave a shake of his head.

Jing Chun asked, "Were not Gongsun Yan and Zhang Yi great

men? As soon as they showed their wrath the feudal lords trembled with fear, and when they were still the empire was spared the conflagration of war. If such people were not great, who else is?"

Mencius replied in a dispassionate way: "How can they be thought great men?"

Jing Chun was listening with all ears.

Mencius asked, "Have you never studied the rites? When a man comes of age, his father gives him advice. When a girl marries, her mother gives her advice, and accompanies her to the door with these cautionary words:'When you go to your new home you must be respectful and circumspect. Do not disobey your husband.' It is the way of a wife to consider obedience and docility the norm.

"A man lives in a spacious dwelling, occupies his proper position, and goes along the highway of the empire. When he achieves his ambition he shares his good fortune with the people; when he fails to do so he practices the Way alone. He cannot be led into excesses when wealthy and honored or deflected from his purpose when poor and obscure, nor can he be made to bow before superior force. This is what I would call a great man."

Jing Chun exclaimed, "What an independent character you have, sir! The things you say sound so out of the ordinary to us dullards. No wonder they call you a modern sage!"

"Not at all," said Mencius. "Well, we must press on with our journey. Shall we say goodbye here?" There they parted.

Mencius and his disciples proceeded on their way, and on the third day they arrived at Shiqiu in the State of Song. As it was getting late they put up at an inn for the night.

Just as they had finished their supper, a man dropped in and requested an interview with Mencius. He introduced himself as Song Keng, whom Mencius knew by name only. He was one of the philosophers at Qi Xia, who had advanced the theory that men did not really desire much and that they could avoid fighting if only they could refuse to feel humiliated in the face of insult. Very soon a conversation took place between the two.

Song Keng said, "I have heard that hostilities have broken out between the states of Qin and Chu. I am going to see the king of Chu and try to persuade him to bring an end to them. If I fail to find favor with the king of Chu I shall go to see the king of Qin and try to persuade him instead. I hope I shall have success with one or other of the two kings."

Mencius said, "So far as I know, both kings are aggressive rulers. Therefore it will be no easy job to persuade them. I do not wish to know the details of how you will go about it, but may I ask the gist of your argument? How are you going to persuade the kings?"

Song Keng replied, "I shall explain to them the unprofitability of war."

"Your purpose is lofty indeed, but your line of reasoning is wrong. If you dangle profit before the kings of Qin and Chu, and they call off their armies because they are drawn to profit, then it means that the soldiers in their armies retire because they are drawn to profit. If a subject, in serving his prince, cherished the profit motive, and a son, in serving his father, and a younger brother, in serving his elder brother, did likewise, then it would mean that in their mutual relations, prince and subject, father and son, elder brother and younger brother, all cherished the profit motive to the total exclusion of morality. The prince of such a state would be sure to perish. If, on the other hand, you placed morality before the kings of Qin and Chu and they called off their armies because they were drawn to morality, then it would mean that the soldiers in their armies retired because they were drawn to morality. If a subject, in serving his prince, cherished morality, and a son, in serving his father, and a younger brother, in serving his elder brother, did likewise, then it would mean that in their mutual relations, prince and subject, father and son, elder brother and younger brother, all cherished morality to the exclusion of profit. The prince of such a state would be sure to become a true ruler. What is the point, sir, of mentioning the word 'profit'?"

"I benefit more from one consultation with you than from ten years of reading," Song Keng quoted a proverb to show his appreciation for the illuminating talk. Then he left.

Nothing happened that evening, and the next morning they continued their journey.

One day they came to a county called Pinglu. On hearing of their arrival, the local governor Kong Juxin met them at the west gate of the county seat, whence he escorted them to the county guesthouse.

As soon as the travelers were settled in, the governor paid Mencius a visit. The following dialogue ensued:

The governor: "I am a man of no administrative ability. I have failed in my position as the county head. I feel very bad about that.

Would you, sir, explain to me how to run a government, as I know that you are so learned and farsighted in this?"

Instead of an answer, Mencius put a question to him: "If one of your spear men failed three times in one day to report for duty, would you or would you not dismiss him?"

The governor: "I would not wait for the third time."

Mencius said pointedly: "But you yourself have failed to report for duty many times. In years of famine close on 1,000 of your people suffered, the old and the young being abandoned in the gutter, the able-bodied scattered in all directions."

The governor: "I was most distressed and keenly regretted that. But it was not within my power to do anything about it."

Mencius: "Supposing a man were entrusted with the care of cattle and sheep. Surely he ought to seek pasturage and fodder for the animals. If he found that this could not be done, should he return his charges to their owner or should he stand by and watch the animals die?"

The governor: "I understand. I am guilty of this."

A few days later Mencius and his disciples arrived home in the State of Zou.

Zhang was overjoyed to see her son back after this long separation. Mencius, on the other hand, could not help a rush of mixed feelings of grief and joy when he saw the much-aged woman with her hoary hair. Hot tears sprang to his eyes as he cried out with infinite poignancy: "Mother Dear!"

All the while Zhang studied her son's weather-beaten, careworn face with her caressing eyes, comforting him the best she could: "A man's future lies abroad, he mustn't bury himself in obscurity. And now you are home again, that's my consolation, isn't it? You should be proud of what you have achieved so far, and I feel honored too. So don't let family affections tie you down."

Mencius said with a long sigh: "I have stayed away from you too long and I have not done enough for you as a dutiful son. My heart aches at the thought of it. Forgive me, dear Mother!"

Presently Zhongzi interrupted to inform his father that His Excellency Mr Chunyu Kun had gone to the school and was waiting for him.

Accordingly Mencius bade a hurried good-bye to his mother and went to meet his friend at the school.

Chunyu Kun said, "I trust you have been well since we last parted?"

"I am all right, thank you," replied Mencius. "And I hope you are doing well?"

Chunyu Kun said, "I have been wondering why you didn't tell me when you were leaving Wei."

"I was in a hurry at the time. Please do not take it to heart."

"I have brought you good news, sir. The crown prince of Qi is now on the throne."

"What kind of a ruler is he, sir?"

"Pi Jiang is very understanding and considerate. And he is knowledgeable about the rites. He will turn out to be a good and wise king, I am sure. I am planning to leave Wei for Qi to aid him."

Mencius then inquired, "What about Prime Minister Zou Ji? Don't you mind him, though?"

"He is dead," said Chunyu Kun

"In that case," said Mencius, "I would not mind going with you to try me luck."

"When will you start?"

"Before I leave I will call on my old friends Duanmu Yan and Xiahou. Then I will visit and offer sacrifices to the tombs of my father and Mr Gongsun Benzheng."

Zhongzi then informed him that both Duanmu Yan and Xiahou were already dead. This sad news threw Mensius into a pensive mood.

Now, about the new ruler of Qi, historically known as King Xuan. When he learned that Chunyu Kun had returned to Qi from Wei, he at once summoned him to court and reinstated him in his former office as minister. Shortly afterwards, he paid a visit to Mencius at the Metropolis Inn.

After they had exchanged courtesies, King Xuan said, "Venerable Master, Duke Huan of Qi and Duke Wen of Jin figured prominently on the political scene during the Spring and Autumn period. Can you tell me their story?"

"None of the followers of Confucius," answered Mencius, "spoke of the history of Duke Huan and Duke Wen. It is for this reason that no one in after ages passed on any accounts, and I have no knowledge of them. If you insist, perhaps I may be permitted to tell you about becoming a true king."

King Xuan asked, "How virtuous must a man be before he can become a true king?"

Mencius replied, "He becomes a true king by bringing peace to the people."

"Can someone like myself bring peace to the people?" asked the king.

"Yes, you can."

"How do you know that I can?"

Mencius replied, "I heard the following story from someone:

"A king was sitting in the upper part of the hall, when someone led an ox through the lower part. The king noticed this and asked, 'Where are you taking that ox?' 'The blood of the ox is to be used for consecrating a new bell', was the reply. 'Spare it. I cannot bear to see it shrinking with fear, like an innocent man going to the place of execution,' said the King. 'In that case, should the ceremony be abandoned?' queried the man. 'That is out of the question. Use a lamb instead.' said the king. I wonder if this could be true?"

"It is," said King Xuan.

Mencius rejoined with "The heart behind your action is sufficient to enable you to become a true king."

"But why? I still do not understand."

Mencius said, "The people all thought that you grudged the expense. But, for my part, I have no doubt that you were moved by pity for the animal."

"You are right," said the king. "How could there be such people? Qi may be a small state, but I am not so miserly as to grudge the sacrifice of an ox. It was simply because I could not bear to see it shrnk with fear that I used a lamb instead."

"You must not be surprised that the people thought you miserly," said Mencius. "You used a small animal in place of a big one. How were they to know? If you were pained by the animal going innocently to its death, what was there to choose between an ox and a lamb?"

The King laughed and said, "What was really in my mind, I wonder? It is not true that I grudged the expense, but I did use a lamb instead of the ox. I suppose it was only natural that the people should have thought me miserly."

"Thre is no harm in this," said Mencius. "It is the way of a benevolent man. You saw the ox but not the lamb."

"Precisely so."

Mencius then explained: "The attitude of a gentleman toward animals is this: Once having seen them alive, he cannot bear to see them die. And once having heard their cry, he cannot bear to eat their flesh. That is why the gentleman keeps his distance from the kitchen."

The king began to regard Mencius with fresh eyes, and he said with a feeling of profound respect: "The *Book of Songs* says, 'The heart is another man's,' But it is I who have surmised it.' This describes you perfectly. For though the deed is mine, when I looked into myself I failed to understand my own heart. You described it for me, and your words struck a chord in me. What made you think that my heart accorded with the way of a true king?"

Mencius said, "Should someone say to you: 'I am strong enough to lift 100 *jun** but not a feather; I have eyes that can see the tip of a fine hair but not a cartload of firewood,' would you accept the truth of such a statement?"

"No."

"Why should it be different in your own case?" Mencius asked. "Your bounty is sufficient to reach the animals, yet the benefits of your government fail to reach the people. That a feather is not lifted is because one fails to make the effort; that a cartload of firewood is not seen is because one fails to use one's eyes. Similarly, that peace is not brought to the people is because you fail to practice kindness. Hence your failure to become a true king is due to a refusal to act, not to an inability to act."

"If you say to someone: 'I am unable to do it' when the task is one of striding over the North Sea with Mount Tai under your arm, then this is a genuine case of inability to act. But if you say, 'I am unable to do it' when it is one of breaking off a twig for an elder, then this is a case of refusal to act, not of inability. Hence your failure to become a true king is not the same in kind as 'striding over the North Sea with Mount Tai under your arm', but the same as 'breaking off a twig for an elder'."

The king still looked puzzled.

Mencius went on, "Treat the aged of your own family in a manner befitting their venerable age and extend this treatment to the aged of other families; treat your own young in a manner befitting their tender age and extend this to the young of other families, and you can roll

---

* Ancient unit of weight (equal to 15 kg).

the empire on your palm. The *Book of Songs* says, 'He sent an example for his consort/And also for his brothers, /And so ruled over the family and the state.' In other words, all you have to do is take this very heart here and apply it to what is over there. Hence one who extends his bounty can bring peace to all within the Four Seas; one who does not cannot bring peace even to his own family. There is just one thing in which the ancients greatly surpassed others, and that is the way they extended what they did. Why is it then that your bounty is sufficient to reach animals yet the benefits of your government fail to reach the people?"

"I don't know," said King Xuan helplessly. "Why?"

Mencius said, "It is by weighing a thing that its weight can be known, and by measuring it that its length can be ascertained. This is so with all things, but particularly so with the heart. Your Majesty should measure his own heart."

The king lowered his head in thought.

Mencius probed: "Perhaps you find satisfaction only in starting wars, imperiling your subjects and incurring the enmity of the other feudal lords?"

"Oh, no!" said King Xuan. "Why should I find satisfaction in such acts? I only wish to realize my supreme ambition."

"May I be told what that is?"

The king smiled, offering no reply.

Chapter Forty-Seven

Mencius Urges King Xuan to Practice Benevolent Government; Master and Disciple Discuss the Way of Self-Cultivation as Befits a Sage

As mentioned in our last chapter, when asked about his supreme ambition by Mencius, King Xuan merely smiled but gave no answer. Thereupon, Mencius pursued, "Is it because your food is not good enough to gratify your palate, and your clothes not good enough to gratify your body? Or perhaps the sights and sounds are not good enough to gratify your eyes and ears and your close servants not good enough to serve you? Surely any of your various officials could make good these deficiencies—it cannot be because of these things?"

King Xuan agreed: "No. It is not because of these things."

"In that case," said Mencius, "one can guess what your supreme ambition is: You wish to extend your territory, to enjoy the homage of the states of Qin and Chu, to rule over the empire and to bring peace to the barbarian tribes on the four borders."

King Xuan smiled and nodded.

Mencius went on, "If you count on that to fulfill your ambition, then you are as good as looking for a fish by climbing a tree."

This stunned the king, and it was several moments before he ventured to ask, "Is it as bad as that?"

"It is likely to be worse," said Mencius. "If you look for a fish by climbing a tree, though you will not find it, there is no danger of this bringing disasters in its train. But if you seek the fulfilment of an ambition like yours by such means as you employ, after putting all your heart and soul into the pursuit, you are certain to reap disaster in the end."

King Xuan asked, "May I hear the whys and the wherefores?"

Mencius said, "If the men of Zou and the men of Chu were to go to war, who do you think would win?"

"The men of Chu," said the king decisively.

Mencius rejoined, "That means that the small is no match for the

big, the few no match for the many, and the weak no match for the strong. Within the empire there are nine areas of 10,000 square li, and the territory of Qi makes up one of these. For one to try to overcome the other eight is no different from Zou going to war with Chu."

The king appeared offended and sullen.

Mencius asked, "Why not go back to fundamentals? Now if you should practice benevolence in the government of your state, then all those in the empire who seek office would wish to find a place at your court, all tillers of land to till the land in outlying parts of your realm, all merchants to enjoy the refuge of your market places, all travelers to go by way of your roads, and all those who hate their rulers to lay their complaints before you. This being so, who could stop you holding sway over the empire?"

King Xuan replied, "I am dull-witted and cannot see my way ahead. I hope you will help me towards my goal and instruct me plainly."

Mencius regarded the king with a doubting gaze.

King Xuan urged, "Though I am slow, I shall do my best to follow your advice."

Mencius said, "Only men of education can have constant hearts in spite of a lack of constant means of support. The people, on the other hand, never have constant hearts if they are without constant means. Lacking constant hearts, they will go astray and fall into excesses, stopping at nothing. To punish them after they have fallen foul of the law is to set a trap for the people. How can a benevolent man in authority allow himself to set a trap for his people? Hence, when determining what means of support the people should have, a good and wise ruler ensures that these are sufficient, on one hand, for the care of parents, and, on the other, for the support of wife and children, so that the people always have sufficient food in good years and escape starvation in bad. Only then does he propel them towards goodness; in this way the people find it easy to follow him.

"Nowadays, the means laid down for the people are sufficient neither for the care of parents nor for the support of wife and children. In good years life is always hard, while in bad years there is no way of escaping death. Thus simply to survive takes more energy than the people have. What time can they spare for learning about the rites and duty?"

"What is the way I should take, sir?" asked the king in distress.

"Why not go back to fundamentals?" Mencius asked. "If the mulberry is planted in every homestead with five *mu** of land, then those who are 50 can wear silk; if chickens, pigs and dogs do not miss their breeding season, then those who are 70 can eat meat; if each lot of a hundred *mu* is not deprived of labor during the busy seasons, then families with several mouths to feed will not go hungry. Exercise due care over the education provided by village schools and discipline the people by teaching duties proper to sons and younger brothers, and those whose heads have turned grey will not be carrying loads on the roads. When the aged wear silk and eat meat and the masses are neither cold nor hungry, it is impossible for their prince not to be a true king."

King Xuan beamed with delight, saying, "I am extremely satisfied with this long discourse of yours, sir. I will come and seek your instruction again the next time I am free. Good-bye till then."

Back from seeing off the king, Mencius received Gongsun Chou in his room. Following is their dialogue:

Gongsun Chou: "If you, Master, were raised to a position above the ministers in Qi and were able to put your doctrines into practice, it would be no surprise if through this you were able to make the king of Qi a leader of the feudal lords or even a true king. If this happened, would it cause any stirring in your heart?"

"No!" replied Mencius definitely. "My heart has not been stirred since the age of 40."

Gongsun Chou: "In that case you far surpass many an ancient."

Mencius reacted with a nonchalant air, saying, "That is not difficult. Gao Zi succeeded in this at an even earlier age than I."

Gongsun Chou gazed at his teacher eagerly as he said: "Excuse me, sir, but I wonder if you could tell me something about the heart that cannot be stirred, in your case and in Gao Zi's case?"

Mencius: "According to the philosopher Gao, 'If you fail to understand words, do not worry about this in your heart. If you fail to understand in your heart, do not seek satisfaction in your *qi*.' It is right that one should not seek satisfaction in one's *qi* when one fails to understand in one's heart. But it is wrong to say that one should not worry about it in one's heart when one fails to understand words."

Gongsun Chou: "Why is that?"

---

* A *mu* is about 1/6 of an acre.

Mencius: "The will is commander over the *qi*, while the *qi* is that which fills the body. The *qi* halts where the will arrives at. Hence it is said, 'Take hold of your will and do not abuse your *qi*.' "

Gongsun Chou shook his head as if to say, "I do not quite understand."

"The will and the *qi* act on each other," Mencius gesticulated as he continued. "The will, when blocked, moves the *qi*. On the other hand, the *qi*, when blocked, also moves the will. Now stumbling and hurrying affect the *qi*, yet in fact palpitations of the heart are produced."

Gongsun Chou: "May I ask what your strong points are?"

Mencius: "I have an insight into words. I am good at cultivating my 'flood-like *qi*'."

Gongsun Chou: "May I ask what this 'flood-like *qi*' is?"

"It is difficult to explain," Mencius gave an ingenuous smile. "In other words, it can be subtly appreciated, but not expressed verbally. Well, let me try, if you insist.

"This is a *qi* which is, in the highest degree, vast and unyielding. Nourish it with integrity and place no obstacle in its path, and it will fill the space between Heaven and Earth. It is a *qi* which unites righteousness and the Way. Deprive it of these, and it will collapse. It is born of accumulated righteousness and cannot be appropriated by anyone through a sporadic show of righteousness. Whenever one acts in a way that falls below the standard set in one's heart, it will collapse. Hence I said that Gao Zi never understood righteousness because he looked upon it as external. You must work at it and never let it out of your mind. At the same time, while you never let it out of your mind, you must not forcibly help it to grow, either. You must not be like the man from Song, who pulled at his rice plants because he was worried about their failure to grow. After he had done so, he went on his way home. 'I'm worn out today,' said he to his family. 'I have been helping the rice plants to grow.' His son rushed out to take a look —and there the plants were, all shriveled up. There are few in the world who can resist the urge to help their rice plants grow. There are some who leave the plants unattended, thinking that nothing they can do will be of any use. They are the people who do not even bother to weed. There are others who help the plants to grow; they are the people who pull at them. Not only do they fail to help them, but they do the plants positive harm."

Gongsun Chou: "What do you mean by 'an insight into words'?"

Mencius: "From biased words I can see wherein the speaker is blind; from immoderate words, wherein he is ensnared; from heretical words, wherein he has strayed from the right path; from evasive words, wherein he is at his wits' end. What arises in the mind will interfere with policy, and what shows itself in policy will interfere with practice. Were a sage to rise again, he would surely agree with what I have said."

Gongsun Chou: "Zai Wo and Zi Gong excelled in rhetoric; Ran Niu, Min Zi and Yan Hui excelled in the exposition of virtuous conduct. Confucius excelled in both and yet he said, 'I am not versed in rhetoric.' Now you, Master, excel in both rhetoric and virtuous conduct; surely you are a sage already?"

"What an extraordinary thing for you to say of me!" protested Mencius heatedly. "Zi Gong once asked Confucius, "Are you, Master, a sage?' Confucius replied, 'I have not succeeded in becoming a sage. I simply never tire of learning nor weary of teaching.' Zi Gong said, 'Not to tire of learning is wisdom; not to weary of teaching is benevolence. You must be a sage to be both wise and benevolent.' A sage is something even Confucius did not claim to be. What an extraordinary thing for you to say of me!"

Gongsun Chou: "I have heard that Zi Xia, Zi You and Zi Zhang each had one aspect of the Sage (Confucius) while Ran Niu, Min Zi and Yan Hui were his replicas in miniature. Which would you rather be?"

Mencius: "Let us leave this question for the moment."

Gongsun Chou: "How about Bo Yi and Yi Yin?"

Mencius: "They followed paths different from that of Confucius. Bo Yi was such that he would serve only the right prince and rule over the right people. He took office when order prevailed, and relinquished it when there was disorder. Yi Yin was such that he would serve any prince and rule over any people, would take office whether order prevailed or not. Confucius was such that he would take office or remain in a state, would delay his departure or hasten it, all according to circumstances. All three were sages of old. I have not been able to emulate any of them, but it is my hope and wish to follow the example of Confucius."

Gongsun Chou: "Were Bo Yi and Yi Yin as much equals of Confucius as that?"

Mencius waxed solemn in countenance as he said, "No. Ever since man came into this world, there has never been one to equal Confucius."

Gongsun Chou: "Was there anything common to the three of them?"

Mencius: "Yes. Were they to become ruler over a territory hundred of square li, they would have been capable of winning the homage of the feudal lords and taking possession of the empire. But had it been necessary to perpetrate one wrongful deed or to kill one innocent man in order to gain the empire, none of them would have consented to it. In this they were alike."

Gongsun Chou: "In what way were they different?"

"Zao Wo, Zi Gong and You Ruo were intelligent enough to appreciate the Sage," said Mencius. "They would not have stooped so low as to show a bias in favor of the man they admired."

Gongsun Chou: "No, I don't think they would."

Mencius: "Just imagine how they admired Confucius. Zai Wo said, 'In my view, the Master surpassed greatly Yao and Shun.' Zi Gong said, 'Through the rites of a state he could see its government; through its music, the moral quality of its ruler. Looking back over 100 generations he was able to appraise all the kings, and no one has ever been able to show him in the wrong in a single instance. Ever since man came into this world, there has never been another like the Master.' You Ruo said, 'That is true not only of men. The unicorn is the same in kind as other animals, the phoenix as other birds; Mount Tai is the same as small mounds of earth, the Yellow River and the Sea are no different from water that runs in the gutter. The Sage, too, is the same in kind as other men. Though one of their kind, he stands far above the crowd. Ever since man came into this world there has never been one greater than Confucius.' There is considerable truth in what they said, I think."

That night, his old friend Kuang Zhang came to see him.

After an exchange of courtesies Kuang Zhang began, "You, Master, possess superior abilities equaled by no one in the world. I have a mind to recommend that His Majesty appoint you to some important position. How would you like that, sir?"

Mencius replied, "His Majesty does have supreme ambition. But I wonder if he is a man of his word."

Kuang Zhang smiled and said, "You sound as if you had doubts about his resolve. Or, should I say, for the time being you prefer to take a wait-and-see attitude. Am I right?"

Mencius said, "To run a state well one has to make enduring and unremitting efforts in practicing benevolent government. One who is to accomplish anything at all must have lofty ambition and a constant heart. A man of inaction is to be pitied. But a man of inconstant heart is contemptible!"

Kuang Zhang said: "I know what you have in mind when you say that, sir."

The next morning Zhuang Bao came to see Mencius.

Zhuang Bao eyed Mencius sheepishly as he greeted him: "How have you been, Master?"

"I am honored by your visit, Your Excellency," said Mencius.

Zhuang Bao informed him: "The king received me and told me that he was fond of music. I was at a loss what to say." As Mencius made no response, he added, "May I ask, Master, what you think of a fondness for music?"

Mencius answered, "If the king has a great fondness for music, then there is perhaps hope for the State of Qi."

Mencius fell silent, and. Zhuang Bao, finding the atmosphere incongenial, took a hasty leave.

One day King Xuan of Qi had an interview with Mencius in his inner chamber at the palace. He put on an amiable smile and said, "I found your words most subtle and profound, Master. I would like to hear more of your wisdom. That is why I have invited you here today."

"Is it true that Your Majesty told Zhuang Bao that you were fond of music?" Mencius asked.

King Xuan explained, "It is not the music of ancient times that I am capable of appreciating; I am merely fond of popular music."

Pleased with the topic, Mencius said cheerfully: "If you have a great fondness for music, then there is perhaps hope for the State of Qi. Whether it is the music of today or the music of antiquity makes no difference."

Resting his puzzled eyes on Mencius, the king protested, "I can make no sense of your remark. Would you kindly explain it for me?"

Mencius asked, "Which is greater, enjoyment by yourself or enjoyment in the company of others?"

"In the company of others, of course," was the reply.

Again Mencius asked, "Which is greater, enjoyment in the company of a few or enjoyment in the company of many?"

King Xuan said, "In the company of many, of course."

"Well, let me tell you about enjoyment," Mencius went on. "Now suppose you have a musical performance here, and when the people hear the sound of your bells and drums and the notes of your pipes and flutes they all with aching heads and knitted brows say to one another: 'In being fond of music, why does our king bring us to such straits that fathers and sons do not see each other, and brothers, wives and children are parted and scattered?' Again, suppose you were hunting here, and when the people heard the sound of your chariots and horses and saw the magnificence of your banners they all, with aching heads and knitted brows, said to one another: 'In being fond of hunting, why does our king bring us to such straits that fathers and sons do not see each other, and brothers, wives and children are parted and scattered?' The reason would simply be that you failed to share your enjoyment with the people."

King Xuan admitted, "Yes, that was how I enjoyed myself previously. But how should I go about it the next time?"

Mencius said, "On the other hand, suppose you were having a musical performance here, and when the people heard the sound of your bells and drums and the notes of your pipes and flutes they all looked pleased and said to one another: 'Our king must be in good health, otherwise how could he have music performed?' Again, suppose you were hunting here, and when the people heard the sound of your chariots and horses and saw the magnificence of your banners they all looked pleased and said to one another: 'Our king must be in good health, otherwise how could he go hunting?' The reason would again simply be that you shared your enjoyment with the people. Now, if you shared your enjoyment with the people the whole empire would surely submit to you."

The king ruminated over these words for some time, then he raised another question:

"Is it true that the park of King Wen was 70 square li?"

"It is so recorded," said Mencius.

"Was it really as large as that?"

"Even so, the people found it small."

King Xuan said, "My park is only 40 square li, and yet the people consider it too big. Why is this?"

Mencius explained, "True, King Wen's park was 70 square li, but it was open to woodcutters as well as catchers of pheasants and hares.

As he shared it with the people is it any wonder that they found it small? When I first arrived at the borders of your state I inquired about the major prohibitions before I dared enter. I was told that within the outskirts of the capital there was a park of 40 square *li* in which the killing of a deer was as serious an offence as the killing of a man. This turns the park into a trap of 40 square *li* in the midst of the state. Is it any wonder that the people consider it too big?"

The king mused a long while, close-eyed, and then, with his eye-lids slowly opening, he spoke in a short-winded manner: "Master, you have been staying in Qi for over two months now. Now do my subjects impress you?"

Mencius had a momentary impulse to unbosom himself, then he thought better of it and changed his mind. He gulped and no words came.

Thereupon the king prompted him, saying, "Say what you really think, Master. Don't hold it back. I am listening."

Mencius said, "From antiquity till the present there have been good versus evil ministers under all rulers."

King Xuan asked, "Which of my subjects, do you think, are good ones and which are bad?"

Mencius replied tactfully: "Of the Qi officials whom I know personally, the governor of Pinglu, Kong Juxin, may be considered a likable fellow, for he knows his limitations."

"What have you found in him?" asked the king.

Mencius recounted to the king his conversation with the governor, then commented favorably, saying, "He knew his limitations. What is more, he owned up to his mistakes, which is praiseworthy."

"Is it as praiseworthy as all that?"

"Yes, it is."

"Why?"

"He who readily owns up to his mistake can readily correct it."

"Is it not more praiseworthy of him if he does not make any mistake at all?"

"That is impossible."

"Why?"

"No man is infallible. To err is human."

"According to you, it is not important if one makes a mistake; what is important is that one can correct it as soon as a mistake is made. Am I right?"

"Right. It is not wrong to correct a mistake when you see it," said Mencius with avidity. "In this connection, men of virtue in the past set us fine examples. Take Zi Lu, one of Confucius' 72 major disciples, for example. When anyone told him that he had made a mistake, he was delighted. Another example was Emperor Yu. When he heard a fine saying he bowed low before the speaker. The great Shun went even further. He was ever ready to fall into line with others, giving up his own ways for theirs, and glad to take from others that by which he could do good. From the time he was a farmer, a potter and a fisherman to the time he became emperor there was nothing he did that he did not take from others. To take from others that by which one can do good is to help them do good. Hence there is nothing more important to a gentleman than helping others do good."

"Well spoken!" cried the king. "Then will you kindly point out my mistake, sir?"

Mencius said with good humor: "Suppose a subject of Your Majesty's, having entrusted his wife and children to the care of a friend, were to go on a trip to the State of Chu, only to find, upon his return, that his friend had allowed his wife and children to suffer cold and hunger, then what should he do about it?"

King Xuan said, "Break off ties of friendship."

Mencius continued, "If the chief judge was unable to keep his guards in order, then what should be done about it?"

"He should be removed from office," said King Xuan.

Mencius then posed the question: "If the whole realm within the four borders was ill-governed, what should be done about it?"

The king blushed with embarrassment, then turned to look right and left, as if he had heard nothing. Then he asked Mencius in an absent-minded way: "If I employ as many virtuous and loyal men as there are to be my ministers, what should be done then?"

Mencius said, "As the saying goes, 'Though the peach does not speak, the world wears a path beneath it.' All Your Majesty has to do is show sincerity, and men of virtue throughout the empire will flock to you."

King Xuan smiled incredulously. "That is easier said than done, isn't it?" he scoffed.

"It is not so difficult as you think, Your Majesty. It all depends on how you approach the matter. If the ruler of a state will advance good and wise men, he may have to promote those of low position over the heads of those of exalted rank and distant relatives over near ones. That in doing so he must exercise great caution goes without saying. Hence, when your close attendants all say of a man that he is good and wise, that is not enough; when the counselors all say the same, that is not enough; when everyone says so, then you should have the case investigated. If the man turns out to be good and wise, then and only then should he be given office. When your close attendants all say of a man that he is unsuitable, do not listen to them; when the counselors all say the same, do not listen to them; when everyone says so, then have the case investigated. If the man turns out to be unsuitable, then and only then should he be removed from office. When your close attendants all say of a man that he deserves death, do not listen to them; when the counselors all say the same, do not listen to them; when everyone says so, then have the case investigated. If the man turns out to deserve death, then and only then should he be put to death. In this way, it will be said, 'He was put to death by the whole country.' Only by acting in this manner can one be father and mother to the people."

After meditating for some time King Xuan further asked, "Master, if I want to practice benevolent government, what should I do in the first instance?"

Mencius said, "First, reduce tax rates, and reward and encourage farming and weaving; second, be friends with those who are loyal and virtuous and keep your distance from those who fawn upon you, or even dismiss them; third, open schools to enrol a large number of students to whom rituals and ceremonies are taught; fourth, take the aged and the young under sheltering care, aid those who have no kith and kin and cannot support themselves; and fifth, encourage handicrafts, trades and business transactions."

King Xuan said with a smile: "You reel off such a long list of things to be done, sir. But what is the urgent task for the present, may I ask?"

Mencius replied, "In today's world the kings of Qin, Chu and Wei are warlike rulers. Theirs are big states, too. So, Your Majesty must be vigilant..."

Their conversation was interrupted by the entrance of Prime Minister Chu Zi, He looked alarmed and bewildered as he reported to the king: "There is a woman at the gate who demands an interview with Your Majesty. The guards cannot stop her. She is now blundering her way in here. What is to be done with her, Your Majesty?"

"What does she look like?" asked the king.

"As plain as you can imagine," answered Chu Zi.

The king gave a vigorous throw of his wide sleeves, a customary gesture of impatience, as he shouted, "Throw her out!"

But the command had hardly issued from his lips, when the woman had already glided into the room. She made a curtsy to the king, saying, "Here is homage to Your Majesty from a common woman."

The king fixed his eyes on her. The woman gave her name as Zhong Lichun. She looked in her early 40s. Indeed she is as ugly as ugly can be, thought the king, with her scanty-haired flat head, her beak-like nose and her deep-socketed eyes. To crown all, she was dark-complexioned; she walked with a stoop and her neck was anything but slender. The king was shocked at what he saw, and it was some time before he had recovered himself enough to ask, "You, woman! What have you come here for?"

Unabashed, Zhong Lichun replied, "To offer myself to Your Majesty as his consort."

The king stared at the strange woman, stupefied. Mencius and Chu Zi too could hardly believe their ears.

Chapter Forty-Eight

Drawn to the Beauty of Virtue, King Xuan Takes an Ugly Woman As His Wife; In a High Position As Minister of Qi, Mencius Forgets Not His Duty As a Son

As related in the last chapter, King Xuan was shocked to hear that the ugly woman Zhong Lichun wanted to marry him, and Mencius and Prime Minister Chu Zi could not believe their ears. All the attendants and ladies-in-waiting, too, wagged their heads and clicked their tongues at the effrontery of this brazen hussy.

The woman, however, took no notice of all this; she took a seat calmly, scanned all those present, and then articulated clearly: "My Sovereign Lord, you are over 40 years of age now. It is high time you accomplished something great for your state and people. You must not fritter away your prime of life with nothing achieved."

Her words struck all as unusual, and they began to regard her with fresh eyes.

Chu Zi said to her: "Can't you see that it is by no means easy to be the king's consort?"

Zhong Lichun retorted, "I should say it can be difficult and it can be easy."

"What do you mean?" asked Chu Zi.

Zhong Lichun said, "As the supreme ruler of a state, His Majesty bears a great burden upon his shoulders; one single word of his may entail the rise or the fall of a whole nation. Some ancient wise man said, 'To govern means to guide aright.' If the king sets a correct example, all his subjects will follow suit and no one will dare disobey. His personal conduct is of paramount importance. For him to guide aright calls for assistance from his ministers at court and support from his consort at home. In this connection, I would say it is difficult to be a king's consort. On the other hand, should the king have a weakness for pretty faces, the consort could easily indulge his whims; so what is so difficult about it?"

Chu Zi gazed keenly at the woman, saying: "So you want to have

a try in spite of the difficulties?"

Zhong Lichun answered without hesitation: "Precisely."

As King Xuan found that the woman talked sense, he could not help asking, "Since you have a great opinion of yourself, will you please tell me what I should do to begin with?"

Zhong Lichun explained, "Your Majesty is a parent to the common people. As such, you should very much take to heart their livelihood. In my opinion, though Qi is a major state, there are underlying dangers."

"Such as?" queried Chu Zi.

Zhong Lichun replied, "Such as the danger of invasion from the mighty states of Qin and Chu. To be ready for that eventuality we must have a strong armed force and keep our treasury fully supplied with revenue. His Majesty must keep sycophantic courtiers away and listen only to those who are loyal but outspoken. Employ good and wise men and put them in key positions. Last but not least, rescind excessive taxes and levies so that the common people may the sooner live a life of plenty."

"Well said! Well said!" cried King Xuan.

Zhong Lichun then asked: "Am I not fully qualified to be your consort?"

"Oh, that..." The king was thrown into confusion, and he looked to Mencius on his left and Chu Zi on his right for help. "But I have had a consort already," he bleated.

"That I know," said Zhong Lichun. "But she died six months ago."

The king gave a gasp, knowing not what to say.

Zhong Lichun went on, "Is His Majesty in love only with moonlight mirrored in the water? Or flowers reflected in a glass?"

"Oh no, no, no!" protested the king. "I love much better a wife who has brains and strong common sense."

"Then you can have no better choice than in me, Your Majesty."

King Xuan cried, "Impossible! Aren't you the woman from Wuyan Town who is said to be the plainest-looking creature on earth? How could I..."

Zong Lichun was nonchalant: "So what? I can assure Your Majesty that once I became your consort I would do a good job in looking after the rear palace so that you could give all your time to state affairs without fear of disturbance in the rear."

King Xuan again turned to Mencius and Chu Zi for help, and the last two nodded their heads.

Thereupon the king gave his reluctant consent with a wave of his hand. "Wait on Lady Zhong and see her properly settled in the rear palace," he ordered his maids-in-waiting.

Thus Zhong Lichun was to all intents and purposes accepted by the king.

Mencius held up his clasped hands and bowed to King Xuan: "Congratulations!"

King Xuan put on a strained smile, saying, "She has a head on her shoulders. That is what I appreciate in her."

On the wedding night, Zhong Lichun declared to her husband the king: "As far as my looks are concerned, I fall far short of being a queen. But as far as my talent and virtue are concerned, I am fully qualified to be one. Do you not agree, Your Majesty?"

"Yes, I do," replied King Xuan, "and that is why I have taken you as my consort."

"This shows that Your Majesty sets more store by talent and virtue than appearance."

"Right."

"That being so, I would like to lay down three rules for you to observe."

"Nonsense!" Incensed by the remark, King Xuan shouted. "How dare you to try to lay down rules for me, the supreme ruler of a state!"

"Please calm yourself, my lord," said Zhong Lichun, not intimidated in the least. "It is just because I respect you as the supreme ruler that I wish to set three rules for your benefit. Otherwise I will not be worthy of my title of consort."

"Name your three rules, then!" The king said, between laughter and tears.

"Rule One," Zhong Lichun began in all seriousness, "Your Majesty must practice benevolent government for better or worse and give first consideration to the betterment of your country and people. Rule Two, loyal and virtuous ministers are pillars of society and valuable assistants, whereas the crafty and adulatory ones are the enemies of the people. Hence you must rely on the former and keep your distance from the latter. Can Your Majesty do that?"

"Every word rings true". admitted the king. "Surely I can and will do as you say."

"So Rule Three, keep away from sensual delights and exercise moderation in your sexual life. Will Your Majesty be able to do that?"

The king fell silent, looking displeased.

Zhong Lichun continued, "The Qi court for long has had a fondness for magnificent display, grand palaces, high living. If this fondness goes unchecked it may alienate the common people from its ruler."

"But," said King Xuan, "some time ago, in a talk with me, Mencius expressed the wish that I should share my enjoyment with the people."

Zhong Lichun said, "It is indeed a good thing to share your enjoyment with the people, and for that matter it should be encouraged. But I do not mean that kind of enjoyment. What I mean is sensual indulgence."

King Xuan protested, "But appetite for food and sex is natural. What's wrong with it?"

Zhong Lichun cautioned him: "There is a limit to everything. Going too far is as bad as not going far enough. Over-indulgence in that sort of thing can only harm one's health, Your Majesty. You cannot hope to run your government efficiently unless you have a sound body, don't you think?"

From that time on, King Xuan began to put more time and energy into affairs of state, and Qi became stronger and more prosperous than ever.

In the spring of 318 B.C., by courtesy of King Xuan, Mencius moved into the king's winter palace—the Snow Palace. One day King Xuan, accompanied by Chu Zi, Tian Ji and Chunyu Kun, went to see Mencius there.

On learning of their arrival, Mencius led his disciples to welcome them at the front gate. He showed his guests round the garden, which was planted with multi-colored peonies. As he browsed among the flowers, delighting in one variety after another, the king suddenly raised a question to his host: "Master, does even a good and wise man have such enjoyment as this?"

"Yes, he does," replied Mencius. "Should there be a man who is not given a share in such enjoyment, he would speak ill of those in authority. To speak ill of those in authority because one is not given a share in such enjoyment is, of course, wrong. But for one in authority over the people not to share his enjoyment with the people is equally wrong. The people will delight in the joy of he who delights in their joy, and will worry over the troubles of he who worries over their troubles. He who delights and worries on account of the Empire is certain to become a true king."

The King hung on these words, fascinated.

Mencius went on, quoting from history as he did so: "Once, Duke Jing of Qi consulted Yan Zi: 'I wish to travel to Zhuangfu and Zhaowu, then follow the sea coast south to Langya. What must I do to be able to emulate the travels of the former kings?' 'This is indeed a splendid question!' answered Yan Zi. 'When the Emperor goes to the feudal lords, this is known as 'a tour of inspection'. It is so called because its purpose is to inspect the territories for which the feudal lords are responsible. When the feudal lords go to pay homage to the emperor, this is known as 'a report on duties". It is so called because its purpose is to report on duties they are charged with. Neither is undertaken without good reason. In spring the purpose is to inspect the plowing so that those who have not enough for sowing may be given help; in autumn the purpose is to inspect the harvesting, so that those who are in need may be given aid. As a saying of the Xia Dynasty puts it: 'If our king does not make his excursions, how can we have rest? If our king does not go on tours, how can we have help? Every time he travels he sets an example for the feudal lords.' Nowadays the state of things is different. A host marches in attendance on the ruler, and stores of provisions are consumed. The hungry are deprived of their food, and there is no rest for those who are called to toil. They look askance, grinding their teeth with hatred. Complaints are heard everywhere. They are being driven to desperation. The lords misuse the people, going against Heaven's will. And behind their vermilion gates. food and drink flow like water. Drifting, lingering, rioting and intemperance—these excesses amongst the feudal lords are a cause for concern. By 'drifting' is meant going downstream with no thought of returning; by 'lingering', going upstream with no thought of returning; by 'rioting', being insatiable in the hunt; by 'intemperance', being insatiable in drink. The former kings never indulged in any of these excesses. It is for you, my lord, to decide on your course of action.' Duke Jing was pleased. He made elaborate preparations in the capital and then went to stay on the outskirts. Then he opened up the granaries and gave to those who were in need. He summoned the Grand Musician and told him: 'Make me music which expresses the subject.' The result was the *Zhishao* and *Jueshao*. Here is the text:'What harm is there in curbing the lord?' To curb the lord is to love him. Now, if Duke Jing had not cared for his subjects, how could they have sung his praises?"

King Xuan said with a broad grin: "An erudite scholar you are indeed! There is nothing under the sun you do not know. I get a wealth of knowledge every time I talk to you."

"You praise me more than I deserve, I'm afraid," demurred Mencius.

King Xuan then changed the subject. "Someone has advised me to pull down the Hall of Light," he said. "Should I or should I not do so?"

Mencius replied, "The Hall of Light is the hall of a true king. If Your Majesty wishes to practice kingly government, then he should not pull it down."

"May I hear about kingly government?" asked King Xuan.

Mencius said, "Formerly, when King Wen ruled over Qi, the old capital of the Zhou Dynasty, tillers of land were taxed one part in nine; descendants of officials received hereditary emoluments; there were inspections but no levies at border stations and market places; fish traps were open for all to use; punishment did not extend to the wife and children of an offender. Old men without wives, old women without husbands, old people without children, young children without fathers—these four types of people are the most destitute and have no one to turn to for help. Whenever King Wen put benevolent measures into effect, he always gave them first consideration. The *Book of Songs* says, 'Happy are the rich; /But have pity on the helpless.'"

"Well spoken!" cried King Xuan.

"If you consider my words well spoken, then why do you not put them into practice?" queried Mencius.

"I have a weakness," the king confessed. "I am too fond of money."

Mencius said, "In antiquity Gongliu was fond of money too. The *Book of Songs* says, 'He stocked and stored; /He placed provisions /In bags and sacks. /He brought harmony and so glory to his state. /On full display were bows and arrows, /Spears, halberds and axes. /Only then did the march begin.' It was only when those who stayed at home had full granaries and those who went forth to war had full sacks that the march could begin. You may be fond of money, but so long as you share this fondness with the people, how can it interfere with your becoming a true king?"

'But I have another weakness," the king said. "I am fond of women."

"That makes no difference either. In antiquity, King Tai Wang was also fond of women. He loved his wife and concubines. That did not prevent him from becoming a true king. The *Book of Songs* says, 'Gugong Danfu*/Early in the morning galloped on his horse/Along the banks of the river in the West/Till he came to the foot of Mount Qi. /He brought with him the Lady Jiang, /Looking for a suitable abode.' At that time, there were neither girls pining for a husband nor men without a wife. You may be fond of women, but so long as you share this fondness with the people, how can it interfere with your becoming a true king? If your Majesty is fond of women, knows conjugal happiness, and thereby shares this happiness with the people, then what is there to prevent him from practicing benevolent government? Your taking Lady Zhong as your consort shows that you love a woman more for her virtue than her physical charms, does it not?"

King Xuan said, "You are admirable, Master! Besides being an erudite scholar, you are a good mind-reader, too."

After Mencius ushered his guests into his parlor, their conversation continued.

King Xuan said, "As a common saying puts it, 'It takes the green leaves of a plant to set off the beauty of its red blossoms.' I have come to realize the truth of that saying more and more. May I ask, in what way can I win the whole-hearted support of my subjects in a common endeavor to build my country?"

"It all depends on you, My Lord," said Mencius. "If a prince treats his subjects as his hands and feet, they will treat him as their belly and heart. If he treats them as his horses and hounds, they will treat him as a stranger. If he treats them as mud and weeds, they will treat him as an enemy. Confucius said, 'The commander of the forces of a large state may be carried off, but the will of even a common man cannot be taken from him.' Benevolence is the finest abode and righteousness is the broadest road. So long as you treat your subjects as your hands

---

* I.e., King Tai Wang

and feet while practicing benevolence and righteousness, they will certainly follow you and even die for your cause."

King Xuan went on, "Somehow I feel that I am stupid, and that I have made blunders in my work. Perhaps I lack the wisdom necessary for a competent ruler?"

Mencius consoled him: "Do not be puzzled by your lack of wisdom, My Lord. Even a plant that grows most readily will not survive if it is placed in the sun for one day and exposed to the cold for ten. The trouble with you is that you lack a constant heart and an iron will. Now take the game of *weiqi* for example. If one does not give one's whole mind to it, one will never master it. As is well known, Yi Qiu is the best player in the whole country. Get him to teach two people to play. One of them concentrates his mind on the game and listens only to what Yi Qiu has to say, while the other, though he listens, dreams of an approaching swan and wants to take up his bow and corded arrow to shoot at it. Now, even though this man shares the lessons with the first, he will never be as good. Is this because he is less clever? The answer is, 'No.'"

That day King Xuan returned to the palace, full of praise for Mencius. He told Lady Zhong as soon as he joined her: "Mencius is a marvel! He has everything at the tip of his fingers. His remarks always drive the point home. It is a pity that he is no longer young and that he is not a native of Qi. Or I would employ him as High Minister in my government."

Lady Zhong said: "I only pity those muddle-headed princes who don't recognize talent when they see it."

"I do treasure such a talent as his."

"But why do you not employ him? There is no time to be lost."

"In what office shall I put him?"

"High Minister would best suit him, perhaps?"

"All right. Let us make him High Minister."

And so, at the next morning's audience King Xuan announced his appointment of Mencius as High Minister to his court.

In the meantime, Mencius was calling Yuezheng Ke to task in the Snow Palace. The latter had just returned from a trip to Lu.

"When did you come back?" asked Mencius.

"Only yesterday, sir."

"Why did you not come to see me as soon as you arrived?"

"I had not found a place to lodge."

"Where did you learn that one should only visit one's elders after finding a place to lodge?"

Yuezheng, shame-faced, said, "I have committed an error, sir."

At this moment Chu Zi came striding in. He made a deep bow to Mencius and said with a beam of delight: "Congratulations! Congratulations!"

Taken by surprise, Mencius asked, "Why? What for?"

Chu Zi: "I have come with a decree from His Majesty to the effect that you have been appointed the king's High Minister. Isn't that cause for congratulations, sir?"

At this, Mencius led Chu Zi to his parlor, where the two took their seats as host and guest.

Chu Zi gave Mencius a curious look before he remarked, "People say that you are out of the common run. Are you at all different from the rest of us mortals?"

Mencius countered this with "In what way should I be different from other people? Even Yao and Shun were the same as everyone else,"

Chu Zi said with an embarrassed smile: "You indeed live up to your reputation as a man who has the gift of the gab." With that, he left to report to King Xuan that his mission had been fulfilled.

Soon afterwards, Mencius went to see King Xuan at the palace, taking Gongsun Chou and Gao Zi along with him. After expressing his thanks for his appointment, Mencius said, "Now that Your Majesty has placed me in a government post, I will certainly do my utmost to assist you in administration. But for a long time to come I cannot afford to leave my mother in far-off Zou. She is advanced in years and I am her only son. Considering this, I am planning to have her join me in Qi so that I can attend to her and cheer her remaining days. I therefore beg your leave to get this done."

King Xuan said, "A dutiful son, you are indeed! I quite appreciate your filial sentiments. I grant you permission."

The king then asked about Gongsun Chou and Gao Zi. Mencius introduced them as his disciples, and particularly emphasized the fact that they were both men of Qi.

"They are among the top ten of my students," he noted.

"What do they specialize in?" asked the king.

"They are versed in the rites, music and administrative affairs."

King Xuan commented, "Heaven has favored the State of Qi with so many talented people that if they were all employed in important positions, a rich and powerful Qi would be certain!"

Mencius had counted on the king saying something more specific after this, but to his disappointment, the king came to a sudden stop and no more.

The next morning Mencius started off for home. It took him several days before he reached Zou, and when finally he joined his mother, he told her what he had come for. Zhang said, "Now you have had your wish fulfilled. From now on you should concern yourself more with the future of the state and the empire. Help the king to practice benevolent government."

Mencius promised to do so.

Zhang asked, "Can I take Duanping with me to Qi?"

"As you wish, Mother."

"All my life," Zhang reminisced, "I have never left Zou even once. Once I leave here it will have to be once and for all, I'm afraid. So before departure, I must visit your father's grave and perform the sacrificial rites."

"I understand," said Mencius. "But please do not feel sad, Mother. You look advanced in years, it is true, but you are still hale and hearty."

Zhang indicated the apricot and peach trees, saying as she did so: "You see all those leaves on the trees, don't you? However hard now the wind is blowing them, they will not fall off. If it were late autumn, things would be entirely different. I am over 90 now. The least buffeting will carry me to my grave."

The following morning the whole family—Zhang, Mencius, and his son and daughter-in-law—went to Mengsun Ji's grave, where they performed the sacrificial rites and prayed.

In due course, Mencius had his mother settled in Qi, and three times everyday he called on her.

One day Zhang said to him: "My son, don't let these filial duties interfere with your work. You have to attend to the affairs of state and the instruction of your disciples, which are more important."

Mencius replied, "I lost my father in childhood, and it was you, Mother, that brought me up. You endured all kinds of hardships to rear and educate me. Without you I could not have become what I am today. All these years I have stayed away from you, traveling around the empire, and I seldom had time to wait on you, for which I can never forgive myself. Now that we are united once and for all I must make up for lost time by staying in your company at every opportunity I can snatch. Do you not agree, dear Mother?"

Zhang said, "From antiquity, the two virtues of loyalty and filial piety have been regarded as integral. If only you can serve your country and people with loyalty, I am content with my lot, my son."

"Dear Mother! Whatever you say, I owe you more than I can repay."

"Now you are in office," Zhang reminded him, "you hold a heavy responsibility. This provides you with the opportunity to urge the king to implement his promise of benevolent government. And once this is realized, more parents—and no less than I—will enjoy family happiness. By then you will have repaid me a hundredfold."

"I will do everything I can to fulfil your cherished wish, dear Mother."

"That is the best comfort you can afford me, my son."

At a morning audience, with all the ministers and officials present, King Xuan addressed Mencius as follows: "Master, I know for a certainly that in performing your duties as a minister you stick to your principle of benevolence and righteousness, and at home you serve your mother with utter devotion. I beg to ask, what is the relationship between dutifulness to one's parents and benevolence?"

Mencius explained, "The essence of benevolence is the serving of one's parents; the essence of dutifulness is obedience to one's elder brothers; the essence of wisdom is to understand these two and to hold fast to them; the essence of the rites is the regulation and adornment of them; the essence of music is the joy that comes of delighting in it. When joy arises how can one stop it? And when one cannot stop it, then one begins to dance with one's feet and wave one's arms about without knowing it. This accounts for the fact that men of virtue in olden times were inevitably men of loyalty and filial piety."

King Xuan asked, "Who of the ancients may be considered the most outstanding?"

"Emperor Shun", replied Mencius. "He did everything that was possible to serve his parents, and succeeded, in the end, in pleasing the Blind Man*. Once the Blind Man was pleased, the empire was transformed, and the pattern for the relationship between father and son was set. This is the supreme achievement of a dutiful son."

Just then, a palace guard came running up to announce that an emissary from the State of Teng was requesting an audience.

---

* Emperor Shun's father.

Chapter Forty-Nine

Mencius' Mother Dies in Qi, and Mencius Honors Her with a Splendid Funeral;
Defeated by the Allied Forces of Six States, a Bellicose Monarch Draws a Bitter Lesson

As related in our last chapter, an envoy from the State of Teng requested an audience with King Xuan. The envoy presented himself, saying: "I have been delegated to inform Your Majesty that the reigning prince of Teng has passed away."

Shocked at this, King Xuan gave a long sigh and said, "How sad! Died so young! And he was such a good king too." While Mencius, grieved, offered to go on a mission of condolence for the king.

"You are a man after my own heart, Master," said King Xuan. "You are well acquainted with the rites and ceremonies. Well, but who can be your deputy?"

Zhuang Bao stepped forward. "Your Majesty," he suggested, "I think the governor of Gai, Wang Huan, can be the deputy. He knows the rites and ceremonies thoroughly." The king agreed to his recommendation, and Wang Huan was at once summoned.

Thus Mencius and Wang Huan started on their mission to Teng. But throughout the journeys to and from Teng, though aboard the same carriage, Mencius never exchanged a word with his companion.

On a later occasion, this incident intrigued Gongsun Chou, and he asked Mencius: "Your position as High Minister is by no means insignificant, and the distance between Qi and Teng is by no means short, yet throughout the journeys between the two states you never discussed official business with Wang Huan. Why was that?"

Mencius said, "It was not right not to have talked with him when I should have. Neither was it right to have talked with him when I should not have. He was self-opinionated and arrogated to himself the whole affair. What was there for me to say?"

Gongsun Chou commented, "With such a man as the governor, the people under him are bound to suffer."

"I should think so!" Mencius gave a sigh. "It is very hard for a

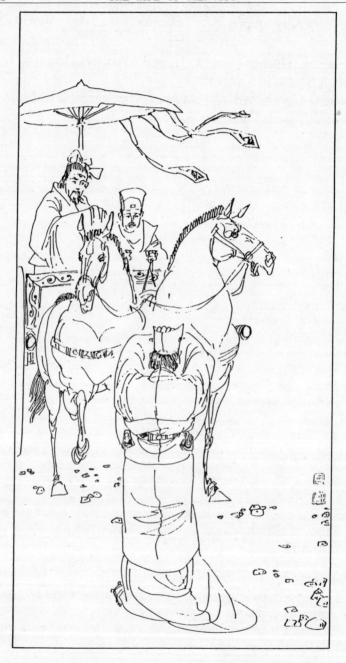

man to know himself. The average man tends to have a higher opinion of himself than his nature warrants. Is this a human weakness or what? So, it is highly important to know one's limitations. Confucius said, 'The best neighborhood is where benevolence is to be found. Not to live in such a neighborhood when one has the choice cannot by any means be considered wise.' Benevolence is the high honor bestowed by Heaven and the peaceful abode of man. Not to be benevolent when nothing stands in the way is to show a lack of wisdom. A man neither benevolent nor wise, devoid of courtesy and dutifulness, is a slave. A slave ashamed of serving is like a maker of bows ashamed of making bows, or a maker of arrows ashamed of making arrows. If one is ashamed, there is no better remedy than to practice benevolence. Benevolence is like archery: An archer makes sure his stance is correct before letting fly the arrow. And if he fails to hit the mark, he does not resent his successful competitor; he simply seeks the cause within himself. Pitiable is the man who, being incompetent does not examine himself but regards with spite those who are superior to him."

Gongsun Chou asked, "You can educate them a bit—men of Wang Huan's type, can't you, sir?"

Mencius replied, "The trouble with people is that they are too eager to assume the role of teacher. Look at the way he carries himself: as if he were on the top of the world. Educate him indeed! Better let him educate himself."

"What do you mean, sir?"

"An opinionated man never draws his lesson until he meets with rebuffs more than he can swallow."

"Suppose he does not do so even then, what will happen?"

"Then ruination befall him."

When next morning Mencius reported to the king on his recent mission to Teng, the latter praised him profusely, saying, "You have been of immense help to me since you joined my court, sir. My only worry at the moment is possible aggression from some more powerful state. Are there any good ways of promoting friendly relations with the neighboring states?"

"There are," answered Mencius. "Only a benevolent man can submit to a state smaller than his own. This accounts for the submission of King Tang to the Ge state and King Wen to the Kun tribes. Only a wise man can submit to a state bigger than his own. This accounts for the submission of Tai Wang to the Xunyu tribe and Gou

Jian to the State of Wu. He who submits to a state smaller than his own delights in Heaven; he who submits to a state bigger than his own is in awe of Heaven. He who delights in Heaven will continue to enjoy the possession of his own state."

King Xuan said, "Great are your words. But I have a weakness: I am fond of valor."

"In that case," said Mencius, "I beg you not to be fond of small valor. Looking fierce, putting your hand on your sword and saying, 'How dare he oppose me!' is to show the valor of a common fellow which is of use only against a single adversary. You should make it something great."

"Please continue," said the king.

Mencius did so: "The *Book of Songs* says, 'The King blazed in rage /And marshalled his troops /To the enemy advancing on Ju /And added to the good fortune of Zhou /In response to the wishes of the empire.' This was the valor of King Wen. In one outburst of rage King Wen brought peace to the people of the empire. If there was one bully in the empire, King Wu felt this to be a personal affront. This was the valor of King Wu. Thus he, too, brought peace to the people of the empire in one outburst of rage. Now if you, too, will bring peace to the people of the empire in one outburst of rage, then the people's only fear will be that you are not fond of valor."

His face wreathed in smiles, King Xuan said, "Your words have enlightened me greatly on the subject. Thank you very much."

As Mencius walked out of the palace he lifted his head and saw that the foliage was already tinted yellow. It is autumn again, he thought, lovely autumn, the season of harvest. The idea suddenly occurred to him: Why not take Mother out on a ride to the outskirts to enjoy the golden autumn today? So thinking, he quickened his pace.

Meanwhile, Zhang and Duanping were in the courtyard, tending their chrysanthemums, which were just in bud. Zhang beamed with delight on seeing her son come back earlier than usual. "You look so happy, son," she said. "Is there any good news for me?"

"Dear Mother," said Mencius, "I want to take you out for a ride outside the city so that you can enjoy yourself a bit. You'll find the countryside in autumn a feast for the eyes."

Bristling with a mother's pride, Zhang responded cheerfully, saying, "That would be wonderful!" But just as she said this, she tottered, and Mencius and Duanping, frightened, hastened on to support her between them.

"I'm dying. Put me to bed, quick!" she pleaded in a pained, weak voice.

With tears in their eyes, Mencius and Duanping put her to bed and inquired anxiously: "Where do you feel the pain, Mother?"

Zhang said, "Don't cry, you two. I should feel content with my lot, having a good son and a nice daughter-in-law. There is only one wish left in me..."

Mencius and Duanping asked together: "What is it, Mother?"

Zhang said, "When I die, be sure that my coffin is taken back to Zou. And let me be buried with your father at the foot of Nine-Dragon Mountain."

Mencius and Duanping nodded their heads.

"But Zhongzi...and Tao Qin.." Her voice faded away, and then she was no more. She died in peace at the age of 91.

Word of the death of Mencius' mother soon reached King Xuan, and he had his Prime Minister Chu Zi pay a visit of condolence to Mencius, taking a gift of 20 yi of gold for the funeral expenses.

Mencius accepted the gold with thanks, and with it he made Chong Yu have a coffin of fine quality made by top-grade carpenters. Then he and Duanping personally conducted the coffin back to their hometown in Zou. There, according to his mother's wish, Mencius had her buried with her husband. The funeral was solemnly carried out, with Mencius' disciples taking part.

On his way back to Qi, Mencius stopped at Ying. Chong Yu begged to put a question to him and said: "Some days ago, you did not think me unworthy and entrusted me with the task of overseeing the carpenters. As the work was urgent, there was something I dared not ask about. May I ask about it now? The wood of the coffin seemed to be excessively fine in quality. Was it really so?"

Mencius explained, "In high antiquity there were no regulations governing the inner and outer coffins. In middle antiquity, it was prescribed that the inner coffin was to be seven inches thick, with the outer coffin to match. This applied to all conditions of men, from emperor to commoner. This was not simply for show. For it is only in this way that one can express fully one's filial love. However, if such wood is not available, one cannot have the satisfaction of using it; neither can one if one is not able to afford the cost. When both conditions are fulfilled, the ancients always used wood of find quality.

Why should I alone be an exception? Furthermore, does it not give one some solace to be able to prevent the earth from coming into contact with the dear departed who is about to decompose? I have heard it said that a gentleman would not for all the world skimp expenditure on his parents."

At this point our story switches to the State of Yan, Qi's northern neighbor. Its old King Yi had died in 321 B.C., and his son Zi Kuai had succeeded to his throne for only a couple of years when suddenly he relinquished his power to his prime minister Zi Zhi. The event sparked off an armed conflict which engulfed the whole state, as Prince Shi Bi, titled Grand Marshal of Peace and Harmony, staged a rebellion, denouncing the abdication as illegal. Terror reigned in the capital of Yan. The whole of the state was in a turmoil. The event had its repercussions in Qi, too. At court a number of officials, headed by Zhuang Bao, thought this was a good chance to annex Yan and urged King Xuan to go to war.

One day, Shen Tong, a Qi minister, paid a visit to Mencius in the Snow Palace. In the course of the conversation, he raised the question at issue: Is it all right to launch a war against Yan?

Mencius answered in no uncertain terms: "Yes, it is."

Nonplussed, Shen Tong asked again: "But why?"

Mencius said: "King Zi Kuai had no right to give the throne of Yan to another; neither had Minister Zi Zhi any right to accept it from Zi Kuai."

As the minister showed no sign of approval, Mencius further explained, "Supposing there were a gentleman here whom you liked, and you were to take it upon yourself to give him your emolument and rank without informing the king, and the gentleman, for his part, were to accept these from you without royal sanction. Would this be permissible?"

"Absolutely no!"

"There you are, you see: The case of Yan is no different."

Back among his colleagues, Shen Tong told them all Mencius had said.

After a long period of planning, in the spring of 315 B.C. King Xuan declared war on Yan. Qi's troops, with 4,000 chariots, under the command of General Zhuang Bao, marched into Yan without encountering any resistance, and within 40 days pressed on its capital, Ji. The

Yan soldiers put up no resistance but opened the city gates to let the invaders in. Thus, the Qi troops easily stormed the palace. They killed Zi Kuai and Zi Zhi, and 4,000 Yan soldiers were taken prisoner. The victors carried off the Yan state treasures.

News of victory soon reached King Xuan, and with a triumphant air he asked his ministers: "I would like to seize the whole territory of Yan in our first flush of victory. What do you say to that, Ministers?"

A flurry of excitement ran over his audience. Some approved; others deplored the idea. A heated debate ensued.

Chu Zi said, "Your Majesty, this is no small matter. Please think twice before making a decision."

"Yes, Your Majesty must weigh all the options," agreed Chunyu Kun.

Tian Ji and Kuang Zhang chorused, "Do think twice, Your Majesty."

The audience thus adjourned without reaching a final decision. Back in his rear palace, King Xuan put his question to Lady Zhong, who replied, "This is a matter concerning your personal honor as well as the future of Qi. Like playing chess, one wrong move and you will lose the whole game. Please don't make a hasty decision ... But now I come to think of it, why don't you take up the matter with Mencius?"

Thereupon, the king summoned Mencius, to whom he said, "Some advise me against annexing Yan, while others urge me to do so. The occupation of a state of 10,000 chariots by another of equal strength in a matter of 40 days is a feat which could not have been brought about by human agency alone. If I do not annex Yan, I am afraid Heaven will send down disasters. What would you think if I decided on annexation?"

Mencius replied, "If, in annexing Yan, you please its people, then annex it. There are examples of men in antiquity following such a course of action. King Wu was one. If, in annexing Yan, you antagonize its people, then do not annex it. There are also examples of men in antiquity following such a course. King Wen was one. When a state of 10,000 chariots attacks another of equal strength and your army is met by the people bringing baskets of rice and bottles of drink, what other reason can there be than that the people are fleeing from water and fire? Should the water become deeper and the fire hotter, they would have no alternative but to turn elsewhere for succor."

King Xuan was locked in an indecision as he passed his hand over his forehead, saying, "I do appreciate your instruction, but I need time to think it over before I make any decision."

Disappointed with the king's weak attitude, Mencius returned to the Snow Palace in low spirits.

Before long, Zhuang Bao, Qi's occupation force commander in Yan, dispatched a staff officer to send back to Qi the 4,000-odd prisoners-of-war and cartloads of booty. King Xuan had the treasures carried to his rear palace, where he inspected each, to his intense delight. As for the POWs, he issued the order: "Make them slaves! Let them work for us as corvee laborers."

His disposal of the booty and prisoners-of-war quite horrified his ministers, yet they dared not say anything to oppose his wishes. The braver of them, such as Chu Zi and Chunyu Kun, therefore, sought Mencius' help. The latter, when he heard of this, grew indignant, saying, "A wise ruler learns a good lesson from history. From antiquity up to the present, there has been none who maltreated his prisoners but has met his day of retribution. He kills the father of another and the other will pay him back in the same coin. He kills the elder brother of another and the other will do the same to him. The result is the same as if he killed his own father or elder brother with his own hand. Now these Yan soldiers went to war at the order of their king. If they did anything wrong, the blame must lie with the man who gave the order. They are innocent. As for a victorious army given to plunder and robbery, this is indeed outrageous!"

Subsequently, Mencius went to the palace, demanding an interview with the king.

At that moment, King Xuan was totally absorbed in viewing the treasures from Yan. Annoyed at the interruption, he waved an impatient hand to his guard, saying, "Tell him to come in!"

Mencius, having taking a seat, said bluntly: 'I hear a host of war prisoners have been brought here. Is it true, Your Majesty?"

Restored to his good humor, King Xuan replied, "Yes it is. Quite a number of them, some 4,000, I believe.

"And many treasures into the bargain?" queried Mencius, with raised eyebrows.

"Right. Some 1,000 pieces."

"I would advise Your Majesty to send back to Yan all these prisoners and treasures as soon as you can," urged Mencius.

"May I ask why, sir?" was the king's surprised retort.

Mencius replied with dignity: "Because they do not belong to Qi."

"But Yan is under my control," protested the king. "Prisoners or treasures, they are all mine."

Aware that he was flogging a dead horse, Mencius said no more, and soon he left.

The following day, soon after the morning audience was over, Chunyu Kun came to see Mencius and asked him about the result of his talk with the king.

Mencius said with indignation: "It is not worth the trouble to talk to a man who has no respect for himself, and it is not worth the trouble to make a common effort with a man who has no confidence in himself. The former attacks morality; the latter says, 'I do not think I am capable of abiding by benevolence or of following righteousness.' Benevolence is man's peaceful abode and righteousness his proper path. It is indeed lamentable for anyone not to live in his peaceful abode and not to follow his proper path."

Chunyu Kun asked, "Is it true that you encouraged Qi to march on Yan, sir?"

"No." said Mencius with finality. "When Shen Tong asked me on his own account, 'Is it all right to march on Yan?' I answered, 'Yes.' And they marched on Yan. Had he asked, 'Who has the right to march on Yan?' I would have answered, 'A Heaven-appointed officer has the right to do so.' Suppose a man killed another, and someone were to ask, 'Is it all right to kill the killer?' I would answer, 'Yes.' But if he further asked, 'who has the right to kill him?' I would answer, 'The chief judge has the right to kill him.' As it is, it is just one tyrannical Yan marching on another Yan. Why should I have encouraged such a thing?"

Chunyu Kun suggested, "Perhaps you should have advised the king against invading Yan in the first place, Master."

Mencius replied, "How can one get a cruel man to listen to reason? He dwells happily amongst dangers, looks upon disasters as profitable and delights in what will lead him to perdition. If a cruel man listened to reason there would be no annihilated states or ruined families. There was a boy who sang, 'If the blue water is clear /It is fit to wash my chin-strap. /If the blue water is muddy /It is only fit to wash my feet.' Confucius said, 'Listen to this, my little ones. When clear, the water washes the chin-strap, when muddy, it washes the feet. The water brings this difference in treatment upon itself.' Only when a man invites insult will others insult him. Only when a family invites destruction will others destroy it. Only when a state invites invasion will others invade it. The *Book of History* says, 'When Heaven sends down calamities, there is hope of weathering them; when man brings them upon himself, there is no hope of escape.' His Majesty refuses to listen to reason because he lets profits blind his eyes; he is inviting trouble upon himself."

In 311 B.C., the former King of Yan's son by a concubine, named Zhi, ascended the throne. Historically known as King Zhao of Yan, Zhi began his government with a program of political reforms. He promoted what was beneficial and abolished what was harmful. He threw his net wide for men of talent to staff his government with. He sent out diplomats to influence the kings of Qin, Wei, Han, Zhao and Chu. His ultimate ambition was to drive out Qi's occupation forces and avenge Yan's humiliation by conquering Qi.

These attempts of King Zhao made the king of Qi uneasy. One day King Xuan said to his consort: "Even a fierce tiger cannot hold its own against a pack of wolves. What chance of success is there for Qi if the other six states combine their forces to attack us? That is my fear. What do you think, my dear?"

Zhong Li-chun said "There is no need to fear, My Lord. It will take time for them to get united, and that will be no easy job for them, either. In the meantime, we can do a lot of work to forestall them too. Besides, you can go and canvass opinions among your ministers and counselors. Or better still, go and ask Mencius about it."

The king was delighted. "You are absolutely right, my dear," he said. "That is exactly what I will do."

"Good advice is hard on the ears," said Zhong Li-chun, "You must listen to those who dare to speak their minds, My Lord."

Thereupon, King Xuan drove to the Snow Palace, and there Mencius received him in the proper manner, but not so warmly as before.

King Xuan said, "At the moment, most of the feudal lords are plotting in collusion with Yan to oppose Qi. What measures should I take to meet the threat, Master?"

Mencius advised him: "I have heard of one who gained ascendancy over the empire from the modest beginning of a territory of 70 square li. Such a one was Tang. I have never heard of anyone ruling over 1,000 square *li* being frightened of others. The *Book of History* says,

'In his punitive expeditions Tang began with Ge.' With this he gained the trust of the empire. When he marched east, the western barbarians complained, and when he marched south, the northern barbarians complained. They all said, 'Why does he not come to us first?' The people longed for his coming as they longed for a rainbow in a time of severe drought. Those who were going to market did not stop; those who were plowing went on plowing. He punished the rulers and comforted the people, like a fall of timely rain, and the people rejoiced greatly. The *Book of History* says, "We await our Lord. When he comes we will be revived.' Now then you went to punish Yan whose ruler practiced tyranny over his people, the people thought you were going to rescue them from water and fire, and they came to meet your army, bringing baskets of rice and bottles of drink. But what did your Qi army do to them? They killed the old and bound the young, destroyed the ancestral temples and appropriated the valuable vessels. How atrocious! Even before this, the whole empire was afraid of the power of Qi. Now you double your territory without practicing benevolent government. This will provoke the armies of the whole empire."

The king got so angry at this, that his whole frame shook and he glowered at his accuser.

Feigning indifference, Mencius went on, "If Your Majesty should wish to extricate himself from the present difficult situation, there is only one way."

"What way?"

"Release all the captives, and send them back together with the captured treasures. Also, withdraw your troops from Yan, wholly and completely."

The king at once thought of his newly acquired treasures. He said not a word.

In 310 B.C. eventually King Zhao succeeded in driving out Qi's occupation forces from Yan, thanks to foreign assistance.

Rueful about the irrevocable mistake he had made, King Xuan beat his breast and stamped his foot, saying with a sigh: "I am ashamed to face Mencius!"

Mencius sent in his resignation to King Xuan, and he and his disciples prepared to leave Qi for Zou.

Chapter Fifty

**Abandoning Office, Mencius Returns Home and
Devotes His Last Years to Teaching and Writing;
In Memory of Their Dear Departed, Wan Zhang
Leaves Words with His Fellow Students at Parting**

Having resigned his post, Mencius made ready to leave Qi with his disciples. But just as he mounted his carriage and was about to start off, who should come up but his old friend Chunyu Kun. Mencius dismounted and exchanged greetings with him.

With a reproachful look on his face, Chunyu Kun announced, "He who puts reputation and real achievement first is a man who tries to benefit others; he who puts reputation and real achievement last is a man who tries to benefit himself. You are numbered among the Three Ministers, yet you have failed to make any reputation and real achievement either in your services to your prince or in your services to the people. Is that all that one can expect of a benevolent man?"

Not easily ruffled, however, Mencius explained calmly: "Even when in a low position, a man was not willing, as a good man, to serve a bad ruler. Such was Bo Yi. Another went five times to Tang and five times to Jie. Such was Yi Yin. Yet another was not ashamed of a prince with a tarnished reputation, nor was he disdainful of a modest post. Such was Liu Xiahui. These three followed different paths, but their goal was one. What is meant by 'one'? The answer is, 'Benevolence'. All that is to be expected of a gentleman is benevolence. Why must he be exactly the same as other gentlemen?"

Chunyu Kun answered, "In the time of Duke Mu of Lu, Gongyi Zi was in charge of affairs of state, and Xie Liu and Zi Si were in office, yet the State of Lu dwindled in size even more rapidly than before. Are good and wise men of so little benefit to a state?"

Mencius retorted, "Yu was annexed for failing to employ Baili Xi, while Duke Mu of Qin, by employing him, became leader of the feudal lords. A state which fails to employ good and wise men will end by suffering annexation. How can it hope to suffer no more than a reduction in size?"

Chunyun Kun rejoined, "Formerly, when Wang Bao settled on the River Qi the residents on the west bank of the Yellow River became skillful at singing. When Mian Ju settled in Gao Tang the local people likewise became well-known for their songs. The wives of Hua Zhou and Qi Liang, being supreme in the way they wept for their husbands, transformed the practice of a whole state. There cannot be any good and wise men alive nowadays, otherwise I am bound to know of them."

Mencius smiled and said, "Confucius was minister of justice of Lu, but his advice was not followed. He took part in a sacrifice, but afterwards was not given a share of the meat of the sacrificial animal. Thereupon, he left the state without waiting to take off his ceremonial cap. Those who did not understand him thought he acted in this way because of the meat, but those who understood him realized that he left because Lu failed to observe the proper rites. For his part Confucius preferred to be slightly at fault in thus leaving rather than to leave for no reason at all. The doings of a gentleman are naturally above the understanding of the ordinary man."

Chunyu Kun said wistfully: "With your extraordinary ability and profound knowledge, sir, you are capable of doing great things for the empire. But now you abandon your office as minister and choose to go home. Surely you are not resigned to your fate as a complete failure?"

"Times! Fate!" said Mencius sadly. "All my life I have traveled round the empire, from one state to another, trying to do my bit in an effort to restore peace and order in a troubled world. Alas, I was born under an ill star! Where is there a good and wise prince to be found in this dislocated empire?"

"But," said Chunyu Kun, "your disciples are mostly brilliant persons from the various states. Do you not want them to take office?"

"It is not that I do not want them to, but there has been no chance at all. Yuezheng Ke is the only exception. When I heard about his employment by the Prince of Lu I lay awake the whole night for sheer joy."

Chunyu Kun exclaimed, "So you are determined to quit official-dom once and for all? Is there no feeling of regret in your heart?"

Mencius looked up at the sky and sighed. "Only when a man will not do some things is he capable of doing great things," were his last words to Chunyu Kun. Then the two friends parted.

And so Mencius and his disciples started on their journey back to

Zou. That day they had covered 30 *li* when they stopped at Zhou for the night. It so happened that Mencius fell a prey to melancholy thoughts the following day, and as his disciples did not want to disturb him, they stayed on two more days in Zhou. On the evening of the third day there came an elder who requested an interview with Mencius. By the weak light of an oil lamp, Mencius found his visitor dressed in the style of a Confucian scholar. He had a square face and big ears, and a pair of well-shaped eyes shone brilliantly under his thin eye-brows. He sat upright and began to speak, but Mencius made no reply and lay down, leaning against the low table.

The visitor was displeased. "Only after observing a day's fast" said he, "dare I speak. You, Master, simply lie down and make no effort to listen to me. I shall never presume to present myself again."

Calm and collected, Mencius said, "No offence is meant, sir. Please be seated. I shall speak plainly to you. Confucius once said, 'Those whose ways are different cannot make plans for one another.' You do not do your best to make King Xuan of Qi change his ways, but go out of your way to detain me. Now, I venture to ask, are you refusing to have anything to do with me, or am I refusing to have anything to do with you?"

Crestfallen, the man beat a hasty retreat.

Gao Zi, who happened to be present, did not like the way Mencius had treated his visitor. He immediately followed the man out, and saw him as far as the outer gate where he bowed to him and asked him about his name.

"I am Yin Shi," said the other. "May I ask your name, sir?"

Gao Zi introduced himself.

Yin Shi beamed upon hearing the name and said, "I have long heard about you. You do look unworldly with your stately and prepossessing appearance. No wonder the Master once spoke so highly of you."

Gao Zi replied, "My Master is in a bad mood these days. Please do not take to heart..."

Yin Shi cut him short with "Please do not mention this, as I know the character of the Master very well." A pause and he added, "Still there is one thing about him which I don't quite understand. Can you help me?"

"With pleasure," said Gao Zi.

Yin Shi continued, "If the Master did not realize that King Xuan of Qi could not become a Tang or a King Wu he was blind, but if he came realizing it, he was simply after advancement. He came from afar to see the king, and left because he met with no success. If he is bent on going, then go quickly he should, shouldn't he? Why is he taking so long about it?"

Later, Gao Zi told Mencius of this.

Mencius said, "How little does Yin Shi understand me! I came from afar to see King Xuan because I wanted to. Having met with no success, I am leaving, not because I want to but because I have no alternative. True. it took me three nights to go beyond Zhou. But even then I felt that I had not taken long enough. I had hoped against hope that the king would change his mind. I was sure he would recall me. It was only when I went beyond Zhou and the king made no attempt to send for me that the desire to go home surged up in me. Even then it was not as if I had abandoned the king. He is still capable of doing good. If he had employed me it would not simply have been a matter of bringing peace to the people of Qi, but of bringing peace to the people of the whole empire as well. If only the king would change his mind! That is what I hope for every day. I am not like those petty men who, when their advice is rejected by a prince, take offence and show resentment all over their faces, and, when they leave, travel all day before they put up for the night."

When he was told of this later Yin Shi sighed, "Indeed, I understand Mencius too little!"

One day, when Mencius and his party had crossed the border of Qi and were entering Lu, Chong Yu, who was driving the carriage for Mencius, suddenly exclaimed, "Master, you look somewhat unhappy. I heard from you the other day that a gentleman reproaches neither Heaven nor man."

Mencius cast him a mere glance but made no reply.

Chong Yu said again: "It seems to me that you have not been your usual self since we left Qi."

Mencius gave a long sigh, then said, "This is one time; that was another time. Every 500 years a true king should arise, and in the interval there should arise one from whom an age takes its name. From King Wu of Zhou to the present it is over 700 years. The 500 mark has been passed and the time has long been ripe. It must be that Heaven does not as yet wish to bring peace to the empire. If it did, who is there in the present time other than myself to act as Heaven's instrument? Why should I be unhappy?"

"How will future generations appraise you, sir?" asked Chong Yu.

Mencius replied, "That is something I cannot forecast. Everybody can say what he has to say, since everybody has got a tongue in his head. There is unexpected praise; equally, there is perfectionist criticism."

Chong Yu asked, "Is one permitted to talk about others' shortcomings?"

"No", said Mencius. "a gentleman publicizes others' merits; he never rakes up others' faults. He who publicizes others' shortcomings will have to take the consequences."

A few days' continuous traveling brought the party to the Sishui River. Mencius told Chong Yu to halt, after which he jumped down from the carriage and walked to the bank of the river. He stood gazing steadily at the river as it ran its turbulent way toward the west. His gaze followed its course until it rounded a big curve and then turned south. A brain-wave occurred to him, and suddenly he saw the whole situation in a new light. "So water can change its course when it is forced to," he thought aloud. "Nevertheless, its seaward course can never be changed. Now, my fatal weakness is..."

Xu Bi came up. "Master," he said, "more than once Confucius expressed his admiration for water by saying, 'Water! Oh, water!' What was it he saw in water?"

Mencius answered, "Water from an ample source comes tumbling down, day and night without ceasing, going forward only after all the hollows are filled, and then draining into the sea. Anything that has an ample source is like this. What Confucius saw in water is just this and nothing more."

Gongsun Chou asked, "If King Xuan sticks to his wrong way of government, turning a deaf ear to warnings, what will happen to Qi, do you think?"

Mencius replied, "If the king does not realize his mistake in good time and change his policies accordingly, Qi is bound to fall."

His prediction turned out to be true. In 284 B.C., by combining the forces of Qin, Wei, Han, Zhao and Chu, King Zhao of Yan sent out an allied force under the command of Grand Marshal Yue Yi to attack Qi. Very soon they took its capital, along with 70 other cities. But this was to come.

After a brief sojourn at the Sishui River, Mencius and his disciples at last returned to Zou via the capital of Lu. He settled down to teaching for the rest of his life.

One day Wan Zhang told Gongsun Chou: "There is one thing of which I want to have your opinion. Mencius has been a teacher all his life. He inherits the traditions of the Duke of Zhou and Confucius, and has opened up a new path for Confucianism. His lectures and talks often contain great wisdom which throws much light on the ideas of Confucius. Politically he may be a failure since he has not the good fortune of meeting with an enlightened and wise ruler by whom his political philosophy can be adopted. That is his tragedy. But as a thinker and an educationist he has made considerable achievements. His words and deeds should be recorded as a valuable legacy we can leave to our descendants. So I have an idea...."

Gongsun Chou immediately took him up, saying, "I know what you are going to say—that we must do the work while our teacher is still hale and hearty, right?"

"Exactly so."

"Let's go and see him about it."

"He is not well right now. Better wait."

One day Mencius was taking a stroll in his courtyard, when Wan Zhang and Gongsun Chou came up to greet him.

Wan Zhang said, "Brother Gongsun and I have discussed a plan to edit a book based upon your words and deeds with which to educate future generations. Would you help us?"

"Good!" said Mencius. "I have lived in bad times and throughout my life I have never come across a good and wise prince who recognized my true worth. However lofty my ideals, I have no way of attaining them, alas! It would not be a bad idea if my philosophy could be preserved in written form so that future generations, on reading it, may draw some useful lessons of their own."

"Shall we begin right now?" suggested Gongsun Chou.

Mencius consented with alacrity.

Thereupon Wan Zhang and Gongsun Chou went off to fetch Gongdu Zi, Peng Geng, Xianqiu Meng, Xu Bi, Wulu Zi, Gao Zi, Chong Yu, Chen Zhen, Cheng Dai and others. When they came Wan Zhang told them of his plan, which won their general approval.

"Where shall we begin?" Someone asked.

Mencius said, "Let us start with my meeting with King Hui of Liang."

"Well", said Wan Zhang, "I could read my sentences out and see if you think them all right, sir."

Mencius fondled his beard with both hands, his face brightening up as he expressed his hearty approval.

Wan Zhang began to articulate the first sentence that had formed in his mind: "Master Meng went to see King Hui of Liang..."

"Stop!" interrupted Mencius. "That will not do. Better say, 'Meng Ke went to see King Hui of Liang'."

"But sir," protested Wan Zhang, "Confucius' disciples always start their passages with 'The Master said' and so on."

"Confucius was the Supreme Sage and the Foremost Teacher," said Mencius solemnly. "Since man came into this world there has been no one to compare with him. All his life he was earnest in what he was doing and careful in his speech. He never went beyond reasonable limits and always abided by the golden mean. What is more, the *Analects* was recollected and edited by his disciples after his death, whereas this book of ours is a joint effort with myself participating. The two are entirely different. Who am I to be compared with Confucius?"

Gongdu Zi was about to argue the point, when Wan Zhang tipped him a wink to stop him.

"Why is it necessary to begin with your meeting with King Hui of Liang, sir?" asked Wan Zhang.

Mencius said, "Because he began his interview by asking me how I could profit his state. His mention of the word 'profit' prompted me to deep thought."

Xianqiu Meng said, "Confucius said, 'The mind of the superior man is conversant with righteousness; the mind of the inferior man is conversant with profit.' Allow me to ask, sir: Does a superior man ever have something to seek after, if not profit?"

Mencius replied, "Yes, he does. But there is a world of difference between what a superior man aims to gain and what an inferior man aims to gain. All an inferior man seeks after is material wealth or the gratification of the flesh. The superior man, on the other hand, is given to intellectual pursuits: the pursuit of knowledge and the pursuit of moral perfection. If everybody strives to be a superior man then the most comfortable abode will be filled with benevolent people and the broadest road will be thronged with kind people."

Peng Geng asked, "In recording your words and deeds, what

points of attention are we expected to observe?"

After a moment of reflection, Mencius said, "I want people of later generations to have a correct understanding of me. To achieve this, you should record my words and deeds truthfully, the way Confucius wrote his *Spring and Autumn Annals*. Remember, tell the truth, only the truth and nothing but the truth. Avoid empty verbiage, words devoid of substance do more harm than good. Lastly, don't make any mistakes in copying or recopying. That will be all." He paused for a moment. As he did so, he cast a caressing glance over his students, then continued, "Yu, an emperor of the Xia Dynasty, disliked delicious wine but was fond of good advice. Tang, an emperor of the Shang Dynasty, held to the mean, and adhered to no fixed formula in the selection of able men. King Wen treated the people as if he were tending invalids, and pursued the Way without the least relaxation. King Wu never treated those near him with familiarity, nor did he forget those who were far away. The Duke of Zhou sought to combine the achievements of the Three Dynasties and heeded outspoken criticisms from his subordinates. These are good examples worthy of emulation when you are going about the present job."

All the students exclaimed in chorus: "We shall bear your words in mind, sir!"

From that day on, Mencius became deeply involved in the team work with his students in reminiscing, holding talks and recording. By the autumn of 304 B.C. the work was completed. Delighted that one of his most cherished wishes had been fulfilled, Mencius one day said to his students: "We have been cooped up in a room pen-pushing far too long. Let us go for an outing for a change of scene, shall we? See what a fine autumn day it is!"

At this, Chong Yu immediately went to the stable, whence he led two strong horses and harnessed them to a carriage.

Mencius stepped into the carriage, his students walking behind, and the excursion party headed northeast. They had traversed 10 *li* when they arrived at the foot of Mount Siji. There Mencius left his carriage and made his way up the mountain. He walked briskly, to the great delight of his students, who followed closely. Half way, Mencius turned round and addressed his followers in a cheerful voice: "The landscape here is enchanting. After my death, let me be buried here!" He was not joking; when he said that, it was with a resolute air. The students looked at him in surprise, but he took no notice.

Mencius looked to the horizon, then said with a sigh: "From Yao and Shun to Tang it was over 500 years. Men like Yu and Gao Yao knew Yao and Shun personally, while those like Tang knew them only by reputation. From Tang to King Wen it was another 500 years or so. Men like Yi Yin and Lai Zhu knew Tang personally, while those like King Wen knew him only by reputation. From King Wen to Confucius it was over 500 years. Men such as Tai Gong Wang and Sanyi Sheng knew King Wen personally, while those like Confucius knew him only by reputation. From Confucius to the present it has been over 100 years. In time, we are so near to the age of the Sage, while in place, we are so close to his home, yet if there is no one who has anything of the Sage, well then, there is no one who has anything of the Sage. Alas! It is indeed lamentable! It is indeed lamentable!"

Back at the school, Wan Zhang and Gongsun Chou lost no time jotting down the above remarks of Mencius and using them as the concluding paragraph of his forthcoming book.

One day in the spring of 303 B.C., when Mencius was on his way home after school, his son Zhongzi ran to him, telling him in tears: "Mother is very ill!" Mencius hurried to her sick-bed and asked anxiously: "How do you feel, Duanping dear?"

Duanping opened her eyes slowly, a ghost of a smile appeared at the corners of her mouth but no words came. Mencius stooped and put his ear to her mouth but could hear nothing but indistinct mumbling. Suddenly she cast her eyes in the direction of the western chamber and fixed them there. Her daughter-in-law Tao Qin accordingly darted her eyes in the same direction, and from one object to another, finally her eyes came to rest on a white cloth bundle. She went snatching up the bundle and asked in a whisper: "Is this that you want, Mother?" The woman nodded with a smile.

Mencius took the bundle and unwrapped it. Lo and behold! Two strips of bamboo on which were inscribed in big and vigorous characters his handwriting exercises from many years ago. A flood of warm feeling surged within him, as he thought back to his youthful struggling days when he used to copy down Confucius' sayings to spur himself on. Now these relics of my early struggles have been kept intact to this day, thought Mencius. A sure sign of her utter devotion to me, too! His eyes swimming with tears, Mencius could not help reading aloud from the bamboo strips:

"The young should inspire one with respect. How do we know

that their future will not equal our present?"

"When the Great Way prevails, the empire will become a Community of All the People."

A sweet smile flitted across Duanping's face, as she listened to the end, and then she breathed her last.

A proper funeral was held on the western side of the Mount Siji. One wintry day in 302 B.C., while outside was a world of ice and snow, Mencius was in his classroom conducting a discussion on morality among his students.

Chen Zhen asked, "What are the most outstanding features which distinguish a man of virtue, sir?"

Mencius replied, "A man of virtue differs from other men in that he retains his heart. He does so by means of benevolence and righteousness."

Chen Zhen asked again: "Does a man of virtue sometimes succumb to outside influences, say, something that may disturb his peace of mind?"

"A man of virtue is free from vexations," explained Mencius. "He never does anything that is not benevolent; he does not act except in accordance with the rites. Even when unexpected vexations come his way, the man of virtue refuses to be perturbed by them."

Chong Yu asked, "Sir, how is a person to cultivate his heart?"

Mencius said, "There is nothing better for the cultivation of the heart than to reduce the number of one's desires. When a man has but few desires, even if there is anything he fails to restrain in himself, it cannot be much. But when he has a great many desires, even if there is anything he manages to restrain in himself, it cannot be much."

Then it was Chen Dai's turn to raise a question: "I venture to ask, sir, what are 'good words'?"

"Words which are simple, while their meaning is far-reaching, are good words."

"What is a good way, sir?"

"The way of holding on to the essential while giving it wide application is a good way. The words of a gentleman never go beyond the simple everyday truth, yet in them is to be found the Way. What the gentleman holds on to is the cultivation of his own character, yet this brings order to the empire. The trouble with people is that they leave their own fields to weed the fields of others. They are exacting toward others but indulgent toward themselves."

Wulu Zi asked, "How do you view the problem of human nature?"

"In talking about human nature," said Mencius, "people in the world merely follow former theories. They do so because these theories can be explained with ease. What they dislike in clever men is that they bore their way through. If clever men could act as Yu did in guiding the flood waters, then there would be nothing to dislike in them. Yu guided the water by imposing nothing on it that was against its natural tendency. If clever men can also do this, then great indeed will their cleverness be. In spite of the height of the heavens and the distance of the heavenly bodies, if one seeks out former instances, one can calculate the solstices of 1,000 years hence without stirring from one's seat."

Suddenly his eyebrows gathered in a tight knot and he clasped his breast with both hands, and gave a pained groan.

"What's the matter, sir?" exclaimed his students, in alarm.

"I felt a sharp pain in my breast, for some reason!" responded Mencius weakly, his face deathly pale.

His students escorted him home, and from that day he was bedridden, with the students taking turns to attend on him. One day Mencius felt that he was getting worse, and so he summoned Zhongzi to his bedside and said, "Fetch me my bamboo strips and put them up on the wall!" This was promptly done.

Presently Mencius had his students gather round him, and then said with feeling: "Over the past centuries, people with lofty ideals have committed themselves to this ideal of a World Community of All People. But such a magnificent and worldwide project certainly cannot be accomplished in one lifetime or even for a few generations to come. After my death, it is my earnest hope that you will go on running schools to admit as many pupils as you can. Let the superb traditions of the former sages be carried on from generation to generation."

All the students listened in heartbroken silence.

"It may be Heaven's will that I have not found a good and wise king in my lifetime. But I am sure the day will come when..." A death-rattle cut him off, his head jerked to one side and he was no more. He died at the age of 83. It was the 25th day of the 11th month by the lunar calendar in 301 B.C.

The whole State of Zou mourned his death. He was buried next to his wife Tian Duanping, on the side of Mount Siji.

The students built huts around the burial ground, in which they stayed for their three-year mourning vigil, in the same manner as Confucius' disciples had done for their master. Likewise, they planted cypresses and junipers around and tended them daily with loving care. They continued copying the book known to posterity as the *Mencius* until each of them had a copy.

On the day which marked the end of the mourning period Wan Zhang emerged from his hut with two large bundles of bamboo strips in his hands.

"My dear fellow students," Wan Zhang said gravely, "a World Community of All People remained a lifelong ideal for our teacher as well as for Confucius. It should be ours, too. Soon we shall say good-bye to one another. I would like to take this opportunity to present you each with a little gift. Here are some bamboo strips, on each of which I have written a seven-word motto. Please accept them as souvenirs of our friendship and may its message be an inspiration to our future work. Thank you!"

Wan Zhang's parting speech met with warm applause and hearty thanks.

The students then all kowtowed before Mencius' grave, saying in chorus: "For a World Community of All People!", as if they were making a vow to their dear departed. Their vow echoed through the valley and reverberated farther and farther....

图书在版编目(CIP)数据

孟子传:英文/曲春礼著.—北京:外文出版社,1998

ISBN 7 – 119 – 01460 – 9

Ⅰ.孟… Ⅱ.曲… Ⅲ.章回小说 – 中国 – 当代 – 英文 Ⅳ.I247.4

中国版本图书馆 CIP 数据核字 (98) 第 05628 号

责任编辑　吴灿飞

封面设计　唐　宇

插图绘制　马　骥

外文出版社网页:

http://www.flp.com.cn

外文出版社电子邮件地址:

info@flp.com.cn

sales@flp.com.cn

孟　子　传

曲春礼　著

张增秩　译

*

©外文出版社

外文出版社出版

(中国北京百万庄大街 24 号)

邮政编码 100037

北京外文印刷厂印刷

中国国际图书贸易总公司发行

(中国北京车公庄西路 35 号)

北京邮政信箱第 399 号　邮政编码 100044

1998 年(28 开)第 1 版

1998 年第 1 版第 1 次印刷

(英)

ISBN 7 – 119 – 01460 – 9 /G·23(外)

06800(精)

7 – E – 3099 S